SIMMARIES

To the present and future students of St Mary's University: this is your heritage

SIMMARIES

THE HISTORY OF ST MARY'S UNIVERSITY, TWICKENHAM

JOANNA BOGLE

GRACEWING

First published in England in 2020
by
Gracewing
2 Southern Avenue
Leominster
Herefordshire HR6 0QF
United Kingdom
www.gracewing.co.uk

ISBN 978 085244 954 7

Typeset by Gracewing

Cover design by Bernardita Peña Hurtado

Printed in Wales by Cambrian Printers Ltd

CONTENTS

Acknowledgements...vii

Foreword ix

1 The History of St Mary's University, Twickenham 1

    Hammersmith: "Pope's Corner"..1

    The founding of the College 3

    The early years...5

    The Graham Years..9

    A new Century..15

    The First World War 19

    The move to Strawberry Hill...24

    The inter-war years 29

    The Second World War 36

    The Post-war years 42

    The 1960s...49

    The 1970s...58

    The 1980s and 90s 64

    Another new century 70

    Looking ahead 74

2 Sport at Simmaries 81

3 The Strawberry Hill story...85

ACKNOWLEDGEMENTS

My very warmest thanks to the wonderful library team at St Mary's University, who during the lengthy course of this project have been unfailingly kind, helpful, and enthusiastic. Grateful thanks, too, to Sarah McKenna Ayres for her help and support, especially with the photographs.

Heartfelt gratitude to Fr Nicholas Schofield at the Westminster Diocesan Archives in Kensington, and to the team at the London Borough of Richmond Archives at the Old Town Hall in Richmond.

Photographs in this book are courtesy of St Mary's University and Tiger Bean Media.

FOREWORD

S t Mary's University is a well-known institution playing a major part in the life of Britain and welcoming many students from overseas. Today it sits in its splendid setting at Strawberry Hill alongside the Thames, with its magnificent sports facilities.

What is perhaps less well-known is its history. Its beginnings, in the early years of Queen Victoria's reign, were at Brook Green, in what was then the semi-rural suburb of Hammersmith. It survived through two world wars and much social change, and in the 21st century enjoyed a part in a Papal visit.

It is in many ways a rather heroic story. The early students were young men, from families who were themselves not at all well-off, who trained as teachers for what were then known as Catholic Poor Schools. They knew they would earn very little money and would work under difficult conditions. Some of the first to graduate spent their lives teaching children whose families were desperately poor and often illiterate, in Britain's rapidly growing industrial cities. Thus were laid the foundations of a network of Catholic schools across the country, a rich inheritance for the generations that followed.

Over the years, and most notably following its move to Twickenham in the 1920s, St Mary's flourished and grew. Its expansion to University status in the 21st century has opened a new era. We should honour the heritage that has been passed to us. Think of the teachers trained over the decades, the literature, science, music, history, sport and so much more that has been shared with their pupils down all those years. Think of the sacrifices made, not least by those whose names are on the chapel war memorials, faithfully recalled each November. Above all, think of the Christian faith that is not only the inspiration from which St Mary's sprang but its living roots today. St Mary's expresses the life of the Church, standing on unchanging and glorious truths that dignify human life and point us all to eternity.

St Mary's story has now entered its next chapters and has a vital role as a Catholic University. As Pope Benedict XVI reminded us when he spoke here in 2010:

> The task of a teacher is not simply to impart information or to provide training in skills intended to deliver some economic benefit to society; education is not and must never be considered as purely utilitarian. It is about forming the human person, equipping him or her to live life to the full—in short, it is about imparting wisdom. And true wisdom is inseparable from knowledge of the Creator, for "both we and our words are in his hand, as are all understanding and skill in crafts" (Wis 7:16).

I trust this book will spark many memories among Simmarians from across the years. It will also help today's students to understand the story of which they are now a part. Above all, I hope this narrative will give us confidence as we look ahead and, with love and gratitude, entrust the future of St Mary's to God's good care.

✠ Vincent Cardinal Nichols
Archbishop of Westminster

1

The History of St Mary's University, Twickenham

Today's students tend to call it "Uni". Generations of past students spoke of it with pride as "Simmaries". The locals call it "The College". And Catholics across Britain know it as Strawberry Hill. It is St Mary's University, Twickenham.

A sign at Strawberry Hill railway station—about 45 minutes from London on the line from Waterloo— announces that this is the home of St Mary's University. The campus faces on to Waldegrave Road. At first sight, the main hub seems to be the large refectory where crowds of young people chatter over pasta or burgers and chips. Alongside stands a large modern chapel, beneath which is another hub—the library where heads are bent over computers or mobile phones, or nodding in armchairs. And beyond lie wide green lawns, a vast sports hall and running-track, and the sudden vista of a turret with battlements and a wrought-iron staircase fronted by gilded griffins.

The story of St Mary's began in the mid-19th century and looks set to flourish in the 21st, with chapters that include heroic work among the urban poor, a gothic mansion, lists of casualties in two world wars, a Papal visit, and the London Olympics.

In one sense, there seems little to connect the University today with its earliest years in the vanished Britain of Queen Victoria's reign. Yet there is a direct line, a running story, which does precisely that, and it seems a story worth telling.

Hammersmith: "Pope's Corner"

The College—named in honour of the Blessed Virgin Mary, under the old English style of St Mary—began life at Brook Green, Hammersmith, in 1850. This suburb of West London had at this period acquired the name of "Pope's Corner": for something over two centuries it had become a place where Catholics lived and ministered, running schools, a convent, and homes for the impoverished elderly and for orphans.

The connection with Catholicism seems to have started in the mid-17th century. Following the Reformation and subsequent events, various anti-Catholic laws made celebration of the Mass illegal in Britain. Catholics had to gather secretly, priests went abroad to be trained, and any sort of public Catholic activity brought penalties.

The laws applied across Britain. But London, as the capital city, housed the embassies of various foreign countries, some of them Catholic, with their own chapels. The Portuguese Ambassador had a summer residence, Cupola House, complete with chapel, at Hammersmith—then a rural area—and Queen Catherine of Braganza, Portuguese-born wife of Charles II, also had a summer home there. Catholics could thus attend Mass at

Hammersmith and a good many settled in the area. The Sacred Heart nuns established a convent from the 1660s onwards, next door to the Ambassador's residence, and ran a boarding-school.

Mrs Carpue, described as "a devout and charitable lady" married to "a gentleman of small fortune, descended from a Spanish family"[1] opened a school for girls at Brook Green in 1760. The Carpues were a notable Catholic family—their son, born at Hammersmith, would become a well-known surgeon and public figure.[2] Most of the girls at the Brook Green school seem to have been of modest means—the fees of several of them were paid out of the charitable funds of Bishop Richard Challoner (1691–1781), Vicar Apostolic of the London District. The headmistress for many years was Mrs Bayley, who died in 1818 and she was succeeded by Miss Gray. Brook Green House was a good-sized property standing in its own grounds and with a couple of adjoining cottages. Bishop Challoner's successor Bishop James Talbot lived and died at Brook Green House.[3]

A Catholic enterprise of this sort had to operate beneath the gaze of the public authorities—until successive Catholic Relief Acts were passed by Parliament towards the end of the 18th century, running a Catholic school was illegal. In 1829, the Catholic Emancipation Act brought major changes, removing the final vestiges of the penal laws, and a new era opened.

It was a time of change: the victories at Trafalgar (1805) and Waterloo (1815) had established a strong sense of British confidence and identity, and a new century seemed to open up new ideas. Britain's naval and military victories had shown how much the nation needed strong forces, and a sense of unity and purpose at home. These would not be well served by continued attempts to crush the religious practices of a significant number of the population: the penal laws against Catholics were causing particular unrest in Ireland. And, in any case, the chances of a restoration of Catholic monarchy had receded following the failure of the 1745 attempt and the subsequent death in exile of Prince Charles Edward Stuart in 1788.

The face of Britain was changing: new cities were emerging, such as Liverpool with its trans-Atlantic trade. There was rapid industrialisation: factories brought people flocking into the cities, leaving behind the older way of life centred on farming and villages. Railway travel would soon bring further changes. Catholic Emancipation was discussed against this background of change— but it provoked considerable debate, and it was the situation in Ireland that convinced the Duke of Wellington—with his considerable estates in that country—to support it. It was introduced by Robert Peel, who spoke for four and a half hours in the House of Commons to persuade Members to support the measure, eventually achieving success.

> The Bill was a Government measure, and with it the official opposition wholeheartedly in support, it went rapidly through all its stages. On its second reading in the Commons it had a majority of 180 and on its third of 178 (320–142). This was on 30th March, and the next day it was read a first time in the House of Lords. Wellington, speaking on the second reading, made no secret that it was the condition of Ireland that alone had moved him... Finally, on 13th April 1829, it received the royal assent, given 'very reluctantly' ...[4]

The founding of the College

In 1837 with the death of William IV, the throne passed to a teenage girl, who took the name Victoria. When she married her cousin Prince Albert of Saxe-Coburg, and produced a large family, the future felt secure. There was no serious faction calling for a Catholic claimant to the throne, and fanatical anti-Catholicism, though still present, seemed less relevant to the nation's actual political life. Following the Act of 1829, Catholicism thrived openly—churches were being built and Catholics were increasingly taking their place in community life. The "Oxford Movement" in the Church of England brought an immense interest in the history of the Church and tended to emphasise a continuity with the centuries of Christian faith rather than the notion of a crucial and necessary break at the Reformation. There were some much-discussed conversions to Catholicism, notably that of John Henry Newman in 1845.

The 1840s famine in Ireland in which so many died of starvation brought large numbers of refugees to Britain, the vast majority of whom were Catholic. They were usually poor, often illiterate, and always desperate to find work and homes. "During the Famine years, of the later 1840s, the existing volume of Irish immigration was suddenly increased, and although not all the Irish who arrived were Catholics—for there were quite sizeable groups of Protestants from north east Ulster in some English cities—most were".[5] The expansion of English Catholics was also "continuous and self-generating" at this time, following Emancipation and full freedom for Catholic life and worship.[6] Catholic numbers in England thus grew "from about 80,000 in the 1760s to three quarters of a million in 1851."[7]

Cardinal Nicholas Wiseman, as Vicar Apostolic of the London District, wrote a letter to his flock, asking them to support an initiative to open schools for the impoverished children of London:

> It would be hard to state the limits of our wants in this respect within this metropolis. Sad and terrible, but not exaggerated, accounts have been lately set forth of the condition of its poorest children. Thousands of them are growing up in perfect ignorance of every duty to God, to society, to their fellow-creatures and to themselves; without faith, without law, without principle, without one germ of usefulness, or one ray of distant hope, without a consolation in this world, or a belief to sustain them in another; trained to vice, educated in dishonesty, apprenticed to crime, early ripened in depravity, a present disgrace, and a future curse, to the society that now neglects them God only know—for probably these victims of early misery have never learnt it—how many of them are children of Catholic parents and baptised in our holy Church. Yet our present schools are full, and many anxious applicants for admission are excluded. How, then, are these wretched little ones to be provided for?[8]

This was part of a nationwide appeal, as letters from the other vicars-apostolic went to their areas too. Donations poured in, and the Catholic Poor Schools Committee was able to begin its work of funding such Catholic schools as existed and of establishing new ones.

Meanwhile, in Rome the decision had been taken to re-establish a full structure of Bishops in Britain, and Cardinal Wiseman announced this with a letter addressed "from out the Flaminian Gate" to his flock. In emotional language, it spoke of "the crowning day of long hopes", and of all the great English saints of the past looking down from heaven with joy: "Catholic England has been restored to its orbit in the ecclesiastical firmament, from which its light had long vanished and begins now anew its course of regularly adjusted action around the centre of unity, the source of jurisdiction, of light and vigour."

A flurry of anti-Catholic fervour produced some "No Popery" rallies and a law rushed through Parliament banning Catholics from using the ancient diocesan titles—Canterbury, York, and so on. The new Catholic dioceses thus took their names from the reality of the geography of Britain in the 19th century: Westminster, Liverpool, Birmingham.

Cardinal Wiseman became the first Archbishop of Westminster and wrote an *Appeal to the Reason and Good Feeling of the English People* on the subject of the Catholic Hierarchy. Widely publicised, it emphasised that he sought to be a pastor and shepherd, not a political ruler or statesman, and that "Westminster" meant the city and its people, not Parliament and officialdom: "under the Abbey of Westminster there lie concealed labyrinths of lanes and courts, and alleys and slums, nests of ignorance, vice, depravity, and crime, as well as of squalor, wretchedness, and disease; whose atmosphere is typhus, whose ventilation is cholera; in which swarms of huge and almost countless population, nominally at least, Catholic; haunts of filth, which no sewage committee can reach—dark corners, which no lighting board can brighten."[9]

This—plus public lectures given by Wiseman at St George's Cathedral in Southwark and elsewhere—did much to reduce opposition to Catholic projects. Meanwhile concern about the lack of education for the poor was widely shared in official circles: grants of public money were made available for the establishment of Catholic schools and formal recognition was given to their establishment. In 1848 the first of Her Majesty's Inspectors for Roman Catholic Schools was appointed, a Mr T. W. Marshall, with the approval of the Catholic Poor Schools Committee which had been created in 1847 through Wiseman's initiative. The Committee chairman was the Hon Charles Langdale, and the Secretary Mr Scott Nasmyth Stokes—who would later go on to become one of HM Inspectors for Catholic schools.[10]

In 1849 the Committee bought, for £3,140, the property at Brook Green which had been known for the previous few years as "Miss Gray's young ladies academy".

Brook Green House was of a good size and had its own chapel, together with about three acres of land. A Catholic architect, Gilbert Blount, was commissioned to turn the property into a Catholic teacher-training college, renovating the whole house and creating dormitories and a lecture hall, and for the students, together with a "practising school" to be attended by 100 boys.[11] Meanwhile, the college itself would come into existence, with students being recruited and sent for training at the Brothers of Christian Instruction (Freres d'Instruction Chretienne) at Ploermel in Brittany. The Abbe Jean-Marie de Lammenais—founder of the Brothers— supervised this, and he and Cardinal Wiseman can be counted as the effective founders of St Mary's College. The second annual report of the Catholic Poor Schools Committee lists the names of twelve men, seven of whom "assumed the habit on the Feast of the Assumption 1849".

These twelve men could be said to be the very first students of what is now St Mary's Catholic University, so it is fair to record their names. Some wore the habit as Brothers, the others were still laymen:

John Kennelly	Jon Nolan
Michael McNamara	William Williams
Daniel Cusak	Patrick Downey
William Martin Eden	John Friar
Albert Herbert	John Jackson
John Callaghan	William Aird

In 1850 the buildings at Brook Green were ready for use, and the students—six from Ploermel, plus some more—moved in, with a French brother from Ploermel, Brother Melanie, in charge. Others who remained temporarily at Ploermel would join them later. The idea was that all the students would take formal religious vows and become Brothers of Christian Instruction, but this plan was dropped as insufficient young men came forward in response to this call, and from 1854 the College was opened up to lay students

Brook Green House had been transformed. A report for the Catholic Poor Schools Committee noted:

> a thorough repair throughout, together with alterations in the dormitories, lecture-rooms, chapel, refectory, and kitchen has converted the old premises into a substantial and commodious residence for students: while the range of new buildings, comprising an excellent Practising School, with classrooms on the ground floor, surmounted by dormitories and chambers, is allowed to reflect much credit on Mr Blount, the architect.[12]

The early years

The first students in 1850, taking religious vows, became the Brook Green Brotherhood, and the records list sixteen of them, although there may have been more as full lists of students at the College only exist from 1854 onwards. With the decision to admit laymen, the pattern and tradition of St Mary's was established: by 1860 there were no Brothers at the College.

St Mary's was established as a College for men, and would continue as such for nearly a hundred years. (There were by now also colleges for women at Liverpool and at St Leonards-on-Sea). Its initial years as a specifically religious foundation left a strong mark and for the next hundred years a strongly religious way of life set the tone for all students, with daily Mass, meals eaten together, and strict discipline concerning behaviour, timekeeping and leisure hours.

In 1851 the College had its first Principal, Fr John Melville Glenie. Born in 1816, he came from a distinguished Church of England family—his father was involved with the establishment of the Anglican Church in Ceylon, becoming the first Archbishop of Colombo—and studied at St Mary's Hall (later Oriel College), Oxford. Ordained into the Church of England in 1841, he became a Catholic in 1845—one of the many Oxford Movement clergy who did so. He taught at the seminary at Oscott, Birmingham, before being appointed to St Mary's.

The need for training teachers was evident: previously, Catholic schools, like their Anglican counterparts, had been run by a system of pupil-teachers, often of varied ability and with no specific training. These were now offered the possibility of entering for a

Queen's Scholarship Examination, which would allow them, on passing, to enter the College for a full course of training, free of charge. Other men could also apply for training, and subject to passing an entrance examination could attend, paying their own way. The schools in which they would teach were similarly funded, in part, with public money. There was at yet no law insisting that all children attend school, but increasing numbers were doing so: by the mid-1850s the majority of Britain's children were attending some form of school, mostly provided by the Anglican or Catholic churches. Compulsory education would become the law in an Act of 1870, which would also create what became known as Board Schools—non-denominational schools catering for children up to the age of 12 which became the formal leaving-age—and continue funding church-based schools.

The re-establishment of the Hierarchy, and the emergence of an increasingly confident Catholic community in Britain including some leading figures with ancient titles, gives the wording of the Trust Deed for St Mary's, signed on July 16th 1851 a somehow Medieval feel. It announces a Trust "dated 16th July 1851 and made between the Earl of Arundel and Surrey, the Earl of Shrewsbury, the Hon Charles Langdale and Charles Townley, of the one part, and William Jos. Amherst, Charles James O'Neal and the Hon Thomas Honer and fifteen others…" The College at Brook Green was to be "for ever appropriated and used as a Training College for Roman Catholic Schoolmasters" and its school would be "at all times open to the inspection of the Inspectors of Schools appointed by the Privy Council of Education."[13]

The Catholic Poor Schools Committee set out information for prospective students:

1. The age of admission from eighteen to twenty-three years
2. The sum of £51 will be required on entering. Titles to partial or entire exemption from this will, in peculiar cases, be entertained by the Principal.
3. The elements of a good English education indispensably necessary.
4. A certificate as to past and present health from a medical man.
5. A certificate from one or more of those under when the candidate has received instruction.
6. A certificate of conduct from the parish priest.[14]

The first year seems to have had its problems: "At the close of 1851, the few students who had then remained for twelve months in the house were submitted to an examination before Mr Marshall; and considering the disadvantages under which they had laboured, it is very creditable to one of them to have gained the certificate of merit."[15]

In addition to the "practising school" for poor boys, in which St Mary's students would practice their teaching skills, it was also planned that there would be "in a different part of the establishment a school for the sons of the middle class, who receive a sound and healthy English education. Boarders cannot as yet be accommodated; but as a day-school, the attempt will be valued by the inhabitants of the neighbourhood. Religious teaching is surely not less important for the class from which employers will spring, than for that which produces the labourer."[16]

Fr Glenie would be Principal of St Mary's for ten years, resigning in 1861.[17] He established the College firmly in the life of the Church in Britain: numbers of students grew steadily through the decade.

The Catholic Poor Schools Committee, in its Report for 1856, gave a glowing account of St Mary's and especially of its high moral character, centred on the tradition established by the Lammenais brothers: "It is under the management of Rev Father Glenie and his brethren of the Poor Schools, all of them on the rule of a strict religious teaching order, which has had the blessing of God on its labours for centuries…"[18]

The Committee reported the College as having accommodation for 50 students: "Of themselves they indicate a fresh epoch in Catholic history in England."[19] They certainly worked hard. At the end of 1858 the Rev R. G. Macmullen, the Diocesan Inspector, and the Rev Father Knox, of the London Oratory, conducted an examination in religious knowledge. Questions to be answered by first-year students included:

> Explain accurately the distinction between "contrition" and "attrition".
>
> What heresies have impugned the verity of our Lord's human (1) Body (2) Soul and by what arguments would you support these truths?
>
> Is the existence of wickedness in the Church no argument against her sanctity? Show how this is.
>
> State what you know of the Maccabees.
>
> Explain the following: "Amen I say to you, that there hath not risen among them that are born of women a greater than John the Baptist yet he that is lesser in the kingdom of heaven is greater than he."
>
> What is the meaning of the words "born out of due time" as applied by St Paul to himself?

Candidates for scholarships had to grapple with "Explain the nature, cause and effects of original sin" and "Are any interior dispositions whatever required on the part of the recipients of the sacraments of the dead in order to their valid reception? If so, what are they?" plus a searching and detailed knowledge of Scripture including "Mention the principle types and figures of Our Blessed Lady in the Old Testament" and "Draw a plan of the tabernacle in the wilderness, and describe the several parts of it and the objects which it contained."[20]

Fr Glenie was succeeded in 1861 by Fr James Rowe, of the London Oratory. The Oratorians were a new Order in England, having been established by John Henry Newman: the London Oratory was established in 1849 initially in King William Street and later in what had been the quiet village of Brompton not far from Hammersmith. By 1860 Brompton Oratory was a thriving church in the rapidly growing suburb that would become known as South Kensington. Its Provost was Father Frederick William Faber (1814–1863), another Oxford Movement convert, well known as a preacher and author of several popular hymns.

Fr Rowe was based at the Oratory and, along with two other Oratorian priests, travelled daily to Hammersmith by (horse-drawn) cab, at a total annual cost of £77. There seems to have been some dispute about how this was listed in the accounts, as in 1863 Rowe was writing to the Committee of the Council about it:

> "Sir
>
> I have the honor [21] to acknowledge the receipt of your letter of the 26 instant and beg to apologise for the errors in the account and to thank you for your kindness in allowing it to be corrected for me. A sum of £77 paid by myself and two lecturers from the Oratory for cabs has been included under the head of tuition as Mr Hamilton agreed with me that it would be most properly entered under this head…"[22]

This dispute seems to have been fairly typical of the College's relationship with the

Council—throughout Rowe's insistently formally courteous letters there rings a note of frustration and irritation. The previous year, 1862, had seen some of St Mary's students fail their Certificate examinations:

> I have the honor to acknowledge the receipt of the Class List of the students of this College and beg to enclose the addresses of those who have left.
>
> The places obtained more particularly by the students of the 1st year have caused much surprise to the Vice Principal, Lecturers, and myself. The greatest pain has been taken with them and although few in number we believe them to be as painstaking and intelligent a set of students as have ever been in the College.
>
> If any clue can be given to us as to the cause of their failure, so that we may devote special attention to the matter in future, I shall be extremely grateful for the kindness.[23]

The College was indeed quite small at this time, although still steadily growing: when Fr Rowe became Principal there were just seven students in the first year, and just over 40 in the College as a whole. The students lived according to a strict timetable that began each day with morning prayers at 6.30am followed by Mass. They were not allowed to leave the College without permission and were allowed just one half-day on Wednesdays and another on Sundays, but had to return by 7.30pm. Meals seem to have been somewhat bleak—bread and dripping was the staple fare for breakfast and for supper—and living conditions poor, with accommodation in dormitories with minimal privacy.[24]

In 1862 the Catholic Poor Schools Committee reported on the achievements of St Mary's thus far:

> The Hammersmith Training School has been opened eight years for the training of secular teachers. There are at present 67 students in training; and during the eight years it has sent out 102 teachers, who have passed the certificate examinations. Of this number, 65 are employed at present in teaching poor-schools; 7 are teaching in private schools; 8 are dead; 4 are Brothers of Charity; 7 are out of a situation; 1 is in ill-health and 10 have given up teaching.[25]

Fr Rowe was assisted by his vice-principal Fr Thomas Graham, who was resident at the College. There were six other members of staff: F. Bolton, E.G. Bagshawe, R. Walker and J. Green as lecturers, H. Hardon the master of the Practising School, J. de Vries music master and a gentleman simply listed without initial as Austin, Drill Sergeant. Fr Rowe, along with Bolton, Bagshawe and Walker are listed as receiving no salary, presumably because they gave their services as members of the Oratory. The Drill Sergeant received £15 per year and the Music Master £20.[26]

The students attended lectures—and were expected pass examinations—in geography. arithmetic, English, algebra, English history, and two languages with a choice of Latin, Greek, French or German. They also regularly displayed their own teaching skills by taking classes at the "practising school" attached to the College. This continued to be a boys-only school, and several of the pupils came from a nearby Catholic orphanage, St Joseph's Home. Other pupils, from local Catholic families, paid a penny a week to attend the school.[27]

Writing from "Hammersmith RCL School" in 1867 Fr Rowe had to respond to another query raised by the Council on Education:

I have the honour to acknowledge the receipt of your letter of 23rd inst … In compliance with your letter the practice of supplying bread to the Home shall at once be discontinued.

With reference to the last paragraph of your letter I would observe that it has always been my earnest desire to follow any suggestion made to me by HM Inspectors of Schools or other officials of the Committee of Council on Education. They however on their part have constantly expressed to me that it is not the wish of My Lords to have their officers interfere in Minute details of Management and so, although I shall be unable at present to make use of the machine I nevertheless believe I can by baking bread at home provide better and perhaps cheaper bread than I could procure from a contractor. I must in respect of the College, decline to adopt the suggestion you have been so good as to make to me…[28]

In 1869/70 government plans for the future of education brought changes in the funding of Catholic schools. The system of grants that dated from the 1840s had served Catholic schools well. It had been established on the (correct) assumption that churches were able and willing to start and run schools, and simply arranged for funds to be made available for these. By the 1860s the majority of children in Britain were receiving some form of basic education, mostly in church-run schools. But the political mood was now strongly in favour of establishing the principle of free, compulsory publicly-funded education for all children. How would the church schools fit into this new system? Cardinal Manning, who had succeeded Cardinal Wiseman as Archbishop of Westminster, called for a united approach on the subject and urged co-operation between the Catholic Poor Schools committee and the Anglican National Education Union. There was concern that the newly-planned Board Schools would threaten the principle of public funding for church-based education.

In the event, denominational schools continued to receive funding under the 1870 Education Act and would continue to play a major role in education in Britain. In his involvement in this major public issue, Manning established a clear principle about the role of the churches in a healthy society—one to which Catholic colleges such as St Mary's could refer in the future. "Manning believed that state support for—but not control of—the intermediate role of the churches in education was critical to the essential character of the liberal state."[29]

The Graham Years

Fr Rowe's vice-principal Fr Thomas Graham had been one of the early students at the College, joining the Brothers of Christian Instruction at St Mary's in 1852, taking the name Brother Nicholas. Born in 1832 in Ayrshire, he came from a Catholic family originally from Co. Tyrone. He completed his studies at the College and qualified as a teacher, but meanwhile had sensed another calling, and went on to train for the priesthood. He was ordained for the diocese of Westminster in September 1860: as a diocesan priest he reverted to his original Christian name of Thomas.

Fr—later Canon—Graham became Principal in 1869 in succession to Fr Byrne and would be one of the most important figures in the College's development, serving for 30 years and dying in 1899 just months after his retirement. It is to his long tenure that we owe most of the detailed records of the College that give a strong sense of what life there was like in the 19th century. The daily timetable that he drew up allowed very little time for any slacking:

St Mary's Hammersmith

ORDER OF THE DAY

6am Rise
6.30am Morning prayers and meditation
Holy Mass and Hymn after Mass
8am Breakfast, Making Beds and Recreation
8.45 to 10.45 Lectures
10.45 to 11 Recreation
11 to 1pm Lectures
1pm Dinner and Short Visit to B. Sacrament
Recreation
2.30—4.30 Practising School
Private Study
Criticism Lesson or Laboratory Work
4.30 to 5pm Tea and Recreation
5 to 7pm Private Study
(Drill 1 hour on Monday)
7.45 to 9.45 Drawing (Monday and Friday)
Written Examination (Saturday)
Private Study (Tuesday Wednesday and Friday)
10 Night Prayers and Bed
Sundays
7 am Rise
7.30 Morning Prayers, Meditation and Holy Communion
9am Missa Cantata
1.45–2.45 Watching before B. Sac. (optional)
3pm Sermon and Benediction[30]

The Sunday reference to Holy Communion perhaps needs explanation. Communion would not be received at the later, sung Mass, because at that time Church rules decreed that anyone receiving Communion should fast from midnight. Hence it was received each Sunday, separately from Mass, early in the morning. At the sung *Missa Cantata*, the priest alone would receive Holy Communion.

The College was now an established part of an increasingly confident Catholic community in Britain. Through the 1870s, it grew in numbers and in status, and became known as a popular and successful teacher-training college. In 1870, as mentioned, attendance at school—or evidence of full-time education at home—became compulsory for all children in Britain between the ages of 5 and 12. In practice, most children had been attending school with some regularity during the preceding three or four decades, but the 1870 Act established Board schools to cater for the children who were not attending church-based schools. The Catholic

Bishops, and the Catholic Poor Schools Committee, were vigorous in calling for adequate funding for Catholic schools, arguing that no Catholic child should be obliged to go to a Board school, where a non-Catholic version of Christianity might be taught.

The College was not only in receipt of public funds but was also allowed to make use of other public educational facilities as required. To supplement the rather meagre collection of books at the College library, students were able to get tickets to use the libraries at the newly-opened museums at South Kensington—initially the students obtained their own tickets individually but this proved cumbersome and at the suggestion of the museum authorities, the College sent a list, at the start of term, of all students who wished to use this facility, to the Science and Art Department in Whitehall, and the tickets were then duly posted to them.[31]

It is worth noting the background of some of the young men who attended the college at this time. Many came from very poor families. John Jordan, born in 1854 arrived at St Mary's in 1870 aged just 16. His parents had fled to Britain from famine-stricken Ireland in the 1840s. They were illiterate and signed their marriage certificate with an X. After studying at Hammersmith, Jordan's first job included a period teaching at a "half-time school", so named because the children—all under 12—worked at a factory in the morning and then had a couple of hours of education in the afternoon. He would later weep in recalling how the children would often fall asleep from sheer exhaustion, and he did not have the heart to wake them as they were so exhausted. Such part-time schools were eventually made illegal. Jordan went on to become headmaster of St Etheldreda's school in Ely Place, and later worked for Archbishop Peter Amigo in Southwark.[32]

The early years at Hammersmith also established a pattern which would continue over the next century and beyond—that of family members succeeding one another at the college, and links being established through marriages. John Jordan's daughter Ursula married Harold Canty, who in turn studied at Hammersmith and went on, after serving in the First World War and rising to the rank of major, to teach at Guardian Angels primary school at Mile End, and then to become the first headmaster of St Augustine's primary school at Beckenham Hill.[33]

In an evidently rousing address given at a public meeting in Newcastle in January 1879 the Marquis of Ripon, chairman of the Catholic Poor School Committee reported:

> There is at Hammersmith a training college for masters. The whole expense of that institution, except what the Government generously gives, is provided by the Poor Schools Committee. I rejoice to say that the institution is doing excellent work. I was not long ago at the Education department, speaking to a friend of mine connected with the management of the department—and the best judge, I may say, in the country—and he told me that the Education Department thought more and more highly, as the time went on, of the Catholic Training College at Hammersmith. And, gentlemen, I have something to do with the men who have been trained at that college since I became Chairman of the Poor School Committee. I have made it my business, as far as possible, to become acquainted with the Catholic schoolmasters of the country, with a view to learning something of their feelings and forming some judgement of their capabilities; and it is only just that I should bear my testimony and say that I have found them a most intelligent and zealous body of men, doing good work for their country and for their Church throughout the length and breadth of the land.[34]

A decade later the same note of success was struck, with the annual report of what was now simply known as the Catholic Schools Committee, noting that "The marks obtained for students for skill in teaching have given them on the average of the last twelve years the fifth place among the eighteen colleges for masters; twice they were second and twice first." It quoted the School Guardian, the educational journal of the National Society (the main Anglican organisation running schools) as saying "The Roman Catholic Training College at Hammersmith is not large, but it does good work, and in one subject—reading and repetition—is unrivalled."[35]

The training was certainly academically rigorous. The Education department's formal announcement of the Syllabus for Male Candidates for the December 1891 Examination for Certificates in Residential Colleges and for Acting Teachers includes English, Geography, Penmanship, Arithmetic, Algebra, English History, and a choice of two languages from Latin, Greek, French and German. In English History students were expected to know the outlines of history from 1066 to 1815 with dates and general knowledge of the most memorable events, plus the reigning houses and dynastic changes, and then, in more detail, the history from 1789 to 1820 with reference to constitutional changes, the most important laws, naval and military operations, the industrial condition of the people and the literature of the period.[36]

Careful records were kept of every student's progress, examination results and general behaviour. When the students went to teach in the "Practising School" they were watched and their skill—or otherwise—noted. A report was then made in the College Record by the Principal. A sample from "Men of 1892" gives a flavour:

> Plunkett. Sympathetic, kindly, patient and industrious. Still he does fairly effective work.
>
> Reeve. He works industriously and (indecipherable) thorough and vigilant.
>
> Rocca. Animated, cheerful, and kindly in manner. He is interested in his work thorough, is earnest and teaches very well.
>
> Shen (Sher?) Kindly sympathetic and patient. He works industriously and gives fairly good lessons. Very reliable.
>
> Sherlock. Sympathetic and patient with untiring energy. He stimulates the boys to vigorous efforts.
>
> Taylor. Slow and unimpressive. But anxious and industrious.
>
> Waring. A particularly attractive winning manner and most sympathetic. Thoroughly interested in his work and vigilant and patient. He readily awakens the interest of his class and gets good work out of the boys.
>
> Webster. Vigorous and earnest and thorough. He makes the boys work well.
>
> Wilson Edw. Intelligent, industrious, thorough. Sympathetic and attractive in manner, he readily gains the co-operation of the boys.
>
> Wilson Wm. Animated and earnest. He takes a pleasure in teaching and gives good lessons. He is vigilant and he gets the boys to work well with him.[37]

There were some tensions. The very strict discipline centred on the threat of expulsion. Fr Graham's notes record seven dismissals in the period 1871–1887: the reasons given include "disobedience and insubordination" "sloth, neglect of studies, public houses" and "general misconduct and insubordination". In February 1894 he expelled a student named McCarthy for what seem to have been a series of offences—but this time the other students rallied to the expellee's support:

> For over a fortnight we have been unable to pursue our studies and now that you have informed us that you cannot allow John McCarthy to return to his duties in this College we are less inclined for work than before for then we had bright hopes of his return. His offence—speaking after night prayers in the dormitory—may be of itself a serious one but it was one of *indirect* insubordination and when compared with those of *direct* insubordination, immorality, scaling the wall at night and being absent without leave it is but a trivial one and we think that if he returns he has been amply punished, but if not he has been extremely unjustly treated. We have appealed to other authorities to consider the matter and we feel quite justified in taking that course.
> The accompanying protest has been presented to the Catholic Poor School Committee and failing satisfaction from that body it is intended to present a copy of it to Mr Acland.

The letter ends "We remain, your obed'nt servants" and has 17 signatures.

The protest to the Committee puts their case even more strongly, noting that the previous year some men were "merely reproved" for being absent from the College overnight.

> In laying our arguments before the Rev Principal the latter has treated us rather as children than as men and consequently he has not heard all we have to say about the matter. Against McCarthy's most unfair dismissal we again wish to vehemently protest and feel sure that you will lend an attentive ear to the above statements of the undersigned students who have been made utterly miserable and unfit for study by the painful exclusion of McCarthy.

It was to no avail. Graham's notes indicate that the student had been in trouble the previous year and had been "gated and warned". Later his allowance had been temporarily stopped (the students had to deposit a modest sum at the start of term which was then given back to them as pocket money from time to time on request). It is not quite clear what he had been doing that was so offensive—correspondence seems to suggest that some of the students, against regulations, used a key to the Science Room in order to study there in the evenings, and he may have been among these. His family wrote a pleading letter but it seems to have fallen on deaf ears. Fr Graham wrote to the McCarthy parents in January 1895: "I can hold out no hopes of receiving him back … meanwhile I am willing to do anything else I can for your son in any way. I will make the report to the Council officer of such a character as not to prevent him taking on [illegible] as Assistant on the 1st year's Certificate, if you agree to it. No doubt I may be blamed for this, but it is as much as I can do."[38]

There were happier chapters in College life. An annual Prizegiving, presided over by, variously, the Duke of Norfolk, the Cardinal Archbishop of Westminster, or Lord Howard of Glossop, was evidently a grand affair. In 1893 cash prizes of £4, £3, £2 and £1 went to William Price, George Bennett, Richard Curry, Thomas Wilkinson and John Brady for Religious Knowledge. Bennett seems to have been something of a star pupil, as he also won "Lord Howard's Prize of a Silver Watch for good conduct and general proficiency" as well as several other prizes. The ceremony began with music—Mendelsohn's Night Song—and concluded with Benediction and Light Refreshments.

Everyday life was regimented and not particularly comfortable, but there was evidently a strong community spirit. Domestic work was carried out by lay brothers of the Xaverian Order—these were men who were not priests but simply monks living under religious vows. They were popular with the students, and the atmosphere within the College seems to have been such as to evoke nostalgic memories later even while the absence of everyday comforts was also recalled.

Several decades later, former student A. P. Braddock, writing in *The Simmarian* magazine, January 1968[39] remembered "the 'smoke-hole' downstairs recreation room, the out-of-doors 'loo', places which could disgrace a slum". The dormitories all had names: "The Strand", "The Lane" and "The Dogs", this last above the Practising School. Each student had his own cubicle, but space and privacy for studying seems to have been limited. The Refectory

> was not so bad, but it was in the basement; it was well-lighted and clean but on the whole rather dingy. As the original tradition of a teaching religious fraternity in the College persisted to my time, there was a rostrum at one end of the room occupied by students in turn during meals to read passages from some improving book. In my time the work was *Apologia Pro Vita Sua* by J. H. Newman. The College and Practising School staff dined with the students.

He recalled that "We were well fed, although the origin of the meat was suspect." They thought it might be horse: there was a College joke that when one of London's horse omnibuses drew up outside and rang its bell, the meat on the plates jumped in response. They thought it tasted odd: "I believe it was boiled for the broth with which we were served before it was roasted for our main joint."

In 1896 a new building was added to the College, created a larger and more airy Refectory, a chemistry laboratory, a Common Room for the students and more bathrooms. At the end of the academic year the domestic arrangements were also changed: "The Xaverian brothers left—replaced by a Matron with a staff of women. Although the students had gone, I had remained at the request of Canon Graham to take charge of the Gate. So I witnessed the Brothers' departure. It was a saddening experience: all were sorry to leave and one was in tears."

The Matron was a Miss G. M. Harper and she took charge in 1898, appointing Margaret Davis, aged 29, as Head Cook at £25 a year, assisted by Upper Housemaids Susan Malony and Mary McDermott at £25 a year each, Under Housemaid Monica Cook at £20 and 18-year-old Kate Haley as kitchen maid at £14. The work proved demanding, and she later appointed an assistant cook, Margaret O'Callaghan, at £20. From the names, it seems that the staff were mostly Catholic—probably it would be expected that they would attend Mass and other services as appropriate. They evidently worked hard: Miss Harper was writing to Canon Graham in 1898 to say that "Since I accepted the post of Matron I have felt that the work will never be done with two housemaids only. You see, they would only break down and always be discontented."[40]

Miss Harper evidently expected high standards of work. Braddock, already quoted, recalled "The domestic affairs did not settle down quite easily after the women took charge, but I was in the Second Year by this time and saw little of the difficulties that arose, except a silly strike when the Matron declared that the tablecloths were not good enough to be put on the dining-tables and without warning attempted to serve dinner on well-scrubbed tables."

The atmosphere and spirit of this era, the first decades of St Mary's life, was recalled by a subsequent Principal, Fr Vincent McCarthy (1930–41) in the centenary issue of *The Simmarian* in 1950: "My first Simmarian contact was with the veterans of the Past, some of whom told me that they had arrived at Hammersmith on horseback! They impressed me as being real Apostles, who regarded the work of a Catholic teacher not as a career but as a vocation. "In their day, there was no fixed or certain salary. They depended for their remuneration on what the parish priest could collect for them. They entered on the work of Catholic teaching not for what they could get out of it but for what they could put in to it."[41]

Certainly a number of the Simmarians of the 19th century went on to make their mark in many fields. *St Mary's College Centenary Record* (1950*)* notes that several became Members of Parliament, Mayors, local councillors, or Justices of Peace: "Mr M. Conway (1863–64), a Liverpool teacher, became MP for North Leitrim in 1886 as one of the famous Parnellite band, Mr W. O'Malley (1870–71) was elected for Galway County in 1898."[42] Among other notable early Simmarians were "Mr D. Fallon (1872–73) who became a professor in the Royal University of Malta, and Mr T. K. Dealy (1879–80) who entered the Hong Kong civil service and was afterwards Director of Education there. He became a Justice of the Peace and a member of the Council and Senate of Hong Kong University. Later he became a professor at the University of Grenoble ... Mr E. A. Ray (1880–81) was professor of English at the University of Stockholm and Swedish correspondent of a London daily. He was created a Knight of Vasa for this educational service and his writings about Sweden... Mr A. P. Braddock MA (1896–98) lecturer in Education at the College from 1903 to 1919, then became Director of the Men's Training Department at the University of Birmingham. He was nominated to the Council of the University in 1933..."[43] T. Clancy (1877–78) became the first Catholic President of the National Union of Teachers and J. P. Callaghan (1895–96) was a prominent JP in Liverpool and A. Webster (1891–92) and T. Marsh (1892–93) in Wigan."[44]

Others travelled further afield: J. Lillie (1882–83) edited a newspaper in Bangkok, T. Donovan (1871–72) was head of a Catholic college there and J. James (1880–81) became tutor to Prince Svasti of Siam, accompanying him on a tour of Europe and bringing him to a prizegiving at Hammersmith in 1893.[45]

A good many became priests and this would continue in the years to follow. The archives of St Mary's have various lists of these.

A new Century

The end of the 19th century brought changes. In 1899 Canon Graham retired—and died not long afterwards, at nearby Nazareth House, a care home for the elderly run by the Sisters of Charity. The running of St Mary's was handed over to the Vincentians, a major religious order. They would shape the college for the next several decades, establishing its style and presence in the Catholic life of Britain on a notable scale.[46]

The Vincentians take their name from their founder St Vincent de Paul who established a band of priests in France in the 17th century, for the instruction of the poor and for supporting and instructing parish clergy. Vincentian priests carry the initials CM after their names, for Congregation of Mission.

The annual report of the Catholic Schools Committee for 1896 formally announced the change:

> 1. The care and management of St Mary's Training College, Hammersmith, is hereby entrusted to the Congregation of the Mission.
> 2. The Principal and Directors of the said College shall be appointed by the Superior of the aforesaid Congregation and shall likewise be removeable by him...
> 5. The Principal shall have full control over the Professorial Staff. It shall belong to him to appoint and dismiss them. It shall likewise belong to him to dismiss students for causes of grave misconduct. But he shall notify to the Committee the reason for such dismissal.[47]

This gave immense authority to the Principal, who seems to have been answerable to no one except perhaps his religious superiors. Lay staff would be at a serious disadvantage as having no effective means of sharing in any College decisions or of redressing any perceived injustice. The system would remain in place for several decades, and only be challenged in the very different Britain of the late 1960s.

Fr William Byrne CM was appointed to St Mary's on August 18th 1899 and seems immediately to have made some drastic changes. In his report made in August 1900 he noted that the new term had begun with a spiritual retreat. This—presumably compulsory—time of silent prayer, interspersed with talks and exhortations on spiritual matters, opportunities for confession, etc—was followed by an announcement was made about "new rules and restrictions that were deemed necessary" which he reported as being received "with a good grace", putting this down to the effects of the retreat. As the rules seem to have been fairly strict since the College's foundation, this tightening up seems to indicate a certain ruthlessness. But there was also some compensation for the students: he also noted the need for "major works required for the comfort of the house". On September 8th an inspection of the College was made by one of Her Majesty's Inspectors of schools, a Mr Barrett, who drew attention to the inadequate library, and the need to improve the students' accommodation and classrooms.

However, the most dramatic changes came with the dismissal of members of the academic staff . The former vice-principal Fr J. Coury remained only until October 1900 and was then replaced with a Vincentian, Fr J. Gilmartin CM. Mr Langton the Prefect of Discipline remained until Christmas 1899 and was then replaced. Two other members of staff, Mr Enright and Mr Edward Mooney, were given three months' notice in the summer of 1899, were reinstated for a few months, and were then dismissed, and both protested vigorously. Mooney wrote to Fr Byrne in August 1900:

> I received your cheque for Salary for August as well as your subsequent communication summarily removing me from the Staff of the Training College and enclosing a cheque for two months and a half salary less £3/15- which you say has been deducted from the Government fund for superannuation. I must inform you that I shall be compelled to use every available means of effecting protest against the arbitrary and iniquitous action you have thought right, and your cheque I shall retain simply as a payment on account.

Fr Byrne seems to have been unfazed by any suggestion that he had acted unjustly or wrongly. Both men appealed to the Catholic Schools Committee, to which Fr Byrne simply noted that "considering it necessary to begin the new scholastic year with a new Staff, the gentlemen were informed that their services would not be needed after that date". Enright succeeded in getting a year's salary as compensation "in consideration of his long service to the Catholic Schools Committee" and wrote a grateful letter, but Mooney, who had begun a public campaign with pamphlets, and letters to the Catholic press, was treated coldly, the Committee noting "that the Secretary be instructed to write to Mr Mooney and state that the offensive tone of his letter entirely precludes them from considering it."[48] Poor Mooney—a married man with a family, who received his arbitrary dismissal letter on his return from a family holiday—eventually capitulated, wrote an apologetic letter in October 1900, and received a year's salary.

Fr Byrne's ruthlessness is evident throughout his early reports in the College records. On May 19th London erupted into rejoicing, in hearing the news of the relief of the town of Mafeking in the Boer war then raging in South Africa. Byrne reported tersely "Gave a day for Mafeking. Students demanded with insistence to be let out to see the illuminations but were steadily refused. They went to study only under threat of expulsion."

But if he was ruthless, he was certainly dedicated, and had the interests of his students at heart. In any event, the Board of Education seemed satisfied with Fr Byrne's leadership. Its official report on March 14th 1901 stated:

> This College is now in the prospect of becoming thoroughly efficient. The Principal is energetic and takes a real interest in the welfare of his students. He is ably seconded by his staff. The students are working quietly and are making satisfactory progress in their studies. A healthy tone again prevails, Mr Morton and Mr McVicker teach their subjects in clear and interesting manner ... the premises have been greatly improved during the past year.[49]

The premises certainly seem to have required considerable improvement: a list compiled by Byrne of repairs to be done in June 1900 included basics such as proper lavatory seats, tarmac for the playground of the Practising School, cleaning of the washbasins, and un-blocking of the waste pipe of the "drinking trough". Improvements and building works continued over the next years. The Board of Education's Report on April 8th 1902 noted that "The older part of the premises is still in need of thorough renovation" although it added that "As regards diet, recreation and health the arrangements are highly satisfactory."[50]

Numbers of students continued to rise—from 56 in 1901 to 64 the next year. Several were now reading for degrees: the 1902 report comments that "The conduct and tone of the students is praiseworthy and there is among them a larger proportion than usual of men of ability and promise." A number of students came from Malta and the Report notes in a perhaps slightly patronising way that they are "studious and gentlemanly in their be-haviour" and that "their progress in English is remarkable".

Renovation work in the 1900s included modernisation of the dormitories. Byrne wrote to the Board of Education "We shall remove the cubicles from their present position along the walls where they shut out the air and light, and place them in the middle of a partition which would run along the centre of the Dormitory from end to end ..." The cubicles were extremely small: 7-foot by 6 -foot with a 6-foot partition between each one. Seeking formal permission for the necessary work, Byrne was told: "Arrange the cubicles as you propose. The matter lies entirely within your proper jurisdiction", and in reply to a query as to whether or not the men should have the additional privacy of curtains across the cubicle entrances, it was suggested that the men themselves might be consulted, via their Prefects.

As part of the renovations in 1903–4, the old Brook Green House—which had been a Catholic school and stronghold of recusant life in the 18th century—was pulled down. This marked the end of a link with that pre-Emancipation Catholicism which had been part of Hammersmith since the days of Charles II's Catholic Queen, Catherine of Braganza. Now it was replaced with a new north wing to the College buildings, enabling a general re-ordering and better use of space for the steadily increasing numbers.

The 1902 Education Act consolidated the position of Catholic schools, ensuring funding from local rates and allowing for the opening of more schools catering for children over the age of 12 and this meant that St Mary's had a greater importance than ever before, and its long-term future was assured. The Act ensured that "from henceforth the training of teachers was to be freed from the limitations imposed upon it by its previous inclusion in the Elementary system, and the College courses, equipment and outlook began to move steadily up to university level.[51]

The Act had been controversial, as it established a place, as of right, for both Catholic and Church of England schools within the publicly-funded system. This was very unpopular with members of the Non-Conformist churches—at that time a substantial lobby—who felt that large numbers of children would be indoctrinated with specific religious ideas at public expense and without regard to the feelings of others. The cry of "Rome on the rates" raised deep feelings—for many people, the Catholic Church was still a fearsome and even alien organisation posing a danger to the nation and its heritage. But for St Mary's, the Act opened an era of growth and development: College numbers grew steadily to meet the demand for well-trained teachers, and there was a mood of confidence.

Although the College regime was strict, and much was expected of the students—long hours of lectures and study, daily attendance at Mass and prayers, obedience to restrictive rules governing social life and so on—the young men at Hammersmith seem on the whole to have enjoyed their college years. London was the prosperous city at the heart of a great empire and had an air of confidence as the new century opened. It must in fact have been rather exciting for a young man from a provincial town or city to find himself in London, with food and accommodation provided, and the whole of the city to explore and enjoy. Most had very limited funds and all were fully committed to the rather austere regime at St Mary's and to the project of training as schoolmasters in Catholic schools at the service of the Church and the nation—but they seem to have enjoyed their leisure time.

They could go to pubs and to concerts if they had enough money—although the College was extremely strict about the hour at which they must return—and there were also the Royal events and military parades of Edwardian London, the parks and gardens and the shops, galleries and museums.

A former student, looking back on those years, would later recall:

> The horse-bus still lumbered along the London streets touting for custom as it went. Hardly luxury travel, but it was cheap. A ride from Hammersmith to Sloane Square cost but a penny … A visit to a theatre was a rare treat, looked forward to with keen anticipation … And a drive home in a hansom cab with rubber tyres, and bells on the horse's collar, the cabby with a top hat, taking pride in a smart turn out … brought a happy evening to a close. It was a simpler and more leisurely world. Little could the easy-going, care-free middle classes, from whom the bulk of entrants to Simmaries

were recruited at that period, suppose that these halcyon days … would disappear in the later Edwardian days, never to return.[52]

Fr Byrne was succeeded as Principal in 1909 by Fr Andrew Moynihan, who served until 1912. He had poor health and only served for three years. But one innovation during his time as Principal was the establishment of a gym and the appointment of a Physical Training teacher. Thus was born what was in later years to be a major part St Mary's: for much of the 20th century, it was famous for producing PT—or, as it soon became known—PE (Physical Education) teachers. It was also Fr Moynihan who established an annual Reunion for former students, and encouraged "Simmarian Clubs" in London, Manchester, Salford and Liverpool—these would become very important in the lives of many Simmarians, keeping up links and news, especially during two world wars.

When Fr Moynihan retired in 1912 he succeeded by Fr Edward Sheehy, who was thus principal at the outbreak of war in 1914.

The First World War

The College, full of young men, was naturally caught up in the drama of that summer, with numbers of the students rushing to enlist. The general mood—along with that of the rest of Britain—seems to have been one of excitement, even eager anticipation, at the prospect of fighting. The College history notes:

> Many Simmarians joined the forces and fought throughout the conflict … St Mary's itself was … gravely affected and it looked for a time as if it must close down Many students felt it their duty to enlist, as also did Messrs Canivet, Punchard and Harris of the staff; Mr Canivet was later killed in France and Mr Punchard became a prisoner in Turkey. Fathers Leonard and Gill went as chaplains to France and other members of staff took up various kinds of war work.

In September 1915 there were 112 students, but a number of them soon volunteered for the Forces. "The Board of Education was anxious to keep Training Colleges functioning as far as possible and made arrangements with the Army Council by which certain categories of students could be accepted. Thus St Mary's was able to keep open. At the same time the numbers steadily dwindled to seventy-four in 1916 and forty-two in 1917."[53]

In the early weeks and months of war, Catholics in London were particularly caught up in the plight of Belgian refugees who fled to Britain as the German army marched through their country. Stories of their suffering and the loss of their homes filled the British newspapers and, because of their shared religious faith, Catholic institutions and parishes were particularly eager to offer help and hospitality.

Few of St Mary's students in 1914 can possibly have imagined the long-drawn-out horror of the trench warfare, slaughter on the Somme and at Gallipoli, and more, that lay ahead. But their mood of patriotic service remained steady even as the war became more and more grim and the death toll rose. Past students had joined the forces in large numbers, and news began to arrive at Hammersmith of their deaths in action:

> By 1915 hundreds [of past students] were in the forces, many had been wounded and the first names of those who made the supreme sacrifice began to come in. News also

came that the first London teacher to be decorated with the DCM was a Simmarian, Mr W. Price … Simmarians were fighting on the various fronts and one, Wilfrid Thompson, is said to have been the first Christian soldier to enter Jerusalem (as the 'point' of the first patrol) after centuries of Turkish possession.[54]

Former students who were serving in the forces often visited the College when on leave, sometimes staying for a weekend, and were made especially welcome.

The First World War would take a great toll of St Mary's students. A total of 64 were killed—a substantial number for a small institution. The College—and now the University—has always been proud of the men who died serving their country in the two world wars.

The War Memorial in the chapel at St Mary's University records the names of the Simmarians who fell in 1914–1918:

Roll of Honour 1914–1918

David Aherne	George McGuinness
John Bamborough	William McGuinness
Frederick Bottomley	John McHugh
James Byrne	Francis Mckee
Hugh Callan	Francis Metcalf
Auguste Canivet	Charles Morgan
Patrick Carey	Mitchell Mulholland
George Carruthers	Arthur Murdoch
Francis Clare	Philip Murrey
John Cleary	James Noone
Noel Coakeley	Michael O'Callaghan
Vincent Cody	James Ormerod
Arthur Coleman	John Parker
Edward Colcannon	James Potter
Cecil Cotter	Harold Poulain
John Cotton	Wiliam Power
Stephen Cunningham	Francis Purcell
Thomas Dagg	Robert Randerson
John Donovan	James Riley
William Doonan	Joseph Sedgwick
Ernest Dupres	Herbert Shaw
John Dwyer	John Shaw
Robert Gribbon	Hugh Smith
William Gurney	Edward Standen
Reginald Hickey	Joseph Standen
Vincent Jolley	Walter Sullivan
Leo Kelly	William Swarbrick
James Lally	Cyril Thompson
George Light	George Watson
Bernard Mahoney	Douglas Wilby
Alexander McCarthy	Alfred Wilkinson
William McGrath	G. Wilson

A number of those serving won honours for courage and are listed here with the years of their College service:

Military Cross

W. Bowman 1900–02; F. J. Haney (with bar) 1903–05; F. L Lofthouse 1906–08; T. C. Farmar 1907–09; P. O. Norton 1907–09; B. J. Halliday 1909–11; P. Heenan 1910–12; D. Ahearne 1912–14; W. E. Sullivan 1912–14; T. D. Conway 1913–15; W. Bowerbank 1914–16.

Distinguished Conduct Medal

W. J. Price 1892–993.

Military Medal

C. A. Nagle 1906–08; J. Aspinall 1907–09; R. Moakler 1911–13; A. Redmond (with bar) 1914–16.

Mentioned in Despatches

F. Hourahane 1908–10; W. Swarbrick 1909–11; P. Heenan 19–10–12; W. Bowerbank 1914–16.

Croix de Guerre

A. Bradshaw 1906–08; P. Heenan 1910–12; F. O'Sullivan.

A later history of St Mary's notes:

> The list of those who died in the first war gives an interesting picture of the spread of Simmarians throughout the armed forces. Mostly they served in the county infantry but there were some in the Yeomanry and other cavalry regiments, others in the various Guards battalions and at least one in the Medical Corps … of the sixty-four who died twelve were officers and at least eight were NCO of various ranks … One of the sixty-four was in the Sportsman's Battalion of the Royal Fusiliers, joining up in January of 1915. He was in France by 15 November 1915, and was captured on 30 July 1916 in the fierce fighting in Delville Wood on the Somme. He died of influenza in the great outbreak in 1918 in a POW camp in Stettin.
>
> Another of the list was among the 20,000 casualties of the infamous First Day of the Somme, 1 July 1916. Several of the Simmarians were in the various Pals battalions and others in the battalions of the Lancashire Fusiliers who served with distinction in Gallipoli. One joined the London Irish and, having served in France, Macedonia and Palestine, was killed on 23 October 1917 in the attack on Jerusalem. Two inseparable brothers, having trained as teachers at St Mary's, emigrated to Canada and then returned to Europe with the famous Princess Pat's Canadian Light Infantry. The brothers joined together and had consecutive military numbers. One was killed in shell fire in the Ypres Salient in 1916 and the other was severely wounded by the same shell and was eventually invalided from the army …[55]

During the war College the small number of students—and the tragic news constantly arriving of the deaths of past and present Simmarians—made for a particularly strong sense of community.

A limited staff and varied attainments among the students hampered class work and College life went on against a background of grave public anxiety, air-raids, serious food shortages, and other deprivations; though it was still possible in the early years of the war for students to have a good night-out for 2s, a seat in the pit of the Hammersmith Palace for 6d, a packet of twenty-five Jones's Special cigarettes for 9d, and sausage and chips, roll and butter and tea for another 9d at "The Cess" a foreign café in Hammersmith Road much frequented by war-time Simmarians.[56]

Dr P. J. McNamara who would later become a lecturer in geography at Strawberry Hill, was a student from 1917–1919 and later recalled that there were only 32 men there. This meant that there was a strong sense of community. They tended to do everything together: he remembered a theatre visit where they walked from the college in double-file, parting with a flourish to let a pretty girl pass through, every student raising his hat as she did so.[57] On such outings they frequently sang College songs, of which a repertoire was developing, and gave occasional ritual shouts—it must have been quite a sight.

By now the name "Simmaries" seems to have been well established among the students. Earlier, they had tended to refer to "Coll", and the authorities, those of both the Church and the public officialdom, department level spoke of the "Hammersmith Training College". It is not quite clear when "Simmaries" took over as the general name used by students and staff alike, but by the 1900s it seems to have been in fairly common use among the students, where it seems to have started. At some point in the 1920s the spelling occasionally changed to "Simmeries", although past and present students remained as "Simmarians", as did the names of College societies and publications.

Wartime brought no let-up in College discipline. Early rising, compulsory attendance at Mass and obedience to all the restrictions on evenings out were still very much the rule. When peace came, the rules and timetable continued in just the same style—which must have been tiresome for men returning from war service who were suddenly expected to live like schoolboys. Discipline was enforced by the Dean—a new appointment following the College's expansion in the 1900s— who had the specific task of ensuring that the students obeyed all the regulations. Former student William Maguire, who was at the College from 1919–20, would later recall "You couldn't be in College half an hour without being conscious of him. He supervised all meals, he checked you in to Chapel in the morning and evening, he kept an eye on you the whole time."[58]

But there was a sense that change was coming: everything from women's fashions to the increased use of motor transport indicated as much. Old certainties had faded: men had seen death and destruction on a massive scale—whole stretches of countryside reduced to mud in which bodies sank and which resembled, at night, a terrifying moonscape lit only by the flares that indicated continued shooting bringing further deaths. Confidence in leaders and rulers was dented: it was clear that predictions made by those in authority had not proved accurate, that decisions had not always been wise. It was also becoming clear that post-war conditions were going to be grim: a slump and widespread unemployment brought poverty to many of those who had served loyally in the forces and who now returned home to find that they could not support their families in peacetime.

Among the changes were those that affected the Church and its institutions. Catholics in Britain had emerged with a changed status. The war had brought people together across previous religious divides, and the work of Catholic chaplains in the front-line had been much admired.

Fr Nicholas Schofield notes: "The war did much to dispel the negative myths that were still in circulation about Catholics. Many were impressed by the courage and devotion of the chaplains and began to realise the power of the sacramental system".[59] Soldiers wrote home about priests who braved gunfire to hear confessions and anoint the sick and dying, and who celebrated Mass at makeshift altars in the trenches. And in the post-war months and years as so many families were in mourning for sons, brothers, husbands and fathers, the Catholic understanding of praying for the dead no longer seemed alien or frightening.

The education scene was changing, too. In 1914 the official school leaving age was 12, and only six per cent of pupils were in school at the age 16.[60] An Act of Parliament in 1918 raised the official school leaving age to 14: this meant that teacher-training needed to be further developed and expanded.

For St Mary's the next years also began a new chapter, one that was to bring the College to a new prominence in national life. In 1917 Fr John Campbell succeeded Fr Sheehy as Principal at St Mary's, and would serve for the next four years. Because of the war, only twelve men planned the College as 1918 opened: but after the Armistice in November everything changed and Fr Campbell arranged for a special plan to be made for men who were leaving the Army and wanted to train as teachers. By September 1919 there were over 120 students in the college, 84 of whom were ex-soldiers.[61]

As the 1920s opened, numbers of students at St Mary's rose to an all-time high to accommodate the need for more and more teachers for the new secondary schools. In 1921 there were 132 students and three years later this had risen to 134. Some now had to be non-resident, as the College dormitories could only accommodate 125.

Prominent among the new students who arrived at the College as the First World War ended were the men who came to be known as the "Twelve Apostles". The Board of Education had launched a special project to attract new teachers: men who had served in the Forces could attend a shortened course which would begin immediately on de-mobilisation. The twelve men who took up the places thus offered at St Mary's were given new study-bedrooms—already the curtained-cubicle dormitories were beginning to be recognised as inadequate and old-fashioned.

The Twelve became something of a legend in the College: William Maguire—who would later be ordained and become Vice-Principal of the College— John Flanagan, Thomas Clancy, Pat Halpin, 'Robbe' Robertson, Tom Bentley, Alfred Gilman, Reg Dunn, Ossie Lord, and Tom O'Leary. Several of these became headmasters or inspectors of schools. One, Reg Dunn, was to have a tragic story: badly wounded in the war, he later became caught up in the horrors unfolding in Ireland as the brutality of the Black and Tans emerged. He was arrested following the murder of the man in charge of the Black and Tans, Sir Henry Wilson, and was executed in 1922.[62]

Some of the staff who had served for many years were now retiring: T. McNeil who had himself studied at the College from 1882–83 and had served as headmaster of St Mary's school in Cadogan Street, Chelsea, before returning to spend over 30 years teaching music at the College, and C. E. McVicker had taught mathematics at the College since 1900. There were new arrivals as the staff team expanded: "To cope with new demands after 1920 the teaching staff was substantially increased by 1925, the following members joining it in those years: Father W. F. Hastings CM, Mr WH Terry, Father JC Thompson CM, Mr PF Burns, Dr JP Dowling, Dr A Wilmore, Mr Ralph Smith, Mr FW Pearson, Mr LA Rozelaar, Father JM Thompson CM, and Dr JJ Doolan".[63]

Above all, in 1921 St Mary's had a new principal—succeeding Fr Campbell was Fr John Doyle, who would be a decisive figure in the College's history. It was he who presided over the move from Hammersmith and took St Mary's to the place with which it would become synonymous—Strawberry Hill.

The move to Strawberry Hill

It was clear that expansion on any large scale at Hammersmith was not possible. Sport had always played a large part in college life and the limited space for athletics was increasingly irksome. Within the College buildings, every possible space was used for student and staff accommodation, lectures, and meals.

Next door stood Cadby Hall, the headquarters of a large and nationally-famous chain of restaurants, J. Lyons and Co. Every town of any significance in Britain throughout the first decades of the 20th century had a "Lyons Tea shop", where the waitresses—known as "nippies" served customers speedily—hence their name as they nipped about in their neat uniforms and white caps—with simple items from a popular menu. A typical Lyons lunch might consist of scrambled eggs on toast with a cup of tea, perhaps followed by a slice of cake. Lyons remained a standard part of British life until the late 1970s, eventually giving way to Wimpy bars and later to the Costa Coffee, Starbucks, and Nero chains that were to dominate from the start of the 21st century.

In the years immediately after the First World War, J. Lyons and Co, rapidly expanding, became increasingly keen to acquire the St Mary's site. It became clear that selling the site would be extremely advantageous for the College. The funds thus raised would be substantial—there could be a move to a new site with room for expansion, a whole new chapter beginning for the new century that was now starting. Students and staff alike had an affection for the Hammersmith buildings, but they were in many ways, despite various improvements over the years, cramped and old-fashioned lacking adequate bathrooms and lavatories, or pleasant rooms for relaxation and eating.

But where should the College go? With sport a priority, plenty of open land was needed—if any move was in the offing, access to sports fields without a lengthy journey was essential.

An unusual option presented itself: Strawberry Hill House in the London suburb of Twickenham. The house, with a fine view of the Thames, was built by Horace Walpole in the 18th century and became famous as his personal project of Gothic revival architecture.

It was now up for sale, and in many ways was peculiarly well-suited as a new home for St Mary's. The Gothic style fitted well with the Catholic traditions of the College and would provide a fitting setting for an institution which had now become an established part of both the education and the Catholic scene in Britain.

The move to Strawberry Hill was of course a major turning-point in the history of St Mary's. It came at a time when life in Britain was changing rapidly: much had been ushered in by the war, from votes for women to jazz music and the possibilities of air travel. Arriving swiftly would be cinemas, BBC radio, and rapidly expanding suburbs.

The Hammersmith site was sold to J. Lyons at massive profit for St Mary's. In due course the buildings there—including the chapel which had been regarded as a fine building of its type, and the dormitories that had been renovated only some twenty years earlier—would be demolished. Stained glass from the chapel was carefully removed and taken to Strawberry Hill where it would eventually find a place in a new chapel. No trace of the College remained by a decade later[64], and "Lyons HQ at Hammersmith" became instead a major feature of London in the 1920s and 30s, and a major employer in the area.

The deal between St Mary's and J. Lyons was so successful for the College that it was often joked that Fr Doyle had perhaps missed his true vocation: had he not become a priest, he would have made an excellent negotiator for some major commercial company.

The move to Strawberry Hill began as 1923 ended, but would not be fully accomplished until the summer of 1925 when the necessary building work had been completed. A rather fine old brown book with broken leather binding records the events in the Principal's own hand. While the normal life of the College went on a usual at Hammersmith, Fr Doyle went regularly to Strawberry Hill to make plans and review progress. The tone of his regular entries in the book is one of satisfaction—and occasional frustrations at delays in the building work—with a sense of history unfolding:

> 1923 Feast of the Immaculate Conception BVM [the College feast-day] Dec 8th. Rev James Doyle, Principal, celebrated Mass at The Mansion, Strawberry Hill. It was the first Mass to be celebrated there. The Principal was accompanied by six students as representatives of the student body, viz:
> M.J. Russell (First Prefect)
> Thomas L. Murray (Librarian)
> Michael Doherty (First Captain)
> Stuart J. Byrne (Secretary)
> Juniors: Leo McHale, James P. Bates. The juniors were chosen by vote of their fellows.
> The Mass was said in the Gallery.[65]

But there was no slacking at Hammersmith—and while there were many developments as the plans for Strawberry Hill went ahead, the daily regime does not seem to have changed much since before the Great War:

> 1924 January 15 Tuesday. College reopened after Christmas vacation.
> January 23rd, Wed. Mr Pugin Powell, Architect, presented today the final plans for the new college at Strawberry Hill.
> March 4th Shrove Tuesday. A whole holiday. The students were invited to a parish dance at the Town Hall, Hammersmith. The Principal decided to allow ("experimenta causa") such senior students as should so desire, to attend. The dance was over at 11.30pm and those students who wished to attend returned in excellent order to the College at the prescribed time—12 o'clock. The others were in at 10.30.
> The College entertained to dinner Mr James Marley MP (returned as Labour member for St Pancras division at the last general election). He was a student here 1913–1915. Members of the lay staff (not all) were invited to meet him. Previous to dinner Mr Marley addressed the students in the library.
> March 5th. At Mr Marley's request a whole holiday was granted to the students today. Leave was granted at night until 9.30.

March 17th St Patrick's Day. A whole holiday. The students rose at 8 o'clock. A certain number of students attended a dance at St Augustine's parish hall, Queen Street Hammersmith. They were directed to be back in College at 10pm but by a special request, the Principal extended their leave until 11 pm.

Finally in the summer of 1925 the College move took place. The Principal's hand-written account tells the story:

> 1925. June 21st Sunday. This afternoon 4–6 there was held by the Principal and staff an "At Home"—in order to give to members of the 'past' an opportunity of seeing the College for the last time. Between 40 and 50 past students availed of the invitation … there was tea in the students' library about 5. At 6 solemn Benediction and Te Deum after which the Principal gave an address in the Library.
> Yesterday morning during work on the East window the MHS [Most Holy Sacrament] was removed from the Chapel to the Priests' Oratory. Today the same was carried out. June 22nd Monday The large East window in the Chapel was begun to be removed today. The study-hall desks, also, were removed from the College.
> June 23rd. This morning the last Mass was celebrated in the College chapel. [underlined in original].
> June 24th 1925. A temporary altar was erected in the library where Mass was celebrated this morning. Attendance at Mass was left optional. After Mass the Ciborium was again removed to our Oratory. Examination in Principles of Teaching.
> Special accommodation has to be found for the students from Northern Ireland who are next academic year coming to the College. Our day-to-day arrangements etc have been completed for the purchase of the property known as Waldegrave Park, Waldegrave Road, adjoining the new college. The purchase of this property is being made by the Congregation of the Mission by which Congregation the property will be leased for the accommodation of said students.[66]

Then, written in red, is "Probatio et Assertio Authenticiatis 4 Parte R.D. Praesidis" and, in a different handwriting, and dated July 1st, "Ego perlegi et pro authenticitis habeo documenteo a R. D. [illegible—could be Hastings] Scripta annis 1923–1925 Deobus annis 1923–1925".[67] It is not clear to what this refers. Is it simply a formal statement by Doyle, confirmed by R. D., that the record thus far written is authentic? Or does it in some way refer specifically to the arrangements for the Northern Ireland students? A special plan had to be made for their accommodation. Ireland had just—following a civil war—been divided and the Northern counties remained part of the United Kingdom while the southern part became an independent republic. Catholics from Northern Ireland seeking to train as teachers would now be trained in Britain rather than at a college in the south.

The diary then continues:

> June 24th. Wednesday. The bell which was founded and hung in 1857 in the Chapel turret was removed from its place today before midday.
> June 30th. Note: The process of removing and dismantling has been going on during the last ten days. The Chapel is now practically entirely denuded; also the students' library, one dormitory, corridors, Priests Community room, Study Hall, handwork-room, Physics laboratory, gymnasium. Meanwhile work on the new building is proceeding very slowly. The roof-beams are fixed, but of slating or plastering there is no sign.[68]

Two empty pages follow this. Perhaps the Principal was too much engaged in all the travelling between Hammersmith and Twickenham, and planned to fill in the gap in due course? In any case, the diary returns in August:

> 1925. August 5th The new college. The building—so far as the shell is concerned—is nearly complete. The roof is on except in one section ... the chapel walls are up as far as the clerestory and most of the stonework of the East window is in position ... meanwhile considerable difficulties are being experienced in regard to lathers and plasterers as well as certain supplies. A number of the students rooms on the upper corridor are finishes. The date for return for second-year students remains fixed for September 15th.
>
> August 27th Cross placed in position in Chapel building by Fr Doyle, Principal.
>
> September. The progress of the building is still slow. The stair-case outside chapel has been finished during last week or so. It will, however, be impossible to put any of the students in new buildings on their return. The old building [ie the Horace Walpole mansion] has consequently been prepared to receive them. The Gallery is fitted up as a temporary chapel, the "Ball-room" as a study-hall the library as a dining-hall: the rooms on the upper and lower corridor of the Waldegrave wing as well as those in the tower as bed rooms. The hostel no. 17 Waldegrave Park is to accommodate some English students as well as those of the Northern Ireland students who are second-year men.
>
> Later on when things have settled down the hostel is to accommodate the Northern Ireland students exclusively. The playing fields are being dressed level and walks cut etc etc
>
> Sept 14th Mr Mann HMI came to College to day officially to inspect the property and the accommodation prepared for the students.[69]

The delays continued, and the students had to be contacted and told they should not return to college until October 19th and then this was changed again to October 22nd. On October 12th Fr Doyle was still lamenting that "The Refectory is little more than half-floored (blocks); over sixty bedrooms are completed (no light or water); the classroom is still untouched; nothing is being done to the chapel ..."

But eventually all was ready, the students returned to college, and academic life at the new St Mary's began. The first College Feast-Day in these new surroundings was evidently celebrated with great seriousness:

> 1925. December 8th Conceptio Immaculata BMV. Students rose at 7.45. Mass 8.15. High Mass at 10. Cel[ebrant] Fr Russell Deacon: Fr Leonard Subdeacon Fr John Thompson. After the First Gospel the Principal preached: he recalled the importance of this first feast of the Immaculate Conception in the new College: the necessity of consecrating ourselves anew to Our Lady through whose patronage so much good was done and growth accomplished in the Hammersmith College and from whom even more can confidently be expected here.
>
> The main part of the Mass was by Palestrina: but the Gloria and Credo were plainsong, sung alternately by choir and congregation.
>
> The students were given the usual special dinner at 1.15 and tea at 5. They were free until 11 pm. The staff dinner took place at 7.30. All the priests and members of the lay staff were present.[70]

There is a sad note at the bottom of the page: "Mr McShee who came as a junior this yr and had to leave through delicacy after 10 days or so, died today RIP."[71]

St Mary's sporting tradition began to flourish new at Strawberry Hill:

> December 17th. Thursday. Sports competition was held this afternoon for the junior students and for the Northern Irish. These competitions are a somewhat new departure; their object is to estimate the abilities of new men with a view to the Inter-Collegiate sports and to training for same…The members of the Choir were given a special 'High Tea' in recognition of their good work this term. They had their tea at 5.45. The general body of students were given leave to attend at Westminster Cathedral Hall a concert given under the auspices of the Catholic Athletic Association. About 40 students availed themselves of this permission: they returned to College about 11.30pm.[72]

With the attractive new surroundings, and the opening up of new opportunities in Britain's expanding school system, the 1920s ushered in what seems to have been a flowering at St Mary's. As at Hammersmith, the students formed a strongly-knit community, and were subjected to a good many rules: essentially the College, with its compulsory daily attendance at Mass and its enforcement of strict rules about evening activities and social events, was run as if it was a seminary.

The memories of those who studied at Strawberry Hill over the next two decades include recollections of rules enforced by the Dean and his omnipresence at meals and around the College generally. Students had no say in the timetabling of College activities or events. There was no question of their having any choice of food at mealtimes—although there are references to treats being provided for them on special occasions—and there was no café or snack bar. Permission had to be sought to attend some out-of-college activity such as a dance or a concert. There seems to have been no question of girlfriends being allowed to visit the College—there were no casual social evenings that would have offered this possibility.

Presumably the young men went to pubs and shops and cinemas locally—and London with its theatres was just a train ride away. But most had little in the way of spending-money, and they generally seem to have remained on the St Mary's campus, busy with their studies and—the dominating feature of College life—with sport.

Already established as a serious sporting institution, St Mary's now began to make a name for itself training Physical Education teachers and winning matches and sports' trophies of every kind. The Simmaries songs that were roared out after sports matches became part of a strong College tradition, along with a number of specific rituals, chants, and shouts at meal-times. Some of these had begun at Hammersmith but would be cemented into the life of the College at Strawberry Hill—and would be imposed on newcomers in due course, sometimes with difficult consequences as we will see.

The Catholic identity of the College, and the fact of its unusual and attractive site by the Thames, all gave the institution a special status. Local people came to be fond of it, and for students, being a Simmarian was a source of real pride, and gave a sense of identity which would be lasting.

The strong sense of community meant that sorrows and triumphs alike were shared, and deep friendships were forged. Towards the end of the summer term of 1926 a student drowned while swimming in the Thames at Teddington, and the whole College was caught up in the tragedy:

1926 June 30th. This Evening at about 5 o'clock John Robinson, a first-ear student (aged 19) was drowned while bathing in the Thames opposite the College stretch. Another student J. Battle who was with him did his best to rescue him. Mr Robinson had been out at school practice during the day and had gone straight for a swim on his return. Requiescat in Pace...

July 2nd Friday. It had been arranged to have a supper for the students this evening, followed by a concert. The usual prizes, also, were to have been distributed. Owing to the upset caused by Mr Robinson's death, the concert and prize-distribution were cancelled. The students were given the 'extras' which had been provided for the supper but no member of staff was present.

July 3rd The Principal had asked last evening for volunteers to search the river at low water for Mr Robinson's body. The police had given up diving since Thursday afternoon. This morning nearly all the students rose at 4.30 and a large number of them went on the river swimming and diving from Teddington to Eel Pie Island but the body was not found.

July 4th Sunday. This morning at 7.45 the body was found at Teddington. Information to this effect was received by the Principal about 12.30. In the afternoon he formally identified the remains at Kingston. Mrs Robinson was communicated with by phone message to Middlesborough Cathedral.

July 6th. Inquest at Kingston. The Principal gave evidence.

July 7th. Wednesday. Solemn Requiem was sung (by Fr John Thomson). Mrs Robinson and relatives were present. The funeral took place at Kingston at 10; the remains had rested at the undertaker there and the funeral started from his premises. The first-year students had no school practice, they walked processionally behind the hearse. The six priests of the staff preceded the hearse. The Principal performed the funeral rites.

July 8th No Te Deum this evening had been arranged. Informal distribution of prizes and awards by the Principal in the Students Refectory after their Tea at 5.[73]

In its new setting, St Mary's was ready to expand, and from the 1920s onwards numbers of missionaries arrived to train as teachers. They received training from public funds: Britain had a worldwide empire and took imperial duties seriously. Education in Africa was considered to be of great importance, and funds were available for the work. A letter to the Principal, from a Fr Bidwell at St Mary's, Cadogan Street, Chelsea, reported that

> The Tanganyika Govt [ie the British colonial administration in the territory then known as Tanganyika—today independent as Tanzania] are willing that the missionaries who depend on them should take their course at the Training College instead of at the London Day training college, and the Colonial Office has asked me for definite suggestions. Would it do to suggest that the course agreed upon by you and Dr Nunn should begin at St Mary's College after the Easter vacation and that all Catholic Missionaries should attend there from that date?[74]

The inter-war years

St Mary's in its new home in Strawberry Hill was very much at the heart of the thriving network of Catholic schools in Britain. Known for its sporting achievements, successful in training teachers for schools that were increasingly popular and successful, and centred on a notable building which made its own unique contribution to Britain's architectural and cultural history, it was also an institution that was a matter of pride for the Catholic community as a whole—a sign that the days when Catholicism was something marginal to British life were over.

In 1930 a new wing was added to the College, with lecture rooms on the ground floor and students' study bedrooms above, together with a large room for drama presentations and concerts. It was all a far cry from the old Hammersmith days of cramped dormitories with small curtained cubicles: students now had comfortable accommodation and some degree of privacy for both rest and study. The hall for drama was known by its Latin name as the "Aula" and the block as a whole was simply called the New Wing.

The College saw no need to present itself as anything other than a strictly-run institution, in the care of the Vincentian Fathers and abiding by its own rules and procedures. The number of students continued to be small enough for all to be known to one another, at least by sight. There was pride in the growth and success of the institution from its early days at Hammersmith, and a strong sense that a tradition had been developed into which each new student needed to be initiated.

St Mary's had various courses available, but all were aimed at training men to teach in Catholic schools. Some could apply after a period as a pupil-teacher, during which they received £52 towards their future college fees. After making an application to St Mary's, would-be students attended an interview. One would later recall:

> The interviews were held in various centres around the country. Mine was in Manchester. There were all sorts of rumours as to the criteria on which selection was based. I never found out what they were except that I failed to satisfy them the first time and I was not accepted. Whatever they were, they must have been variable because I satisfied them the following year and entered Simmaries in 1933.
> At that time there were 105 students in the first and second years and 23 in the third year. Included in both these numbers were 40 Irish students, four Maltese, four from the Channel Islands and 28 brothers belonging to various religious orders. The total was 233. The third year students were the egg-heads, taking a London University external degree, or graduates doing a one-year Dip ed. Course, The rest of us were known, in Simmarian parlance, as "certif men."[75]

Sport was of such central importance that it dominated refectory arrangements before important inter-collegiate events. Tables were rearranged so that athletes were given a central space to themselves and served better food in the weeks beforehand: "I cannot recall any other students objecting to these special dietary arrangements for the inter-coll team, drawing the obvious conclusion that the rest of us were, by inference, under-fed: with few exceptions we all looked like whippets."[76]

Central to Simmarian life were the College songs, associated chiefly with sporting events. The songs—and various associated shouts called out at mealtimes in a ritual way—were not seen some amusing or optional addition to College life but were taken rather seriously. The songs had to be sung in a certain way, and ritual shouts done at a set time and in a set order.

One song went to the tune of *Marching through Georgia*:

Gather round your leader, boys
We'll sing another song
Sing it with the spirit that has been with us so long

Sing it as we've always sung it
Boldly, loud and strong
As we go marching along.

Chorus
Hurrah! Hurrah! Hurrah for Simmaries
Hurrah! Hurrah! There's none so fine as these
As the men who come from Simmaries
And sing Simmarian songs
As we go marching along.

The Coll has left old Hammersmith
And wandered to the "Hill"
But we will have the "Pawst" to know
That we're Simmarians still
And though we've changed our domicile
Our spirit still can kill
As we go marching along.

The reference to "the Pawst" also had a more solemn meaning, referring specifically to those who had fallen in war. At the end of a meal, there would be a knock on the table followed by a shout of "Two more for the Pawst!" to which the reply was "Ypres! Ypres!" This was a way of honouring those who had been killed at Ypres, Passchendale and the other battles of the First World War and was taken seriously: it was always done at the conclusion of any singing or other "College shouts".

All of this was connected with an emphasis on the College's history, to reinforce every possible sense of tradition. The "shouts" seem chiefly to have been at mealtimes, especially before or after sporting events. But they could also take place at other times, for example at meetings of the student body: to show disagreement there could be a shout of "All together boys" after which all could shout "He's a bloody liar!". Shouts seem to have been traditionally done in a Northern accent—or was there a North/South rivalry with each accent deriding the other?

It was a tradition to spell out S-I-M-M-A-R-I-E-S followed by a shout, in mock-Latin, of "Ee Nicodeema Eee Faveo Simmaries". And then "What about the Prinny?" meaning the Principal, and then "the Dixie" (meaning the Dean) "the Matron" and so on, each receiving a shout of "Ee Nicodeema Ee faveo Simmaries".

The tone of the songs was hearty and sometimes ironic, or with references to the College's dreary food or other restrictions, with a rather heavy humour:

This is a Coll of fair renown
Yo ho! Yo ho!
Yo ho yer buggers, Yo ho yer buggers
We're fed up with kippers and prunes and cheese
And dirty potatoes and beans and peas
And now we haven't long to stay
We'll pip Cerif and then away
And then a train for London town (substitute Liverpool, Newcastle etc)
I hope to hell the bugger breaks down
Yo ho yer buggers …

There were also other songs, shared among the rest of the sporting fraternity and with a vaguely saucy connotation:

> Adam was the first man, the father of the race
> And late investigation showed he used to go the pace
> He lived with Eve in Eden with nothing on at all
> And he went the pace the fastest when the leaves began to fall …

One of these became special to St Mary's, named at "The Coll Chorus" and had to be sung while a procession was formed, led by the senior student, each man putting a hand on the shoulder of the student in front:

> I am a simple country yokel
> La-di-da-dida (after each line)
> And from Lancashire I came
> To see the sights of London town
> I took a walk down Leicester Square
> There I met a damsel fair
> We had drinks and she did pay
> She fairly stole my heart away …[77]

As part of this sense of tradition, a reunion of past students was held each year. These reunions had started in the 1900s at Hammersmith, with an annual dinner for former students, and at Strawberry Hill the programme was expanded to include an afternoon garden party to which the men could also bring their wives and families. The extensive grounds made for a full afternoon of games and races for the children and an outdoor buffet tea, and then in the evening a dinner and dancing until midnight.

A programme for Whit Monday (Pentecost Monday, then a public holiday) 20th May 1929 reads:

> 2.30 Games
> 4.30 Tea
> 6.30 Benediction
> 7.00 Dinner
> Tickets 5/-. Wines extra. Ladies will be welcomed.

Later on, the reunions were held during the summer holiday, so that overnight accommodation could be offered in the vacated students' rooms.

College life clearly centred around sport, but there were also other activities. The "Seniors" welcomed the first-year students with a concert in the September term. The committee organising the 1929 event, held on November 7th, was chaired by E.G. Pilkington and members were H. O'Brien, F. Mulhall and J. McBride. The concert included a one-act play *The ghost of Jerry Blunder,* and a three-act play *Loaves and Fishes.* The Juniors were evidently expected to show their appreciation by presenting a concert of their own, and they did so in style, with a programme announcing the Patrons of the event—the Principal and other Vincentian fathers teaching at the College—and the committee members "Messrs P. Spiuteri, P. A. Lamont, F. A. Murray, B. H. Malone, E. Burrows and J. Logan."[78]

Daily meals were eaten at set times, with students being allocated set places in the dining-room. There was no question of there being any choice in the matter of food, and both quantity and quality seem to have been rather poor. Ritual accompanied all the meals, even when there were no formal shouts or songs. Above all, there was constant surveillance of the students, with the idea of noting and controlling behaviour. The Dean was omnipresent, and at meals each table was supervised by a Prefect who seems to have been regarded, in a jocular way, as a sort of jailer. William Glynn, a student from 1933 to 1935, would later recall:

> I can clearly visualize the lay-out of the refectory, and even remember the names of some of my table-companions in our junior year: 'Kip' Lennon (Liverpool) Fred Fenlon (Bebington) Sean Egan (London) PD Duggan (Cumberland) Bernard Goggin (Liverpool) Tom Devine (Oldham) Bill Hamon (Jersey).
>
> I think there were seventeen tables in the refectory, that is nine on one side and eight on the other., with a wide aisle down the middle from the entrance doors to the kitchen doors. Each table seated twelve, six chairs on each side, one chair at the end of the table being reserved for the prefect ('nark') who served out the food which was brought up the aisle by the "nippies". The supplies came directly from the kitchen and matron stood inside the kitchen doors and supervised the coming and going of the girls. No verbal exchanges, except possibly concerning food, were permitted between us and these maidens. Prisoners of war gave more information to their captors than the nippies gave to us. However, they seem to have been chosen for qualifications other than their beauty, so ogling and chatting-up and the like were absent. In any case, in addition to the eyes and ears of the matron, there were also those of the Dean (Fr Maguire in my time) who stood by a large long-mirrored chiffoniere on one side of the entrance doors. Those of us who were romantically inclined had to wait until Saturday and Sunday evenings to assuage our aspirations, though our straitened finances made this pastime somewhat fanciful, especially as we had to be back for night prayers at 8.15pm, so we could hardly plumb the depths of moral turpitude in so limited a period ...
>
> Desire for food more than for anything else occupied our waking hours, and sometimes our dreams: so Saturday evening was the occasion when we resorted to the flesh-pots of Twickenham or Richmond where we patronised the local cafes (the cheap ones) and also swigged cheap beer in the four ale bars. (There was no bar in college and incidentally only one phone-box ...)
>
> In the refectory no food was refused except on one notorious occasion when the cabbage on two adjacent tables was found to contain some two-inches long multicoloured boiled caterpillars. These were promptly impaled on forks and held up for general inspection. This was a signal for all tables to send back the dishes of cabbage. Matron promptly slammed shut the kitchen doors. One nippy failed to make it in time: a combined table-shout 'Love's locked out' alerted matron to the girl's peril. The dean ordered us all out of the refectory and shut the doors from the inside. He re-opened them about twenty minutes later and we returned to our places...I cannot remember what food was on the table except that there was no cabbage, nor were there any recriminations afterwards from the dean.[79]

It is rather odd that he seems to have assumed there would be "recriminations" for the students when they had done nothing wrong! Surely, on the contrary, an apology should have been made to them following the discovery of boiled insects in their food?

The emphasis on student discipline pervades all reminiscences of this period—there is even a sort of grim pride in describing the bizarre attitudes of the College administration.

Why, for example, would it have been wrong for a student to become friendly with one of the young women serving in the refectory? (Even if they were not pretty!) Many good Catholic marriages have begun in just this way. And why should the notion of any romantic involvement be linked to "moral turpitude"? Young Catholic men, training to be teachers, might reasonably have been expected to meet young women in a perfectly wholesome and good way at, for example, a Catholic parish dance or similar event in a London suburb such as Twickenham, with a good marriage as the natural and happy result. Perhaps it is in these earlier decades of the 20th century that the seeds of the massive social changes of three decades later were sown, as a new generation in the 1960s shrugged off restrictions and attitudes seen as anachronistic and unjust—and then went too far in assuming that there should be no restrictions of any kind on students' lives.

But these years at Strawberry Hill forged strong friendships among the students, deep loyalty and a great attachment to the College. They stayed in touch after they had left, as the College archives' wealth of newsletters and notes of local gatherings of former students attest, and they returned to the College in good numbers for reunions and for special occasions. As teachers, they had been trained to see themselves as following a vocation rather than merely holding a job. They also took on positions of responsibility within the Catholic community and the country at large—and great numbers served loyally in the Armed Forces in wartime.

The sense of tradition was of course strongly linked to the College's Catholic identity, and was felt by local people as well as by the College community. Local Catholics were proud of St Mary's and the fact that it occupied the most impressive building in the area. There were good links with the Catholic parishes in Twickenham, Richmond, and Kingston.

In 1929 Catholics in Britain celebrated the centenary of Catholic Emancipation, and a garden party was held at St Mary's that summer, attended by the Archbishop of Westminster Cardinal Francis Bourne and many other Bishops, along with various leading figures in Catholic life.

During the 1920s and 30s, the College grounds were used each summer for a Corpus Christi Procession organised by the nearest local Catholic parish, St James in Twickenham. A special feature of this event was the attendance of members of the exiled Portuguese Royal Family, who lived in Twickenham. They were not the first exiled foreign royalty to make their home locally—the nearby Orleans House had provided a refuge for French royalty in an earlier generation. The Portuguese royals played a notable part in local life, the former King Manoel even becoming chairman of the Twickenham stamp collecting society.

For St Mary's, this link with Portugal actually went back to Hammersmith days, when Catholic activity at Brook Green had been associated with the nearby presence of the Portuguese Ambassador in the 17th century: now, two centuries later, the hospitality was, as it were, being returned. A description of the Corpus Christi event on June 22nd 1930 lists HM Queen Augusta Victoria and His Highness Prince Franz Joseph in the procession, followed by the College choir, students, Knights of St Columba, and parishioners of St James and of other local parishes.[80]

Fr Doyle—who had steered the College so successfully through the move to Strawberry Hill and then presided over notable years of growth and achievement, retired in September 1930. In addition to the move, his major achievement was the establishment of the Degree courses at the College—enabling students to graduate from the University of London—and the strengthening of the relationship with the Board (later Ministry, now Dept) of Education. He was honoured with tributes from many in the Church and in the world of education. The University of London, and many leading Catholic schools, sent messages of thanks. He had been respected and admired far beyond the Catholic scene: Rev H. B. Workman of the Wesleyan Education Committee wrote that Doyle was "a great friend, a far-sighted administrator, and a perpetual joy". The Rev G H Dix from the Anglican College of St Mark and St John in Chelsea was also a friend, and after a gathering at which Doyle had been a guest wrote to thank him for a "singularly felicitous speech". At Strawberry Hill, the Bishop of Portsmouth presided at a special dinner in Doyle's honour. Fr Doyle was succeeded as Principal by Fr Vincent McCarthy.

Although the everyday fare at the College in the 1930s was rather grim, there were occasional treats, and the College Feast on December 8th, celebrating the Immaculate Conception, always seems to have been a good spread. St Cecilia's Day on 24th November was usually celebrated in style, honouring the patron saint of music, to thank the College choir members for their efforts during the year. A menu card from 1931 suggests a hearty, if somewhat unimaginative meal:

Thick Scotch broth
Roast turkey, stuffed sausages, ham,
Braised celery, Brussels sprouts, mashed potatoes
Garden fruits
Tangerine
Walnuts
Coffee, cigarettes, twilight crackers[81]

In 1935 a young Vincentian priest, Fr Kevin Cronin, arrived at the College to lecture in History. He had been ordained for just three years and had spent these in Paris. He would be part of a small team of priests at the College during the war years and would later go on to become Principal.

St Mary's was proud of its reputation, and throughout the 1930s it grew in numbers and in status. Its Governing Body was composed of members of the Catholic Education Council of England and Wales, with two additional members nominated by the Senate of the University of London. But everyday control was very much in the hands of the Principal, appointed by the Vincentian Order. He conducted interviews of prospective students—and there seems to have been no appeal against his decision on whether to admit some one or not—and he controlled the College finances and oversaw academic matters and the regulations governing students' lives. A letter to the University of London, outlining these arrangements, adopts a perhaps slightly defensive tone:

In 1899 the Catholic Education Council entrusted the administration of the College to the Vincentian Order.
The Principal of the College is appointed by the Governing Body from among a number of nominees submitted by the Vincentian Order. The selection made by the Governing Body is submitted to the Board of Education in the usual way. The Principal is responsible to the Governing Body for the administration of the College generally.
The Vincentian Order, as such, does not interfere with the administration of the College, but the Principal, who has on his staff a number of resident colleagues

belonging to the Order, is guided in his decisions by those colleagues, who form the College Council. In matters of general academic interest the entire staff, lay and clerical, meet in conference.

While the Principal bears the burden of actual responsibility in academic and disciplinary matters, he always consults the College Council and his Governing Body before making any decisions of grave moment in these departments ... In financial matters the Principal acts as Treasurer and pays from current income (consisting of grants from the Board of Education and of students' fees) accounts for salaries, provisions, repairs, rates, taxes etc. He is under obligation to submit, annually, for scrutiny to the Board of Education and to the Catholic Education Council a statement of accounts certified by an independent firm of chartered accountants ...[82]

A formal visitation of the College by a delegacy from the London University seems to have been satisfied, noting in February 1938: "Throughout our visit, we were most favourably impressed by the evidence of efficiency, of the keenness of the students and of their cheerful spirit. This was made abundantly clear to us by the talk that we had with the senior students ..."[83]

During the 1930s, grants for students were not generous, and were not widely available, and many would-be students had to withdraw after being accepted by the College, because they had been unable to obtain a grant from their local authority. This, along with other issues concerning the funding of education, would be much discussed in the years to come, especially in post-war planning. But first came war.

The Second World War

In September 1939 St Mary's was preparing for the new academic year. In due course students arrived, and for the first few months after the outbreak of war on September 3rd College life continued more or less as normal—except that some of the Senior students had left to join the Forces.

College traditions continued, and indeed by 1940 had assumed a slightly savage quality. Desmond McMahon arrived as a new student in January of that year:

The first day at Simmaries stands out in my mind. It was a very cold day in January and there was a liberal coating of snow in Manchester when we entrained for London. With various emotions of excitement, trepidation, feigned self-confidence and wonder we entered the College during the afternoon. Later on, we were summoned to the Refectory for Tea. Everyone appeared to be excessively polite to everyone else in the new intake during the early part of the meal. This attitude was shattered part-way through when the few Senior students who were present at the meal suddenly banged the table alarmingly, three times, and bawled out in unison "Who are these handsome strangers?" A group of our new College mates on another table, with rather more courage than sense, responded with even more gusto by banging the table ferociously with the bread board and roared out "We are the Ovaltinies" [a popular advertising slogan at the time]. The Seniors did not seem to appreciate this readiness of response. I was facing their table and they appeared to be scarlet with rage at being upstaged by their callow juniors.

As a result of this spontaneous response we were all summoned to the Library after the meal to be instructed as the error of our ways. On assembly in the library we were addressed, or raved at, by the Senior Fuzz leader who was seated in the manner of Semaris when he wasn't leaping about. He frothed at the mouth and called the whole of our intake unmentionable names. He roared and he ranted and reminded us that although we may have been Prefect, House Leaders, School Captains and the like in our previous existence we were now just base material (he had a name for it).

During his frantic appearance I idly wondered why he had not been locked away by the College authorities, as a safety precaution, or packed away in some suitable institution. One of our number questioned the right to call us such terrible names. The result had to be seen to be believed. The Fuzz Leader yelled and roared, stamped and went scarlet in the face before his straining vocal chords screeched out "OUTSIDE THE CAN!" We were all summoned to watch the discipline involved which certainly restrained others from stepping out of line so early in our College days.[84]

While this ill-tempered bullying could have been regarded as simply something that had to be endured, the night provided a real danger—although this time with no deliberately cruel intent:

> We were required to sleep in bunks in an underground air raid shelter which had been dug in the wood between the College and the playing field. The weather was terribly cold and someone with a misguided sense of kindness and scant knowledge of science, it would appear, had arranged for coke braziers to heat these enclosed bunkhouses. When the call for Mass came the following morning there was great difficulty in awakening about a dozen of our number and during Mass about sixteen fainted and were taken out with various degrees of carbon monoxide inhalation. It did little to ease our troubled minds to hear it said that if the call to morning Mass had been half an hour later some of our number could well have succumbed.[85]

The war hit home at St Mary's, as it did to the rest of Britain, in the Autumn of 1940. The London "blitz" brought repeated bombing raids by the Luftwaffe, and Twickenham's turn came in September:

Fr Cronin later (1969) remembered that the New Wing received a direct hit: "That night we were the twentieth fire in the district and by the time the firemen got around to us the whole building was in flames. The New Wing was destroyed so completely that the entire fabric right down to the ground floor was burned. The ground floor had to be replaced [after the war] but the outer shell remained. The present [1969] Senior Common Room was destroyed...Another firebomb came through the drawing room and burned a large hole in the floor...The Long Gallery also suffered: a hole was burned in the floor...One bomb fell in the Entrance Hall of the Walpole House and burned much in that area In all, during the war this place was a ruin."[86]

St Mary's was fortunate: no one was killed and the New Wing could eventually be rebuilt. Walpole's mansion was not badly damaged. In the same raid, another local house, very near the College, was completely destroyed: Radnor House, built in the 18th century and something of a rival to Strawberry Hill, took a direct hit and was reduced to rubble. The site is now Radnor Gardens, a public park.

Former student Tom Carter would later recall that after this bombing "the students were sent home and several were enlisted for military service. However sufficient repair work was carried out to enable the college to re-open though the hot water system supplying hot water to the students' rooms was to remain out of action until the day after the war."[87]

The daily routine during the war years was much as it had been for the previous decades: students were expected to attend Mass at 7am, and breakfast followed at 8, and then lectures until lunch at 1pm. The afternoon was devoted to games and Physical Education, with Tea at 5pm. Dinner was at 7pm and the evening was free for study or leisure activities—but no one was expected to leave the College, and there was a Lights Out rule at 11pm. At weekends, students were permitted to go out but had to be back by 11pm on Saturdays, 10.30pm on Sundays, which must have seriously restricted any social life.

A total of 96 rooms were lost through the bombing in 1940. Fr Cronin remembered:

> We dug a shelter in the grounds, just under the trees on the far side of the lawn, and we used the ground floor underneath the Waldegrave Drawing Room as a sleeping area.
>
> Without a doubt I would say that these war years, with the catacombs under the Drawing Room, was the time that I enjoyed most during my period at Strawberry Hill. The men came that much younger to College—17 years and 3 months; they were already engaged in para-military training, in the Home Guard and the RAF. They left us rather early: examinations hardly mattered. We were constantly interrupted by air-raids—even during examinations. There was a type of enjoyment that we experienced at that time, which I have never experienced since. We really did not have any problems—except the problem of surviving and getting enough to eat.[88]

A University of London Air Squadron was initiated at St Mary's. Tom Carter recalled "The College was our base and cadets from Borough Road were part of our squadron. We had a CO whose name was Fl. Lt Geoghan (he was later killed in action) and a Flight Sergeant Wireless Operator-Air Gunner, plus LAC Tye. Flight Lt Alec Calvert enjoyed the role of Drill Sergeant trying desperately to find volunteers for a demonstration squad."[89]

A detachment of the Home Guard was also established at St Mary's. Initially, this seems to have been perceived as a rival to the Air Squadron, but it soon attracted recruits and, according to *The Simmarian* "lent a military touch to the lawn as it paraded on Wednesdays and Saturdays".[90]

College traditions continued with "Table shouts" at meals: One of them focused specifically on the longing of the (mostly northern) students to get home—and away from dreary College food and restrictions. "On the passing of every ten days a bread board would strike the table thrice, a prolonged *shhss* would issue from the occupants and as the ref fell silent a shout of '909 days' or whatever was applicable, to the Vac. 'Any more for the North?' The whole body would respond 'E.U.R.'." (Was this "Here you are" or a sort of exaggerated Northern "Eeee, you are"?) "The other regular shout would be usually on a Saturday lunch time prior to the College teams going forth to defend the honour of the College in various codes. The shout would call for success to all the teams and the unison response would be 'Second that!' "[91]

There were now a number of local groups of former Simmarians around Britain, and these worked hard to maintain contact during the war years. The Merseyside group established a *War Bulletin*, typed out and circulated by carbon copies—paper rationing was now in force and a printed newsletter was not possible. The *Bulletin* has the same hearty, slightly ironic tone that marks the student memories: the bleak food and strict regime at St Mary's evidently prepared men well for war service, and even news from men who were prisoners of war had a light treatment.

> B. J. Robinson is a posh lad—he's a 2nd Lieutenant. What'll he do with all the money he earns? Buy saving stamps of course!" (Bulletin 9th Nov 1941)
>
> Jim Doyle is in Egypt. He and Tom Kelly are signallers together. They have become experts in Night Ops—bugs and ants. Any more for the Mediterranean Cruise? What, no takers?" (16th Nov 1941)
>
> Larry Kavanagh is in Stalag 4B [ie prisoner-of-war]. I wonder if he would prefer Jimmy Quinns. Don't ask soft questions. (7th Dec 1941)
>
> Jim Geraghty RAF has spent more time on his knees than he did in Coll. His job is polishing floors. He'll make a great husband. (14th Dec 1941)

The editor was W. F. "Bill" Cogley, who ran the *Bulletin* from his home at 34 Woodville Avenue, Liverpool 23. The ultra-cheery tone masks what was evidently very dedicated work. The Merseyside Simmarian Club sent a small Christmas gift to every member serving in the Forces. And among the news items were solemn ones, reporting the deaths of men in action. As 1942 opened, the Bulletin reported death of a former Merseyside Simmarian Club President—and chairman of its football and cricket teams—Hugh "Sandy" Shennan. In all, a total of 71 Simmarians fell in World War II: long columns of names on the War Memorial in the present University chapel. The names, along with those from the First World War, are recalled each November when a Remembrance Service is held on the square outside the chapel.

The College continued to have its usual clubs and activities: the *Simmarian* magazine for June 1940 lists the Altar Society (caring for the chapel, preparing for Mass etc) the Literary and Debating Society, Historical Society, Gaelic Circle, Billiards Society and Photographic Society, as well as clubs for rugger, soccer, hockey, swimming, tennis, badminton, cross-country running, and athletics.

In 1941 Fr McCarthy was succeeded as Principal by Father Gerald Shannon. He had already been on the staff for a number of years and would serve as Principal until 1948. Other Vincentian priests on the staff were Fr John Hurley, Fr Calahan, Fr Kevin Cronin, and Fr T. Downing. They continued to live, as the Vincentian priests had done throughout the 1930s, in the Walpole mansion, which remained mainly for their use although the Gallery served as an Art Room for the students, who also used the Waldegrave rooms, one of which had become the college Library.

Throughout the war years, windows had to be covered by black-out curtains in case any light helped enemy aircraft intent on bombing. St Mary's, like every other institution, appointed its own teams to look out for fire-bombs and to check that the black-out was observed. This last seems to have been an unpopular task: The *Simmarian* magazine (June 1941, page 9) observed "Another interesting post which has arisen is the Black Out Nark, a typical wartime product. His duty is to see that the College is properly blacked-out and to receive reproach, opprobrium and even savage invective."

Roll of Honour 1939–1945

Robert Abbott	1933–1935	Patrick Lavin	1929–1931
John Ambler	1933–1936	Harold Leigh	1931–1933
Robert Anderson	1935–1937	William Mallen	1931–1933
James Bannon	1938–1940	Joseph McArdle	1931–1932
Francis Brindley	1940–1942	William McCormack	1934–1937
Robert Carroll	1936–1939	Thomas McDonough	1936–1939
John Chisholm	1930–1932	Joseph McEvoy	1932–1934
William Cleary	1940–1942	Edward McGlone	1928–1930
Thomas Collins	1937–1939	Alphonsus McGlynn	1929–1931
Francis Connolly	1940–1941	John McGough	1936–1938
Cornelius Cronin	1930–1933	Francis McKeown	1931–1934
Thomas Cross	1934–1936	William McMahon	1939–1940
Henry Daly	1939–1941	Thomas Melia	1932–1934
George Dawson	1934–1936	Francis Nevin	1938–1940
Terence Donovan	1933–1935	John Nugent	1933–1935
Bernard Dorn	1932–1935	James Nyland	1939–1941
Patrick Duggan	1933–1935	Anthony O'Brien	1940–1942
Francis Easton	1932–1934	Thomas O'Shaughnessy	1932–1934
Kenneth Edwards	1936–1938	Edward Penlington	1939–1940
Joseph Egan	1935–1937	John Quigley	1937–1939
Frederick Fineron	1932–1934	Jean Rabet	1931–1933
George Finlay	1939–1940	Roland Riddehough	1941–1942
Charles Fleming	1934–1936	Thomas Ronchetti	1936–1938
Vincent Flynne	1935–1938	Peter Sands	1940–1942
Matthew Fox	1935–1937	Raymond Shellard	1935–1937
Edwin Furlong	1939–1941	Bernard Sheriff	1938–1940
Charles Gallagher	1931–1933	Charles Smith	1934–1936
Francis Garrick	1934–1936	Francis Smith	1939–1940
Thomas Gleeson	1938–1940	John Tanner	1938–1940
William Goodyer	1931–1933	James Timmons	1935–1937
James Goulding	1936–1939	Thomas Timney	1933–1935
Henryk Grynkiewicz	1936–1939	John Walsh	1932–1935
Ignatius Hand	1935–1937	John Ward	1937–1940
George Howard	1926–1929	Henry Wharton	1931–1933
Frank Hutchinson	1938–1940	David Whelan	1937–1939
Henry Kershaw	1930–1933	John Whelan	1932–1934

The University Air Squadron (No 3 Squadron University of London Air Service), already mentioned, played a big part in daily College life. Flight Lieutenant Geoghan was succeeded by Flt Lieutenant Luff as Commanding Officer and the *Simmarian* magazine noted that "Under his Command the squadron has flourished during the year and is now an integral part of Simmarian life."[92]

And there were visits from former students serving in the Forces: "Throughout the year we have had many visits from Simmarians in HM Forces, all looking fit and well as they came into the ref[ectory] and experienced the ordeal and honour of being greeted with "Two More for the Pawst". Those we have seen and the many more we have heard about are to be found in all branches of the services and are scattered in many quarters and battle-fronts."

Every month, two special Masses were celebrated in the College chapel: one for former students serving in the Forces, and another a requiem Mass for those who had died, news of which reached the College through their families and via the various local Simmarian clubs and newsletters.

Following the Blitz of 1940/41 and the abandonment of German invasion plans, it was not until 1944 that St Mary's was once again under direct attack, when London was hit by a fresh wave of bombing. A former student would later recall some

> short but noisy attacks. They were of such a nature that that we were roused from our beds and had to make our way to underground shelters in the wooded area behind the lawns and the soccer pitch. In order to facilitate a speedy but disciplined entry to these shelters, each shelter was numbered and each student was allocated a numbered shelter. A student was designated to get to each subterranean entrance as soon as the warning was given and then call out into the night the shelter's number. Quite often the good order disintegrated massive anti-aircraft barrages exploded overhead and rained murderous shrapnel…
> Then doodlebugs [flying bombs] and the students were sent home. The Seniors stayed for they were into their Finals. I believe that General Absolution was given to them that they might be better prepared for a more searching exam should that occur.[93]

Sport continued to be central to Simmarian life, both for students at the College and for former students whose reunions through local groups usually centred on sporting fixtures. The war put a temporary halt to many official sporting events: priority went to troop movements and necessary transport of goods and serves rather than to people travelling to leisure activities, however important. Thus for colleges, the major sporting event of the year, competing for the shield at Inter-Collegiate College athletics championships, was put in abeyance "for the duration". Competitions were still held—and St Mary's continued to excel—but with leading athletes away in the Forces, and a general sense that wartime solidarity precluded other loyalties, the passionate rivalry with Borough Road seems to have been, at least officially, put aside.

While the main focus of the war was in Africa, the Merseyside Simmarian Club's *Bulletin* jostled news of members fighting there, and on duty at home, with wry comments about wartime shortages and the way in which life at St Mary's had helped to train people for these.

Jack Macaulay reports that he had a smashing leave, met many of the lads and returned to do guard duty on Downing Street. Here he saw the PM and nearly followed him for the end of his cigar. Simmarian habits stick all right, don't they? (25th Jan 1942)

Tom Kelly is a signaller attached to an Armoured Brigade in Libya. Actually, he is in the thick of the fighting. Here's hoping he gives Rommel what for. (1st March 1942).

But people were also already thinking about the future and the sort of Britain that would emerge from the war. Discussion about education still reflected old tensions about the role of Church-based schools and colleges. Bill Cogley mused in his *Bulletin* (6th June 1943) about the contradiction in the minds of people who 'are prepared to send our young men far away to die for the rights of minorities' while apparently unconcerned about the rights of minorities—by which he essentially meant Catholics—at home.

This last referred to the debates emerging about the funding of Catholic and Church of England schools and colleges. The National Union of Teachers was opposed to such funding, and a rival National Association of Schoolmasters had been established which was more sympathetic to voluntary schools—but now this seemed to be changing its attitude too.

The Post-war years

Meanwhile, as the war ended, a new intake of students arrived at Strawberry Hill. During the war years, students had come straight from school, aged 17—but this new intake was rather different. It consisted of men who had served in the Forces and were now returning to take up careers in civilian life. They would be responsible for significant changes. Former pupil G. X. Sullivan would later recall:

In 1946 my year was the last to come straight from Grammar School to College. I was 17 when I started and of course at that age we students knew it all. We duly went through the initiation procedure meted out to the "Junior" year. We were harangued by the Fuzz leader, we were taught the chants and the Coll chorus, we had to write down and learn the songs, we had to perform the antics, obey our "elders" and suffer the programs. We didn't enjoy it, but it was part of the way of life at Simmaries and without it we would not have been Simmarians. It did have the effect of moulding us into a body, as does any form of group persecution. We went on to win all before us on the sports field, and eventually to hand on all the traditions. We elected our Fuzz leader, prefects and house secretary.

The day came when we were seniors. We knew we had one disadvantage in that there was an imbalance in the two years in college at any time: our year was about 80 students, the other about 110. But this numerical inferiority did not seem a problem. The problem we did not realise was, our "Juniors" were all ex-servicemen who had fought in the war and were several years older than any of us. However, we intended carrying on the traditions and that is what we did. We were told the practice must cease, but we could not see why—probably this had happened every year, we didn't know. The practice did not cease, and we were addressed by the Principal in Room 1. He told us that unless the perpetrators of the last incident owned up by 6pm and these traditional practices ceased, the entire year would be sent down. (A typical incident might be that the entire contents of some one's room might be removed—temporarily).

We "knew" that they couldn't send an entire year down.

At 6.00pm we re-assembled to call the Principal's bluff. He told us that after breakfast we had to leave college with our cases packed! We talked of marching to Westminster Cathedral to see the Cardinal. After all, we were the only Catholic Teacher Training College for men in England!

At first, as we travelled in groups to Cardiff, Lancashire, Yorkshire, the NE, the spirits were still kept up, but as we travelled to our own homes and towns we knew we had to face the music at home on our own. There was no one when I got home. Security wasn't a big thing in those days, and I soon got into my house. There I waited for my mother (my father had died in the war).

Two months at home was a blessing in disguise. I had a geography and a PE thesis to write … Early in December I received a letter from a fellow student saying if I wrote to the Principal and said I'd be a good boy I'd be allowed to return. This I did and I was.

Thus died the initiation rites that had been followed throughout the 1920s and 30s. The College would continue to have a strong sense of tradition and identity, but the post-war mood was distinctly different.

The ending of the initiation rites caused resentment among traditionalists, and was also seen by some as being a matter of injustice on the part of a College in the south of England towards Northerners. Tom Sharp, writing about his family's four-generation link with St Mary's fifty years later, would recall:

My younger brother Gerald entered Strawberry Hill in 1946 and I became his junior when entering with all other ex-servicemen in 1947. The then Principal Dr Shannon used this unique period to wipe out all the ritual and initiation ceremonies which united both years of the student body. The tripartite rift which ensured between the Principal and the 46 and 47 years caused the "sending down" of all the 1946 students for a whole term.

Ever since the birth of Simmaries there has always been a large student intake from the Liverpool/Lancashire area and the Newcastle/Durham /Northumberland area. Simmarians in all these areas were fuming and very angry that Dr Shannon had carried out his threat and sent delegations to College to protest. The Dr was undeterred and only allowed the student year to return on written promises by parents. Needless to say, Dr Shannon was replaced in 1948 by Rev Fr Cronin, a quiet and understanding priest who was indeed a friend to all.[94]

It seems unlikely that Dr Shannon's ending of the ritual humiliations was the reason for his retirement: he was a popular and effective principal and his successor continued the pattern of change.

The *St Mary's College Centenary Record* explains:

In 1947 there was a large influx of ex-servicemen into the College, and in 1948 the great majority of the students were of this class. New arrangements in the life of the College were made in view of the maturity and experience of these students. Many of the rules were relaxed, attendance at daily Mass was not insisted upon, and students were allowed to make use of their time for study outside of class according to their own discretion. Many of these students were married men, and Simmarians soon got used to the presence of wives and babies on the touch-line at College games.[95]

A College Union—later called the Students' Union—was established, its Constitution stating that its aim was "to foster in every way possible the interests of the College and of its students as members of a Catholic Training College … and to foster in every way the Catholic and professional purposes of the College."[96]

Changes were also happening on a wider front. In June of that year, an important meeting of the Governors was held in London, at 15 Baker Street, Piccadilly. It was formally agreed that an application should be made to the University of London for St Mary's to be admitted as a constituent college of the University.

This marked a definite change in direction for the College—a sign at once of its maturity as it approached its centenary, and a recognition of the realities of the education scene in Britain in the mid-20th century. The application to the University was accepted, for an initial period of three years. St Mary's was to be part of a new Institute of Education, and this was inaugurated in style with a ceremony at the University on December 19th 1949, with the band of the Grenadier Guards in attendance. Fr Twomey represented St Mary's at this event.

Along with the rejoicing and the sense of a landmark having been reached, there were signs indicating a new direction for the future. The University had regularly carried out visitations to the College and these invariably resulted in a glowing report. The visitation in November 1949 carried the usually warmly complimentary remarks about the College's work: "The college initiates its students into a dignified and well conceived way of life, preparing them effectively, especially from the academic point of view, for their professional life as teachers." But the report also raised something new:

> Most of us are not convinced that the staff are allowed to play all the part they might do in the selection of students for entry. Little reliance seemed to be placed upon Interviewing Panels for the admission of students, the Principal in most cases doing the selection himself, making use in a small proportion of cases of deputies (eg the Vice Principal)…[97]

This concern about the lack of involvement of the staff was held within the College itself. In 1949 the staff consisted to the Principal, bursar, dean, five lecturers and ten full-time and four part-time staff. There were 270 students. In March of that year the lay staff petitioned for the appointment of a lay vice-principal. Their request, noted in a Memorandum produced by the Principal, urged that:

> it would improve the status of the lay lecturers as a whole…
> It would be more in accordance with the custom obtaining in other men's training colleges
> It would be a tangible recognition of the devoted service given by lay staff, and would be an extra incentive to such service
> As the Vice-Principalship carries with an extra emolument of from £50 to £150 per annum, it would have an appreciable effect upon the pension claims of those Lecturers who had occupied the post.

The Memorandum reports that the Principal "summoned" (interesting choice of word!) the six senior lecturers to discuss the proposal with him and "drew their attention" to the following:

1. 'The 1899 agreement, according to which the administration of the College must be in the hands of the Vincentian Congregation, precludes such an innovation.

2. While during the past fifty years the College had been administered by a succession of Vincentian Principals, it would be more true to say that it had in fact been directed by the Vincentian community as whole. This Community had an educational tradition peculiar to itself, which was the reason why it had been entrusted by the Governors with the running of the College in the first instance. The introduction of a lay Vice-Principal would, therefore, effect a radical alteration in the distinctive character of the College and its management.

3. None of the lay lecturers was resident in the College, whereas all the priests resided there.

Dr Cronin clearly, however, recognised the justice of the request that had been made, and announced the that from henceforth the College would have two vice-principals:

> The priest would function, as hitherto, as the Principal's Deputy in all matters connected with the administration. The lay Lecturer would be in charge, under the Principal, of academic and tutorial affairs. This would necessitate no fundamental alteration in the Instrument of Government of the College. It would have this advantage, among others, of providing a director of the Tutorial system of internal studies, which had greatly extended in recent years, in accordance with the directions of the Ministry. It was besides understood that the arrangement should involve no addition to the salary bill, as the combined emoluments of the two Vice-Principals should not exceed that of a single Vice-Principal in a College such as ours.[98]

This was perhaps the first indication of a slow—and later rather fast—change of style at St Mary's, in which the strong role of the Principal would give way to a broader style of management. Eventually, following the tumultuous years of the 1960s, much larger questions would be raised—with campaigns among the students themselves demanding to be consulted, and with a whole new approach to the whole idea of how a Catholic College could and should be run.

Meanwhile, the change of style was evident in many ways. A report in 1950 noted that "Father Cronin has given every encouragement to the College Union, and under his guidance it continues to function smoothly to the satisfaction of all concerned. The lay staff now take lunch with the priests and students from Monday to Friday each week of term."[99] The food had also improved. Clearly the days of caterpillars in the cabbage and a stern Dean supervising all meals were in the past.

And there was the matter of rebuilding the College following wartime damage. "Restoration was necessary, and this took place with the rebuilding pf the New Wing which began in 1948" Fr Cronin would later recall "It occurred to many of us that, as we were rebuilding the students' accommodation, we could just as easily add another storey—so the 'Queen Mary' [the green-coloured vaguely nautical rooftop rooms on the New Wing] was added. This building was ready for our centenary in 1950 and it was one of our showpieces.

> We were fortunate in getting as our architect Sir Albert Richardson in 1946. The architect for the old building had been Sebastian Pugin Powell, a grand-nephew of the

old Pugin, who had built the Houses of Parliament, and who had been responsible for the Victorian Gothic revival. In 1946 Sir Albert had been Professor of Architecture in the University of London, and had just retired and started a small firm. The governors of the College, who included two University governors, were very interested in him … Sir Albert was an extraordinary man, he exuded personality, he was full of good nature, he was passionately dedicated to the cause of architecture …[100]

The new chapel was—and is—the dominant building on the St Mary's site, soaring up over the campus, with steps sweeping up to its doors. Its main windows were designed by Gabriel Loire and made in his studio at Chartres. The style of the whole building emphasises light and space. Some items from the old chapel—an altar table, and some sanctuary furniture, were given a place in the crypt, and the old chapel's stained glass filled the windows of the stairs leading from the crypt to the main chapel. Beneath the chapel the architect created the college library. This would later be expanded with a further building alongside.

In this post-war reconstruction, the opportunity was taken to deal with some overdue repairs and maintenance to the original Walpole mansion. The College authorities seem to have become, rather belatedly, aware that the mansion's use for accommodation—all the priests lived there, and the Gallery was also used as an art studio for the students—had meant sacrificing its importance as a building of historic significance. It had been allowed to decay, and Sir Albert insisted that repairs were carried out. There had also been considerable damage inflicted by the fire hoses during the wartime bombing. Sir Horace Walpole's unique gothic gem was in danger of being lost to the nation, and repair work was urgently needed. A grant from the Ministry of Works enabled this to be done, with £40,000 being spent over ten years, beginning with some emergency work on the roof.

The old gothic mansion, and the adjoining Waldegrave Suite which links it the modern buildings, thus came back into use after the neglect of the war years. GX Sullivan—whose exploits with Simmarian traditions we have already described—had an extraordinary experience at this time:

> One evening in October 1946 a fellow student and I were alone reading in the Library (as it then was). This is the Waldegrave Drawing room. In the silence we heard a noise coming from the tower side of the end wall of the Library. Eventually, we decided to investigate, and although it was out of bounds we went down the corridor towards the tower. In the small ante-room there is a door opening onto the iron staircase to the lawn— this door was closed. There was no sound to explain our original query but in the dark silence of that October evening, suddenly a door in the corridor around the Tower opened, a shaft of light shone through and the door closed leaving darkness again; but immediately the iron stair door opened and then closed, just as though some one had walked through both doors and down to the lawn. We turned and fled down the corridor back tour rooms. We didn't return until daylight next day. Everything was quite normal.[101]

The mood in the immediate postwar years at St Mary's was a mix of "settling back" into the normality of College life after disruption, and a confident sense of moving forward: the plans for the new chapel and the Queen Mary wing symbolising the latter. Becoming a constituent College of the new Institute of Education at London University marked an important step, and was a sign of further developments to come. St Mary's needed to grow—demand for teachers was high following the 1944 Education Act, and Catholic schools were thriving and popular.

At St Mary's, the sense of continuity was strong, and was connected to the strong sense of identity held by Catholics in Britain generally. Tom Marsh, already quoted, was proud of the fact that his grandfather and father were both at the Hammersmith college, the latter becoming College organist—he himself sang in the choir at Strawberry Hill in the 1940s and found sheet music with his father's name on it.[102]

Sport remained central to the College ethos. Gerry Creagh, who was at St Mary's from 1948–1950 remembers the victory of the Irish rugby team: "The year before, Ireland had won the Triple Crown in Belfast so we wanted them to win again. Huge numbers of the students and staff at St Mary's at that time were Irish. We all went to the Rugby ground at Twickenham—it cost a shilling for the 'dug-out' places—and Ireland won 19-nil. Of course we all celebrated, down at The Fox pub. The next day at Mass Father Twomey announced 'Today is the first Sunday after Twickenham.'"[103]

The Catholic Church in Britain was flourishing—substantial numbers at Mass, a steady annual rise in baptisms, marriages, and ordinations. A year of celebratory events took place in 1950 to mark the centenary of the restoration of the Hierarchy—and of course at St Mary's the year also marked the College's own centenary.

The local newspaper, the *Richmond the Twickenham Times* reported the centenary celebrations, which centred on a grand opening of a new accommodation block for students. Although the mood was celebratory, the Cardinal Archbishop had a rather grim message, perhaps reflecting the fears induced by the Cold War and the oppression of the Church by the Communist authorities then consolidating their grip across Eastern Europe::

> The centenary of St Mary's College Strawberry Hill, the Roman Catholic training college for men teachers, was celebrated on Wednesday June 1 when Cardinal Griffin, Archbishop of Westminster, blessed and opened a new students' wing.
> Cardinal Griffin said that "We are all fighting a battle for freedom against the possible usurpation of the rights of the Church and of the parents by the State". He described the Education Act 1944 as a hotch-potch which, as far as denominations went, only dealt with children actually in school. It took no account he said of the new generation which had arisen since the War ...
> After Pontifical High Mass, Cardinal Griffin presided at a luncheon at which the Minister of Education, Mr George Tomlinson MP was a guest of honour.
> The new students wing which came into use immediately after the opening ceremony, contains a students' common room and 70 study-bedrooms. It replaces an extension opened by the late Cardinal Bourne in 1930 and damaged during the war by enemy action.[104]

In fact the 1944 Education Act would prove to work well for Catholic schools, allowing for generous funding while giving the Church free rein over the curriculum. The next years would be a time of confidence in the Catholic community in Britain, and the mood at St Mary's reflected this.

In 1954 Horace Walpole's Chapel in the Woods was refurbished to become a shrine to Our Lady of Strawberry Hill, with a statue of Mary designed to show her as a teacher. Simmarians from Northern Ireland raised funds for this. The chapel's original stained glass was removed and found a new home in a church at Bexhill in Sussex. A new stained glass by Harry Clarke was commissioned, together with a statue, and the shrine was formally dedicated to mark 1954 as a Marian Year, as declared by Pope Pius XII.

Students who came to St Mary's in the 1950s found a College that relished its status in the Catholic community: to be a Simmarian was a badge of honour and many past students were now headmasters or long-serving and dedicated teachers at successful schools. The rebuilding following the war had emphasised continuity rather than change, and the College's fine setting near the river and with beautiful grounds was a matter for pride: it was the most notable institution in the area.

During these years St Mary's remained, of course, a men's college—but there were some women students.

Fionuala Fenlon was 20 and just completing a two year course, (1956–58) leading to a qualification in teaching, at St Paul's College, Newbold Revel, when she heard of a new programme at St Mary's. This course had been devised by Fr Patrick Dunning. The aim was to prepare teachers for the education of Catholic children in a changing post-war world. Students on the course had already qualified as teachers. Some came straight from their teacher training colleges, others had some years of teaching experience. Most of the men on the course had experienced National Service and were older than most of the women. Men were in the majority. Fionuala would later remember that the women sat in the front row of the small lecture room, while the men sat together, at the back. There was a dedicated women's student common room, where afternoon tea was served at 4 o'clock. The women students were accommodated off-site, with a local landlady. All tuition and boarding costs were met— part of the state provision for the post-war bulge in pupil numbers.

After the prescriptive timetable of her teacher training college, Fionuala was amazed at the freedom offered at St Mary's in timetable and syllabus content. One example: tea had been served in the women's junior common room, but only she and one other young woman had appeared. They were perturbed by the absence of their fellow students, and so they "covered" their absence by dirtying the cups and plates. They feared that absence would bring retribution, as it would have done at their previous college.

Women's training colleges at this time often replicated the regime of a boarding school (and anyone below 21 was still legally a minor.) St Mary's syllabus was another area of new discovery for the women: scriptural studies which showed the Old Testament as a precursor to the New, an emphasis on Catholic social teaching as revealed in the encyclical *Rerum Novarum*, fresh insights into the liturgy.

Fionuala long cherished a particular memory of Fr Dunning. One evening, a group of the women students had returned, after class, and were playing music in one of the lecture rooms. While they played and sang along to songs from "My Fair Lady" and "South Pacific," Fr Dunning was above in his study. He came down to discover the source of the disturbance. However, instead of issuing the expected rebuke, following his appearance in the doorway, he sat down to discuss different sorts of music.[105]

In the summer of 1959 the work on Strawberry Hill House—repairing wartime damage and doing other necessary restoration—had finally been completed, and a celebration "Evening at Strawberry Hill" was held for special guests on June 3rd. The commemorative programme for the event noted that "The recent re-building of Walpole's Little Cloister at the main entrance, together with the re-decoration of the Waldegrave Drawing Room, have brought the work to a point which, it was felt, afforded an occasion for inviting some of the many friends of the College to see what has been done". Sir Albert Richardson spoke about his work, and guests were able to look around the mansion, after which there was a lecture on the life of Lady Waldegrave by a local author, Osbert Wyndham Hewett. [106]

The 1960s

There was a sense that changes were on the way as the 1960s opened. Notes from a meeting of the Academic Board give a flavour of the decade to come:

> Appearance and attitude of students: Mr Hopper said he has recently noticed a lack of courtesy among students. Gone are the days when they saluted him: now they look through him or past him. On a recent occasion he thought the multicoloured clothes of College athletes unbecoming. He has spoken his mind to some offenders. Mr Kane deplored the popularity of jeans, carpet slippers and open-necked shirts.
> The Principal said that much is done to impress upon students the importance of good behaviour. Our students are not seriously ill-mannered outside the College. Their behaviour in college is a matter for himself and Dr Dunning. He has already spoken to the Committee of Management about excessive ebullience at the College sports. Dr Dunning expressed surprise at the complaint and said that on several occasions he had been complimented on the good behaviour of the students.[107]

But the general mood of the College was still very conservative. A student handbook from the early 1960s has a solemn tone:

> St Mary's is a Catholic Training College: its fundamental purpose is to serve the Catholic Schools by the production of good Catholic teachers, and all its activities are directed towards this end, Students at St Mary's shall bear in mind always the lofty character of the career for which they are training and shall order their lives in the light of the high religious and professional ideals which that career implies. Catholic teachers are responsible before God for the spiritual and temporal wellbeing of the children who are committed to their care. The duty of students in College is so to advance themselves in grace and wisdom, in religious zeal and professional efficiency, that they may become leaders of the Catholic schools in their all-important work for Faith and country.[108]

The Simmarian, February 1962 notes the regulation that students must be in their rooms by 11pm on weekdays, midnight on Saturdays, although there was no longer a "lights out" rule and they were permitted to visit one another's rooms and talk.

Attendance at Mass on Sundays and Holydays of Obligation was compulsory— post-war changes had established that weekday Mass and/or Benediction was now optional. On major feasts, students had to attend the main High Mass—on other Sundays, they could opt for an earlier Mass which would leave the rest of the day free. They were also expected to take part in an annual spiritual retreat. Everyday life also operated within strict rules:

> Attendance at lectures is compulsory. If a student be absent from any Lecture, the Lecturer should be notified without delay. No change shall be made in the approved course of any student unless there shall have been prior consultation with the Lecturers concerned and the appropriate Tutor ... punctuality is required of students at all times

... Permission for absence from College must be sought at all times and students absent from College must give their temporary addresses.

The kitchen quarters, domestic quarters, staff common room and staff residence must be considered as out of bounds to students. The portion of the Lawn which lies in front of the Waldegrave Room and Walpole House has been regarded traditionally as reserved to members of staff.[109]

And a note about the Students Union sets a tone which would sit oddly with the student events of the late 1960s: "The Union shall be under the patronage of Our Lady Seat of Wisdom. Its meetings shall open with the prayer 'Under Thy Protection' and with the invocation 'Seat of Wisdom, pray for us.'"[110]

The Academic staff in the early 1960s were as follows:

Principal Very Rev K. P. Cronin
Vice Principals Rev P. J. Dunning (also head of history)
WA Maguire Esq who also taught geography)
Bursar Rev E. Sweeney
Chaplain Rev D. P. Cleere
Student Activities Moderator Rev L. O'Dea

Latin was taught by Fr C. McGowan, Handcrafts by Mr W. F. Beardmore, Music Mr J. P. Rush, Physics Mr B. J. Hopper, Philosophy Rev F. V. Morris, English Rev M. P. Ryan, Maths Mr A. G. Vosper, French Mr D. J. Bahatchet, Chemistry Mr P. A. Duffy, Biology Mr W. J. Fyfc, Art Mr R. H. I. de Castelnau-Bucher.

The students had a wide range of sports clubs—from Rugby and soccer to canoeing, fencing, volleyball, swimming and judo. There were also clubs for those interested in drama, country dancing, mountaineering, film, photography, art, folk song, and more. There were French and Hispanic clubs, a Legion of Mary, and even a Scout club.

In 1960 Fr Cronin was honoured for his services to education by being created CBE—a Commander of the British Empire. He went to Buckingham Palace to receive the honour in frock-coat and black top hat. It was a sign that St Mary's, and Catholic education in general, had definitely come of age—the years when Catholics were regarded as suspect or were marginal to the life of the nation were over. The next years were to see developments that would affect both Church and nation in new ways.

Kevin Cook, who was a student at St Mary's from 1962–65 remembers this period as one of social change combined with a sense of tradition:

Most students came straight from school and didn't have 'A' levels. The normal thing was to study geography and PE (Physical Education) and get a certificate which qualified you to teach in a Catholic school. But you could also take a different course and get a degree—studying as an external student at London University.

Physical Education included studying the human body and how it worked, and students went to Kings College Hospital to examine leg and arm muscles, using the bodies in the mortuary. Cheerier visits were the regular Friday trips to the sports centre at Crystal Palace for swimming and tennis, learning how to coach these sports.

We still all ate together for meals. There were Halls of Residence for students and for the first year at College a place at one of them was offered. After that, you had to look for local accommodation. But if you volunteered to be on the Committee of Management for one of the Halls that got you a place there. I remember that every Sunday members of the Committee would walk across to the Mansion to have a glass of sherry with Father Cronin—that was all part of his way of keeping in touch with the students.

Fr Cronin was keen on buying pictures for the College—I think as an investment. Lionel Peres, one of the students on the Committee of Management, volunteered to drive him around to art galleries to make these purchases, often of modern art: one was Graham Sutherland's "Green Toad".

A considerable body of the students came from Ireland, and there was often a ceildh on Saturday or Sunday nights: girls would come from Assumpta and from Digby Stuart, the two nearest Catholic colleges for women. A lot of marriages started that way and fifty years later were still going strong with Golden Wedding invitations being sent around …[111]

He had an experience in the Waldegrave Suite that echoed that of the students back in 1946, already noted. "Part of my job as a Committee member was to check the lights, and when I went in to the Billiard Room, the billiard balls were rolling across the table, but there was no one there."[112]

Work was progressing on the large new college chapel during these years. The old chapel had become much too small and was packed to discomfort on Sundays. It later became the students' bar and, later again, part of the drama department: it is still (2019) in use by the latter.

A legend developed about the funding of the new chapel: it was said that Fr Cronin had been unable to get Government funding for the project as it was deemed to be of specifically religious rather than educational value. So he applied instead successfully for funding for a library, which in due course became the foundations of the chapel, with steps sweeping up to the impressive doors.

The new chapel was formally opened on 8th December 1963—the College feast day— by Archbishop George Beck of Liverpool. He had played a major role in Catholic education for the preceding two decades, as the 1944 Education Act was implemented.

The opening of the chapel was marked with great celebrations. Joseph Frederick Scott, who had been a student at St Mary's, and later returned to teach mathematics there, eventually becoming vice-principal, was appointed a Knight of St Gregory in a ceremony presided over by Archbishop Beck. Scott had become known as an expert on the history of mathematics on which he wrote extensively. In the evening there was a formal dinner— shrimp cocktail, tomato soup, roast turkey with Brussels sprouts, Christmas pudding, and mince pies, all formally described in French on the menu card—with speeches by the Archbishop, the Mayor of Twickenham Alderman A. Denham JP, and Fr Cronin.[113]

In the early 1960s the College Literary Society launched its own magazine, *Cresset* with essays, poetry and short stories on a variety of topics. Run entirely by volunteers, its success seems to have taken its founders by surprise, writing about the "sparkling success of the first issue of the magazine: We can only report that, largely owing to popularity, it encouraged a flood of creative writing inside the College, thus enabling us to increase by half the amount of material included". [114]

The team were evidently good businessmen too—the magazine carried a number of advertisments from local shops and restaurants, and these give a flavour of the Twickenham of the period:

> Page and Taylor 'Twickenham's Family Store' Highest value men's and boys' outfitting, school wear overalls, fancy linens, materials, dress fabrics, hose.
>
> Rawalpindi Grill 62 King Street (opposite Odeon). Lunch at 4/11 in English and Continental Dishes. Our speciality Chicken Mussala, Persian Dishes and Kobab. (comment: is this was today would be called Kebab?)
>
> Smith tailor, 158 Waldegrave Road Teddington. Evening Dress Hire Service. Your own materials made up. Suits made to measure from £16.16/0.
>
> For the most comprehensive stocks of High Class Modern, Antique and Reproduction FURNITURE go to Phelps Ltd. Linoleums and Underlays—curtain runway and all ACCESSORIES: new and secondhand bedsteads—divans—bedding—carpets and underfelts. Your old furniture accepted in part exchange.
>
> Morris (Colin Farrow) THE man's shop of Twickenham 6 Heath Road. The latest trends in Fashion Casual or Formal for the Man of the Moment.

Pubs and restaurants included the Waldegrave Arms ("The Waldy") and The Anglers which announced itself as a "favourite Simmarian restaurant. Peggy and Harry will welcome you to their friendly atmosphere—Simmaries Riverside Haunt."

The 1960s, a decade synonymous with change, were now getting under way. Changes at St Mary's during this time centred on two things. The first was the postwar expansion in education, bringing with it the decision to admit more students to the College and widen its scope, and the second was the wave of social change that swept all of Britain and the Western world in the second half of the decade.

In the 1950s the need for more places at teacher-training colleges had brought an obvious suggestion: why not expand St Mary's and open it to women students as well as to men? Fr Cronin the Principal made an extended visit to the USA where there were a number of Colleges open to both men and women, returned after a three-month stay with a favourable report, and the decision was made: St Mary's would "go mixed". Fr Cronin would later take up the story:

> In 1963 we were able to undertake this development, as the second stage of our major expansion was being planned. The first stage had brought our number from 400 to about 700. In 1963 we were asked to expand to 1,000 students. We planned, therefore, that the additional 300 students should be women students, and that something like one-third of our students in future should be women.[115]

The first women students arrived in 1966. A new residential block for women was built for them, named Clive Hall, after the 18th century actress Kitty Clive who lived at Strawberry Hill. She was a rather good role model for modern Catholic women: a Catholic, a successful actress, and a campaigner for fair rates of pay for those working on the stage. She became a friend of Horace Walpole, who gave her a house on his estate.

Through the 1960s the numbers of women students at St Mary's steadily grew. Further hostels for them were established in Waldegrave Park, and one in East Twickenham, run by a group of religious sisters, the Daughters of Mary Immaculate.

Fr Cronin wrote reflectively to former students, as the women students were settling into their second term:[116]

> Whenever I have met pastmen in the past few months, I am certain that the second sentence will be something like
>
> "Well Father, how's it going?"
>
> I don't even have to ask what 'it' is. I know it can only mean one thing—the much debated and now finally realised enterprise of introducing women into Simmaries ... Last September, the first women students arrived. It was, no doubt about it, a major change in the character of the College, and a break with tradition. The members of the College staff and student body who told us with various intonations of voice that 'the college would never be the same again' were quite right, but none of us could have expected that a change of such a radical nature would have been effected so easily and so smoothly. For a few days, the old-timers amongst us found it strange to walk along the corridors or around the playing-fields and to meet at every turn groups of girls talking, laughing, lounging about and generally acting as if they were at home in the place. The novelty lasted for perhaps forty-eight hours and then we took the entire thing for granted. It seemed the most natural thing in the world and of course it is.

He discussed how the young women were coping with it all:

> One characteristic is their extreme good sense. There are only 160 of them in a student body which this year topped the 1100 mark and they would have been pardoned if this had gone a little to their heads. They don't seem to have reacted like that at all. All the various officers of the College who have dealt with them have found them eminently reasonable and co-operative. Take the question of dress, for instance. From the beginning there was no regulation on this subject and while some of the staider members of our community are inclined to look askance at the crop of miniskirts that appeared in a short time, the overall position is best reflected in the special commendation expressed at a staff meeting at the end of the first term on the subject of the women's dress and, to use an old fashioned word, 'deportment'. They were commended for their good taste and sense of restraint in this matter.
>
> A second and perhaps surprising characteristic is that they genuinely feel Simmarians. They feel very proud of being members of this College. They accept wholeheartedly the traditions of the place. They are not, and again it is surprising that we can say this so soon, a body within a body...They understood clearly that they were the first women students in what had been traditionally a men's college and that it would not be easy for many of the older community to accept the change. They might have decided to combat the old diehards and enforce their rights to be recognised. Instead, they sympathised with the traditional feelings and tactfully eased themselves in without raising issues.

The fashion for adopting a sense of grievance or victimhood was clearly not in vogue among the pioneering women at Simmaries in 1966 and both they and the College as an institution seem to have profited very considerably from a cheerful and pragmatic approach, while still assuming the inevitability of change.

The women's arrival coincided with a general new style at St Mary's. The old disciplinary system, with a Dean who constantly watched the students at meals and other communual gatherings had been abandoned. The *Simmarian* in April 1967, under "College News" noted that the last Dean, Fr Eugene Sweeney had been appointed in 1944 but in due course his role "was no longer considered to be either necessary or appropriate to the modern situation" and he became Bursar. In 1965 he left to become Bursar at All Hallows College in Dublin.

Women now also became members of staff: the first four to be appointed were Miss Constance O'Hara, Mrs Lazell, Mrs Rathbone and Miss Margaret Hogan. The first three ran the various women's hostels: they had an active "housemother" role which in turn would be challenged over the next years as students voiced dislike of rules about visitors and other restrictions. Miss Hogan became Vice-Principal, with special responsibility for women students. This was an innovation: all senior posts at the College had until that time been held by clergy.

Other big changes included a hair-dressing salon, and also new dining arrangements: the old formal meals with set places and no possibility of any choice in the matter of food gave way to a cafeteria style, with students serving themselves from a range dishes and sitting where they wished. Student accommodation had also undergone a transformation "Students' bed-sitting rooms were quite simple box-like affairs until recently. The modern student's room is quite spacious by contrast and is far more attractive."[117]

Fr Cronin's comment about the women students quickly identifying with the College and becoming Simmarians is borne out by the memories of the women themselves. Mary Martin arrived in 1968, and after studying for a Teacher's Certificate stayed on to convert it into a degree : "We were the third intake of women students. It was great—we all truly loved it, there was a wonderful community feeling and it stayed with you. Wherever you went in the world, if you met some one who was also a Simmie, there was an immediate bond, immediate friendship:

> We lived in a hostel in Waldegrave Park, and Mrs Davies was the warden—she also taught art at the College. There were various rules about when boys could visit and we broke them of course, and so all visits were banned for a while.
> The hostels had been allocated to students alphabetically, and to this day some of my best friends all have names starting with M, because they date back to that time—we've all stayed in touch. Girls whose names started O and P were in the hostel next door.
> I think there was definitely a feeling, among parents, that St Mary's was a safe place. I know that my father wanted me to be at a small Catholic college rather than a big university. I was a shy, rather obedient sort of girl—I'd been Head Girl at school and so on.

It was of course long before the days of emails or mobile phones. Contact with home was by letter, collected from the Porter's Lodge, and by telephone from a line of phone boxes near the students' bar.

> On Sunday nights the chapel was packed—absolutely packed—for Mass, with music set to folk tunes. You had to get there early to get a seat.
> Friday nights were spent in the bar—that's where everyone gathered and where social life happened. It had been the chapel before the new one was built. We didn't really go out to London much—we were students and didn't have much money. But the big thing was to go out for an Indian meal at the Rawalpindi in Twickenham— we had wonderful evenings there.
> Our lecturers included Mr Enright who taught philosophy and chain-smoked all the way through, lining up the cigarette-butts in front of him—rather odd to watch. And

there was drama, which seemed to me very exciting, with modern plays that seemed quite daring.[118]

Two of the new women students were elected to the College's Committee of Management: Shelagh Martin and Carole de Monte. Both, like many of the other students, male and female, came from Liverpool, and St Mary's would for the next few years continue to have a "Northern" feel—but this too was changing as numbers increased.

Symbolic of a new style at St Mary's in the mid-1960s was a suggestion that would have sounded like an April Fool to earlier generations of students: that attendance at certain lectures in the 3rd year should be voluntary.

Meeting of the College Academic Board lst April 1966

Diverse views were expressed on the question of voluntary attendance at lectures in Third Year. Mr Bucher feared that many students would not attend and that carefully prepared weekly lectures, scheduled to continue to the end of the course, would lose their value.

Mr Kenney thought that voluntary attendance at lectures would have the merit of placing the onus of decision on the students themselves ... Mr White felt that, where large numbers of students are involved, lectures described as compulsory are not so in fact..

The Principal stated that, in this matter, pressure is being exerted by the Institute and the Ministry and, while inviting an expression of opinion, he suggested a trial followed by a progress report ... Proposal that all 3rd yr lectures should not be compulsory in the final term: carried by 30 votes to 22.

A similar discussion took place at a Special Meeting on Curriculum Courses: should some courses—currently Divinity, English and Mathematics—be required?

Recommendation that the purpose of the basic curriculum should be clarified. Also consider a system based not on simple subjects but on broad curriculum area. Such a system might well be

Literary—to include English, Philosophy, Divinity, Library Studies etc

Environmental—to include History, Sociology, Geography and General Science etc

Expressive—to include Drama, Physical Education, Art, Music and Handcrafts.[119]

Not long after this, the whole nature of the Academic Board itself came up for discussion. Everything was changing. A major overhaul was suggested: the new structure would include the Principal and two vice-principals along with lecturers with senior responsibilities, other principal lecturers, and some members elected by the teaching staff as a whole. The Board would take decisions which would be binding on the College as a whole, and would report to the full teaching body at regular intervals. In due course a similar plan to this was adopted, in line with other universities.[120]

Female students, the exit of the Dean, some lectures to be non-compulsory ... and St Mary's also now had a Student Bar! It was created in what had formerly been the chapel, and which still retained its gothic arches. Mario Greening was President of the Simmarian Union from 1964–1967 and would later describe the scene: "... the President of the Students' Union is ceremoniously pulling the first pint. Being a Simmarian he downs it in one with obvious relish. 'Gentlemen' he proclaims 'The bar is now open.' A gentle yet firm movement begins in our ranks towards the waiting pumps, which turns suddenly into a stampede as the President speaks again … 'Gentlemen, the bar is free' ." [121]

Student social life centred on the student bar and on local pubs—although the nearest pub, the Alexander Pope, then called the Pope's Grotto, was for a while out of bounds to Simmarians—and the Rawalpindi Indian restaurant, the "Pindi". Another popular destination in the 1960s was Eel Pie Island on the Thames, which had become a centre for emerging pop groups. One of the leading singers at a group that just beginning to make its name locally was Mick Jagger, son of Joe Jagger, who was head of PE at St Mary's.

Joe Jagger was a popular member of staff, and PE was of course central to College life. His son was then studying at the London School of Economics. Kevin Cook, already quoted, remembers that another member of staff, Nigel Press, had a teenage son, also called Michael, and Joe Jagger asked him "How do you get a teenager to listen to advice? My son Mick just isn't interested in studying: all he thinks about is this music and the group he is forming."

1968 would see student unrest across Western Europe. Fr Cronin at St Mary's, commenting at the start of that year, could sense an era of immense change, but reflected on things at St Mary's in a calm spirit.

> In the Universities which are also undergoing rapid expansion the dons debate in their common rooms whether this is really all for the better or not and many of them have concluded that "more means worse". I have often had this question put to me by visiting pastmen. Is the College really better now for all these modern amenities than it was when there were just 200 students here and life was simpler? Is the modern Simmarian student better than the older one? I think it is probably too soon to ask this question and it is certainly too soon to try to answer it. A College that has just trebled in size in the short span of six years must have been shaken up pretty thoroughly in the process and could not be expected to stabilise itself and accommodate to the new conditions as yet. But whether or not one likes change of this sort, it certainly was inevitable. If the rest of the world is changing, if the pattern of College life is going through this sort of revolution elsewhere, it would have been impossible for us to have stood still. [122]

It was certainly not just a question of modern amenities, growth in student numbers, or becoming mixed. Massive social change was in the daily atmosphere, in the lives of students and their families, and in the laws and customs of Britain.

At St Mary's this chiefly manifested itself in the attitudes of the students. Most were certainly not wedded to any strongly revolutionary ideas: they tended to be fairly dedicated Catholics planning to teach in Catholic schools. The most popular subjects in which to specialise at St Marys continued to be Geography and Physical Education. The students seem, on the whole, to have followed a moderate line on the issues of the day, with politics playing no very large part in their lives. However, they certainly reflected a growing sense of opposing any restriction on their social lives or in their living arrangements—and they followed a standard student demand in wanting some representation in the College's administrative structures. The days when the Rector could announce a policy affecting everyday student life, and a Dean enforce it, were over. Students were asking for official representation on governing bodies, and formal arrangements through which their opinions and ideas on academic and other issues could be made known.

In December 1968 the authorities at St Mary's agreed with student requests and issued a statement, under the signature of Fr Cronin the Principal: "The College Governors met yesterday December 10th under their Chairman Cardinal Heenan and among other items of business considered a formal request from the Committee of Management on behalf of the student union for student representation on the governing body:

> The Governors agreed this in principle. I was instructed to proceed first with arrangements to secure staff representation on the Board and when this has been achieved, representatives of the students.

The National Union of Students was by now taking a very strident line, and the Students' Association of the University of London Institute of Education was affiliated to it. A letter earlier that year went to every college of the Institute, including, of course, St Mary's:

> 25th April 1968
> Dear Principal…
> You will have seen from the press a few weeks ago that the ULIESA Executive spoke out in opposition to violent forms of demonstration as a means of solving difficulties. Clearly this is not a problem that we have had to face as yet within ULIESA Colleges, but I think it is important that we try to observe objectively the circumstances surrounding these demonstrations, particularly their causes … Many of the demonstrations have resulted from a feeling of frustration among students; a feeling that their views are ignored or considered inconsequential (I think it is fair to note that young people have been bitterly disappointed that the right to vote at 18 has not, after all, been granted) …[123]

Teachers were also becoming more militant, and encouraging student-teachers to join them. The National Union of Teachers and the National Association of Schoolmasters planned a one-day strike on 20th November 1968 with a rally in London's Royal Albert Hall, and students at St Mary's were being urged to take part. This would mean that those who were doing their teaching practice at various schools would be urged to take the day off and join the other strikers. An emergency meeting of the Academic Board was called to discuss this. In the end it seems that few Simmarians decided to become involved—or, at any rate, to do so in any very public way. But it was also clear that many were sympathetic to the strikers and certainly that the College's Student Union was strongly so.

The College made headlines in the spring of 1969 for a quite different reason: thieves made off with a haul of valuable paintings. Fr Cronin had, as described earlier, gathered a large collection of modern art, and the paintings were on display around the College and in the Walpole mansion. One night thieves broke in and stole a number of them—but some found their way back. The local newspaper reported the story:

> Five stolen paintings were returned to St Mary's teacher-training college, Strawberry Hill this week—because of the sharp eyes of the Very Rev Kevin Cronin.
> Five days after the theft in April Fr Cronin, the Principal, and Mr Robert Lazell, the bursar, went shopping for chandeliers in Kensington.
> In the window of an antique shop, Fr Cronin spotted two ivory figures which looked familiar. They were part of the haul of nine items taken from the college.
> Mr Lazell phoned Mr John Fagg, principal lecturer at St Mary's art department to come and examine the ivories. He gave positive identification and Teddington police were called. Det Michael Calon said yesterday "It was a million to one chance The art dealer

told police he had paid £1,000 for the ivory figures and seven paintings and had resold three for £1,500. Police traced the man who had sold the works, recovered all but two of the paintings stolen from St Mary's....This week the paintings were returned to St Mary's College. Their condition? One had been cleaned while it was away.[124]

In 1969 Fr Cronin retired. His years as Principal had seen the biggest single change since the move to Strawberry Hill: the College was now mixed and had substantially expanded, offering degree courses as a matter of routine and with new accommodation and a range of facilities for students. Fr Cronin's retirement was marked by the presentation of a portrait, specially commissioned. He was succeeded by Fr Thomas Cashin. He too would oversee many changes at St Mary's.

The 1970s

Life for Simmarians was by this time completely different from that known by their predecessors in the 1930s or 40s. Evenings at local pubs were now the norm, as were meals at the "Pindi" restaurant, already mentioned. On summer evenings, while some rock-music enthusiasts would head for Eel Pie Island, most students were content to remain in or around the College grounds.

A student in the 1960s was Peter Postlethwaite, who went on to become a well-known actor. He studied PE and drama at St Mary's, and then went on to develop a strong acting career beginning at the Everyman Theatre in Liverpool and going on to become famous in a wide range of television dramas. He died in 2011.

Josephine Siedlecka, a student from 1969–72, remembers idyllic days:

> We had the run of Strawberry Hill House, and Alexander Pope's grotto was just down the road. We would read poetry by the river on summer evenings.
> There were also occasional formal events, including an annual Ball for which the girls would wear long dresses and the boys black-tie evening dress. Graduation was also a formal occasion, held for many years at London's Royal Albert Hall.
> That was the really special thing, the Ball that marked the end of the academic year. Everyone dressed up—there were some really lovely dresses—and of course there was this fabulous setting, the mansion and the grounds, on a summer evening. All this made for great memories. And the friendships have lasted and lasted—I still meet regularly with a big group formed to stay in contact from those years, and we all still get on well and enjoy each others' news and company.

Among the staff, she recalled Joan Reilly who taught English literature, specialising in the 18th century— "really inspirational"—and the matrons at the various hostels who supervised the domestic arrangements and looked after the girls' welfare. Meals were eaten in the cafeteria "It was all rather boring by today's standards—lots of fish fingers and mass-produced steak-and-kidney pies."[125]

The majority of the students at this time came from Britain or Ireland, with groups also arriving from Malta and Gibraltar. From 1977 until 1983 there were regular exchange students from the USA, from the Universities of South California, St Thomas Minneapolis, and St Clara and Marymount in New York.

The overall numbers of students steadily expanded, from some 600 in the middle 1960s and over a thousand ten years later. The academic approach also shifted: in the early 1960s many students did not have "A" levels, and only a minority were intent on getting a degree. This altered during the decade. In 1967 it became possible to stay on for a fourth year and convert the Teacher's Certificate into a B.Ed degree. External degrees from London University—a BA or a BSc—had been available from 1920. as the college opened up new links and expectations generally were raised.

Bill McLoughlin, who had arrived at the College two years earlier to teach Physical Education became a leading figure in developing the B. Ed in this subject, and went on to become a leading gymnastics coach, taking teams to the Olympics and to major international sporting events over the next decades. At St Mary's he became known for his inspirational saying such as "Those who say it cannot be done should not interrupt those who are doing it." [126]

He would remain at St Mary's until his retirement in 1995—and beyond, as he continued to coach and help new generations of gymnasts. Student life in the 1960s was much more free from discipline than at any time in the College's history. But there was still a strong sense of identity, and students continued to refer to themselves as "simmarians", or, increasingly, to "simmies" or "sims".

The social changes of the 1960s only really manifested themselves at St Mary's in the 1970s. The Students Union became gradually more left-wing and militant in style during the latter part of this decade, although it does have to be said that for most students its political activities seem to have been largely irrelevant to their lives. Attendance at Union meetings tended to be small—sometimes so small that it was not possible, under the rules, to take specific decisions. There was much greater interest when the Union tackled matters that were directly related to the College and to the practicalities of student life.

On October 16th 1970 the Union called an Emergency Meeting. The style was still formal, and Catholic. The traditional opening prayer was said and then "it was followed by the President calling on Mr Cranny to propose the motion". This called for a boycott of extended teaching practice, in line with an approach being taken by the National Union of Teachers, but was defeated. A few days' latter the Union was dealing with matters that were evidently of more direct concern:

> 22nd October. Dining hall Committee meeting with Mr Cresswell.
> Sandwiches as an alternative to the main course will be available on Saturdays and Sundays after the success of a pilot scheme last year.
> A welcome back to CHIPS from this week after endless meals of creamed potatoes. Creamed potatoes will now be available at BOTH hatches which should prevent delays as people with salads need no longer hold up the hot meals queue.

The role of the Student Union seemed to have been established through discussion with the college authorities, presumably in order to safeguard the specifically Catholic nature of St Mary's. But this did not fit well with the leadership of the Union, or so it seems from a statement in the Union newsletter:

> Have you ever thought just how much you belong to this place, how great a say you have here, or how much you are really worth in the college? The concept of student power here in this College was amongst the refreshing crop of insights into aspects of our corporate life here, which was harvested in the debates of last week. I am thinking

of the SRC meeting last Wednesday when Paddy Rooney was in the awkward position of explaining the place of the Students Union in St Mary's College. His main gist was that 'we are not an independent students' union'. This was, as we all know, over the enticing red herring of whether we could or should hold a meeting at 10.30 on Thursday morning. This would have been in the face of a specific ban by the Principal, an understanding (three years old, no less) with the staff and the unwillingness of the President. But it did demonstrate that we are not as independent as many other student unions. Perhaps we have relied too long on the benevolent liberalism of our hosts.[127]

The Students Union ran a small publication *The Weekly Record* which in 1970 gave voice to what were evidently real concerns on practical matters. Women students in 1970 were obliged to pay a deposit of £5—a considerable sum for a student at that time—for use of an iron and £5 for an electric kettle. A group wrote in to the *Record*:

> Surely it is not too much to ask to be supplied with these basic necessities. We appreciate that we have washing facilities but feel they are completely inadequate without this essential piece of equipment. Is there any way in which the Students Union, or any more powerful organisation, can help us acquire an iron without excessive expenditure?

The signatories were Mary Ridgers, Maria Bolgen, Marie Hoare, Mary Burns, Sian Cook, M. Ryan and Arlene McNair.

Another student had a bigger complaint but did not want to sign her name, confining herself to the initials "KC". She disliked the restrictions in the girls' hostels, operated under the direction of a warden, and complained that the atmosphere was one of "moral blackmail and repression" and was "not like a boarding school … but more like a remand home". The argument was that most of the women living in the hostels were aged 19 or over, and therefore were legally adults and should not be made to live under restrictions in this way. [128]

These complaints related to the whole question of what the College authorities called "Mixed Visiting"—essentially the question of whether or not friends could be invited in to the various hostels run by the College. An agreement between the College authorities and a Committee of Management laid down rules in a memo dated 21 January 1969:
Students will be allowed to entertain their parents/guardians/family members in their rooms at the following times:

> Monday-Thursday 1.00pm—10.30pm
> Friday-Saturday 6pm-11pm
> Sunday 11 am- 10.30pm
> Each guest must be met by his/her host either in a reception or common room or where this facility is not provided, at the entrance to the hall or hostel.
> The latter regulation is felt to be a most important one as it is hoped that it would prevent unwanted intrusion.

It was also suggested that hostels might, at their own discretion, provide a signing-in register—and it was urged that "extreme consideration should be taken with regard to dress of students in particular those who wish to take showers or baths".

Josephine Siedlecka, already quoted, remembers strict rules: "During my time at St Mary's, two girls were rusticated for having men in their rooms. In fact, it was all entirely innocent—they were sitting together drinking coffee and chatting. But the rules were strict and that was that."[129]

But over the next few years it became clear that this gently paternal tone, with its understanding that students needed guidance and rules, was somewhat against the mood of the times. In November 1975 the Students Union launched a campaign for "24 hour mixed visiting" and abolition of all rules and regulations at the hostels, and urged students to back the campaign by showing that the old rules were not needed: "The only way we can have any success in this is if we can show that the students here are behaving in a responsible, mature way. We can't have any chance of success if we don't have this responsible action." It was suggested that the way ahead was for each hostel to have a "student house committee" to regulate domestic arrangements if required. It seems that something of this sort was eventually adopted—and in any case over the next decades the whole system of hostels was altered.

The College authorities were certainly trying to keep pace with the needs and demands of students. In November 1971 *The Simmarian* reported:

> During the Summer an extension to the Dining-room in the form of a coffee-bar/lounge was completed; it is hoped that this will provide quiet surroundings for those who find the Junior Common Room and Bar somewhat noisy. Work is still proceeding with the extensions to the Library and Religious Studies building, both of these should be completed by Christmas.

Changes were also taking place in the Catholic Church in the 1960s and 70s. Mass could now be celebrated in English and audibly, with people encouraged to say or sing the appropriate parts of the prayers. This proved popular with students and Sunday evening Masses in the large chapel were crowded throughout this period.

"You had to be there very early to get a seat" Josephine Siedlecka remembers. "It was always packed. We all went to Mass quite naturally: I don't remember whether it was compulsory or not, but that wasn't the issue anyway. Everyone went, and you had to squeeze in and find a place."[130]

But some enthusiasts evidently went too far, experimenting with replacing Scripture readings with poetry and adding secular music. A letter to *The Weekly Record* describes an experimental Mass at St Mary's:

> I attended the Folk Mass last Sunday. Various thoughts go through my mind when reflecting on it
> What is the aim of a Folk Mass?
> 1. Is it to worship God?
> 2. Is it a gimmick to get young people to attend Mass?
> Is a Folk Mass merely a theatrical performance, in the eyes of the participants, or is it a liturgical rite aimed at the depths of one's soul?
> Last Sunday's readings in the Lectionary were dropped in favour of an Autumn theme. Why? Why substitute a theme on Autumn—which to my mind is one for Advent, in the Church's Liturgical Cycle—for a very great and necessary theme in our times, namely Prayer, contained in last Sunday's readings from the Lectionary?
> Why was the first reading a poem from a secular source? Could not an appropriate reading be found in the many books of man's religious experiences, eg the Bible, the

Koran, the Hindu sacred writings? Furthermore, does it mean that we will eventually be singing "Adios Amigo" or "Should auld acquaintance be forgot?" as an exit hymn? I am interested in liturgical renewal. That's why I went to the Folk Mass. I do not wish to hurt anyone's feelings. However, I am very interested in truth, with regard to liturgy.

The letter was from a Redemptorist priest, Fr Liam Keegan. It drew a lengthy reply from the College chaplain Fr Kevin Rafferty who insisted that Robert Frost's poem on Autumn and Simon and Garfunkel's song "The leaves they are a falling" could

> raise religious questions about the transitoriness of human life and on the particular Sunday in question they were a good introduction to the biblical reading on the promise of eternal life … It is my belief that for the particular congregation here at Strawberry Hill folk music can capture a mood of sorrow or of repentance or of joy in the readings on a particular day; it can create a sense of fellowship and community; it can in its own right lead to prayer and be prayer …[131]

Meanwhile, there were various plans and hopes for the future of St Mary's. A series of meetings were held discussing the possibilities for a merger with the Maria Assumpta College—a women's college based in Kensington. Eventually this scheme was abandoned: a formal statement from St Mary's Academic Board on June 12th 1975 announced that the Board "having considered the Agreed Statement of the representatives of St Mary's and Maria Assumpta College…relating to the operation of a single institution on two sites for an indefinite period, greatly regrets that it does not regard the proposals contained therein to be academically feasible."

Fr Desmond Beirne was appointed Principal in 1976. He would be the last in the long tradition of Vincentian priests holding the position, and would be the one to hand over to a lay principal. During his time as Principal, the college continued to expand and, with more and more students seeking to do degrees, the decision was taken to link with the University of Surrey, based at Guildford. This broke with a long association with London University. In 1983 the first students under the new system received their degrees from Surrey, and starting in 1986, graduates went to Guildford Cathedral for their degree ceremonies. Later, the degree ceremonies for St Mary's were moved to Westminster Cathedral.

During the 1970s a major feature of life at St Mary's was fund-raising for various projects in poorer countries, following the launch of St Mary's Overseas Concern—or SHOC as its became known. Over the years, there would be strong links forged with some of the institutions funded through this project in Africa and Asia. Later the group's fund-raising was extended to include projects at home as well as abroad and it became St Mary's Overseas and Community Concern, SHOCC.[132]

Dr Mary Eaton joined St Mary's in 1976 as a lecturer, and would in due course become the college's third female vice-principal, following Drs Mary Hogan and Moya Cosgrove. A criminologist, she studied for her PhD (at the London School of Economics) while lecturing at St Mary's in sociology. "The Vincentians were a wonderful community and really cared for everyone. From the moment I arrived on the staff, I really sensed this care—you were truly loved. There was a strong sense of community in every way."

The College was now some 2,000-strong, and those who worked or studied there at this time all seem to share a strong sense of affection and loyalty, and to recall examples of kindness, understanding and care from the Vincentians and the staff.

Gerard Batty studied at St Mary's from 1979 to 1983, gaining a degree from London University. "I can honestly say these were among the happiest four years of my life. The whole place had a Catholic atmosphere, a strong sense of belonging—this was partly due to the chaplains, who were there alongside us and the Faith was part of our lives." Het met his wife, Tina, there. She was not a Catholic but lived nearby, at Tolworth and had chosen St Mary's because of its good reputation: she was received into the Church while at the college. "The Sunday evening Mass, 5.30pm, was so beautiful— people loved it, my parents sometimes used to come from London to be there. Tina was received into the Church at that 5.30pm Mass, and we would go together."[133]

Rugby was a major part of life for the men, and the week had its own routine: Mondays and Tuesdays were filled with lectures, Wednesday morning saw the chapel filled for an (optional) Mass and an afternoon of sports. "Then on Wednesday night there was the Rugby teams getting together and drinking—'carnage' we called it—and on Thursday and Friday lectures again and then the weekend, with its Friday and Saturday discos, and its packed Sunday evening Mass, Film Club and socialising."

At Christmas, students filled two coaches going to London to sing carols at charity fund-raising event at St Martin-in-the-Fields church. There was also a Christmas Ball, with a drinks reception in the Waldegrave Drawing Room. Summer brought the annual Strawberry Fayre, with "crazy chariot" races with vehicles made from odds and ends, and Cream Teas served in the Waldegrave rooms by girls dressed in old-fashioned mob caps and pinafores, with funds going to St Mary's Overseas Concern.

Gerard Batty remembers that although students enjoyed the formal events in the old mansion, they tended to avoid it at night because it felt rather scary.

> There were stories of ghosts in the old mansion, and the picture of Lady Waldegrave was said to hold a secret—if you looked at it from a particular angle she seemed to have a scarred face. I think people rather enjoyed the spooky stories.[134]

The overriding mood of the college was of a very strong community atmosphere. Sport brought people together with strong bonds that would remain lifelong, and the cultural and social activities filled up the days so that loneliness was not a problem. "I think the chaplains played a big part in that: they were available, there was always some one to whom you could talk."

The residences were strictly separated but in practice men visited the women's halls and vice versa. "I was in Old Hall, with the college administration alongside and the lecture halls below– the other men's residence were across the grounds, and the women's were in the neighbouring road. Each had its warden—some were quite strict and there was a lot of talk about trying to circumvent their rules."[135]

Leafing through programmes and magazines for the various College clubs and societies gives a flavour of the life: in November 1978 the College choir presented Handel's *Messiah* in the chapel, and the student magazine announced a range of sports and social activities and carried film reviews and various feature articles. There seems to have been something of a gulf, however, between most of the student activities in music, sport and drama, and the Students' Union which nominally represented the student body.

"To be honest, the Union was not something that interested most of us" Josephine

Siedlecka recalls "Its politics all seemed separate from the rest of us. We all had our own ideas, and the Union didn't really relate to us."[136]

It is clear that the politics and ideas of the Union itself were not popular: a General Meeting of students gathered only twenty people, far below the 165 necessary to be quorate. A campaign against the rents charged for student accommodation, and plans for a "rent strike", had to be abandoned. Union activities seem to have been dominated by a political faction that most students did not feel was relevant to them: various campaigns in the 1970s revolved around killing seals in Scotland and opposition to Israeli policies in the Middle East, along with (September 1977) a call for people to join picket lines in the strike at the Grunwick printing works. None of this seems to have resonated with most of the students. [137]

The Union's chief role was to provide space for social activities. But this too brought problems as there was clearly a small rowdy element. *The Weekly Record* for 9 October 1978 had a special message from the Editor, Derek Hayward : "Last Wednesday saw the worst night this term as regards mess around college. For those of you who don't know, the patio and refectory, the toilets outside the Union Hall and the college were in such a state that the regular workers and cleaners refused to clean such a disgusting mess. Of course the causes were evident but the culprits were, as usual, keeping a low profile. In my short while at St Mary's I have seen the situation get worse every year, and each time NUPE [the trade union for cleaners] complain something is meant to be done but it never ends in the way that would be most desirable...Last Wednesday's fracas was worsened by the fact that those running the disco and Jazz night were not conscious of the fact that they had to clean up the mess left behind. A deposit is charged by the Social Committee (which is returnable) to ensure that all is left in a satisfactory manner. But this was neglected on Wednesday resulting in the fact that the NUPE workers refused to clean up. As far as I am concerned, if any function is held and is subsequently carried out in an unsatisfactory manner, the club of society in the wrong should suffer; this Union is far too soft on such matters and it is time to put the foot down before the college authorities do it..."

A few weeks later there was an editorial plea to stop the practice of urinating into beer glasses, noting that they were made of plastic and could carry germs even after being washed. A plaintive letter reported how gate-crashers had ruined a 21st birthday party—students could rent a room for a private gathering for £15 but strangers had arrived to ruin this particular event which had to close early. In the same issue of the *Weekly Record* (19 Jan 1979) a group of 3rd year girls complained about the use of obscene language in the refectory.

The 1980s and 90s

The St Mary's Student Union Handbook for 1984–85 includes recipes, presumably aimed at helping students to live within a limited budget. Among its list of recommended foodstuffs to have on hand was instant coffee, something that a later generation with its espresso machines and frequent buying of café lattes would find somewhat bleak. The political line remained left-wing. Student Union President Paul Alford in the 1989–90 handbook announced "an unequivical [sic] stance" against government plans for student loans and "categorically opposed the introduction of Clause 28 ... on the issues of homosexuality"[138]

But the Union also listed a range of clubs and activities, giving information about a "Simms pro-life" group, a St Vincent de Paul Society, St Mary's Overseas Concern, and groups promoting pilgrimages to Lourdes, and the handbook included a message from the Chaplain—his office was F.203 in the Old House—with an announcement about the regular Sunday Mass time of 6pm. There was clearly a mix—sometimes an awkward one?—of views and ideas at Simmaries, reflecting the nature of what the College sought to be for the years ahead. It was no longer just a College training Catholic teachers who would work in Catholic schools: it was now moving towards offering a range of studies culminating in degrees in different subjects.

The 1987–88 Prospectus offered courses in Religious Studies, Sociology, Principles and Practice of Industry and Commerce, Multicultural Education and Teaching English as a Second Language among other subjects.

It was still a small college, however —some 500 students finishing their studies each year with certificates in various subjects— and one with a sense of common values and a shared Catholic tradition. The massed carol singing in London each year was a great event and each year and a report in the prospectus described it in traditional Simmarian cheery terms: "Father Loftus, the College Chaplain, mustered his troops for the annual Carol Singing in Trafalgar Square. The choir whimpered and gargled their way to the end of term having bribed, cajoled, threatened (?) and sung to the tune of £10,500. Two hundred or so lost voices seemed a small price to pay."[139]

There was a strong loyalty which for many proved lifelong. Francesca Byrne arrived in 1986 to study Drama and English and would later return as a member of staff, by which time the College had grown and was part of Surrey University. As a student in the 1980s she was one of 32 studying drama—when teaching in 2001 she had a class of 150. Recalling her student days she listed people who were still close friends, and remembered "the Going Down Ball with all the Laura Ashley ballgowns! We had a sherry reception and a string quartet with a dance in the Waldegrave Drawing Room." The friendly atmosphere, she said, was still the same when she came back as a member of staff "I was away from College for five years before returning. It didn't take long before I felt at home here again."[140]

The Senate and Council of the University of Surrey formally awarded St Mary's "affiliated college status" in 1990. For the next decade and a half, the name of Surrey University was on the College letterhead and notice-boards. In May 1991 the Duke of Kent, as Chancellor of Surrey University, visited St Mary's.

There had always been links with Ireland at St Mary's, and the 1991–2 Prospectus offered a new Degree in Irish Studies. Under the direction of James O'Hara, the Degree was described as "an exciting initiative for St Mary's, and ... a reflection of the growing interest being shown in Irish Studies generally...Students will be involved in the study of geography, history, language, literature, politics, religion and sociology. [141]

In 1990 an official report from Her Majesty's Inspectorate on "Professional Training for intending Primary and secondary School Teachers" at St Mary's reported in its section on Religious Education:

The BA QTS [Qualified Teacher Status] secondary and PGCE [Post Graduate

Certificate of Education] secondary courses are carefully designed, with a fitting place for catechetical issues but a key aim of preparing students to regard RE as a part of the basic curriculum in all schools. The courses are appropriate to the needs of secondary specialists. In particular they address the challenge and opportunity presented by an ethnically diverse multi-faith society and give thorough consideration to the implications of the 1988 Education Reform Act and the organisation of acts of worship.[142]

This slightly jargon-laden report reflects the changing situation of Britain, attitudes towards Religious Education, and the specific position of a Catholic college. St Mary's was no longer simply training Catholic teachers for Catholic schools. Some would teach in state schools with a non-denominational basis—and whereas at one time that would have meant some general instruction in the basics of Christianity, it was increasingly felt that other religions should be introduced into the curriculum. Over the next decades, the demographics of many of Britain's cities would change dramatically, with some areas becoming overwhelmingly Moslem following massive immigration.

In addition, many Catholic schools at this time were uncertain about how to teach the basics of Catholic doctrine, or indeed about whether it should be taught at all. During the 1970s and 80s there was much debate about this, and young people at St Mary's had attended Catholic schools where there was often some confusion. At St Mary's, as elsewhere, the theology offered at times seemed to reflect some of the confusion of the era. The publication in 1992 of the *Catechism of the Catholic Church* would prove useful in renewing Religious Education and establishing ways of ensuring a grounding in the essentials of the Catholic faith.[143]

In changing times, an added challenge was that fewer and fewer men were coming forward to train as priests, and religious orders were beginning to make plans based on this. In the case of St Mary's, the widening of the scope of the College's work also brought a sense that a new era was beginning.

In 1992 Father Beirne retired as principal: the decision had been taken to hand the College over to lay leadership. He had been a popular principal and had carried forward the strong traditions that had been established. His retirement brought to an end over a century of Vincentian administration of the College. They had shaped its style and forged its traditions, and hundreds of teachers across Britain—and overseas—had been trained under their care.

St Mary's first lay principal was Dr Arthur Naylor. His appointment in 1992 would see the start of the major expansion and changes leading to the establishment of St Mary's as a university in its own right. A graduate of Glasgow University, he had worked for some years as a lecturer in Scotland, and served on a number of bodies connected with teacher-training.

On his first visit in 1991 he stayed with the Vincentian fathers in the original Walpole Mansion, and met Fr Cronin, who was living there in retirement. "They were gracious and gave me a wonderful welcome. We all understood that an era was ending, but we knew there was a tradition that should be passed on."

Naylor's task as Principal was not only to continue the policy of expansion so that the College now offered a range of courses in addition to its initial and continuing role in teacher training, but also to help foster its new identity as a Catholic institution open to all while still retaining a Catholic spirit and ethos.

Such an identity would be in keeping with the idea of the Church as offering a strong spiritual message in a country and culture rapidly becoming confused. But it would not be easy to achieve. There was a worry that much-cherished Simmarian traditions could be completely lost. Opening up St Mary's to students of all faiths and none –in due course the first Moslems would begin to arrive—made for a radical departure from the days when all students shared a common culture of ideas and values which had shaped them from childhood.

Dr Naylor recalls:

> When I arrived in 1992 the evening Mass was still absolutely packed. This was partly because most of the students came from other parts of Britain and naturally did not go home at weekends: there had been this long tradition of students coming from Lancashire and Liverpool and the northern heartlands of Catholicism. They lived at the College throughout the term and there was a strong sense of community. After the evening Mass there would usually be showing of a film, and everyone would troop off to that together.
>
> There was also, throughout the decade, a strong bond with old Simmarians, many of whom would come back each year for the Easter Triduum. They would stay in the students' accommodation—available, of course, because the students went home for the holidays—and at the end of the three days things would finish with a big celebration lunch. These were men of the World War II generation and many were getting elderly— but they came with great enthusiasm.
>
> It's worth noting that St Mary's was built some fifty years before Westminster Cathedral, and its role in the story of the Catholic community is huge. In its earliest years, in the 19th century, most of the men came from poor homes, and at St Mary's they received a fully rounded education: only academic but physical—all that sport—and spiritual. St Mary's helped to foster a growing Catholic middle class, men whose impact on the wider culture was huge as they took their place in public life in many fields.[144]

The policy in the 1990s and into the new century was to focus on developing St Mary's as a centre of Catholic theology while running degree courses in a wide variety of subjects. Sport would also dominate in new ways, with new running tracks, sports halls etc catering for large numbers of students.

The sense of history and tradition remained strong. The winter 1993 issue of *The Simmarian* was published as a booklet, crammed with memories and with news of current activities.

It noted the death of "One of the last surviving Hammersmith Simmarians, Thomas Sarsfield Clancy" on 31 May (1993). Clancy was "the last of the legendary Twelve Apostles…" [ie the men who entered the College immediately after World War I and went on to become leading figures in Catholic education in Britain]. He joined the Royal Navy immediately on leaving school in 1917, and on demobilisation at the end of the war going straight to St Mary's at Brook Green.

In same issue, Bill Glynn a student in 1933–35 offered memories, recalling a fight between students and local lads at The Kings Head pub in Twickenham which resulted in the students being banned for a while, and also various domestic arrangements.

The nickname "nymphs" was given to the ladies who cleaned the students' rooms but they were actually "quite respectable local matrons of 40 and upwards. They used to call us 'duckie'. These ladies were quite separate from the domestic staff in the Vincentian apartments. They cleaned each room at 9.30 each morning" The rooms were simple, having a bed, a wardrobe, a washbasin that had cold water only, and electric light with low wattage.[145]

Tom Marsh, a student in 1947–49 already quoted listed "Four generations of Simmarians":

> The first (Thomas) Marsh was at St Mary's College, Brook Green Road, Hammersmith in 1892/93. He was my grandfather ... I knew him as the headmaster of St William's school, Ince ...
>
> My father, Thomas P. Marsh was at St Mary's Hammersmith in 1919–1921 after serving in the army ... a brilliant pianist and organist and became College organist. In 1947 I found sheet music in the choir still bearing his signature. He earned extra money playing for dancing while his friend R. Fairclough was a cartoonist who sold his work to the local and national press ...

This 1993 *Simmarian* also had news of current events: student president Annie Richardson described the opening of Cashin and Cronin halls of residence, named after previous College principals: "They seem to be more like hotels, with en-suite bathroom, pine beds and enough space for a family of ten. The first years who are lucky enough to live there are very happy." The two new halls were opened by Cardinal Basil Hume.

> There was news of Dr Naylor's appointment, with a note about the College's mission: St Mary's is a Catholic College of Higher Education with a distinctive mission. The mission aims of the College are inspired by the charism of the Congregation of the Mission. There is a strong emphasis on encouraging the students to be Christian leaders and on developing gospel values, especially with regard to the needs of our disadvantaged neighbour. The College remains committed to those values and attitudes which are as important and relevant now as at any point in the past.[146]

As Principal, Dr Naylor inherited a system of having two vice-principals, one Executive and the other Academic. This dated back to the discussions in the late 1940s when lay staff sought to have a greater role in the running of St Mary's, the College being at that time wholly in the care of the Vincentian priests and non-ordained staff having a much lower status. The Academic vice principals were, from that time on, always non-ordained, beginning with Robert E. Mills in 1949 and continuing with Dr Joseph F. Scott, William Maguire, H.V. Sheppee and finally Anthony Kenney, appointed in 1978. He would be the last Academic Vice-Principal, being appointed Deputy Principal in 1999. This role absorbed that of both the Academic and the Executive Vice-Principals. The last of the Executive vice-principals, Miss Moya Cosgrove, appointed in 1984, was also the first to be a lay person.

Dr Mary Eaton was appointed vice-principal in 1993. Her connection with the College went back, as mentioned, to the 1970s. As a lecturer, she had worked for many years with the Vincentian Fathers and remembers the warmth and friendliness that was combined with slightly old-fashioned courtesy and approach:

> I was invited to a dinner-party and they were glad when I accepted, saying that this would 'make it 50–50'. But this didn't mean female/male, it meant 50–50 clergy/laity! I was the only lady present. But it was all delightful—fun and friendly and relaxed. I was

a sociologist and a feminist yet I couldn't have felt more at home or been more welcomed. The Vincentians really were a most wonderful community.[147]

It was during the 1990s that the long-established custom of having tea served daily in the Senior Common Room slowly dwindled:

> It was delightful: we'd have sandwiches, and different sorts of cake on different days— somehow a sort of tradition established itself. It was a good opportunity to relax and talk with colleagues. But then eventually this gave way to having a coffee-machine— and then the new Dolce Vita café opened, and everyone found it easy and convenient to go there ...[148]

With many other Simmarians, Dr Eaton maintains (2019) a strong connection with St Mary's and frequently attends Mass in the College chapel: "You never really stop being a Simmarian. It's a place that binds you together, draws you into a real community. And I continue to be impressed with some of the young people I meet."

In 1994 a purpose-built Chaplaincy centre was opened by Bishop Patrick O'Donohue, chairman of the Governors of the College, across from the chapel and next to the old Chapel in the Woods by the College's boundary wall. With slightly church-style pointed windows, it was designed as a place where the chaplain would have an office and where students could also gather to chat or have an informal lunch after weekday Masses.

In December 1996 Cardinal Basil Hume opened a new extended library building alongside the chapel and a commemorative stone was laid at its entrance to mark the event.

A 1997 reunion for men who studied at St Mary's from 1945–47 resulted in a booklet in which they told their stories and shared some memories. Kevin Finn recalled "the dock strike—we ate anything—rice loaf sandwiches on Sundays" and also "our swim down the Thames from Teddington Lock to Eel Pie Island" and the bitter winter of 1947 which saw the students walking across the lake at Hampton Court. The Simmarians who told their stories included a number who had gone on to become headmasters, editors of educational or religious journals, and authors of books. The style and approach of the contributions reflected an academic approach, with a strong schoolmasterly message: in a not untypical contribution, Dr Gerry Forrest, whose career included teaching in Pakistan, director of research at the Joint Matriculation Boar, and gaining a doctorate at Keele University appealed to fellow teachers in forming a STEUAC: a Society to Encourage The Use of Apostrophes Correctly.[149]

Meanwhile, in presenting itself to prospective students, the College emphasised its friendliness and small size—"2000 students—no long walks between lectures!" and its attractive setting. Its 1996–97 Prospectus offered "A warm welcome to all students—of all ages, nationalities and backgrounds" who during their college years would "sample the many attractions of the local area—riverside pubs, theatres, Hampton Court, Kew Gardens."[150] There was also a strong spiritual tone, with the Prospectus offering a message from the Chaplain Fr Perry Gildea describing the chaplaincy's work as "fostering the religious and spiritual welfare of the college community,...not solely concerned for the interests of Catholic or Christian students or staff, but the human well-being and spiritual welfare of students of all denominations and indeed those of no denomination whatever the need."[151]

This reassuring tone jostled alongside with other material on offer in the prospectus: the Sociology department's section stressed fashionable references to "gender, class, race, ethnicity, ideology and values" while the geography department emphasised "the world debt problem" and "the destruction of the tropical rain forests".[152] It was a time of acronyms: PGCE, CCRS, QTS, SWELTEC.[153] But a message from the Students' Union, Matt Adshead, stressed "a sense of unity arising out of the warmth of feeling to be experienced within a close-knit community. St Mary's is famous for its uniquely positive, warm and friendly atmosphere. Intimacy and fellowship become key words at the expense of the feelings of anonymity so often endured in less personal institutions."[154]

Another new century

In the millennium year 2000 St Mary's marked its own 150th anniversary. Among the celebrations, two long-serving members of staff who worked in secretarial and administrative positions, Jean McGinley and Eileen Walker, were given honorary degrees in the December graduation ceremony. During the year, the College bought several acres of playing fields formerly owned by the Shell company's Lensbury Club at Teddington. This new sports facility was formally named St Mary's, Teddington Lock.

The reputation of St Mary's for sports, already high, was growing all the time. In 2001 a young sportsman born in Magadishu, Somalia, started training at St Mary's running track Mohammed "Mo" Muktar Jama Farah would go on to become the most decorated athlete in British athletics history. He trained at the College from 2001 to 2011, and was awarded the CBE in 2013 and knighted in 2017.

In 2001 *The Simmarian* carried a message from Dr Naylor announcing that the previous year had seen almost 2,500 undergraduates at the College, the largest student population in its history. Work had started on a new Centre for Excellence in Initial Teacher Training—costing around £3.6 million, funded with a grant from the Higher Education Funding Council. Bishop Patrick O'Donohue, who had been chairman of the Governors for some years, had been appointed Bishop of Lancaster, a diocese with strong links to St Mary's. He was replaced as chairman by Bishop George Stack, an auxiliary in the diocese of Westminster. The newsletter also noted the death of the former head of French, Dr David Balhatchet, who had retired in 1983. He had gone on to gain a D. Phil at Oxford, and also been made a Bard by the Cornish Language Board.[155]

As the twenty-first century got into its stride, there were still active Simmarian Clubs in Liverpool, Manchester, the North East, and Leeds as well as Ireland and Gibraltar. The Simmarian Old Boys Football Society flourished and in 2001 decided to add golf to its activities.

In 2002 St Mary's awarded Honorary Fellowships to various people, including former Simmarian Anna-Marie Ashe, a journalist broadcasting with the London News Network who was a student from 1973–77 and Bishop Mark Jabale, who studied at the College in 1960–61 and went on to become a Benedictine monk, headmaster, a rowing coach, and in due course Bishop of Menevia.

February 2005 saw St Mary's receiving a Royal visitor: Prince Philip came to present sports awards under a scheme called "Competitive Edge" which aimed to encourage more young people to play Rugby. Some 400 young people from local schools gathered to greet him: the "Competitive Edge" scheme was a joint initiative between St Mary's and the London Borough of Richmond on Thames education authority.

Honorary Fellowships were again awarded in 2005, this time to former students Rebecca Romero, who won a silver medal for rowing in the 2004 Olympics, Jonathan Holloway founder of the Red Shift Theatre Company, and Antonia Watson founder of a housing charity for homeless Irish people in London. A former popular member of staff, Vincentian Father Philip Walshe was also made an Honorary Fellow. The presentation was made by Bishop George Stack at a ceremony in the Waldegrave Drawing Room.

By now a great change in national policy was coming into effect, centred on the idea that something like 50 per cent of all young people in Britain should attend university. New universities began to be named everywhere, forged out of colleges formerly specialising in various forms of further education. Catholic teacher-training colleges spent the 1990s examining options for the future: to close, to merge with other colleges, to enlarge? There were meetings, conferences, decisions, announcements. In the end, the decision was that St Mary's would seek university status.

From 2007 St Mary's University College could award its own degrees. The majority of students were by now studying subjects unconnected with teacher-training or with the Catholic faith. There were also by now a number of post-graduate students taking part-time degrees in a range of subjects including theology and bioethics. This ensured a continuing Catholic atmosphere at one level. Meanwhile rising numbers of students arrived each year to take degrees in subjects ranging from media studies to sports management, without any particular interest in the College's Catholic status. But a major event in 2010 sealed St Mary's place in English Catholic life and history for all time: the visit of Pope Benedict XVI in September 2010.

Pope St John Paul II had visited Britain in 1982, making history.[156] In 2010 Pope Benedict XVI followed him—and this time it was a State Visit, as he had been officially invited by the Queen. There was much media controversy, due to the Pope's role in upholding the teachings of the Catholic Church, with publicity about counter-demonstrations, and suggestions that crowds supporting the Pope would be thin. In the event, the visit brought massive enthusiastic crowds and the Pope, far from being the angry figure caricatured by campaigners, arrived as a gentle fatherly priest.

The team planning the Papal visit had visited St Mary's with the thought that it might be suitable for a gathering of Catholic school pupils. The plans expanded and in the event the College was used for three major gatherings: representatives of different faiths—including the Chief Rabbi, and leading figures from the Sikh, Hindu, and Moslem communities—met the Pope in the Waldegrave Drawing Room. Members of religious orders from across Britain met him in the Chapel. And some 4,000 children from Catholic schools met him at a "Great Assembly", an open-air event held in the sports area.

2010 was in fact the 110th anniversary of the College's founding. Pope Benedict's style fitted into the mood of the day, with children's excitement at being part of a vast crowd mingling with a sense that something of serious importance was happening.

"It is not often that a Pope, or indeed anyone else, has the opportunity to speak to the students of all the Catholic schools of England, Wales and Scotland at the same time" he told the gathering "And since I have the chance now, there is something I very much want to say to you."

> I hope that among those of you listening to me today there are some of the future saints of the twenty-first century. What God wants most of all for each one of you is that you should become holy. He loves you much more than you could ever begin to imagine, and he wants the very best for you. And by far the best thing for you is to grow in holiness.
>
> Perhaps some of you have never thought about this before. Perhaps some of you think being a saint is not for you. Let me explain what I mean. When we are young, we can usually think of people that we look up to, people we admire, people we want to be like. It could be someone we meet in our daily lives that we hold in great esteem. Or it could be someone famous. We live in a celebrity culture, and young people are often encouraged to model themselves on figures from the world of sport or entertainment. My question for you is this: what are the qualities you see in others that you would most like to have yourselves? What kind of person would you really like to be?[157]

The Pope also addressed a gathering of teachers and others involved in education—including the Secretary of State for Education—in the sports hall. Quoting from the Book of Wisdom, he reminded them:

> As you know, the task of a teacher is not simply to impart information or to provide training in skills intended to deliver some economic benefit to society; education is not and must never be considered as purely utilitarian. It is about forming the human person, equipping him or her to live life to the full—in short it is about imparting wisdom. And true wisdom is inseparable from knowledge of the Creator, for "both we and our words are in his hand, as are all understanding and skill in crafts."[158]

At St Mary's, a commemorative stone by the chapel entrance, and a fine mosaic in the chapel itself mark the Papal visit—and the event, coming at the College's 210th anniversary and when the college was seeking full university status and a new role, held great significance. In a way that no one in 1850 could possibly have imagined, Simmaries in the 21st century was an institution playing a confident role in national life.

Dr Naylor had been due for retirement in January 2010, but stayed on in an honorary capacity for the Papal visit. "Watching the Pope speak to that great crowd, gathered at St Mary's, I found myself thinking that all the old Simmarians—the men who loved this place, who had such loyalty—were somehow there in spirit. The day belonged to them, too."[159]

On Naylor's retirement the local newspaper, the *Richmond and Twickenham Times*, noted:

> Since taking over Dr Naylor has seen a large expansion in student numbers, and has also overseen the beginning of a project to restore Strawberry Hill, the historic house of St Mary's grounds.
>
> He has also seen many sporting milestones, with the university college set to host the South African Olympic team prior to the 2012 Games.
>
> He said "I would like people to say that over that time, a time of growth, expansion and change, St Mary's maintained its ethos and character, its commitment to high academic standards and, as has been the case since its foundation in 1850, to wider access to education at all levels...I think that, overall, what I like most about where we are is [that] we have tried to keep true to what we are about. Education is central to what we

do, and theology is important as a church university college."[160]

Following Dr Naylor's retirement. Prof Philip Esler was appointed Principal, and served until 2013. Australian-born Prof Esler trained as a lawyer in Sydney and later became an academic, serving as Chief Executive of Britain's Arts and Humanities Research Council and from 1995 to 2010 as Professor of Biblical Criticism at St Andrew's University. His time at St Mary's was brief and he went on to chair a department in New Testament Studies at the University of Gloucestershire. On 23rd January 2014 St Mary's became a full University in its own right, with a charter from the Privy Council. Dr Naylor, who had been appointed interim Principal following Prof Esler's departure, became St Mary's first Vice Chancellor. He was succeeded a few months later by Francis Campbell, who had concluded a distinguished service in the Diplomatic Corps with six years as Britain's Ambassador to the Holy See. In 2015 Cardinal Vincent Nichols, Archbishop of Westminster since 2009, was installed as Chancellor.

The year 2012 was the year of the London Olympic Games, and a landmark in the story of St Mary's sporting tradition. Professor Dick Fisher, head of St Mary's Department of Sport, Health and Exercise Science would later recall:

> The 2012 Games united the nation and something similar happened at St Mary's. Academics, administrator, and support staff from across the institution engaged in one way or another. For example, looking after Olympians from ten nations based at St Mary's, through our Olympic Lecture series, a torch relay around local Primary and Secondary schools, by students (each school arranged a special reception for it) and supporting Simmarians past and present in the Games. We won more gold medals than Australia! And came top for London Higher Education institutions.[161]

Professor Fisher was the first non-Catholic to join the senior management team at St Mary's:

> I was very comfortable supporting the institution's mission and values—attended all the important Masses as a mark of respect for what the place was all about. At the 2012 Graduation, my last, Philip Esler allowed me to give the main address in his place—I told the students that they and I were leaving and would follow very different paths—but St Mary's would always be with us.[162]

The creation of St Mary's as a university was part of a major restructuring of all higher education across Britain: former colleges and polytechnics became universities and it was suggested that half of all Britain's young people should attend universities and receive degrees. It was something entirely new. St Mary's had one major advantage in this time of change: a name and tradition that rested on faith and a strong spiritual heritage.

The sense of history at St Mary's remains strong among its alumni. In 2014, the year that the new era began, the Liverpool Simmarian Club marked its 110th anniversary, and ten members joined other former students for a celebration. The following year, newly-appointed Principal Francis Campbell visited Liverpool to attend their annual Mass, concelebrated by two former Simmarians Fr Alex Fleming (1944–46) and Fr. Godric Timney OSB (1971–72). At the Mass, all former Liverpool Simmarians were remembered including two who had recently died, Jack Griffiths (1944–45) and Gerry Wright (52–54) who had served for many years as President of the Club.[163]

Meanwhile, on another continent, former staff members were being honoured through the work of St Mary's Overseas Concern: former Geography lecturer Amy Hemmings and former Vice-Principal Antony Kenney had left money to the charity, and a Catholic secondary school in Muthebeni, Kenya unveiled a plaque with their names.[164]

In 2018 one of St Mary's best known lecturers, Dr Christopher Harper Bill, died. A distinguished medieval historian, he had begun working at St Mary's in 1973 and had taught generations of students, retiring in 1997. Like many other former members of staff, he had maintained strong links with St Mary's throughout his retirement.

Looking ahead

Today St Mary's University's describes itself as "a strong and welcoming community of students and staff … committed to the highest standards in teaching across the wide range of undergraduate and postgraduate courses we offer. In addition, we have a vibrant research culture and environment".[165] There are undergraduate degree courses in subjects ranging from English literature to theology, from communications and marketing to sports sciences, from creative and professional writing to acting, from drama and education to visual design. There are over 6,000 students and activity swirls around the refectory, the library, the Student Union, the lecture halls and the sports halls and running tracks—and, in summer, around the extensive grounds. There is still an emphasis on teacher-training, and St Mary's retains its strong association with sport at every level: top-level sports activities take place throughout the year, and in the summer term local primary schools arrive to make use of the sports fields and running tracks.

Prof John Charmley and Rt Hon Ruth Kelly are pro-vice-chancellors, responsible for respectively for research and enterprise and academic strategy. A Board of Governors forms the backbone of the structure: chairmen over the decades from the 1970s have been Cardinal John Heenan, Bishop Patrick O'Donohue, Bishop George Stack and—currently serving—Bishop Richard Moth.

The facilities at St Mary's today, with vast sports halls, beautiful grounds, theatres for music and drama, a refectory serving a range of good meals, a student bar and a coffee shop, and splendid formal rooms for great events, would make the first students of the old College at Brook Green gasp. Nor could they, in their wildest dreams, have imagined the aspects of student life that are now normal, from video conferencing and internet-based submission of essays to the international outlook that takes students on "gap year" trips around the world.

The majority of St Mary's students today are not Catholic: for most of them, the Church is essentially unknown territory. Only a tiny number—perhaps a dozen—will be found at a weekday Mass, and on Sundays the chapel is not more than half-filled: most students in any case live off-campus, many some distance away.

The idea at St Mary's in this new era is that the University with its Catholic heritage and tradition exists to serve the wider community and to present a message of hope and truth in a changing world. Thus it has a strong theology department, good numbers of students including several taking post-graduate degrees. Links have been developed with seminaries training young men for the priesthood, and from 2019 this will include courses for them at St Mary's.

The University also plays a major role in the wider life of the Church in Britain: it hosts Catholic events, retreats, talks, and conferences and in recent years these have ranged from a gathering of FOCUS—the USA-based Federation of Catholic University Students to a conference celebrating the 50th anniversary of the encyclical *Humanae Vitae*. A small community of Augustinian sisters offers commitment to prayer in the chapel daily, and is active in the chaplaincy: a praying presence on the campus.

The Benedict XVI Centre flourishes with talks and lectures on aspects of Catholic social teaching under the leadership of Dr Philip Booth. Pope Benedict XVI's link with the university is also fostered at Benedict XVI House, a student residence where young people commit to living in community with a shared regular life of prayer and service.

In 2018 Bishop Philip Egan, Bishop of Portsmouth, gave a lecture in the Waldegrave Suite, on the theme of John Henry Newman's *Idea of a University*, a reminder of the breadth and depth to which a Catholic University should aspire, with theology seen not as an optional extra but as something at the core of academic work. That Autumn, Lord Kerr spoke at the launch of the University's new Law School, and in London, at the Mansion House, home of the City's Lord Mayor, the Department of Business, Law and Society launched its project on business ethics.

The task of St Mary's for the future is to marry its rich Catholic heritage with the needs of new generations growing up in a Britain where the Church is seen as something old and unimportant, catering for a small minority of people and of no particular relevance. The spiritual hunger produced by such an outlook is evident and a strong institution with confidence in its Catholic tradition has much to offer.

St Mary's motto is *Monstra te esse Matrem*—"Show thyself a mother". The idea of St Mary's as a mother of many children has been central from the start: students have always felt a strong sense of belonging. To nurture, to teach, to inspire and to point towards eternal truths—these are among a mother's tasks. They have probably never been so important as in the Britain of the 21st century. As St Mary's looks ahead, there is a sense of a rich heritage to cherish, new adventures ahead, and work to be done.

It is the honour and responsibility of a Catholic University to consecrate itself without reserve to the cause of truth. This is its way of serving at one and the same time both the dignity of man and the good of the Church, which has "an intimate conviction that truth is (its) real ally … and that knowledge and reason are sure ministers to faith"[166] Without in any way neglecting the acquisition of useful knowledge, a Catholic University is distinguished by its free search for the whole truth about nature, man and God. The present age is in urgent need of this kind of disinterested service, namely of proclaiming the meaning of truth, that fundamental value without which freedom, justice and human dignity are extinguished.

Pope St John Paul II, *Ex Corde Ecclesiae* (1991), 4.

Notes

1. E. H. Burton, *The Life and Times of Bishop Challoner* (New York: Longmans, 1909), p. 18.

2. Joseph Constantine Carpue 1764–1846, pioneering surgeon and promoter of vaccination.

3. Information from parish archives, Holy Trinity church, Brook Green.

4. P. Hughes, *The Catholic Question 1688–1829* (London: Sheed and Ward, 1929), pp. 311–312.

5. E. Norman, *The English Catholic Church in the Nineteenth Century* (Oxford: Clarendon Press, 1984), p. 217.

6. J. Bossy, *The English Catholic Community 1570–1850* (London: Darton Longman and Todd, 1966, 1975), p. 306.

7. H. Chadwick, "Newman's Significance for the Anglican Church" in D. Brown (ed.), *Newman: a Man for our time* (SPCK, London: 1990), p. 60.

8. Pastoral Letter of Nicholas Wiseman *To our dearly beloved, the faithful of the London District*, July 1848. In First Annual Report of the Catholic Poor School Committee, London 1848. p. 35.

9. Wiseman, http://www.choleraandthethames.co.uk/cholera-in-london/cholera-in-westminster/the-devils-arce/ accessed 29 April 2017.

10. St Mary's College Centenary Record, 1950.

11. Second Annual Report, Catholic Poor Schools Committee.

12. *St Mary's College Centenary Record*, 1950.

13. Copy of Trust deed in archives SMH/3/25 in box 35.

14. Fourth annual report of Catholic Poor Schools Committee, London 1851, p. 8.

15. *Ibid.*

16. *Ibid.*, p. 9.

17. He went on to become parish priest of the Church of the Assumption, Deptford.

18. Ninth annual report, p. 8.

19. Ninth annual report, p. 8.

20. Appendix to tenth annual report of the Catholic Poor Schools Committee. London 1857, pp. xxv–xxvii

21. At this stage he used the old spelling, today regarded as American. He also occasionally used the old-fashioned f for s, eg in "addrefses". This changed over the decade that he was at St Mary's—later letters use the spelling "honour".

22. *Register of Letters 1862–1872* in archives SMH/4/1/ record number 74, in box 33.

23. *Register of Letters 1862–1872* in archives SMH/4/1/ record number 74, in box 33.

24. *St Mary's Centenary Record* 1950.

25. Fifteenth annual report of Catholic Poor Schools Committee, p. 18.

26. Fifteenth annual report of Catholic Poor Schools committee, p. lxvi.

27. There were now a large number of local Catholic families. The church of Holy Trinity, Brook Green, was opened in 1853, the foundation stone having been laid by Cardinal Wiseman in 1851, a year after St Mary's College opened. Holy Trinity had a school for girls and very small children, while the boys went to the Practising School at the College.

28. *Register of Letters 1862–1872* in archives SMH/4/1/ record number 74, in box 33.

29. J. Von Arx, "Cardinal Manning and the Education Act of 1870". In S. Gilley (ed.), *Victorian Churches and Churchmen* (Catholic Record Society: 2005), p. 11.

30. Undated, College archives SMH/3/20 box 35.

31. Letter from G. J. Duncombe, 12th September 1872, to The Principal, Roman Catholic Training College, Hammersmith. SMH 3/6 record number 135, box number 33 location 8A.

32. Information from Philip McCarthy, great-grandson of John Jordan, interviewed April 2019.

33. Information from Philip McCarthy. The links continued: his father-in-law Peter Scanlan attended St Mary's at Twickenham in 1949 and went on to teach in Uganda and later in Bristol.

34. Catholic Poor Schools Committee report 1869, p. 34.

35. Forty first annual report of Catholic Schools Committee 1878, p. 12.

36. Archives, St Mary's University Box 35 SMH/3/20.

37. Archives, SMH 3/20.

38. Archives, SMH/3/20 Box 35.

39. *Simmarian* (Jan 1968), p. 21.

40. Correspondence, undated but clearly 1898. In archives SMH3/22.

41. *The Simmarian*, jubilee issue 1950 *Salute to the Simmarians! The memories of a former Principal.*

42. *St Mary's College Centenary Record* (1950), p. 120.

43. *Ibid.*, p. 118.

44. *Ibid.*, p. 120.

45. *Ibid.*

46. Archives SMH 3/25 box 35.

47. Annual report, Catholic Schools Committee, archives PRI 3 20–39.

48. Committee report, undated, archives SMH/325 box 35.

49. Archives SMH 3/26 box 35.

50. Board of Education Report 1902 archives SMH box 35.

51. *St Mary's College Centenary Record* 1950, pp. 34–35.

52. Harold Clarke, student 1913–1915, in *St Mary's College Centenary Record*, 1950, pp. 32–33.

53. W. A. Maguire, *St Mary's College Centenary Record*, 1950, pp. 40–41.

54. *St Mary's College Centenary Record*, 1950, p. 41.

55. *150 Years of St Mary's College*, ed K. Breen, Freeland Haynes Marketing Communications, undated but presumably published in 2000, p. 43.

56. W. A. Maguire, *St Mary's College Centenary Record*, 1950, p. 41.

57. *Simmarian* magazine Feb 1962. In college archives.

58. *Simmarian* magazine Feb 1962, page 4. In college archives.

59. Fr Nicholas Schofield, *British Catholics and the Great War*, FAITH magazine July/August 2017.

60. Information from a display at the Imperial War Office, 2018, giving a portrait of Britain on the outbreak of war in 1914.

61. *St Mary's College Centenary Record*, 1950, p. 42.

62. *150 Years of St Mary's College*, 2000, p. 44.

63. *St Mary's College Centenary Record*, 1950, p. 46.

64. Today (2019) a walk around the area reveals no trace whatever of the College, not even an exterior wall.

65. Log Book in archives, record number 874 location 3C MH/11/1.

66. *Ibid.*

67. *Ibid.*

68. *Ibid.*

69. *Ibid.*

70. *Ibid.*

71. *Ibid.*

72. *Ibid.*

73. Log Book in archives, record number 874 location 3C MH/11/1.

74. Archive PRI/3/7 record number 131 box 43.

75. Former student William T. Glynn, in *The Simmarian* spring 1990, p. 32.

76. Former student William T. Glynn, 1933–35, in *The Simmarian* winter 1988, pp. 46–47.

77. In archives 334 box number 29, location 6D, booklet compiled 1981 with a note saying: "Tradition has always been an integral part of Simmaries life, whether it be in the Religious, Academic, or Sporting field … In 1932 began a series of victories in the Inter College athletics meeting, winning the Shield annually until 1948. Though the Shield was not at stake in the war years, meetings were held at Strawberry Hill from 1940 to 46, each of which we won! This explains the pride of students of those days. Our thanks are extended to The Irish Simmarian Union, J. Wallwork (25–27) Wilf Sudlow (40–42) Joe Burns (46–48) Frank Lepnis (49–51) for the use of their copies of songs which will be preserved in the archives. April 1981."

78. In archive PRI1/3/7 record number1131 box 43.

79. *Simmarian* Spring 1990, p. 32.

80. Brochure in archives PRI/3/9.

81. Archives ref PRI/3/16.

82. Archives PRI/3/19.

83. Archives PRI/3/19.

84. Archives SIM/5/I box 20.

85. Archives SIM//5/I box 20.

86. *Thirty Four Years at Strawberry Hill*, in *The Historian,* magazine of the St Mary's History Society, 1969.

87. *Simmarian* magazine winter 1992, p. 48.

88. *34 Years at Strawberry Hill*, 1969.

89. Carter, *Simmarian* magazine winter 1992 p. 48.

90. *The Simmarian*, 144, quoted on page 37 of *150 Years of St Mary's College*, 2000.

91. Anon. archives PRI SIM 5/1 box 20.

92. *Simmarian* June 1943, p. 3.

93. Archives SIM 5/1 box 20.

94. Tom Marsh, *The Simmarian*, winter 1993.

95. *St Mary's College Centenary Record* 1950 p. 80.

96. *St Mary's College Centenary Record* 1950, p. 81.

97. Archives PRI/3/28.

98. *Memorandum on the proposed appointment of a second vice-principal of St Mary's College Strawberry Hill* 3rd March 1949. Westminster diocesan archives, Kensington.

99. *St Mary's College Centenary Record,* 1950, p. 81.

100. *Thirty Four Years at Strawberry Hill,* in *The Historian,* magazine of St Mary's Historical Society, 1969.

101. G. X. Sullivan, student 1946, writing in *The Simmarian,* winter 1987, p. 45.

102. He met his future wife at St Mary's when she came with others from Maria Assumpta College for a drama event—and in the 1990s their daughter enrolled at St Mary's, *The Simmarian,* winter 1993.

103. Interview with author, 2017.

104. Newspaper cutting in London Borough of Richmond local history collection, Old Town Hall, Richmond.

105. Fionuala Fenton's memories, told to Dr Mary Eaton and reprinted here in a memo to the author, February 21 2019.

106. London Borough of Richmond local history collection, Old Town Hall, Richmond.

107. St Mary's archives, Meeting of Academic Board 2 June 1961, location 3C.

108. Student handbook, p. 20, St Mary's archives, undated. Box number 63.

109. Student handbook p. 22.

110. Student handbook p. 25.

111. Interview with author 2018.

112. Interview with author 2018.

113. Menu card in London Borough of Richmond local history collection, Old Town Hall, Richmond.

114. *Cresset*, 1963, in London Borough of Richmond local archives, Old Town Hall, Richmond.

115. *The Simmarian* newsletter April 1967, p. 3.

116. *The Simmarian* newsletter April 1967.

117. The *Simmarian* April 1967.

118. Interview with author July 2018.

119. St Mary's archives ACB 3/1.

120. St Mary's archives ACB 3/1.

121. *Simmarian* winter 1979 page 11.

122. *The Simmarian* Jan 1968.

123. Archives PRI 3 20–39.

124. *Richmond and Twickenham Times*, 1969, London Borough of Richmond history collection, Old Town Hall, Richmond.

125. Interview with author, 2018.

126. Tribute to Bill McLaughlin, St Mary's University Twickenham www.stmarys.ac.uk/news/2014/01.

127. Archives DPY /1/1–5.

128. Archives DPY /1/1/1–5.

129. Interview with author 2018.

130. Interview with author 2018.

131. *Weekly Record*, 1970s, in archives, STU 3/3).

132. Kevin Cook, already quoted, was involved with SHOCC from its first years, and it still flourishes: at a 2017 Reunion Dinner he spoke about recent visits to various projects funded by the organisation in various parts of the world. A quiz about St Mary's history rounded off the dinner and raised further funds for SHOCC.

133. Interview with author, April 2019.

134. Interview with author, April 2019.

135. Interview with author, April 2019.

136. Interview with author, 2018.

137. Archives STU/3/3/ box 68.

138. Archives STU/3/3/ box 68. The "Clause 28" law prevented homosexual groups from lobbying in schools but has since been revoked.

139. St Mary's College Prospectus 1987–88, p. 30.

140. Interview in *The Simmarian* Spring 2001.

141. St Mary's College prospectus 1991–1992, p. 32.

142. Local history collection Richmond ref acc ic11 964, Old Town Hall, Richmond.

143. See *Religious Education Curriculum Directory for Catholic schools and colleges in England and Wales*. Catholic Bishops Conference of England and Wales 2012.

144. Interview with author, March 2019.

145. *The Simmarian*, 1993, local history collection Richmond ref acc ic11 964. Old Town Hall, Richmond.

146. *The Simmarian*, 1993, local history collection Richmond ref acc ic11 964. Old Town Hall, Richmond.

147. Interview with author February 2019.

148. *Ibid.*

149. *1945–1947 In their own words… St Mary's University College Strawberry Hill September 1997*, booklet in private collection.

150. St Mary's University College prospectus 1996–97, p. 3.

151. St Mary's University College prospectus 1996–97, p. 6.

152. *Ibid.*

153. Postgraduate Certificate in Education, Catholic Certificate of Religious Studies, Qualified Teacher Status, South West London Teacher Education Consortium

154. *St Mary's University College Prospectus 1996–97*, p. 16.

155. *Simmarian* issue number 13, winter 2001.

156. The original plan for Pope John Paul's visit had included a gathering at St Mary's, but the site was deemed not to be sufficiently secure—the Pope had been the victim of two assassination attempts, one in Rome in 1981 and another in Fatima a year later. Digby Stuart College at Roehampton was chosen instead.

157. Pope Benedict XVI, *Address to Pupils* (17 September 2010).

158. Pope Benedict XVI, *Address to Teachers and Religious* (17 September 2010).

159. Interview with author, March 2019.

160. *Richmond and Twickenham Times* January 2010 in London Borough of Richmond local history archives, Old Town Hall, Richmond.

161. More on this in the Sport at Simmaries section.

162. Interview with author, May 2019.

163. *Simmarian* winter 2015.

164. *Simmarian* winter 2015.

165. See current (2019) website and brochures.

166. J. H. Newman *The Idea of a University* (London: Longmans, Green and Company, 1931), p. 11.

The Quadrangle of the original St Mary's Training College, Brook Green, Hammersmith. No trace of it now exists.

Early Students at Hammersmith, 1880s.

Very Rev James Rowe, Cong. Orat.,
1861

Early Principals of
St Mary's College

Very Rev Canon Thomas Graham DD,
1869

Very Rev William Byrne CM,
1899

Rev Andrew Moynihan CM,
1909

Rev Edward Sheehy CM,
1912

Rev John Campbell CM,
1917

Rev John Boyle CM,
1921

Early Principals of
St Mary's College

Rev Vincent McCarthy CM,
1930

Rev Gerald Shannon CM,
1941

Rev Kevin Cronin CM,
1948

Rev Thomas Cashin CM,
1969

An early aerial view of St Mary's, Strawberry Hill, with the newly-built College buildings adjoining the Waldegrave and Walpole buildings.

The old chapel at St Mary's, Strawberry Hill, in use until the Second World War and now a drama studio.

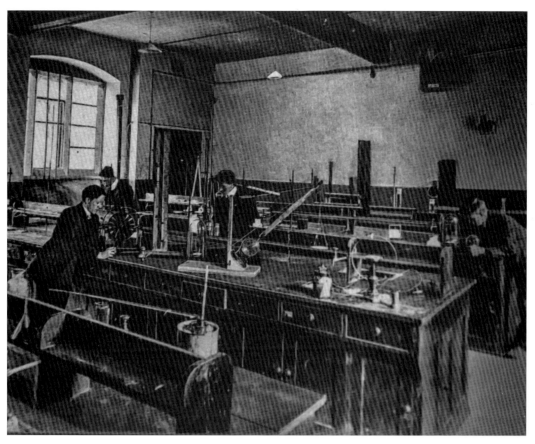

Early science laborator at St Mary's, Strawberry Hill

At Strawberry Hill, 1930s: the College was a substantial size by this time.

Athletics team with the Inter-Collegiate shield, 1937.
There was deep annual rivalry with Borough Road College for this coveted trophy

Post-war hockey team with Fr Kevin Cronin: major matches against other colleges were not possible during the Second World War but restarted as soon as peace came.

College staff, 1940: the Principal, Rev Vincent McCarthy, front row centre.

College staff, 1950: the Principal, Rev Kevin Cronin, front row centre.

Centenary celebrations, 1950: dinner in the Waldegrave Drawing Room, Strawberry Hill.

In the 1950s, students used the Waldegrave Drawing Room as a Library.

2

Sport at Simmaries

For most students, most of the time, sport has been the dominating fact of life at St Mary's. From the earliest days at Brook Green, Hammersmith, when the College had its own gymnasium built under the leadership of Fr Moynihan in the 1900s, right through to today's top-quality running track and sports halls, sport has been central.

Athletics at St Mary's began with an inaugural meeting of athletic clubs of the Metropolitan Training Colleges (namely London's teacher training colleges) at Stamford Bridge in June 1898.[1] A notable runner was Bob Randerson, who held the student record, running 100 yards in just 10.2 seconds. Later he volunteered for service in the First World War, and was killed in 1914.

Over the next years, and throughout the first half of the 20th century, there was much rivalry between St Mary's and the Borough Road College. The Inter-Collegiate trophy or "Inter Coll" was the coveted prize each year and in the 1930s St Mary's won it for six years in succession. Activities included running, discus throwing, long jump, and javelin-throwing. The rivalry was interrupted by World War II but continued afterwards, St Mary's winning again until Borough Road made a breakthrough in 1949.

Football was important from the beginning. The *St Mary's College Centenary Record* published in 1950 notes the names of students who went on to play for some of the most famous football teams in Britain. "The pitch behind the College in Brook Green could hardly be expected to provide opportunity for serious practice. Yet it is an amazing fact that at no time did interest wane, and by about 1910 soccer was the principal topic of conversation in the college." Among top College footballers, Matthew McCabe joined Glasgow Celtic and went on to become the founder of the Scottish Schools Football, League John Gilroy became a well-known referee, Tom Maley played for Glasgow Celtic, Richard Currey played for Fulham, and Jack Casey joined Chelsea and West Ham.[2] The move to Strawberry Hill saw Rugby and cricket added to the sports available, and then followed tennis cross-country running, hockey and basket-ball.

College songs, College dinners, gatherings of old Simmarians, wartime get-togethers, local Simmarian clubs—all of these centred on sport from the College's earliest days. Being active and sporty was part of being Simmarian. Several generations of Simmarians studied "Geography and PT" as their main subjects at St Mary's, and went on to become teachers of physical education at schools across Britain and overseas.

Andrew Reid-Smith, a student at St Mary's 1990–91, currently head of the Sports Department at St Mary's, noted in 2017 that the old rivalry between St Mary's and Borough Road—the latter now part of the Brunel University at its Uxbridge campus—has been re-ignited in recent years with the annual Varsity event with a full day of competitive sport including Rugby, table tennis, football and even cheerleading. It takes place alternately at St Mary's and at Uxbridge.

For the first century and a half at St Mary's, all sport apart from Physical Education was essentially carried out through voluntary clubs run by the students themselves. Today, students can actually study and take part in sports as part of their degree course.

> It's all much more professional: you can study sports leadership and sports management, and also gain qualifications in coaching and so on. There are courses in sports science, in sports rehabilitation, and sport in the community. A significant proportion of students are involved in sport in one way or another.
> Sport has really defined St Mary's. Joe Jagger was a pivotal figure in the development of Physical Education in the postwar period, and helped to make it central.[3]

In the 1960s the sports department was run by Dr John Gane, a former Simmarian and the first person in Britain to gain a doctorate in Physical Education. Leading names from that era include Dudley Cooper, who began teaching Physical Education at St Mary's at the age of 25 and became a long-serving staff member.

The sense of tradition at St Mary's still echoes: Claire McLaughlin, current (2019) senior lecturer in Sports Rehabilitation, is the daughter of Bill McLaughlin, a legendary figure in sport at St Mary's who retired in 1995 after some 30 years teaching Physical Education.

The athletics track at St Mary's is named in honour of Sir Mo Farrah, who trained at St Mary's from 2001 to 2011. The current Sports Hall was opened by Sebastian Coe in October 2011 and a commemorative plaque marks this.

In the 2012 London Olympics St Mary's played a major role, including the preliminary work for the bid for the Games to come to Britain. Professor Dick Fisher, as Head of St Mary's Preparations, was a member of the Steering Group writing the specifications that formed part of the bid.

The pre-Games training was then held at St Mary's, with ten countries sending their teams to Strawberry Hill during the weeks before the start of the Games. Medal winners in the Olympics and the Paralympics thus looked back to the tracks at St Mary's as part of their memories. David Weir, winner of fur gold medals in the Paralympics, was one of these.

Fisher had been created Professor in 2007 in tribute to his work for sport at St Mary's. He was Honorary President of the European Physical Education Associations, had pioneered work in developing education for coaching in athletics, and received an award for "a sustained and distinguished contribution to the physical education profession".[4]

Among famous names associated with sport at St Mary's over recent decades are Gordon Pirie, John Bicourt, Bill , Annette Stapleton. David Bedford OBE, Matt Wells, Moe Sbihi and Rebecca Romero MBE.

Notes

1. *St Mary's Centenary record*, 1950, p. 100.
2. *150 years of St Mary's College*, p. 28.
3. Interview with author, 2017.
4. *The Simmarian*, issue 19, 2007.

Aerial view of St Mary's University campus today, with its extensive running-track dominating the scene.

Aerial view: today the original Walpole mansion—the white turreted building to the right—is in the care of the Strawberry Hill Trust.

The new Chapel, completed in 1950. The architect was Sir Albert Richardson.

The Chapel: exterior front.

The Chapel: interior showing the west window.

The Queen Mary wing, with a cloister connecting it to the chapel

Students in the garden by the Waldegrave rooms.

Horace Walpole's Chapel in the Woods.

The statue of Our Lady, shown as a teacher, in the Chapel in the Woods.

Snow dramatically highlights the white turreted Walpole mansion.

Cardinal Basil Hume, Archbishop of Westminster, at the opening of a new library extension, 1996.

*Cardinal Cormac Murphy-O'Connor, Archbishop of Westminster,
at the Mass marking St Mary's 150th anniversary, May 2000.*

Pope Benedict XVI with Chief Rabbi, Jonathan Sacks, in the Waldegrave Drawing Room. State Visit to Britain 2010.

The Duke and Duchess of Cambridge with the Duke of Sussex at St Mary's University.

Sir Mo Farah at the new running track, 2010.

21st century: the new sports building.

Francis Campbell, Vice-Chancellor of St Mary's University, appointed in 2014.

Graduation, 21st century style: students celebrate at Westminster Cathedral.

3

THE STRAWBERRY HILL STORY

The name "Strawberry Hill" is rather charming, and has now been adopted by the whole district, but in fact the original name of the house was more prosaic: "Chopp'd Straw House".

It was an old farmhouse standing not far from the Thames at a particularly beautiful spot on the outskirts of Twickenham. The acquisition of this house by Horace Walpole in the eighteenth century, and its subsequent transformation into a "gothick"[1] mansion, would change the whole area, making use of its natural beauty to create a house and park that would also transform ideas about art and architecture.

Horatio—usually called Horace—Walpole was born in 1719, the youngest son of Britain's first Prime Minister, Sir Robert Walpole. He was educated at Eton and Cambridge, and in due course his father's patronage brought him various official positions which gave him an income. He also later became a Member of Parliament. He wrote a number of pamphlets and essays, and what would become known as a "gothic" novel, *The Castle of Otranto*, establishing a new trend in writing.

Twickenham in the early eighteenth century was fashionable because of its lovely setting by the Thames. It offered the possibility of country living while not being too far from London. There were a number of fine houses with large gardens and land leading down to the river. Curiously, in view of its subsequent history, this area in the 18th century had quite a Catholic flavour—the aptly named poet Alexander Pope (1688–1744), of a recusant family, lived nearby, having in 1719 acquired a house later known as Pope's Villa.

Horace Walpole rented Chopp'd Straw House for the 1747 season. The name was a sort of local joke: the house was built by a coachman to Lord Bradford and it was said that he paid for it by selling the hay he was given for the horses and feeding them on chopped straw instead. It was a timber-framed farmhouse built in the 17th century and by Walpole's arrival it had been extended and rebuilt by various tenants. These included William Talbot, Bishop of Durham, who substantially extended the house to accommodate his large family and made it rather grander, and the playwright and Poet Laureate Colley Cibber. Walpole rented the house from a subsequent owner, Mrs Chevenix, who owned a shop in London's Charing Cross selling toys and china and glass ornaments. He loved the setting of the house and felt that it had huge possibilities, and in due course bought it from the Chenevix family.

Walpole seems to have felt that the name "Chopp'd Straw House" was not very suitable for a gentleman's residence, and must have been glad to discover that the land around the house had been known as Strawberry Shot, presumably because strawberries had been grown there. And so the house and estate were renamed Strawberry Hill. Walpole gradually acquired more land as it came on to the market, eventually owning almost fifty acres around the house.

Walpole "decided to adapt the original Chopp'd Straw Hall rather than demolish it and start afresh, and his first alterations created a balanced, symmetrical elevation to the south 'front'. He added a bay to the central part of the elevation with an even arrangement of windows to either side. At this stage the house would have looked fairly classical and fashionable; what was different was the use made of gothic elements—quatrefoil windows, ogee door and window detailing, pinnacles to give the house a fairy-tale skyline, battlements around the roof—all elements usually reserved for grand buildings but here used to enhance a tiny house."[2]

Walpole had embarked on what was to become his major project. His fascination with gothic architecture would make him the fore-runner of the great Gothic Revival of the 19th century which, particularly through the work of Augustus Welby Pugin, would give Britain some of its most important public buildings, notably the Houses of Parliament. Undoubtedly, Walpole's "Gothick" opened the way for the developments of the 19th century, although it is interesting to note that he shared none of the Catholic beliefs that underpinned Pugin's work: as an MP he opposed any liberalising of the anti-Catholic laws of his era and tended to see the Catholic Church as simply an instrument of oppressive political power.

At Strawberry Hill, Walpole collected together a "Committee of taste" to create a mansion that would be a delight to the eye and also a place of comfort, pleasure and relaxation for himself and his friends. He never married and this was not designed as a family home. Instead it was a gothick fantasy-house, filled with curiosities and objects of interest and beauty.

The later Gothic Revival architects tended to dislike Walpole's house because its style was essentially artificial: the gothic trimmings were just that, decorations in wood, plaster or papier-maché, not solid stonework that genuinely supported the arches and windows. Walpole was not a professional architect, Pugin on the other hand was: his pillars and arches were all designed and built in stone as part of the essential structure of his massive gothic churches and public buildings. Walpole's mansion was a place of decoration: but it was of good quality and would survive the next two centuries well. He ordered painted glass from an Italian designer—it showed coats of arms and Medieval figures, along with flowers and birds, and gave the windows and rooms a church-like feel. He created a Gallery with a fan-vaulted ceiling, in which he would in due course entertain friends to lavish parties. In the Great North Bedchamber a gothic fireplace pointed up to a richly decorated ceiling, beneath which a vast four-poster bed had its own rich canopy. In the Library, completed in 1754, books lined the walls in great gothic arches, and the fireplace was framed by sweeping spires giving the general effect of a sanctuary or chancel with portraits on either side.

Walpole added a great tower—the Round Tower—complete with battlements, with another turreted Beauclerk Tower alongside. This completed the general Medieval appearance, and added gravitas to the whole scene. Strawberry Hill was now no longer merely a gentleman's residence but something of a castle—while still retaining its sense of light and delicacy through its gothic windows and finely-carved arches. People flocked to see it—not just friends who were invited to stay and who made their own contribution to the project with their designs, knowledge of history, gifts and information, but also members of the public who could buy tickets and come on a tour. Walpole eventually became irritated by these last groups, as they took up a good deal of time, intruded on his peace, and sometimes seem to have damaged, or even stolen, things as they made their way around the rooms, poking and stroking and chattering as they went. He had strict rules drawn up; people had to book in advance, and parties should be no larger than four and were requested not to bring children.[3]

Walpole filled the house with paintings and enjoyed deciding where each would be placed: "All this morning I have been busy in placing Henry VII in the State Bedchamber and making a new arrangement of pictures. It is really a very royal chamber now and much improved. Besides the family of Henry VIII over the chimney as before, and Queen Maintenon over one of the doors, there are Henry VII and Catherine of Braganza, on one side of the bed: Henry VIII and Henrietta Duchess of Orleans on the other."[4]

Outside, Walpole created a Prior's Garden with Medieval-style beds of herbs, and planted a grove of trees to frame the lovely view down to the river. A seat, designed like a vast seashell occupied one pleasant shady corner, along a walk that went around the grounds to the "chapel in the woods". This was completed in 1773 and modelled on a sixteenth-century chantry chapel in Salisbury Cathedral. It was built of brick, faced with stone, and in it Walpole placed various religious items shipped from Rome and elsewhere. He had his favourite pets buried there, and placed memorial tablets recording them. He never used the chapel for Christian worship—it was a place to be viewed and enjoyed as a curiosity and a delight for its charm and beauty.

By the time Horace Walpole died in 1797, Strawberry Hill was a famous landmark. It had played a major role in the artistic, cultural and even political life of the nation: here ideas were discussed, books, essays, poems and pamphlets written and printed—Walpole had his own printing press—and men and women of prominence met there. Walpole himself—who on inheriting the family title in 1791 became the 4th Earl of Orford—was a nationally known figure, partly through his *Otranto* novel and partly through the house and the people who gathered there.

Among those associated with Strawberry Hill during the Walpole years were the actress and singer, and incidentally a Catholic, Kitty Clive who retired to live in a cottage in the grounds, the antiquarian John Chute who designed many of the rooms, the abolitionist campaigner Hannah More, and the poet Thomas Gray, author of *An Elegy written in a Country Churchyard*, whose friendship with Walpole went back to their youth.

There was a substantial—and hard-working—staff keeping Strawberry Hill house clean, warm, and comfortable over the years, and in Walpole's old age their duties also had to include carrying him about as he suffered badly from gout.

As he had no children, he left the house to his cousin, the sculptress Anne Seymour Damer, whose work he had encouraged. She knew the house well and had often stayed there when young: on inheriting it she took responsibility for keeping it open to the public, and continued the ticket sales and tours instituted by Walpole. She and her mother moved in and made it their home: she revived the printing press and also arranged for theatrical performances in the house. But it was evidently difficult—and expensive—to maintain and after her mother's death in 1810 she handed it over to Lady Waldegrave. Thus, in the first years of a new century, Strawberry Hill embarked on a new beginning.

The Waldegrave connection with Horace Walpole was quite distant and was through an illegitimate line via his brother Sir Edward Walpole. Lady Waldegrave was Sir Edward's granddaughter. It was her grandsons who would pave the way for the most significant owner of Strawberry Hill since Walpole's acquisition of Chopp'd Straw House a hundred years earlier.

In early 1839 the famous English tenor, John Braham, came to sing at Strawberry Hill, and brought with him his 18-year-old daughter Frances (b.1821). The two Waldegrave brothers, John and Edward, were immediately fascinated by her beauty, and on May 25th of that year she married the older brother, John. It would be a short marriage: after only six months John died, and in September 1840 Frances married the younger brother, Edward. As English law forbade marriage to a deceased husband's brother, the ceremony took place in Scotland.

If the circumstances of their marriage were unusual, what followed was even more dramatic. While living at Strawberry Hill, Edward—now the 7th Earl Waldegrave—became involved in a drunken brawl, and was sentenced by the Twickenham magistrates to six months in prison. Frances, who seems to have been a woman of unusually strong character, went to live with him in London's Queen's Bench prison. On his release, Edward announced that, because he had been treated so badly in Twickenham, he was selling the entire contents of Strawberry Hill House and retiring to another Waldegrave family property in the country.

The Great Sale of 1842 became a major national event. Tickets had to be obtained, and a Private Viewing of all the many items—the great collection lovingly built up by Horace Walpole—began on March 28th. Huge crowds came to view the curios—ornaments, books, pamphlets, prints, pictures, furniture, items of historical interest or of mere whimsy, a completely unique collection that fascinated all who visited, and the newspapers that reported it all. The catalogue ran to eight editions, and the sale took over a month in a special temporary auction hall on the lawn at Strawberry Hill, raising £33,000.[5]

It seems that Edward's idea was that the empty and abandoned Strawberry Hill House would stand as a reproach to Twickenham, and would break the family's link with the place—in fact the link would become stronger over the next years. He died in 1846, and the house, along with other Waldegrave family estates in Somerset, were left to Frances.

She was still only in her twenties, and it must have been an enormous responsibility. Her life now took another turn: in 1848 she married a man nearly thirty years her senior, George Granville Harcourt. Together, they moved to Strawberry Hill, and she began to establish the house as a centre of political life and hospitality. At the Great Sale she had rescued various Waldegrave family portraits by paying for them to be bought anonymously. These were now brought back to Twickenham and she began an immense project of extending, altering and renovating the house.

Under Lady Waldegrave—she retained the name through her marriage to Harcourt and also her remarriage, following widowhood, to a Liberal MP, Chichester Fortescue—Strawberry Hill was substantially remodelled and enlarged. Among much else, she added an extra wing and remodelled the main house to create a large entrance hall. Walpole's great Round Tower and Beauclerk Tower were each raised by a further storey—necessary in order to keep the whole building properly in scale. A circular drive was created at the front of the house.

Today, the rooms connecting Walpole's original mansion with the 20th-century college buildings are known as the Waldegrave Suite, and Lady Waldegrave's portrait gazes down on guests who gather for graduation celebrations, conferences, lectures and formal dinners.

The rooms are known as the Drawing Room, the Billiard Room, the Ante Room and the Senior Common Room, and in addition to being approached via the main college building, they can be entered through what is known as the Iron Staircase leading up from the garden.

Although she married four times, there was never any suggestion of anything remotely improper about Lady Waldegrave: she was known as a kindly, intelligent, generous and dignified woman, whose devotion to each of her spouses was genuine. Her aim at Strawberry Hill seems to have been to create a place where important matters of state and public policy were discussed and ideas circulated in an atmosphere of goodwill and hospitality. Local legend credits her with the establishment of a railway station at Strawberry Hill—certainly the purpose of the new railway line reaching out in this direction was to serve the great house, as there was no suburban housing in this part of Twickenham in the 19th century.

Frances Waldegrave died in 1879, and in 1883 the estate was bought by Baron Herbert de Stern (b.1851), a banker from a prominent Portuguese family. He was a leading philanthropist who used his immense wealth in aid of the National Gallery in London. He was created Baron Michelham in 1905. Strawberry Hill became his family home and when he died in 1919 it passed to his son, Hermann, who sold it to the Catholic Education Council in 1923.

The Waldegrave and Michelham families continue to have links with Strawberry Hill and are invited to events at St Mary's University.

Strawberry Hill House—or "The Castle" as it is often called locally—is now in the care of the Strawberry Hill Trust. With funding from various sources the house has been restored to Horace Walpole's original vision, and is open to the public, attracting thousands of visitors every year. Teams of experts in textiles, printing, art, architecture, and eighteenth-century history have worked to restore or recreate pictures, prints, wallpaper and furnishings and to display the history and stories of the house, including its domestic arrangements and its gardens. The latter have received particular attention, and Walpole's woodlands walks and Prior's Garden have been revived for new generations to enjoy. Relays of volunteers work in the house and gardens: sewing enthusiasts create eighteenth-century costumes for schoolchildren to wear as part of history projects, gardeners dig and plant in the grounds, and throughout the year there are events ranging from a popular annual quiz to moonlit walks. A busy restaurant serves meals and teas and hosts an annual Christmas market. Special guests through the year include well-known actors, gardening experts and leading historians, all working to bring alive the events and atmosphere of the Walpole and the Waldegrave eras.

Websites

http://www.strawberryhillhouse.org.uk (accessed 21 Jan 2018)

Notes

1.   "Gothick" spelled with a 'k' is the usual way of differentiating the light-hearted, even frivolous, style of gothic favoured by eighteenth-century architects and designers (of which Strawberry Hill is a prime example), from the more archaeologically 'correct' versions of the nineteenth-century Gothic Revival, promoted by architects such as A.W.N. Pugin and George Gilbert Scott.

2.   A. Chalcraft and J. Viscardi. *Strawberry Hill: Horace Walpole's Gothic Castle* (London: Francis Lincoln 2007), p. 17.

3.   J. Iddon, *Horace Walpole's Strawberry Hill—a History and Guide* (St Mary's University College, 1996), p. 27.

4.   Chalcraft and Viscardi. *Strawberry Hill*, p. 107.

5.   Iddon, *Horace Walpole's Strawberry Hill*, p. 15.

The Marshall Children's
Animal
ENCYCLOPEDIA

CONSULTANT: PROFESSOR PHILIP WHITFIELD

MARSHALL PUBLISHING • LONDON

A Marshall Edition
Conceived, edited and designed by
Marshall Editions Ltd
The Orangery
161 New Bond Street
London W1Y 9PA

First published in the UK in 1999 by
Marshall Publishing Ltd

ISBN 1 84028 018 2

Originated in Singapore by Master Image
Printed in Germany by Mohndruck Graphische
Betribe GMBH

Main contributor: Jinny Johnson
Other contributors: Steve Setford, Roger Few,
Professor Philip Whitfield
Consultants: *Mammals:* Dr Sara Churchfield,
King's College, University of London
Birds: Dr Malcolm Ogilvie, formerly of the Wildfowl
and Wetlands Trust
Reptiles and Amphibians: Professor Barry Cox, formerly
of King's College, University of London
Fish: Professor Philip Whitfield, Head of the Division of
Life Sciences, King's College, University of London
Insects, spiders and other invertebrates: Dr Bryan Turner,
King's College, University of London

Senior Designer: Caroline Sangster
Assistant Designer: Nelupa Hussain
Design Manager: Ralph Pitchford
Art Director: Simon Webb
Managing Editor: Kate Phelps
Editors: Claire Berridge, Annabel Reid
Proof reader: Lindsay McTeague
Editorial Director: Cynthia O'Brien
Picture Research: Zilda Tandy
Production: Janice Storr, James Bann

Contents

INTRODUCTION AND HOW TO USE THIS BOOK
4–5

Mammals 6–65

What is a mammal?	8–9
Monotremes and marsupials	10–13
Insect eaters, sloths and colugos	14–17
Bats	18–21
Focus on vampire bats	20–21
Primates	22–27
Carnivores	28–37
Focus on tigers	30–31
Seals, whales and dolphins	38–45
Focus on Antarctic seals	40–41
Hoofed mammals	46–57
Focus on elephants	48–49
Rodents and rabbits	58–65

Why do zebras have stripes? 66–67

Birds 68–113

What is a bird?	70–71
Game birds and ground birds	72–77
Waders, waterbirds, cranes and seabirds	78–89
Focus on penguins	86–87
Owls and birds of prey	90–95
Focus on eagles	94–95
Birds of the trees and masters of the air	96–103
Focus on hummingbirds	100–101
Songbirds	104–13
Focus on birds of paradise	108–9

How do animals communicate? 114–115

Reptiles 116–37

What is a reptile? 118–19
Crocodiles, alligators, turtles
    and tortoises 120–27
Focus on Nile crocodiles 122–23
Lizards and snakes 128–37
Focus on chameleons 132–33

Amphibians 138–53

What is an amphibian? 140–41
Newts and salamanders 142–45
Frogs and toads 146–53
Focus on arrow-poison frogs 150–51

Why are some animals poisonous?
154–55

Fish 156–97

What is a fish? 158–59
Hagfish, lampreys,
    sharks and rays 160–63
Focus on skates, rays
    and seabed sharks 162–63
Sturgeon, gars and relatives 164–65
Eels, tarpon and herring 166–67
Carp, bream and piranhas 168–69
Catfish and relatives 170–71
Electric eel, salmon, hatchetfish
    and pike 172–73
Cod, anglers and cusk-eels 174–75
Perchlike fish 176–85
Focus on tuna 180–81
Flyingfish, lanternfish and lizardfish
    186–87

Guppies, grunions and relatives 188–89
Oarfish, squirrelfish and relatives 190–91
Seahorses, scorpionfish and relatives
    192–93
Flatfish 194–95
Coelacanth, lungfish, triggerfish
    and relatives 196–97

Why do some animals work together?
198–99

Insects, spiders and other invertebrates 200–255

What is an invertebrate? 202–3
Cockroaches, earwigs, crickets,
    grasshoppers and relatives 204–7
Mantids, dragonflies and relatives
    208–11
Bugs, lice, fleas and beetles 212–19
Focus on stag beetles 216–17
Flies, moths and butterflies 220–27
Focus on sphinx moths 224–25
Bees, wasps, ants and termites 228–35
Focus on honeybees 232–33
Spiders and scorpions 236–43
Focus on orb weavers 240–41
Snails, slugs and other
    land invertebrates 244–45
Sea creatures 246–55
Focus on rock clingers 252–53

Why do animals build nests? **256–57**

INDEX 258–63

LIST OF ABBREVIATIONS 263

AKNOWLEDGEMENTS 264

Introduction

The land, air and waters of our world are filled with an astonishing variety of life and more than 1.5 million kinds, or species, of animals have been named so far. All of these animals can be divided into two main groups – vertebrates and invertebrates.

Fishes, amphibians, reptiles, birds and mammals are all vertebrates, which means they have a backbone in their body. Invertebrate animals, such as insects, spiders and snails, do not have a backbone. Scientists believe that most species of vertebrates, such as mammals and birds, are already known, but there may be millions of species of insects and other small invertebrates that still await discovery. This illustrated encyclopedia provides an invaluable catalogue of all the major types of animal from whales to fleas.

The Earth has a number of natural zones, or habitats, divided according to the climate and the plants and animals that live there. The habitats are shown on this **map**. The colours are the same as for the habitat symbols (see page 5).

Key to map (see page 5 for full key)

Temperate grassland

High ground

Coral reefs

Tropical grassland

Desert, semi-desert and scrub

Tropical evergreen forest

Northern forest

Deciduous forest and seasonal forest

Coast

Tundra and polar

Map of the world's main natural habitats

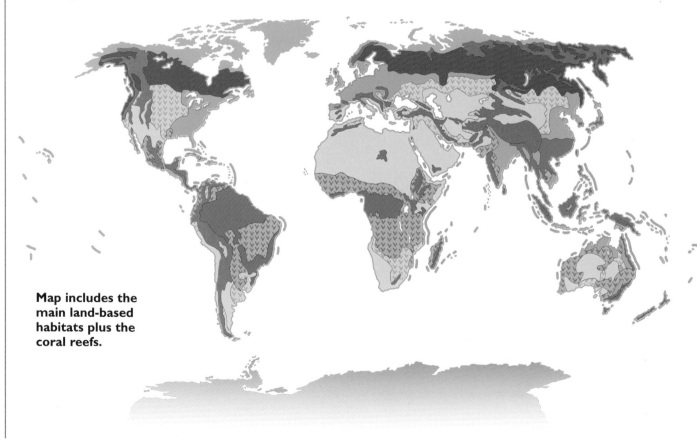

Map includes the main land-based habitats plus the coral reefs.

How to use this book

This encyclopedia of animals is divided into six chapters: mammals, birds, reptiles, amphibians, fish, and insects, spiders and other invertebrates. Each chapter contains an introduction, pages that describe the features of each type of animal (such as a mammal), catalogue pages that illustrate and give the facts about many different species, and focus pages that look in more detail at particular animals. There are also five special double-pages featuring information on animal adaptation and behaviour.

Habitat
The symbols show the habitats in which the species or insect family lives. The key is below.

Size
The approximate size of the animal is given in metric and imperial measurements. See page 263 for a list of the abbreviations in the book.

Range
This lists the areas of the world in which the species is found.

Scientific name
Most species of animals have a common name, such as Viriginia opossum, which can vary from place to place. All species have a scientific or Latin-based name, which always stays the same. It is shown in *italics*. In the insects and spiders section, the family name is given instead of the scientific name. The **number of species** is the number in that family.

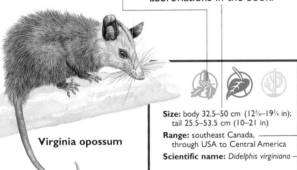
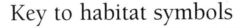

Virginia opossum

Size: body 32.5–50 cm (12¾–19¾ in); tail 25.5–53.5 cm (10–21 in)
Range: southeast Canada, through USA to Central America
Scientific name: *Didelphis virginiana*

Key to habitat symbols

Oceanic includes open sea and oceans, top and middle layers of water

Temperate grassland includes steppe, prairie, pampas, bush, open country, moors, heaths, plains and lowlands

Coastal waters includes estuaries and the seabed

High ground includes hills, foothills, plateaus, volcanoes and mountains

Coral reefs

Tropical grassland also called savanna

Desert includes rocky areas, sandy areas, semi-desert, scrub, brushland, arid (dry) and semi-arid land

Tropical evergreen forest includes tropical and subtropical rainforests, bamboo and mangroves

Worldwide used for insects and spiders only

Temperate used for insects and spiders only

Tropical used for insects and spiders only

Inhabited areas and agricultural land includes gardens, orchards, parks, farmland, cultivated land, fields, plantations, pasture, towns and cities, hedgerows and roadsides

Fresh water includes rivers, lakes, ponds, lagoons, streams, creeks, wetlands, marshes, swamps, inland waters, flood plains, springs, ditches, dams, river banks and underground water in caves

Northern forest includes taiga, northern (boreal) and coniferous forests

Deciduous forest and seasonal forest includes temperate and tropical seasonal forests

Deep sea

Coast includes mudflats, shores, cliffs, islands and tidal areas

Tundra and polar includes Arctic and Antarctic regions, pack ice and ice floes

Mammals

Human beings are just one of about 4,000 mammal species. Mammals come in all shapes and sizes and are found in almost every part of the world, from the frozen Arctic to the hottest deserts, the densest forests and the biggest oceans. There are many different kinds of mammal, each with its own way of life. The tiger, for example, hunts prey in the depths of the forest, while dolphins swim through the sea, moles burrow underground, bats fly through the air, horses gallop across the ground, and monkeys swing through the trees.

Fossils show that the first mammals evolved more than 200 million years ago from a group of mammal-like reptiles, when dinosaurs still roamed the Earth. The earliest mammals were small shrewlike animals, which fed on insects and dinosaur eggs. When dinosaurs began to die out about 65 million years ago, mammals took their place as the dominant creatures. Their ability to adapt to very different habitats helped mammals to spread throughout the globe.

A female **polar bear** dozes with her cub in the sunshine on the Arctic ice. One of the reasons why mammals are so successful is that they take greater care of their young than other animals, protecting them until they are old enough to fend for themselves.

Atlantic bottle-nosed dolphin

What is a mammal?

Mammals are a very diverse group of animals, but they all have certain things in common. They are warm-blooded, have lungs to breathe in air and a bony frame called a skeleton to support their bodies and protect their internal organs. Most also have relatively large brains, good senses and hair or fur.

Indian elephant

Mammals are warm-blooded animals, meaning that they can keep their body temperature constant, whatever the temperature of their surroundings. When they are too hot, many mammals sweat to cool down. **Elephants** cannot sweat, so they keep cool by staying in the shade, bathing in water and letting heat radiate from their huge ears.

Senses

Mammals generally have well-developed senses of sight, hearing, smell, taste and touch. These senses help them to locate food, avoid predators, find a mate and much more. The sense organs are often found in the head, near the brain.

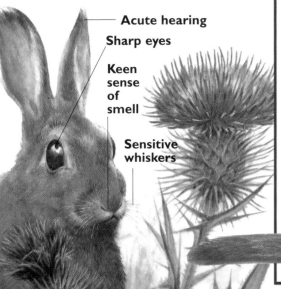

Acute hearing

Sharp eyes

Keen sense of smell

Sensitive whiskers

Types of mammal

Most mammals give birth to live young. In the majority of mammals, known as eutherians, the babies grow inside the mother's womb. They are supplied with food and oxygen by a special organ called the placenta, and are well developed when they are born. The babies of some mammals, called marsupials, are very undeveloped at birth and crawl into a special pouch, where they can grow stronger in safety. Monotreme mammals are unusual in that they lay eggs, instead of producing babies.

MONOTREME

SHORT-BEAKED ECHIDNA

Female carries egg in a groove on her belly

Coat of protective spines

Echidna has no teats – milk oozes from pores in skin

MARSUPIAL

RING–TAILED WALLABY

BABY WALLABY FEEDING IN POUCH

Large head

Young wallaby clings to teat

Poorly developed legs

Powerful legs for bounding along fast

Long thick tail for balance

Suckling

Instead of having to gather food for her babies like other animals, a female mammal is able to make her own baby food. She has special mammary glands (also called breasts or udders) that produce milk, which the babies suck from teats. This is called suckling. The milk contains sugar, fat, proteins and vitamins, which the babies need to grow and stay healthy.

Female wild boar with young

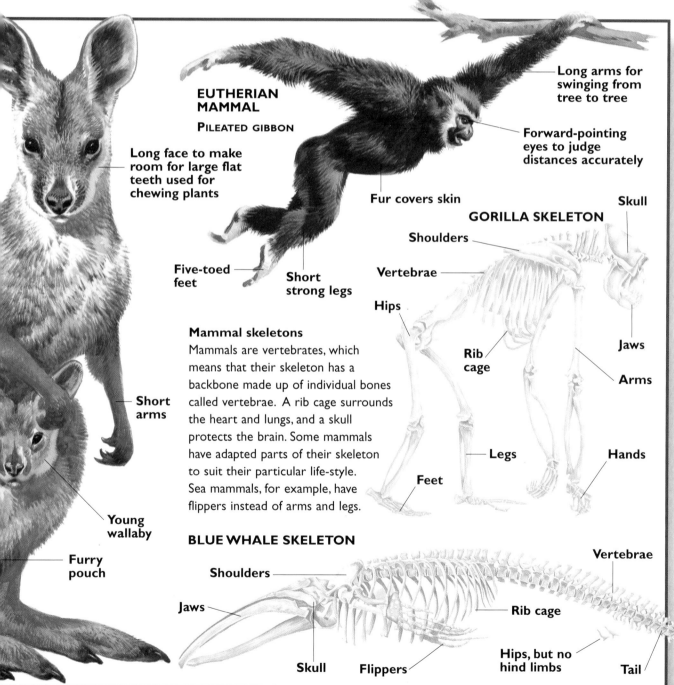

EUTHERIAN MAMMAL

PILEATED GIBBON

Long arms for swinging from tree to tree

Forward-pointing eyes to judge distances accurately

Fur covers skin

Long face to make room for large flat teeth used for chewing plants

Five-toed feet

Short strong legs

GORILLA SKELETON

Skull

Shoulders

Vertebrae

Hips

Rib cage

Jaws

Arms

Legs

Hands

Feet

Mammal skeletons

Mammals are vertebrates, which means that their skeleton has a backbone made up of individual bones called vertebrae. A rib cage surrounds the heart and lungs, and a skull protects the brain. Some mammals have adapted parts of their skeleton to suit their particular life-style. Sea mammals, for example, have flippers instead of arms and legs.

Short arms

Young wallaby

Furry pouch

BLUE WHALE SKELETON

Shoulders

Jaws

Vertebrae

Rib cage

Skull

Flippers

Hips, but no hind limbs

Tail

Monotremes and marsupials

In most mammal species, the young develop inside their mother's body for a long time before they are born. But monotremes and marsupials are different. Just like their reptile ancestors, monotremes lay eggs. However, when the eggs hatch, the young feed on their mother's milk like other mammal babies. Milk oozes from enlarged skin pores because the females have no teats. Marsupials give birth to very undeveloped babies: some are no bigger than a grain of rice, and all are hairless and blind. Once they are born, a young marsupial develops in a furry pouch on the underside of its mother's body.

Monotremes

Monotremes consist of echidnas (sometimes called spiny anteaters) and platypuses. A female echidna lays a single soft-shelled egg and puts it in a special groove on her belly. The egg is covered in a sticky substance for 7 to 10 days until it hatches. The platypus is one of the few venomous mammals: males have a spur on each hind foot, which they use to inject poison into an enemy. A female platypus lays two or three eggs at the end of a long tunnel, which take up to two weeks to hatch.

Long-beaked echidna

Size: body 45–77 cm (17¾–30¼ in); virtually no tail
Range: New Guinea
Scientific name: *Zaglossus bruijni*

Long-beaked echidna

Echidnas have long slender snouts. They have no teeth and weak jaws, so they lap up ants, termites and other small creatures with their sticky tongues and crush them against the roof of their mouths.

Platypus

The platypus spends most of the day in a riverside burrow. At dawn and dusk it comes out to feed on the riverbed, using its sensitive bill to probe the mud for insects, worms, grubs, crayfish and frogs. Its bill is a skin-covered framework of bone.

Platypus

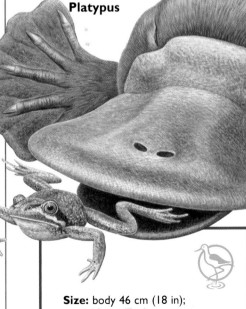

Size: body 35–50 cm (13¾–19¾ in); tail 9 cm (3½ in)
Range: Australia, Tasmania, southeast New Guinea
Scientific name: *Tachyglossus aculeatus*

Short-beaked echidna

The echidna's spiny coat protects it from attackers. When threatened, it either curls itself up into a ball or, if it is on soft soil, digs straight downwards so that only its spines are visible. In this way, its soft spineless face and underparts are protected.

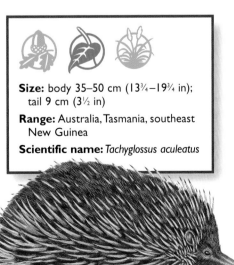

Short-beaked echidna

10

Size: body 46 cm (18 in); tail 18 cm (7 in)
Range: Australia, Tasmania
Scientific name: *Ornithorhynchus anatinus*

Marsupials

The word marsupial means "pouched mammal". A tiny marsupial baby has to wriggle its way through its mother's fur to reach her pouch. Once inside, it latches on to a teat and drinks her milk. The teat swells up inside the baby's mouth and keeps the baby fastened to its milk supply. The pouch gives the baby a safe place in which it can grow and develop until it is ready to face the outside world. There are more than 250 different marsupial species, most of which live in Australia and on the neighbouring islands, but a few species are found in the Americas.

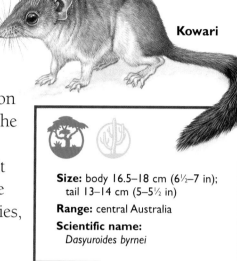

Kowari

Size: body 16.5–18 cm (6½–7 in); tail 13–14 cm (5–5½ in)
Range: central Australia
Scientific name: *Dasyuroides byrnei*

Water opossum

The water opossum is the only marsupial that lives in water. It emerges from its river bank burrow to swim and search for fish, shellfish and other small water creatures, which it carries back to the bank to eat. It swims with its webbed hind feet, and steers with its long tail. Its oily fur repels water, keeping it dry.

Water opossum

Size: body 27–33 cm (10½–13 in); tail 36–40 cm (14¼–15¾ in)
Range: Mexico, Central and South America
Scientific name: *Chironectes minimus*

Kowari

At home in grasslands and deserts, these marsupials live alone or in small groups in an underground burrow. At night, they hunt among the tussock grass for insects, lizards and birds to eat. Kowaris breed in winter and produce litters of five or six young.

Virginia opossum

This is the sole North American marsupial. It often scavenges for food in refuse tips and rubbish bins. To escape a predator such as a dog, bobcat, eagle or mink, the opossum may "play dead", lying on its side with its tongue hanging out and its eyes shut or staring into space. Thinking it is already dead, the predator may lose interest, giving the opossum vital seconds to make its escape.

Virginia opossum

Size: body 32.5–50 cm (12¾–19¾ in); tail 25.5–53.5 cm (10–21 in)
Range: southeast Canada, through USA to Central America
Scientific name: *Didelphis virginiana*

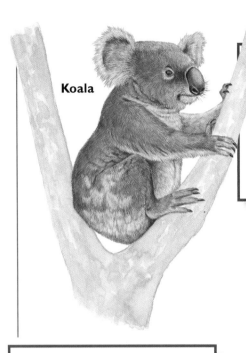

Koala

Size: body 60–85 cm (23½–33½ in); virtually no tail

Range: eastern Australia

Scientific name: *Phascolarctos cinereus*

Koala

The koala spends up to 18 hours each day asleep. The rest of the time it feeds on the leaves of eucalyptus trees. It has a long gut, which enables it to digest the tough leaves and deal with the leaves' poisonous chemicals. Special pouches in its cheeks store the leaves until it needs to eat them.

Brush-tailed possum

Size: body 32–58 cm (12½–22¾ in); tail 24–35 cm (9½–13¾ in)

Range: Australia, Tasmania; introduced into New Zealand

Scientific name: *Trichosurus vulpecula*

Brush-tailed possum

In its natural woodland habitat, the brush-tailed possum feeds on flowers, leaves, fruit, insects and young birds. In populated areas, it makes its home on buildings and feeds on rubbish. It has one young once or twice a year.

Size: body 70–120 cm (27½–47 in); virtually no tail

Range: eastern Australia, Tasmania

Scientific name: *Vombatus ursinus*

Wombat

The wombat feeds on grass in forests and scrubland and can go without water for months at a time. In high summer, this burly mammal spends the day sheltering from the heat in a long deep burrow. The female gives birth to a single young, which stays in her pouch for three months. Once out of the pouch, it forages with her for several months before leaving to live independently.

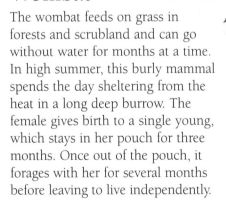

Wombat

Tasmanian devil

About the size of a small dog, the Tasmanian devil has powerful jaws which enable it to crush the bones of its prey. This stocky marsupial moves slowly, but is very cunning. Its keen sense of smell is used to locate prey in the dark and take it by surprise. It feeds on reptiles, birds, fish and small mammals.

Size: body 52–80 cm (20½–31½ in); tail 23–30 cm (9–11¾ in)

Range: Tasmania

Scientific name: *Sarcophilus harrisii*

Brown bandicoot

The brown bandicoot hunts by following the scent of its prey. It lives in areas of dense vegetation, where it can hide from larger predators such as eagles and foxes. It feeds on worms, insect larvae and underground fungi. It will even eat scorpions, biting off the poisonous tail before consuming them.

Size: body 30–33 cm (11¾–13 in); tail 7.5–18 cm (3–7 in)

Range: southern and eastern Australia, Tasmania

Scientific name: *Isoodon obesulus*

Tasmanian devil

Brown bandicoot

Size: body 1–1.6 m (3¼–5¼ ft); tail 90–110 cm (35½–43½ in)

Range: central Australia

Scientific name: *Macropus rufus*

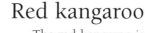

Red kangaroo

The red kangaroo is the largest marsupial. It usually bounds along with huge leaps, on its back legs only, reaching speeds of up to 56 km/h (35 mph). It lives in Australia's hot dry deserts and grassland. The female gives birth to a single baby called a joey, which emerges from her pouch after two months. Whenever danger threatens, the joey dives back into her pouch out of harm's way.

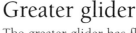

Size: body 30–48 cm (11¾–19 in); tail 45–55 cm (17¾–21¾ in)

Range: eastern Australia

Scientific name: *Petauroides volans*

Greater glider

The greater glider has flaps of skin running between its wrists and ankles. To get from tree to tree in the eucalyptus forests where it lives, it leaps into the air and spreads out its arms and legs. The skin flaps act like a kind of parachute, allowing it to glide to its destination.

Red kangaroo

Musky rat-kangaroo

This tiny kangaroo is unusual because it regularly gives birth to twins. Unlike other kangaroos, it prefers to move around on all fours like a rabbit. Both males and females produce a strong musky smell, but no one knows why they do this.

Lumholtz's tree kangaroo

The tree kangaroo spends most of its time high up in the forest trees, where it eats leaves and fruit. It can even sleep up there, crouched on a thick branch. It is endangered because its rainforest habitat is shrinking as a result of logging.

Bridled nail-tail wallaby

The nail-tail gets its name because it has a small fingerlike nail hidden in thick hair at the tip of its tail. It has a strange way of hopping, moving its arms in circles as it bounces along. Heavy grazing by sheep and cattle has destroyed much of the scrubland where it used to live and feed, and so this wallaby is now an endangered species.

Musky rat-kangaroo

Size: body 23–34 cm (9–13½ in); tail 13–17 cm (5–6¾ in)

Range: northeastern Australia

Scientific name: *Hypsiprymnodon moschatus*

Lumholtz's tree kangaroo

Size: body 45–67 cm (17¾–26¼ in); tail 33–66 cm (13–26 in)

Range: eastern Australia

Scientific name: *Onychogalea fraenata*

Bridled nail-tail wallaby

Size: body 52–80 cm (20½–31½ in); tail 42–93 cm (16½–36½ in)

Range: northeastern Australia

Scientific name: *Dendrolagus lumholtzi*

13

Insect eaters, sloths and colugos

Although these animals are not all related to each other, many of them feed almost exclusively on insects and they are perhaps among the oddest-looking mammals of all. The insect eaters include armadillos, anteaters, pangolins, aardvarks, moles, tenrecs, shrews, and hedgehogs. Sloths and colugos are plant eaters and spend most of their time in the trees.

Anteaters, armadillos, pangolins, aardvarks and sloths

Anteaters and armadillos are edentate mammals. The word edentate means "toothless", which is misleading, as only the anteaters are truly toothless. In fact, some armadillos have up to 100 teeth, although they are only small and peglike. These mammals do not need big biting teeth because they feed on ants and termites, which they lick up with their tongues. Sloths are also edentates, but they feed on leaves instead of insects, chewing them very slowly. They eat, sleep, mate and even give birth hanging upside down in trees. Pangolins and aardvarks have similar life-styles to armadillos and anteaters, even though they are not closely related.

Three-toed sloth

Size: body 50–60 cm (19¾–23½ in); tail 6.5–7 cm (2½–2¾ in)
Range: northern South America
Scientific name:
 Bradypus tridactylus

Three-toed sloth

The three-toed sloth is the slowest living mammal, managing a top speed of just 2 m (6½ ft) per minute on the ground. The hairs of its fur have grooves on them, in which tiny plants called algae live. These give the fur a greenish tinge, which camouflages the sloth, hiding it from predators such as eagles and jaguars.

Giant anteater

This anteater sniffs out ants' nests and termite mounds, breaks them open with its claws and thrusts its long sticky tongue inside. Ants and termites become glued to the tongue, which is covered with tiny spines. It is careful never to destroy a nest or eat all the ants, so it can return there to feed in the future.

Size: body 1–1.2 m (3¼–4 ft); tail 65–90 cm (25½–35½ in)
Range: Central and South America, down to northern Argentina
Scientific name:
 Myrmecophaga tridactyla

Giant anteater

14

Giant armadillo

Giant armadillo

Like other armadillos, the giant armadillo's body is covered with horny plates. It weighs up to 60 kg (132 lb) and is very strong, so it can easily burrow into ants' nests or smash open termite mounds with its front limbs. Unlike the nine-banded armadillo, it can only partly roll into a ball – it usually runs from danger.

Size: body 75–100 cm (29½–39½ in); tail 50 cm (19¾ in)

Range: South America, from Venezuela through to northern Argentina

Scientific name: *Priodontes maximus*

Nine-banded armadillo

When threatened, this armadillo rolls up into a ball so that its soft belly is protected and only its armour-plated back is exposed. It spends most of the day asleep in the safety of a burrow, which it digs with its strong front claws, kicking away loose soil with its hind legs.

Nine-banded armadillo

Size: body 45–50 cm (17¾–19¾ in); tail 25–40 cm (9¾–15¾ in)

Range: southern USA, Central and South America

Scientific name: *Dasypus novemcinctus*

Aardvark

The aardvark looks as if it is made up from parts of other animals, with its kangaroolike tail, piglike body and rabbitlike ears. The aardvark feeds on termites at night. During the day, it sleeps in its burrow, which it digs with its strong feet. The burrow may be very long and complex, with numerous openings.

Aardvark

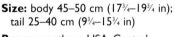

Size: body 1–1.6 m (3¼–5¼ ft); tail 44.5–60 cm (17½–23½ in)

Range: Africa, south of the Sahara

Scientific name: *Orycteropus afer*

Northern tamandua

The tamandua is a tree-dwelling anteater. On the ground, it moves slowly and clumsily, but in the trees of the forest it is an agile climber, using its tail as a fifth limb to grip. If it is attacked, it strikes out with its sharp powerful claws. The female tamandua gives birth to a single baby, which travels around the rainforest on its mother's back.

Giant pangolin

This the only mammal covered in scales. When it is feeding on ants' nests, thick eyelids protect its eyes from bites, and special muscles seal off its nostrils to keep out the ants. It can roll itself up into a ball if threatened, or lash out with its tail, which is clad in razor-sharp scales.

Giant pangolin

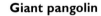

Size: body 54–58 cm (21¼–22¾ in); tail 54.5–55.5 cm (21½–21¾ in)

Range: southern Mexico, through Central and northern South America

Scientific name: *Tamandua mexicana*

Size: body 75–80 cm (29½–31½ in); tail 50–65 cm (19¾–25½ in)

Range: eastern and central Africa

Scientific name: *Manis gigantea*

Northern tamandua

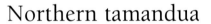

Moles, tenrecs, shrews hedgehogs, solenodons and colugos

Moles, tenrecs, shrews and hedgehogs feed almost exclusively on insects and small creatures such as worms, centipedes, snails and spiders. Many of these mammals have long narrow snouts in order to reach into the small spaces where insects hide. They also have sharp teeth and claws. They have poor eyesight, but an excellent sense of smell. Colugos and solenodons are not related but are both unusual mammals. Colugos can glide through the trees using special flaps of skin. Solenodons have a poisonous bite – a very rare feature in mammals.

Streaked tenrec

The streaked tenrec is covered in protective spines. The female produces a litter of 7 to 11 babies. If she feels threatened, she raises a small patch of spines on her back and vibrates them rapidly. This makes a clicking noise to warn her young of approaching danger.

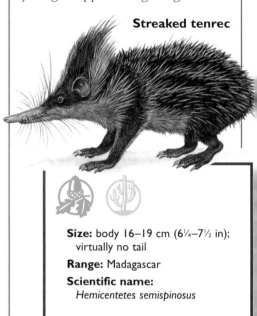

Streaked tenrec

Size: body 16–19 cm (6¼–7½ in); virtually no tail
Range: Madagascar
Scientific name: *Hemicentetes semispinosus*

Western European hedgehog

The hedgehog roots around in hedgerows and undergrowth for small creatures to eat, making piglike grunts as it goes. If it is attacked, the hedgehog curls itself up into a ball, so that its prickly coat deters predators. In cold climates, it hibernates through the winter.

Western European hedgehog

Size: body 13.5–27 cm (5¼–10½ in); tail 1–5 cm (⅓–2 in)
Range: western Europe; introduced into New Zealand
Scientific name: *Erinaceus europaeus*

Giant golden mole

The giant golden mole hunts above ground for beetles, small lizards, slugs and worms. When disturbed, it heads straight for the safety of its burrow – even though it is blind, it always knows exactly where the entrance is. No one knows quite how it does this.

Giant golden mole

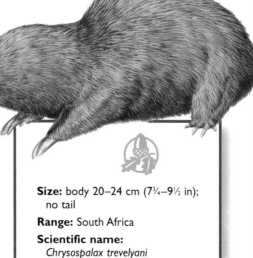

Size: body 20–24 cm (7¾–9½ in); no tail
Range: South Africa
Scientific name: *Chrysospalax trevelyani*

European mole

This small mammal spends almost its entire life underground, digging tunnels with its broad spadelike front legs. It has poor eyesight, but good hearing. It feels its way around and finds worms and insects to eat by detecting the vibrations in the ground caused by their movements.

Size: body 9–16.5 cm (3½–6½ in); tail 3–4 cm (1¼–1½ in)
Range: Europe, eastern Asia
Scientific name: *Talpa europaea*

European mole

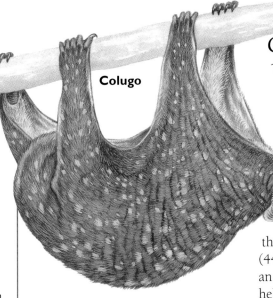

Colugo

Colugo

The forest-dwelling colugo, also known as the flying lemur, has flaps of skin running from its neck to the tip of its tail. By leaping into the air and stretching its arms and legs to open out the flaps, it can glide for 135 m (440 ft) between the trees. It is an agile climber, but is almost helpless on the ground.

Size: body 38–42 cm (15–16½ in); tail 22–27 cm (8¾–10½ in)
Range: Philippines
Scientific name:
  Cynocephalus volans

Common tree shrew

This squirrel-like creature is an excellent climber. It normally lives alone or with its mate, and feeds on ants, spiders, seeds, buds and probably small birds and mice. It nests in holes in trees or among tree roots, where the female gives birth to a litter of one to three young.

Common tree shrew

Size: body 14–23 cm (5½–9 in); tail 12–21 cm (4¾–8¼ in)
Range: southern Asia
Scientific name:
  Tupaia glis

Short-eared elephant shrew

Short-eared elephant shrew

Elephant shrews get their name because of their extraordinary trunklike noses. They walk on all fours, but when they need to move fast, they hop on their back legs like miniature kangaroos. They live in dry open country. They feed on termites, seeds, fruit and berries in the daytime, but shelter from the midday sun in burrows.

Size: body 9.5–12.5 cm (3¾–5 in); tail 9.5–14 cm (3¾–5½ in)
Range: southern Africa
Scientific name:
  Macroscelides proboscideus

Armoured shrew

The armoured shrew has an incredibly strong backbone and is said to be able to support the weight of a grown man without being crushed! It lives in forests, where it feeds on insects and other small creatures.

Cuban solenodon

The solenodon probes the forest floor at night in search of food such as insects, fungi and roots. It can also climb trees to reach fruit, berries and buds. It kills lizards, frogs and small birds with a venomous bite. The venom is produced by glands in its lower jaw.

Size: body 28–32 cm (11–12½ in); tail 17–25 cm (6¾–9¾ in)
Range: Cuba
Scientific name:
  Solenodon cubanus

Cuban solenodon

Size: body 12–15 cm (4¾–6 in); tail 7–9.5 cm (2¾–3¾ in)
Range: central Africa
Scientific name:
  Scutisorex somereni

Armoured shrew

17

Bats

Bats are the only flying mammals. They power themselves through the air on smooth wings of skin, making sudden mid-air turns and spectacular twists. Most bats spend the day asleep, hanging upside down, out of reach of predators. At night, they are ready to launch themselves into the air to hunt for food. Some bats find their food and navigate in the dark by echolocation. They make high-pitched sounds that bounce, or echo, off nearby objects and are picked up by the bats' ears. The bats use the echoes to locate their prey and avoid obstacles.

Greater false vampire bat

Spear-nosed bat

Spear-nosed bat

The spear-nosed bat will eat insects and fruit, but prefers the flesh of mice, birds and small bats. The spear-nosed bat, in turn, is preyed upon by false vampire bats. It has a broad spear-shaped flap of skin sticking up from its nose. Huge flocks of these heavy-bodied bats like to shelter in buildings and caves. Flocks emerge at dusk to fly to their feeding grounds. The female gives birth to a single baby, either once or twice a year.

Size: body 10–13 cm (4–5¼ in); tail 2.5 cm (1 in); wingspan 44–47 cm (17¼–18½ in)
Range: Central America and northern South America
Scientific name: *Phyllostomus hastatus*

Size: body 6.5–8.5 cm (2½–3¼ in); no tail; wingspan 23–30 cm (9–11¾ in)
Range: India to Myanmar, southern China, Malaysia
Scientific name: *Megaderma lyra*

Greater false vampire bat

The greater false vampire is one of the largest of all bats. It feeds mainly on insects and spiders, but also preys on rodents, frogs, fish and even other bats. It roosts in caves in groups of 3 to 50 bats. Other bats stay away from the cave, presumably to avoid being eaten. Unlike true vampire bats, false vampire bats do not drink blood.

Ghost bat

The ghost bat, a type of false vampire bat, gets its name from the eerie colour of its pale fur at night. It flies over all kinds of terrain, from forest to desert, and feeds on mice, birds, geckos and other bats. By day, it roosts in caves, rocky clefts and old mine shafts, but it is easily disturbed by people. It is now rare because quarrying (removing stone) has destroyed some of its most important roosts.

Size: body 11.5–14 cm (4½–5½ in); no tail; wingspan 40–60 cm (15¾–23½ in)
Range: northern and western tropical Australia
Scientific name: *Macroderma gigas*

Ghost bat

Greater fruit bat

The largest wings in the bat world belong to the greater fruit bat. By day, they roost in trees in flocks of several thousand bats, taking flight at dusk to find juicy fruit to eat or sweet flower nectar to lap up. Fruit trees are able to reproduce as their pollen, sticking on to the bats' fur, is moved from flower to flower. Fruit seeds they spit out or pass in their droppings take root and grow into new fruit trees.

Size: body 35–40 cm (13¾–15¾ in); no tail; wingspan 1.5 m (5 ft)
Range: southern and Southeast Asia
Scientific name: *Pteropus giganteus*

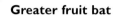

Greater fruit bat

Tube-nosed fruit bat

The scroll-shaped nostrils of this bat stick out on each side of its head like a pair of snorkel tubes. They probably help the bat to find ripe fruit, such as guavas, figs and even young coconuts. Using its sharp teeth, the bat chews the fruit to extract the juice. It drops the unwanted pulp on the ground.

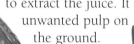

Tube-nosed fruit bat

Size: body 7–12 cm (2¾–4¾ in); tail 1.5–2.5 cm (⅝–1 in); wingspan 20–28 cm (7¾–11 in)
Range: Southeast Asia, New Guinea, northern Australia
Scientific name: *Nyctimene major*

Size: body 11–13 cm (4¼–5 in); tail 2.5–4 cm (1–1½ in); wingspan 33–35 cm (13–13¾ in)
Range: Europe, Asia, northern Africa
Scientific name: *Rhinolophus ferrumequinum*

Greater horseshoe bat

The greater horseshoe bat feeds on beetles, swooping down to snatch them off the ground with pinpoint accuracy. It roosts in caves, trees and the roofs of old buildings. But as caves are explored, trees felled and buildings pulled down, the bat finds it harder and harder to find suitable homes. It is now almost extinct in northwestern Europe.

Greater horseshoe bat

Common long-eared bat

This bat's ears are nearly as long as its head and body combined. The bat uses its sensitive ears to detect the calls and movements of insect prey, and to find its way by echolocation. The long-eared bat hibernates in caves during winter. In summer, it roosts in colonies of 50 to 100 bats in buildings and trees, feeding at night mainly on moths.

Size: body 4–5 cm (1½–2 in); tail 3–4.5 cm (1¼–1¾ in); wingspan 23–28 cm (9–11 in)
Range: northern Europe eastwards to China and Japan
Scientific name: *Plecotus auritus*

Common long-eared bat

19

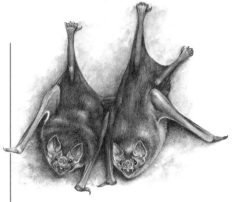

Roosting bats

The common vampire bat is a cave dweller, clinging to cave roofs and roosting in total darkness in colonies of up to 1,000 bats, but usually nearer to 100. It is a wary bat and usually only emerges on very dark moonless nights.

The body of the **common vampire bat** is 9 cm (3½ in) long, and its wingspan is 18 cm (7 in). It has no tail, a snub nose and short pointed ears. It has fewer teeth than most bats because it has no need to chew or grind up food.

Vampire bats

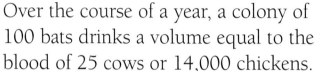

The only mammals to feed entirely on blood are vampire bats, which live in the tropical countries of Central and South America. The common vampire bat, *Desmodus rotundus*, preys on sleeping animals – usually cattle and horses – and sometimes even people. The two other vampire species, *Diaemus youngi* and *Diphylla ecuadata*, prey on large birds such as chickens. The common vampire feeds on its victim for about 30 minutes. The victim does not lose a dangerous amount of blood, but the bat's bite can spread disease and infection. Over the course of a year, a colony of 100 bats drinks a volume equal to the blood of 25 cows or 14,000 chickens.

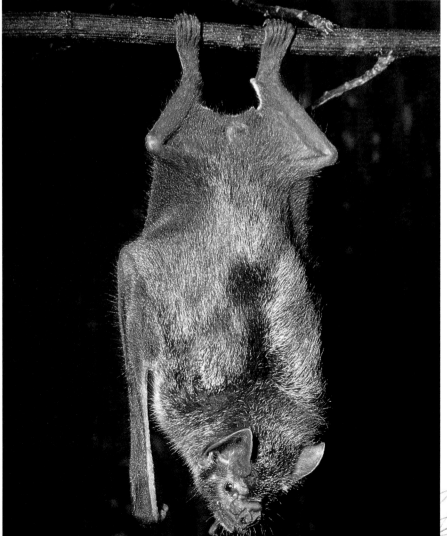

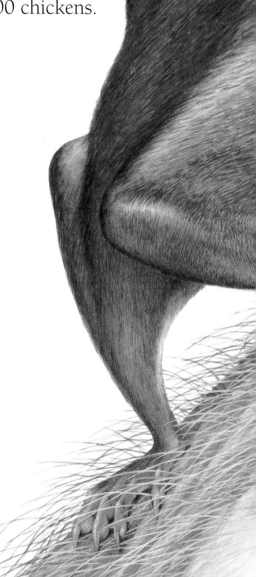

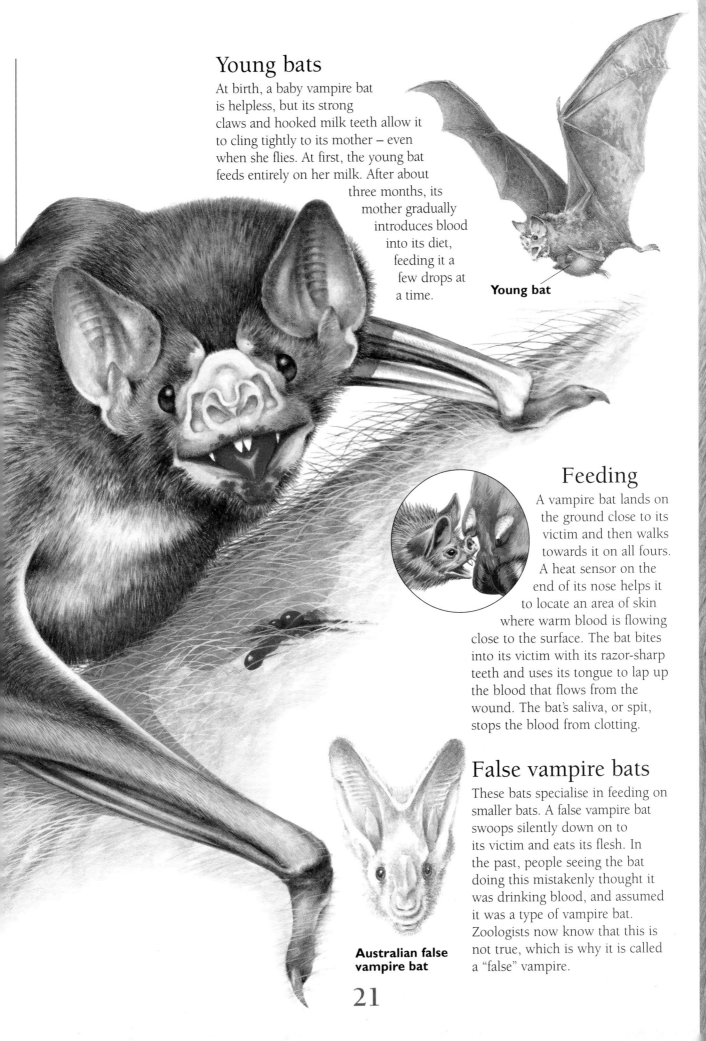

Young bats

At birth, a baby vampire bat is helpless, but its strong claws and hooked milk teeth allow it to cling tightly to its mother – even when she flies. At first, the young bat feeds entirely on her milk. After about three months, its mother gradually introduces blood into its diet, feeding it a few drops at a time.

Young bat

Feeding

A vampire bat lands on the ground close to its victim and then walks towards it on all fours. A heat sensor on the end of its nose helps it to locate an area of skin where warm blood is flowing close to the surface. The bat bites into its victim with its razor-sharp teeth and uses its tongue to lap up the blood that flows from the wound. The bat's saliva, or spit, stops the blood from clotting.

False vampire bats

These bats specialise in feeding on smaller bats. A false vampire bat swoops silently down on to its victim and eats its flesh. In the past, people seeing the bat doing this mistakenly thought it was drinking blood, and assumed it was a type of vampire bat. Zoologists now know that this is not true, which is why it is called a "false" vampire.

Australian false vampire bat

21

Pygmy marmoset

Primates

Humans, monkeys, apes, lorises, tarsiers and lemurs all belong to a group of about 200 species called primates. These mammals tend to have relatively large brains, making them intelligent and quick to learn new skills. Many primates have opposable thumbs, which means that their thumbs can move across their palms to press against their fingers, allowing them to grasp objects firmly. Some also have opposable big toes. Most primates live in trees, and they have forward-pointing eyes to help them judge the distance between branches.

Size: body 14–16 cm (5½–6¼ in); tail 15–20 cm (6–7¾ in)

Range: South America: upper reaches of Amazon River area

Scientific name: *Cebuella pygmaea*

Pygmy marmoset

As the pygmy marmoset is one of the smallest of all the primates, it is often attacked by large birds, so it tries to keep out of sight and therefore danger. It moves either in short dashes or by creeping along very slowly, sometimes staying very still to avoid being spotted.

Lemurs, aye-ayes, lorises, bushbabies, tarsiers, marmosets and tamarins

Lemurs, aye-ayes, bushbabies, lorises and tarsiers are found in parts of Africa and southern Asia. They have smaller brains than monkeys and apes, and their skeletons resemble those of small, tree-dwelling shrewlike animals, which were probably the first primates to evolve. The fast-moving marmosets and tamarins of the South American rainforests are among the most attractive-looking primates of all and often have colourful fur and unusual "hairstyles".

Slender loris

This creature's opposable thumbs and big toes enable it to grip tightly on to branches as it moves slowly and carefully through the trees on its long thin legs. It feeds on insects, lizards, birds and eggs, creeping up on its prey and then snatching it with both hands.

Size: body 18–26 cm (7–10¼ in); virtually no tail

Range: southern India, Sri Lanka

Scientific name: *Loris tardigradus*

Size: body 45 cm (17¾ in); tail 55 cm (21¼ in)

Range: Madagascar

Scientific name: *Lemur catta*

Ring-tailed lemur

The ring-tailed lemur climbs up to the tops of trees to bathe in the early morning sunshine after a cold night. It marks out its territory with smelly secretions from scent glands. In the mating season, two rival males will rub their tails with this scent and have a "stink fight" by wafting their smelly tails in the air.

Ring-tailed lemur

Slender loris

22

Golden lion tamarin

This beautiful primate gets its name from the silky lionlike mane that covers its head and shoulders. It lives in family groups and at night shelters in hollows in old trees. It is a nimble creature and leaps from branch to branch searching for insects, lizards and birds to eat.

Golden lion tamarin

Size: body 19–22 cm (7½–8¾ in); tail 26–34 cm (10¼–13½ in)
Range: southeastern Brazil
Scientific name:
  Leontopithecus rosalia

Emperor tamarin

The emperor tamarin is easily recognised by its long drooping "moustache". Small troops of these tamarins dart through the trees looking for insects, fruit, tender leaves and even flowers to eat. They will also lap up sap flowing from damaged parts of trees and steal birds' eggs.

Emperor tamarin

Size: body 18–21 cm (7–8¼ in); tail 25–32 cm (9¾–12½ in)
Range: western Brazil, Peru, Bolivia
Scientific name:
  Saguinus imperator

Greater bushbaby

The bushbaby gets its name because its call sounds like a child crying. It eats plants but also preys on reptiles and birds, pouncing and killing its victims with one bite. A night hunter, the bushbaby's keen eyes can focus on prey in moonlight or starlight.

Greater bushbaby

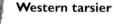

Size: body 27–47 cm (10½–18½ in); tail 33–52 cm (13–20½ in)
Range: southern Africa
Scientific name:
  Otolemur crassicaudatus

Western tarsier

The tarsier's huge eyes make it a ruthless night-time hunter, but the eyeballs are so big that they cannot move in their sockets. To make up for this, the tarsier can turn its head right round. It also has large batlike ears to detect the sounds of its small prey.

Western tarsier

Size: body 8.5–16 cm (3¼–6¼ in); tail 13.5–27 cm (5¼–10½ in)
Range: Southeast Asia: Sumatra and Borneo
Scientific name: *Tarsuis bancanus*

Size: body 36–44 cm (14¼–17¼ in); tail 50–60 cm (19¾–23½ in)
Range: Madagascar
Scientific name:
  Daubentonia madagascariensis

Aye-aye

Aye-aye

The aye-aye taps on trees with its long middle finger, listens for the sound of insects moving under the bark and then uses the same finger to hook the insects out. Local tradition says that if you see this strange-looking animal you will have bad luck. Sadly, it is often killed.

Old World monkeys

There are about 80 species of monkeys in Asia and Africa. These monkeys are known as Old World monkeys. They have close-set downward-pointing nostrils. On their buttocks are pads of hard skin that allow them to rest their weight on their bottoms comfortably while they sleep sitting upright. They tend to be larger than the New World monkeys of the Americas. Unlike the New World monkeys, they do not have prehensile (gripping) tails. Most Old World monkeys are active in the daytime and sleep at night. They have excellent eyesight, hearing and sense of smell.

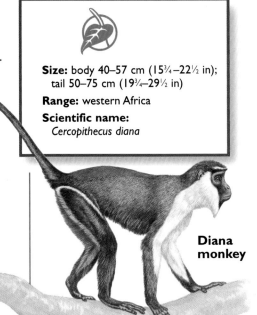

Size: body 40–57 cm (15¾–22½ in); tail 50–75 cm (19¾–29½ in)
Range: western Africa
Scientific name: *Cercopithecus diana*

Diana monkey

Mandrill

The forest-dwelling mandrill is unmistakable, with its flaming red nose and blue cheeks. A female mandrill gives birth to a single baby, which she carries about with her, either on her back or clinging to her belly. Adults are bad tempered and aggressive and have even been known to attack humans.

Size: body 55–95 cm (21¾–37½ in); tail 7–10 cm (2¾–4 in)
Range: western central Africa
Scientific name: *Mandrillus sphinx*

Diana monkey

This elegant colourful monkey is an excellent climber and spends almost all its time high up in the trees of the rainforest. Troops of up to 30 monkeys live together, led by an old male. They feed mainly on plants, but also eat insects and the eggs and young of birds.

Japanese macaque

Japan's mountain forests are home to macaque monkeys. In cold winters, these monkeys warm themselves in volcanic springs, where water heated deep below ground bubbles up to the surface to form steaming pools. They eat fruit, leaves, insects and small animals.

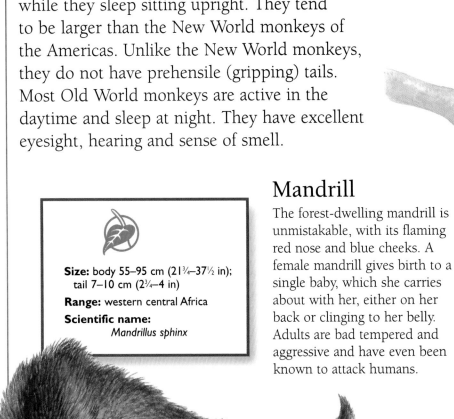

Mandrill

Japanese macaque

Size: body 50–75 cm (19¾–29½ in); tail 7–12 cm (2¾–4¾ in)
Range: Japan
Scientific name: *Macaca fuscata*

Proboscis monkey

The male proboscis monkey has a long fleshy nose, which straightens out when he makes his loud honking call. The nose probably acts like a loudspeaker, amplifying his call to warn other monkeys of danger. It also goes red or swells when he is angry or excited. The female has a much smaller nose and a quieter cry. The proboscis monkey lives in mangrove swamp jungle, where it climbs nimbly through the trees using its long fingers and toes to grip the branches.

Proboscis monkey

Size: body 53–76 cm (20¾–30 in); tail 55–76 cm (21¾–30 in)

Range: Southeast Asia: Borneo

Scientific name: *Nasalis larvatus*

Olive baboon

Orderly troops of up to 150 olive baboons move around Africa's savanna, eating leaves, shoots, seeds, roots, bark, fruit, insects, eggs and lizards. These large heavily built baboons also hunt small mammals such as young antelopes. They spend much of their time grooming each other's fur, removing dirt, parasites and dead skin to keep it clean. They mainly live on the ground, but sleep at night in trees or on rocks.

Size: body 46–70 cm (18–27½ in); tail 42–80 cm (16½–31½ in)

Range: western, central and eastern Africa

Scientific name: *Procolobus badius*

Red colobus

This monkey lives in troops of 50 to 100 animals. The troop contains many small family groups, each consisting of a male and several females with their young. The red colobus makes spectacular leaps between the branches of trees as it searches for fruit, leaves and flowers to eat. Chimpanzees sometimes band together in hunting parties to prey on the red colobus.

Red colobus

Size: body up to 1 m (3¼ ft); tail 45–75 cm (17¾–29½ in)

Range: western, central and eastern Africa

Scientific name: *Papio anubis*

Olive baboon

Allen's swamp monkey

This little-known monkey lives near rivers and in swamps. Though it eats mainly leaves and fruit, it also goes into the water to snatch crabs and even fish. It, in turn, is hunted by local people for meat and because it sometimes raids farmers' crops. It is now an endangered species.

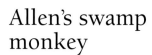

Allen's swamp monkey

Size: body 40–50 cm (15¾–19¾ in); tail 45–55 cm (17¾–21¾ in)

Range: Congo and Zaire

Scientific name: *Allenopithecus nigroviridis*

New World monkeys

The monkeys that live in the lush rainforests of Central and South America are known as New World monkeys. Their long tails help them to balance when they are high off the ground. Many – such as the capuchin, howler and spider monkeys – have prehensile (gripping) tails, which they can wrap around branches and use like an extra limb. They have long fingers, strong feet that grip well and are excellent runners and leapers. Unlike their Old World relatives, they have broad nostrils that open to the sides and no sitting pads on their buttocks.

Woolly spider monkey

This monkey moves around the rainforest by using its long arms and prehensile tail to swing from branch to branch. Numbers are falling because their rainforest home is being destroyed, giving them little refuge from hunters who kill them for meat.

Woolly spider monkey

Size: body 61 cm (24 in); tail about 67 cm (26¼ in)

Range: southeastern Brazil

Scientific name: *Brachyteles arachnoides*

Red howler

Red howler monkeys live in the rainforest in troops of up to 30. Sometimes, all the males in a troop join together in a dawn chorus of howling that can be heard 3 km (1¾ miles) away. The howling tells other monkeys to stay away from their territory. The male howler monkey has a large throat with a special chamber that amplifies its call.

Red howler

Size: body 80–90 cm (31½–35½ in); tail 80–90 cm (31½–35½ in)

Range: South America

Scientific name: *Alouatta seniculus*

White-fronted capuchin

This intelligent monkey is always picking up things, hoping that they may be edible. It feeds on shoots, fruit, insects, young birds and birds' eggs. It soaks its hands and feet in urine and uses the scent to mark its territory as it moves through the trees.

White-fronted capuchin

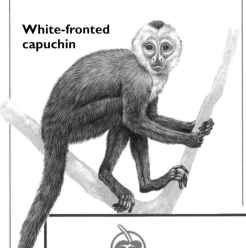

Size: body 30–38 cm (11¾–15 in); tail 38–50 cm (15–19¾ in)

Range: South America: upper reaches of Amazon River area

Scientific name: *Cebus albifrons*

Monk saki

The monk saki has long shaggy hair around its face and on its neck, and a thick bushy tail. This shy wary monkey lives high in the trees and never ventures down on to the ground. It usually moves on all fours, but may sometimes walk upright on a large branch. It can make huge leaps between branches. These monkeys spend their time in pairs or small family groups.

Monk saki

Size: body 35–48 cm (13¾–19 in); tail 31–51 cm (12¼–20 in)

Range: South America: upper reaches of Amazon River area

Scientific name: *Pithecia monachus*

26

Gibbons and great apes

Gorillas, chimpanzees and orang-utans are called great apes. They are our closest living relatives. After humans, they are the most intelligent of all the primates and can even be trained to use simple sign language. Gibbons are tree-dwelling apes of southern Asia. They are smaller than great apes, so they are known as lesser apes. Apes live in family-based groups. They usually walk on all fours, using the knuckles of their hands rather than the flat palms, but they can walk upright, on their hind legs.

Orang-utan

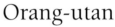

Size: height standing 1.2–1.5 m (4–5 ft); no tail
Range: Southeast Asia: Borneo and Sumatra
Scientific name: *Pongo pygmaeus*

Chimpanzee

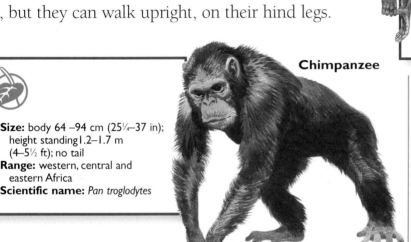

Size: body 64–94 cm (25¼–37 in); height standing1.2–1.7 m (4–5½ ft); no tail
Range: western, central and eastern Africa
Scientific name: *Pan troglodytes*

Orang-utan

After the gorilla, the orang-utan is the second largest primate. It builds a platform of sticks to form a tree nest in which it sleeps, which may be a different one each night. A female orang-utan gives birth to a single baby, which clings to her fur as she moves around in the treetops.

Lar Gibbon

The lar gibbon lives in trees and rarely descends to the ground. As it swings through the trees and runs upright along branches, it has to look out for weak or dead branches, because a fall from this height could be fatal. They live in small family groups.

Lar gibbon

Chimpanzee

The chimpanzee mainly eats plants, but occasionally insects and meat. It makes many noises, gestures and facial expressions. It has learned to use everyday objects as simple tools. Stones, for example, are used to smash open nuts, wads of leaves to mop up drinking water, and sticks to prise grubs out of rotten wood and to extract ants and termites from their nests.

Gorilla

Gorillas spend most of their time on the ground. They feed on leaves, buds, stalks, berries, bark and fern. They live in troops of up to 30 animals, made up of a leading adult male, a few young males and several females and their young. Young gorillas travel on their mother's back until they are two or three years old.

Size: body 42–58 cm (16½–22¾ in); no tail
Range: Southeast Asia
Scientific name: *Hylobates lar*

Size: height standing 1.4–1.8 m (4½–6 ft); no tail
Range: western central Africa
Scientific name: *Gorilla gorilla*

Gorilla

Carnivores

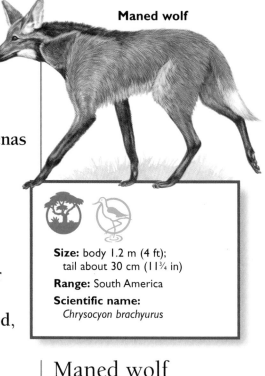

Maned wolf

This group of flesh-eating mammals includes dogs, bears, raccoons, mustelids, mongooses, civets, hyenas and cats. Most carnivores have finely tuned senses of sight, hearing and smell, so they can find their prey before it detects them. Their agile bodies enable them to catch their prey using very little energy. The main difference, however, between carnivores and other mammals is that they have special teeth that can shear flesh from bone, the way scissors cut paper. Some carnivores have adapted their diet to include other food, such as seeds, fruit, roots and insects.

Size: body 1.2 m (4 ft); tail about 30 cm (11¾ in)
Range: South America
Scientific name: *Chrysocyon brachyurus*

Dogs

All domestic dogs are descended from wolves. Wolves and other wild dogs have long legs for chasing prey and sharp teeth for killing it. A dog's most important sensory organ is its nose, which it uses to detect the scent of prey, find a mate, identify other animals and even tell whether they are afraid or relaxed. Wild dogs hunt animals as small as mice and as large as moose. Some wild dogs, such as foxes, live on their own, while others, such as wolves and hunting dogs, live, travel and hunt in family groups called packs. Pack members share their food and defend each other.

Maned wolf

The maned wolf is similar to the red fox in appearance, but with longer legs and a longer muzzle. A wary creature, the maned wolf lives in remote areas and hunts mainly at night. It preys on large rodents, birds, reptiles and frogs.

Bush dog

With its stocky legs, short tail, squat body and broad face, the bush dog looks more like a small bear than a dog. It inhabits grasslands and open forests, hunting in packs at night for rodents. It spends most of the day underground in a den, which may have been stolen from another animal, such as an armadillo.

Hunting dog

Hunting dogs hunt together as a pack. The pack chases a group of animals, such as wildebeest, separates one from the fleeing herd and then moves in for the kill. They once stalked prey throughout the African savanna but, because so many were shot by farmers who thought they would attack their cattle, today they are found in only a few scattered places.

Size: body 80–110 cm (31½–43½ in); tail 30–40 cm (11¾–15¾ in)
Range: Africa, south of the Sahara to South Africa
Scientific name: *Lycaon pictus*

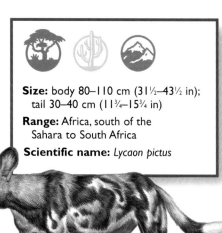

Hunting dog

Size: body 57.5–75 cm (22¾–29½ in); tail 12.5–15 cm (5–6 in)
Range: Central and South America
Scientific name: *Speothos venaticus*

Bush dog

Arctic fox

The Arctic fox can withstand temperatures as low as -50°C (-58°F) on the icy windswept tundra. It feeds on ground-dwelling birds, lemmings and other small rodents, and the leftovers from polar bears' meals. In winter, its white coat acts as a camouflage against the snow and ice, so it can creep up unseen on its prey. When the snow melts, its coat turns brown or grey and it blends in with the rocks and plants.

Size: body 46–68 cm (18–26¾ in); tail up to 35 cm (13¾ in)

Range: Arctic regions of Europe, Asia, North America

Scientific name: *Alopex lagopus*

Fennec fox

The fennec is the smallest of the foxes. Its large ears, up to 15 cm (6 in) long, allow heat to escape from its body, keeping the fox cool in the hot deserts where it lives. It hunts at night for small rodents, birds, insects and lizards. During the day it shelters in burrows in the sand.

Fennec fox

Size: body 37–41 cm (14½–16¼ in); tail 19–21 cm (7½–8¼ in)

Range: northern Africa, Middle East

Scientific name: *Vulpes zerda*

Red fox

Size: body 46–86 cm (18–33¾ in); tail 30.5–55.5 cm (12–21¾ in)

Range: North America, Europe, northern Africa, northern Asia

Scientific name: *Vulpes vulpes*

Red fox

The red fox has adapted to many different environments, from forests and grasslands to mountains, deserts and even towns and cities. Red foxes live and hunt alone and only come together to breed and rear their young. They usually prey on rodents, rabbits and other small animals, but they will also eat fruit, vegetables, earthworms and fish.

Grey wolf

The largest of all the wild dogs, the grey wolf preys on hoofed mammals, such as bison, moose and musk oxen. Packs vary from 5 to 20 dogs, led by the strongest male. Each pack has its own hunting territory of up to 1,000 km² (386 sq miles). The wolves howl loudly to warn other packs to stay away from their territory.

Grey wolf

Size: body 1–1.4 m (3¼–4½ ft); tail 30–48 cm (11¾–19 in)

Range: Canada, northern USA, eastern Europe, Asia

Scientific name: *Canis lupus*

Siberian tiger

Caspian tiger

Indo-Chinese tiger

Sumatran tiger

Tiger types

The coloration and size of these animals vary according to where they live. Tigers from northern areas, such as Siberia, are larger and paler than those from tropical areas, such as Sumatra. The largest of all is the Siberian tiger. Many types of tiger are now rare, including the Siberian, Indo-Chinese and Sumatran, and some, such as the Caspian, have not been seen for many years

Hunting

At dusk, tigers set out to hunt buffalo, deer, wild pigs and other forest animals. They can only run fast for short distances, so they rely on their cunning and stealth to catch their prey. Their striped coat camouflages them against the background of trees and long grass, enabling them to sneak up on their victims without being seen. When they are close enough, they sprint forwards and pounce on the unsuspecting animal.

Tigers

The tiger is the biggest and strongest of all the wild cats. At the beginning of the 20th century, there were hundreds of thousands of tigers living throughout the forests of Asia. Hunting and the destruction of forests have had such a devastating effect on their numbers that there are now just 6,000 to 9,000 wild tigers left, mainly living in parts of India, China, Indonesia and Siberia.

Tigers live alone, roaring loudly to tell other tigers to keep away from their territory, which they mark out with scent, droppings and scratches on tree trunks. They hunt large mammals, usually at night, and sometimes travel up to 20 km (12 miles) in search of food. As few as one in every ten hunts may be successful, so when they do make a kill they gorge themselves on as much meat as they can eat. Despite stories of "man-eating" tigers, they rarely attack humans.

30

Tiger cubs

Tigers can be born at any time of the year in litters of between two and six cubs. They are blind for the first 10 days and their mother suckles the cubs for up to eight weeks. Not until they are about 18 months old do they hunt for themselves, and they stay with their mother for two to three years. The father takes no part in their rearing. Cubs are sometimes killed when another male tiger takes over their father's territory. If the cubs are killed, the female mates again.

Unlike domestic cats, **tigers** like to be near water and will take a dip to cool off on a hot day. They are good swimmers and may cross rivers or swim between islands in search of their prey. Tigers can occasionally be seen climbing trees.

Raccoons, bears and pandas

Both the bear and raccoon families developed from doglike ancestors millions of years ago. Bears are the largest flesh-eating land mammals, but they will eat almost anything, including plants and insects. Raccoons – and their relatives the coatis and olingos – are long-tailed carnivores, which like to spend much of their time in trees. There are two different types of panda: the giant pandas are classified with the bears and the red pandas with the raccoons. Some zoologists think that pandas should be classified in a separate family of their own.

Olingo

Size: body 35–48 cm (13¾–19 in); tail 40–48 cm (15¾–19 in)
Range: Central America and northwestern South America
Scientific name: *Bassaricyon gabbii*

Olingo

The olingo lives mostly in the trees, using its long tail to help it balance as it runs along branches and leaps from tree to tree. It lives alone or in pairs, but joins up with other olingos to look for food. It mostly eats fruit, but also feeds on insects, small mammals and birds.

Coati

With its long nose, the coati probes into holes and cracks in the ground, searching for insects, spiders and small animals to eat. Groups of up to 40 animals hunt both day and night, resting during the hottest part of the day. After mating, the female goes off alone to give birth to a litter of between two and seven young in a cave or a tree nest.

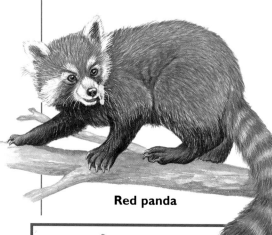

Red panda

Size: body 51–63.5 cm (20–25 in); tail 28–48 cm (11–19 in)
Range: Himalayas, from Nepal to Myanmar, southwestern China
Scientific name: *Ailurus fulgens*

Raccoon

The raccoon runs and climbs well, and swims if necessary. It is most active at night. As well as catching prey such as frogs, fish, mice and birds, it often raids rubbish bins, searching for edible items with its long sensitive fingers. It has a peculiar habit of washing food before eating it. Its thick fur keeps it warm during winter.

Raccoon

Size: body 41–60cm (16¼–23½ in); tail 20–40 cm (7¾–15¾ in)
Range: southern Canada, USA, Central America
Scientific name: *Procyon lotor*

Size: body 43–67 cm (17–26¼ in); tail 43–68 cm (17–26¾ in)
Range: southeastern USA, Central and South America
Scientific name: *Nasua nasua*

Red panda

The red panda looks more like a raccoon than a giant panda. It sleeps during the day, curled up on a branch with its tail over its eyes or its head tucked into its chest. It feeds during the night, mainly on bamboo shoots, although it will also eat grass, roots, fruit, acorns, mice, birds and birds' eggs.

Coati

Polar bear

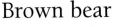

Polar bear

With a thick layer of fat beneath its skin to keep it warm, a polar bear is perfectly comfortable roaming across the Arctic ice in freezing temperatures. Cubs are born in dens dug by their mother in deep snow. They stay with her for about 28 months, learning how to hunt seals and fight.

Size: body 2.2–2.5 m (7¼–8 ft); tail 7.5–12.5 cm (3–5 in)
Range: ice sheets and coastal waters of Arctic Ocean
Scientific name: *Ursus maritimus*

Brown bear

Also known as the "grizzly", the brown bear mostly eats leaves, berries, fruit, nuts and roots, and sometimes insects, rodents and fish. It also hunts large mammals such as moose and musk oxen. The bear may hide the dead prey under dirt and leaves until it is ready to consume it.

Brown bear

Size: body 1.5–2.5 m (5–8 ft); small tail
Range: Europe, Asia, North America
Scientific name: *Ursus arctos*

Sun bear

The sun bear spends the day sleeping and sunbathing. It searches for food at night, using its long tongue to lick honey out of bees' nests and termites from their mounds. With its curved claws it hooks fruit from branches and tears off tree bark to uncover tasty grubs.

Size: body 1.1–1.4 m (3½–4½ ft); no tail
Range: Southeast Asia
Scientific name: *Helarctos malayanus*

Sun bear

Spectacled bear

This mountain bear has light rings around its eyes and across its muzzle, making it look as if it is wearing spectacles. It makes a tree nest by building a platform of branches. It forages for food at night and spends the day resting in its nest.

Spectacled bear

Size: body 1.5–1.8 m (5–6 ft); tail 7 cm (2¾ in)
Range: Andes Mountains of western South America
Scientific name: *Tremarctos ornatus*

Giant panda

Size: body 1.2–1.5 m (4–5 ft); tail 12.5 cm (5 in)
Range: remote mountain regions of central China
Scientific name: *Ailuropoda melanoleuca*

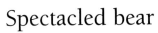

Giant panda

The giant panda has to feed for up to 15 hours each day to survive, during which time it consumes up to 20 kg (44 lb) of bamboo. The panda has a thumblike bone in its hands that allows it to grip its food. Unfortunately, there are only about 1,000 giant pandas left in the wild.

33

Mustelids, civets and mongooses

All of these mammals are small- to medium-sized carnivores. Most of the mustelids, which include stoats, badgers, otters, skunks and wolverines, have a long supple body, short legs and a long tail. There are about 65 species of mustelids living throughout most of the world except Australia and Madagascar. The 34 or so species of civets are tree-dwelling hunters that are active at night. They live in southern Europe, Africa and Asia. The 37 species of mongooses are fast-moving ground dwellers. They live in Africa and Asia.

Eurasian otter

Size: body 55–80 cm (21¾–31½ in); tail 30–50 cm (11¾–19¾ in)
Range: Europe, northern Africa, Asia
Scientific name: *Lutra lutra*

Eurasian otter

The slender-bodied otter moves fast both in water and on land. It uses its strong tail to push itself along in water and its short thick fur keeps its skin warm and dry. Its nostrils and ears can be closed off when it is in water. The otter lives in a burrow in the river bank. Rarely seen during the day, it comes out at night to find fish, frogs, voles and other water creatures to eat.

Eurasian badger

Families of Eurasian badgers live in huge burrows called setts. These burrows have several entrances and networks of underground passages and chambers. Badgers are generally active at night, coming out of the sett around dusk. They eat large quantities of earthworms as well as other small animals, plants, fruit and nuts.

Stoat

Size: body 23–28 cm (9–11 in); tail 8–12 cm (3¼–4¾ in)
Range: Europe, Asia, North America
Scientific name: *Mustela erminea*

Stoat

The agile stoat is a skilled hunter. It kills with a powerful bite to the back of the prey's neck. Rodents and rabbits are its main victims, but it also kills other mammals as well as birds, fish and insects. In the northern part of its range the stoat loses its dark fur at the beginning of winter and grows a pure white coat. Only the tail tip stays black.

Wolverine

Wolverine

A powerful heavily built animal, the wolverine is extremely strong for its size and can kill prey larger than itself. It spends most of its life on the ground but it will climb trees to find birds' eggs and berries. Young are born in spring. They suckle for about two months and remain with their mother until they are about two years old, when she drives them away to find their own territory.

Size: body 65–86 cm (25½–33¾ in); tail 17–26 cm (6¾–10¼ in)
Range: Siberia, Scandinavia, North America
Scientific name: *Gulo gulo*

Size: body 56–81 cm (22–32 in); tail 11–20 cm (4¼–7¾ in)
Range: Europe, Asia
Scientific name: *Meles meles*

Eurasian badger

Sea otter

This otter feeds on shellfish and uses rocks as tools to help it open the hard shells. The otter lies on its back in the water and places a rock on its chest. It bangs its prey against the rock until the shell breaks, revealing the soft flesh inside.

Sea otter

Size: body 1–1.2 m (3¼–4 ft); tail 25–37 cm (9¾–14¼ in)
Range: Bering Sea, Californian coast of North America
Scientific name: *Enhydra lutra*

African palm civet

This civet has short legs and a long thick tail. It is a skilled climber and spends much of its life in trees, where it rests during the day. It usually hunts at night, catching insects and small creatures such as lizards and birds. It also eats many kinds of fruit and leaves. The female gives birth to litters of two or three young at any time of year.

African palm civet

Size: body 43–60 cm (17–23½ in); tail 48–62 cm (19–24½ in)
Range: central Africa
Scientific name: *Nandinia binotata*

Size: body 35 cm (13¾ in); tail 25 cm (9¾ in)
Range: Middle East, Asia; introduced into West Indies, Hawaii, Fiji
Scientific name: *Herpestes auropunctatus*

Indian mongoose

The mongoose eats almost any food it can catch, including snakes, scorpions and insects. It is popular among humans because it hunts pests such as rats and mice. As a result, the mongoose has been introduced into areas outside its normal range.

Indian mongoose

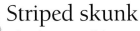

Meerkat

Meerkats are a type of mongoose. They are sociable animals and several families may live together. During the day, while most of the group forages for food such as insects, lizards, birds and fruit, some meerkats watch out for birds of prey. They give a shrill call to alert the others to any danger.

Meerkat

Size: body 25–30 cm (9¾–11¾ in); tail 19–24 cm (7½–9½ in)
Range: southern Africa
Scientific name: *Suricata suricatta*

Striped skunk

Skunks are well known for the foul-smelling fluid they spray when threatened. The fluid comes from glands near the tail. The strong smell makes it difficult for an enemy to breathe and irritates its eyes. The striped skunk is active at night, when it searches for food.

Size: body 28–38 cm (11–15 in); tail 18–25 cm (7–9¾ in)
Range: North America
Scientific name: *Mephitis mephitis*

Striped skunk

Cats and hyenas

Cats are ruthless hunters. Their strong legs enable them to catch their prey in a brief, rapid chase or with a lightning-quick pounce. They have bendy backbones that allow them to twist and turn easily when chasing prey. When they pounce, their claws extend and grip their victim's flesh, but when the cat is walking or running, the claws retract into the toes so they are not damaged. Most cats have coats patterned with spots or stripes to camouflage them as they stalk prey. There are 36 species of wild cats, from big cats such as lions and tigers to smaller ones such as lynxes.

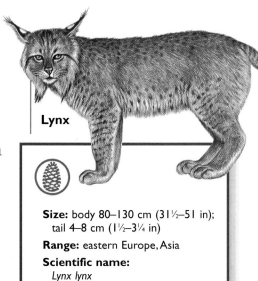

Lynx

Size: body 80–130 cm (31½–51 in); tail 4–8 cm (1½–3¼ in)
Range: eastern Europe, Asia
Scientific name: *Lynx lynx*

Lynx

The lynx lives alone in forests and woodland and hunts hares, rabbits, rodents, small deer and birds such as grouse. The tufts on its ears help it to hear in dense forests, where sound does not travel well. The lynx has excellent eyesight – it can spot a mouse 75 m (250 ft) away.

Wild cat

The wild cat looks similar to a domestic cat, but is larger and has a shorter, thicker tail. It is a good tree climber, but stalks most of its prey on the ground, catching small rodents and ground-dwelling birds. In courtship, males howl and screech to attract a female mate.

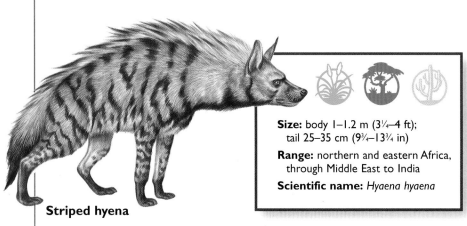

Striped hyena

Size: body 1–1.2 m (3¼–4 ft); tail 25–35 cm (9¾–13¾ in)
Range: northern and eastern Africa, through Middle East to India
Scientific name: *Hyaena hyaena*

Mountain lion

Deer are the main prey of this stealthy hunter. Having stalked its victim, the mountain lion pounces and kills it with a swift bite to the neck. It then drags the carcass to a sheltered place, where it can feed undisturbed. It lives in lowland swamps, forests and grasslands, and also on mountain slopes up to 4,500 m (15,750 ft).

Striped hyena

Although hyenas have a doglike body, they are actually related to cats. They specialise in feeding on carrion (dead animals), especially the leftovers of kills made by big cats such as lions. Striped hyenas also prey on young sheep and goats, small mammals, birds, lizards, snakes and insects.

Wild cat

Mountain lion

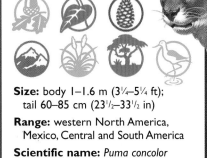

Size: body 1–1.6 m (3¼–5¼ ft); tail 60–85 cm (23½–33½ in)
Range: western North America, Mexico, Central and South America
Scientific name: *Puma concolor*

Size: body 50–65 cm (19¾–25½ in); tail 25–38 cm (9¾–15 in)
Range: Europe, Africa, Middle East, India
Scientific name: *Felis silvestris*

Leopard

The leopard hauls the bodies of large prey up into trees and out of reach of scavenging hyenas and jackals. Its stunning coat is dappled with spots to camouflage it among the leaves of the trees and the long grass below. It will sometimes leap straight out of a tree on to passing prey.

Size: body 1.3–1.9 m (4¼–6¼ ft); tail 1.1–1.4 m (3½–4½ ft)
Range: Africa, south of the Sahara, Middle East, southern Asia
Scientific name: *Panthera pardus*

Size: body 1.4–2 m (4½–6½ ft); tail 67–100 cm (26¼–39½ in)
Range: Africa, south of the Sahara, northwestern India
Scientific name: *Panthera leo*

Snow leopard

The solitary snow leopard feeds mainly on wild sheep and goats. Its broad furry feet stop it sinking in the snow on high mountain slopes. It can make huge leaps between rocky crags, using its tail for balance.

Size: body 1.2–1.5 m (4–5 ft); tail about 91 cm (36 in)
Range: Himalayas Mountains of central Asia
Scientific name: *Uncia uncia*

Snow leopard

Lion

Lions live in grassland or scrub country in family groups called prides. A pride normally contains up to 3 males, 15 females and their young. The females do most of the hunting, often stalking antelopes and zebras in pairs or larger groups. The males' role is to defend the pride's territory.

Jaguar

Lion

Cheetah

The cheetah is the fastest land mammal, able to accelerate from 0–96 km/h (0–60 mph) in just three seconds. It has little stamina, so will try to position itself as close as possible to its prey and catch it with an explosive burst of speed. If this attempt fails, it usually gives up.

Jaguar

The largest South American cat, the jaguar cannot run fast for very long, so it relies on getting close to its prey to make a successful kill. It is a good swimmer, and feeds on fish and turtles, as well as on deer and other land animals. The female has litters of one to four cubs and defends them from any intruder – including the father.

Size: body 1.5–1.8 m (5–6 ft); tail 70–91 cm (27½–36 in)
Range: southern USA, Central and South America
Scientific name: *Panthera onca*

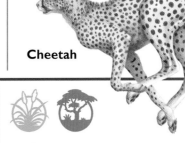

Cheetah

Size: body 1.1–1.4 m (3½–4½ ft); tail 65–80 cm (25½–31½ in)
Range: Africa, south of the Sahara, Middle East to eastern Asia
Scientific name: *Acinonyx jubatus*

Seals, whales and dolphins

Millions of years ago, the ancestors of seals, whales and dolphins left the land to live in the sea. Their bodies adapted to life in the water, becoming sleek and streamlined, while their limbs developed into paddle-shaped flippers. Under their skin, these marine mammals have a thick layer of fat called blubber to keep them warm. They spend much of their time under water, often diving to great depths in search of food. But because they have lungs, and not gills like fish, they have to surface regularly to breathe air.

Seals, sea lions and walruses

With their torpedolike bodies, these marine mammals are skilful swimmers and divers. They can slow down their heartbeat during dives to enable them to stay under water for long periods. Unlike whales and dolphins, which give birth under water, seals, sea lions and walruses come ashore to have their babies. Seals and walruses swim by pushing themselves through the water with their tail-like hind flippers, but sea lions use their long front flippers.

California sea lion

This is the fastest swimmer of all the seals and sea lions, capable of speeds of 40 km/h (25 mph). It can also move fast on land by tucking its back flippers forwards under its body. In the breeding season, huge colonies gather on the rocky southwestern shores of the USA.

California sea lion

Size: 1.7–2.2 m (5½–7¼ ft)
Range: Pacific coasts, from Canada to Mexico
Scientific name: *Zalophus californianus*

Size: 1.4–1.8 m (4½–6 ft)
Range: southern Pacific and Atlantic oceans
Scientific name: *Arctocephalus australis*

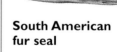

South American fur seal

South American fur seal

This seal eats fish, squid, penguins and small marine creatures. The female gives birth to a single pup. She stays with it for 12 days, then goes off to sea to feed, returning regularly to suckle her young pup.

Size: 2.2–3.5 m (7¼–11½ ft)
Range: Arctic Ocean, occasionally north Atlantic Ocean
Scientific name: *Odobenus rosmarus*

Walrus

Walrus

Walruses live in the Arctic, where they feed on shellfish. They have sharp tusks, which they use to drag themselves out of the water and also for fighting. Their four flat flippers make them excellent swimmers. On land, walruses move with great difficulty. They spend much of their time sleeping on the ice in large groups.

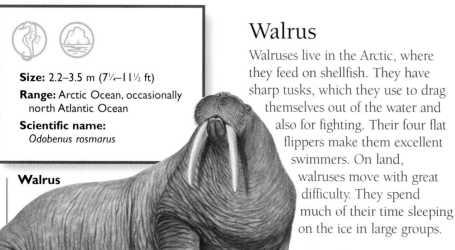

Leopard seal

Size: 3–3.5 m (10–11½ ft)
Range: Southern Ocean
Scientific name:
  Hydrurga leptonyx

Leopard seal

The leopard seal is the fiercest hunter of all seals, with large tooth-studded jaws for grasping prey and tearing it apart. The leopard seal preys on penguins by catching them under water just as they launch themselves off the ice. It also hunts other smaller seals, as well as fish, squid and shellfish.

Harp seal

The harp seal has a grey body with a black head and stripe across its back. In the breeding season, rival males fight over females using their teeth and flippers. After mating, the females form groups on the ice to give birth. The pups grow rapidly as they feed on their mother's nourishing fat-rich milk.

Size: 1.6–1.9 m (5¼–6¼ ft)
Range: north Atlantic Ocean and Arctic Ocean
Scientific name:
  Pagophilus groenlandica

Harp seal

Size: 2.4–2.8 m (7¾–9¼ ft)
Range: northern Pacific Ocean
Scientific name:
  Eumetopias jubatus

Steller sea lion

Steller sea lion

This is the largest of the sea lions, and it catches fish, squid and octopus. A large male may even eat smaller seals such as fur seals. The beaches where the Steller sea lion breeds are sometimes so crowded that young pups are crushed as males hurry across them to mate with females. A seal mother often goes to sea to find food for herself and her pup. When she comes back, she makes a warbling sound to attract nearby pups, and then smells and touches them until she finds the one that belongs to her.

Harbour seal

Like all seals, the harbour seal spends most of its life in water, coming to land only to mate and give birth. Harbour seal pups are well developed when they are born. They can swim from birth, and can dive for up to two minutes when just two or three days old. The harbour seal feeds on fish and squid.

Size: 1.4–1.8 m (4½–6 ft)
Range: north Atlantic and northern Pacific oceans
Scientific name:
  Phoca vitulina

Harbour seal

Antarctic seals

The world's coldest and most remote continent is Antarctica, most of which is permanently covered in thick ice. With wind speeds sometimes exceeding 320 km/h (200 mph) and temperatures plummeting as low as -89°C (-128°F), it is so inhospitable that few animals can survive there. Even the surrounding seas freeze over. However, the seas are rich in food and are able to support many animals, including seals. There are six species of Antarctic seals: southern elephant, Ross, leopard, crabeater, Weddell and southern fur seals. The southern elephant seal is the world's largest seal, with males weighing up to 4,000 kg (8,800 lb). Seals usually give birth in late winter. By late spring, the seal pups are strong enough to find their own food in the Antarctic waters. For many hundreds of years, seals have been killed for their fur and blubber, and some species are now almost extinct.

Crabeater seal

Surprisingly, crabeater seals do not eat crabs. They actually feed on small shrimplike creatures called krill, which they filter from the water through their teeth. They detect nearby krill with their long downward-curving whiskers. Killer whales often attack crabeater seals, and many carry scars on their bodies that tell of lucky escapes. Crabeater seals can move as fast as 25 km/h (16 mph) on land.

Elephant seal

In the breeding season, a male southern elephant seal guards a group of 40 to 50 females, with whom he mates. If a rival male challenges him, he takes up a threatening pose and roars loudly. The skin bag on his nose inflates to amplify the sound. If the challenger does not back off, a bloody battle occurs. A female elephant seal gives birth to a single pup, which she suckles for about a month. During this period she herself does not eat but lives off the energy already stored in her blubber.

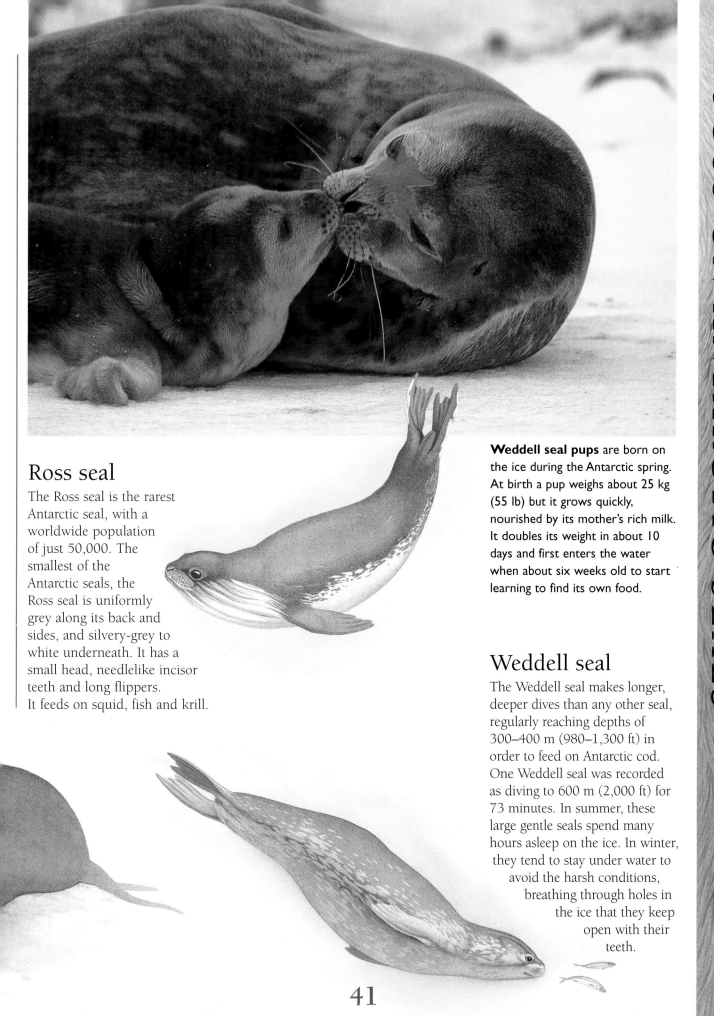

Ross seal

The Ross seal is the rarest Antarctic seal, with a worldwide population of just 50,000. The smallest of the Antarctic seals, the Ross seal is uniformly grey along its back and sides, and silvery-grey to white underneath. It has a small head, needlelike incisor teeth and long flippers. It feeds on squid, fish and krill.

Weddell seal pups are born on the ice during the Antarctic spring. At birth a pup weighs about 25 kg (55 lb) but it grows quickly, nourished by its mother's rich milk. It doubles its weight in about 10 days and first enters the water when about six weeks old to start learning to find its own food.

Weddell seal

The Weddell seal makes longer, deeper dives than any other seal, regularly reaching depths of 300–400 m (980–1,300 ft) in order to feed on Antarctic cod. One Weddell seal was recorded as diving to 600 m (2,000 ft) for 73 minutes. In summer, these large gentle seals spend many hours asleep on the ice. In winter, they tend to stay under water to avoid the harsh conditions, breathing through holes in the ice that they keep open with their teeth.

41

Whales, dolphins and porpoises

Whales are the largest sea mammals. There are two kinds of whale: toothed and baleen. Dolphins and porpoises are small, toothed whales. Baleen whales have bristly plates in their mouths instead of teeth. When they feed, they take gulps of water. Baleen plates act like filters, so the water drains away but the fish, krill and plankton stay in the whale's mouth. Toothed whales can locate other sea creatures by echolocation. They send out high-pitched clicking sounds and detect the echoes as they bounce back from objects. Whales swim with up-and-down strokes of their tails, using their flippers to steer.

Dall's porpoise

These porpoises are larger and heavier than most porpoises and inhabit deeper waters. They live in groups of up to 15. Schools of 100 or more porpoises may gather to migrate north in summer and south in winter. Mothers suckle their calves for as long as two years.

Dall's porpoise

Size: 1.8–2.3 m (6–7½ ft)

Range: warm northern Pacific waters

Scientific name: *Phocoenides dalli*

Killer whale

The largest of the dolphin family, the killer whale is a fierce hunter that feeds on fish, squid, sea lions, birds and even other whales. It sometimes snatches seals from the shore or tips them off floating ice into its mouth. It lives and hunts in travelling family groups of up to 40 animals.

Size: 7–9.7 m (23–32 ft)

Range: worldwide, especially cooler seas

Scientific name: *Orcinus orca*

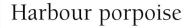

Harbour porpoise

Harbour porpoise

These porpoises feed on fish such as herring and mackerel. They dive for up to six minutes when hunting prey, which they pinpoint using echolocation clicks. Before breeding, they perform long courtship rituals, caressing each other as they swim side by side. Calves are born 10 to 11 weeks after mating. While a mother suckles her calf, she lies on her side on the water surface, so the calf can breathe easily.

Size: 1.4–1.8 m (4½–6 ft)

Range: northern Atlantic and Pacific oceans, Black and Mediterranean seas

Scientific name: *Phocoena phocoena*

Killer whale

Common dolphin

This beautifully marked dolphin has pointed flippers, a curved fin and a long beak. They live in groups of between 20 and 100 dolphins. Several dolphins will join together to help injured or sick companions. These curious, playful sea mammals are often seen swimming alongside ships, leaping and rolling in the water. They feed on fish and squid.

Common dolphin

Size: 2.1–2.6 m (7–8½ ft)

Range: warm and tropical oceans worldwide

Scientific name:
Delphinus delphis

Ganges dolphin

Size: 1.5–2.4 m (5–7¾ ft)

Range: India: Ganges and Brahmaputra river systems

Scientific name:
Platanista gangetica

Ganges dolphin

One of only five species of freshwater dolphin, the Ganges dolphin lives in muddy rivers in India. It is blind – its eyes have no lenses in them – and uses radarlike echolocation signals to find its prey of fish and shrimps.

Atlantic bottle-nosed dolphin

The curving line of this dolphin's mouth makes it look as if it is always smiling. It feeds mainly on bottom-dwelling fish, and is a skilful echolocator, producing up to 1,000 clicking noises a second. The bottle-nosed dolphin is often taught to perform tricks in zoos.

Size: 3–4.2 m (10–14 ft)

Range: warm and tropical oceans worldwide

Scientific name:
Tursiops truncatus

Atlantic bottle-nosed dolphin

Blue whale

The world's largest mammal, the blue whale can weigh 145 tonnes (tons) and measures 32 m (105 ft). This giant feeds on huge quantities of tiny shrimplike creatures called krill, consuming up to 4 tonnes (tons) each day in the summer. The blue whale is in danger of extinction, as there are only a few thousand left in the world's oceans.

Blue whale

Size: 25–32 m (82–105 ft)

Range: all oceans

Scientific name:
Balaenoptera musculus

White whale

White whale

White whales, also called belugas, often live together in small groups called pods. They communicate with a variety of sounds, such as whistles, clicks, clangs, twitters and moos. Polar bears prey on belugas that get trapped by the Arctic ice. In winter, big herds of belugas migrate south.

Size: 4–6.1 m (13–20 ft)

Range: Arctic Ocean and subarctic waters

Scientific name: *Delphinapterus leucas*

Cuvier's beaked whale

This is one of 18 whale species with a distinct beak. It has a tapering scarred body, marked by oval patches where parasitic lampreys have fed on it. It dives for up to 30 minutes to feed on squid and deep-water fish.

Cuvier's beaked whale

Size: 6.4–7 m (21–23 ft)

Range: all oceans, temperate and tropical waters

Scientific name: *Ziphius cavirostris*

Sperm whale

Size: 11–20 m (36–66 ft)

Range: all oceans

Scientific name: *Physeter catodon*

Grey whale

This whale stirs up the seabed with its snout and uses its baleen plate to sieve out tiny creatures to eat. It makes a round trip of 20,000 km (12,430 miles) between its summer feeding waters off Alaska and the warmer shallower waters off the coast of Mexico, where it breeds during winter.

Size: 12.2–15.3 m (40–50 ft)

Range: northeast and northwest Pacific Ocean

Scientific name: *Eschrichtius robustus*

Grey whale

Narwhal

The narwhal is related to the white whale, but has only two teeth. One of the male's teeth grows into a spiral tusk up to 2.7 m (8¾ ft) long, which sticks through its top lip. The tusk is probably used to impress females and fight rivals in the breeding season. Females sometimes have a short tusk.

Size: 4–6.1 m (13–20 ft)

Range: high Arctic Ocean

Scientific name: *Monodon monoceros*

Narwhal

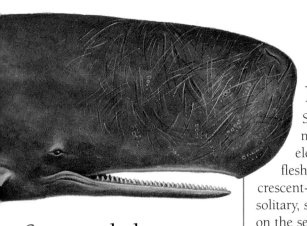

Dugong

Surprisingly, dugongs and manatees are related to elephants. The dugong is fleshy and streamlined, with a crescent-shaped tail. It is shy and solitary, spending much of its life on the seabed feeding on seaweed and seagrass. A female dugong gives birth to a single baby in the water and helps it to the surface.

Dugong

Size: up to 3 m (10 ft)
Range: east African coastal waters, Indian Ocean, Red Sea to northern Australia
Scientific name: *Dugong dugong*

Sperm whale

The sperm whale has a huge head filled with a waxy substance called spermaceti. The spermaceti helps the whale to alter its buoyancy – its ability to float. This enables it to reach depths of more than 1,000 m (3,280 ft) in search of squid to eat.

American manatee

American manatee

Manatees live in bays, river estuaries and shallow coastal waters. They are fine swimmers and can reach speeds of 25 km/h (16 mph). They use their flattened tails as paddles and sometimes walk along the bottom of the ocean on their flippers, grazing on seagrass.

Size: up to 3 m (10 ft)
Range: Atlantic Ocean, from Florida to Guyana
Scientific name: *Trichechus manatus*

Size: 8–10 m (26–33 ft)
Range: all oceans, temperate and polar areas
Scientific name: *Balaenoptera acutorostrata*

Minke whale

Minke whale

The minke whale is a pint-sized relative of the humpback and blue whales. Like them, it has distinctive grooves along its throat. In polar regions, the minke feeds mainly on plankton, but in warmer waters it eats fish and squid as well.

Humpback whale

The humpback whale is famous for the amazingly complex songs it sings to keep in touch with other whales and to attract mates. It often sings for hours on end, only pausing to take a breath of air. These songs travel great distances through the water.

Size: 14.6–19 m (48–62½ ft)
Range: all oceans
Scientific name: *Megaptera novaeangliae*

Humpback whale

45

Hoofed mammals

Some mammals have toes that end in hard coverings called hooves. Hooves are made of keratin – the same substance as nails and claws. Long ago, all hoofed mammals had five toes. As they evolved, they lost the use of some toes to enable them to run faster. Hoofed mammals are classified according to whether their feet have an odd (one or three) or an even (two or four) number of working toes. Elephants are the only hoofed mammals that still have five working toes.

Pigs, peccaries and hippopotamuses

A pig is easily recognised by its long muscular snout, which ends in a round flat disc. The piglike peccary lives only in the Americas, while the hippo, the larger cousin of pigs and peccaries, is found in Africa. Pigs, peccaries and hippos are even-toed hoofed mammals, with four toes on their feet (peccaries have only three on their hind feet). They have simpler stomachs than other even-toed hoofed mammals.

Wild boar

Wild boar

The wild boar is the ancestor of the farmyard pig. With its long snout it roots around the woodland floor for plants and insects to eat. It also digs up bulbs and tubers. Young boars have stripy coats which blend in with the trees and hide them from predators.

Size: body 1.1–1.3 m (3½–4¼ ft); tail 15–20 cm (6–7¾ in)
Range: southern and central Europe, northern Africa, Asia
Scientific name: *Sus scrofa*

Size: body 2.8–4.2 m (9¼–14 ft); tail 35–50 cm (13¾–19¾ in)
Range: Africa, south of the Sahara
Scientific name: *Hippopotamus amphibius*

Size: body 1.1–1.4 m (3½–4½ ft); tail 35–50 cm (13¾–19¾ in)
Range: central and southern Africa
Scientific name: *Phacochoerus aethiopicus*

Warthog

The warthog is not a pretty sight. It has long legs, curving tusks and a long broad head with two pairs of large wartlike protruberances. It lives in small family groups on the African savanna and on treeless plains, where it feeds on short grasses and herbs. In the hottest part of the day, it shelters in its burrow, which is often the disused burrow of an aardvark. Its main enemies are lions and leopards.

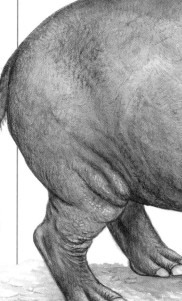

Warthog

Size: body 75–90 cm (29½–35½ in);
tail 1.5–3 cm (⅝–1¼ in)

Range: southwest USA, Mexico,
Central and South America

Scientific name: *Tayassu tajacu*

**Pygmy
hippopotamus**

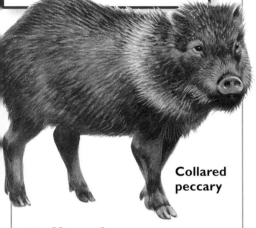

**Collared
peccary**

Size: body 1.7–1.9 m
(5½–6¼ ft); tail 15–21 cm (6–8¼ in)

Range: western Africa, from
Guinea to Nigeria

Scientific name:
Hexaprotodon liberiensis

Collared peccary

A light neckband gives collared peccaries their name. They live in groups of up to 15 animals, marking their territory with scent produced by musk glands on their backs. They eat roots, herbs, grass, fruit, worms and insect larvae. They can run fast enough to escape from predators such as jaguars and pumas.

Pygmy hippopotamus

This small hippopotamus lives around swamps, but spends most of its time on dry land. The pygmy hippo is in severe danger of becoming extinct as its forest habitat is cut down. It is also at risk from hunters, who kill the animal for its meat.

Bearded pig

The bearded pig has a long body and narrow head. It gets its name from the mass of whiskers on its chin. It lives in rainforests, scrub and mangrove swamps. Fallen fruit, rats and insect larvae are this pig's main food. It often follows monkeys to pick up any fruit that they might have dropped. Females give birth to two or three piglets.

**Bearded
pig**

Hippopotamus

Hippopotamus

The hippo is one of the world's largest land mammals, with only the rhino and the elephant weighing more. It lives near rivers and lakes, and spends up to 16 hours each day wallowing in the water to keep cool. It emerges at sunset to graze on riverside plants and eat fallen fruit. It can swim well, but often prefers to walk along the river bottom. A hippo can hold its breath under water for up to five minutes.

Size: body 1.6–1.8 m (5¼–6 ft);
tail 20–30 cm (7¾–11¾ in)

Range: Malaysia, Sumatra,
Borneo

Scientific name: *Sus barbatus*

47

Elephants

African

Asian

Weighing as much as 5,900 kg (13,000 lb) and standing up to 4 m (13 ft) tall at the shoulder, the elephant is the largest land mammal. There are two elephant species: one lives in Africa, the other in India and Southeast Asia. An elephant's flexible trunk – a long nose fixed to its upper lip – contains up to 100,000 muscles and is used for smelling, feeling, breathing, feeding and making loud trumpeting calls. The elephant uses its tusks for fighting, stripping bark off trees and digging for water. Elephants live on grassy plains and desert scrubland, and in river valleys and swamps. They can reach the age of 78. Females and young elephants live in family herds, while mature males roam.

Two species

The African elephant is larger and heavier than its Asian cousin, with bigger, more rounded ears. It has two fingerlike projections on the end of its trunk, while the Asian has one. Both male and female African elephants have tusks, but only Asian males do.

Elephants at work

For thousands of years, humans have trained elephants to lift, push and drag heavy objects. In forestry work, elephants are sometimes taught to use their tusks to raise heavy logs like a fork-lift truck.

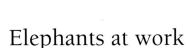

Big appetite

An African elephant eats about 150 kg (330 lb) of grass, leaves, twigs, bark, roots and fruit every day. In order to consume such a large amount, it has to spend three-quarters of its time feeding.

A **baby elephant** does not need to forage for food because it drinks its mother's milk for at least two years. Sometimes, other adult females in the herd also suckle it.

Showers and mud baths

As well as releasing heat through their large flappy ears, elephants also keep cool by giving themselves a shower. They suck up water with their trunks and spray it over their bodies. With practice, an elephant can reach every part of its body by swinging its trunk and blowing at just the right moment. Elephants sometimes wallow in mud or throw dust over themselves, which coats their skin and protects them against insects and sunburn. It also stops moisture evaporating from their skin.

Camels

The camel family consists of the dromedary, the bactrian camel, the vicuña and the guanaco. They are cud-chewing animals, and their feet have just two toes on each foot. The desert-dwelling dromedary and bactrian camels have broad flat pads under each foot to help them walk over the soft sandy soil. Vicuñas and guanacos can breathe the thin air on high mountain pastures, and their thick woolly coats enable them to endure the chilly temperatures at high altitude.

Vicuña

Vicuña

Vicuñas are humpless camels. They live in small family herds in the Andes Mountains of South America, where they feed on grass and small plants. Each herd is guarded by an adult male. He warns the rest of the herd of danger by whistling loudly to them.

Size: body 1.4–1.6 m (4½–5¼ ft); tail 15 cm (6 in)

Range: Andes Mountains, from Peru to northern Chile

Scientific name: *Vicugna vicugna*

Dromedary camel

Deer, giraffes, pronghorns and bovids

This group of even-toed hoofed animals all chew the cud, which means that they have complex stomachs. When they eat, they briefly chew leaves and grasses and swallow them. The animal then brings the partly digested food back up into its mouth and chews it properly. Giraffes, pronghorns and bovids (cattle, antelopes, sheep and goats) have horns on their heads, while deer have antlers. Horns are permanent growths, but antlers drop off and grow again each year.

Size: body 2.2–3.4 m (7¼–11 ft); tail 50 cm (19¾ in)

Range: northern Africa, Middle East; introduced into Australia

Scientific name: *Camelus dromedarius*

Dromedary camel

Dromedaries are well suited to life in the desert. Their ears and nostrils can close to keep out sand, while their tough lips enable them to eat thorny desert plants without being injured. They use their humps to store fat, which their bodies break down into water and energy when food and drink become scarce.

Water chevrotain

Water chevrotain

The tiny water chevrotain is about the size of a hare, with a hunched back, small head and thin legs. It lives in forests near water and spends the day resting in thick undergrowth. At night, it comes out to forage for grass, leaves and fruit. It also eats crabs, worms, insects, fish and small mammals. If danger threatens, it dives deep into the water to escape.

Size: body 75–85 cm (29½–33½ in); tail 10–15 cm (4–6 in)

Range: western and central Africa

Scientific name: *Hyemoschus aquaticus*

Forest musk deer

Size: body about 1 m (3¼ ft);
tail 4–5 cm (1½–2 in)
Range: Himalayas to central China
Scientific name:
Moschus chrysogaster

Forest musk deer

The male musk deer has a scent gland on the underside of its body. This oozes a strong-smelling liquid called musk, which the deer uses to send signals to females in the breeding season. The musk deer has a coat of long thick bristly hairs and two tusklike teeth on its upper jaw. It feeds on lichens, shoots, buds, grass, moss and twigs.

Red deer

Male and female red deer live in separate herds. The males' antlers drop off each spring and are replaced by a new, larger set. In the breeding season, males use their antlers to fight each other for the right to mate with the females. The older males usually win.

Red deer

Size: body 1.6–2.5 m (5¼–8 ft);
tail 12–25 cm (4¾–9¾ in)
Range: northern Africa, Europe, Asia, North America; introduced into New Zealand
Scientific name: *Cervus elaphus*

Moose

Male

Moose

The moose (also known as the elk) is the largest of all the deer species. It has massive antlers, a broad overhanging muzzle and a flap of skin that dangles from its throat. In winter, the moose eats pine cones, and shovels away the snow with its hooves to find mosses and lichens too. It swims well, and in summer it will often wade into lakes and rivers to feed on water plants. Males bellow to attract the females.

Size: body 2.5–3 m (8–10 ft);
tail 5–12 cm (2–4¾ in)
Range: northernmost parts of Europe, Asia, North America
Scientific name: *Alces alces*

Caribou

The caribou, or reindeer, is the only deer species in which both males and females have antlers. (it is usually only the males). The caribou feeds mainly on lichens in winter. In summer it travels north to feed on the rich grass and plants of the tundra. The females and young live in herds, but adult males often live alone.

Caribou

Size: body 1.2–2.2 m (4–7¼ ft);
tail 10–21 cm (4–8¼ in)
Range: northern Europe, northern Asia, Greenland, northern North America
Scientific name: *Rangifer tarandus*

51

Size: body 3–4 m (10–13 ft); tail 90–110 cm (35½–43½ in)
Range: Africa, south of the Sahara
Scientific name:
  Giraffa camelopardalis

Giraffe

Giraffe

The giraffe lives on Africa's savanna. With its amazingly long legs and neck, it stands nearly 6 m (19½ ft) tall, making it the tallest living mammal. Its great height enables it to feed on leaves and buds at the tops of trees, and to spot approaching danger.

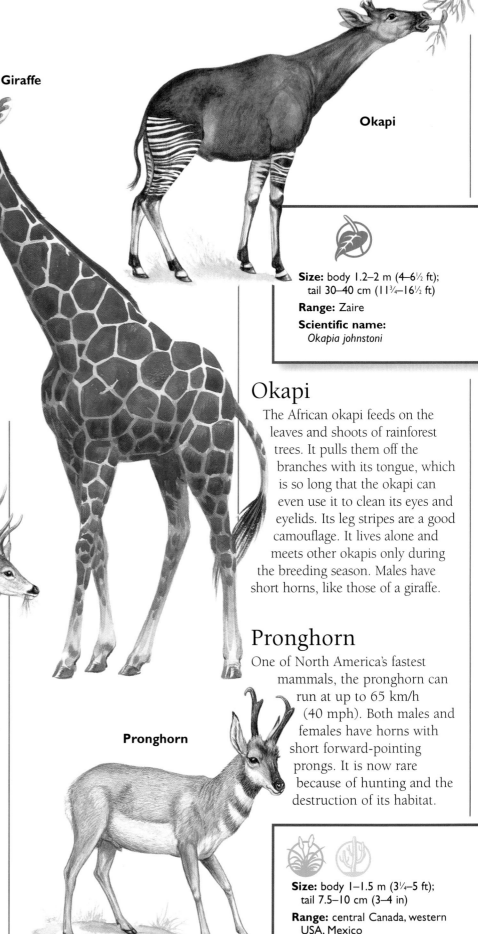

Okapi

Size: body 1.2–2 m (4–6½ ft); tail 30–40 cm (11¾–16½ ft)
Range: Zaire
Scientific name:
  Okapia johnstoni

Okapi

The African okapi feeds on the leaves and shoots of rainforest trees. It pulls them off the branches with its tongue, which is so long that the okapi can even use it to clean its eyes and eyelids. Its leg stripes are a good camouflage. It lives alone and meets other okapis only during the breeding season. Males have short horns, like those of a giraffe.

Size: body 1.1–1.3 m (3½–4¼ ft); tail 10–15 cm (4–6 in)
Range: South America
Scientific name:
  Ozotoceros bezoarticus

Pampas deer

Pampas deer

This deer used to live only in tall pampas grass, but today it is also found in woodland because so much grassland is now used for farming. It rests during the day and feeds at dusk. There are only a few hundred pampas deer left and it is therefore a protected animal.

Pronghorn

One of North America's fastest mammals, the pronghorn can run at up to 65 km/h (40 mph). Both males and females have horns with short forward-pointing prongs. It is now rare because of hunting and the destruction of its habitat.

Pronghorn

Size: body 1–1.5 m (3¼–5 ft); tail 7.5–10 cm (3–4 in)
Range: central Canada, western USA, Mexico
Scientific name:
  Antilocapra americana

Blue wildebeest

In the dry season, huge herds of these large cowlike antelopes walk great distances across the African savanna in search of fresh grass and watering holes. Young wildebeest calves are born during the wet season, when the herds split up and food is more plentiful.

Size: body 1.7–2.4 m (5½–7¾ ft); tail 60–100 cm (23½–35½ in)
Range: southern Africa
Scientific name:
Connochaetes taurinus

Blue wildebeest

Bongo

The shy, forest-dwelling bongo hides among the bushes and trees during the daytime. At dawn and dusk it comes out to feed on leaves, bark and fruit. When it runs, the bongo tilts its head so that its horns lie along its back, to prevent them catching on branches.

Size: body 1.7–2.5 m (5½–8¼ ft); tail 45–65 cm (17¾–25½ in)
Range: central Africa
Scientific name:
Tragelaphus eurycerus

Bongo

Asian water buffalo

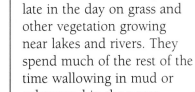

Water buffalo feed early and late in the day on grass and other vegetation growing near lakes and rivers. They spend much of the rest of the time wallowing in mud or submerged in the water, with only their muzzles showing. They use their long curved horns to defend themselves against tigers.

Asian water buffalo

Size: body 2.5–3 m (8¼–10 ft); tail 60–100 cm (23½–35½ in)
Range: India, Southeast Asia; introduced into other places
Scientific name: Bubalus arnee

Wild yak

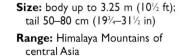

Size: body up to 3.25 m (10½ ft); tail 50–80 cm (19¾–31½ in)
Range: Himalaya Mountains of central Asia
Scientific name: Bos grunniens

Wild yak

Despite its size, the yak is surprisingly sure-footed as it grazes on remote mountain slopes. Its long thick ragged hair almost reaches to the ground. It also has a woolly undercoat to help protect it against freezing temperatures.

Size: body 1–1.2 m (3¼–4 ft);
tail 10–20 cm (4–7¾ in)
Range: South Africa
Scientific name:
Pelea capreolus

Rhebok

Size: body 2.1–3.5 m (7–11½ ft);
tail 50–60 cm (19¾–23½ in)
Range: North America
Scientific name:
Bison bison

European bison

Rhebok

The rhebok is a small graceful antelope with a soft woolly coat. It lives on grassy hills and high plains with low bushes and scattered trees. This wary animal bounces away with a jerky run if it is disturbed. In the breeding season, the males stage fierce mock battles, but do not harm each other.

Lechwe

The lechwe lives around lakes, swamps and flood plains. It spends much of its time wading in shallow water, where it feeds on grasses and water plants. Its long wide hooves are ideal for plodding through mud, but prevent it from moving quickly on dry land. When threatened by lions, hyenas or other predators, it hides under water, with just its nostrils showing.

American bison

American bison

There were once 60 million bison roaming over the Great Plains of North America, but so many were killed by European settlers in the 19th century that only about 20,000 remain. These magnificent animals are now only seen in national parks and reserves. They live in herds and feed on grass.

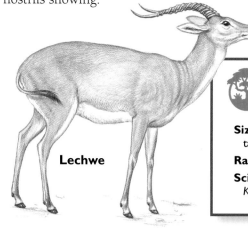

Size: body 2.1–3.5 m (7–11½ ft);
tail 50–60 cm (19¾–23½ in)
Range: eastern Europe
Scientific name:
Bison bonasus

European bison

The European bison feeds on leaves, ferns, twigs, bark and acorns found in the forest. In 1919, the species died out in the wild, due to hunting and deforestation. Six European bison were released from captivity into the wild, where they bred and thrived. There are now about 300 European bison in the wild.

Lechwe

Size: body 1.3–1.7 m (4¼–5½ ft);
tail 30–45 cm (11¾–17¾ in)
Range: southern Africa
Scientific name:
Kobus lechwe

Arabian oryx

The desert-dwelling oryx can endure long periods without water. It gets all the moisture it needs from the grass and shrubs it eats.

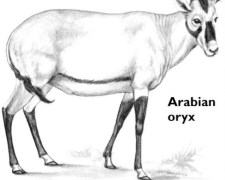

Arabian oryx

Size: body 1.6 m (5¼ ft); tail 45 cm (17¾ in)
Range: Saudi Arabia
Scientific name:
  Oryx leucoryx

Addax

The addax is one of the few large animals that live in the Sahara Desert region, where it feeds on plants such as cacti. Its wide hooves stop its feet from sinking into the desert sand. It is now extremely rare because it has been hunted for sport and for its horns and skin.

Addax

Size: body 1.3 m (4¼ ft); tail 25–35 cm (9¾–13¾ in)
Range: northern Africa
Scientific name:
  Addax nasomaculatus

Impala

At home in light woodland or on the African savanna, the glossy-coated impala has long elegant spiral-shaped horns. When running, it can make leaps of up to 10 m (33 ft) in order to escape predators. It also seems to do this just for fun.

Impala

Size: body 1.2–1.6 m (4–5¼ ft); tail 30–45 cm (11¾–17¾ in)
Range: southern Africa
Scientific name:
  Aepyceros melampus

Saiga

The saiga lives on high grassy plains called steppes. Its trunklike nose has special hairs and glands to filter sand and dust from the air. In winter, it grows a thick woolly coat to protect it from the icy steppe winds.

Saiga

Size: body 1.2–1.7 m (4–5½ ft); tail 7.5–10 cm (3–4 in)
Range: central Asia
Scientific name:
  Saiga tatarica

Chamois

In summer, the nimble chamois grazes on mountain tops, often leaping between rocky crags to find food. It has sturdy legs and hooves with special spongy pads underneath to help its feet grip slippery surfaces. In winter, it moves lower down the mountainside to feed on lichens, mosses and shoots.

Size: body 90–130 cm (35½–51 in); tail 3–4 cm (1¼–1½ in)
Range: Europe to the Middle East
Scientific name:
  Rupicapra rupicapra

Chamois

Size: body 1.9–2.3 m (6¼–7½ ft);
tail 9–10 cm (3½–4 in)

Range: northern Canada,
Greenland

Scientific name:
Ovibus moschatus

Musk ox

Musk ox

On the freezing tundra landscape of the Arctic, musk oxen dig through snow and ice with their hooves to reach mosses, lichens and roots. If attacked by wolves, they form a defensive circle around their young, with their horns pointing outwards.

Horses and tapirs

Along with rhinoceroses, horses and tapirs make up a group of odd-toed, hoofed mammals. Animals in the horse family, including zebras and asses, live in herds and feed mainly on grass. Their feet have only one toe with a single hoof on the end. This enables them to run fast. Tapirs are short stocky creatures with four toes on their front feet and three on the hind feet. Rhinoceroses have three toes on each foot, short legs, large heads and horns.

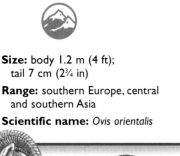

Size: body 1.2 m (4 ft);
tail 7 cm (2¾ in)

Range: southern Europe, central
and southern Asia

Scientific name: *Ovis orientalis*

Mouflon

Mouflon

The mouflon has long inward-curving horns. In order to survive in the rugged mountains where it lives, it eats virtually any vegetation it can find – including poisonous plants, such as deadly nightshade.

Grevy's zebra

Herds of grazing zebras roam Africa's savanna. Zebras need to drink frequently, so they spend most of their time near water holes. Their coats are striped to confuse predators.

Size: body 2.6 m (8½ ft);
tail 70–75 cm (27½–29½ in)

Range: eastern Africa

Scientific name:
Equus grevyi

Grevy's zebra

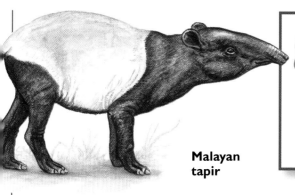

Malayan tapir

Size: body 2.5 m (8 ft); tail 5–10 cm (2–4 in)

Range: Southeast Asia

Scientific name: *Tapirus indicus*

Black rhinoceros

The black rhino's hooklike upper lip helps it to grab leaves, buds and shoots from small trees and bushes. It makes up for its poor eyesight with good senses of hearing and smell. If it ever feels threatened, it will charge. Despite its size, it can reach a speed of 48 km/h (30 mph).

Malayan tapir

The Malayan tapir is a shy, solitary animal that lives in humid swampy forests. It swims well and rushes into the water to hide when it feels threatened. The Malayan tapir prefers to feed on aquatic vegetation, but also eats the leaves, buds and fruit of some land plants.

Black rhinoceros

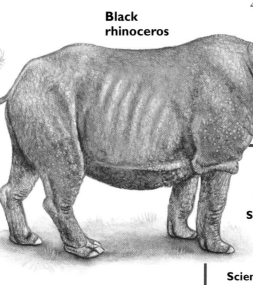

Przewalski's horse

This short sturdy horse is the ancestor of all modern horses. It was once common on the dry plains of Mongolia, where it grazed on grass and leaves. It has not been seen in the wild since 1968 and now lives only in zoos.

Size: body 3–3.6 m (10–12 ft); tail 60–70 cm (23½–27½ in)

Range: eastern and southern Africa

Scientific name: *Diceros bicornis*

Sumatran rhinoceros

This the smallest and hairiest member of the rhinoceros family. There are only a few hundred wild Sumatran rhinos left. It is hunted for its horns, which are used in traditional medicine, and the forests where it lives are being chopped down.

Przewalski's horse

Size: body 2.5–2.8 m (8–9¼ ft); tail about 60 cm (23½ in)

Range: Southeast Asia

Scientific name: *Dicerorhinus sumatrensis*

Size: body 1.8–2 m (6–6½ ft); tail 90 cm (35½ in)

Range: Mongolia, western China

Scientific name: *Equus przewalski*

Sumatran rhinoceros

Rodents and rabbits

Rodents are a large group of small- to medium-sized mammals which include such groups as squirrels, rats and beavers. There are at least 1,800 species of rodents and they are found all over the world in every kind of habitat. Most feed on plants and they have a single pair of sharp incisor teeth, which allows them to chew through the toughest food. Pikas, rabbits and hares are another successful group of plant-eating mammals called lagomorphs. They also have sharp incisors for chewing plant food.

Pikas, rabbits and hares

Pikas are smaller than rabbits and have short rounded ears and no tail. There are about 21 different species, most of which live in north and central Asia, although two species also live in North America. Rabbits and hares are common in the Americas, Europe, Asia and Africa and have been successfully introduced into Australia and New Zealand – about 47 species in all. Most of the fast-moving rabbits and hares have long narrow ears, small fluffy tails and well-developed back legs.

European rabbit

Rabbits live in burrows which they dig near to one another. There may be a couple of hundred rabbits in a colony, called a warren. Grass and leafy plants are their main food, but they also eat grain and can damage young trees. Females have several litters a year.

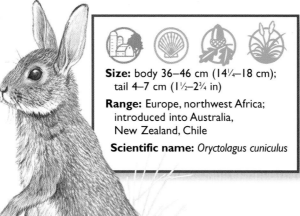

European rabbit

Size: body 36–46 cm (14¼–18 cm); tail 4–7 cm (1½–2¾ in)
Range: Europe, northwest Africa; introduced into Australia, New Zealand, Chile
Scientific name: *Oryctolagus cuniculus*

Northern pika

Pikas live in family groups, which shelter in dens among rocks or tree roots. Grass and juicy plant stems are their main food. In summer, they gather extra food which they pile up in little haystacks to keep for the winter months. Pikas can tunnel through snow to reach their food stores.

Northern pika

Size: body 20–25 cm (7¾–9¾ in)
Range: northern Asia
Scientific name: *Ochotona alpina*

Snowshoe hare

The snowshoe hare is dark brown in summer but turns white in winter. Only the tips of its ears remain dark. Its light coat helps it to hide from enemies in its snowy home. Usually active at night and in the early morning, the snowshoe hare eats grass in summer and twigs and buds in winter.

Snowshoe hare

Size: body 36–52 cm (14¼–20½in); tail 2.5–5 cm (1–2 in)
Range: Canada, Alaska, northern USA
Scientific name: *Lepus americanus*

Squirrels, beavers, pocket gophers, pocket mice and springhares

These animals are all rodents. The squirrel family includes animals such as woodchucks, prairie dogs and chipmunks. Pocket gophers live in North America and spend most of their lives underground. Pocket mice are found in North and South America. Some are mouselike and live in dense forest. Others bound across arid plains on long hind legs. The single species of springhare can also leap like a kangaroo. The two species of beaver spend much of their lives in water.

Size: body 11.5–18 cm (4½–7 in); tail 11.5–18 cm (4½–7 in)
Range: India, Sri Lanka
Scientific name:
Funambulus palmarum

Indian striped palm squirrel

Indian striped palm squirrel

These active little squirrels leap about in palm trees during the day, feeding on palm nuts, flowers and buds. Rival males fight for females, but after mating have nothing further to do with females or young. The females produce about three litters a year, each containing about three young.

Woodchuck

The woodchuck, or ground hog as it is sometimes known, eats plenty of plant food in summer and gets fat. At the first sign of frost it goes into its burrow and sleeps through the winter, living on its store of body fat.

Size: body 45–61 cm (17¾–24 in); tail 18–25 cm (7–9¾ in)
Range: North America
Scientific name:
Marmota monax

Woodchuck

Black-tailed prairie dog

Size: body 28–33 cm (11–13 in); tail 7.5–10 cm (3–4 in)
Range: central USA
Scientific name:
Cynomys ludovicianus

European red squirrel

Red squirrels use their sharp teeth to feed on conifer cones in winter, but in summer they also eat mushrooms and fruit. Where food is plentiful, females may have two litters of about three young a year. The young are born in a tree nest called a drey.

Black-tailed prairie dog

Prairie dogs live in huge underground burrows, called towns. A town may house several thousand animals. They come out during the day to feed on grass and other plants, and warn each other of any danger with sharp doglike barks.

Size: body 20–24 cm (7¾–9½ in); tail 15–20 cm (6–7¾ in)
Range: Europe, Asia
Scientific name:
Sciurus vulgaris

European red squirrel

59

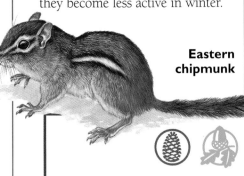

Plains pocket gopher

This gopher's name comes from its two deep fur-lined cheek pouches. These can be crammed full of food (mostly roots) to carry back to the nest. Gophers spend most of their lives underground in burrows which they dig with their sharp front teeth and strong paws.

Plains pocket gopher

Size: body 18–24 cm (7–9½ in); tail 10–12.5 cm (4–5 in)
Range: central USA
Scientific name: *Geomys bursarius*

Desert kangaroo rat

Kangaroo rats belong to the pocket mouse family. This desert species spends the day in a burrow and comes out at night to find food such as seeds. It is well adapted to dry areas and may live its whole life without ever drinking. It can carry food in cheek pouches.

Size: body 12–16.5 cm (4¾–6½ in); tail 18–20 cm (7–7¾ in)
Range: western USA
Scientific name: *Dipodomys deserti*

Desert kangaroo rat

Eastern chipmunk

The lively little chipmunk belongs to the squirrel family. It shelters in burrows it digs under logs and boulders and comes out in the morning to forage for nuts, berries and seeds. During autumn, chipmunks store food for the winter. They do not hibernate but they become less active in winter.

Eastern chipmunk

Size: body 13.5–20 cm (5¼–7¾ in); tail 7.5–11.5 cm (3–4½ in)
Range: eastern North America
Scientific name: *Tamias striatus*

Size: body 73–130 cm (28¾–51 in); tail 20–30.5 cm (7¾–12 in)
Range: North America
Scientific name: *Castor canadensis*

Springhare

Size: body 35–43 cm (13¾–17 in); tail 36–47cm (14¼–18½ in)
Range: southern Africa
Scientific name: *Pedetes capensis*

American beaver

One of the largest rodents, the American beaver weighs up to 27 kg (60 lb). Beavers eat leaves, bark and twigs and always live near water. They build a dam across a stream with branches and mud, which creates a lake. A shelter, or lodge, is also made of branches and used to store food.

Springhare

When alarmed or travelling a long way, the springhare bounces along on its long back legs like a kangaroo. When feeding, it moves on all fours. The springhare spends much of the day in its burrow and comes out at night to forage for bulbs, roots and grain as well as some insects.

American beaver

New World rats and mice

There are at least 400 species in this group of rodents, found in all kinds of habitats from the northern woodlands of Canada to the deserts and forests of South America. They adapt well to different conditions – fish-eating rats which live near rivers and lakes even have partially webbed feet. Most New World rats and mice are small – the largest, the giant water rat, measures 30 cm (11¾ in). Plant material is their main food, although some also feed on insects.

Size: body 12–22 cm (4¾–8¾ in); tail 8–18 cm (3¼–7 in)
Range: Canada to Mexico
Scientific name:
  Peromyscus maniculatus

Deer mouse

Arizona cotton rat

Cotton rats sometimes occur in such numbers that they are considered pests. They feed on plants and small insects, but may also take the eggs and chicks of bobwhite quails as well as crayfish and crabs. The female has her first litter of up to 12 young when just 10 weeks old.

Arizona cotton rat

Size: body 12.5–20 cm (5–7¾ in); tail 7.5–12.5 cm (3–5 in)
Range: USA
Scientific name:
  Sigmodon arizonae

Deer mouse

Agile little mice, deer mice run and hop through grass and dense vegetation. They build nests underground or in tree holes and feed on insects as well as seeds, nuts and acorns. Young deer mice start to breed at only seven weeks old. They may have several litters a year, each containing up to nine young.

Hamsters and mole-rats

Hamsters and mole-rats are both burrowing rodents. Hamsters are found from Europe across the Middle East to central Asia. There are about 18 species, all of which have a rounded body and short tail. They have large cheek pouches, which they use for carrying food back to the burrow. There are two groups of mole-rats: one group includes two species of east African mole-rats and four species of bamboo rats from Southeast Asia. All are plant eaters. The other group includes eight species, which all live in Africa. The most unusual is the virtually hairless naked mole-rat.

Common hamster

The hamster lives in a burrow with separate areas for sleeping and storing food. It feeds mainly on seeds, grain, roots, green plants and insect larvae. In late summer, it gathers extra food to store for the winter. From October to March or April, the hamster hibernates, waking from time to time to feed on its food stores.

Size: body 22–30 cm (8¾–11¾ in); tail 3–6 cm (1¼–2¼ in)
Range: western Europe, central Asia
Scientific name: *Cricetus cricetus*

Common hamster

Size: body 36–48 cm (14¼–19 in); tail 10–15 cm (4–6 in)
Range: Southeast Asia
Scientific name:
Rhizomys sumatrensis

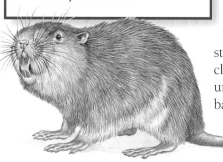

Bamboo rat

Bamboo rat

This rat has a heavy body, short legs and a short, almost hairless tail. Its front teeth are large and strong and it uses these and its claws for digging. It burrows underground near clumps of bamboo – the roots of this plant are its main food. It also eats other plants, seeds and fruit.

Naked mole-rat

Size: body 8–9 cm (3¼–3½ in); tail 4 cm (1½ in)
Range: eastern Africa
Scientific name:
Heterocephalus glaber

Naked mole-rat

This little rodent has a life-style more like that of an insect than a mammal. They live in a colony of up to 200 animals, ruled by one female, or queen. She is the only one to breed. Worker mole-rats dig burrows and gather food such as roots for the whole colony to eat. A few non-workers tend the queen.

Swamp rats, gerbils, lemmings and voles

There are 11 species of African swamp rats. They do not always live near water or swampy areas, but they are all good swimmers. Lemmings and voles are plump-bodied rodents which live in North America and northern Europe and Asia. All feed mainly on plants and they usually live in large groups or colonies. There are about 120 species. Gerbils live in Africa and in central and western Asia. All are well adapted to desert conditions and are able to survive with very little water. Their long hind legs and feet help keep their bodies well away from hot sand.

Norway lemming

The Norway lemming is busy day and night, feeding on grass, leaves and moss. In winter it clears pathways under the snow so it can still run around foraging for food. Lemmings start to breed in spring under the snow and may produce as many as eight litters of six young each during the summer.

Norway lemming

Swamp rat

Swamp rat

This plump, active rat feeds on seeds, berries, shoots and grasses. It often goes into water and even dives to escape enemies – many larger creatures feed on these rats. It usually makes a nest of leaves and twigs above ground but may sometimes shelter in a burrow left by another animal.

Size: body 13–20 cm (5–7¾ in); tail 5–17 cm (2–6¾ in)
Range: southern Africa
Scientific name:
Otomys irroratus

Size: body 13–15 cm (5–6 in); tail 2 cm (¾ in)
Range: Scandinavia
Scientific name:
Lemmus lemmus

62

Great gerbil

This gerbil manages to survive in the Gobi Desert, with its hot summers and icy winters. During the summer, it builds up stores of 60 kg (130 lb) or more of plant material in its burrow so that it has plenty of food for the winter months.

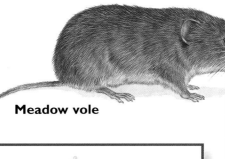

Meadow vole

Size: body 9–12.5 cm (3½–5 in); tail 3.5–6.5 cm (1¼–2½ in)
Range: North America
Scientific name:
   Microtus pennsylvanicus

Size: body 16–20 cm (6¼–7¾ in); tail 13–16 cm (5–6¼ in)
Range: Middle East and Asia
Scientific name:
   Rhombomys opimus

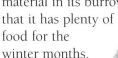

Great gerbil

Meadow vole

The meadow vole manages to live in many kinds of habitat. Grass, seeds, roots and bark are its main food and it moves along runways which it clears and keeps trimmed in the grass. It makes a nest on the ground or a burrow under the runways.

Old World rats and mice

This large group of almost 500 species of rodents contains some of the world's most common and widespread mammals. Rodents such as the brown rat and house mouse have adapted to life all over the world in many different kinds of conditions and will eat a wide range of foods. Many of this group are considered pests by humans because they damage grain and root crops as well as stored food. Some, such as the brown rat, also carry diseases such as salmonella.

Size: body 25–30 cm (9¾–11¾ in); tail 25–32 cm (9¾–12½ in)
Range: worldwide
Scientific name:
   Rattus norvegicus

Brown rat

Wood mouse

The wood mouse is one of the most common small rodents in Europe. It comes out of its nest under the roots of trees in the evening and forages for seeds, insects and berries. The female usually produces young between April and November, but may breed through the winter if there is plenty of food.

Brown rat

This rat is a serious pest. It has followed humans all over the world and lives wherever people settle. An extremely adaptable animal, it eats any scraps of waste food. It breeds all year round and produces about eight litters of 8 to 10 young each in a year.

Size: body 8–13 cm (3¼–5 in); tail 7–9.5 cm (2¾–3¾ in)
Range: Europe, Asia
Scientific name:
   Apodemus sylvaticus

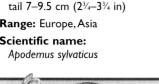

Wood mouse

Dormice and jerboas

There are about 21 species of dormice living in Africa, Europe and northern Asia. In autumn most dormice eat extra food to build up reserves of fat in the body. They then hibernate – sleep through the winter – living on their fat but waking from time to time to feed on stored food. Jerboas are small rodents with long back legs used for jumping. There are 49 species of jerboas, living in North America, eastern Europe and Asia.

Great jerboa

This lively rodent leaps through the desert on its long back legs. At night, it searches for seeds and insects to eat, which it finds by combing through the sand with the long slender claws on its front feet. During the day the jerboa shelters in a burrow.

Great jerboa

Desert dormouse

This dormouse is active at night, catching insects to eat. It also feeds on plants and makes stores of plant food for the winter months. It digs a burrow in which it shelters during the day and may also use it for hibernation. This rodent was first discovered in 1938.

Size: body 7–8.5 cm (2¾–3¼ in); tail 7–9.5 cm (2¾–3¾ in)
Range: central Asia: Kazakhstan
Scientific name: *Selevinia betpakdalensis*

Desert dormouse

Size: body 9–15 cm (3½–6 in); tail 16–22 cm (6¼–8¾ in)
Range: northern Asia
Scientific name: *Allactaga major*

Porcupines, chinchillas, guinea pigs, capybaras and hutias

These widely varied animals all belong to small families of medium to large rodents. Porcupines are instantly recognised by the long sharp spines covering parts of the body and tail. There are two families: one occurs in Africa and Asia, and the other in North and South America. Chinchillas and guinea pigs are all ground-living rodents which live in South America. The capybara too lives in South America and is the only species in its family. The 12 species of hutias all live on West Indian islands.

Chinchilla

Size: body 22–38 cm (8¾–15 in); tail 7.5–15 cm (3–6 in)
Range: northern Chile
Scientific name: *Chinchilla laniger*

Chinchilla

With its large eyes, long ears and bushy tail, the chinchilla is an appealing animal. They live in colonies of 100 or more and feed on plants. They usually sit up to eat, holding their food in their front paws. Females are larger than males. They breed in winter and have two litters of up to six young.

Crested porcupine

Size: body 71–84 cm (28–33 in);
tail up to 2.5 cm (1 in)
Range: Africa
Scientific name:
Hystrix africaeaustralis

Crested porcupine

The spines on the back of the crested porcupine are up to 30 cm (11¾ in) long. If threatened, the porcupine charges backwards, driving these sharp spines, which detach easily from its body, into its enemy. This porcupine shelters in a burrow during the day and comes out at night to feed.

Tree porcupine

The body of the tree porcupine is covered with short thick spines. Its tail is prehensile, which means it has special muscles that grip easily, acting like an extra limb. Tree porcupines usually feed at night on leaves, plant stems and fruit.

Size: body 30–61 cm (11¾–24 in);
tail 33–45 cm (13–17¾ in)
Range: Bolivia, Brazil, Venezuela
Scientific name:
Coendou prehensilis

**Tree
porcupine**

Hutia

The hutia feeds mostly on fruit and leaves, but it also eats some insects and small reptiles. It is a good climber and may search for food in trees. Active during the day, it shelters in a burrow or rock crevice at night. Unfortunately, hutias are now rare because they are preyed on by mongooses and dogs introduced into the West Indies by humans.

Hutia

Size: body 30–50 cm (11¾–19¾ in);
tail 15–30 (6–11¾ in)
Range: Caribbean: Bahamas
Scientific name:
Geocapromys ingrahami

Guinea pig

Size: body 20–40 cm (7¾–15¾ in);
no visible tail
Range: Peru to Argentina
Scientific name:
Cavia tschudii

Guinea pig

Also known as the cavy, the wild guinea pig has a chunky body, short legs and small ears. They live in family groups, which may join together to form colonies of up to 40 animals. At dawn and dusk, guinea pigs come out of their burrows to eat grass and leaves.

Capybara

The largest living rodent, the capybara has a strong body and large head. It spends much of its time in water and is an expert swimmer and diver. Its feet are partially webbed, and when swimming only its eyes, ears and nostrils show above the water. It eats mainly plants, including water plants, and is usually active at dawn and dusk.

Capybara

Size: body 1–1.3 m (3¼–4¼ ft)
Range: Panama to eastern
Argentina
Scientific name:
Hydrochoerus hydrochaeris

65

Why do zebras have stripes?

A zebra's stripes, the humps on a camel's back, the "fishing rod" on the head of an angler fish and the leaflike wings of an insect may seem extraordinary features, but they all make the animals that have them better able to survive in their environment. These types of features are called adaptations and include the special markings or colours, known as camouflage, that allow creatures to hide from predators or prey. Other features help animals to survive in extreme conditions such as hot deserts or freezing polar lands.

Some insects look remarkably like the leaves of the trees and bushes they live among, making it very hard for their enemies to spot them. The bright green wings of this **leaf insect** are leaf-shaped and have veinlike markings. The edges even look as if they have been nibbled by other insects.

The **bactrian camel** is one of the biggest animals in the desert and special features help it cope with life there. Wide flat feet stop it from sinking into soft sand. Large humps store fat to help it survive food shortages. When it gets the chance, the camel can drink a huge quantity of water at one go.

The bold black and white stripes of the **zebra** are not for camouflage, since they make the animal very obvious in the grasslands of Africa. Because the pattern of the stripes is slightly different in each individual, experts think that they enable the zebras to recognise their own family group. This helps keep them together and so safer from predators.

The flap of skin like a fishing rod on the **angler fish's** head is a special structure for catching prey. Other fish come near to investigate what could be a morsel of food. The angler opens its huge mouth and swallows the prey.

Birds

Birds are among the most successful of all the world's animals, and have conquered air, land and water. They are found all over the world, including the icy lands of Antarctica and on the remotest islands. They live at heights of more than 8,000 m (26,250 ft) in the Himalayas and at 40 m (130 ft) below sea level around the shores of the Dead Sea.

There are about 9,000 different species of birds, ranging in size from tiny hummingbirds, weighing only a few grams (ounces), to huge eagles and fast-running ostriches. Despite their differences, all birds lay eggs. It would be impossible for birds to carry their growing young inside their bodies as mammals do because they could become too heavy to fly. The baby bird is protected inside a hard-shelled egg, which is usually kept warm, or incubated, by the parents, in a nest. The incubation period – the time taken for a chick to grow inside the egg and break out of the shell – varies from about 10 to 12 days in small birds, such as warblers and wrens, to as many as 84 days in albatrosses.

These **seagulls** are in flight off the coasts of the Channel Islands. Coastal birds such as gulls do not spend much time actually in the water, but they do depend on the sea for most of their food. Gulls are the scavengers of the shore. They eat waste from fishing boats and take food from rubbish dumps, as well as eating fish.

Royal flycatcher

What is a bird?

A typical bird has a strong but light body, two legs and a pair of wings. The wings are, in fact, modified forelimbs. All birds are covered with feathers – and are the only creatures to have feathers. The feathers are made of keratin, a protein that also makes up the scales on reptiles and the hair and nails of humans and other mammals.

Not all birds fly. The world's largest bird, the **ostrich**, is too heavy to take to the air. Instead it runs fast on its long legs.

A bird's **wings** are shaped for different kinds of flight. The long broad wings of hawks and vultures allow these birds to soar for hours on air currents over land. The long wings of the albatross are suited to the different wind conditions over oceans. Agile, fast-flying birds such as swifts and swallows have slender pointed wings. The hummingbird's wings can move in almost any direction, while the pheasant's wings are for slower, flapping flight.

Albatross

Swift

Hummingbird

Swallow

Hawk

Vulture

Pheasant

Bird anatomy

Here is a powerful martial eagle poised to snatch its prey. Its strong wings keep its body in the air and its tail feathers are spread to help it steer during flight. Its strong talons are held ready to crush its prey, which it will then tear apart with its hooked beak. All birds have wings, beaks and claws that are shaped for their particular life-style.

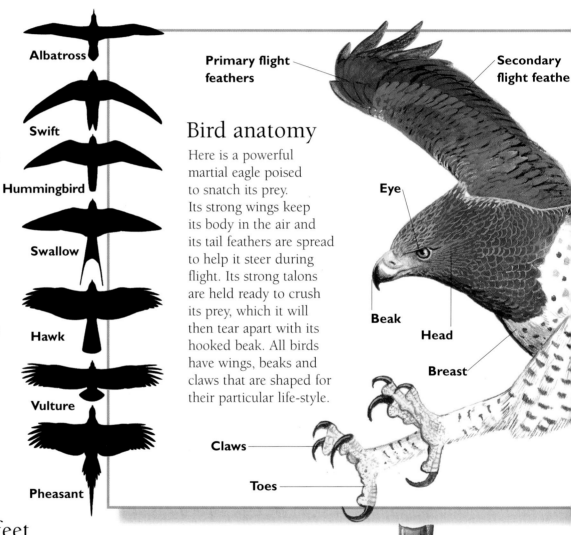

Primary flight feathers

Secondary flight feathe

Eye

Beak

Head

Breast

Claws

Toes

All types of feet

Perching birds, such as crows, all have four-toed feet, three toes facing forwards and one backwards. Seabirds, such as cormorants, have webbed feet. The ostrich's two-toed foot is suited to running, and the eagle's strong toes and claws are used for killing prey.

Carrion crow

Harpy eagle

Ostrich

Great cormorant

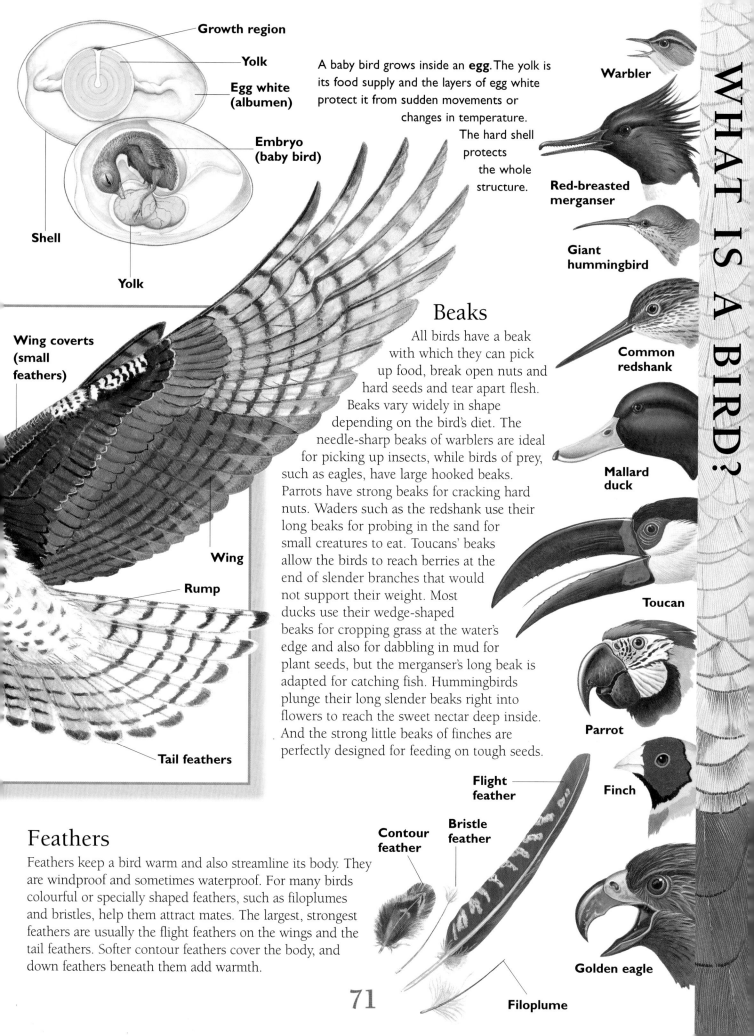

Growth region

Yolk

Egg white (albumen)

Embryo (baby bird)

Shell

Yolk

A baby bird grows inside an **egg**. The yolk is its food supply and the layers of egg white protect it from sudden movements or changes in temperature. The hard shell protects the whole structure.

Warbler

Red-breasted merganser

Giant hummingbird

Common redshank

Mallard duck

Toucan

Parrot

Finch

Golden eagle

Wing coverts (small feathers)

Wing

Rump

Tail feathers

Beaks

All birds have a beak with which they can pick up food, break open nuts and hard seeds and tear apart flesh. Beaks vary widely in shape depending on the bird's diet. The needle-sharp beaks of warblers are ideal for picking up insects, while birds of prey, such as eagles, have large hooked beaks. Parrots have strong beaks for cracking hard nuts. Waders such as the redshank use their long beaks for probing in the sand for small creatures to eat. Toucans' beaks allow the birds to reach berries at the end of slender branches that would not support their weight. Most ducks use their wedge-shaped beaks for cropping grass at the water's edge and also for dabbling in mud for plant seeds, but the merganser's long beak is adapted for catching fish. Hummingbirds plunge their long slender beaks right into flowers to reach the sweet nectar deep inside. And the strong little beaks of finches are perfectly designed for feeding on tough seeds.

Flight feather

Contour feather

Bristle feather

Feathers

Feathers keep a bird warm and also streamline its body. They are windproof and sometimes waterproof. For many birds colourful or specially shaped feathers, such as filoplumes and bristles, help them attract mates. The largest, strongest feathers are usually the flight feathers on the wings and the tail feathers. Softer contour feathers cover the body, and down feathers beneath them add warmth.

Filoplume

71

Game birds and ground birds

Not all birds are high fliers. Many spend most of their lives on the ground, where they scratch around to find food. Some of the most interesting ground-living birds are the ratites, or running birds, a group which includes species such as the ostrich, rhea and emu. None of these birds can fly. They do have wings but these are too small to be used for flight. The ratites lead peaceful lives, feeding on seeds, leaves and plant shoots. Game birds, too, spend most of their time on the ground, but they can fly when necessary and often roost in trees at night.

Game birds

This large and varied group has more than 260 different species and includes pheasants, grouse, guineafowl and mallee fowl. Most have well-rounded bodies and short strong legs. The domestic fowl is a typical example. They are known as "game birds" because certain species, such as grouse and pheasants, have long been hunted and shot in some parts of the world for sport and food. Pheasants and other game birds scratch around for seeds and berries with their stout legs and strong claws. They usually make simple nests on the ground.

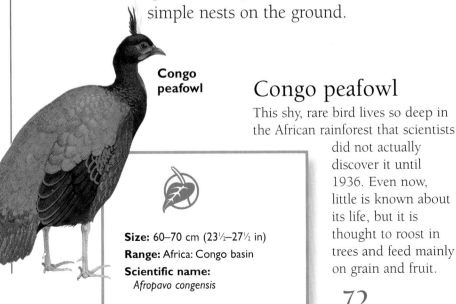

Congo peafowl

Congo peafowl

This shy, rare bird lives so deep in the African rainforest that scientists did not actually discover it until 1936. Even now, little is known about its life, but it is thought to roost in trees and feed mainly on grain and fruit.

Size: 60–70 cm (23½–27½ in)
Range: Africa: Congo basin
Scientific name:
Afropavo congensis

Ptarmigan

In summer the ptarmigan has mottled brown and grey feathers. But in winter the ptarmigan moults and grows plumage that is pure white, except for its tail feathers. This white winter coat helps the ptarmigan hide from its enemies in its snowy Arctic home.

Ptarmigan

Size: 33–39 cm (13–15½ in)
Range: Arctic
Scientific name:
Lagopus mutus

Indian peafowl

Size: male 2.2 m (7¼ ft) with train; female 86 cm (33¾ in)
Range: India, Sri Lanka
Scientific name:
Pavo cristatus

Size: 24–28 cm (9½–11 in)
Range: western USA
Scientific name:
  Callipepla californica

California quail

Temminck's tragopan

Size: 64 cm (25¼ in)
Range: China, Southeast Asia
Scientific name:
  Tragopan temminckii

California quail

California quail move and feed in flocks, eating leaves, berries, seeds and some insects. Both males and females have an unusual head plume, but only the male has black and white markings on the face.

Pheasant

Pheasants came originally from Asia but have now been introduced into many other countries. The female is plainer than the male, with brown plumage. Wild pheasants eat seeds, buds and berries.

Temminck's tragopan

The favourite home of this beautiful bird is cool mountain forest. The male is striking and colourful, while the female has brownish feathers. At the start of the breeding season, the male bird courts the female by displaying his brilliant plumage. She lays three to six eggs. Tragopans eat seeds, buds, leaves, berries and insects.

Pheasant

Indian peafowl

The male peafowl (peacock) is one of the most magnificent of all birds. It has colourful feathers, and its glittering train, adorned with "eyespot" markings, can be spread by raising the tail beneath. With his train fanned out, the male struts around to attract the plainer female (peahen). She has brown and green feathers and a small crest. In the wild, peafowl feed on seeds, berries, leaves and insects. They have been introduced into parks and gardens all over the world.

Junglefowl

The junglefowl is the ancestor of the domestic chicken. The female is smaller than the colourful male and has brown and chestnut feathers. Junglefowl move in flocks of about 50 birds, searching for grain, grass, seeds and insects to eat. In the breeding season the female scrapes a shallow nest in the ground near a bush and lines it with leaves. She lays five or six eggs.

Size: male 76–89 cm (30–35 in);
  female 53–64 cm (20¾–25¼ in)
Range: Asia
Scientific name:
  Phasianus colchicus

Junglefowl

Size: male 63–75 cm (24¾–29½ in);
  female 40–45 cm (15¾–17¾ in)
Range: Southeast Asia
Scientific name:
  Gallus gallus

73

Greater prairie chicken

Prairie chickens feed mainly on leaves, fruit and grain. In the summer they also catch insects, particularly grasshoppers. In the breeding season, male birds attract females by blowing out their orange neck pouches and raising their crests. They give booming calls and stamp their feet as they display. Females lay 10 to 12 eggs.

Size: 41–51 cm (16¼–20 in)
Range: northern Europe, northern Asia
Scientific name:
 Tetrao tetrix

Black grouse

Black grouse

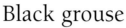

In spring, male black grouse perform a group display, called a lek, to attract female birds. Every morning they gather at a special place to dance, call and spread their beautiful tails before the watching females. The females mate with the best dancers and lay clutches of 6 to 11 eggs.

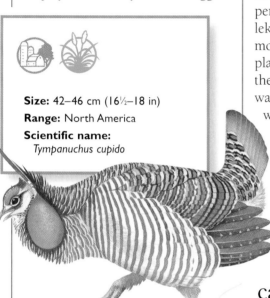

Size: 42–46 cm (16½–18 in)
Range: North America
Scientific name:
 Tympanuchus cupido

Greater prairie chicken

Turkey

The wild turkey has a lighter, slimmer body and longer legs than domestic farm turkeys. It has bare skin on its head and neck. The turkey can fly well for short distances but finds most of its food on the ground. It eats seeds, nuts and berries and also catches small creatures such as insects and lizards.

Western capercaillie

This magnificent turkeylike bird is the biggest of all the grouse. It feeds mainly on pine needles and pine seeds in winter. Its diet changes in summer, when it eats the leaves, stems and juicy fruit of cranberry, bilberry and other forest plants.

Size: male 86 cm (33¾ in); female 58 cm (22¾ in)
Range: northern Europe
Scientific name:
 Tetrao urogallus

Female

Turkey

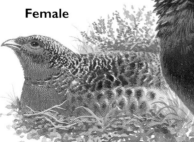

Western capercaillie

Male

Size: 91–122 cm (36–48 in)
Range: USA, Mexico
Scientific name:
 Meleagris gallopavo

Ground birds

The long-legged running birds, such as ostriches, rheas, cassowaries and emus, live in dry grasslands and semi-desert. They cannot fly and often have to travel far to find food so it is important for them to be fast runners. They also rely on running to escape from danger. Kiwis have shorter legs and move more slowly on the ground, and they cannot fly either. Also included in this section are ground-living birds from other families, such as the curassow, tinamou, great bustard, satin bowerbird and Pallas's sandgrouse. All of these birds can fly, but spend most of their lives at ground level.

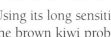

Satin bowerbird

Great curassow

Great curassow

The great curassow finds food, such as fruit and leaves, on the ground but flies up into the trees to roost. If in danger, it runs away rather than flies. The male has a loud booming call.

Size: 94 cm (37 in)
Range: Mexico to Ecuador
Scientific name:
 Crax rubra

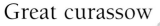

Size: 46 cm (18 in)
Range: South America
Scientific name:
 Tinamus major

Great tinamou

Great tinamou

Dense rainforest is the home of the great tinamou. This bird can fly but is weak and clumsy in the air. If in danger it usually remains still, relying on its brownish colouring to keep it hidden. It spends most of its time on the ground, eating berries, seeds and insects. Females lay up to 12 greenish-blue or violet eggs, which are among the most beautiful of all birds' eggs.

Satin bowerbird

The male bowerbird builds a "bower" (chamber) on the ground to attract females. The bower is made of sticks and decorated with bright blue flowers and berries. If a female comes near, the male dances in his bower, flapping his wings and puffing up his feathers.

Size: 27–33 cm (10½–13 in)
Range: eastern Australia
Scientific name:
 Ptilonorhynchus violaceus

Brown kiwi

Using its long sensitive beak, the brown kiwi probes in the undergrowth for insects, worms and berries. Its keen senses of smell and hearing help it find food. Like other kiwis, this bird has tiny wings under its hairlike body feathers and cannot fly.

Brown kiwi

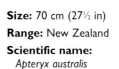

Size: 70 cm (27½ in)
Range: New Zealand
Scientific name:
 Apteryx australis

75

Size: 35–40 cm (13¾–15¾ in)

Range: central Asia to China and Mongolia

Scientific name: *Syrrhaptes paradoxus*

Pallas's sandgrouse

The male sandgrouse often flies long distances to find water for his chicks. On his belly are special feathers which soak up water like sponges. Once he finds a water hole, the sandgrouse wades in to soak his belly feathers. He then flies back to the nest where the chicks eagerly drink the water.

Pallas's sandgrouse

Common cassowary

The common cassowary lives in the tropical rainforest. It cannot fly and scientists think it may use the large horn casque, located on the top of its head, to help it break through the undergrowth as it searches for fallen fruit to eat. Males and females look similar, but females are slightly larger and have brighter plumage. They have extremely strong legs with very sharp-toed feet, which they use as weapons if attacked.

Common cassowary

Great bustard

The great bustard is one of the world's heaviest flying birds. A large male weighs up to 18 kg (40 lb) but can still fly. Females are much lighter – up to 5 kg (11 lb) – and do not have bristly "whiskers". Great bustards move in flocks as they search for plants, seeds and insects to eat. They have strong legs and can run fast.

Great bustard

Size: male up to 104 cm (41 in); female 75 cm (29½ in)

Range: parts of south and central Europe, across Asia to Japan

Scientific name: *Otis tarda*

Size: 1.5 m (5 ft) tall

Range: New Guinea, northern Australia

Scientific name: *Casuarius casuarius*

Size: 2 m (6½ feet) tall

Range: Australia

Scientific name: *Dromaius novaehollandiae*

Emu

The emu is the second largest bird in the world and, like the ostrich, it cannot fly. It runs at speeds of up to 48 km/h (30 mph) on its long legs as it looks for food in the Australian bush. Fruit, berries and insects are its main foods, and it also eats grass and other crops. The female lays 7 to 10 eggs, which the male keeps warm (incubates).

Size: 107 cm (42 in)

Range: parts of Africa, south of the equator

Scientific name: *Bucorvus cafer*

Emu

Greater roadrunner

Greater roadrunner

True to its name, the greater roadrunner runs at speeds of up to 20 km/h (12 mph) on itsbig strong feet. It can fly but does not often do so. This speedy bird eats ground-living insects as well as birds' eggs, lizards and even snakes.

Size: 50–60 cm (19¾–23½ in)
Range: southwest USA, Mexico
Scientific name:
Geococcyx californianus

Greater rhea

Size: 70 cm (27½ in)
Range: South America
Scientific name:
Cariama cristata

Red-legged seriema

Red-legged seriema

The graceful seriema rarely flies but runs fast to escape from any danger. It kills snakes and lizards with its sharp bill and also feeds on seeds, leaves and insects. The nest, made from sticks, is built in a tree. The female lays two or three eggs which the pair take turns to incubate.

Size: 1.5 m (5 ft) tall
Range: South America
Scientific name:
Rhea americana

Southern ground hornbill

Most hornbills live in trees, but these birds spend much of their lives on the ground. They wander around in pairs or family groups, searching for insects, reptiles and other small animals to eat.

Greater rhea

The largest birds in South America, greater rheas are fast runners but cannot fly. They usually live in groups of up to 30 birds. At breeding time the male rhea mates with several females. He makes a shallow nest on the ground and incubates all their eggs together.

Southern ground hornbill

Ostrich

The ostrich, the world's largest living bird, is too big and heavy to fly. Instead it runs fast and can reach speeds of up to 70 km/h (43 mph). Ostriches feed on plants and seeds but also catch small reptiles. Ostrich eggs are larger than any other bird's eggs. One weighs about 1.5 kg (3¼ lb).

Ostrich

Size: 1.75–2.75 m (5¾–9 ft) tall
Range: Africa
Scientific name:
Struthio camelus

Waders, waterbirds, cranes and seabirds

A huge variety of birds live in and around water. Wading birds, such as sandpipers, plovers and jacanas, spend much of their lives on sea coasts or by rivers and lakes further inland. Waterbirds, such as herons, flamingos and ducks, spend more time actually in the water and many are excellent swimmers. Lakes, ponds, rivers and marshlands provide plenty of plant and animal foods and birds can nest among bankside reeds. Seabirds depend on the ocean for their food and many can swim and dive to perfection.

Redshank

This common bird lives near almost any kind of water. It breeds on moorland and marshes, but spends the winter on shores, mudflats, meadows and estuaries. Insects are its main food, but it also eats other small creatures such as crabs and snails. It lays eggs in a grass-lined nest on the ground.

Redshank

Size: 28 cm (11 in)

Range: Europe, Asia, northern Africa

Scientific name:
Tringa totanus

Waders

Most wading birds, or shorebirds, are small to medium-sized, ranging from the smallest plovers, only 15 cm (6 in) long, to curlews measuring almost 60 cm (23½ in) in length. Wading birds usually feed on the ground and most are fast runners. Their beaks are various lengths and shapes for probing to different depths in mud and sand looking for food. All are strong fliers, and many perform long migrations every year between winter feeding areas and the place where they lay eggs and rear young in spring and summer.

Avocet

The avocet has an unusual beak that curves upwards. It catches insects and small water creatures by holding its long beak slightly open and sweeping it from side to side on the surface of mud or in shallow water. In deeper water it dips its head below the surface to find food.

Avocet

American golden plover

The golden plover is a champion long-distance traveller. It breeds on the Arctic tundra of North America. After breeding, it flies about 13,000 km (8,000 miles) south to spend the winter months in South America. It feeds mainly on insects and other small creatures such as snails.

American golden plover

Size: 23–28 cm (9–11 in)

Range: Arctic North America (summer); South America (winter)

Scientific name:
Pluvialis dominica

Size: 42 cm (16½ in)

Range: Europe, Asia

Scientific name:
Recurvirostra avosetta

Jacana

Jacana

The jacana is best known for its amazing feet. The toes and claws are very long so that the bird's weight is spread over a large area. This allows the jacana to walk on unsteady surfaces, such as floating lily pads, as it looks for food.

Size: 25 cm (9¾ in)
Range: southern USA, Central America
Scientific name: *Jacana spinosa*

Lapwing

The lapwing is also known as the "pee-wit" because of the shrill call it makes during its display flight. A common bird of farmland and other open areas, it eats insects as well as worms, snails and some seeds.

Lapwing

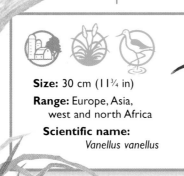

Size: 30 cm (11¾ in)
Range: Europe, Asia, west and north Africa
Scientific name: *Vanellus vanellus*

Common oystercatcher

The oystercatcher has a long blunt beak, which it uses to prise shellfish such as cockles and mussels off seashore rocks and to chisel open their hard shells. It also eats insects and worms, which it finds on farmland.

Common oystercatcher

Size: 46 cm (18 in)
Range: almost worldwide
Scientific name: *Haematopus ostralegus*

American woodcock

Although it is a kind of sandpiper, the American woodcock spends more time inland than other wading birds. It feeds mainly on earthworms, which it finds by probing the soil with its long beak. Females make their nests under trees or bushes and lay up to four eggs.

American woodcock

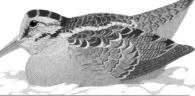

Size: 28 cm (11 in)
Range: North America
Scientific name: *Scolopax minor*

Eskimo curlew

Huge flocks of eskimo curlews used to migrate every year from the northern tundra to South America, where they spent the winter months. Today, the bird is almost extinct because so many have been shot by hunters. A few are still seen and shooting is now banned, but it is probably too late to save the eskimo curlew.

Eskimo curlew

Size: 28–33 cm (11–13 in)
Range: northern Canada, Alaska
Scientific name: *Numenius borealis*

79

Waterbirds and cranes

Waterbirds such as egrets, storks, ibises and flamingos are all large birds with long necks and legs. They stand in water while feeding and take food with their beaks. Ducks, geese and swans swim on the water as they look for food, and some even dive beneath the surface. Most have strong legs and webbed feet to help them swim. Other birds found in fresh water include cranes, grebes and divers, or loons. Cranes are long-legged birds that wade in shallow water to find food. Fast-swimming grebes and divers feed mainly on fish, which they chase and catch under the water with their pointed beaks.

Tundra swan

This swan lays eggs and rears its young on the Arctic tundra. In autumn, it flies south, usually returning to the same place year after year. Tundra swans feed on plants in shallow water.

Tundra swan

Size: 1.1–1.4 m (3½–4½ ft)
Range: North America, northern Europe, Asia
Scientific name: *Cygnus columbianus*

Canada goose

This goose breeds in the north and migrates south in autumn. Birds use the same routes year after year and tend to return to their birthplace to breed. The female lays about five eggs in a shallow nest scraped on the ground. Her mate stays nearby while she incubates the eggs for 25 to 30 days. Canada geese feed on water and land plants.

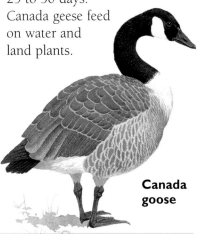

Canada goose

Size: 56–110 cm (22–43½ in)
Range: North America; introduced into Europe and New Zealand
Scientific name: *Branta canadensis*

Glossy ibis

The beautiful glossy ibis is the most widespread member of its family. It lives around lakes and marshy areas and eats insects and water creatures, which it picks from the mud with its long bill. Glossy ibises breed in colonies, sometimes of thousands of birds. The female lays three or four eggs in a nest in a tree or reed bed. Both parents incubate the eggs and care for the young once they hatch.

Size: 55–65 cm (21½–25½ in)
Range: Central America, Africa, Europe, Asia, Australasia
Scientific name: *Plegadis falcinellus*

Glossy ibis

Mallard

The mallard is the ancestor of most domestic ducks. It has been introduced into Australia and New Zealand and can even live on ponds in city areas. It eats plants as well as insects and other small creatures and is often seen feeding tail-up in shallow water.

Mallard

Size: 41–66 cm (16¼–26 in)
Range: Northern Hemisphere
Scientific name: *Anas platyrhynchos*

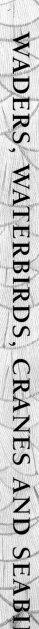

Sunbittern

In its courtship display, the sunbittern spreads its wings and fans its tail to reveal colourful feathers. It spends most of its life searching shallow water for prey, such as insects and fish, which it seizes in its sharp beak.

Size: 51 cm (20 in)
Range: Europe, Asia, Africa, Australia, New Zealand
Scientific name: *Podiceps cristatus*

Great crested grebe

This beautiful bird does not often fly and is rarely seen on land, where it moves awkwardly. Before mating, great crested grebes perform an elegant courtship dance on the water. During the dance they wag their heads and present each other with pieces of weed.

Size: 46 cm (18 in)
Range: southern Mexico to Bolivia and Brazil
Scientific name: *Eurypyga helias*

Great crested grebe

Sunbittern

Mandarin duck

Mandarin duck

The colourful mandarin duck is most active at dawn and dusk when it feeds on seeds, acorns and rice as well as insects, snails and small fish. Mated pairs stay together year after year. They perform elaborate courtship displays using the sail-like feathers on their sides.

Common crane

Size: 43–51 cm (17–20 in)
Range: eastern Asia, China, Japan; introduced worldwide
Scientific name: *Aix galericulata*

Size: 33 cm (13 in)
Range: worldwide, except Australasia
Scientific name: *Gallinula chloropus*

Moorhen

Common crane

The common crane is famous for its dancing display. The birds walk in circles, bowing, bobbing and tossing small objects over their heads. Cranes nest on the ground or in shallow water. After breeding they fly south to spend the winter in northern Africa, India or Southeast Asia.

Size: 1.1–1.2 m (3½–4 ft)
Range: Europe, Asia
Scientific name: *Grus grus*

Moorhen

A lively bird, the moorhen lives on fresh water almost anywhere, including city parks. Pond weeds, fallen fruit and berries are its main food, and it also catches insects. It makes its nest in reeds or in bushes at the water's edge.

Red-throated diver

This graceful bird has a slender beak and a red patch on its throat. It flies well and, unlike other divers, can take off easily from small areas of water. An expert swimmer, it feeds on fish, which it catches under water. It makes a variety of calls, including growling sounds and high-pitched wails. The female lays two eggs in a nest on the ground.

Red-throated diver

Size: 53–69 cm (20¾–27¼ in)
Range: North America, northern Asia, northern Europe
Scientific name: *Gavia stellata*

Size: 71–91 cm (28–36 in)
Range: Colombia, Venezuela
Scientific name: *Chauna chavaria*

Northern screamer

Northern screamer

Although related to ducks and geese, the northern screamer does not have webbed feet and seldom swims in open water. It has a loud trumpeting call which it uses as an alarm signal to warn others of danger. This noisy bird lives in the rivers and swamps of a small area in the north of South America. Here it walks around over floating leaves, its long toes helping to spread its weight. Females lay four to six eggs in a nest made of plants.

Common eider

Size: 56–71 cm (22–28 in)
Range: North Pole
Scientific name: *Somateria mollissima*

Great egret

This egret, also known as the American egret, lives in marshy areas and eats fish, insects and other small creatures. It finds its food either by waiting in the water until it spots something or by slowly stalking its prey. In the breeding season adults have a mostly black beak. The rest of the year it is yellow. Breeding pairs make a nest in a tree or clump of reeds. The female lays two to five eggs and both parents take it in turns to incubate the clutch.

Great egret

Size: 90–120 cm (35½–47 in)
Range: worldwide, except much of Europe
Scientific name: *Egretta alba*

Common eider

Like most ducks, the common eider lines her nest with downy feathers plucked from her breast. The down of the eider is particularly warm and soft. It has long been collected by humans for making items such as duvets and sleeping bags. Eiders live mainly on shellfish and other small creatures.

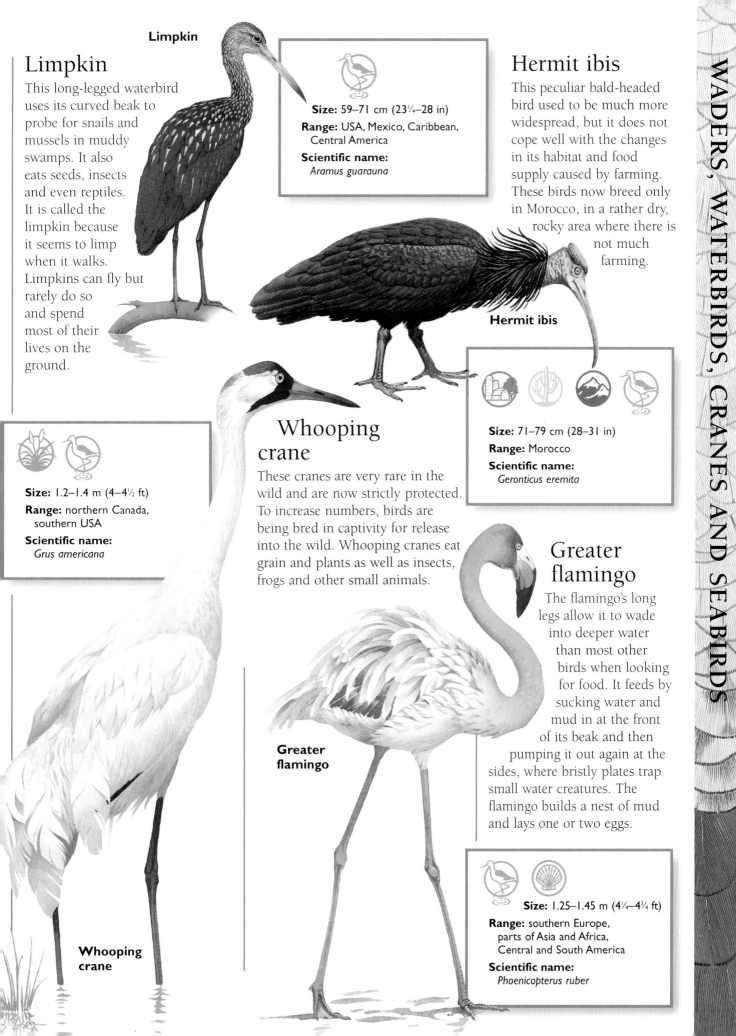

Limpkin

Limpkin

This long-legged waterbird uses its curved beak to probe for snails and mussels in muddy swamps. It also eats seeds, insects and even reptiles. It is called the limpkin because it seems to limp when it walks. Limpkins can fly but rarely do so and spend most of their lives on the ground.

Size: 59–71 cm (23¼–28 in)
Range: USA, Mexico, Caribbean, Central America
Scientific name:
Aramus guarauna

Hermit ibis

This peculiar bald-headed bird used to be much more widespread, but it does not cope well with the changes in its habitat and food supply caused by farming. These birds now breed only in Morocco, in a rather dry, rocky area where there is not much farming.

Hermit ibis

Size: 71–79 cm (28–31 in)
Range: Morocco
Scientific name:
Geronticus eremita

Whooping crane

These cranes are very rare in the wild and are now strictly protected. To increase numbers, birds are being bred in captivity for release into the wild. Whooping cranes eat grain and plants as well as insects, frogs and other small animals.

Size: 1.2–1.4 m (4–4½ ft)
Range: northern Canada, southern USA
Scientific name:
Grus americana

Greater flamingo

The flamingo's long legs allow it to wade into deeper water than most other birds when looking for food. It feeds by sucking water and mud in at the front of its beak and then pumping it out again at the sides, where bristly plates trap small water creatures. The flamingo builds a nest of mud and lays one or two eggs.

Greater flamingo

Size: 1.25–1.45 m (4¼–4¾ ft)
Range: southern Europe, parts of Asia and Africa, Central and South America
Scientific name:
Phoenicopterus ruber

Whooping crane

Seabirds

Life at sea is harsh and demanding for birds. Many seabirds, such as albatrosses, terns and gannets, are powerful fliers. They cover long distances over the open ocean as they search for food. Some spend almost the whole year in the air, only coming to land to mate, lay eggs and raise their chicks. There are some seabirds, though, that cannot fly at all. Penguins are the best-known examples. They are expert swimmers and divers.

Dovekie

Dovekie

Vast numbers of these birds, also known as little auks, live in the Arctic. In the summer, they breed in colonies of millions on Arctic coasts and cliffs. Dovekies can fly but they also swim and dive well. They feed on small fish and other small creatures such as shellfish.

Size: 20 cm (7¾ in)
Range: Arctic and north Atlantic oceans
Scientific name:
Alle alle

Snowy sheathbill

These birds are eager scavengers of any food they can find. They haunt penguin colonies to seize eggs and chicks, and search the rubbish tips of Antarctic research stations. Sheathbills also feed on fish and shellfish. They swim well and can fly, but spend most of their time on the ground.

Size: 39 cm (15½ in)
Range: Antarctic coasts and South Atlantic islands
Scientific name:
Chionis alba

Snowy sheathbill

Great cormorant

The cormorant swims by using its webbed feet to push itself along. It eats mainly fish and catches prey during underwater dives that may last a minute or more. The cormorant usually brings fish to the surface and tosses them in the air so they can be swallowed headfirst. The cormorant makes a nest in a tree or on the ground. The female lays three or four eggs and both parents care for the chicks.

Great cormorant

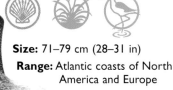

Size: 71–79 cm (28–31 in)
Range: Atlantic coasts of North America and Europe
Scientific name:
Larus marinus

Great black-backed gull

One of the largest gulls, this bird is a fierce hunter which spends more time at sea than other types of gull. It chases and kills other seabirds, such as puffins, and takes their eggs and young. It also eats fish and scavenges on waste. The young of these gulls have speckled brown feathers.

Young great black-backed gull

Common tern

Size: 33–41 cm (13–16¼ in)
Range: eastern North America, northern Europe
Scientific name: *Sterna hirundo*

Common tern

A coastal bird, this tern feeds on shrimps and other small sea creatures. It catches its food by hovering above the sea until it spots something, then diving rapidly into the water to seize the prey in its sharp beak. Terns nest in large colonies on islands and cliffs. The female lays two or three eggs in a nest scraped in the ground.

Size: 80–100 cm (31½–39½ in)
Range: coasts of North America, Europe, Africa, Asia, Australia
Scientific name: *Phalacrocorax carbo*

Great skua

A strong bird with a hooked bill, the great skua is a fierce hunter. It not only attacks other birds to steal their prey but also kills and eats puffins, kittiwakes and gulls, and preys on their eggs and young. It also eats unwanted fish thrown overboard from fishing boats.

Great skua

Size: 51–56 cm (20–22 in)
Range: north Atlantic Ocean
Scientific name: *Catharacta skua*

Brown pelican

The brown pelican is the smallest pelican and different from the rest of its family. It is a seabird and feeds by diving for fish, making high-speed plunges into the water from heights of more than 9 m (30 ft). When it dives, it holds its wings back and curves its neck, straightening it just before entering the water. Once in the water, it opens its mouth and catches the fish in the pouch below its beak. It returns to the surface to eat. This bird lays two or three eggs in a nest on the ground.

Brown pelican

Size: 1.3 m (4¼ ft)
Range: Pacific and Atlantic coasts of North and South America
Scientific name: *Pelecanus occidentalis*

Herring gull

The herring gull is the most common gull on North American and European sea coasts. It catches small fish, steals eggs and young from other birds and scavenges on waste. It also flies inland to find worms and other creatures on farmland. Herring gulls nest on cliffs, islands or beaches. They make nests of weeds and grass in a hollow in the ground or in a tree. The female lays two or three eggs which are cared for by both parents.

Herring gull

Size: 55–66 cm (21¾–26 in)
Range: most of Northern Hemisphere
Scientific name: *Larus argentatus*

Penguins

Penguins are better suited to life in the sea than any other bird. Expert swimmers and divers, they use their strong flippers to push themselves through the water. On land, penguins walk upright and have an awkward gait. They cannot fly.

Most penguins live around the Antarctic and on islands near the Antarctic Circle and have to survive in freezing conditions. They have a dense covering of glossy waterproof feathers, which keep them both warm and dry. A thick layer of fat beneath the feathers also helps to keep out the cold.

There are about 17 different kinds of penguin. The smallest is the little, or fairy, penguin, which measures about 40 cm (15¾ in). The biggest is the emperor penguin, which stands about 1.15 m (3¾ ft) tall. All look very similar, with black or grey feathers on the back and white ones on the belly.

Friendly behaviour

Penguins are sociable birds and usually live in huge colonies on land and in the sea. Penguins usually keep the same mate for several years. When a breeding pair meets, they rub their heads in greeting. They also preen each other's feathers.

Penguin prey

Squid and fish are the main food of the king penguin and other large penguins such as the emperor. Smaller penguins, such as the gentoos and chinstraps, catch much smaller prey, such as shrimplike krill.

Underwater hunter

The king penguin dives deep to catch prey and often plunges to 45 m (150 ft) or more. The deepest recorded dive is 250 m (820 ft). The penguin uses its webbed feet and tail for steering as it dives.

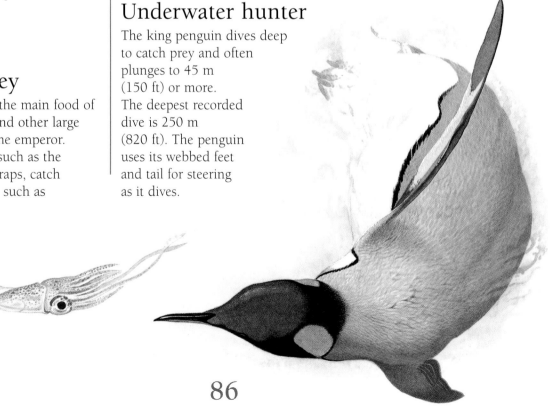

Tobogganing

Not at their best on land, penguins slip and slide as they waddle over the frozen ground. Often the birds lie down on their bellies and toboggan over the ice – an easier way to move. Once in the water, most penguins swim at speeds of 5–10 km/h (3–6 mph).

Taking care of young

At the beginning of winter, the female emperor penguin lays one egg on land. Her partner then incubates the egg on his feet for about 64 days. When the chick hatches he keeps it warm on his feet, wrapped in a fold of skin.

Adélie penguins nest in large colonies around the Antarctic coasts. Eggs are laid in late November and incubated first by the male and then the female for a total of 35 days.

Little penguin

Galápagos penguin

This is the only penguin that lives near the equator. The Galápagos Islands are bathed by a cool current, making the area suitable for a cold-loving penguin. The Galápagos penguin feeds mainly on small fish. It nests in small groups and females lay two eggs in a cave or a hole in volcanic rock.

Red-tailed tropicbird

Red-tailed tropicbird

This elegant seabird is an expert in the air, but it moves awkwardly on land.
It usually nests on ledges or cliffs in a position that allows for easy take-off. Fish and squid are its main food. Females lay a single egg on the ground. Both parents incubate the egg and care for the chick.

Size: 40 cm (15¾ in) tall
Range: Antarctic coasts
Scientific name:
  Eudyptula minor

Size: 50 cm (19¾ in) tall
Range: Galápagos Islands
Scientific name:
  Spheniscus mendiculus

Galápagos penguin

Little penguin

The smallest of all the penguins, the little penguin lives around coasts and islands, looking for small fish and other food in shallow waters. It nests in a crevice or burrow. The female lays two eggs which both parents take turns to incubate for between 33 and 40 days.

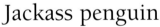

Wandering albatross

Jackass penguin

The jackass penguin lives in a warmer climate than most other penguins. It comes to land to breed and nests in a burrow or under rocks to avoid the hot African sun. It is active on land only at night.

Size: 1.1–1.35 m (3½–4½ ft)
Range: southern oceans
Scientific name:
  Diomedea exulans

Size: 69 cm (27¼ in) tall
Range: coasts of South Africa
Scientific name:
  Spheniscus demersus

Jackass penguin

Wandering albatross

This seabird has the longest wingspan of any bird – up to 3.4 m (11 ft). It spends most of its life soaring over the open ocean, sometimes flying up to 500 km (300 miles) in a day.

Size: 90–100 cm (35½–39½ in)
including tail
Range: Indian and Pacific oceans
Scientific name:
Phaethon rubricauda

Size: 14–18 cm (5½–7 in) cm
Range: northeast Atlantic
Ocean
Scientific name:
Hydrobates pelagicus

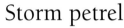

Storm petrel

This seabird eats fish
and squid, which it
catches as it swoops low
over the water, as well as food
scraps thrown from ships. The
storm petrel spends most of its
life at sea but comes to land in
the breeding season to nest in a
burrow or rock crevice.

**Storm
petrel**

Size: 29–36 cm (11½–14¼ in)
Range: north Atlantic
Ocean
Scientific name:
Fratercula arctica

**Atlantic
puffin**

Atlantic puffin

This puffin uses its colourful beak
to catch fish and can hold as many
as a dozen fish at a time. An expert
swimmer and diver, the puffin can
also fly well. Its short legs are set
well back on the body
and it waddles clumsily
when it comes to land to
nest. The female puffin lays
one egg, sometimes two, in an old
burrow or in a hole she digs herself.

Northern gannet

A sturdily built seabird
with a strong beak, the
northern gannet soars
over the ocean, searching
for fish and squid. When it
spots prey, the gannet
plunges 30 m (100 ft) or
more into the water to seize the
catch and bring it to the surface.

Size: 87–100 cm (34¼–39½ in)
Range: north Atlantic Ocean
Scientific name:
Sula bassana

Northern gannet

Great frigatebird

This large seabird has a
wingspan of more than 1.8 m
(6 ft) and a big hooked beak.
It spends most of its life in the
air and does not often land on
the water. It catches food by
snatching prey from the surface
of the water or by threatening
other seabirds until they
drop their meals. Large
colonies nest together
on oceanic islands.

**Great
frigatebird**

Size: 86–100 cm (33¾–39½ in)
Range: Indian and Pacific oceans
Scientific name:
Fregata minor

Owls and birds of prey

Long-eared owl

Most birds of prey hunt and kill other creatures to eat. Although this is a varied group of birds, ranging from tiny falcons to huge condors, they all have features in common. These include keen vision to spot food from the air, strong feet with sharp claws, and a hooked beak for tearing prey apart. Eagles, hawks and buzzards are all birds of prey. Owls, too, kill other animals to eat but, unlike hawks and eagles, they usually hunt at night.

Long-eared owl

The long tufts on the head of this owl are feathers not ears. But this bird does have excellent hearing, which helps it catch prey such as voles and mice. This owl lays its eggs in a nest abandoned by a bird such as a crow.

Size: 33–40.5 cm (13–16 in)
Range: North America, Europe, northwest Africa, Asia
Scientific name: *Asio otus*

Owls

There are 170 or so kinds of owl found over most of the world, except on a few islands. Most look similar, with their large disclike faces and huge eyes. Typically, an owl sits on a branch watching and listening for the slightest movement of prey. When it hears something, it pinpoints the direction of the prey with its extraordinarily acute hearing before flying down to pounce. The edges of an owl's feathers are soft and fluffy, not hard like those of most birds. This cuts down the noise of flight so the hunter can fly almost silently in the darkness.

Size: 52–65 cm (20½–25½ in)
Range: Arctic
Scientific name: *Nyctea scandiaca*

Snowy owl

Snowy owl

The snowy owl hunts during the day, as well as at night, for birds and for mammals such as mice, hares and lemmings. The female owl is up to 20 per cent bigger than the male and has dark markings on her mainly white feathers. She lays 4 to 15 eggs.

Barn owl

Barn owl

The barn owl is easily recognised by its pale heart-shaped face. During the day it roosts in a sheltered spot. At dusk it comes out to hunt for food, usually small creatures, such as rats and mice.

Size: 34 cm (13½ in)
Range: worldwide, except temperate Asia and many Pacific islands
Scientific name: *Tyto alba*

Birds of prey

Birds of prey hunt in a variety of ways. Some, such as goshawks and sparrowhawks, live mainly in forests and woodlands and hunt in the cover of trees. They move from one leafy perch to the next, ready to dash out to catch their prey in a sudden attack. Others, such as buzzards and eagles, soar over open country, watching for victims. Not all birds of prey are killers. Vultures are scavengers – they eat carrion, the bodies of creatures that are already dead.

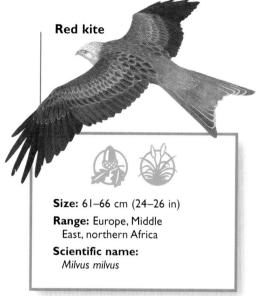

Red kite

Size: 61–66 cm (24–26 in)
Range: Europe, Middle East, northern Africa
Scientific name:
Milvus milvus

Red kite

This large bird of prey has long wings and a forked tail. It hunts in woodland and open country and often hovers briefly as it searches for prey, such as rats, birds and reptiles. Like vultures, it also eats carrion. The red kite nests in a tree and the female lays up to five eggs.

Northern goshawk

A powerful, fast-moving hunter, the northern goshawk can catch creatures such as hares and pheasants. It flies through the forest, weaving in and out of trees as it chases prey. It kills its victims with its strong sharp talons and eats them on the ground.

Size: 1–1.15 m (3¼–3¾ ft)
Range: Africa, Middle East
Scientific name:
Aegypius tracheliotus

Lappet-faced vulture

Like all vultures, this bird feeds mostly on carrion. It has huge wings, on which it soars long distances searching for food, and a powerful hooked beak, which cuts easily into the flesh of dead animals. This vulture lays one egg in a nest at the top of a tree.

Lappet-faced vulture

Northern goshawk

Size: 51–66 cm (20–26 in)
Range: North America, Europe, northern Asia
Scientific name:
Accipiter gentilis

Size: 46–61 cm (18–24 in)
Range: North and Central America, West Indies
Scientific name:
Buteo jamaicensis

Red-tailed hawk

Red-tailed hawk

A powerful, aggressive bird, this hawk can live anywhere from forest to desert. It hunts other birds in the air or swoops down on rabbits, snakes and lizards from a high perch. It makes a nest of twigs high in a tree or cactus plant. The female lays one to four eggs. Both parents take turns to incubate the eggs.

91

Golden eagle

The magnificent golden eagle has a hooked beak, extremely sharp eyesight and strong feet with long curved claws. When hunting, the eagle soars over land, searching for food. Once it spots prey, it dives down and kills its victim on the ground.

Size: 76–89 cm (30–35 in)
Range: North America, Europe, northern Asia and Africa
Scientific name: *Aquila chrysaetos*

Golden eagle

Size: 1.5 m (5 ft) tall
Range: Africa, south of the Sahara
Scientific name: *Sagittarius serpentarius*

Secretary bird

This long-legged bird spends much of its life on the ground, where it may walk 30 km (20 miles) or so every day. It runs to catch prey such as small mammals, birds, insects and reptiles. It kills larger animals by stamping on them. Pairs make a nest of sticks and turf on top of a tree. The nest is lined with grass and leaves. The female lays two or three eggs.

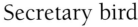

Secretary bird

Osprey

This bird of prey flies above water looking for fish to catch. When the bird catches sight of a fish, it plunges down, holding its feet out to seize the prey. The soles of the osprey's feet are studded with small spines to help it grip its slippery catch.

Size: 53–62 cm (20¾–24½ in)
Range: almost worldwide
Scientific name: *Pandion haliaetus*

Osprey

Common kestrel

The kestrel belongs to the falcon family. It hunts by hovering above the ground on fast-beating wings to watch for prey. If it spots something, such as a small mammal, the kestrel drops down to the ground and snatches the prey with its sharp-clawed feet.

Common kestrel

Size: 31–35 cm (12¼–13¾ in)
Range: Europe, Asia, Africa
Scientific name: *Falco tinnunculus*

Peregrine falcon

One of the fastest fliers, the peregrine is an expert hunter, which preys on other birds. It makes a spectacular high-speed dive towards its prey, often a pigeon or dove, and seizes it in mid-air. It kills the prey with its powerful talons and takes it to the ground to eat.

Size: 38–51 cm (15–20 in)
Range: almost worldwide
Scientific name: *Falco peregrinus*

Peregrine falcon

Madagascar fish eagle

With a total population of less than 100, this fish eagle is one of the rarest birds. It usually hunts around shallow estuaries and coastal swamps, where it plunges down to catch fish with its strong feet.

Size: 68–79 cm (26¾–31 in)
Range: northwest Madagascar
Scientific name:
Haliaeetus vociferoides

Madagascar fish eagle

Size: 79 cm (31 in)
Range: Mexico, Central and South America
Scientific name:
Sarcorhamphus papa

King vulture

With its brightly patterned bare-skinned head, the king vulture is one of the most colourful of all birds of prey. Although it may occasionally kill some prey for itself, it feeds mostly on carrion – animals that are already dead. The king vulture is one of the few birds that uses its sense of smell to find food.

King vulture

Rough-legged buzzard

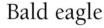

Rough-legged buzzard

The rough-legged buzzard hovers over the tundra as it hunts for prey, such as lemmings and voles. It nests in the far north, laying up to four eggs in a nest of twigs made in a tree or on a rocky ledge. After the breeding season, this buzzard flies south for the winter.

Bald eagle

The national bird of the United States, the bald eagle is now rare over much of the country. Fish is one of its main foods, and eagles gather around Alaskan rivers to catch exhausted salmon as they migrate up river. The eagle's nest is made of sticks and is one of the largest birds' nests.

Size: 50–60 cm (19¾–23½ in)
Range: North America, northern Europe and Asia
Scientific name:
Buteo lagopus

Size: 81–102 cm (32–40 in)
Range: North America
Scientific name:
Haliaeetus leucocephalus

Bald eagle

93

Eagles

Eagles are large birds of prey with strong hooked beaks, sharp talons and big golden eyes. There are about 60 kinds of eagle living all over the world.

Typically, a hunting eagle soars over the land for long periods, searching for food. With its keen eyesight, an eagle spots prey from a great distance and then makes a rapid dive to the ground to seize and kill the animal with its talons. But some eagles hunt in different ways. Harpy eagles chase their prey through the trees, and sea eagles seize fish from the water.

Eagles usually build their nests in trees or on cliffs. The nests are made of sticks and branches and may be used year after year.

A snake hunter

Like other snake eagles, the crested serpent eagle feeds mostly on snakes and other reptiles. This eagle generally hunts by perching in a tree to watch for prey on the ground then dropping down on to it. The eagle's short strong toes have a rough surface that helps it to grip its wriggling catch.

Rainforest eagle

The world's biggest and most powerful eagle, the harpy, lives in the South American rainforest. Instead of soaring high in the air, this eagle makes short flights from tree to tree, looking for prey. The harpy preys mostly on monkeys, sloths and tree porcupines. When it spots a victim, such as a monkey, the harpy chases it through the trees at high speed until it is close enough to catch the monkey in its strong talons.

94

Fish-eating eagle

Fish is the main food of the sea eagle. The bird soars over the ocean looking for prey. It then swoops down to the water surface to seize a fish in its talons. Sea eagles also catch other creatures and rob smaller birds of their prey. They may also dive repeatedly at swimming birds such as ducks until they are exhausted and easy to catch. There are several different types of sea eagle. The largest is the Steller's sea eagle, which lives on Siberian coasts.

A **bald eagle** is feeding her hungry chicks. The young stay in the nest for about 10 weeks. They often fight each other and sometimes the weakest of the brood is killed.

Birds of the trees and masters of the air

One of the many advantages of flight is that it allows birds to fly up into trees. There, among the branches, they find havens from ground-living hunters, as well as safe places to roost and make nests. Many birds also gather much of their food in trees. Pigeons and parrots feed mostly on seeds, nuts and fruits. Others, such as woodpeckers and cuckoos, eat insects that they find on leaves and tree trunks. Some birds are more skilful fliers than others. Hummingbirds, for example, are true masters of the air and perform extraordinary aerial acrobatics. Swifts are so used to life in the air that they rarely, if ever, walk on land.

Crested tree swift

Size: 20.5 cm (8 in)
Range: Southeast Asia
Scientific name:
 Hemiprocne longipennis

Crested tree swift

This swift catches insects in the air to eat. It makes a tiny cup-shaped nest from thin flakes of bark, glued together with spit. There is room for just one egg, which both parents take turns to incubate.

Nightjar

The nightjar becomes active at sunset, when it takes to the air to dart after moths and other night-flying insects. The nightjar's tiny beak opens very wide and is fringed with bristles that help to trap its prey.

Size: 26 cm (10¼ in)
Range: Europe, Asia, northern Africa
Scientific name:
 Caprimulgus europaeus

Nightjar

Potoo

The potoo feeds by night, flying out from a perch to capture insects in its large beak. By day, it sits upright and very still on a broken branch or stump. With its head and beak pointing upwards, the potoo looks like part of the tree and so is hidden from its enemies. It lays its single egg on top of a tree stump.

Potoo

Size: 41 cm (16¼ in)
Range: West Indies, Central America, tropical South America
Scientific name:
 Nyctibius griseus

96

Ruby-throated hummingbird

Size: 9 cm (3½ in)

Range: Canada, USA; winters in Central America and West Indies

Scientific name: *Archilochus colubris*

Ruby-throated hummingbird

Like all hummingbirds, the ruby-throated bird plunges its beak deep inside flowers to feed on nectar. After breeding in Canada and the eastern United States, this amazing small bird travels some 800 km (500 miles) to winter in Central America and the West Indies.

Sand martin

The sand martin is also known as the bank swallow. A lively bird, it darts in the air as it chases and snaps up insects. It lives in a burrow which it digs into sand banks near water, using its beak and feet. Martins lay up to eight eggs in a nest at the end of the burrow.

Sand martin

Size: 12–14 cm (4¾–5½ in)

Range: parts of Europe, Asia and North America; winters in South America, Africa and Southeast Asia

Scientific name: *Riparia riparia*

Barn swallow

The barn swallow eats insects, which it catches in the air or snatches from the surface of water. Both male and female help to make a nest of mud and grass on the wall of a building. The female lays four or five eggs.

Barn swallow

Size: 19.5 cm (7¾ in)

Range: almost worldwide

Scientific name: *Hirundo rustica*

Poorwill

Size: 18–21.5 cm (7–8½ in)

Range: North America

Scientific name: *Phalaenoptilus nuttallii*

Poorwill

Named after its call, which sounds like "poor-will", this bird hunts insects at night. It is the only bird known to hibernate and each autumn it finds a rock crevice in which to spend the winter. Its body temperature falls and its heart and breathing rates slow down, so that it uses as little energy as possible.

White-throated swift

Swifts are fast and expert fliers. They catch insects, eat, drink and even mate in the air. Their legs and feet are tiny, and they rarely walk. The white-throated swift makes a cup-shaped nest from feathers and grass, glued together with spit. The nest is built in a crack or crevice in a cliff or mountainside. The female lays four or five eggs.

Size: 15–18 cm (6–7 in)

Range: western USA, Central America

Scientific name: *Aeronautes saxatilis*

White-throated swift

Rufous-tailed jacamar

Size: 23–28 cm (9–11 in)
Range: Mexico, Central America, South America
Scientific name:
Galbula ruficauda

Quetzal

Quetzal

The beautiful male quetzal has a train of long tail feathers that wave and flutter as he flies and performs courtship displays. These feathers are shed after each breeding season and are then regrown. The ancient Mayan and Aztec peoples of Central America and Mexico believed the quetzal was a sacred bird, and its feathers were highly prized. The female does not have a red breast or long train.

Size: 30 cm (11¾ in); tail feathers 61 cm (24 in)
Range: Mexico, Central America
Scientific name:
Pharomachrus mocinno

Rufous-tailed jacamar

This brightly plumaged long-billed bird sits on a branch, watching for insects. When it spots something, it darts after the prey and snatches it in mid-air. The jacamar then flies to a perch and may bang the insect against a branch to kill it before eating it. The female jacamar digs a breeding tunnel in the ground and lays two to four eggs. Both birds incubate the eggs for 19 to 23 days. The parents feed and care for their young until they can fly, at about three weeks old.

Victoria crowned pigeon

The world's largest pigeon, the Victoria crowned pigeon has been hunted heavily and is now rare. This beautiful bird usually feeds on the ground, eating fallen fruit, seeds and berries. If disturbed, it flies off to perch in a tree.

Victoria crowned pigeon

Blue-crowned motmot

This bird has an unusual tail which has two long central feathers with racquet-shaped tips. With its tail swinging from side to side like a pendulum, the motmot sits on a branch, watching for prey. It darts out from its perch to catch insects, spiders and lizards and returns to eat them.

Hoopoe

This bird catches insects and other small creatures in trees and on the ground. It makes a nest in a hole in a tree or wall or on the ground. The female lays two to nine eggs and is fed by her mate while she incubates them for 16 to 19 days.

Hoopoe

Size: 28 cm (11 in)
Range: Europe, Asia, Africa
Scientific name:
Upupa epops

Size: 58.5–73.5 cm (23–29 in)
Range: New Guinea, Biak and Yapen islands
Scientific name:
Goura victoria

Blue-crowned motmot

Size: 38–41 cm (15–16¼ in)
Range: Mexico, Central America, South America
Scientific name:
Momotus momota

Size: 23 cm (9 in)
Range: Africa
Scientific name:
Lybius bidentatus

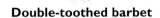
Double-toothed barbet

Belted kingfisher

This kingfisher is an agile flier. It watches for prey from a tree overhanging a river or stream, then dives down to seize a fish or frog from the water. A breeding pair digs a long nesting tunnel in a river bank. The female lays five to eight eggs in a nest made at the end of the tunnel.

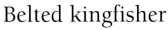

Pileated woodpecker

Ants and termites are the main food of this woodpecker. Clinging tightly to a tree trunk with its sharp claws, the bird hammers into the bark with its strong beak to find prey. It also feeds on fruit. The female bird lays four eggs in a tree hole nest.

Double-toothed barbet

This barbet has two sharp toothlike structures on its beak. It perches in trees and bushes, feeding on figs, bananas and other fruit, and also darts out to catch flying termites.

Belted kingfisher

Size: 38–48 cm (15–19 in)
Range: North America
Scientific name:
Dryocopus pileatus

Size: 28–35.5 cm (11–14 in)
Range: North America
Scientific name:
Megaceryle alcyon

Collared dove

This extremely common dove lives close to people in both towns and countryside. The collared dove feeds mainly on seeds but it also eats berries, other plant foods and scraps put out by humans.

Collared dove

Size: 31.5 cm (12½ in)
Range: parts of Europe and Asia
Scientific name:
Streptopelia decaocto

Size: 28 cm (11 in)
Range: Europe, Asia, Africa
Scientific name:
Merops apiaster

European bee-eater

True to its name, this bird eats bees, as well as wasps. It rubs its prey on a branch to remove the venom from the sting before eating the insect. Bee-eaters nest in long tunnels, often dug in a river bank.

Pileated woodpecker

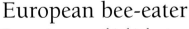
European bee-eater

Hummingbirds

Beautiful hummingbirds are more agile in the air than any other group of birds. They are named after the humming sound made by the rapid beating of their wings as they hover in front of flowers while they feed. Their wings beat so fast that they are almost invisible. The birds can fly upwards, sideways, downwards and even backwards. Hummingbirds live only in North, Central and South America, mostly in the warmest parts. They measure from just over 5 cm (2 in) to about 20 cm (7¾ in) long, but the tail feathers make up as much as half of this length. Many have colourful, glittering plumage and decorative head crests and tail feathers. Females usually have duller plumage than males. The sweet nectar contained in flowers is the main food of hummingbirds. Most have long beaks, which they plunge deep into flowers to reach the nectar.

White-tipped sicklebill

The long, strongly curved beak of the white-tipped sicklebill is perfect for taking nectar from deep flowers such as heliconias.

The smallest bird

The bee hummingbird is the world's tiniest bird. The male is only about 5 cm (2 in) long, including its beak and tail. Females are about 0.5 cm (¼ in) longer.

The longest beak

The sword-billed hummingbird has a longer beak than any other hummingbird. The beak allows the bird to reach nectar inside the deepest tube-shaped flowers. This bird also eats insects, which it catches in the air.

A colourful hummingbird

The male crimson topaz is one of the most beautiful hummingbirds, with colourful plumage and long curving tail feathers. It takes nectar from a wide range of flowers and also catches insects. The female bird has mostly green feathers.

Courtship display

This hummingbird, known as the marvellous spatuletail, has only four full-grown tail feathers, two of which have a long bare shaft ending in a broad wedge shape, or spatule. During courtship displays the male shows off these decorative feathers as he flies to and fro in front of the female.

A male **violet sabrewing** hummingbird hovers on rapidly beating wings as he feeds on nectar from a ginger flower. Like many hummingbirds, this bird has shimmering feathers.

101

Red-crested turaco

The red-crested turaco lives in trees and does not often come down to the ground. It is a poor flier, but runs, hops and climbs well among the branches. It eats fruit and also insects.

Red-crested turaco

Size: 61 cm (24 in)
Range: South America: Amazon and Orinoco basins
Scientific name: *Opisthocomus hoazin*

Hoatzin

Although it lives in trees, the hoatzin is a poor flier. It clambers along branches, feeding on fruit, buds and leaves.

Hoatzin

Size: 40.5 cm (16 in)
Range: Africa
Scientific name: *Tauraco erythrolophus*

Common cuckoo

The cuckoo does not make a nest but lays her eggs in the nests of other birds. She usually lays 8 to 12 eggs, all in different nests. The young cuckoos hatch in about 12 days and are bigger and stronger than the host's young, which they eject from the nest so they get all the food.

Common cuckoo

Size: 33 cm (13 in)
Range: Europe, northern Africa, Asia
Scientific name: *Cuculus canorus*

Size: 85 cm (33½ in)
Range: Mexico, Central America, northern South America
Scientific name: *Ara macao*

Scarlet macaw

Great Indian hornbill

This hornbill lives high in the rainforest, eating fruit and catching small animals. The female hornbill is smaller and does not have such a large beak as the male. In the breeding season, she lays one to three eggs in a hole in a tree. Once she has laid her eggs, the male seals up the nest hole, leaving only a slit-like opening. The male brings her food and passes it through this slit. The female stays walled up until the young are hatched and old enough to leave the nest.

Great Indian hornbill

Size: 1.5 m (5 ft) tall
Range: India, Southeast Asia, Sumatra
Scientific name: *Buceros bicornis*

Scarlet macaw

These spectacular birds are usually seen in pairs or flocks of up to 20 birds. At sunrise the birds fly, screeching noisily, from their roost sites to feeding areas. There they feast on seeds, fruit and leaves high in the trees. At dusk they return to their roosts.

Toco toucan

Although the toucan's colourful beak is up to 18 cm (7 in) long, it is not solid, so it is not as heavy as it looks. Inside the largely hollow beak are crisscrossed rods of bone that give it strength. The toucan feeds on fruit. It picks up food in the tip of its bill, then tosses the morsel into its mouth.

Size: 61 cm (24 in)
Range: eastern South America
Scientific name:
Ramphastos toco

Toco toucan

Rainbow lorikeet

Rainbow lorikeet

The pattern of the colourful feathers of the rainbow lorikeet varies slightly from bird to bird. Screeching, chattering flocks of up to 100 lorikeets fly among the branches, eating fruit, insects, pollen and nectar.

Size: 26 cm (10¼ in)
Range: Indonesia, New Guinea, Australia
Scientific name:
Trichoglossus haematodus

Size: 18 cm (7 in)
Range: Australia; introduced into USA
Scientific name:
Melopsittacus undulatus

Budgerigar

Eclectus parrot

The male eclectus parrot has mostly green feathers, while the female is bright red with a blue belly. Both feed mainly on fruit, nuts, flowers and nectar. They usually make a nest in a hole high in a tree. The female lays two eggs and incubates them for about 26 days.

Female

Male

Eclectus parrots

Size: 35 cm (13¾ in)
Range: New Guinea, northeast Australia
Scientific name:
Eclectus roratus

Sulphur-crested cockatoo

These noisy parrots gather in huge flocks to feed on seeds, fruit, palm hearts and insects. In the breeding season the cockatoos separate into pairs or family groups. A pair makes a nest in a tree and both parents incubate the two or three eggs.

Sulphur-crested cockatoo

Budgerigar

Best known as cage birds with many colour variations, these small fast-moving parrots usually have mainly green feathers in the wild. Flocks of budgerigars search the ground for seeds.

Size: 50 cm (19¾ in)
Range: Melanesia, New Guinea, Australia
Scientific name:
Cacatua galerita

Songbirds

About half of all the kinds of bird in the world are included in the group known as songbirds. There are more than 4,000 different kinds and they live all over the world, except at the poles. While not all sing as sweetly as the lark or the nightingale, the males of most species are normally able to sing sequences of musical notes. They sing when courting mates or defending their territory. Female singers are rare, but females of a few species such as song sparrows and robins do sometimes sing.

Songbirds are also called perching birds and have feet that are adapted to their habit of perching on trees and posts. Their feet have four toes – three that point forwards and one backwards – and are ideally shaped for holding on to twigs, reeds and even wires.

Northern wren

The tiny northern wren has a plump body and a short tail, which it nearly always holds cocked up. Its main foods are insects and spiders, which it finds on low plants. In spring, the wren makes a nest in a hollow tree stump or among tree roots. The female lays five to eight eggs, which she incubates.

Size: 8 cm (3¼ in)
Range: North America, Europe, northern Africa, Asia
Scientific name:
Troglodytes troglodytes

Northern wren

Size: 16 cm (6¼ in)
Range: Europe, Asia, northern Africa; winters in tropical Africa
Scientific name:
Luscinia megarhynchos

Nightingale

Nightingale

Best known for its beautiful song, the nightingale sings both night and day. It eats insects such as ants and beetles, which it finds in undergrowth and on the ground. In summer, it also eats berries and fruit. The female makes a nest of leaves on or close to the ground and lays four or five eggs.

Red-whiskered bulbul

This bulbul is named after the tufts of red feathers at each side of its head. Male and female look alike, but young birds have white whiskers. Flocks of these lively, noisy birds gather to feast on fruit trees, where they eat both ripe and unripe fruit. They also eat the insects they come across while feeding. The female lays two to four eggs in a cup-shaped nest made of grass, roots and stalks.

Size: 20.5 cm (8 in)
Range: Southeast Asia, southern China, Nepal, India; introduced into USA and Australia
Scientific name:
Pycnonotus jocosus

Red-whiskered bulbul

Black-capped chickadee

Size: 16.5–19 cm
(6½–7½ in)

Range: North America, Central America

Scientific name:
Sialia sialis

European robin

In many areas the robin is a shy forest bird, but in Britain and parts of Europe it lives in gardens and is often quite tame. Insects, spiders, worms and snails are the robin's main food, but it also eats berries, small fruit and scraps of food put out by humans.

Size: 12–15 cm (4¾–6 in)

Range: North America

Scientific name:
Parus atricapillus

Eastern bluebird

Eastern bluebird

The eastern bluebird feeds mainly on insects and berries. The male performs acrobatic flight displays to court his mate. Both birds then build a nest of grass and twigs in a hole in a tree. Eastern bluebirds lay three to seven eggs. Both parents feed the young chicks for up to 20 days after they hatch.

Size: 14 cm (5½ in)

Range: Europe, northern Africa, Asia

Scientific name:
Erithacus rubecula

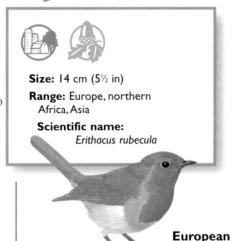

European robin

Black-capped chickadee

This little bird has a call which sounds like "chick-a-dee-dee-dee". It feeds on caterpillars and other insects as well as seeds and berries. The chickadee makes its nest in the soft wood of a dead tree, where it lays 5 to 10 eggs.

Northern mockingbird

One of the best-known American songbirds, the mockingbird is the state bird of five US states. The male sings night and day and often mimics other birds and sounds. Mockingbirds feed mainly on insects such as grasshoppers and beetles, but also eat spiders, snails, small reptiles and fruit. They lay three to six eggs at a time.

Willow warbler

The willow warbler catches insects in the air or picks them from leaves. In winter, when there are fewer insects in the north, it flies south to Africa. Willow warblers nest on the ground or in a low bush. They lay six or seven eggs.

Size: 21.5 cm (8½ in)

Range: Europe, Asia; introduced almost worldwide

Scientific name: *Sturnus vulgaris*

Starling

Starling

Starlings are common in both country and city areas and have been introduced into countries outside their natural range. Only a century ago, 60 birds were released in New York. Now, the starling is one of the most common birds in North America. Starlings eat insects, worms, snails, fruit, berries and seeds.

Size: 23–28 cm (9–11 in)

Range: North America

Scientific name:
Mimus polyglottos

Willow warbler

Size: 11 cm (4¼ in)

Range: northern Europe and Asia; winters in Africa and southern Asia

Scientific name:
Phylloscopus trochilus

Northern mockingbird

Purple honeycreeper

Groups of purple honeycreepers feed on fruit, especially bananas, and insects in trees. They also perch by flowers and suck nectar from them with their long curved beaks. The female honeycreeper builds a neat cup-shaped nest in the fork of a tree or bush. She lays two eggs, which she incubates for 12 to 14 days.

Purple honeycreeper

Size: 10 cm (4 in)
Range: Trinidad, South America
Scientific name:
Cyanerpes caeruleus

Pine grosbeak

A type of finch, the pine grosbeak uses its heavy bill to crush the stones of fruit such as cherries and plums. It also eats seeds, buds and insects. A breeding pair makes a nest in a tree and the female lays four eggs.

Pine grosbeak

Size: 20 cm (7¾ in)
Range: northern Europe, northern Asia, North America
Scientific name:
Pinicola enucleator

Cardinal

Only the male cardinal has brilliant red plumage. The female is mainly brown, with a red beak. Cardinals eat foods such as insects, fruit, seeds and buds. They also visit bird feeders in gardens.

Size: 20–23 cm (7¾–9 in)
Range: North America, Central America
Scientific name:
Cardinalis cardinalis

Cardinal

Northern parula

This little warbler feeds mainly on caterpillars and other insects that it finds in trees. It creeps over the branches and hops from perch to perch as it looks for prey. It makes its nest in hanging tree lichen or Spanish moss. The female usually lays four or five eggs, which she incubates for 12 to 14 days. Both parents feed and care for the young when they hatch.

Northern parula

Size: 11 cm (4¼ in)
Range: North America
Scientific name:
Parula americana

Snow bunting

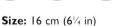

Size: 16 cm (6¼ in)
Range: Arctic region, northern Europe, North America
Scientific name:
Plectrophenax nivalis

Snow bunting

The snow bunting breeds farther north than any other land bird. To escape the cold, it sometimes burrows in the snow. After breeding, it flies south for the winter. Seeds, insects and grasses are its main food.

House sparrow

The house sparrow has been introduced worldwide and is an extremely common and adaptable bird. A few birds were taken to New York in 1850 and they have now spread all over North and South America. Seeds are the sparrow's main food, but it also eats insects and scraps put out by humans.

House sparrow

Size: 14.5 cm (5¾ in)
Range: Europe, Asia; introduced worldwide
Scientific name:
Passer domesticus

Zebra finch

Size: 9 cm (3½ in)
Range: Australia
Scientific name:
Poephila guttata

Zebra finch

Large flocks of zebra finches feed in trees and on the ground on seeds and insects. In dry areas these birds wait for rain before breeding. They make a domed nest low in a tree or bush and the female lays four to six eggs.

Golden oriole

Most of the golden oriole's life is spent high in the trees, feeding on insects and fruit with the help of its sharp beak. Its nest is like a tiny hammock made of grass and hung from a forked branch. Golden orioles lay three or four eggs.

Golden oriole

Size: 24 cm (9½ in)
Range: Europe, Asia, northwest Africa
Scientific name:
Oriolus oriolus

Scarlet tanager

Red-billed quelea

Size: 19 cm (7½ in)
Range: eastern North America
Scientific name:
Piranga olivacea

Red-billed quelea

Size: 12.5 cm (5 in)
Range: Africa, south of the Sahara
Scientific name:
Quelea quelea

Red-billed quelea

In huge flocks of thousands of birds, red-billed queleas move like clouds across the sky. They feed on grain crops and can destroy whole fields. Queleas breed in colonies and they lay two or three eggs at a time, in a kidney-shaped nest which hangs from a branch and has a side entrance.

Scarlet tanager

The scarlet tanager usually nests in woodlands, where it eats bees, wasps and other insects and their larvae, as well as fruit. After breeding, male tanagers moult their scarlet feathers and become olive green like the female birds.

American dipper

This little bird lives around mountain streams. It can swim under water and even walk on the bottom of the stream as it searches for insects and other small creatures. The female dipper makes a domed nest of moss and grass in a crevice in a stream bank. She lays three to six eggs.

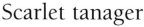

Size: 18–22 cm (7–8¾ in)
Range: North America
Scientific name:
Cinclus mexicanus

American dipper

Birds of paradise

Birds of paradise are named for their beautiful plumage and are among the most spectacular of all birds. While some are mainly black, with bright patches of shimmering iridescent feathers, others are coloured brilliant blue, red and yellow. Many have long, strangely shaped feathers on their head or tail.

There are more than 40 different species, ranging in size from about 13 to 107 cm (5 to 42 in) long. Most live in the rainforests of New Guinea, but a few birds of paradise are found in the nearby Moluccan Islands and the forests of northeast Australia. Fruit is their main food, but they also catch insects, spiders and, occasionally, frogs and lizards. Only the males have the colourful and decorative head and tail feathers for which birds of paradise are famed. The females look quite different, with dull, usually brownish plumage.

Ribbon-tailed bird of paradise

The male ribbon-tailed bird of paradise has patches of shining green feathers around his head and ribbonlike tail feathers nearly 1 m (3¼ ft) long. He twitches these tail feathers from side to side as he displays to females.

King of Saxony bird

Two wirelike plumes, up to 50 cm (19¾ in) long, extend from the male bird's head. During courtship, he holds them high and bounds up and down, hissing loudly. As the female approaches, the male sweeps his long head feathers down in front of her. He follows her, and they mate.

An upside-down display

The blue bird of paradise hangs upside down in an effort to attract females. His long tail streamers form a graceful arc over the cascade of magnificent blue plumage. He swings to and fro while making a grating call.

A group display

Most birds of paradise display alone, but the raggianas gather in groups. When females appear, the males hop around, flapping their wings and calling excitedly. Each then tries to outdo the others in showing off his glorious plumage. At the peak of the display, the birds make a series of high-pitched calls.

Tail plumes

Wilson's bird of paradise has two coiled tail feathers. They are held at right angles to the body when the bird displays.

The striking colours and magnificent tail plumes of the **greater bird of paradise** are a spectacular sight as it perches on a branch in the rainforest.

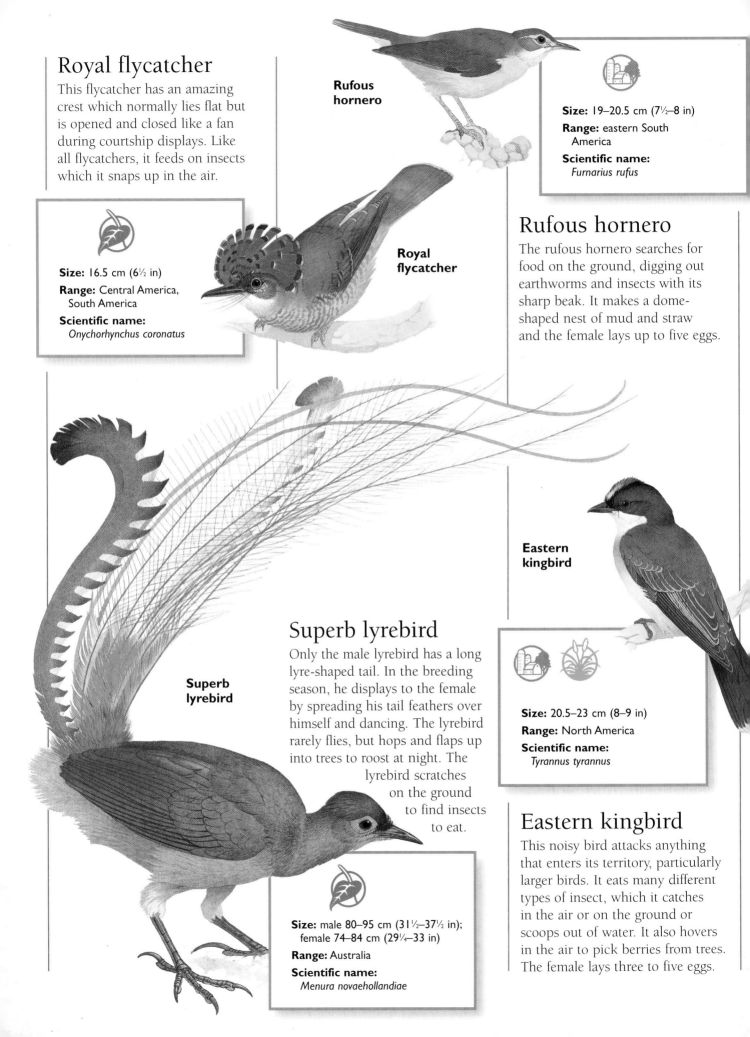

Royal flycatcher

This flycatcher has an amazing crest which normally lies flat but is opened and closed like a fan during courtship displays. Like all flycatchers, it feeds on insects which it snaps up in the air.

Size: 16.5 cm (6½ in)
Range: Central America, South America
Scientific name: *Onychorhynchus coronatus*

Rufous hornero

Size: 19–20.5 cm (7½–8 in)
Range: eastern South America
Scientific name: *Furnarius rufus*

Royal flycatcher

Rufous hornero

The rufous hornero searches for food on the ground, digging out earthworms and insects with its sharp beak. It makes a dome-shaped nest of mud and straw and the female lays up to five eggs.

Eastern kingbird

Superb lyrebird

Superb lyrebird

Only the male lyrebird has a long lyre-shaped tail. In the breeding season, he displays to the female by spreading his tail feathers over himself and dancing. The lyrebird rarely flies, but hops and flaps up into trees to roost at night. The lyrebird scratches on the ground to find insects to eat.

Size: male 80–95 cm (31½–37½ in); female 74–84 cm (29¼–33 in)
Range: Australia
Scientific name: *Menura novaehollandiae*

Size: 20.5–23 cm (8–9 in)
Range: North America
Scientific name: *Tyrannus tyrannus*

Eastern kingbird

This noisy bird attacks anything that enters its territory, particularly larger birds. It eats many different types of insect, which it catches in the air or on the ground or scoops out of water. It also hovers in the air to pick berries from trees. The female lays three to five eggs.

Size: 15 cm (6 in)
Range: Malaysia, Sumatra, Borneo
Scientific name:
  Pitta granatina

Garnet pitta

Garnet pitta

Both male and female garnet pittas have bright feathers, but young birds are a dull brown. This bird spends much of its time on the ground, catching ants, beetles and other insects. It also eats seeds and fruit and can fly short distances.

Wire-tailed manakin

Size: 11.5 cm (4½ in)
Range: South America
Scientific name:
  Pipra filicauda

Wire-tailed manakin

Only the male manakin has dramatic black, red and yellow plumage, but both male and female have long wiry tail feathers. The male shows off his bright colours in courtship displays. These birds usually feed alone, searching for insects and fruit in forests and cocoa plantations.

Torrent tyrannulet

This bird lives by fast-flowing streams. It often plucks insects from slippery rocks surrounded by foaming water, drenching itself in the process. A breeding pair makes a cup-shaped nest, usually hanging over water. The female lays two eggs which she incubates while the male stays nearby. Both parents feed the young on insects.

Torrent tyrannulet

Size: 10 cm (4 in)
Range: Central America, South America
Scientific name:
  Serpophaga cinerea

Cock of the rock

In the breeding season, the brilliantly coloured male cocks of the rock perform group displays, competing for the attention of the plainer females. They leap into the air, make noisy calls and flick their wings. These birds feed mainly on fruit.

Size: 38 cm (15 in)
Range: northern South America
Scientific name:
  Rupicola peruviana

Long-billed woodcreeper

Long-billed woodcreeper

Using its long beak, this woodcreeper searches the leaves of rainforest plants for insects and spiders to eat. It also finds prey under the bark of trees. An expert climber, it uses its stiff tail for support as it clambers around trees. The female lays two eggs in a nest in a tree hole and incubates them for about 14 days.

Size: 35.5 cm (14 in) including bill
Range: northern South America
Scientific name:
  Nasica longirostris

Cock of the rock

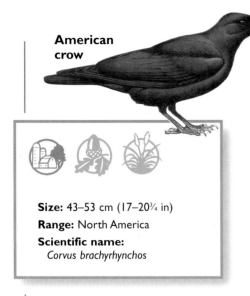

American crow

Size: 43–53 cm (17–20¾ in)
Range: North America
Scientific name:
Corvus brachyrhynchos

American crow

This large black bird eats almost anything it can find, including insects, spiders, frogs, and birds and their eggs. It also scavenges on waste food. A nest of sticks and twigs is made in a tree or bush. The female lays three to six eggs in it.

Size: 16 cm (6¼ in)
Range: Europe, Asia, North America, northern Africa
Scientific name:
Eremophila alpestris

Shore lark

Shore lark

Only the male bird has black tufts of feathers on his head. He raises them during courtship displays or when defending territory. Shore larks eat seeds, buds, insects and other small creatures. A simple nest of plant stems, surrounded with pebbles, is made on the ground. The female lays four eggs.

Black-billed magpie

The magpie eats insects, spiders and snails but also flies up into trees to snatch young birds from their nests. A breeding pair makes a large nest in a tree or bush. The female lays five to eight eggs and incubates them while the male keeps her supplied with food.

Black-billed magpie

Size: 44–57 cm (17¼–22½ in)
Range: Europe, northern Africa, Asia, North America
Scientific name:
Pica pica

Northern shrike

The northern shrike keeps watch for prey from a perch and makes short flights to catch insects. It also hovers in the air, waiting to pounce on small birds and mammals. Usually, the shrike carries its catch back to a perch to eat, but when food is plentiful it stores the extra insects, spiked on a thorn or sharp twig.

Northern shrike

Size: 24 cm (9½ in)
Range: North America, Asia, Europe, northern Africa
Scientific name:
Lanius excubitor

Water pipit

The water pipit makes its nest in high mountain areas, usually close to rushing streams. In winter, harsh weather drives it down to damp lowland meadows. Water pipits eat water worms and insects, which they catch by wading into shallow pools and on to mudflats.

Water pipit

Size: 15–18 cm (6–7 in)
Range: Europe, Asia
Scientific name:
Anthus spinoletta

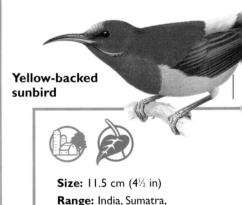

Yellow-backed sunbird

Size: 11.5 cm (4½ in)
Range: India, Sumatra, Borneo, Malaysia
Scientific name:
Aethopyga siparaja

Yellow-backed sunbird

This sunbird eats flower nectar as well as insects. It hovers in front of tube-shaped flowers and reaches into them with its long tongue. When feeding from big blooms such as hibiscus, it pierces the petals to get the nectar at the base.

Cardinal honeyeater

Yellow-throated longclaw

This bird gets its name from the back claw on each foot which is nearly 5 cm (2 in) long. It is often seen on farmland and feeds on insects, which it usually finds in grass. In the breeding season, the male makes a special courtship flight and fans his tail and sings. The female lays three or four eggs in a nest hidden in long grass.

Yellow-throated longclaw

Size: 20.5 cm (8 in)
Range: Africa, south of the Sahara
Scientific name: *Macronyx croceus*

Size: 13 cm (5 in)
Range: islands of Vanuatu, Samoa, Santa Cruz and Solomon
Scientific name: *Myzomela cardinalis*

Cardinal honeyeater

The cardinal honeyeater feeds by sipping nectar from flowers and picking insects from leaves. The female is duller than the colourful male. She has olive grey feathers with red patches. This bird's cup-shaped nest hangs from a forked branch, and the female lays two or three eggs.

Red-tufted malachite sunbird

Red-tufted malachite sunbird

This sunbird lives only on high mountain slopes, where it feeds on the nectar of plants such as giant lobelias and protea flowers. But its main food is insects, particularly flies, which it catches in the air. Both male and female have scarlet tufts at the sides of the breast, but only the male has long central tail feathers. An oval-shaped nest is built in a low bush from plant down (soft hairs) and dry stems. The female lays one or two eggs.

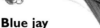
Blue jay

Size: male 25.5–30.5 cm (10–12 in); female 14–15 cm (5½–6 in)
Range: Africa
Scientific name: *Nectarinia johnstoni*

Size: 30 cm (11¾ in)
Range: North America
Scientific name: *Cyanocitta cristata*

Blue jay

Noisy groups of blue jays are a familiar sight in gardens. Seeds and nuts are their main food, and they bury extra supplies to save for the winter. Blue jays also eat insects and even steal eggs and chicks from the nests of other birds. A breeding pair makes its nest in a tree or bush, and the female lays two to six eggs.

How do animals communicate?

Almost all animals have some way of keeping in touch with others of their own kind. Many, such as birds, whales, dogs and monkeys, make a wide range of sounds, each with its own meaning. Other animals communicate by smell. They use scents to announce to others that they are ready to mate or that a particular area is their territory. Sight is also important. Courting lizards nod their heads in a special way and the positions of the ears of animals such as dogs and cats show when they are pleased, angry or frightened.

Like all wild dogs, the **coyote** communicates with barks and yaps as well as by using its tail and ears to show its mood. The coyote's howl is a way of signalling its ownership of a particular territory and warning off rival animals.

A male moth's antennae allow him to detect the scent given off by a female of his own kind from more than 1 km (½ mile) away. The large feathery antennae of the male **silk moth** are especially sensitive.

Wingless female fireflies, called **glow-worms**, signal to males by making a series of flashes. Each species has a different sequence. The flashes are made by a combination of substances in the firefly's abdomen.

Male

Warblers are well known for their songs. The **zitting cisticola** sings during its special song-flight to attract mates. It may go up to 30 m (100 ft) or more above the ground, circling over a wide area.

One of the front claws of the male **fiddler crab** is much larger than the other and brightly coloured. The male crab stands outside his burrow on the seashore and waves this claw to attract the attention of females. Each species of fiddler crab has a slightly different pattern of waves.

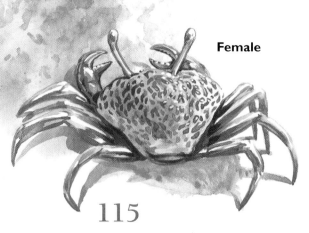

Female

Reptiles

The first reptiles evolved from amphibians about 300 million years ago. In the form of dinosaurs, which first appeared 225 million years ago, reptiles dominated life on Earth for 140 million years.

Today there are more than 6,500 known species of reptiles, including animals such as sea-living turtles, predatory crocodiles, poisonous snakes and fast-moving lizards. They live on all continents except Antarctica. Most hunt other animals to eat but there are some plant-eating turtles, tortoises and lizards.

One of the great advantages reptiles have over amphibians is the structure of their eggs. The eggs have a tough shell to protect the baby reptile and a yolky foodstore to feed it as it grows. This means the eggs do not have to be laid in water where there are many enemies. The eggs are normally laid in the soil, but in some reptiles they are kept inside the female's body so that the young are born as fully formed miniature adults.

The **emerald tree boa** is a bright green snake that spends much of its life in trees, where it wraps its gleaming coils across a branch. It watches for prey, such as birds and bats, which it catches and kills with its sharp fangs. The fastest-moving of all the boas, it is also a good swimmer.

Loggerhead turtle

Iguana

Reptiles are cold blooded and cannot control their own body temperature. As a result, most live in warm climates and bask in the sun to get warm. They usually take cover at midday to avoid overheating.

What is a reptile?

Reptiles are vertebrate animals – like mammals and birds, they have a backbone made up of small bones called vertebrae. Their bodies are covered in tough waterproof scales. Most reptiles live on land, but turtles and some snakes live in water, and crocodiles are adapted to life in both.

Types of reptile

Four groups of reptiles survive today. Turtles and tortoises have short broad bodies, enclosed by a bony shell. Crocodiles and alligators are the only survivors of the group to which dinosaurs belonged. They are hunters and the largest living reptiles. The third group includes lizards and snakes. All snakes and most lizards are predators. The last group has only two living species, the tuataras of New Zealand.

TURTLES AND TORTOISES
EUROPEAN POND TURTLE

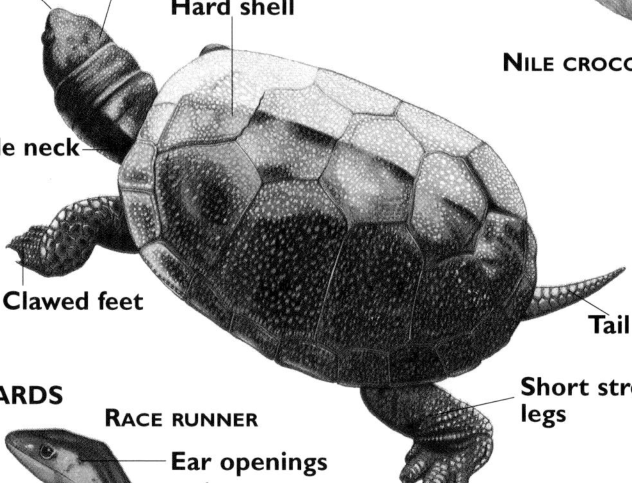

- Hard beak
- Head
- Hard shell
- Flexible neck
- Clawed feet

NILE CROCODILE

- Long tail
- Four-toed back foot
- Tail
- Short strong legs

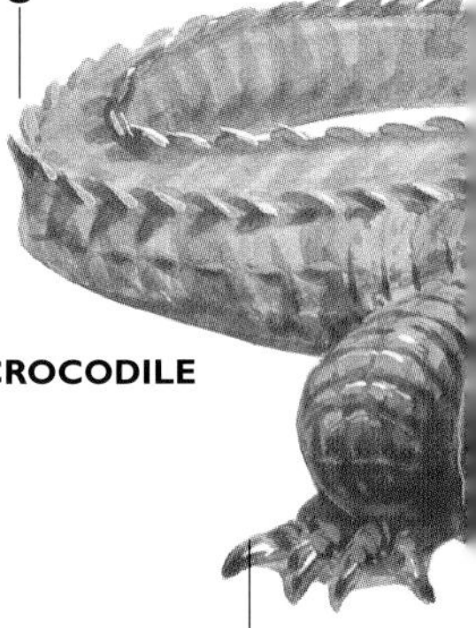

TUATARAS

- Crest on back
- Large head
- **TUATARA**
- Four legs

LIZARDS
RACE RUNNER

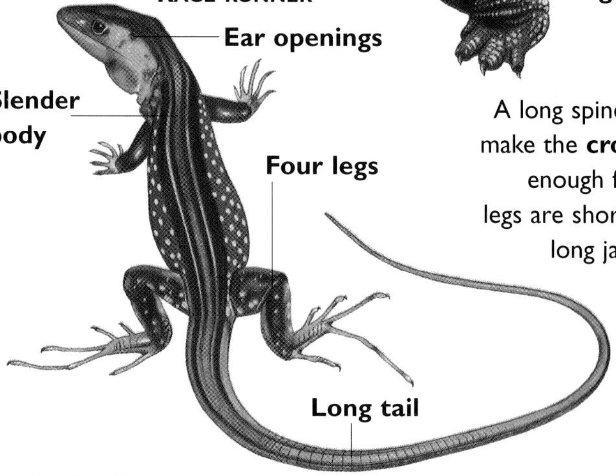

- Ear openings
- Slender body
- Four legs
- Long tail

A long spine and a strong tail help make the **crocodile's** body flexible enough for moving in water. Its legs are short but strong and it has long jaws studded with many sharp teeth.

SNAKES

DARK GREEN WHIPSNAKE

- Slender body
- Forked tongue
- Tail bones

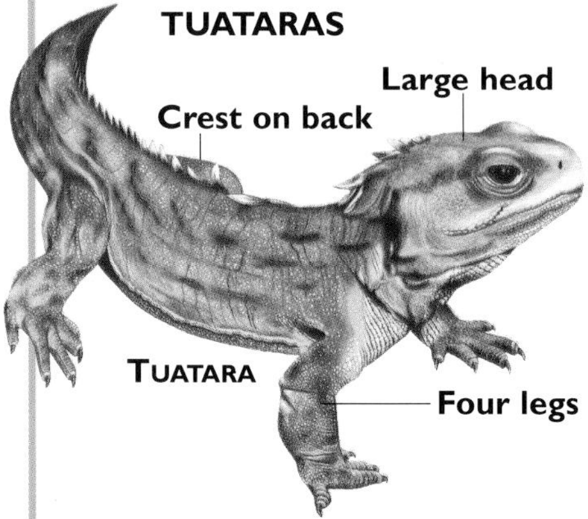

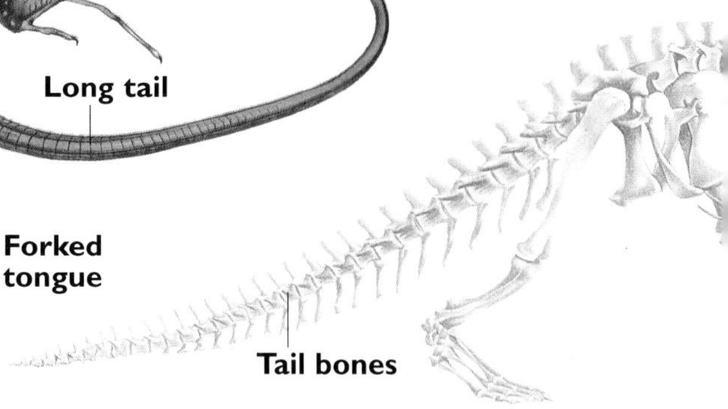

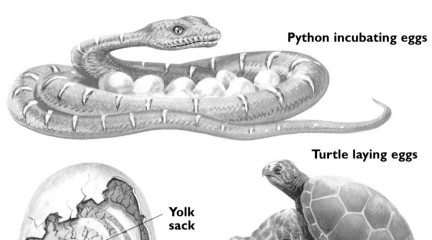

Python incubating eggs

Egg-laying reptiles

Most reptiles lay eggs from which their young hatch, although some give birth to live young. The egg is protected by a tough shell. Inside is a yolk sac that provides food for the developing young. The young grows inside the egg until it is ready to hatch out as a small version of the adult, able to live independently on land.

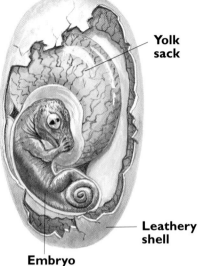

Yolk sack

Leathery shell

Embryo reptile

Turtle laying eggs

Most reptiles, such as **turtles**, simply lay their eggs in a safe place and leave them to hatch by themselves. Some snakes, such as **pythons**, curl around their eggs to keep them warm.

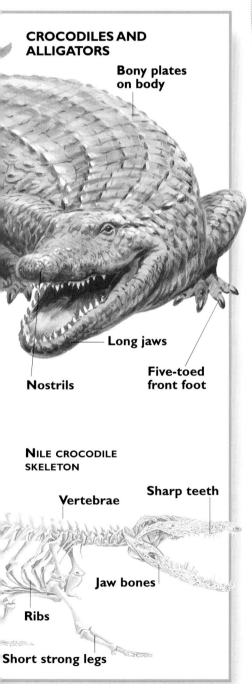

CROCODILES AND ALLIGATORS

Bony plates on body

Long jaws

Five-toed front foot

Nostrils

NILE CROCODILE SKELETON

Vertebrae

Sharp teeth

Jaw bones

Ribs

Short strong legs

Prehistoric reptiles

The first dinosaurs lived about 225 million years ago and were the most successful reptiles ever. Like reptiles today, they had leathery skin and laid eggs. Many, such as *Lambeosaurus*, were plant eaters. Others, such as *Tyrannosaurus rex*, were fierce hunters.

Lambeosaurus with young

Crocodiles, alligators, turtles and tortoises

Both these groups of reptiles are armoured in different ways. A typical turtle has a hard shell, made of plates of horn and bone, which protects its soft body. A crocodile's body is covered with hard scales, with thickened bony plates on the back for extra protection. The turtle group includes freshwater turtles and terrapins, land tortoises and sea-living turtles. The crocodile group includes three families: crocodiles, alligators and caimans, and the gavial, which consists of a single species.

Size: up to 5.5 m (18 ft)
Range: southeast USA
Scientific name:
Alligator mississipiensis

American alligator

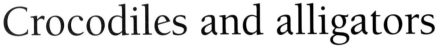

Crocodiles and alligators

There are 14 species of crocodiles, 7 of alligators and caimans, and 1 gavial. All are powerful creatures that live on land and in water and hunt a range of other animals. They live in tropical and subtropical areas. Males and females generally look alike, but males tend to grow larger. Both crocodiles and alligators have a pair of large teeth near the front of the lower jaw for grasping prey. In the crocodiles, these teeth fit into notches in the upper jaw and can be seen when the jaw is closed. In alligators and caimans, the large teeth fit into bony pits in the upper jaw and cannot be seen when the mouth is closed.

American alligator

At one time American alligators came close to extinction because hunters killed so many for their skins. Efforts to protect the species have been very successful and numbers are increasing. These alligators usually mate in spring. The female lays about 50 eggs in a mound of leaves and other plant material and guards the nest while they incubate. The young stay with their mother for up to three years.

Gavial

The gavial has long jaws studded with about 100 small teeth – ideal equipment for seizing fish and frogs under the water. The most aquatic of all the crocodiles, it moves awkwardly on land and rarely leaves the water except to nest. The female lays 35 to 60 eggs at night in the river bank in a pit, which she digs with her back feet. She stays nearby while the eggs incubate for 60 to 80 days. Like all crocodiles, the gavial has been hunted for its skin and is now quite rare.

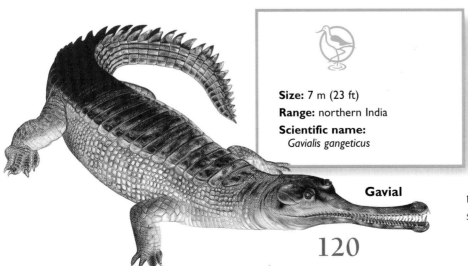

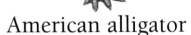

Size: 7 m (23 ft)
Range: northern India
Scientific name:
Gavialis gangeticus

Gavial

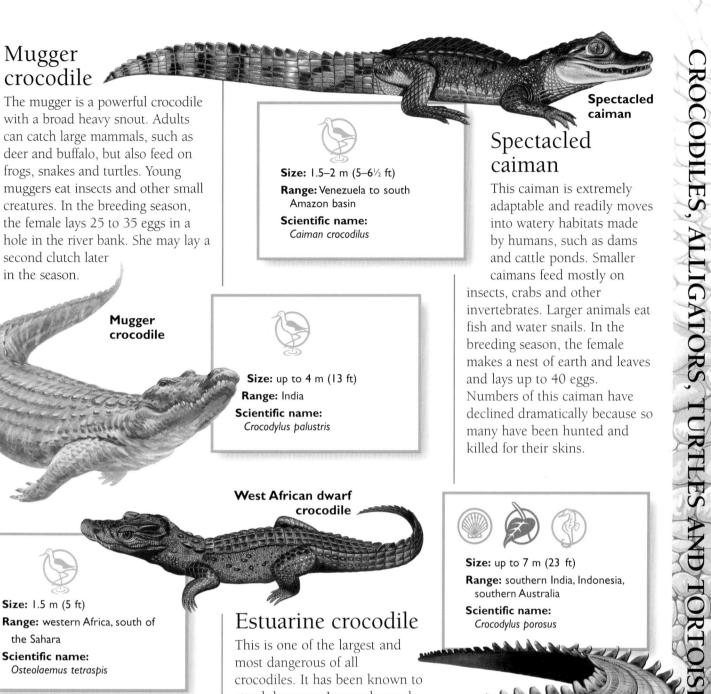

Mugger crocodile

The mugger is a powerful crocodile with a broad heavy snout. Adults can catch large mammals, such as deer and buffalo, but also feed on frogs, snakes and turtles. Young muggers eat insects and other small creatures. In the breeding season, the female lays 25 to 35 eggs in a hole in the river bank. She may lay a second clutch later in the season.

Mugger crocodile

Size: up to 4 m (13 ft)
Range: India
Scientific name:
Crocodylus palustris

Spectacled caiman

Size: 1.5–2 m (5–6½ ft)
Range: Venezuela to south Amazon basin
Scientific name:
Caiman crocodilus

Spectacled caiman

This caiman is extremely adaptable and readily moves into watery habitats made by humans, such as dams and cattle ponds. Smaller caimans feed mostly on insects, crabs and other invertebrates. Larger animals eat fish and water snails. In the breeding season, the female makes a nest of earth and leaves and lays up to 40 eggs. Numbers of this caiman have declined dramatically because so many have been hunted and killed for their skins.

West African dwarf crocodile

Size: 1.5 m (5 ft)
Range: western Africa, south of the Sahara
Scientific name:
Osteolaemus tetraspis

Size: up to 7 m (23 ft)
Range: southern India, Indonesia, southern Australia
Scientific name:
Crocodylus porosus

West African dwarf crocodile

This small crocodile has become rare in recent years because of changes to the rivers and lakes it inhabits and because of ruthless hunting. A slow-moving and not very dangerous animal, it is easy to kill or catch. Little is known about this crocodile's life, but it is thought to be active at night, when it feeds on crabs, frogs and fish. The female lays about 20 eggs in a mound of leaves and other plant material.

Estuarine crocodile

This is one of the largest and most dangerous of all crocodiles. It has been known to attack humans. It spends much of its life in the sea, catching fish, but it also preys on land animals such as monkeys, cattle and buffalo. The female comes to land to lay up to 80 eggs in a mound of plant material.

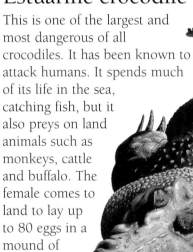

Estuarine crocodile

Nile crocodiles

Unlike most reptiles, the female Nile crocodile is a devoted mother. After mating, the male plays no further part in the rearing of his family. Alone, the female digs a pit near the river with her back legs and lays up to 60 eggs. She covers the nest with soil and stays close by to guard it while the eggs incubate for three months. She does not even leave the nest area to find food during this time. When they are about to hatch, the baby crocodiles call out to their mother from inside their shells. She uncovers the nest so that the young can escape. The mother continues to care for her young until they are six months old, when they are about 45 cm (17¾ in) long and can find food for themselves.

The crocodile's nest

The nest is usually made near water on a sandy beach or river bank and is 20–45 cm (7¾–17¾ in) deep. Once she has dug the nest burrow, the female lies over it and deposits her eggs inside.

Beginning life

When ready to hatch, the young crocodiles are very sensitive to any movements on the earth above them. When they hear their mother's footsteps they call out. Once she has uncovered the nest, each young uses the sharp egg tooth on its jaw to chip its way out of its shell. The mother may help to pull the babies free. Once the hatchlings are out of the eggs they must find shelter from the many predators waiting to catch them. The mother picks the babies up, a few at a time, and carries them to a safe nursery site. She does not close her mouth and the tiny crocodiles look like prisoners behind the bars of her big sharp teeth. She releases her babies in a quiet pool and defends them fiercely.

The **Nile crocodile** does not live only in the Nile River. It is found in rivers and lakes all over tropical and southern Africa. Adults can measure more than 5 m (16½ ft) long.

Fierce hunter

The Nile crocodile is a ruthless hunter. It lurks in the water, often with only its eyes and ears above the surface, waiting for prey to come to the river bank to drink. The crocodile then seizes its prey, drags it into the water and drowns it.

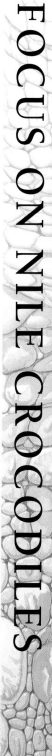

123

Turtles and tortoises

There are about 230 living species of turtles and tortoises. Typically, they have a hard shell made of horn and bone to protect the soft body. The shell is in two parts – the carapace on the back and the plastron underneath. The ribs and most of the vertebrae are attached to the shell, and most turtles and tortoises can pull their head under the shell for protection. Turtles and tortoises have hard beaks made of horn instead of teeth for chewing their food. All turtles and tortoises lay eggs. Most bury them in sand or earth and leave the hatchlings to make their own way out.

Arrau river turtle

Size: 61–76 cm (24–30 in)
Range: northern South America
Scientific name:
Podocnemis expansa

Arrau river turtle

This is the largest of the turtles known as sidenecks – a sideneck retracts its head by moving it sideways under the shell. Females gather in huge numbers on sandbanks to lay their eggs. When the young hatch, they must make their own way to the water.

Wood turtle

This rough-shelled turtle stays near water, but spends most of its life on land. It is a good climber and feeds on fruit, worms and insects. In May or June, females lay six to eight eggs. These may hatch before autumn, but usually the eggs of turtles in the north of their range do not hatch until the next spring.

Size: 12.5–23 cm (5–9 in)
Range: USA
Scientific name:
Clemmys insculpta

River terrapin

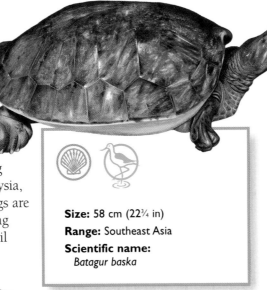

River terrapin

A large plant-eating turtle, the river terrapin, or batagur, lives in salt water as well as in rivers. It nests on sandbanks, so it is easy for people to catch it and dig up its eggs for food. In Malaysia, to save the river terrapin, eggs are taken to hatcheries and young turtles kept safe in pools until they are two years old.

Size: 58 cm (22¾ in)
Range: Southeast Asia
Scientific name:
Batagur baska

Pond slider

Size: 13–30 cm (5–11¾ in)
Range: USA and Central America to Brazil
Scientific name:
Trachemys scripta

Pond slider

The pond slider rarely moves far from water and often basks on floating logs. Young pond sliders feed mainly on insects, tadpoles and other small invertebrate animals, but as they grow they start to feed more on plants. In summer, the female pond slider lays up to three clutches of 4 to 23 eggs each.

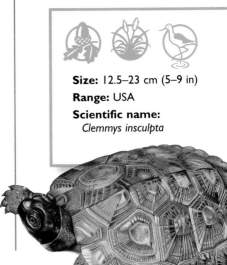

Wood turtle

Galápagos giant tortoise

This huge tortoise may weigh more than 215 kg (475 lb) – males are usually larger than females. It lives on land and feeds on almost any plants it can find. Some have a shell that curves up above the head, allowing the tortoise to reach higher plants. The female digs a pit with her back feet and lays up to 17 eggs. She covers the eggs with soil and leaves them to incubate. The young dig themselves out of the pit when they hatch.

Galápagos giant tortoise

Size: up to 1.2 m (4 ft)
Range: Galápagos Islands
Scientific name:
 Geochelone nigra

Pancake tortoise

This remarkable tortoise has a soft flexible shell. If in danger, it crawls into a rocky crevice and breathes in lots of air, making its body expand so much that it is stuck fast and very difficult to pull out. But this does not protect the animal from hunters who catch large numbers for the pet trade.

Pancake tortoise

Size: 15 cm (6 in)
Range: Africa
Scientific name:
 Malocochersus tornieri

Spur-thighed tortoise

A native of dry, scrubby regions around the Mediterranean Sea – which are being changed by farming and the building of holiday homes – this tortoise is rare because millions have been captured and sold as pets. Some trade still goes on, but is now banned by most countries.

Size: 15 cm (6 in)
Range: northern Africa, southeast and southwest Europe, Middle East
Scientific name:
 Testudo graeca

Schweigger's hingeback tortoise

Schweigger's hingeback tortoise

This tortoise catches some small animals but feeds mainly on plants and spends much of its life hiding among plant debris. Its shell is unique. A hinge allows the rear of the shell to be lowered to protect the animal's hindquarters if it is attacked. Young tortoises do not have a hinge – it develops as they grow.

Size: 33 cm (13 in)
Range: west and central Africa
Scientific name:
 Kinixys erosa

125

Spur-thighed tortoise

Matamata

The irregular shape of this turtle keeps it well hidden as it lies among leaves and other debris on the riverbed. Fleshy flaps at the sides of the head wave in water and may attract small fish. When a fish comes close, the turtle opens its large mouth and water rushes in, taking the fish with it. The turtle closes its mouth, leaving only a slit for the water to flow out.

Size: 41 cm (16¼ in)
Range: northern South America
Scientific name:
Chelus fimbriatus

Hawksbill

Hawksbills have long been hunted for their beautiful shells as well as for their eggs. There are now strict controls on hunting, but numbers are still low. The hawksbill has an unusual diet. As well as eating molluscs and crustaceans, it feeds on sponges. Many of these contain poisons, but they do not seem to affect the turtles.

Size: 76–91 cm (30–36 in)
Range: tropical Atlantic, Pacific and Indian oceans, Caribbean
Scientific name:
Eretmochelys imbricata

Murray river turtle

Murray river turtle

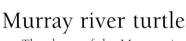

The shape of the Murray river turtle's shell changes as it develops. Newly hatched young have almost circular shells. As they grow, the shell becomes widest at the back, and adult shells are oval. This active turtle feeds on frogs, tadpoles and plants. In summer, the female lays between 10 and 15 eggs in a hole dug in the river bank. The eggs hatch in about 10 or 11 weeks.

Size: 30 cm (11¾ in)
Range: southeast Australia
Scientific name:
Emydura macquarri

Hawksbill

Leatherback

The world's largest turtle, the leatherback weighs about 360 kg (800 lb). Its shell is not covered with hard plates like that of other turtles but made of a thick leathery material. It has weak scissorlike jaws and feeds mostly on jellyfish. Leatherbacks travel long distances between the areas where they feed and their nesting sites. Most breed only every other year. Newly hatched young have small scales on their shells and skin, but these soon disappear.

Leatherback

Size: 1.5 m (5 ft)
Range: tropical Atlantic, Pacific and Indian oceans
Scientific name:
Dermochelys coriacea

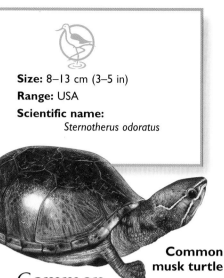

Size: 8–13 cm (3–5 in)
Range: USA
Scientific name:
Sternotherus odoratus

Common musk turtle

Common musk turtle

Also known as the stinkpot, this turtle oozes a strong-smelling fluid from special glands if attacked. It eats insects and molluscs but also feeds on carrion (creatures that are already dead) and small amounts of fish and plants. It rarely strays far from the water.

Spiny softshell

Softshell turtles have rounded, bendy shells with no hard plates. They can move fast on land and in water but spend most of their lives in water. The spiny softshell feeds on insects, crayfish and some fish and plants. It breeds in summer, when the female lays about 20 eggs.

Size: 15–46 cm (6–18 in)
Range: North America
Scientific name: *Trionyx spiniferus*

Spiny softshell

Loggerhead turtle

Size: 76–102 cm (30–40 in)
Range: temperate and tropical areas of Pacific, Indian and Atlantic oceans
Scientific name: *Caretta caretta*

Loggerhead turtle

The loggerhead has a chunky head, which may be as much as 25 cm (9¾ in) wide, and powerful jaws. It can crush even hard-shelled prey such as clams, but it also eats jellyfish and plants. Its heavy shell is very thick at the back, which may protect it from attack by sharks. Loggerheads usually breed every other year and lay several clutches of about 100 eggs each.

Green turtle

This turtle spends most of its life in water, feeding on seaweed and sea grasses. It may travel huge distances to lay its eggs on the beach where it was born. The female drags herself on to the sand, where she digs a pit and lays 100 or more eggs. She covers them with sand and returns to the sea. When the young hatch, they must struggle out of the pit and down to the sea.

Alligator snapping turtle

This turtle can weigh up to 91 kg (200 lb). It has a lumpy shell that makes it hard to see as it lies on the riverbed, watching for prey. It waits with its large mouth open to show a pink fleshy flap on its lower jaw. Passing fish come to try this "bait" and are quickly swallowed or sliced in half by the turtle's strong jaws.

Size: 1–1.25 m (3¼–4 ft)
Range: tropical Atlantic, Pacific and Indian oceans;
Scientific name:
Chelonia mydas

Green turtle

Size: 36–66 cm (14–26 in)
Range: central USA
Scientific name:
Macroclemys temmincki

Alligator snapping turtle

Lizards and snakes

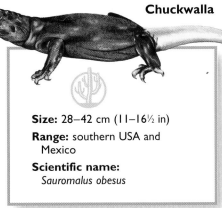

Lizards and snakes belong to a large group of reptiles, all of which have a body covered with scales. There are at least 3,500 kinds of lizard living over most of the world except the far north and Antarctica. Most live on land or in trees, but the marine iguana spends much of its time in the sea. There are about 2,400 kinds of snake. Like lizards, they live mainly in warmer parts of the world and there are none in the far north or Antarctica. Most snakes live on land but there are some freshwater and marine species.

Size: 28–42 cm (11–16½ in)
Range: southern USA and Mexico
Scientific name:
Sauromalus obesus

Chuckwalla

This plump lizard lies among rocks at night and comes out in the morning to bask in the sun and warm its body. A plant eater, it spends the day feeding on leaves, buds and flowers. If in danger, it hides in a rock crevice and puffs its body up with air so it is almost impossible to move.

Lizards

Lizards are the largest group of living reptiles. They range from tiny geckos only 7.5 cm (3 in) long to huge Komodo dragons which measure up to 3 m (10 ft). A typical lizard has four legs, but there are some legless species and others, such as the skinks and snake lizards, which have extremely small limbs. Most have ear openings and movable eyelids. In general, lizards lay eggs in a hole or a safe place under a rock and give them no further attention. But a few types keep their eggs inside their bodies until the young are quite well grown. They hatch almost as soon as the eggs are laid.

Size: 12.5 cm (5 in)
Range: southwest Africa: Namib Desert
Scientific name:
Palmatogecko rangei

Web-footed gecko

Web-footed gecko

This rare desert-living gecko has webbed feet which act like snowshoes to help it run over soft sand. It also uses its feet for burrowing into the sand to hide from enemies or the burning sun. It sits in the burrow with its head facing the entrance, waiting to pounce on insects such as termites.

Leaf-tailed gecko

Leaf-tailed gecko

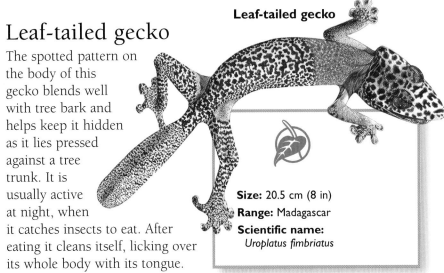

The spotted pattern on the body of this gecko blends well with tree bark and helps keep it hidden as it lies pressed against a tree trunk. It is usually active at night, when it catches insects to eat. After eating it cleans itself, licking over its whole body with its tongue.

Size: 20.5 cm (8 in)
Range: Madagascar
Scientific name:
Uroplatus fimbriatus

Arabian toad-headed agamid

A burrowing lizard, this agamid digs tunnels for shelter or buries itself in the sand. If alarmed, it takes up a defensive position to warn off the enemy – it lifts its tail high, rolls it up and then unrolls it again.

Arabian toad-headed agamid

Size: up to 12.5 cm (5 in)
Range: southwest Asia
Scientific name:
    Phrynocephalus nejdensis

Tuatara

There are only two kinds of tuatara, which are very similar to related animals alive 130 million years ago and known only from fossils. The tuatara lives on the ground and shelters in burrows. It eats insects and other small invertebrates as well as small birds and lizards.

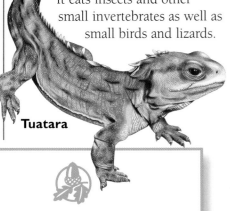

Tuatara

Size: up to 65 cm (25½ in)
Range: New Zealand
Scientific name:
    Sphenodon punctatus

Common iguana

Size: 1–2 m (3¼–6½ ft)
Range: northern and central South America; introduced into USA
Scientific name: *Iguana iguana*

Rhinoceros iguana

This lizard, which gets its name from the pointed scales on its snout, is found only on Hispaniola and its small neighbour Mona Island. It lives among thorn bushes and cacti and feeds mainly on plants, worms and mice. Its survival is threatened by the various animals, such as pigs, dogs, cats and mongooses, that have been brought to the islands. They eat its eggs and young.

Marine iguana

The marine iguana is the only lizard that spends most of its life in the sea, swimming and diving as it searches for seaweed, its main food. When in the water, the iguana uses its powerful tail to push itself along. It has to come to the surface to breathe, but when it dives, its heart rate slows so its body uses less oxygen.

Common iguana

A tree-living lizard, the iguana also swims well. It has sharp teeth and claws and defends itself fiercely when attacked. In autumn, 28 to 40 eggs are laid in a hole in the ground, where they incubate for three months. The newly hatched young are about 20 cm (7¾ in) long.

Rhinoceros iguana

Size: up to 1.2 m (4 ft)
Range: West Indies
Scientific name:
    Cyclura cornuta

Marine iguana

Size: 1.2–1.5 m (4–5 ft)
Range: Galápagos Islands
Scientific name:
    Amblyrhynchus cristatus

Green anole

Size: 9.5–12.5 cm (3¾–5 in)
Range: southwest USA
Scientific name:
Xantusia vigilis

Size: 12–20 cm (4¾–7¾ in)
Range: southern USA
Scientific name:
Anolis carolinensis

Green anole

The anole's long-toed feet help it climb in trees, where it searches for insects and spiders to eat. The male anole has a flap of pink skin on his throat which he fans in a display to attract females. After mating, the female lays one egg on the ground among leaves or rocks every two weeks during the breeding season. The eggs hatch in five to seven weeks.

Desert night lizard

Desert night lizard

This lizard lives among desert plants such as yucca and agave and feeds on termites, ants, flies and beetles. It does not lay eggs but gives birth to one to three live young, which develop inside the female's body and receive all the nourishment they need from her.

Gila monster

Gila monster

This is one of only two poisonous lizards. Its poison is made in glands in the lower jaw, and as the gila bites its prey, poison flows into the wound. Birds, mice and other lizards are its main prey. If food is scarce, the gila can live off fat reserves stored in its tail.

Size: 45–61 cm (17¾–24 in)
Range: southwest USA, Mexico
Scientific name:
Heloderma suspectum

Jungle runner

This very active lizard hunts on the ground. It has a long forked tongue, which it flicks out to search for insects and other invertebrates. The female is smaller than the male and her body is marked with stripes instead of spots.

Size: 15–20 cm (6–7¾ in)
Range: Central America, South America, east of the Andes; introduced into Florida
Scientific name: *Ameiva ameiva*

Western blue-tongued skink

This plump-bodied lizard has a large head and tiny legs. It scuttles around in the daytime, searching for insects, snails and berries. It sometimes takes shelter from the scorching sun in a rabbit burrow. The young grow inside the female's body and are born fully developed.

Size: 45 cm (17¾ in)
Range: southern Australia
Scientific name:
Tiliqua occipitalis

Jungle runner

Western blue-tongued skink

130

Size: 3 m (10 ft)
Range: islands of Komodo, Flores, Pintja and Padar, east of Java
Scientific name:
Varanus komodoensis

Komodo dragon

Komodo dragon

This creature dwarfs most other lizards and is large and strong enough to kill deer, wild boar and pigs. It has a heavy body, long thick tail and strong legs with talonlike claws. Despite its size, it is a good climber and moves surprisingly fast. It swims well and is often found near water.

Frilled lizard

This lizard has a collar of skin which normally lies in folds around its neck. But if the lizard is disturbed, its collar stands up like a frill, making it look larger and more frightening than it really is. It eats insects and other creatures that it finds in trees and on the ground.

Size: 66 cm (26 in) including tail
Range: Australia and New Guinea
Scientific name:
Chlamydosaurus kingii

Frilled lizard

Transvaal snake lizard

With snakelike movements of its long body and tail, this lizard streaks through the grass in search of insects and spiders to eat. Its tiny legs are often held off the ground as it moves. The female's two to four eggs develop inside her body. The fully formed young break from their shells as they are laid.

Size: 40 cm (15¾ in)
Range: South Africa
Scientific name:
Chamaesaura aena

Transvaal snake lizard

Slow worm

The slow worm is a smooth long-bodied lizard, with no visible legs. It moves like a snake and can shed its tail if seized by an enemy. After spending the night under rocks or logs, it comes out in the morning to hunt for prey such as slugs, worms and insects.

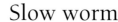

Slow worm

Size: 35–54 cm (13¾–21¼ in)
Range: parts of Europe and Asia, northwest Africa
Scientific name:
Anguis fragilis

Great plains skink

This lizard is unusual because the female guards her eggs carefully while they incubate and turns them regularly to make sure they warm evenly. She also helps the young to wriggle free of their shells and cares for them for about 10 days.

Size: 16.5–35 cm (6½–13¾ in)
Range: USA, Mexico
Scientific name:
Eumeces obsoletus

Great plains skink

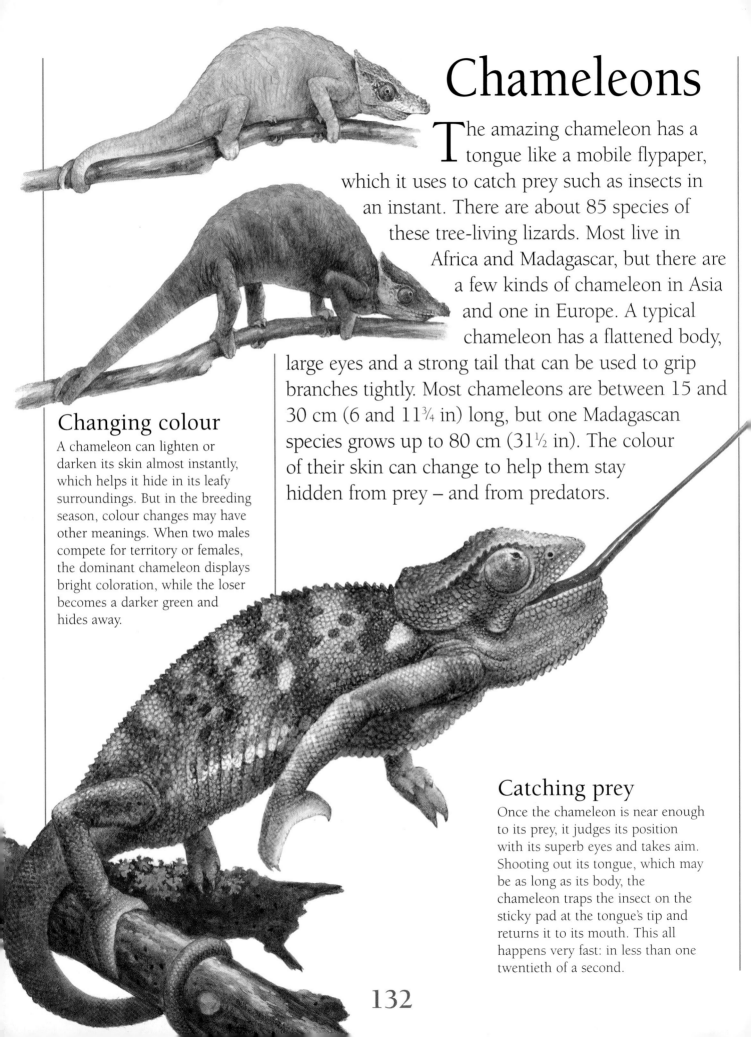

Chameleons

The amazing chameleon has a tongue like a mobile flypaper, which it uses to catch prey such as insects in an instant. There are about 85 species of these tree-living lizards. Most live in Africa and Madagascar, but there are a few kinds of chameleon in Asia and one in Europe. A typical chameleon has a flattened body, large eyes and a strong tail that can be used to grip branches tightly. Most chameleons are between 15 and 30 cm (6 and 11¾ in) long, but one Madagascan species grows up to 80 cm (31½ in). The colour of their skin can change to help them stay hidden from prey – and from predators.

Changing colour

A chameleon can lighten or darken its skin almost instantly, which helps it hide in its leafy surroundings. But in the breeding season, colour changes may have other meanings. When two males compete for territory or females, the dominant chameleon displays bright coloration, while the loser becomes a darker green and hides away.

Catching prey

Once the chameleon is near enough to its prey, it judges its position with its superb eyes and takes aim. Shooting out its tongue, which may be as long as its body, the chameleon traps the insect on the sticky pad at the tongue's tip and returns it to its mouth. This all happens very fast: in less than one twentieth of a second.

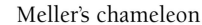

Flap-necked chameleon

This reptile has flaps of skin at the back of its head, which it can extend to threaten a rival of its own species. It spends nearly all its life in trees and only comes down to move to another tree or to lay eggs.

Jackson's chameleon

The male of this species has three large horns on his head. Females have only one small horn on the nose and tiny horns by each eye. The dull green of its skin keeps it camouflaged on lichen-covered tree bark.

Meller's chameleon

The bold markings on this chameleon make it extremely hard to see as it sits motionless on a branch, watching for prey. Meller's chameleon grows up to 58 cm (22¾ in) long.

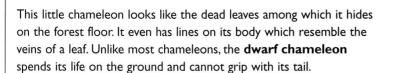

This little chameleon looks like the dead leaves among which it hides on the forest floor. It even has lines on its body which resemble the veins of a leaf. Unlike most chameleons, the **dwarf chameleon** spends its life on the ground and cannot grip with its tail.

Snakes

Snakes have long bodies and no limbs. Even though they have no legs, snakes can still move fast. They wriggle along the ground with wavelike movements of the body, and pointed scales on the underside of the belly help them grip. Snakes range in size from 10 cm (4 in) to about 9 m (30 ft). All have a long forked tongue, but they do not have ear openings or movable eyelids. All snakes hunt other animals for food. Some, such as boas, wrap victims in their strong body coils and squeeze them to death. Others, such as vipers, have a poisonous bite.

Size: 18–38 cm (7–15 in)
Range: southwest USA
Scientific name:
  Leptotyphlops humilis

Western blind snake

A smooth round-bodied reptile, the western blind snake has a blunt head and tail. It lives anywhere there is sandy or gravelly soil and spends much of its time below ground. It eats ants and termites, which it finds by smell, and its body is so slender that it can slide into their nests.

Anaconda

One of the longest of all snakes, the anaconda spends much of its life in slow-moving water, watching for prey. When an animal comes to the water's edge to drink, the anaconda seizes the victim in its coils. Female anacondas produce up to 40 live young, each 66 cm (26 in) long.

Size: 9 m (30 ft)
Range: South America
Scientific name:
  Eunectes murinus

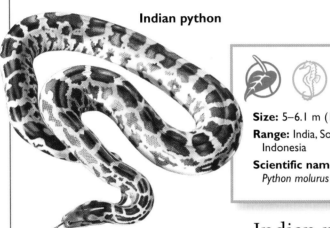

Indian python

Size: 5–6.1 m (16½–20 ft)
Range: India, Southeast Asia, Indonesia
Scientific name:
  Python molurus

Indian python

One of the largest snakes in the world, the Indian python basks in the sun by day or rests in a cave or other shelter. At night, it prowls around, searching for prey such as birds, small deer and boar, or waits near a water hole where animals are sure to come. It stalks close to its prey, then grasps it in its body coils and crushes it to death.

Boa constrictor

The boa constrictor kills prey, such as birds and mammals, by wrapping the victim in the strong coils of its body until it is suffocated or crushed to death. The boa spends most of its life on the ground, but it does climb trees and can grip branches with its tail.

Boa constrictor

Size: up to 5.6 m (18½ ft)
Range: South America
Scientific name:
  Boa constrictor

Anacond

Boomslang

The active, tree-living boomslang is one of the most poisonous snakes in Africa. Its poison flows from special glands on to large grooved teeth in the mouth and then enters the victim's body as the snake chews. The snake normally uses its venomous bite on prey such as lizards, frogs and birds, but it can even kill humans. It rarely attacks unless disturbed.

Size: up to 2 m (6½ ft)
Range: central to South Africa
Scientific name:
Dispholidus typus

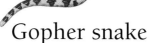

Gopher snake

Gopher snake

This large snake is a good climber and burrower. It feeds mostly on mice, small birds and lizards, all of which it kills with its powerful body coils – the victim is squeezed until it suffocates. Gopher snakes mate in spring and the female lays up to 24 eggs in a burrow or under a log. The young hatch in 9 to 11 weeks.

Size: 1.2–2.5 m (4–8¼ ft)
Range: southwest Canada, USA, Mexico
Scientific name:
Pituophis melanoleucus

Size: up to 1.2 m (4 ft); occasionally up to 2 m (6½ ft)
Range: Europe, northwest Africa, Asia, east to Russia
Scientific name: *Natrix natrix*

Boomslang

Grass snake

Size: 30–50 cm (11¾–19¾ in)
Range: Australia
Scientific name:
Enhydris punctata

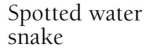

Spotted water snake

Able to move swiftly both in water and on land, this snake preys on creatures such as fish and frogs. Its small eyes face upwards and its nostrils are also on the upper surface of the head. Pads of skin close off the nostrils completely when the snake dives under water. It is mildly poisonous.

Grass snake

The grass snake swims well and hunts fish and frogs in woodland rivers as well as mice on land. It is one of the commonest snakes in Europe. In the breeding season, the male courts the female by rubbing his chin over her body before mating. She lays 30 to 40 eggs in a warm spot.

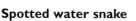
Spotted water snake

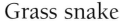

135

Eastern green mamba

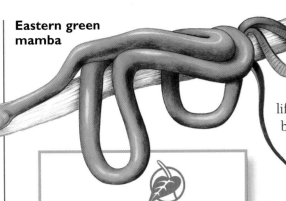

Eastern green mamba

The slender fast-moving mamba spends much of its life in trees, where it hunts for birds and lizards. It has a strong poison. In the breeding season, males take part in ritual fights for females. They wrap their bodies around each other and threaten each other with their heads.

Size: 2 m (6½ ft)
Range: eastern and southern Africa
Scientific name: *Dendroaspis angusticeps*

Sidewinder

This poisonous snake hides under a bush or in a burrow during the day and comes out at night to hunt for mice, rats and lizards. A desert dweller, the sidewinder has a special way of moving over sand. It throws its body into waves, only two small sections of which touch the ground. The snake moves itself sideways by pushing against these two points.

Size: 43–82 cm (17–32¼ in)
Range: southwest USA and Mexico
Scientific name: *Crotalus cerastes*

Paradise tree snake

Size: up to 1.2 m (4 ft)
Range: Philippines to Indonesia
Scientific name: *Chrysopelea paradisi*

Paradise tree snake

This snake is an excellent climber and spends much of its life in trees. Also known as the flying snake, it can launch itself into the air and glide 20 m (65 ft) or more from tree to tree in the rainforest. It does not have much control over its "flight" and cannot glide upwards or steer.

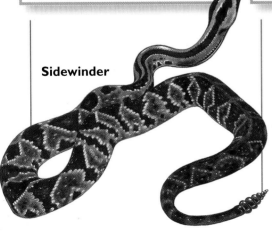

Sidewinder

Banded sea snake

Size: 2 m (6½ ft)
Range: Indian and Pacific oceans
Scientific name: *Hydrophis cyanocinctus*

Banded sea snake

This snake spends all its life in the sea and never goes on land. Its body is slightly flattened and its paddle-shaped tail helps it push itself through the water. It breathes air but can stay under water for up to two hours. Like all sea snakes, it eats fish and has a poisonous bite.

Eastern coral snake

The colourful markings of the coral snake are a warning to enemies that it is highly poisonous. This snake spends much of its time buried in sand or dead leaves. In the morning and late afternoon it moves around searching for small snakes and lizards, which it kills with its poisonous bite.

Size: 56–120 cm (22–48 in)
Range: USA, Mexico
Scientific name: *Micrurus fulvius*

Eastern coral snake

Eastern diamondback rattlesnake

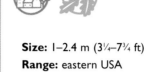

Eastern diamondback rattlesnake

This is the most dangerous snake in North America, with poison that attacks its victims' blood cells. Like all rattlesnakes, it makes a rattling sound with a series of hard hollow rings of skin at the end of its tail. Each ring was once the tip of the tail and a new one is left behind each time the snake sheds its skin.

Size: 1–2.4 m (3¼–7¾ ft)
Range: eastern USA
Scientific name:
  Crotalus adamanteus

Indian cobra

This large very poisonous cobra feeds on mice, lizards and frogs. It can attack or defend itself from a distance by "spitting" out jets of poison. This can cause severe pain if it reaches the eyes of mammals. To threaten enemies, the cobra raises the front of its body and spreads the ribs and loose skin at its neck to form a hood shape. Eyelike markings on the hood confuse the enemy further.

Indian cobra

Size: 1.8–2.2 m (6–7¼ ft)
Range: India, central and Southeast Asia
Scientific name:
  Naja naja

Gaboon viper

The patterns on the Gaboon viper's body help keep it hidden as it lies among dead leaves on the forest floor. It hunts at night, preying on mice, frogs and birds. Its fangs are up to 5 cm (2 in) long, the longest of any viper, and it has powerful poison. The female viper gives birth to litters of up to 30 live young.

Gaboon viper

Size: 1.2–2 m (4–6½ ft)
Range: western Africa, south of the Sahara
Scientific name:
  Vipera gabonica

Saw-scaled adder

An extremely dangerous snake, the saw-scaled adder causes more human deaths in Africa than any other snake. During the day, it lies under a log or rock, sheltering from the sun. At night it feeds on creatures such as mice, lizards and scorpions. In the breeding season, the female lays about five eggs. The young adders are about 20 cm (7¾ in) long when they hatch.

Saw-scaled adder

Size: 53–72 cm (20¾–28¼ in)
Range: northern Africa, Asia
Scientific name:
  Echis carinatus

137

Amphibians

Amphibians were the first vertebrate animals to live on land. They evolved from fish about 370 million years ago, and modern amphibians still spend part of their lives in water. Many also mate and lay their eggs in water. The eggs hatch into water-living larvae that have fins and gills. As they grow, they lose their gills and develop legs and lungs, so that they are able to live on land. Some amphibians such as mudpuppies, however, spend their whole lives in water and keep their feathery gills.

There are about 4,550 species of amphibians known, but new species are being discovered all the time, particularly in tropical areas, and there are likely to be more than 5,000. These consist of two main groups – salamanders and newts, and frogs and toads. There is also a third, smaller, group of legless long-bodied amphibians called caecilians, which look similar to earthworms.

True to its name, the brilliantly coloured **spotted salamander** has a line of irregular spots running down its back from head to tail. Normally a peaceful creature, the male can be aggressive when defending his territory against intruders. The male may bite the nose of a rival.

Oriental fire-bellied toad

139

What is an amphibian?

Amphibians are cold-blooded vertebrates. They cannot control their body temperature and must gain heat by basking in the sun. Although they have lungs, they gain most of the oxygen they need through their skin. The skin is not scaly and must be kept moist.

Taking off

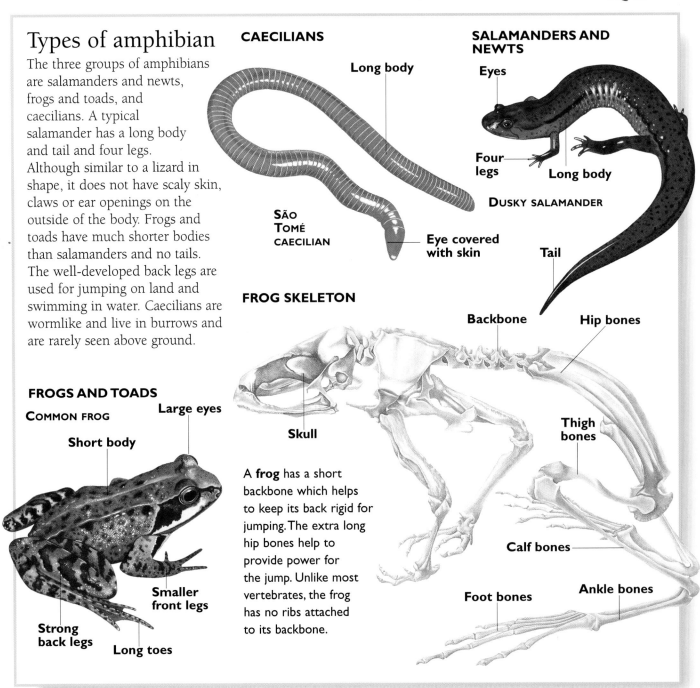

Types of amphibian

The three groups of amphibians are salamanders and newts, frogs and toads, and caecilians. A typical salamander has a long body and tail and four legs. Although similar to a lizard in shape, it does not have scaly skin, claws or ear openings on the outside of the body. Frogs and toads have much shorter bodies than salamanders and no tails. The well-developed back legs are used for jumping on land and swimming in water. Caecilians are wormlike and live in burrows and are rarely seen above ground.

CAECILIANS

Long body

São Tomé Caecilian

Eye covered with skin

SALAMANDERS AND NEWTS

Eyes

Four legs

Long body

Dusky salamander

Tail

FROG SKELETON

Backbone

Hip bones

Skull

Thigh bones

A **frog** has a short backbone which helps to keep its back rigid for jumping. The extra long hip bones help to provide power for the jump. Unlike most vertebrates, the frog has no ribs attached to its backbone.

Calf bones

Foot bones

Ankle bones

FROGS AND TOADS

COMMON FROG

Large eyes

Short body

Smaller front legs

Strong back legs

Long toes

140

Getting ready to land

Back legs fully stretched

Leaping frog

On land, the frog crouches with its long legs folded. The foot, calf and thigh are all about the same length. As the frog leaps, its legs unfold to push it into the air. When stretched right out, the frog's back legs are usually longer than its body.

From egg to adult

A typical frog develops in stages known as a life cycle. The eggs, which have a protective jellylike coating, are laid in water. They hatch into tadpoles, which have a tail and feathery gills. As each tadpole grows, it develops legs and lungs, and the gills disappear. Finally, when it has grown into a miniature version of the adult, the tadpole loses its tail. Not all frogs follow the same cycle. Some keep their developing eggs inside their body.

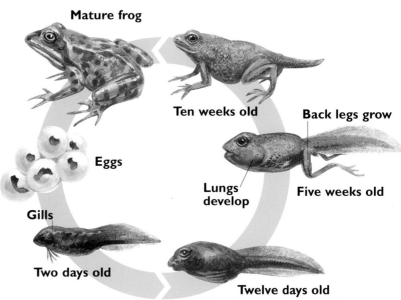

Mature frog

Ten weeks old

Eggs

Gills

Two days old

Back legs grow

Lungs develop

Five weeks old

Twelve days old

Arrow-poison frog

South American false-eyed frog

Spotted salamander

Beware of bright colours

Many amphibians have extremely brightly coloured and patterned skins. This is usually a warning to potential predators that the amphibian's skin contains nasty-tasting secretions. These can cause severe irritation in mammals and some even contain poisons that can kill. The South American false-eyed frog has large eyelike markings on its rear. If attacked, it displays these to fool its enemy into thinking it is larger than it really is.

Prehistoric amphibians

Amphibians such as *Ichthyostega* were the first-known land animals. *Ichthyostega* was a strongly built creature with four legs. Like its fish ancestors, it had a tail fin and bony scales on its belly and tail.

Ichthyostega

Newts and salamanders

There are about 350 species of newts and salamanders divided into 10 groups, or families. Sirens, congo eels, olms and mudpuppies are all long-bodied amphibians with small, almost useless legs. These creatures all live in water and have feathery gills for breathing, which many of them keep throughout their lives.

The lungless salamanders are the largest group of living salamanders. With no lungs, they obtain all their oxygen through their moist skin. There are several other groups of salamanders, most of which have sturdy bodies and well-developed legs. The newt family includes about 49 species. There are water- and land-living newts, but most stay near water.

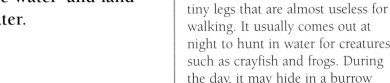

Two-toed congo eel

Size: 45–116 cm (17¾–45½ in)
Range: eastern USA
Scientific name:
Amphiuma means

Two-toed congo eel

The congo eel has a long body and tiny legs that are almost useless for walking. It usually comes out at night to hunt in water for creatures such as crayfish and frogs. During the day, it may hide in a burrow that it digs in the mud or takes over from another creature. Congo eels mate in water and the female lays about 200 eggs in a beadlike string. She curls around the eggs and protects them until they hatch.

California slender salamander

True to its name, this salamander has a long slim body and tail. Its legs and feet are tiny, with four toes on each foot. It generally lives on land and moves by wriggling its body rather than by using its legs. During the day it hides among damp plants, coming out at night to hunt for creatures such as worms and spiders.

Olm

Olm

This strange salamander has a long body and red feathery gills. Its tail is flattened and it has small weak legs. It is almost blind and lives in total darkness in underground streams and lakes. There it rummages in the mud to find food such as worms and small crustaceans. Animal collectors have taken so many of these fascinating creatures from the wild that new areas where they have been found are kept secret.

Size: 7.5–14 cm (3–5½ in)
Range: USA: Oregon, California
Scientific name:
Batrachoseps attenuatus

Size: 20–30 cm (7¾–11¾ in)
Range: former Yugoslavia and Italy
Scientific name: *Proteus anguinus*

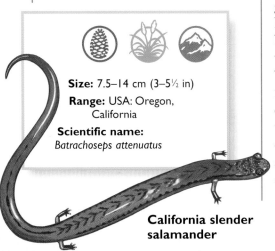

California slender salamander

142

Mudpuppy

The mudpuppy spends all its life in water, so even adults have large feathery gills. It hunts worms, crayfish and insects at night. In the breeding season the female lays up to 190 eggs, each of which is stuck separately to a log or rock.

Mudpuppy

Size: 20–43 cm (7¾–17 in)
Range: southern Canada and USA
Scientific name:
Necturus maculosus

Greater siren

The siren has a long eel-like body and tiny front legs with four toes on each foot. It has no back legs and swims by fishlike movements of its body. During the day, it hides under rocks or burrows into the muddy riverbed. At night, it comes out to catch snails, insect larvae and fish.

Size: 50–97.5 cm (19¾–38½ in)
Range: USA
Scientific name:
Siren lacertina

Greater siren

Red salamander

Size: 9.5–18 cm (3¾–7 in)
Range: eastern USA
Scientific name:
Pseudotriton ruber

Red salamander

The brilliantly coloured red salamander has a stout body and a short tail and legs. It spends much of its time on land, but usually stays near water. Earthworms, insects and smaller salamanders are its main food. After courting and mating, the female salamander lays between 50 and 100 eggs. The larvae hatch about two months later but do not become adults until they are about two years old.

Texas blind salamander

Size: 9–13.5 cm (3½–5¼ in)
Range: USA: south Texas
Scientific name:
Typhlomolge rathbuni

Texas blind salamander

This salamander lives in water in underground caves. It has a pale body, tiny eyes and red feathery gills that it keeps all its life. The Texas blind salamander eats cave-dwelling invertebrates that feed on the droppings left by the bats that roost in the caves.

Spotted salamander

Size: 15–24 cm (6–9½ in)
Range: southeast Canada, eastern USA
Scientific name:
Ambystoma maculatum

Spotted salamander

Spotted salamanders spend most of their time well out of sight, burrowing through damp soil, but every spring they gather in crowds around pools to mate and lay eggs in the water. Sadly, this spectacle no longer occurs in many areas because acid rain has polluted breeding pools.

143

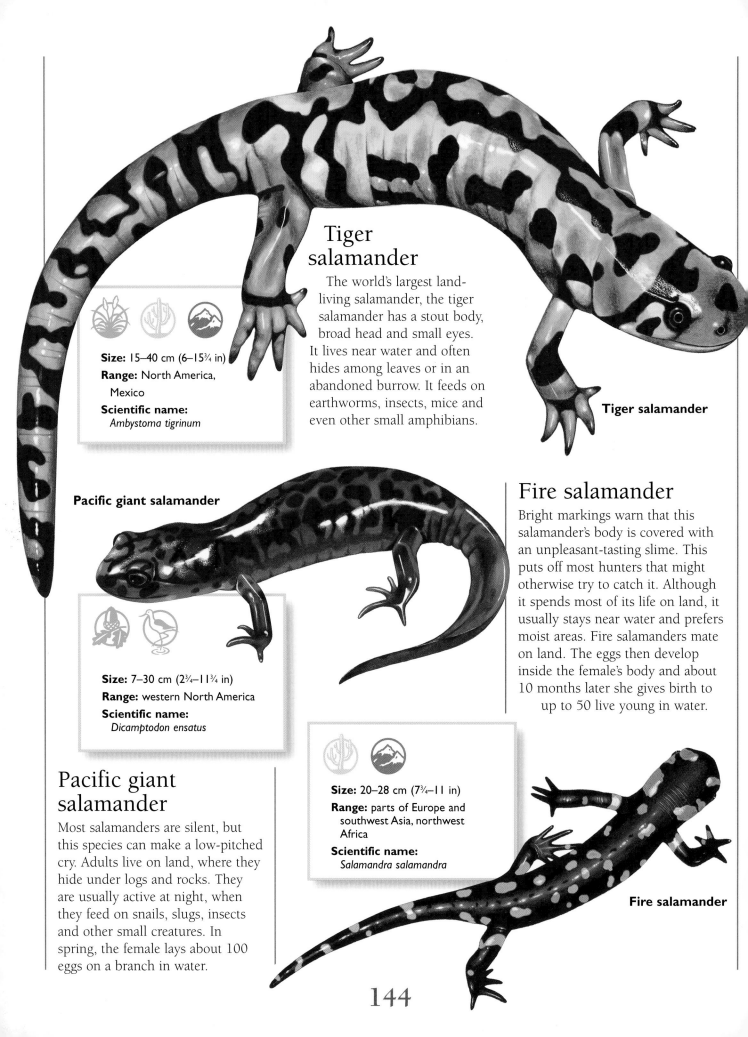

Tiger salamander

The world's largest land-living salamander, the tiger salamander has a stout body, broad head and small eyes. It lives near water and often hides among leaves or in an abandoned burrow. It feeds on earthworms, insects, mice and even other small amphibians.

Size: 15–40 cm (6–15¾ in)
Range: North America, Mexico
Scientific name: *Ambystoma tigrinum*

Tiger salamander

Pacific giant salamander

Size: 7–30 cm (2¾–11¾ in)
Range: western North America
Scientific name: *Dicamptodon ensatus*

Pacific giant salamander

Most salamanders are silent, but this species can make a low-pitched cry. Adults live on land, where they hide under logs and rocks. They are usually active at night, when they feed on snails, slugs, insects and other small creatures. In spring, the female lays about 100 eggs on a branch in water.

Fire salamander

Bright markings warn that this salamander's body is covered with an unpleasant-tasting slime. This puts off most hunters that might otherwise try to catch it. Although it spends most of its life on land, it usually stays near water and prefers moist areas. Fire salamanders mate on land. The eggs then develop inside the female's body and about 10 months later she gives birth to up to 50 live young in water.

Size: 20–28 cm (7¾–11 in)
Range: parts of Europe and southwest Asia, northwest Africa
Scientific name: *Salamandra salamandra*

Fire salamander

144

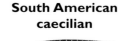

Axolotl

Axolotl

This unusual amphibian is now rare because so many have been collected for the pet trade and predatory fish have been introduced into the lake where it lives. Many axolotls remain as larvae with feathery gills all their lives, but some do become land-living adults without gills.

Size: up to 29 cm (11½ in)
Range: Mexico: Lake Xochimilco
Scientific name:
Ambystoma mexicanum

Warty newt

The male of this large rough-skinned newt develops a jagged crest on his back in the breeding season. Females are often larger than males. Warty newts feed on small invertebrates; they also eat small fish and other amphibians and their eggs.

Warty newt

Size: 14–18 cm (5½–7 in)
Range: parts of Europe
Scientific name:
Triturus cristatus

South American caecilian

South American caecilian

Caecilians are not salamanders but belong to a separate group of blind, burrowing amphibians. This caecilian has a short thick body and, unlike most caecilians, it has no scales on its skin. It spends most of its life underground, where it feeds on earthworms.

Size: 35 cm (13¾ in)
Range: South America, east of Andes
Scientific name:
Siphonops annulatus

Size: 6.5–14 cm (2½–5½ in)
Range: eastern North America
Scientific name:
Notophthalmus viridescens

Hellbender

Despite its fierce name, this large salamander is a harmless creature, which hides under rocks in the water during the day. At night it comes out to hunt crayfish, snails and worms, which it finds by smell and touch rather than sight. In autumn, the female lays up to 500 eggs in a hollow made by the male on the stream bed.

Eastern newt

Size: 30.5–74 cm (12–29¼ in)
Range: USA
Scientific name:
Cryptobranchus alleganiensis

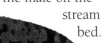

Hellbender

Eastern newt

This newt breeds in early spring. The female lays up to 400 eggs on water plants, and larvae hatch two months later. After a few months, the larvae turn into sub-adults, called efts. They leave the water and spend up to three years on land. They return to the water and grow into adults.

145

Frogs and toads

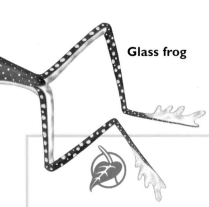

Glass frog

There are more than 3,500 species of frogs and toads. All are very similar in appearance whatever their lifestyle. Typically, an adult frog or toad has long back legs, webbed toes and no tail. The skin is smooth or warty but always moist. Like all amphibians, frogs and toads are at home both on land and in fresh water and can swim, hop and even climb trees. Most feed on small creatures such as slugs, snails and insects, which they catch with their long sticky tongue.

Frogs and toads usually breed in water, laying eggs which hatch into tailed, swimming young known as tadpoles. The tadpoles live in water, breathing through feathery gills at the sides of the head and eating plants. As the tadpoles grow they lose their gills and tail and grow legs. Some weeks after hatching, they develop into tiny frogs.

Size: up to 3 cm (1¼ in)
Range: northern South America
Scientific name:
Centrolenella albomaculata

Glass frog

This delicate little frog lives in small trees and bushes, usually near running water. It has sticky discs on its toes that help it grip when climbing. The female lays her eggs in clusters on the underside of leaves overhanging water. When the tadpoles hatch they tumble into the water below, where they complete their development.

African clawed toad

African clawed toad

This toad moves as fast in the water as any fish and is even able to swim backwards. It uses the claws on its front feet to dig in the mud around pools and streams for food and eats any creatures it can find, even its own tadpoles. The toads mate in water, the male making a soft buzzing sound under water to attract the female. The eggs are attached to water plants and hatch after seven days.

Size: 6.5–12.5 cm (2½–5 in)
Range: South Africa
Scientific name:
Xenopus laevis

Natal ghost frog

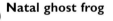

Size: up to 5 cm (2 in)
Range: northeast South Africa
Scientific name:
Heleophryne natalensis

Natal ghost frog

This frog lives in fast-flowing mountain streams. The female lays her eggs in a pool or on wet gravel. Once hatched, the tadpoles move into the streams where they hold on to stones with their suckerlike mouths to stop themselves being swept away.

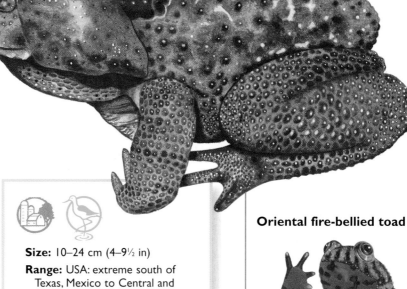

Giant toad

Giant toad

One of the largest toads in the world, the giant toad has been introduced to many areas outside its natural range. This is because it feeds on insects that destroy crops, such as sugar, and so helps to control them. This toad has glands at the sides of its body that make a poisonous liquid that may cause irritation and even death in mammals that try to eat it. Eggs are laid in water where three days later they hatch into tadpoles.

Size: 10–24 cm (4–9½ in)
Range: USA: extreme south of Texas, Mexico to Central and South America
Scientific name: *Bufo marinus*

Oriental fire-bellied toad

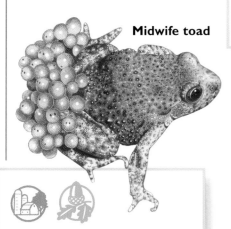

Midwife toad

Size: up to 5 cm (2 in)
Range: western Europe
Scientific name:
   Alytes obstetricans

Western spadefoot

An expert burrower, the western spadefoot toad has a hard spike on each back foot that helps it dig. It spends the day in its burrow and comes out at night to feed. The spadefoot waits for rain to fall before mating. Its eggs are laid in a rain-pool, hatching only two days later.

Size: 5 cm (2 in)
Range: Siberia, northeast China, Korea
Scientific name:
   Bombina orientalis

Western spadefoot

Size: 3.5–6.5 cm (1¼–2½ in)
Range: western USA and Mexico
Scientific name:
   Scaphiopus hammondi

Midwife toad

The midwife toad hides by day under logs or in cracks in walls. At night it feeds on insects and other small creatures. It has unusual breeding habits. After the female has laid her eggs, the male takes them and carries them on his back while they develop. When they are ready to hatch, he places them in shallow water.

Oriental fire-bellied toad

The brilliantly coloured rough skin of this toad gives off a milky substance which irritates the mouth and eyes of any attacker. The female fire-bellied toad lays her eggs on the underside of stones in water. The eggs are laid in small clumps of two to eight and left to hatch by themselves.

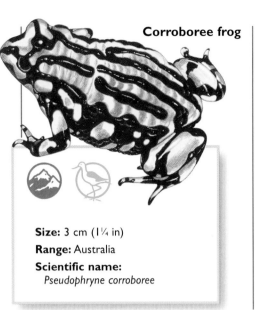

Corroboree frog

Size: 3 cm (1¼ in)
Range: Australia
Scientific name:
  Pseudophryne corroboree

Gold frog

This tiny frog often lives among dead leaves on the forest floor but may also hide in cracks in trees or rocks in dry weather. It has a bony shield on its back and may use this to block off the entrance of its hiding place to keep the atmosphere inside moist.

Gold frog

Size: up to 2 cm (¾ in)
Range: southeast Brazil
Scientific name:
  Brachycephalus ephippium

Marsupial frog

The marsupial frog has an unusual way of caring for its eggs. As the female lays her eggs, the male helps her to pack them into a skin pouch on her back. A few weeks later, she finds some shallow water to release her brood, which have hatched into tadpoles. She uses the long toe on her back foot to open the pouch.

Marsupial frog

Size: up to 4 cm (1½ in)
Range: South America
Scientific name:
  Gastrotheca marsupiata

Corroboree frog

This frog lives on land, but near water, and shelters under logs or in a burrow that it digs itself. In summer, pairs dig a nesting burrow in a bog. The female lays up to 12 large eggs and one parent usually guards the eggs while they develop. The tadpoles usually stay in the eggs until there is enough rain to wash them into a creek, where they hatch at once.

Size: 20 cm (7¾ in)
Range: north and central South America
Scientific name:
  Ceratophrys cornuta

Horned frog

The horned frog is almost as broad as it is long and has a wide head and large mouth. It has small eyes, with a lump on each upper eyelid. Even though it spends much of its life half-buried in the ground, its toes are partly webbed. It feeds on snails, small frogs and mice and probably also eats tadpoles of its own species.

Horned frog

Darwin's frog

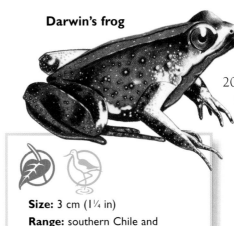

Size: 3 cm (1¼ in)
Range: southern Chile and southern Argentina
Scientific name:
Rhinoderma darwinii

Darwin's frog

This frog has unusual breeding habits. The female lays 20 to 45 eggs on land. Several males stand guard for up to 20 days until the young begin to move around inside the eggs. Each male then gathers up to 15 eggs in his mouth and lets them slide into the large sac under his chin. The tadpoles continue to develop inside the sac. When they have grown into tiny frogs, the males let them go in water.

European green tree frog

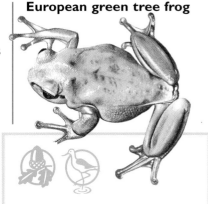

Size: up to 5 cm (2 in)
Range: most of Europe
Scientific name:
Hyla arborea

Natterjack toad

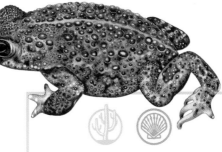

Size: 7–10 cm (2¾–4 in)
Range: western and central Europe
Scientific name:
Bufo calamita

Natterjack toad

The male natterjack has the loudest call of any European toad. His croak carries 2 km (1¼ miles) or more. The natterjack usually lives on land but is often found near the sea and may even breed in salty water. These toads mate at night and the female lays strings of up to 4,000 eggs in shallow water. The eggs hatch into tadpoles in about 10 days.

European green tree frog

This smooth-skinned tree frog spends most of its life in trees. It can change colour with amazing speed, turning from bright green in sunlight to dark grey in shade. The frogs breed in early summer and the female lays up to 1,000 eggs in water.

Spring peeper

Size: 2–3 cm (¾–1¼ in)
Range: southeast Canada, USA
Scientific name:
Hyla crucifer

Arum lily frog

A good climber, this frog has large sticky discs on each toe which help it grip. The underside of its legs is orange but the rest of the body changes colour according to conditions. In bright sun it is light cream, and in shade it turns dark brown. Courting males often climb up on to arum lilies to call to females. They mate in water and eggs are laid on plants.

Arum lily frog

Size: up to 6 cm (2¼ in)
Range: South Africa
Scientific name:
Hyperolius horstockii

Spring peeper

This agile frog can climb trees and jump heights of more than 17 times its own body length. It feeds mainly on small spiders and insects, including flying insects which it leaps into the air to catch. In the breeding season, males sit in trees courting females with their bell-like calls.

Arrow-poison frogs

A rrow-poison frogs are among the most colourful of all amphibians. But for some, their jewel-like appearance is a warning to predators to keep their distance because the skin contains extremely strong poisons. The frogs cannot inject their poison into enemies. It is produced in special glands and simply released into the skin, making a dangerous meal for a predator. Arrow-poison frogs live in the tropical rainforests of Central America. There are about 155 species of arrow-poison frogs but only 55 of these are poisonous.

Golden arrow-poison frog

The poison in the skin of the neon-bright golden arrow-poison frog may come partly from its food, such as small beetles and millipedes. Although so deadly to its enemies, the frog's poison may have a value. Doctors are investigating its use in a medicine for heart-attack patients.

Small but lethal

One of the most deadly of all arrow-poison frogs is *Phyllobates terribilis*. This frog is only 5 cm (2 in) long, but its poison is at least 20 times as strong as that of any other frog and can be lethal for humans even to touch. It is one of only three species traditionally used by local tribesmen for tipping hunting arrows. The arrow is simply rubbed over the frog's body and it is ready to use. The poison remains strong for over a year.

1. The eggs are laid on a leaf

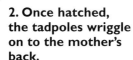

2. Once hatched, the tadpoles wriggle on to the mother's back.

3. She carries them to a leaf-pool high in a tree.

Caring for young

The female flaming arrow-poison frog looks after her tadpoles while they develop into frogs. She carries them up into a tree and places them in groups of about four in tiny pools of water contained in plants. She checks on them every few days and even gives them some unfertilised eggs to eat. The young are not poisonous at this stage, so they are very easy for other creatures to catch and eat.

Among the most beautiful of all arrow-poison frogs is **Dendrobates tinctorius**, with its shiny blue markings. It is one of the 55 poisonous species.

151

Size: 10 cm (4 in)
Range: Southeast Asia
Scientific name:
  Rhacophorus nigropalmatus

Wallace's flying frog

Wallace's flying frog

This frog does not really fly, but glides from tree to tree in the forest. The large webbed feet and flaps of skin on its legs act like a parachute to help it float as far as 12 m (39½ ft) through the air. It can even steer by changing the position of one or more of its feet. Little is known about this frog's breeding habits, but it is thought to lay its eggs in a mass of foam, which protects them while they incubate.

Termite frog

South African rain frog

This plump frog has small legs and a sprinkling of warty lumps on its back. It spends much of its life in underground burrows, which it digs with its strong back feet. It comes above ground only during wet weather to hunt insects and other small creatures.

Size: 5 cm (2 in)
Range: Africa, south of the Sahara
Scientific name:
  Phrynomerus bifasciatus

Termite frog

As its name suggests, termites and ants are the main food of this frog. It digs in burrows or climbs trees to find the insects. Its bright markings warn that its skin contains a nasty-tasting substance which irritates the mouth or skin of predators. Termite frogs breed in shallow pools. The jelly-coated eggs attach to plants or lie at the bottom of the pool until they hatch.

South African rain frog

Eastern narrow-mouthed frog

An excellent burrower, this small frog can disappear into the earth in a moment. It rests in a burrow during the day and comes out at night to hunt for insects such as ants. It breeds in summer when there is heavy rain.

Size: 3 cm (1¼ in)
Range: South Africa, Namibia, Botswana, Zimbabwe
Scientific name:
  Breviceps adspersus

Eastern narrow-mouthed frog

Size: 2–4 cm (¾–1½ in)
Range: southeast USA
Scientific name:
  Gastrophryne carolinensis

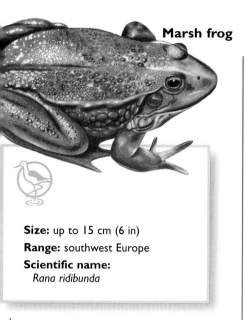
Marsh frog

Mottled burrowing frog

Mottled burrowing frog

This frog has a small pointed head, with a hard snout used for burrowing. It digs head first, pushing into the soil with its snout and clawing its way forwards with its strong legs. The female lays her large eggs in a burrow. When the young hatch, she digs a tunnel for the tadpoles to swim to the nearest water.

Size: up to 3 cm (1¼ in)
Range: northeast South Africa
Scientific name:
Hemisus marmoratum

Size: up to 15 cm (6 in)
Range: southwest Europe
Scientific name:
Rana ridibunda

Marsh frog

This noisy frog spends most of its life in water but comes out on to banks or to float on lily pads. It catches small invertebrates and also eats small birds and mammals. Males call night and day, particularly in the breeding season. The female lays thousands of eggs in several large clusters.

Common frog

Much of this frog's life is spent on land, feeding on insects, spiders and other small creatures. It breeds in spring, when males attract females with their deep croaking calls. They mate in water and the females lay clusters of 3,000 to 4,000 eggs.

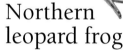

Northern leopard frog

This frog adapts to any watery home and eats almost any creatures it can find. If disturbed when hunting on land, it leaps away to water in a series of zigzagging jumps. In the breeding season, males attract females with low grunting calls. Each female lays about 20,000 eggs, which lie at the bottom of the water until they hatch about four weeks later.

Northern leopard frog

Size: 5–12.5 cm (2–5 in)
Range: most of northern North America, except Pacific coast
Scientific name: *Rana pipiens*

Bullfrog

The largest North American frog, the bullfrog lives in water but also spends time on land at the water's edge. It hunts at night, catching insects, fish, smaller frogs and even birds and snakes. It is a good jumper and can leap nine times its own length. In the breeding season, the female lays up to 20,000 eggs in water.

Size: 9–20.5 cm (3½–8 in)
Range: eastern and central USA
Scientific name:
Rana catesbeiana

Bullfrog

Common frog

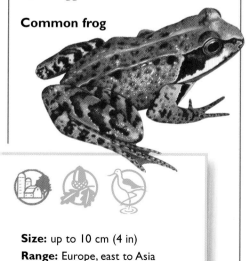

Size: up to 10 cm (4 in)
Range: Europe, east to Asia
Scientific name:
Rana temporaria

Why are some animals poisonous?

Many animals use poison for protection against enemies. By being unpleasant to eat, small creatures such as toads and caterpillars are able to defend themselves against much larger creatures. Many have colourful markings that serve as a warning to others – predators learn to link these bright colours with the unpleasant taste and stay away. Poison is also an effective weapon for hunters. They use it to paralyse or kill their prey before it can escape.

The **Oriental fire-bellied toad** has small poison glands all over its body, which produce an unpleasant-tasting substance. If threatened, the toad reveals the bright scarlet markings on the underside of its body to warn off its attacker.

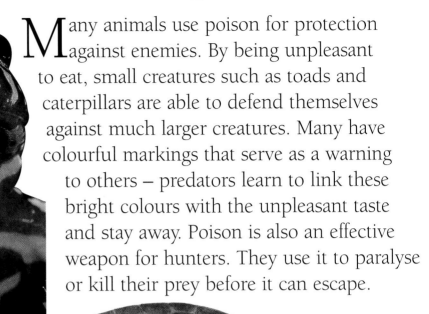

The **cobra** uses its poison to kill its prey. As it bites the victim, poison passes from glands in the mouth, through the special canals in the teeth at the front of the jaw. The snake may also spit out venom to defend itself against enemies.

154

The **scorpion** paralyses and kills prey with its poisonous sting. Near the sharp sting at the end of its body are poison glands. When the scorpion attacks, it swings the sting forward over its body and into the prey. Muscles force poison down into the hollow sting. Some scorpions have poison strong enough to kill a human.

The **monarch butterfly caterpillar** feeds on the poisonous milkweed plant. The poison in the plant does not affect the caterpillar but is stored in its body and makes it taste extremely unpleasant. Its bold stripes warn predators to leave it alone. When the caterpillar becomes a butterfly it remains poisonous.

Fish

There are more than 24,000 species of fish in the world today, more than any other type of vertebrate. They range from tiny species such as the pygmy goby, which is only about 1 cm (⅓ in) long, to giants such as the whale shark, which can measure as much as 12 m (39½ ft).

All fish live in water. There are at least 14,000 species in the sea, and the rest live in freshwater lakes and rivers all over the world. To enable them to breathe, fish have special structures called gills, which allow them to take oxygen from water. Instead of legs, they have fins and a tail to help them push their bodies through water.

Fish feed in a wide variety of ways. Some eat aquatic plants. Others catch tiny animals or strain them from the water through filterlike structures attached to their gills. Many are active, fast-moving hunters, with sharp teeth, while some, such as flatfish and angler fish, lie hidden on the seabed and wait for prey to come close enough to catch.

Like many other kinds of fish, these **bluestripe snappers** swim in a large group called a school or shoal. The exact reasons for schooling are not known, but there is certainly safety in numbers. Many predators are confused by the group, which can turn and change direction with breathtaking speed.

Lionfish

157

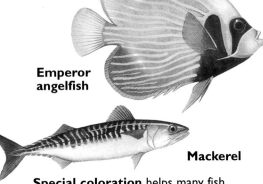

Emperor angelfish

Mackerel

Special coloration helps many fish hide from their enemies. The angelfish's markings and the mackerel's light belly and darker back break up their body outlines and make them harder to see.

GILLS OF BONY FISH

Mouth open   **Mouth closed**

Water

Gills

Gill flap

Gills closed   **Gills open**

How fish breathe

Fish breathe through special structures called gills at the sides of the head. These are made up of large numbers of delicate plates, packed with blood vessels. As water flows through the gills, molecules of oxygen pass into the blood, which is then carried around the body. The gills of a bony fish have one combined opening to the outside, which is covered by a protective flap. In sharks and rays, each gill has its own exit to the water.

GILLS OF SHARK

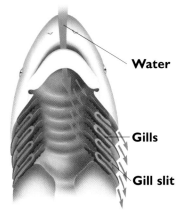

Water

Gills

Gill slit

What is a fish?

Fish were the first vertebrates – animals with backbones – to live on Earth. The earliest fish lived about 500 million years ago. All except for the the group that includes lampreys and hagfish have a backbone made of bones called vertebrae, although in the sharks and rays this is made of cartilage.

Structure of a fish

There are three main groups of fish and their relatives. The most primitive group includes the lampreys and hagfish. These fishlike animals have no jaws, only a suckerlike mouth. The second group includes all the sharks and rays. These are known as cartilaginous fish because their skeletons are made of a gristly substance called cartilage, not bone. The third, and largest, group contains the bony fish. As their name suggests, these fish have skeletons made of bone.

JAWLESS FISHLIKE ANIMAL

RIVER LAMPREY

Fin rays

Tail fin

Suckerlike mouth

A LAMPREY'S SUCKERLIKE MOUTH

Teeth

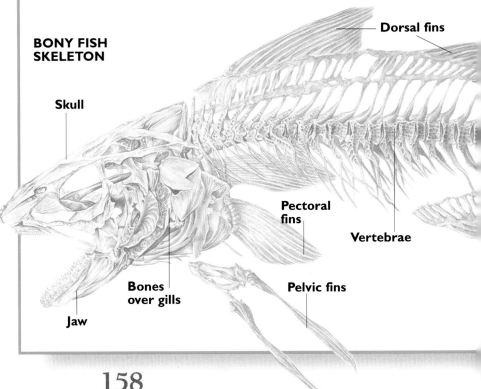

BONY FISH SKELETON

Dorsal fins

Skull

Pectoral fins

Vertebrae

Bones over gills

Pelvic fins

Jaw

Eggs and young

Most female fish lay large numbers of small eggs into the water. Males then release sperm to fertilise the eggs, which float in surface waters or sink to the bottom. The eggs hatch into tiny larvae, many of which are eaten by other creatures. Some survive to develop into juveniles, with a more adultlike body. The juveniles feed and grow into adult fish.

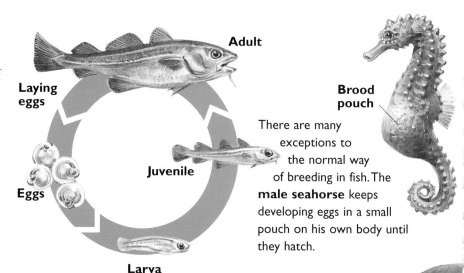

Adult

Laying eggs

Juvenile

Eggs

Larva

Brood pouch

There are many exceptions to the normal way of breeding in fish. The **male seahorse** keeps developing eggs in a small pouch on his own body until they hatch.

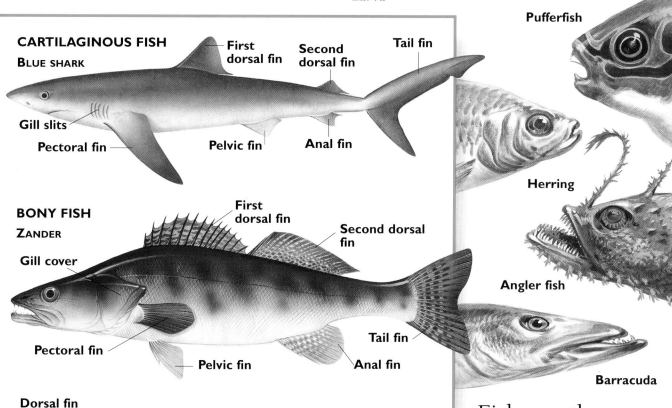

CARTILAGINOUS FISH
BLUE SHARK

First dorsal fin

Second dorsal fin

Tail fin

Gill slits

Pectoral fin

Pelvic fin

Anal fin

BONY FISH
ZANDER

First dorsal fin

Second dorsal fin

Gill cover

Pectoral fin

Pelvic fin

Tail fin

Anal fin

Dorsal fin

Tail fin

Anal fin

Pufferfish

Herring

Angler fish

Barracuda

Like all vertebrates, **fish** have a bony skull and a movable lower jaw. Special bones cover the gills on each side of a fish's head. In the fins there are small bones called fin rays. These bones keep the fins stiff and spread out.

Fish mouths

The mouth of a fish is adapted to suit the food that it eats. Fierce hunting fish, such as the barracuda, have a long snout and lots of sharp teeth for seizing prey. The angler uses its very wide mouth for engulfing prey that it lures near with its fishing rod. Many, such as the pufferfish, have a hard beaklike mouth for crushing hard-shelled creatures. The herring filters tiny animal plankton from the water through special structures linked to its gills called gill rakers.

Hagfish, lampreys, sharks and rays

Hagfish and lampreys are primitive fishlike animals that have no true jaws. Hagfish have a slitlike mouth surrounded by small tentacles. Lampreys have sucking discs for feeding on the blood of other creatures. All hagfish live in the sea, but there are some freshwater lampreys.

Sharks, sawfish, rays and their relatives are all cartilaginous fish – they have skeletons made of cartilage, not bone. There are about 850 known species of cartilaginous fish and all live in the sea. Most are active hunters, equipped with sharp-edged teeth in both jaws. A few of the largest, such as the whale shark, are not hunters. They filter small creatures from the water.

Mako shark

A powerful fish, with a slender body and a pointed head, the mako is a fast-swimming, aggressive hunter. It usually feeds on surface-living fish, such as tuna and mackerel. The female mako gives birth to live young, which develop inside her body.

Mako shark

Size: 3–4 m (10–13 ft)
Range: Atlantic, Pacific and Indian oceans
Scientific name: *Isurus oxyrinchus*

Greater sawfish

Size: 7.7 m (25½ ft)
Range: temperate and tropical oceans
Scientific name: *Pristis pectinata*

Hammerhead shark

The hammerhead has a broad head that extends to each side. There is one eye and one nostril on either side of the elongated head. This spacing of eyes and nostrils may improve the shark's sight and sense of smell.

Size: 4.3 m (14 ft)
Range: all oceans
Scientific name: *Sphyrna zygaena*

Hammerhead shark

Sandy dogfish

A small shark, the sandy dogfish lives on sandy and muddy seabeds, where it feeds on fish and bottom-living invertebrates. The female's eggs are laid in hard cases, which lodge among weeds or other objects. The young dogfish hatch 5 to 11 months later and are about 10 cm (4 in) long.

Sandy dogfish

Size: 60–100 cm (23½–39½ in)
Range: north Atlantic Ocean
Scientific name: *Scyliorhinus canicula*

Greater sawfish

Also known as the smalltooth, the greater sawfish has a long bladelike snout. Each side is studded with 24 or more large teeth. The sawfish lives on the seabed in shallow water and uses its saw to dig in the sand and mud for small invertebrates to eat. It may also swim into a school of smaller fish and lash its toothed saw from side to side to stun prey.

White shark

A large, aggressive hunter equipped with jagged triangular teeth, this shark kills seals, dolphins and even other sharks. It also scavenges dead animals and waste. White sharks have been involved in a number of attacks on humans.

Size: 61 cm (24 in)
Range: Arctic and north Atlantic oceans
Scientific name: *Myxine glutinosa*

Hagfish

Hagfish

The hagfish has no jaws, just a slitlike mouth surrounded by small tentacles. It feeds on crustaceans, but it also eats dead and dying fish. Using its toothed tongue, the hagfish bores into the prey's body and eats its flesh.

Sea lamprey

The adult sea lamprey is a blood-feeding parasite. It has no true jaws and uses its sucking, disclike mouth to attach itself to its victim so firmly that it is almost impossible to remove it. A special substance in its mouth keeps the host's blood flowing so the lamprey can feed. Victims often die from blood loss.

Size: 6 m (19½ ft)
Range: Atlantic, Pacific and Indian oceans
Scientific name: *Carcharodon carcharias*

Size: 90 cm (35½ in)
Range: Atlantic coasts and Mediterranean Sea
Scientific name: *Petromyzon marinus*

Sea lamprey

White shark

Atlantic manta

With its huge pointed pectoral fins, the manta is the biggest of the rays. Like the whale shark, this giant feeds mostly on tiny animal plankton, which it filters from the water. It also eats fish. The manta often basks near the surface with the tips of its pectoral fins out of the water.

Atlantic manta

Size: 12 m (39½ ft)
Range: all oceans
Scientific name: *Rhincodon typus*

Whale shark

Whale shark

The whale shark is the biggest of all fish. Despite its size, it is not a fierce hunter and eats tiny animal plankton that it filters from the water. The shark opens its mouth and takes in a rush of water, which contains lots of small creatures. The water flows out through the gill slits, leaving the plankton in the mouth.

Size: 5.2 m (17 ft) long; 6.7 m (22 ft) wide
Range: Atlantic Ocean
Scientific name: *Manta birostris*

Skates, rays and seabed sharks

There are more than 300 different species of skates and rays found worldwide. Most have an extremely broad flattened body and huge winglike fins, giving them a diamond shape. As they swim, the fish flap their fins up and down, and appear almost to be flying through the water. Skates and rays spend much of their lives on or near the seabed. Their flattened bodies make them hard to see as they lie half-covered with sand. Small openings, called spiracles, on the upper surface of the head allow them to breathe as they lie on the seabed. They feed mostly on molluscs, crustaceans and fish and they also scavenge any dead creatures and other waste that falls to the sea floor.

Sharks are usually thought of as fast-swimming fish in the surface waters of the sea, but some are seabed dwellers. Horn sharks, nurse sharks and carpet sharks lurk on the bottom, moving only to catch passing prey.

Nurse shark

A slow-moving bottom dweller, the nurse shark has lots of short sharp teeth, ideal for crushing shellfish. The sensitive fleshy whiskers on its flattened head are thought to help it find hidden prey on the seabed. This shark spends much of its time on the seabed and tends to crawl away if disturbed, rather than swim.

Skate

The skate's flattened body is covered with tiny spines, and a line of larger spines runs down the middle of the tail. The spines help the skate defend itself against attackers. The female lays her eggs in a leathery case with long tips at each corner, which is left on the seabed. When the young fish hatch, they are about 20 cm (7¾ in) long.

Horn shark

This shark has a long tapering body and a large blunt head. It gets its name from the sharp spines in front of the fins on its back. Active at night, it collects prey such as sea urchins, crabs and worms on the seabed. It crushes hard-shelled food with the large flat teeth at the back of its jaws.

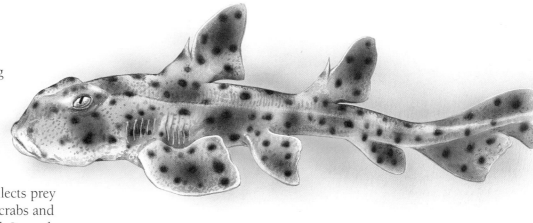

Camouflaged by its colouring and the many flaps of skin at the sides of its body, the **carpet shark** lies on the seabed waiting for prey to come near.

Sting ray

Eagle ray

Sting ray and eagle ray

Both of these fish have long whiplike tails which they use to lash out at prey and enemies. The spines are linked to venom glands and can cause serious injury to humans. Rays have flattened teeth with which they crush the hard shells of prey, such as crabs and molluscs.

Sturgeons, gars and relatives

All of these fish live in fresh water, but most sturgeons spend part of their life in the sea. They travel into rivers to lay their eggs, and the young remain there for several years, feeding and growing before making their first journey to the sea, where they spend their adult lives. Sturgeons are increasingly rare, partly because humans collect the female's unshed eggs to eat as a food called caviar. Gars, bichirs and bowfins are separate groups of fish. They generally occur in areas where there is a dense growth of water plants.

Goldeyes, pirarucus and elephant-snout fish belong to a group of about 220 species of freshwater fish. Most live in the southern half of the world, but there are two species of goldeyes in North America. They all eat fish and insects.

Bowfin

This fish lives in slow-moving waters with dense plant life. In spring, the male clears a hollow in the riverbed and makes a nest of plant roots and gravel. The female then lays her eggs and the male guards them for 8 to 10 days until they hatch.

Bowfin

Size: 91 cm (36 in)
Range: northeast USA
Scientific name: *Amia calva*

Longnose gar

As its name suggests, this gar has extremely long jaws, studded with sharp teeth. It hides among water plants, waiting for fish and shellfish to come near. It then dashes forward and seizes its prey. It lays eggs in spring in shallow water. The eggs are sticky and attach themselves to stones or waterweed so they are not carried away by the water current.

Size: 1.5 m (5 ft)
Range: North America
Scientific name:
Lepisosteus osseus

Bichir

A long-bodied fish covered with hard diamond-shaped scales, the bichir lives among water plants at the edges of rivers and lakes. It has an unusual dorsal fin made up of small flaglike sections, each supported by a bony ray. The bichir feeds mainly on fish, frogs and newts.

Size: 40 cm (15¾ in)
Range: central Africa
Scientific name:
Polypterus weeksi

Bichir

Longnose gar

164

Elephant-snout fish

This fish gets its name from its long trunklike snout. The muscles along its body are adapted to produce weak electric charges which set up an electric field in the water around the body. The fish can sense any disturbances in this field, which helps it find prey at night or in murky water.

Elephant-snout fish

Size: 80 cm (31½ in)
Range: Africa: Nile River
Scientific name:
Mormyrus kannume

Goldeye

The goldeye belongs to a small family of fish known as mooneyes. They have big golden eyes that provide good vision at night, when they are generally active. The goldeye has a large number of small fine teeth and it feeds mainly on insects and their larvae as well as on fish.

Goldeye

Size: 30–40 cm (11¾–15¾ in)
Range: North America
Scientific name:
Hiodon alosoides

Pirarucu

One of the largest freshwater fish in the world, the pirarucu may weigh up to 200 kg (440 lb). It has large scales on its body but none on its head. Other fish and insect larvae are its main food. Pirarucus breed in sandy-bottomed water. The eggs are laid in a hollow in the riverbed and the parents guard them until they hatch.

Size: up to 4 m (13 ft)
Range: South America
Scientific name:
Arapaima gigas

Pirarucu

Common sturgeon

Sturgeons spend most of their lives in the sea, feeding on worms and other invertebrates, but they lay their eggs in rivers. In spring, sturgeons migrate to rivers where each female lays thousands of sticky black eggs. The eggs hatch in about a week. The young fish remain in the river for about three years before travelling to the sea.

Size: 3 m (10 ft)
Range: European coastline
Scientific name:
Acipenser sturio

Common sturgeon

Paddlefish

Size: 2 m (6½ ft)
Range: USA: Mississippi River
Scientific name:
Polyodon spathula

Paddlefish

The paddlefish is a relative of the sturgeon. It swims with its large mouth open and its lower jaw dropped. Small creatures in the water are caught on comblike structures in the fish's mouth. Eggs are laid in spring. Newly hatched fish do not have long snouts, but they develop in two or three weeks.

Eels, tarpons and herrings

Most of these fish live in the sea, but some eels and tarpons spend at least part of their lives in fresh water. There are more than 730 species of eels. They live in all oceans, except in polar areas, and there are a few freshwater species. All have slender bodies and long fins on the back and belly.

The herring group includes more than 350 species, some of which are important food fish, such as herrings themselves, sardines and anchovies. Most are marine and live in schools in surface waters in the open sea or near coasts. The tarpons belong to a small family of marine fish that are related to eels and herrings. They are slender-bodied fish with deeply forked tails.

Sardine

The sardine is similar to the herring but has a more rounded body and larger scales. Shoals of sardines swim in surface waters, feeding on animal plankton. Sardines are a valued food fish and large numbers are caught every year.

Sardine

Size: 25 cm (9¾ in)
Range: European coasts
Scientific name:
 Sardina pilchardus

Alewife

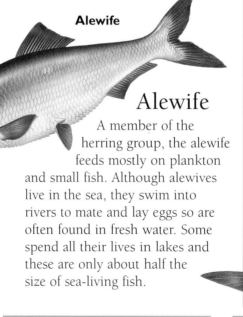

Alewife

A member of the herring group, the alewife feeds mostly on plankton and small fish. Although alewives live in the sea, they swim into rivers to mate and lay eggs so are often found in fresh water. Some spend all their lives in lakes and these are only about half the size of sea-living fish.

Size: 38 cm (15 in)
Range: North American Atlantic coast
Scientific name:
 Alosa pseudoharengus

Tarpon

A strong fast-swimming fish, the tarpon feeds on many types of fish and on crabs. The female lays millions of eggs in coastal waters, but many of the larvae drift into rivers, where they remain until they grow larger.

Tarpon

Size: 1.2–2.4 m (4–7¾ ft)
Range: Atlantic Ocean
Scientific name:
 Tarpon atlanticus

Atlantic herring

Herrings have long been an important food for humans, and large numbers of these fish are caught every year. In the sea, they are also preyed on by birds, other fish, dolphins and seals. Herrings themselves feed on plankton, small crustaceans and fish.

Atlantic herring

Size: 40 cm (15¾ in)
Range: Atlantic and Pacific oceans
Scientific name:
 Clupea harengus

Snipe eel

This deep-sea eel has an extremely long thin body, with fins that run almost its whole length. It has narrow beaklike jaws and sharp backwards-facing teeth which it uses to trap prey such as fish and crustaceans.

Snipe eel

Size: 1–1.2 m (3¼–4 ft)
Range: Atlantic, Pacific and Indian oceans
Scientific name:
    Nemichthys scolopaceus

Spiny-eel

Size: 1.2 m (4 ft)
Range: north Atlantic Ocean
Scientific name:
    Notacanthus chemnitzii

Spiny-eel

The spiny-eel has a long slender body, but it is not a true eel. It has short spines on its back and belly. Little is known about this deep-sea fish, but it is thought to feed head down on the seabed, eating bottom-living animals such as sea anemones.

Moray

Like all of the 100 or so different species of moray eels found in warm seas, this moray has a scaleless, boldly patterned body, powerful jaws and strong sharp teeth. A fierce hunter, the moray usually hides among underwater rocks with only its head showing, watching out for prey such as fish, squid and cuttlefish.

Moray

Size: 1.3 m (4¼ ft)
Range: Atlantic coastal waters and Mediterranean Sea
Scientific name:
    Muraena helena

European eel

Size: 50–100 cm (19¾–39½ in)
Range: north Atlantic Ocean
Scientific name:
    Anguilla anguilla

Conger eel

Conger eel

This eel is common on rocky North Atlantic shores. It usually lives in shallow water, where it hides among rocks and comes out to find prey such as fish and octopus. Conger eels travel to deeper water to mate and lay their eggs. The eggs hatch into small transparent larvae which drift in the sea for a year or two before they develop into small eels.

Size: 2.7 m (8¾ ft)
Range: coastal waters of north Atlantic Ocean
Scientific name: *Conger conger*

European eel

Young eels live in fresh water, where they feed on insects, crustaceans and fish. When they are ready to breed they swim to the sea, where they mate, lay their eggs, then die. The eggs hatch and the larvae drift in surface waters for about three years. They then swim into rivers and the cycle starts again.

167

Carp, bream and piranhas

Carp, bream, roach and their relatives, such as the bigmouth buffalo and the white sucker, belong to a group of about 2,700 freshwater fish. They dominate the streams, rivers and lakes of Europe, northern Asia and North America and are also found in Africa. Most have scales on the body, but not on the head, and a single fin on the back. These fish eat a wide range of prey and some also feed on plant material.

Pacus and piranhas belong to a separate group of freshwater fish, most of which live in lakes and rivers in Central and South America. Some relatives of the piranhas also live in Africa. Flesh-eating piranhas have sharp teeth for chopping flesh from their victims.

Goldfish

The colourful goldfish belongs to the carp family. In the wild, it lives in ponds and lakes where there are plenty of water plants, but it is best known as an ornamental fish, bred for keeping in aquariums and ornamental pools. Goldfish are now found all over the world.

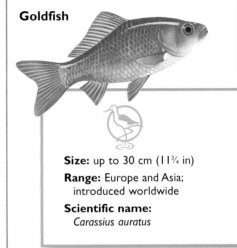

Goldfish

Size: up to 30 cm (11¾ in)

Range: Europe and Asia; introduced worldwide

Scientific name: *Carassius auratus*

Red piranha

Red piranha

Size: up to 30 cm (11¾ in)

Range: northern South America

Scientific name: *Serrasalmus nattereri*

Piranhas are not large fish, but they swim in such large shoals that together they can catch and kill animals much larger than themselves. There are reports of shoals of piranhas stripping animals such as cows of their flesh in minutes.

Pacu

Not all piranhas are fierce hunters. Some are peaceful plant-eating fish, such as the pacu. These fish feed on the many fruits and seeds that fall from the forest trees bordering the rivers where they live. They use their strong teeth to crush them. Plant-eating piranhas are slower swimmers than the hunting species and they do not have such powerful jaws.

Size: 70 cm (27½ in)

Range: South America

Scientific name: *Colossoma nigripinnis*

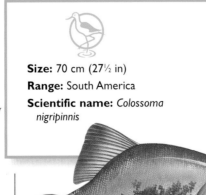

Pacu

Carp

The carp is a sturdy deep-bodied fish. It usually lives in slow-moving water where there is plenty of plant life and feeds mostly on crustaceans and insect larvae as well as some plants. The eggs are laid in shallow water, where they stick to plants until they hatch.

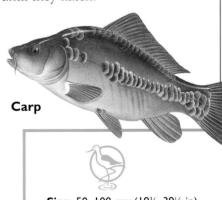

Carp

Size: 50–100 cm; (19¾–39½ in)

Range: southern Europe; introduced into many other areas

Scientific name: *Cyprinus carpio*

Bigmouth buffalo

This powerful fish feeds on crustaceans and insect larvae as well as some plant material. In spring, adults gather in shallow water, where females lay as many as 500,000 eggs. The young fish stay in the shallow breeding area for some months, feeding on plankton.

Size: 1 m (3¼ ft)
Range: North America
Scientific name:
Ictiobus cyprinellus

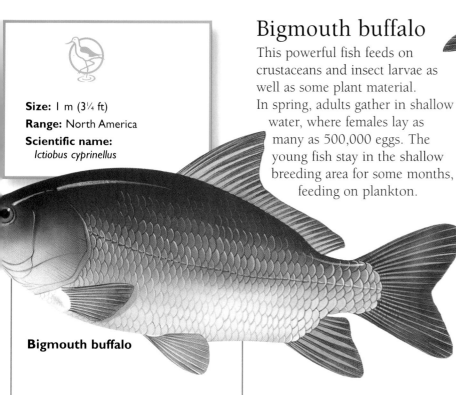

Bigmouth buffalo

Roach

Size: 35–46 cm (13¾–18 in)
Range: Europe and western Asia
Scientific name:
Rutilus rutilus

Roach

This common river fish feeds on insects and their larvae as well as molluscs, crustaceans and plants. It, in turn, is an important food for many fish-eating birds and mammals. Roach breed in shallow water and the eggs stick to plants while they develop. The young hatch in about two weeks.

White sucker

This bottom-living fish has thick suckerlike lips which give it its common name. It feeds on insect larvae, crustaceans and molluscs as well as some plants. White suckers breed in spring, laying their eggs at night in gravel-bottomed streams. The eggs sink to the bottom, where they stay among the gravel until they hatch.

Size: 30–52 cm (11¾–20½ in)
Range: North America
Scientific name:
Catostomus commersoni

White sucker

Tench

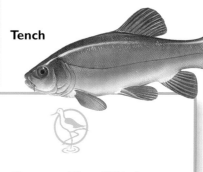

Size: up to 70 cm (27½ in)
Range: Europe and western to central Asia
Scientific name: Tinca tinca

Bream

This fish has a tubelike mouth which it uses to gather insect larvae, snails and worms from the river bottom. It lives in shoals and usually feeds at night. Bream breed in late spring or summer in shallow water. The eggs stick to water plants and hatch in about 12 days.

Tench

A relative of the carp, the tench has a thickset body and rounded fins. The scales on the body are extremely small and covered with mucus. It usually feeds on the river or lakebed on insect larvae, crustaceans and molluscs. Tench breed in shallow water, shedding their eggs on to plants.

Size: 23–28 cm (9–11 in)
Range: Europe, northern Asia
Scientific name:
Abramis brama

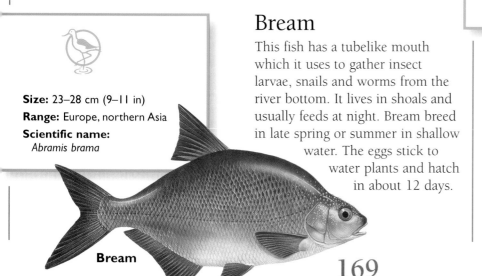

Bream

169

Catfish and relatives

There are more than 2,400 species in the catfish group, ranging from tiny fish just over 2 cm (¾ in) long to giant forms measuring 1.5 m (5 ft) or more and weighing as much as 45 kg (100 lb). Most live in rivers and freshwater lakes in the warmer parts of the world, but there are a number of sea-living species. More catfish live in South America than anywhere else. Catfish do not have ordinary scales, but some have bony plates which cover their bodies like jointed armour. They are bottom dwellers and find their food by touch and taste, digging in the mud of a river or lakebed until the sensitive whiskers, or barbels, around their mouth find prey. The whiskered appearance these barbels give is the reason for the catfish's common name.

Australian freshwater catfish

The fins of this catfish run right around its body from its back to its belly. The spines on its back and on its pectoral fins can cause painful wounds if touched. Sensory whiskers, or barbels, around the mouth help it find food, mainly mussels, prawns and worms.

Australian freshwater catfish

Size: 60 cm (23½ in)
Range: south and east Australia
Scientific name:
    Tandanus tandanus

Surubim

This South American catfish has a long snout and a slender body, marked with dark stripes and blotches. It spends most of its life on the riverbed, where it feeds on invertebrate animals. The sensitive whiskers, or barbels, around its mouth help it find food.

Size: 50–90 cm (19¾–35½ in)
Range: South America
Scientific name:
    Pseudoplatystoma fasciatum

Surubim

Candirú

A tiny delicate catfish, the candirú is a parasite – it lives on the blood of other fish. With small fish, it simply bites the skin and then feeds, but it may get inside the gill system of larger fish and stay there sucking blood. It is usually active at night and buries itself in the riverbed when not feeding.

Candirú

Size: 2.5 cm (1 in)
Range: South America
Scientific name:
    Vandellia cirrhosa

Cascarudo

The body of this little catfish is covered with overlapping bony plates, which help protect it from enemies. In the breeding season, the male fish makes a nest for the eggs among floating plants by blowing bubbles of air and mucus to form a foamy mass.

Size: 18 cm (7 in)
Range: tropical South America
Scientific name:
    Callichthys callichthys

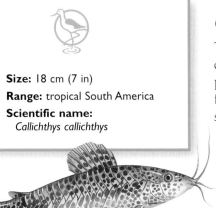

Cascarudo

Glass catfish

As its name suggests, this fish is transparent and many of the internal organs can be seen through the body. It has a long anal fin, a tiny dorsal fin and a slightly lopsided tail fin. It sometimes balances vertically on the lower part of this tail fin. Unlike most catfish, it moves in small schools in surface waters during the day. It has become a popular species with aquarium owners.

Size: 10 cm (4 in)
Range: Malaysia, Indonesia
Scientific name:
Kryptopterus bicirrhis

Glass catfish

Blue catfish

One of the largest catfish in North America, the blue catfish can grow to over 45 kg (100 lb) and is an important food fish. It often lives in faster-moving water than other catfish and is even found in rapids and waterfalls. It feeds on fish and crayfish. Its eggs are laid on the river- or lakebed and both parents guard the nest and then the young.

Size: 1.5 m (5 ft)
Range: USA, Mexico
Scientific name:
Ictalurus furcatus

Blue catfish

Sea catfish

This sea-living catfish is most active at night, when it feeds on crabs, shrimps and fish. They breed in summer and as the eggs are laid, the male takes them in his mouth, where they incubate. He cannot eat during this time. The young fish may also swim into the male's mouth for safety after hatching.

Size: 30 cm (11¾ in)
Range: west Atlantic Ocean
Scientific name:
Aruis felis

Sea catfish

Walking catfish

This catfish lives in ponds or temporary pools that may disappear in long dry periods. When this happens, the fish can move over land to another pool, making snakelike movements of its body and using its pectoral fins as "legs". It feeds on fish and invertebrate animals.

Walking catfish

Size: 30 cm (11¾ in)
Range: India, Sri Lanka, Southeast Asia
Scientific name:
Clarias batrachus

Wels

A large catfish, the wels has a broad head and long anal fin. It lives in slow-moving or still waters and is usually active at night, hiding in plants near the bottom during the day. Fish are its main food, but it also eats frogs, birds and even small mammals such as water voles.

Size: 1–3 m (3¼–10 ft)
Range: central and eastern Europe
Scientific name:
Silurus glanis

Wels

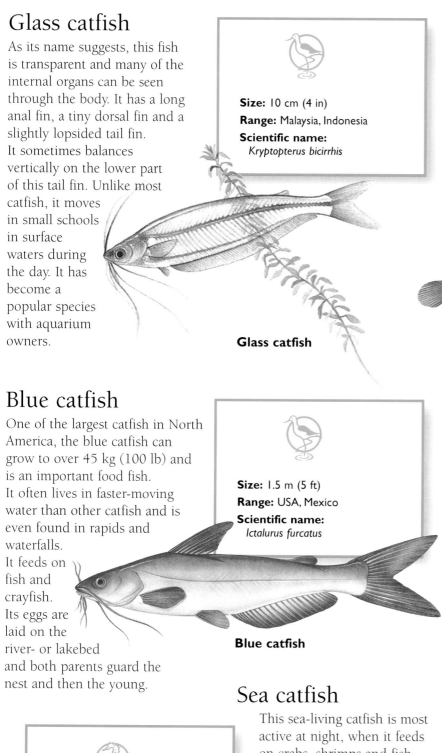

Electric eel, salmon, hatchetfish and pike

The electric eel is the only species in its family. It is not a true eel but has a similar long body and, as its name suggests, is able to produce electric charges.

In a separate group is the hatchetfish, a deep-sea fish which has light-producing organs on its body. These help the hatchetfish recognise its own kind in the darkness of the deep sea and to confuse predators.

The salmon family contains about 76 species which live in both fresh water and the sea. Some migrate from the sea into rivers to lay eggs. The smelts belong to a different group of sea fish but they, too, travel up rivers to breed. Pike are a small group of freshwater fish.

Hatchetfish

This fish normally lives in water 400–600 m (1,300–2,000 ft) deep, but each night it comes up near the surface to find plankton to eat. On its belly are rows of light-producing organs, which give out a pale blue light. This confuses predators about the size and shape of the fish's body, making it harder to catch.

Hatchetfish

Size: 7 cm (2¾ in)

Range: warm and tropical areas of all oceans

Scientific name: *Argyropelecus aculeatus*

Northern pike

A fierce predator, the pike lurks among plants, keeping watch for any prey. Young pike feed mainly on invertebrates, but adults catch other fish and even birds and mammals. Female pike are larger than males and may weigh 23 kg (50 lb) or more.

Northern pike

Size: 1.5 m (5 ft)

Range: northern Europe, Russia, Alaska, Canada, northern USA

Scientific name: *Esox lucius*

Smelt

Smelts are sea-living fish which go into fresh water to breed. In winter, adult fish leave the sea to travel up rivers. In spring, the females shed their eggs on to gravel on the riverbed or on to plants. When the young fish are large enough, they swim to the sea, where they grow and mature.

Size: 30 cm (11¾ in)

Range: north Atlantic Ocean

Scientific name: *Osmerus eperlanus*

Smelt

Electric eel

Special muscles in the electric eel's body release high-voltage electric charges into the water. The eel uses these shocks to kill prey, usually other fish, or to defend itself from enemies. The charge can even give a human a severe shock.

Electric eel

Size: 2.4 m (7¾ ft)

Range: South America

Scientific name: *Electrophorus electricus*

Grayling

A member of the salmon family, the grayling has a high sail-like fin on its back and a forked tail. It eats insects and their larvae as well as crustaceans and molluscs. In spring, the female makes a hollow in gravel in shallow water for her eggs. The eggs hatch three to four weeks later.

Grayling

Size: 46 cm (18 in)
Range: northern Europe
Scientific name:
  Thymallus thymallus

Arctic charr

The Arctic charr spends most of its life in polar seas, feeding on fish and molluscs. When they are ready to breed, they swim into rivers, where the females lay eggs among gravel on the riverbed. The young eventually make their way back to the sea. Some Arctic charr live in lakes.

Size: 25–96 cm (9¾–37¾ in)
Range: Arctic and north Atlantic oceans
Scientific name:
  Salvelinus alpinus

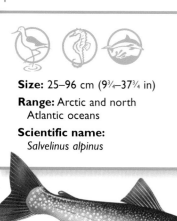

Arctic charr

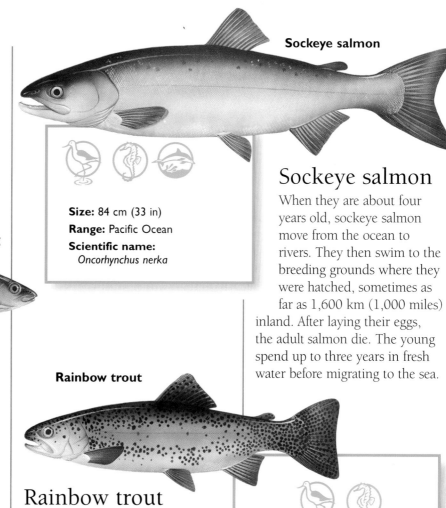

Sockeye salmon

Size: 84 cm (33 in)
Range: Pacific Ocean
Scientific name:
  Oncorhynchus nerka

Sockeye salmon

When they are about four years old, sockeye salmon move from the ocean to rivers. They then swim to the breeding grounds where they were hatched, sometimes as far as 1,600 km (1,000 miles) inland. After laying their eggs, the adult salmon die. The young spend up to three years in fresh water before migrating to the sea.

Rainbow trout

Rainbow trout

Now farmed in large quantities, rainbow trout are an important food fish. In the wild, rainbow trout live in rivers, although some spend part of their lives in the sea. In spring, the female makes a shallow nest in a stream and lays her eggs, which are then fertilised and covered over by the male.

Size: up to 1 m (3¼ ft)
Range: western North America; introduced worldwide
Scientific name: *Salmo gairdneri*

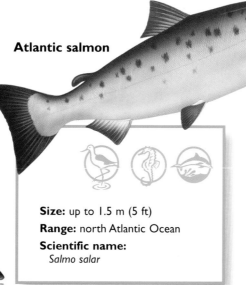

Atlantic salmon

Size: up to 1.5 m (5 ft)
Range: north Atlantic Ocean
Scientific name:
  Salmo salar

Atlantic salmon

Like the sockeye, most Atlantic salmon swim into rivers to breed. The female makes a shallow nest on the riverbed in winter and lays her eggs, which are fertilised by the male. The eggs hatch the following spring and the young spend two to six years in the river before going to sea.

Cod, anglers and cusk-eels

There are about 480 species of fish in the cod group, of which only 5 live in fresh water. The rest live in the sea, mostly in the northern half of the world, and include some of the most popular of all food fish such as cod, haddock, hake and ling. They hunt for their food, preying on other fish and invertebrate creatures. Many have a sensory whisker, or barbel, on the chin which helps them find food on the seabed.

The anglers include about 300 species of fish. All have a large head and an extremely wide mouth filled with rows of sharp teeth. Most have a special spine on the head which they use as a lure to attract prey.

Cusk-eels belong to a separate group and are small eel-like fish.

New Providence cusk-eel

This little eel-like fish was discovered in 1967 and is known only from a few freshwater pools in the Bahamas. It has a broad flattened head and a tapering body, with a continuous back, tail and anal fin. Most of its head is bare of scales, but it does have small scales covering its body.

New Providence cusk-eel

Size: 11 cm (4¼ in)
Range: Bahamas
Scientific name:
Lucifuga spelaeotes

Burbot

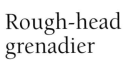

Size: 50–100 cm (19¾–39½ in)
Range: Canada, northern USA, northern Europe, Asia
Scientific name: Lota lota

Rough-head grenadier

A relative of the cod, the rough-head grenadier is a deep-sea fish with a large head and a tapering tail. Its body scales are rough and toothed. Males make loud sounds by vibrating the swim bladder (a gas-filled sac inside the body) with special muscles.

Rough-head grenadier

Size: 90–100 cm (35½–39½ in)
Range: north Atlantic Ocean
Scientific name:
Macrourus berglax

Burbot

One of the few fish in the cod group that lives in fresh water, the burbot hides among water plants by day and comes out at dawn and dusk to feed. Adults eat fish, crustaceans and insects, while young burbot feed on insect larvae and small shrimps. They lay their eggs at night in winter. One female may lay as many as three million eggs.

174

Ling

The ling is most common in rocky-bottomed waters, where it eats fish and large crustaceans. Although usually a deep-water fish, it may live in shallower areas where there are rocks. It breeds in spring and summer and one female may lay as many as 60 million eggs.

Ling

Size: 1.5–2 m (5–6½ ft)
Range: northeast Atlantic Ocean
Scientific name:
Molva molva

Size: 90 cm (35½ in)
Range: north Pacific Ocean
Scientific name:
Theragra chalcogramma

Pollock

Pollock

The pollock has a long tapering body, three fins on its back and two on its underside. Its head and mouth are large and it has bigger eyes than most other cod. Unlike most cod, it feeds in mid-waters, catching crustaceans and small fish.

Atlantic cod

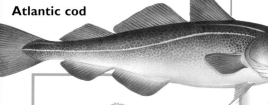

Atlantic cod

The cod has three fins on its back and a single long whisker, or barbel, on its chin. Its mouth is large and it has many small teeth. Cod usually swim in schools in surface waters but will search for food such as fish and worms on the seabed. Cod is an extremely valuable food fish for humans.

Size: 1.2 m (4 ft)
Range: north Atlantic Ocean
Scientific name:
Gadus morhua

Football fish

This deep-sea angler has a round body studded with bony plates, each with a central spine. On its head is a lure, which carries a light-producing organ. It uses this lure to attract prey in the darkness of the deep sea.

Football fish

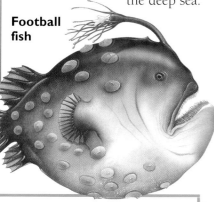

Size: 60 cm (23½ in)
Range: all oceans
Scientific name:
Himantolophus groenlandicus

Haddock

The haddock is a member of the cod family and feeds on bottom-living worms, molluscs and brittlestars as well as fish. It gathers in shoals to spawn and the eggs are left to float in the surface waters until they hatch. Young haddock often shelter among the tentacles of large jellyfish.

Size: 76 cm (30 in)
Range: north Atlantic Ocean
Scientific name:
Melanogrammus aeglefinus

Haddock

Angler

On its large head, the angler has a spine tipped with a flap of skin. It uses this as a fishing lure. The fish lies on the seabed and moves its lure to attract other fish. When something comes within reach, the angler opens its huge mouth and water flows in, together with the prey.

Angler

Size: 1–2 m (3¼–6½ ft)
Range: European coasts
Scientific name:
Lophius piscatorius

Perchlike fish

This is the largest and most varied of all groups of fish, and species live in almost every watery habitat. This group includes at least 9,300 types of fish such as the sea basses, cichlids, gobies and wrasses. They have a wide range of body forms and include fish as different as the barracuda, angelfish, swordfish and siamese fightingfish. Despite their differences, all perchlike fish have one or two fins on the back and most have pelvic fins close to the head. The pelvic fins usually have a spine and five rays.

Orange-throat darter

This little member of the perch family feeds on insects and animal plankton. A breeding male has an orange throat and breast, while the female has a pale throat. The male chooses a nest site in a river and guards the eggs once they are laid.

Orange-throat darter

Size: 8 cm (3¼ in)
Range: central USA
Scientific name:
  Etheostoma spectabile

Perch

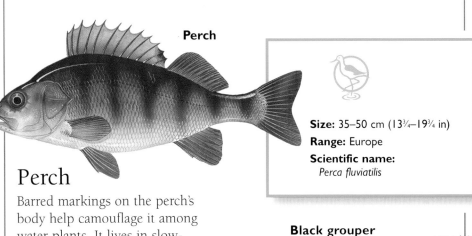

Size: 35–50 cm (13¾–19¾ in)
Range: Europe
Scientific name:
  Perca fluviatilis

Perch

Barred markings on the perch's body help camouflage it among water plants. It lives in slow-moving water and feeds on fish. Perch breed in shallow water in spring. The eggs are shed in long strings which wind around plants or other objects. They hatch in about eight days and the young fish feed on plankton.

Black grouper

Size: 1.2 m (4 ft)
Range: Atlantic coastal waters and Caribbean Sea
Scientific name:
  Mycteroperca bonaci

Black grouper

This common grouper may weigh up to 23 kg (50 lb) when fully grown. It has a large head and irregular dark markings on the sides of its body. It is not a particularly fast-moving fish and tends to lurk among rocks, waiting for prey to swim by. When something comes near, the grouper opens its large mouth and sucks in the prey with a mouthful of water. Young fish usually stay in shallow coastal areas, but adults move into deeper waters.

Greater amberjack

A relative of the pompano, the greater amberjack is a large fish with a sleek body and a deeply forked tail. It feeds on many species of fish and is itself caught as a food fish.

Size: up to 1.8 m (6 ft)
Range: west Atlantic Ocean
Scientific name:
  Seriola dumerili

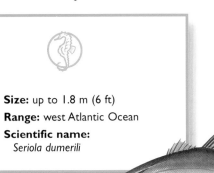

Greater amberjack

Bluefish

An extremely fierce hunter, the bluefish kills more prey than it can eat and feeds on almost any fish, including young of its own species. Shoals of bluefish travel together, often following shoals of prey fish. Young bluefish, which are known as snappers, also form their own shoals.

Bluefish

Size: up to 1.2 m (4 ft)

Range: warm and tropical waters of Atlantic, Indian and western Pacific oceans

Scientific name: *Pomatomus saltatrix*

Pompano

The pompano has a rounded snout and a fairly deep body, which tapers sharply to a forked tail. It feeds mainly on molluscs and crustaceans, which it finds in the mud and sand of the seabed. It is an excellent and valuable food fish.

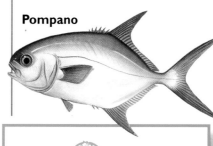

Pompano

Size: 45–65 cm (17¾–25½ in)

Range: west Atlantic Ocean

Scientific name: *Trachinotus carolinus*

Giant sea bass

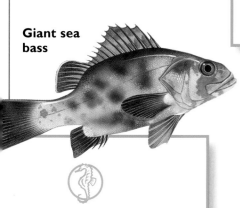

Size: 2 m (6½ ft)

Range: Pacific Ocean

Scientific name: *Sterolepis gigas*

Giant sea bass

This sea bass really is a giant. Some weigh more than 250 kg (550 lb) and live for more than 70 years. They eat fish and crustaceans and are themselves popular as food fish. Young fish are reddish in colour and deeper bodied than adults. They gradually develop the adult appearance by the time they are about 12 or 13 years old.

Size: up to 1.5 m (5 ft)

Range: warm and tropical waters of all oceans

Scientific name: *Coryphaena hippurus*

Dolphinfish

Dolphinfish

The brightly coloured dolphinfish is easily identified by the large fin which runs along its back. The forehead of the male fish becomes steeper as he grows older; otherwise male and female look alike. Dolphinfish move in small shoals and eat fish, squid and crustaceans. They are often seen around patches of floating seaweed, where their prey may hide.

Size: 76 cm (30 in)

Range: west Atlantic Ocean

Scientific name: *Ocyurus chrysurus*

Yellowtail snapper

Snappers are common around coral reefs and are a popular fish for humans to eat. This species is easily recognised by its bright yellow tail and the yellow stripe along each side. It feeds mostly on other fish and small crustaceans.

Yellowtail snapper

Blue parrotfish

Size: up to 1.2 m (4 ft)

Range: west Atlantic Ocean and Caribbean Sea

Scientific name:
Scarus coeruleus

Blue parrotfish

As its name suggests, this fish has beaklike jaws. Its teeth are joined together to form strong plates, which it uses to scrape algae and coral reefs. When young, these parrotfish are light blue. They turn darker blue as they get older. Old males also develop a bump on the snout

Clown anemonefish

This boldly striped fish lives among the tentacles of large sea anemones. It sometimes cleans waste from its host, and it may help to attract other fish for the anemone to catch and eat. The anemone's stinging tentacles do not harm the anemonefish.

Clown anemonefish

Size: 6 cm (2¼ in)

Range: Pacific Ocean

Scientific name:
Amphiprion percula

Queen angelfish

Despite its colourful markings, this angelfish can be difficult to see among the bright corals. It has long fins on its back and belly which extend past the tail fin. It feeds on sponges and other invertebrate animals. Young queen angelfish may act as cleaners – they pick and eat parasites off other fish.

Size: up to 45 cm (17¾ in)

Range: Atlantic Ocean and Caribbean Sea

Scientific name:
Holacanthus ciliaris

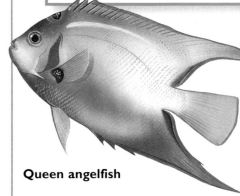

Queen angelfish

Sweetlip emperor

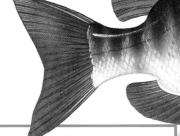

Copperband butterfly fish

Copperband butterfly fish

This fish uses its long beaklike snout to reach into crevices in the coral and find small creatures to eat. The large "eyespot" near its tail fin may confuse predators into thinking the copperband is larger than it really is.

Size: 20 cm (7¾ in)

Range: Indian and Pacific oceans

Scientific name:
Chelmon rostratus

Size: 90 cm (35½ in)

Range: Australia

Scientific name:
Lethrinus chrysostomus

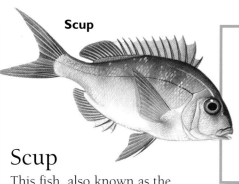

Scup

Scup

This fish, also known as the northern porgy, has a deep body, a strongly forked tail and spines on both its dorsal and anal fins. It finds food such as crustaceans and worms on the seabed. In spring, the adults breed in coastal waters and the eggs float freely until they hatch.

Size: 46 cm (18 in)
Range: Atlantic coast of North America
Scientific name:
Stenotomus chrysops

Size: 35–50 cm (13¾–19¾ in)
Range: Atlantic Ocean and Mediterranean Sea
Scientific name:
Pagellus bogaraveo

Red sea bream

Black drum

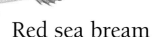

Red sea bream

This fish has a reddish flush to its body and fins, and a dark spot above its pectoral fin. Young red sea bream are paler in colour and may not have a dark spot. The young fish swim in large shoals in shallow waters, feeding on crustaceans. Adults live in smaller groups in deeper waters and eat fish as well as crustaceans.

Size: 1.2–1.8 m (4–6 ft)
Range: west Atlantic Ocean
Scientific name:
Pogonias cromis

Black drum

This large fish can weigh as much as 66 kg (146 lb). A bottom feeder, it eats molluscs and crustaceans, which it is able to crush with the special flat teeth in its throat. Oysters are a favourite food and black drums can cause a great deal of damage to commercial oyster beds. Despite their size, black drums are not a popular food fish.

Size: 40 cm (15¾ in)
Range: east Atlantic Ocean and Mediterranean Sea
Scientific name:
Mullus surmuletus

Sweetlip emperor

This heavy-bodied fish is one of the many that hunt for their food around coral reefs. It has a rather large head for its body, a long snout and no scales on its cheeks. It has deep red fins, dark barring on its sides and red patches around the eyes. It can grow to more than 9 kg (20 lb) and is an extremely popular food fish.

Red mullet

Red mullet

This fish searches for food on the seabed, using the sensory whiskers, or barbels, on its chin to help it find bottom-living invertebrates. Once prey is found, the red mullet digs it out of the sand or mud. It is able to change colour to blend in with its surroundings, varying between day and night.

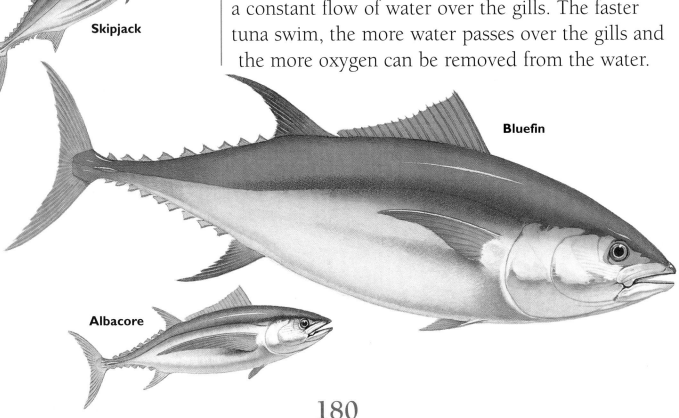

Bigeye

Tuna

Types of tuna

The bluefin is the biggest of the tuna. It can grow up to 3 m (10 ft) long and weigh more than 540 kg (1,200 lb) – as much as seven or eight people. A fast swimmer, the bluefin has been known to cross the Atlantic in 199 days. The bigeye tuna grows to nearly 2.4 m (7¾ ft) long and can weigh more than 180 kg (400 lb). The albacore and skipjack are smaller – up to 1.5 m (5 ft) and 90 cm (35½ in), respectively. The skipjack gets its name from its habit of sometimes "skipping" over the surface of the water as it chases its prey.

Skipjack

Albacore

A mong the fastest of all fish, tuna are shaped for speed and can swim at 80 km an hour (50 mph). They are the most streamlined of all fish, with a pointed head and a torpedo-shaped body tapering to a narrow tail stalk and a crescent tail. The 13 species of tuna live in the surface waters of warm and tropical oceans. All are hunters which feed mainly on fish and squid. Many swim in large schools, but the biggest fish swim in smaller groups or alone.

Tuna rarely, if ever, stop swimming because they have to breathe. They swim with their mouth open so there is a constant flow of water over the gills. Fish obtain oxygen from water, not air; the oxygen is taken out of the water flowing past the gills. Most fish have to pump water over the gills by muscle action in order to obtain oxygen. Tuna, however, must keep swimming at all times to create a constant flow of water over the gills. The faster tuna swim, the more water passes over the gills and the more oxygen can be removed from the water.

Bluefin

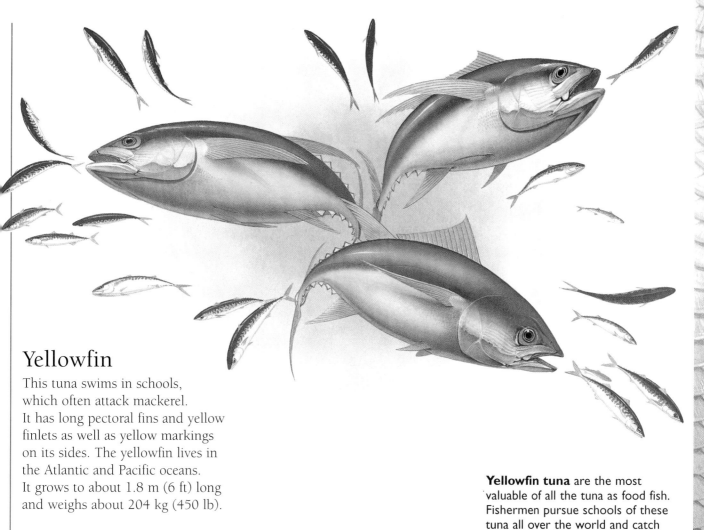

Yellowfin

This tuna swims in schools,
which often attack mackerel.
It has long pectoral fins and yellow
finlets as well as yellow markings
on its sides. The yellowfin lives in
the Atlantic and Pacific oceans.
It grows to about 1.8 m (6 ft) long
and weighs about 204 kg (450 lb).

Yellowfin tuna are the most
valuable of all the tuna as food fish.
Fishermen pursue schools of these
tuna all over the world and catch
large numbers.

Blue tang

This fish has extremely sharp movable spines on each side of its tail which it can raise to wound an enemy. The young are bright yellow with blue markings. This colour changes as the fish matures, becoming blue all over by the time it is an adult.

Size: 30.5 cm (12 in)
Range: west Atlantic Ocean and Caribbean Sea
Scientific name:
  Acanthurus coeruleus

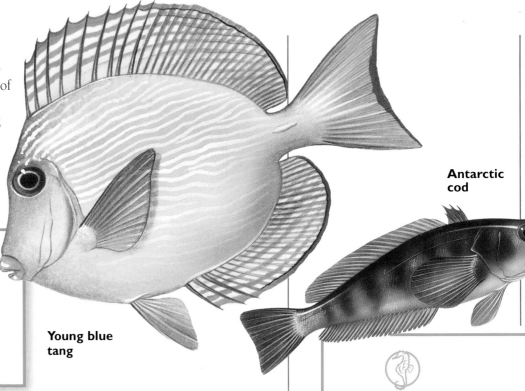

Young blue tang

Antarctic cod

Moorish idol

This spectacular fish has bold stripes and a protruding snout. Its body is deep and it has long swept-back fins. Although it is a relative of the blue tang, the moorish idol does not have tail spines. But the young fish does have a sharp spine at each corner of its mouth. These spines drop off as the fish grows bigger.

Size: 18 cm (7 in)
Range: Indian and Pacific oceans
Scientific name:
  Zanclus cornutus

Moorish idol

Size: 61 cm (24 in)
Range: Antarctic coasts
Scientific name:
  Notothenia coriiceps

Antarctic cod

This fish belongs to a group known as icefish. Many of them have a special substance in their blood that lowers its freezing point. Because of this, the icefish are able to survive at temperatures as low as -1.9°C (28.5°F), at which most fish would freeze to death. This cod is a bottom dweller and eats molluscs, crustaceans and worms as well as some algae.

Atlantic spadefish

This fish has a deep body, which is very flattened from side to side, and sweeping dorsal and anal fins. Its coloration changes as it grows. Young fish are black, becoming silvery grey as they grow, with dark vertical bars down the sides. These become less clear in large adults. Spadefish feed mostly on small invertebrates.

Atlantic spadefish

Size: 46–90 cm
  (18–35½ in)
Range: west Atlantic Ocean
Scientific name:
  Chaetodipterus faber

Dragonet

The male dragonet is a striking fish, with his long blue and yellow fins. The female is smaller and does not have extended fins. Dragonets lie half-buried in the sand on the seabed, watching for bottom-dwelling crustaceans and worms – their main food. They breed in spring or summer and males perform displays with their decorative fins to win females.

Size: 30 cm (11¾ in)
Range: east Atlantic Ocean and Mediterranean Sea
Scientific name:
Callionymus lyra

Dragonet

Northern stargazer

The northern stargazer has a large head with its mouth pointing upwards; its eyes are on top of its head, also facing upwards. This allows the stargazer to lie partly buried on the seabed, with only its eyes and mouth uncovered, watching for prey such as fish and crustaceans. Behind the eyes is a special area of electric organs. These produce electric charges that the stargazer uses to stun prey. Stargazers breed in deeper offshore waters. The young fish drift into coastal waters, where they settle to the bottom-dwelling life of adults.

Size: up to 30.5 cm (12 in)
Range: Atlantic coast of North America
Scientific name:
Astroscopus guttatus

Northern stargazer

Northern clingfish

Northern clingfish

A common fish, the northern clingfish has a smooth body and a broad head. Its dorsal and anal fins are set back near its tail. Like all clingfish, its pelvic fins form part of a sucking disc on its belly. It uses this to cling to rocks or other surfaces to stop itself being washed away by strong tides in the coastal waters where it lives. Molluscs and crustaceans are the clingfish's main foods.

Size: 15 cm (6 in)
Range: Pacific Ocean
Scientific name:
Gobiesox maeandricus

Size: 12 cm (4¾ in)
Range: west Atlantic Ocean, Gulf of Mexico and Caribbean Sea
Scientific name:
Ophioblennius atlanticus

Redlip blenny

Redlip blenny

This fish is identified by the bristles on its rounded snout as well as its red lips and red-tipped fin. It lives on rocky or coral-bottomed seabeds, where it searches for small invertebrates to eat. The female lays her eggs among coral or under rocks and the male guards them until they hatch.

Rock goby

There are more than 1,800 kinds of goby. Most live in the sea, but there are some freshwater species. The rock goby is one of the larger gobies, but is typical of the group, with its big blunt head and rounded tail. Its pelvic fins form a sucking disc which it uses to cling to rocks. It feeds on small invertebrates and fish.

Size: 12 cm (4¾ in)
Range: north Atlantic Ocean and Mediterranean Sea
Scientific name:
Gobius paganellus

Rock goby

Siamese fightingfish

Male Siamese fightingfish are bred in captivity to take part in staged fights, but wild males battle with rivals over territory. In the breeding season, the male blows a bubble nest from air and mucus. When the female lays her eggs, the male fertilises them and spits them into the nest to keep them safe.

Size: 6 cm (2¼ in)
Range: Thailand
Scientific name:
Betta splendens

Siamese fightingfish

Snakehead

Snakehead

Size: 1 m (3¼ ft)
Range: India, China and Southeast Asia
Scientific name:
Channa striatus

Snakehead

This long-bodied fish belongs to a small group of freshwater fish that live in tropical Africa and Asia. It usually lives in oxygen-poor waters and has special structures in its gills which help it take some oxygen from the air. It can even survive out of water as long as it burrows into mud to keep its skin moist.

Man-o'-war fish

Best known for its habit of living among the trailing tentacles of the Portuguese man-of-war, this little fish does not seem to be affected by the jellyfish's stinging cells. It may even prevent them working. The jellyfish seems not to notice the man-o'-war fish but it is possible that the fish removes parasites and other debris from its host's body.

Man-o'-war fish

Size: 22 cm (8¾ in)
Range: tropical areas of Indian, Pacific and west Atlantic oceans
Scientific name:
Nomeus gronovii

Blue marlin

The blue marlin is one of the fastest of all fish and has the streamlined body and crescent-shaped tail typical of high-speed swimmers. It weighs at least 180 kg (400 lb) and has a long beaklike nose, which it may use to stun its prey such as smaller schooling fish and squid.

Size: 3–4.6 m (10–15 ft)
Range: worldwide, tropical and warm seas
Scientific name:
Makaira nigricans

Blue marlin

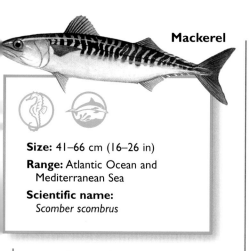
Mackerel

Size: 41–66 cm (16–26 in)
Range: Atlantic Ocean and Mediterranean Sea
Scientific name: *Scomber scombrus*

Mackerel

Mackerel move in large schools and make regular migration journeys. In spring and summer they go north, where they breed; in winter they return south again. A female may produce as many as 450,000 eggs, which float in the water until they hatch about four days later. Adult mackerel eat small fish and crustaceans, while young fish feed mainly on plankton and fish larvae.

Wahoo

Unlike its relatives the mackerel and tuna, the wahoo is not a schooling fish. It usually swims alone or in small groups. It has a longer thinner body than most tunas and a narrow snout, equipped with many strong teeth. A fast swimmer, it can reach speeds of up to 66 km an hour (41 mph) when chasing prey.

Wahoo

Size: up to 2 m (6½ ft)
Range: worldwide in tropical seas
Scientific name: *Acanthocybium solanderi*

Swordfish

The huge spectacular swordfish is a fast, active hunter with a streamlined body and a sickle-shaped fin on its back. It feeds on small fish as well as squid, and it may use its extremely long snout to strike at schooling fish. Young swordfish do not have a long snout; it develops as they grow.

Size: 2–4.9 m (6½–16 ft)
Range: worldwide, warm and tropical seas
Scientific name: *Xiphias gladius*

Swordfish

Size: up to 1.8 m (6 ft)
Range: worldwide
Scientific name: *Sphyraena barracuda*

Great barracuda

Great barracuda

There are about 18 different types of barracuda living in warm and tropical waters of all oceans. The great barracuda is typical, with its long slender body and large jaws and teeth. A fierce predator around coral reefs, it can be dangerous to humans if disturbed. Young barracudas may swim in schools, but larger fish hunt alone.

Sailfish

This fast-swimming fish has a tall sail-like fin on its back and long rounded jaws. It is a fierce predator and eats almost any fish it can find, as well as squid.

Sailfish breed in open sea. The female sheds several million eggs, which float in surface waters until they hatch.

Size: 3.6 m (12 ft)
Range: worldwide, warm and tropical waters
Scientific name: *Istiophorus platypterus*

Sailfish

185

Flyingfish, lanternfish and lizardfish

The flyingfish belongs to a large group of mostly sea-living fish, which also includes halfbeaks, needlefish, sauries and garfish. Most are active near or above the surface of the water. Flyingfish can actually lift themselves into the air with their pectoral fins and use their rapidly beating tails to help them glide short distances over the surface. Lanternfish are deep-sea fish found in all oceans from the Arctic to the Antarctic. They have light-producing organs on the body. The lizardfish and its relative the bummalow both live in shallow coastal waters, where they prey on small fish.

Wrestling halfbeak

This small slender fish feeds on mosquito larvae and so helps to control these pests. Male fish are aggressive and fight one another by wrestling with their long jaws.

Wrestling halfbeak

Size: 7 cm (2¾ in)
Range: Thailand, Malaysia
Scientific name:
    Dermogenys pusillus

Flyingfish

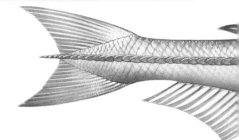

Size: 30 cm (11¾ in)
Range: all oceans
Scientific name:
    Exocetus volitans

Flyingfish

The flyingfish escapes its enemies by leaping up and gliding over the surface of the water, with the aid of its winglike fins. Unlike some other species, this flyingfish has only one pair of "wings".

Size: 45 cm (17¾ in)
Range: Atlantic Ocean
Scientific name:
    Hemiramphus brasiliensis

Lanternfish

This fish has groups of light-producing organs on its body. The arrangement of these is different in male and female fish. The light organs may help the fish to light up the dark depths of the sea to find prey or they may be used to confuse the fishe's enemies. Lanternfish feed on animal plankton.

Ballyhoo

Ballyhoo

This fish cannot leap above the water like its relative the flyingfish, but it can skim over the surface. It moves in schools, feeding on sea grass and small fish, and it may use its long lower jaw to scoop up food from the water surface.

Size: 10 cm (4 in)
Range: north Atlantic Ocean and Mediterranean Sea
Scientific name: *Myctophum punctatum*

Lanternfish

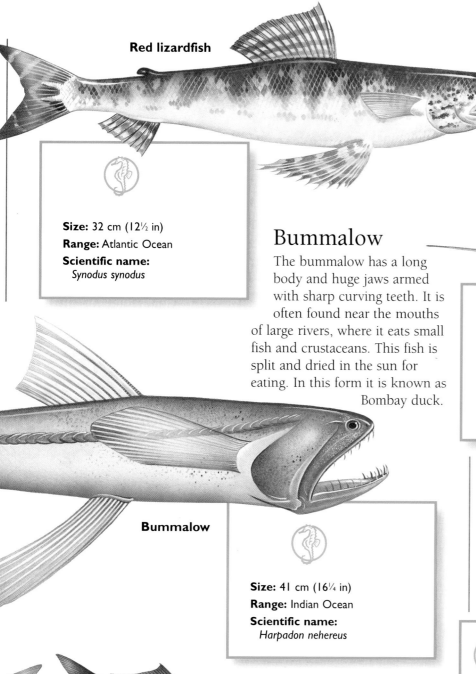

Red lizardfish

Red lizardfish

The red lizardfish has unusually long pelvic fins and often lies on the seabed, supporting its body on these fins. A fierce hunter, it lies in wait for prey, then suddenly darts up from the seabed and catches the victim in its long sharp teeth.

Size: 32 cm (12½ in)
Range: Atlantic Ocean
Scientific name:
Synodus synodus

Bummalow

The bummalow has a long body and huge jaws armed with sharp curving teeth. It is often found near the mouths of large rivers, where it eats small fish and crustaceans. This fish is split and dried in the sun for eating. In this form it is known as Bombay duck.

Bummalow

Size: 41 cm (16¼ in)
Range: Indian Ocean
Scientific name:
Harpadon nehereus

Needlefish

Size: 5 cm (2 in)
Range: South America
Scientific name:
Belonian apodion

Needlefish

This tiny freshwater fish has an extremely slender body, with small fins near its tail. It has a long lower jaw that it uses to scoop up animal plankton.

Size: 94 cm (37 in)
Range: north Atlantic Ocean, Mediterranean and Black seas
Scientific name:
Belone belone

Garfish

Saury

Sauries swim in shoals in surface waters, feeding on small fish and crustaceans. They have beaklike jaws, the lower longer than the upper. Young fish hatch with short jaws of equal length; the long lower jaw develops as they grow.

Size: 40–50 cm (15¾–19¾ in)
Range: north Atlantic Ocean and Mediterranean Sea
Scientific name: *Scomberesox saurus*

Garfish

The slender garfish has long jaws studded with many needlelike teeth. An active hunter, the garfish eats small fish and crustaceans. They breed in coastal waters and the small round eggs attach themselves to floating debris or seaweed.

Saury

187

Guppies, grunions and relatives

Guppies belong to a large group of freshwater fish which contains more than 800 species, including mummichogs, sheepshead minnows, lyretails and the four-eyed fish. Most are surface swimmers which feed on insects and plant matter that has fallen on to the water. They are extremely adaptable and able to survive in stagnant, slow-moving water that is unsuitable for most other fish.

Grunions belong to a group of more than 280 species which includes silversides, sand-smelts and rainbow fish. Most feed on animal plankton and live in large shoals in lakes, estuaries and shallow coastal waters.

Crimson-spotted rainbow fish

This colourful fish is one of about 53 types of rainbow fish found in Australia and New Guinea. In early summer it lays eggs, which become anchored to water plants by fine threads.

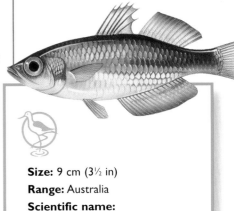

Crimson-spotted rainbow fish

Size: 9 cm (3½ in)
Range: Australia
Scientific name:
 Melanotaenia fluviatilis

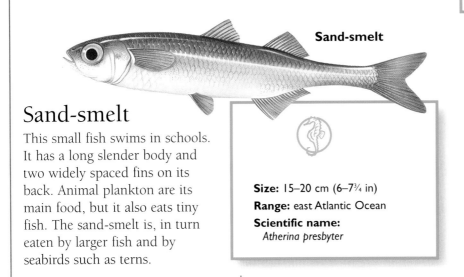

Sand-smelt

Sand-smelt

This small fish swims in schools. It has a long slender body and two widely spaced fins on its back. Animal plankton are its main food, but it also eats tiny fish. The sand-smelt is, in turn eaten by larger fish and by seabirds such as terns.

Size: 15–20 cm (6–7¾ in)
Range: east Atlantic Ocean
Scientific name:
 Atherina presbyter

Hardhead silverside

During the day, the slender body of this little fish looks almost transparent, with a narrow silvery stripe running down each side. When night falls, the colour darkens. Silversides are common fish and they swim in large schools. Their eggs have tiny threads which attach them to water plants while they develop.

Hardhead silverside

California grunion

Grunions time their breeding with the rhythms of the tides. On the night of an extremely high, or spring, tide, they swim ashore and lay their eggs in the sand. The next wave carries the fish back to the sea. Two weeks later, at the next spring tide, the eggs hatch and the young are carried out to sea.

Size: 18 cm (7 in)
Range: Pacific Ocean
Scientific name:
 Leuresthes tenuis

Size: 12.5 cm (5 in)
Range: north Atlantic Ocean
Scientific name:
 Atherinomorus stipes

Four-eyed fish

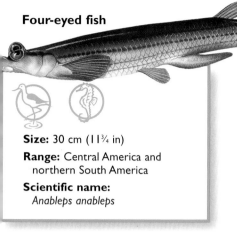

Size: 30 cm (11¾ in)
Range: Central America and northern South America
Scientific name:
Anableps anableps

Four-eyed fish

This unusual fish has, in fact, only two eyes that are divided into two parts. The top part of each eye is for seeing in the air and the lower part is for seeing in water. The two are separated by a dark band. The fish swims at the surface, the water reaching the dividing bands on the eyes. It is able to watch for insect prey in the air or other prey in the water at the same time.

Cape Lopez lyretail

The male lyretail is a brightly coloured fish with large pointed fins. The female is plainer with smaller fins. The lyretail lays its eggs in mud. If there is a long dry season the eggs stop developing until the rains return. The embryos then start to grow again and hatch shortly afterwards.

Size: 6 cm (2¼ in)
Range: Africa
Scientific name:
Aphyosemion australe

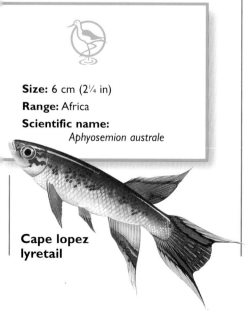

Cape lopez lyretail

Size: 7.5 cm (3 in)
Range: USA coasts
Scientific name:
Cyprinidon variegatus

Sheepshead minnow

Outside the breeding season, male and female sheepshead minnows look similar, but breeding males develop brighter coloration. The female lays her eggs a few at a time and the male fertilises them as they are shed. The eggs have sticky threads on the surface which bind the eggs to each other and to plants.

Sheepshead minnow

Mummichog

The stout-bodied mummichog is a hardy little fish that can survive in salt or fresh water and eats almost any plants and animals it can find. It breeds in spring in shallow water. The male chases his mate and then clasps her with his fins so he can fertilise the eggs as they are laid. The eggs stick together and sink to the bottom in a cluster.

Size: 10–15 cm (4–6 in)
Range: North American coasts
Scientific name:
Fundulus heteroclitus

Mummichog

Guppy

The guppy is an extremely common fish. It is popular with humans because it feeds on mosquito larvae and so helps to control this pest. It also eats other insect larvae, small crustaceans and the eggs and young of other fish. Many colourful forms of the guppy are bred as aquarium fish.

Size: 6 cm (2¼ in)
Range: northern South America
Scientific name:
Poecilia reticulata

Guppy

189

Oarfish, squirrelfish and relatives

All of these fish live in the sea. The pinecone fish, squirrelfish, roughie and beardfish all belong to a group of about 123 species of deep-bodied fish with spiny fins. The John dory belongs to a separate group of deep-bodied fish, many of which live in deep sea. The whalefish is a deep-sea species. The oarfish and opah belong to a rare group of which little is known.

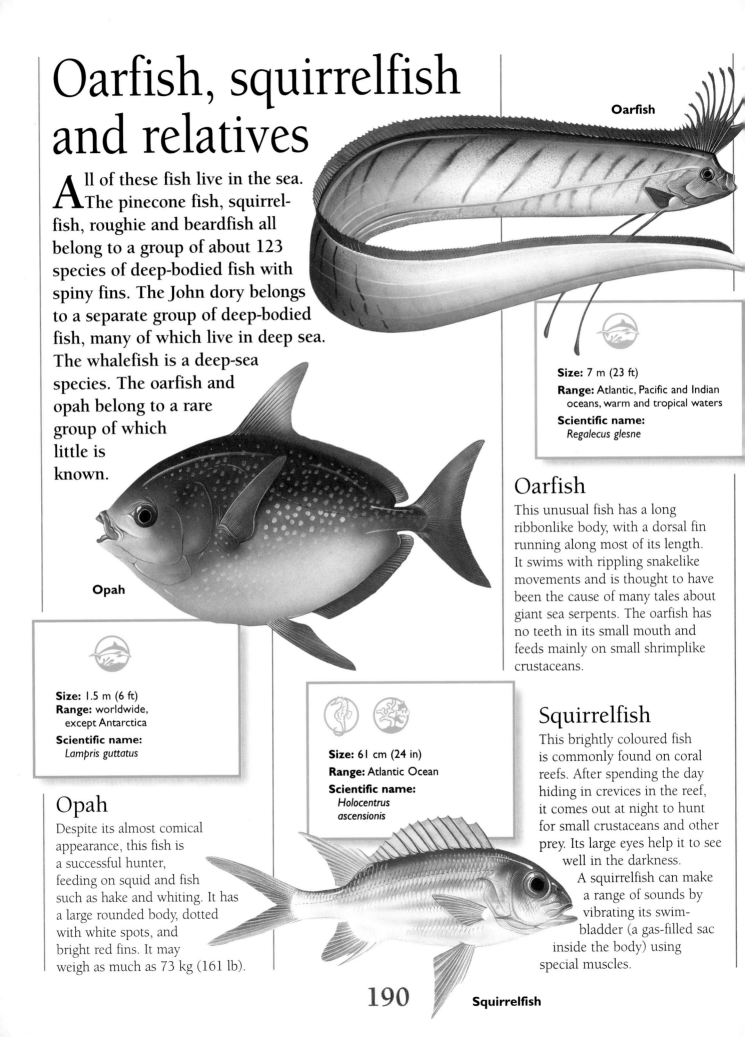

Oarfish

Opah

Size: 7 m (23 ft)
Range: Atlantic, Pacific and Indian oceans, warm and tropical waters
Scientific name: *Regalecus glesne*

Oarfish

This unusual fish has a long ribbonlike body, with a dorsal fin running along most of its length. It swims with rippling snakelike movements and is thought to have been the cause of many tales about giant sea serpents. The oarfish has no teeth in its small mouth and feeds mainly on small shrimplike crustaceans.

Size: 1.5 m (6 ft)
Range: worldwide, except Antarctica
Scientific name: *Lampris guttatus*

Size: 61 cm (24 in)
Range: Atlantic Ocean
Scientific name: *Holocentrus ascensionis*

Squirrelfish

This brightly coloured fish is commonly found on coral reefs. After spending the day hiding in crevices in the reef, it comes out at night to hunt for small crustaceans and other prey. Its large eyes help it to see well in the darkness.

A squirrelfish can make a range of sounds by vibrating its swimbladder (a gas-filled sac inside the body) using special muscles.

Opah

Despite its almost comical appearance, this fish is a successful hunter, feeding on squid and fish such as hake and whiting. It has a large rounded body, dotted with white spots, and bright red fins. It may weigh as much as 73 kg (161 lb).

Squirrelfish

Size: 12.5 cm (5 in)
Range: Indian and Pacific oceans
Scientific name:
Monocentris japonicus

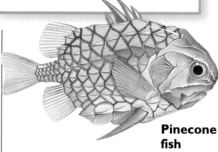

Pinecone fish

Pinecone fish

The body of the pinecone fish is protected by an armour of heavy platelike scales. Its dorsal fin is made up of thick spines and it has more spines on its underside. Under the lower jaw it has two light-producing organs. Pinecone fish move in schools near the bottom of the sea.

Whalefish

The whalefish belongs to a small group of deep-sea fish. It has a big head for its size and no scales on its body. The area at the base of the dorsal and anal fins is thought to glow in the dark. It hunts for its food and seizes prey in its large jaws lined with many tiny teeth.

Size: 14 cm (5½ in)
Range: Indian Ocean
Scientific name:
Cetomimus indagator

Whalefish

Stout beardfish

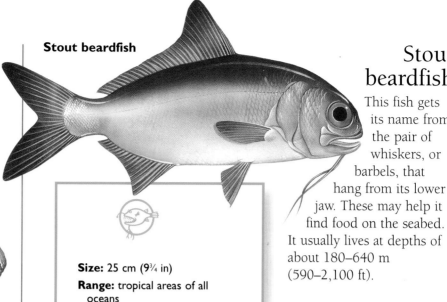

Size: 25 cm (9¾ in)
Range: tropical areas of all oceans
Scientific name: *Polymixia nobilis*

Roughie

Size: 30 cm (11¾ in)
Range: north Atlantic Ocean
Scientific name:
Hoplostethus atlanticus

John dory

The john dory has 9 or 10 thick spines in the front part of its dorsal fin and 3 or 4 on the belly in front of its anal fin. This fish is not a fast swimmer and catches its prey by stealth not speed. It approaches its victims slowly, until near enough to snap them up in its huge mouth. Small fish and crustaceans are the john dory's main foods.

Stout beardfish

This fish gets its name from the pair of whiskers, or barbels, that hang from its lower jaw. These may help it find food on the seabed. It usually lives at depths of about 180–640 m (590–2,100 ft).

Roughie

The brightly coloured roughie has a large head and a deep body. It has sharp spines on its back in front of its dorsal fin and on its belly. Its mouth is large and upturned and its jaws are lined with lots of tiny teeth. Little is known about the habits of this fish, but it is thought to feed on small crustaceans.

John dory

Size: 40–66 cm (15¾–26 in)
Range: east Atlantic Ocean and Mediterranean Sea
Scientific name: *Zeus faber*

Seahorses, scorpion-fish and relatives

Seahorses and sticklebacks belong to a group of more than 260 fish which also includes tubesnouts and pipefish. Sticklebacks have between 3 and 16 spines on their back and are found in the sea and in fresh water. The extraordinary seahorses, with their horselike head, all live in the sea. The stonefish, lionfish, northern sea robin and bullrout belong to the scorpionfish group. This includes nearly 1,300 species, most of which live in the sea. Many of these fish are chunky and spiny.

The flying gurnard belongs to a small group of only seven species of marine fish. Despite their name, these fish have never been seen flying above the surface of the water.

Weedy seadragon

The many leaflike flaps of skin on the body of this strange little seahorse are thought to help it hide from its enemies among fronds of seaweed. The male incubates his mate's eggs on a flap of skin beneath his tail.

Weedy seadragon

Size: 46 cm (18 in)
Range: coasts of southern Australia
Scientific name:
    Phyllopteryx taeniolatus

Size: 5–10 cm (2–4 in)
Range: North America: coasts and fresh water
Scientific name:
    Gasterosteus aculeatus

Dwarf seahorse

This unusual fish moves slowly, gently pushing itself along with movements of its tiny dorsal fin. It can also attach itself to seaweed with its curling tail. In the breeding season, the female lays 50 or more eggs, which she places in a pouch on the male's body, where they incubate.

Dwarf seahorse

Size: 4 cm (1½ in)
Range: west Atlantic Ocean and Caribbean Sea
Scientific name:
    Hippocampus zosterae

Three-spined stickleback

In the breeding season, the male stickleback develops a bright red belly. He make a nest from tiny bits of plants, glued together with mucus. He then displays to attract females to his nest, where they lay their eggs. He fertilises the eggs and guards them carefully until they hatch about three weeks later.

Three-spined stickleback

192

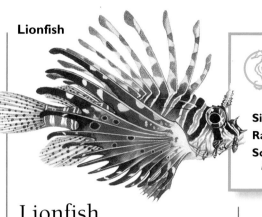

Lionfish

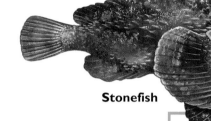

Size: 38 cm (15 in)
Range: Indian and Pacific oceans
Scientific name:
Pterois volitans

Lionfish

With its brightly striped body and large fanlike fins, this fish is one of the most extraordinary in the sea. The spines on its back are poisonous and can be dangerous even for humans. The fish uses its spines to defend itself against its enemies, not to attack prey.

Stonefish

The stonefish's mottled coloration and irregular shape keep it well hidden as it lies half-buried among stones on the seabed. The sharp spines on its back are linked to glands containing a deadly poison, which can even kill any human unlucky enough to tread on a stonefish's spines.

Stonefish

Size: 30 cm (11¾ in)
Range: Indian and Pacific oceans
Scientific name:
Synanceia verrucosa

Bullrout

Also known as the shorthorn sculpin, this fish has spines near its gills and along each side. Females are usually larger than males. A bottom dweller, the bullrout eats seabed crustaceans as well as worms and small fish.

Size: 25–60 cm (9¾–23½ in)
Range: north Atlantic Ocean
Scientific name:
Myoxocephalus scorpius

Bullrout

Northern sea robin

A relative of the lionfish, the northern sea robin spends much of its life on the seabed, often supporting itself on its pectoral fins. It uses the first three rays of its pectoral fins to feel for prey on the seabed. If in danger, the sea robin buries itself in sand, leaving only the top of its head and eyes showing.

Flying gurnard

A bottom-dwelling fish, the flying gurnard uses its long winglike pelvic fins to "walk" over the seabed as it searches for crustaceans to eat. If alarmed, the gurnard spreads its fins wide, showing their blue spots.

Flying gurnard

Size: 30–40.5 cm (11¾–16 in)
Range: west Atlantic Ocean and Mediterranean Sea
Scientific name:
Dactylopterus volitans

Size: 41 cm (16¼ in)
Range: west Atlantic Ocean
Scientific name:
Prionotus carolinus

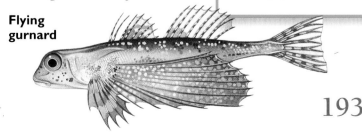

Northern sea robin

Flatfish

The flatfish belong to a group of about 570 species. All but three of these live in the sea. Young flatfish have normal bodies at first, but as they grow their bodies flatten and the eye on one side moves so that both eyes are on the upper surface. A typical flatfish spends much of its life on the seabed, lying with its eyes facing up. Some flatfish have both eyes on the right side; others have them on the left.

Adalah

The adalah is less dramatically flattened than most other flatfish. Some have eyes to the left side, others to the right, but one eye is on the edge of the head, rather than on the side with the other eye. Like other flatfish it spends much of its life on the seabed, but it also swims in mid-waters, looking for fish and other creatures to eat.

Size: up to 61 cm (24 in)
Range: Red Sea, Indian Ocean, west Pacific Ocean
Scientific name: *Psettodes erumei*

Turbot

This extremely broad-bodied flatfish varies in colour, but it usually has speckled markings that help to keep it hidden as it lies on the seabed. Adult turbots feed mostly on fish, but young turbots eat small crustaceans. Turbots breed in spring or summer and females produce as many as 10 million eggs.

Turbot

Size: 1 m (3¼ ft)
Range: east Atlantic Ocean and Mediterranean Sea
Scientific name: *Scopthalmus maximus*

Adalah

California halibut

Size: 1.5 m (5 ft)
Range: Pacific Ocean
Scientific name: *Paralichthys californicus*

California halibut

This halibut has a large mouth and strong sharp teeth. It feeds on fish, particularly anchovies, and is itself eaten by creatures such as rays, sea lions and porpoises. It is also an important food fish for humans. A large individual can weigh up to 32 kg (70 lb).

Summer flounder

Size: up to 1 m (3¼ ft)
Range: west Atlantic Ocean
Scientific name: *Paralichthys dentatus*

Summer flounder

A slender, active fish, the summer flounder feeds on crustaceans, molluscs and fish and will chase prey into surface waters if necessary. But although a fast swimmer, it spends much of its life lying half-buried on the seabed. Its colour varies according to the type of seabed it is on, but it is usually greyish brown, with dark spots.

Plaice

The topside of this flatfish is a rich brown colour, dotted with orange spots. Both eyes are usually on the top, on the right side of the body; plaice with eyes on the left are rare. Plaice breed in spring and the larvae live in surface waters for up to six weeks before starting a bottom-dwelling life. Plaice are an important food fish.

Sole

Normally a night-time feeder, the sole usually spends the day buried in sand or mud. They breed in shallow water and the eggs float at the surface until they hatch. Larvae live at the surface but move to the seabed when they are about 1.25 cm (½ in) long.

Sole

Size: 30–60 cm (11¾–23½ in)
Range: east Atlantic Ocean and Mediterranean Sea
Scientific name: *Solea solea*

Naked sole

Size: up to 23 cm (9 in)
Range: northwest Atlantic Ocean
Scientific name: *Gymnachirus melas*

Naked sole

The naked sole has no scales on its skin and is marked with dark stripes on its uppermost side. The underside is whitish in colour. Most of these fish have both eyes on the right side and the small mouth is also twisted to the right. The naked sole spends most of its life on the seabed, but it is an active hunter and can swim well when necessary.

Blackcheek tonguefish

This flatfish has a body that is broad at the front and tapers to a pointed tail. Its dorsal and anal fins join with the tail fin. Both of its eyes are on the left of the head and its small mouth is twisted to the left side. Like other flatfish, it lives on the seabed and feeds on small invertebrate animals such as worms and crustaceans.

Plaice

Size: 50–91 cm (19¾–36 in)
Range: east Atlantic Ocean and Mediterranean Sea
Scientific name: *Pleuronectes platessa*

Size: 20 cm (7¾ in)
Range: west Atlantic Ocean
Scientific name: *Symphurus plagusia*

Blackcheek tonguefish

Coelacanth, lungfish, triggerfish and relatives

The coelacanth is thought to resemble some of the earliest fish. Common millions of years ago, only one species now survives. Lungfish are related to early air-breathing fish and are thought to be more closely related to amphibians than any other living fish. They have lunglike breathing organs, which they use to take breaths of air at the water's surface. Triggerfish, pufferfish, boxfish and their relatives belong to a group of about 340 species, many of which have round or boxlike bodies. Most live in the sea.

Scrawled filefish

A relative of the triggerfish, this filefish has a long spine on its back and small prickly spines on the scales of its body. It lives on bottom-living invertebrates and seaweeds and feeds nose down on the seabed. It often lurks in clumps of eel grass, where its greenish coloration keeps it well hidden.

Scrawled filefish

Size: 91 cm (36 in)
Range: tropical waters of Atlantic, Pacific and Indian oceans
Scientific name: *Aluterus scriptus*

Porcupinefish

The body of this fish is covered with long sharp spines. They normally lie flat, but if the fish is in danger, it puffs up its body so the spines stand out, making it almost impossible for any predator to catch. It has two teeth in each jaw. The teeth are joined together, making a sharp beak for crushing hard-shelled prey such as molluscs and crabs

Size: 56 cm (22 in)
Range: west Atlantic Ocean and Caribbean Sea
Scientific name:
 Balistes vetula

Size: 91 cm (36 in)
Range: tropical waters of Pacific, Indian and Atlantic oceans
Scientific name:
 Diodon hystrix

Porcupinefish

Queen triggerfish

Queen triggerfish

On the triggerfish's back are three spines. When the first spine is upright, it is locked into place by the second. If in danger, the triggerfish can wedge itself into a crevice with this "locking" spine and is extremely hard to move. It feeds on small invertebrate creatures, particularly sea urchins.

Blue-spotted boxfish

Like all boxfish, this fish has a hard shell around its body, made up of joined plates. Its mouth, eyes, fins and gill openings are the only breaks in the armour, which protects the fish from its enemies. It feeds mostly on bottom-living invertebrate creatures.

Blue-spotted boxfish

Size: 46 cm (18 in)
Range: Indian and Pacific oceans
Scientific name:
 Ostracion tuberculatus

Size: 15 cm (6 in)
Range: India, Myanmar, Malaysia
Scientific name:
Tetraodon cutcutia

Common pufferfish

Common pufferfish

If threatened, this fish can blow its body up until it is almost completely round and very difficult for any predator to swallow. Many kinds of pufferfish are popular food fish, even though some parts of the body are very poisonous. In Japan, chefs are specially trained in the preparation of pufferfish.

Coelacanth

Coelacanths were thought to have been extinct for millions of years until one was caught off the coast of South Africa in 1938. This living species is still very like its fossil relatives. It has a heavy body and fleshy sections at the base of all its fins except the first dorsal fin. It is believed to hunt other fish to eat.

Coelacanth

Size: 2 m (6½ ft)
Range: Indian Ocean: off Comoro Islands and off Indonesian coast
Scientific name:
Latimeria chalumnae

Ocean sunfish

The extraordinary ocean sunfish is a relative of the triggerfish but is quite unlike any other fish. Its body is almost completely round and ends in a curious frill-like tail. Despite its huge size, it has a small beaklike mouth and feeds on small creatures such as animal plankton and tiny jellyfish.

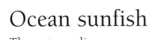

Ocean sunfish

Size: up to 4 m (13 ft)
Range: Atlantic, Pacific and Indian oceans
Scientific name: Mola mola

South American lungfish

This lungfish lives in swamps that dry out for part of the year. During this time, it lives in a burrow that it digs in the mud and breathes air with the help of lunglike organs in its body. When the rains return, the fish comes out of its burrow.

Size: 1.25 m (4¼ ft)
Range: Central South America
Scientific name:
Lepidosiren paradoxa

South American lungfish

Why do some animals work together?

When animals develop close links with creatures of another species both partners can benefit. The cleaner fish, for example, feeds on parasites and tiny scraps of food it finds on the bodies of larger fish. The cleaner fish gains a good meal and the host has its body cleared of debris and harmful parasites. Sometimes only one partner benefits. Cattle egrets follow large mammals such as elephants to feed on the insects disturbed as they pass. The egrets get plenty of food but there is no clear advantage to the elephant.

The **honeyguide** feeds on wax and bee larvae, but it is not able to get into bees' nests by itself. Instead, the bird leads another honey-eating animal such as the **honey badger**, or ratel, to the nest and waits while it smashes open the nest. Both creatures benefit.

Black ants protect groups of the tiny bugs called aphids from other insects. When an ant strokes an aphid's body with its antennae, the aphid produces a drop of a sugary substance called honeydew — delicious food for the ant.

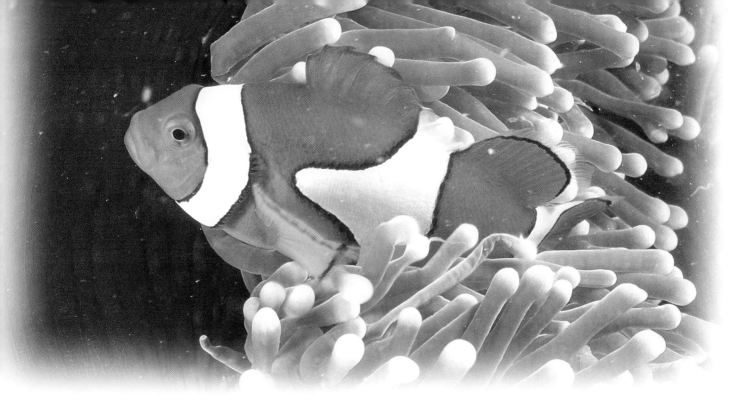

The **clown anemonefish** finds safety from enemies among a **sea anemone's** stinging tentacles. Its own skin is immune to the sting. The clown anemonefish may attract other fish near enough for the anemone to catch.

The **oxpecker** provides a very useful service for the **buffalo** while getting a good meal for itself. The bird eats the ticks and other parasites that live on the buffalo's skin.

199

Insects, spiders and other invertebrates

*Insects outnumber every other creature on Earth.
There are about one and a half million known animal
species in the world, and about one million of those
species are insects. Some experts believe that as many as
30 times this number of insects are yet to be discovered.
Arachnids, like insects, are found all over
the world in every kind of habitat. There are
at least 75,000 species of arachnids, of which spiders are
the biggest group.*

*Insects and spiders are not the only types of
invertebrate animal. On land there are creatures such as
worms, snails, centipedes and millipedes. In the sea
there is an amazing range of at least 160,000 species
of invertebrates, including sponges, clams, mussels,
jellyfish and crabs.*

A gleaming **mint leaf beetle**
settles on a leaf of its main food
plant. Leaf beetles feed on the
leaves and flowers of different
plants and their larvae may
attack the plant's roots. Many
leaf beetles are serious pests
of agricultural crop plants.

Garden snail

What is an invertebrate?

An invertebrate is an animal without a backbone – creatures such as crabs, worms, insects and spiders are all invertebrates. There are invertebrates on land, in the sea and in fresh water, and many insects fly in the air. These animals have an extraordinary range of life-styles and feeding habits.

Arthropods

Arthropods are the largest group of invertebrates and some of the most successful creatures ever to have lived on Earth. They include creatures such as insects, spiders and crabs. One of the reasons for the arthropods' success is that they have a hard external skeleton, called an exoskeleton, which protects the soft body within.

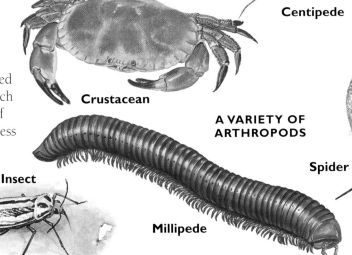

Centipede

Crustacean

A VARIETY OF ARTHROPODS

Spider

Insect

Millipede

An insect's body

An insect is divided into three parts – head, thorax and abdomen. The head carries the eyes, a pair of sensory antennae, which the insect uses to find out about its surroundings, and the mouthparts. These vary in shape according to the insect's diet. On the thorax are three pairs of legs and, usually, two pairs of wings.

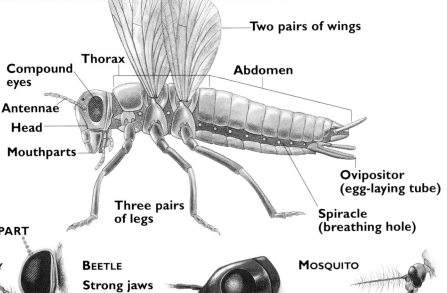

Two pairs of wings

Thorax

Compound eyes

Abdomen

Antennae

Head

Mouthparts

Ovipositor (egg-laying tube)

Three pairs of legs

Spiracle (breathing hole)

DIFFERENT TYPES OF MOUTHPART

HOUSE FLY
Spongy mouthparts for mopping up liquid food

BUTTERFLY
Long coiled tube for sucking liquid food

BEETLE
Strong jaws for cutting and piercing prey

MOSQUITO
Needlelike tube for sucking up food

A spider's body

A typical spider's body is divided into two parts. The head and thorax are joined to make one structure called the cephalothorax. This is linked to the abdomen by a narrow waist. At the front of the head are the spider's jaws, called chelicerae. Behind these is the mouth. Spiders have four pairs of legs. Each one is divided into segments and tipped with two or three claws.

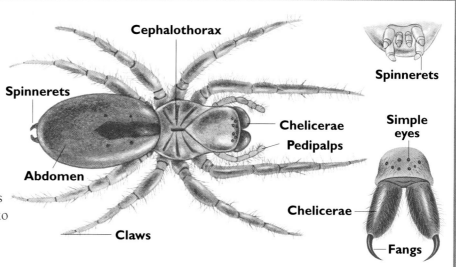

Cephalothorax

Spinnerets

Spinnerets

Chelicerae

Pedipalps

Simple eyes

Chelicerae

Abdomen

Claws

Fangs

Other invertebrate groups

Molluscs

The three main groups of molluscs are the gastropods – creatures such as limpets; the bivalves – clams, scallops and mussels; and cephalopods – squid, cuttlefish octopus and nautilus.

Nautilus

Annelid worms

There are about 11,500 species of these worms living in water and on land. In all of them, the body is divided into a number of segments.

Medical leech

Cnidarians

This group includes creatures such as sea anemones, jellyfish and coral. Most have tubelike bodies with a central mouth surrounded by tentacles.

Comb jellies

Comb jellies have a simple baglike body, with eight lines of tiny hairs arranged down it. These hairs beat to move the comb jelly through the water.

Beroe comb jelly

Lampshells

There are about 260 living species in this group, which dates back some 600 million years. All lampshells have an upper and a lower shell.

Purple jellyfish

Lampshell

Echinoderms

There are four main groups of echinoderms – brittle stars, starfish, sea cucumbers, and sea urchins and sand dollars. Most move around using tiny stilts called tube feet.

Flower urchin

Sponges

Sponges are the simplest many-celled animals. Their shapes vary from tiny cups, tubelike pipes and tall vases to rounded masses. Special filtering cells in their bodies trap food particles in the water.

Glass sponge

Cockroaches, earwigs, crickets, grasshoppers and relatives

While these insects are not closely related, they share certain features. All of them have strong jaws for chewing and mobile heads, and most have large back wings. They also include some of the most ancient of all insect groups – cockroaches have existed on the Earth for about 350 million years. Most of these creatures are familiar to humans, and some are even unwelcome guests in our homes.

Cockroaches, earwigs and bristletails

Although most cockroaches live outdoors, in every kind of habitat from mountains to rainforest, they are best known as indoor pests. Earwigs, found in every garden, are also considered pests, since many feed on plants and flowers. Also common in houses, but less often seen, are the wingless insects known as silverfish, a type of bristletail.

Silverfish

Fast-moving, light-shy silverfish usually live in dark corners indoors, where they eat paper, glue and spilled foods. The long tapering body is covered with tiny scales.

Silverfish

Family: Lepismatidae
Size: 0.8–1.9 cm (⅓–¾ in) long
Number of species: 200

Firebrat

The firebrat is a bristletail. It usually lives indoors near warm places such as ovens or boilers. It is a fast runner and scurries around finding crumbs and scraps of food to eat.

Firebrat

Family: Lepismatidae
Size: 0.8–1.9 cm (⅓–¾ in) long
Number of species: 200

Family: Forficulidae
Size: 0.9–2.5 cm (⅜–1 in) long
Number of species: 450

Common earwig

Common earwig

The female earwig lays her eggs in a burrow and stays close to look after them. Unusually for an insect, she tends her young until they are able to look after themselves.

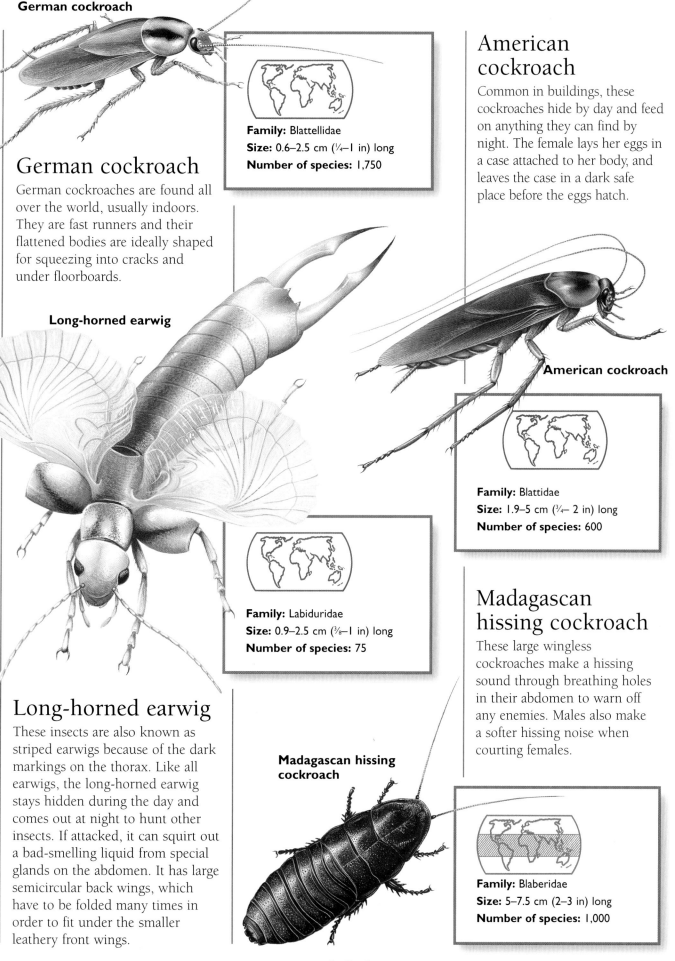

German cockroach

German cockroaches are found all over the world, usually indoors. They are fast runners and their flattened bodies are ideally shaped for squeezing into cracks and under floorboards.

Family: Blattellidae
Size: 0.6–2.5 cm (¼–1 in) long
Number of species: 1,750

American cockroach

Common in buildings, these cockroaches hide by day and feed on anything they can find by night. The female lays her eggs in a case attached to her body, and leaves the case in a dark safe place before the eggs hatch.

Family: Blattidae
Size: 1.9–5 cm (¾– 2 in) long
Number of species: 600

Long-horned earwig

These insects are also known as striped earwigs because of the dark markings on the thorax. Like all earwigs, the long-horned earwig stays hidden during the day and comes out at night to hunt other insects. If attacked, it can squirt out a bad-smelling liquid from special glands on the abdomen. It has large semicircular back wings, which have to be folded many times in order to fit under the smaller leathery front wings.

Family: Labiduridae
Size: 0.9–2.5 cm (⅜–1 in) long
Number of species: 75

Madagascan hissing cockroach

These large wingless cockroaches make a hissing sound through breathing holes in their abdomen to warn off any enemies. Males also make a softer hissing noise when courting females.

Family: Blaberidae
Size: 5–7.5 cm (2–3 in) long
Number of species: 1,000

Crickets, grasshoppers and relatives

More often heard than seen, grasshoppers are best known for their calls, usually made by males when courting females. They make these sounds by rubbing together special parts of their wings or legs. There are two main families of grasshoppers: short-horned, which include locusts, and long-horned, which include katydids. Crickets are relatives of grasshoppers and also make chirping sounds. Stick and leaf insects are famous for their ability to hide themselves by looking like twigs or leaves.

Long-horned grasshopper

As their name suggests, long-horned grasshoppers have long antennae. They feed on plants but also catch and eat small insects. Many are green or brown in colour and can be hard to spot in the trees and bushes where they live.

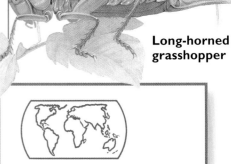

Long-horned grasshopper

Family: Tettigoniidae
Size: 1.2–7.5 cm (½–3 in) long
Number of species: 5,000

Locust

Locusts are a type of grasshopper and are among the most damaging of all insects. Swarms of locusts swoop down on to crops and feed until there are scarcely any leaves left. A swarm may contain as many as 50 billion insects.

Family: Acrididae
Size: 1.2–7.5 cm (½–3 in) long
Number of species: 9,000

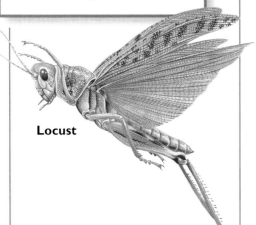

Locust

Short-horned grasshopper

Short-horned grasshoppers have short antennae. Like all grasshoppers, they have powerful back legs and can leap more than 200 times their own length.

Short-horned grasshopper

Family: Acrididae
Size: 1.2–7.5cm (½–3 in) long
Number of species: 9,000

Leaf insect

Leaf insect

These extraordinary insects are shaped just like the leaves they live on, complete with veins. Even their eggs look like the plant's seeds. Leaf insects live in tropical parts of Asia and Australia.

Family: Phylliidae
Size: 5–10 cm (2–4 in) long
Number of species: 50

True cricket

True cricket

True crickets "sing" by rubbing together specially ridged and thickened areas of their front wings to make a high-pitched sound. They are usually coloured green, black or brown and have broad bodies and well-developed feelers at the end of the abdomen.

Family: Gryllidae
Size: 0.9–2.5 cm (⅜–1 in) long
Number of species: 2,000

Mole cricket

Mole cricket

Like tiny moles, these crickets live under the ground, where they burrow with their large spadelike front legs. A covering of fine hairs protects the body from soil. Plant roots are their main food and they often damage crops and trees. They also catch and eat worms and larvae.

Family: Gryllotalpidae
Size: 2–5 cm (¾–2 in) long
Number of species: 60

Katydid

This insect has wings that look like leaves to help it hide among plants. The female katydid has a knifelike ovipositor (egg-laying tube). She uses this to insert eggs into slots that she cuts in the stems of plants.

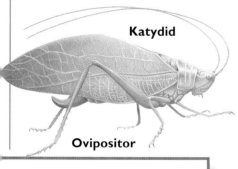

Katydid

Ovipositor

Family: Tettigoniidae
Size: 1.2–7.5 cm (½–3 in) long
Number of species: 5,000

Family: Phasmatidae
Size: up to 30 cm (11¾ in) long
Number of species: 2,000

Stick insect

With its slender green or brown body, the stick insect looks so like a leafless twig that it is hard for hungry birds to see. During the day it clings to a plant, with only its long thin legs swaying gently, as though blown by a breeze. At night the stick insect moves around, feeding on leaves.

Stick insect

Mantids, dragonflies and relatives

These insects are some of the fiercest hunters in the insect world. Mantids are equipped with long front legs, which they extend at lightning speed to grasp their prey. More energetic hunters are the dragonflies, some of the fastest-flying of all insects. They seize their prey in the air or pluck tiny creatures from leaves. Lacewings, antlions, snakeflies and mantidflies are known as nerve-winged insects. They have two pairs of delicate veined wings that can be folded like a roof over the body. Their larvae feed on other small creatures, which they catch in their powerful jaws.

Angola mantis

This mantis is hard to see as it lies on a lichen-covered branch. It remains very still as it watches for food but can reach out to grab its prey in a fraction of a second. Mantid larvae hatch as tiny versions of their parents and start hunting for themselves right away.

Family: Mantidae
Size: 1.2–15 cm (½–6 in) long
Number of species: 1,400

Angola mantis

Praying mantis

The powerful front legs of the praying mantis are its hunting tools. They are lined with sharp spines, which help the insect hold on to its struggling prey as it feeds. Females are usually larger than males and sometimes attack or even eat males during mating.

Flower mantis

Some mantids are coloured to match the flowers that they perch on. This helps them stay hidden from both their victims and their enemies. Mantids usually prey on other insects but they can also catch frogs and small lizards.

Flower mantis

Family: Mantidae
Size: 1.2–15 cm (½–6 in) long
Number of species: 1,400

Praying mantis

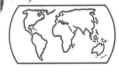

Family: Mantidae
Size: 1.2–15 cm (½–6 in) long
Number of species: 1,400

Family: Perlidae
Size: 0.9–4 cm (⅜–1½ in) long
Number of species: 350

Common stonefly

Stonefly nymphs (young) live in streams, where they feed mostly on plants, although some hunt insects. They can take in oxygen through their body surface but they also have gills, usually behind the first two pairs of legs, which help them breathe in water. Adult stoneflies are poor fliers and spend much of the day resting on stones with their wings folded on their bodies. They live only two or three weeks and most do not feed.

Mantisfly

This relative of the lacewing looks like a small praying mantis and catches prey in the same way. Some mantisfly larvae burrow into the nests of wasps or bees and eat their larvae. Others feed on spider eggs.

Family: Mantispidae
Size: 0.3–2.5 cm (⅛–1 in) long
Number of species: 350

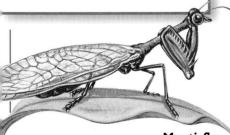

Mantisfly

Family: Raphidiidae
Size: 0.6–2.5 cm (¼–1 in) long
Number of species: 85

Common stonefly

Green lacewing

Green lacewing

Both adult lacewings and their larvae feed on small insects such as aphids. The larvae suck out the body juices of their prey with special mouthparts.

Family: Chrysopidae
Size: 0.9–1.9 cm (⅜–¾ in) long
Number of species: 1,600

Snakefly

The snakefly gets its name from its long snakelike neck, which it lifts as it searches for prey. Both adults and larvae hunt insects such as aphids and caterpillars.

Snakefly

Family: Myrmeleontidae
Size: 0.9–5 cm (⅜–2 in) long
Number of species: 1,000

Antlion

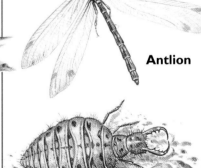

Larva

Antlion

The adult antlion looks like a dragonfly but has longer antennae, with clublike tips. The name antlion comes from the larva, which is a fierce hunter with spiny jaws. The larva digs a pit in sandy soil. When an insect comes near, the antlion tosses soil at it until it falls into the pit.

209

Biddy

Biddies are large dragonflies often seen around woodland streams, where they hover about 30 cm (11¼ in) above the surface of the water. They are usually brownish in colour and have big eyes which meet, or nearly meet, on the broad head, depending on the species. Biddy nymphs are large and they live under water at the bottom of streams, where they feed on insects and tadpoles.

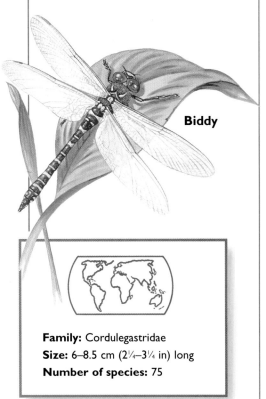

Biddy

Family: Cordulegastridae
Size: 6–8.5 cm (2¼–3¼ in) long
Number of species: 75

Mayfly

Adult mayflies live for only one day: enough time to mate and lay eggs. Most of the mayfly's life is spent in water as a nymph.

Nymph

Adult

Family: Lestidae
Size: 3–5 cm (1¼–2 in) long
Number of species: 200

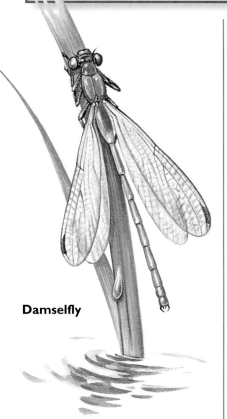

Damselfly

Damselfly

These insects are sometimes known as spread-winged damselflies because they hold their wings partly spread out when at rest. They live around ponds and marshes, where they catch insects such as small flies.

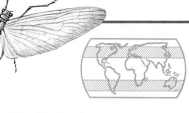

Family: Baetidae
Size: about 1 cm (⅜ in) long
Number of species: 800

Clubtail dragonfly

These dragonflies hunt in a different way from many other dragonflies. The clubtail finds a suitable perch and watches for prey. Once it sights the prey, it darts out to seize it, then returns to the perch.

Clubtail dragonfly

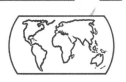

Family: Gomphidae
Size: 5–7.5 cm (2–3 in) long
Number of species: 875

Family: Coenagrionidae
Size: 2.5–5 cm (1–2 in) long
Number of species: 1,000

Narrow-winged damselfly

The males of these slender-bodied damselflies are usually brighter in colour than the females. Their nymphs, like those of all damselflies, live in water and catch small insects to eat.

Narrow-winged damselfly

Family: Libellulidae
Size: 2–6 cm (¾–2½ in) long
Number of species: 1,250

Skimmer

Skimmer

A skimmer is a kind of dragonfly with a wide flattened body that is shorter than its wings. Some have a wingspan of up to 10 cm (4 in). Skimmers are usually seen flying near still or slow-moving water, such as ponds and swamps.

Family: Aeschnidae
Size: 6–12 cm (2¼–4¾ in) long
Number of species: about 1,000

Darner dragonfly

Darners are some of the largest and fastest of all dragonflies. When hunting, the darner zooms back and forth with its legs held ready to seize prey. The male is very territorial – he has a particular area that he patrols and defends. Females are allowed to enter the territory, but other male darners are chased away.

Darter

This type of dragonfly gets its name from its fast darting flight. Like all dragonflies, darters lay their eggs in or close to water. The young are called nymphs or naiads. They look quite different from adults and live in water, catching prey such as tadpoles.

Family: Libellulidae
Size: 2–6 cm (¾–2 ½ in) long
Number of species: 1,250

Darter

Family: Panorpidae
Size: 1.2–2 cm (½–¾ in) long
Number of species: 400

Scorpionfly

This insect gets its name from the curving end of the male's body, which looks like a scorpion's sting. Adults have two pairs of wings and long thin legs. They eat nectar and fruit as well as insects.

Scorpionfly

Darner dragonfly

Bugs, lice, fleas and beetles

These are some of the most numerous of all insects. Beetles form the largest group of insects and account for 40 per cent of known insect species. One of the reasons for their success is that they can adapt to almost any type of food. Bugs, too, feed on a wide range of foods, from plant juices to human blood. Lice and fleas live as parasites, feeding on the blood, skin, feathers or hair of other animals.

Bugs, lice and fleas

Although the name bug is used for insects generally, it also describes a particular group of insects. These include a wide variety of species such as aphids, cicadas and stinkbugs. All have special needlelike mouthparts for piercing food and sucking out the juices. Lice are small wingless insects which live on birds and mammals. There are two types: sucking lice and chewing lice. Fleas, too, are wingless. They have powerful legs to help them leap on to other animals to feed.

Treehopper

Many of these little bugs have strangely shaped extensions on the thorax, which makes them look like the sharp thorns of plants. They feed mostly on sap from trees and other plants.

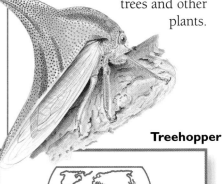

Treehopper

Family: Membracidae
Size: 0.6–1.2 cm (¼–½ in) long
Number of species: 2,500

Aphid

These small soft-bodied insects are familiar to gardeners because they feed on sap from the leaves and stems of plants and can damage them. They reproduce extremely quickly, but many are destroyed by insects such as ladybirds and parasitic wasps.

Aphid

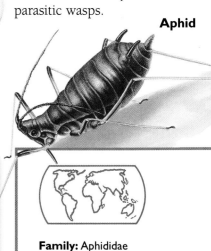

Family: Aphididae
Size: up to 0.9 cm (⅜ in) long
Number of species: 4,100

Cicada

This insect is best known for the shrill, almost constant call of the males. The sound is made by a pair of structures called tymbals, located on the abdomen, which are vibrated by special muscles. Female cicadas usually lay their eggs in slits they make in tree branches. The nymphs young live under the ground and feed on plant roots.

Cicada

Family: Cicadidae
Size: up to 5 cm (2 in) long
Number of species: 2,500

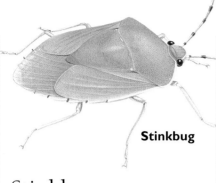

Stinkbug

Family: Pentatomidae
Size: 0.6–2 cm (¼–¾ in) long
Number of species: 5,250

Stinkbug

Stinkbugs get their name from the foul-smelling liquid they squirt at any creature that tries to attack them. The liquid comes from glands on the underside of the stinkbug's body. The stinkbug's mouthparts are inside its beaklike snout. It uses these for piercing the surface of a plant or animal to get at the sap or body juices.

Plant bug

The biggest group of true bugs, plant bugs live in every kind of habitat. Most feed on leaves, seeds and fruit and some are serious pests of food crops such as alfalfa. Other plant bugs are more welcome to farmers since they feed on insects such as aphids, which are also pests. Plant bugs have delicate, often brightly coloured bodies.

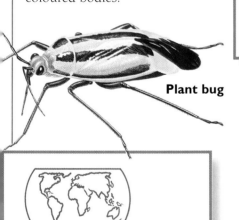

Plant bug

Family: Miridae
Size: 0.3–1.9 cm (⅛–¾ in) long
Number of species: 7,000

Head louse

The head louse is a sucking louse that lives on human heads, feeding on blood. It stays on the head by holding on to hairs with its strong legs and claws, and also glues its small eggs to the hairs of its host.

Hair

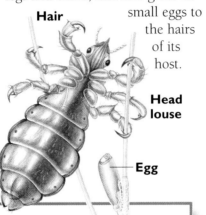

Head louse

Egg

Family: Pediculidae
Size: 0.15–0.3 cm (¹⁄₁₆–⅛ in) long
Number of species: 2

Froghopper

Like tiny frogs, froghoppers hop about on plants as they feed. They lay their eggs on plant stems and when the nymphs hatch they cover themselves with a substance much like spit, or saliva. This comes from glands on the abdomen and mixes with air to form a frothy mass. The froth helps to protect the nymphs and hides them from enemies.

Bedbug

Bedbugs usually stay hidden during the day, then come out at night to feed on the blood of birds and mammals. They do not live on their host but in its home or nest, and their flattened bodies make it easy for them to hide in crevices. Adults can survive for weeks without food.

Bedbug

Family: Cimicidae
Size: up to 0.6 cm (¼ in) long
Number of species: 90

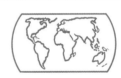

Family: Cercopidae
Size: 0.3–1.2 cm (⅛–½ in) long
Number of species: 1,400

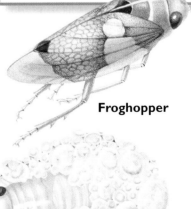

Froghopper

213

Family: Reduviidae
Size: 1.2–5 cm (½–2 in) long
Number of species: 5,500

Assassin bug

Assassin bug

Fierce-looking assassin bugs attack and kill other insects, such as caterpillars, beetles and bees. Once the bug has grasped its prey, it injects some spit, or saliva, which paralyses its victim. The bug then sucks up the prey's body juices. Some assassin bugs also bite large mammals, including humans, to feed on their blood. These bites can be painful and may even carry disease.

Chigoe flea

Like other fleas, chigoes live on the blood of humans and other animals. The flea causes a reaction in the host that makes the skin grow and engulf the insect. The female chigoe lays her eggs while embedded in this way.

Chigoe flea

Family: Tungidae
Size: 0.3–0.6 cm (⅛–¼ in) long
Number of species: 20

Family: Pulicidae
Size: up to 0.6 cm (¼ in) long
Number of species: 200

Family: Psocidae
Size: 0.15–0.6 cm (1/16–¼ in) long
Number of species: 500

Bark louse

Bark louse

Bark lice are not lice at all but small insects called psocids. There are both winged and wingless species. Most live outdoors on or under the bark of trees and bushes and feed on lichen and algae. Others live indoors, feeding on mould or stored food, and are often called booklice.

Cat flea

Cat flea

Like most fleas, the cat flea can jump up to 200 times its length. This helps it leap on to cats to feed on their blood. The spiny combs on the flea's head help to anchor it in the host's fur. The finer the host's fur, the closer together the spines of the comb are. The flea also uses its hooklike claws to hold on to the host's skin. Female fleas lay their eggs in the nest or bedding of the host animal.

Feather louse

Feather lice are chewing lice and live on a wide range of birds. They have two claws on each leg which they use to cling on to their host's feathers. They feed by biting off pieces of feather with their strong jaws. Females lay up to 100 eggs, which they fix to the feathers of the host with a gluey substance made in their own bodies.

Feather

Feather louse

Family: Philopteridae
Size: 0.15 cm (1/16 in) long
Number of species: 2,700

214

Beetles

More than a quarter of a million species of beetles are known and there are certainly many more yet to be discovered. They live in almost every type of habitat, from polar lands to rainforests, and feed on almost every type of food with their strong chewing mouthparts. Typically, beetles have two pairs of wings – the front pair are thick and hard and act as covers for the more delicate back wings. When beetles are at rest, their back wings are folded safely away under the front wings.

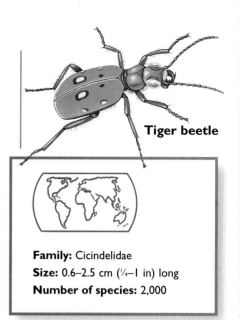

Tiger beetle

Family: Cicindelidae
Size: 0.6–2.5 cm (¼–1 in) long
Number of species: 2,000

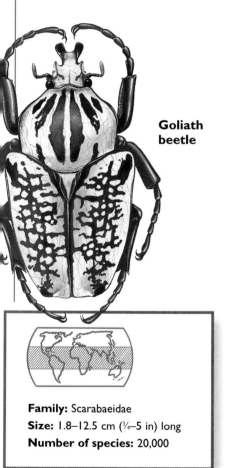

Goliath beetle

Family: Scarabaeidae
Size: 1.8–12.5 cm (¾–5 in) long
Number of species: 20,000

Family: Staphylinidae
Size: up to 4 cm (1½ in) long
Number of species: 27,000

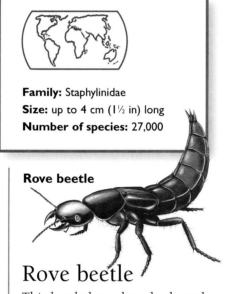

Rove beetle

Rove beetle

This beetle has a long body and short wing cases which cover only a little of the abdomen. When it is disturbed, it holds the back end of its body up, like a scorpion does. Both adult rove beetles and their larvae prey on insects and other small creatures such as worms.

Tiger beetle

The colourful tiger beetle has long legs and is a fast runner. A fierce, active hunter, it catches smaller insects in its strong jaws. The female beetle lays its eggs in the sand. When the larvae hatch, they dig burrows where they hide, waiting to grab passing prey.

Whirligig beetle

Glossy whirligig beetles swim on the surface of ponds and streams, feeding on insects that fall into the water. Their eyes are divided into two parts so that they can see above and below the water surface at the same time. Larval whirligigs eat water insects, but they also hunt other small creatures such as snails.

Goliath beetle

One of the largest and heaviest of all insects is the goliath beetle, found in Africa. Males are the giants; females are smaller and less brightly patterned. These beetles have strong front legs and are excellent climbers. They clamber up into trees in search of sap and soft fruit to eat.

Family: Gyrinidae
Size: 0.3–1.5 cm (⅛–⅝ in) long
Number of species: 750

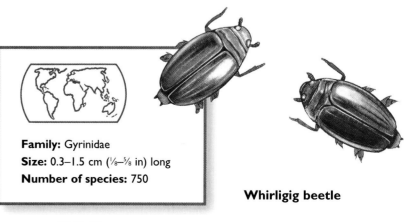

Whirligig beetle

Stag beetles

With their large head and massive jaws, male stag beetles are among the most spectacular of all insects. But despite their fearsome appearance, these insects are harmless and feed mostly on tree sap and other liquids.

There are about 1,250 species of stag beetles, some measuring up to 10 cm (4 in) long. Most stag beetles are black or brownish in colour. They usually live in woodland and are particularly common in tropical areas.

The jaws of the males are branched like the antlers of a stag and, like stags, these beetles take part in fierce battles with one another to win females. They rarely bite, just use their "antlers". Sometimes they damage each other's wing cases. The beetle with the biggest jaws usually wins the contest.

Female stag beetles lay their eggs in cracks in logs or dead tree stumps. When the larvae hatch, they feed on the juices of the rotting wood.

Larva and pupa

Stag beetle eggs hatch into wormlike, C-shaped larvae called grubs. They spend most of their time feeding and grow quickly. As a larva grows, it moults several times – it sheds its skin to allow for the increase in body size. When the larva is full grown, it becomes a pupa – the stage during which the larva changes into an adult beetle. When the process is complete, a winged adult beetle comes out of the pupa.

Female stag beetle

The female stag beetle is smaller than the battling male and does not have such large jaws. However, she can give a much more powerful nip if under threat. The male's mighty jaws are so specialised for fighting that they are almost useless for feeding or biting.

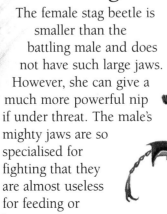

Its wing cases raised, this magnificent **stag beetle** is about to take to the air. When the beetle is not in flight, the tough wing cases, formed from the front wings, protect the more delicate back wings, which are folded underneath.

The helpless loser

If a stag beetle lands on its back after a battle it is very hard for it to right itself again. In this position, it is extremely easy for other enemies, such as birds, to snap the beetle up.

Battling rivals

The beetles usually meet on the branch of a tree. As they struggle, each male tries to lock the other in its jaws – the jaws are just the right shape to fit around the top part of the stag beetle's body. Once one competitor succeeds in grabbing the other, he lifts the loser up and tries to throw him off the branch.

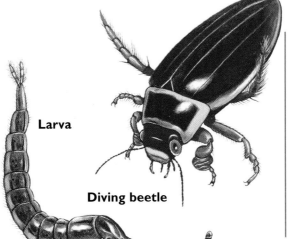

Diving beetle

Diving beetles live in ponds and lakes. They swim by moving their paddlelike back legs together as oars. When they dive, these beetles can stay under for some time, using air trapped under the wing cases. Both adults and larvae hunt prey.

Larva

Diving beetle

Family: Dytiscidae
Size: 0.15–4 cm (¹⁄₁₆–1½ in) long
Number of species: 3,500

Carrion beetle

These brightly coloured beetles and their larvae feed on dead animals, such as mice and birds. Some carrion beetles dig under the bodies, causing them to sink into the ground. They then lay their eggs on the buried decaying creature so that their young have a ready supply of food to eat when they hatch.

Family: Silphidae
Size: up to 4 cm (1½ in) long
Number of species: 250

Carrion beetle

Family: Buprestidae
Size: 2–6 cm (¾–2¼ in) long
Number of species: 14,000

Family: Cerambycidae
Size: up to 18 cm (7 in) long, including antennae
Number of species: 25,000

Longhorn beetle

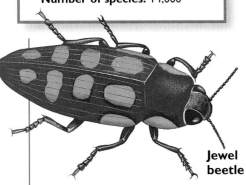

Jewel beetle

Jewel beetle

With their gleaming metallic colours, jewel beetles deserve their name. They live in woodland, usually in tropical areas, where the adults feed on flower nectar and leaves. The larvae bore into dead or living wood as they eat and can cause a great deal of damage.

Longhorn beetle

This beetle has extremely long antennae – up to three times the length of its body. While her mate stands guard, the female longhorn lays her eggs in the crevices in living trees or logs. When the larvae hatch, they tunnel into the wood as they feed and may cause considerable damage to timber and trees. The larvae also eat roots. Adult longhorn beetles feed on pollen and nectar.

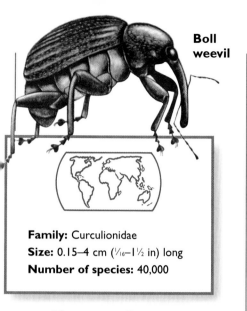

Boll weevil

Family: Curculionidae
Size: 0.15–4 cm (¹⁄₁₆–1½ in) long
Number of species: 40,000

Boll weevil

This insect belongs to the weevil family, all of which eat plants and can cause serious damage. The boll weevil uses its long snout to bore into the seedpods – called bolls – and buds of cotton plants. The female also lays her eggs in holes made in seedpods.

Darkling beetle

Common in dry areas, where they lurk under stones, darkling beetles scurry out at night to feed. They are scavengers and eat many kinds of food, including rotting wood, insect larvae and stored grain. Some desert-living darklings have long legs and can move quickly as they run from one patch of shade to another.

Family: Tenebrionidae
Size: 2–4.5 cm (¾–1¾ in) long
Number of species: 15,000

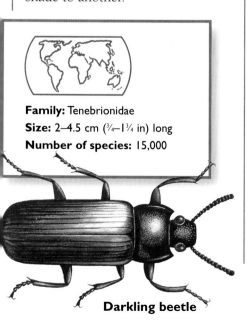

Darkling beetle

Ladybird

The ladybird's round shiny body makes it one of the most easily identifiable of all insects. Adults and larvae feed mainly on aphids, which suck the juices of plants and can be serious pests. Without ladybirds, these insects would be a far greater problem for farmers and gardeners. The ladybird's bright colours warn its enemies that it tastes unpleasant and may be poisonous. Ladybirds often hibernate, sheltering under logs, bark, piles of leaves or in attics.

Ladybird

Family: Coccinellidae
Size: up to 0.9 cm (⅜ in) long
Number of species: 5,000

Firefly

Fireflies, also known as glow-worms, can produce a yellowish-green light in a special area at the end of the abdomen. Each species of firefly flashes its light in a particular pattern to attract mates of its own kind. Male fireflies have wings, but females are often wingless and look like larvae. Fireflies usually glow at dusk and can shut off their light when it is not required.

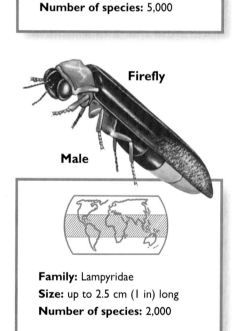

Firefly

Male

Family: Lampyridae
Size: up to 2.5 cm (1 in) long
Number of species: 2,000

Click beetle

The clicking sound made as they leap in the air to right themselves when they fall on their backs, gives these beetles their name. They can jump as high as 30 cm (11¾ in). Adult beetles live on the ground or in rotting wood.

Click beetle

Family: Elateridae
Size: up to 6 cm (2¼ in) long
Number of species: 8,500

Flies, moths and butterflies

Robber fly

F lies are thought of as dirty and disease-carrying, but they do have their value. Like bees, they pollinate plants as they feed and they are an important source of food for many other creatures, such as birds. Also, their scavenging habits help to get rid of decaying waste, such as dung and dead bodies. Butterflies and moths are much more attractive insects. They pollinate plants, too, as they flit from flower to flower, sipping nectar.

Flies

One of the larger groups of insects, with more than 90,000 known species, flies are common almost everywhere. One of the few land-based creatures in Antarctica is a midge, a type of fly. An important feature of flies is that they have only one pair of wings. The hind wings are reduced to small knobbed structures called halteres, which help the fly to balance in flight. Flies usually take liquid food. Many feed on nectar and sap from plants or lap up juices from rotting plants. Some, such as mosquitoes, suck blood from humans and other animals.

Family: Asilidae
Size: 0.6–4.5 cm (¼–1¾ in) long
Number of species: 5,000

Robber fly

A fast-moving hunter, the robber fly chases and catches other insects in the air or pounces on them on the ground. It has strong bristly legs for seizing its prey. Once it has caught its victim, the robber fly sucks out its body fluids with its sharp mouthparts. Larvae live in soil or rotting wood, where they feed on the larvae of other insects.

Midge

Tiny delicate insects, midges fly in huge swarms, usually in the evening, and are often seen near ponds and streams. There are two families of midges, those in the Chironomidae family do not bite, but those that belong to the other family bite other animals, including humans.

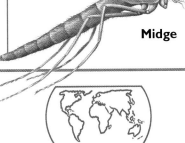

Midge

Horsefly

These flies have particularly large iridescent (shimmering) eyes. Males feed on pollen and nectar, but female horseflies take blood from mammals, including humans. Their bites can be painful and the flies may carry diseases such as anthrax.

Family: Tabanidae
Size: 0.6–2.5 cm (¼–1 in) long
Number of species: 4,100

Family: Chironomidae
Size: 0.15–0.9 cm (¹⁄₁₆–³⁄₈ in) long
Number of species: 5,000

Horsefly

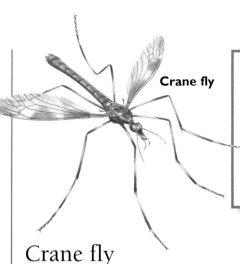

Crane fly

Family: Tipulidae
Size: 0.6–6 cm (¼–2¼ in) long
Number of species: 15,000

Family: Calliphoridae
Size: 0.6–1.5 cm (¼–⅝ in) long
Number of species: 1,500

Crane fly

With their long thin legs, crane flies look like large mosquitoes, but they do not bite or suck blood. The largest have a wingspan of as much as 7 cm (2¾ in). Most adults live only a few days and probably do not eat at all. The larvae feed mainly on plant roots and rotting plants, although some do hunt for their food.

Hover fly

Also known as flower flies, adult hover flies feed on pollen and nectar and are often seen around flowers. They are expert fliers and can hover with ease and even fly backwards. Many species are brightly coloured and look much like bees or wasps. They do not sting, however. Some hover fly larvae hunt insects such as aphids. Others feed on plants or live in the nests of bees or wasps, where they feed on their larvae.

Blowfly

Many blowflies are coloured metallic blue or green. Adults feed on pollen and nectar as well as fluids from rotting matter. Many lay their eggs in carrion – the bodies of dead animals – or in dung, so that the larvae, called maggots, have plenty of food to eat when they hatch.

Blowfly

Housefly

Found almost everywhere in the world, houseflies suck liquids from manure and other decaying matter and from fresh fruit and plants. These insects can be dangerous as they may carry diseases.

Family: Tephritidae
Size: 0.3–0.9 cm (⅛–⅜ in) long
Number of species: 4,500

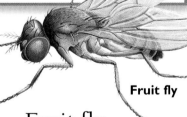

Fruit fly

Fruit fly

These little flies are common around flowers and overripe fruit. Their larvae feed on plant matter and some are serious pests, causing great damage to fruit trees and other crops.

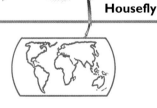

Housefly

Family: Muscidae
Size: 0.3–1.2 cm (⅛–½ in) long
Number of species: 3,000

Family: Syrphidae
Size: 0.6–3 cm (¼–1¼ in) long
Number of species: 6,000

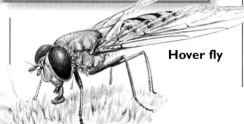

Hover fly

221

Butterflies and moths

Everywhere in the world that plants grow there are butterflies and moths. Known as the Lepidoptera, this is the second largest group of insects, containing about 150,000 species. Caddis flies look similar to butterflies and moths but are in fact a separate group called the Trichoptera.

The young butterfly or moth is called a caterpillar. Caterpillars spend most of their lives feeding on plants and growing fast. When it has reached its full size, a caterpillar becomes a pupa. During this stage, it makes its transformation from wingless larva to winged adult.

Clothes moth

The caterpillars of the clothes moth feed on hair and feathers in animal nests and on the dried corpses of small mammals and birds. Few creatures, other than some beetle larvae, can digest these difficult foods. Because humans use animal wool to make clothes, the caterpillars often come into our homes to feed on cloth. The adult moths are small and brownish in colour, with narrow front wings that are folded neatly over the body when at rest. They do not usually eat anything.

Geometrid moth

Geometrids have slender bodies and fragile wings. When they are at rest, they spread their wings out flat. Their caterpillars are known as inchworms or "loopers" because of the loop shape they make as they move. They eat leaves and may cause serious damage to trees.

Family: Tineidae
Size: wingspan 0.6–2 cm (¼–¾ in)
Number of species: 2,500

Clothes moth

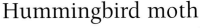

Caterpillar

Family: Geometridae
Size: wingspan 1.2–4 cm (½–1½ in)
Number of species: 18,000

Family: Sphingidae
Size: wingspan 3–15 cm (1¼–6 in)
Number of species: 1,200

Hummingbird moth

Geometrid moth

Hummingbird moth

Many of the scales on the wings of this moth drop off after its first flight, leaving large clear areas. It feeds on flower nectar, using its long proboscis, or feeding tube, to reach deep into the flowers. It hovers as it feeds, making a noise a little like the sound of a hummingbird's wings.

Caterpillar

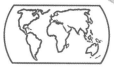
Atlas moth

Atlas moth

These brightly patterned moths are some of the largest in the world. Most have transparent scaleless patches on their broad wings and feathery antennae. The antennae help male moths pick up the scent signals given off by females when looking for mates. Adults have very small mouthparts and do not generally feed during their short lives.

Family: Saturniidae
Size: wingspan 2.5–25 cm (1–9¾ in)
Number of species: 1,100

Cotton boll moth

This moth belongs to one of the biggest families of moths. Most moths in this family fly at night and are dull in colour. The cotton boll caterpillar feeds on cotton seedpods and can damage the plants.

Cotton boll moth

Family: Noctuidae
Size: wingspan 1.2–7.5 cm (½–3 in)
Number of species: 25,000

Larva

Large caddis fly

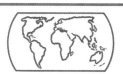

Family: Phryganeidae
Size: wingspan 1.2–2.5 cm (½–1 in)
Number of species: 500

Tiger moth

Tiger moths have broad hairy bodies and boldly patterned wings. The bright markings of these moths, and of their hairy caterpillars, warn birds and mammals that they are unpleasant to eat. The caterpillars feed on plants that are poisonous to vertebrate animals and store the poison for their own protection.

Family: Arctiidae
Size: wingspan 2–7 cm (¾–2¾ in)
Number of species: 2,500

Large caddis fly

Caddis flies look like moths but have hairs not scales on the body and wings. They have short mouthparts for lapping up food instead of a coiled proboscis. The caterpillarlike larvae are usually aquatic and they live and pupate in water in cases made of leaves, stones or twigs.

Family: Saturniidae
Size: wingspan 2.5–25 cm (1–9¾ in)
Number of species: 1,100

Luna moth

This beautiful moth has wings that can measure up to 11 cm (4¼ in) across with long tails trailing from them. It lives in forests and its caterpillars feed on the leaves of trees such as hickory, walnut and birch. The caterpillars pupate in a cocoon on the ground.

Tiger moth

Luna moth

Sphinx moths

Of all butterflies and moths, sphinx moths, also called hawkmoths, are some of the most powerful fliers. Their wings beat so fast that they make a whirring noise. The moths can even hover like hummingbirds in front of flowers as they feed.

Like all moths, adult sphinx moths eat liquid food such as plant nectar. They suck up the food with a special kind of tongue called a proboscis. This structure is hollow in the middle, like a drinking straw, and is kept rolled up under the head when not in use. Sphinx moths have the longest tongues of any moths and can feed on nectar at the bottom of long tubelike flowers.

There are about 1,200 species of sphinx moths, some with wingspans of up to 15 cm (6 in). Most have large heavy bodies and long narrow front wings. Their caterpillars are fat and smooth, sometimes with a hornlike structure at the end of the abdomen.

Bee sphinx moth

A bee sphinx moth plunges its long tongue deep into a flower. With its broad striped body and the large clear areas without scales on its wings, this moth looks amazingly like a bee as it hovers over plants. It flies by day, not at night.

Poplar sphinx moth

The colour and irregular shape of the poplar sphinx moth's wings help it to hide on bark as it rests during the day. Its caterpillars feed on the leaves of trees such as poplar and willow.

Egg

Caterpillar

Egg to pupa

As soon as a caterpillar hatches from its egg it starts to feed, devouring plants with its strong chewing mouthparts. It grows fast and sheds its skin several times as it gets bigger. When fully grown, the caterpillar becomes a pupa. The bee sphinx moth pupates on the ground in a cocoon made of silk.

Pupa in cocoon

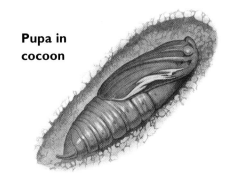

224

Oleander sphinx moth

This is one of the most beautifully patterned of all moths. Its caterpillar feeds on the leaves of plants such as oleander and grows up to 15 cm (6 in) long.
It has bold eyespots on its body, which can fool a predator into thinking it is a much larger creature than it really is.

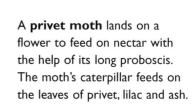

A **privet moth** lands on a flower to feed on nectar with the help of its long proboscis. The moth's caterpillar feeds on the leaves of privet, lilac and ash.

White-lined sphinx moth

The white-lined sphinx moth visits flowers at night to feed. Like most moths, its antennae are very sensitive to smell as well as touch. It can pick up the faintest scents, which helps it to find flowers in the darkness.

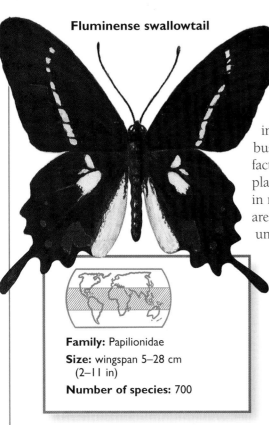

Fluminense swallowtail

Fluminense swallowtail

This beautiful butterfly is one of Brazil's most endangered insects. Drainage of its swampy, bushy habitat to build houses and factories and to lay out banana plantations has caused it to die out in many sites. Even the 10 or so areas in which it still lives are under threat. Conservationists hope to be able to catch some butterflies and establish new colonies in safer places.

Family: Papilionidae
Size: wingspan 5–28 cm (2–11 in)
Number of species: 700

Morpho

Morpho butterflies live in the rainforests of Central and South America. The males are brilliantly coloured – the beautiful iridescence of their wings is caused by the arrangement of the rows of scales which reflect the light. Females are much plainer. Like all Nymphalid butterflies, morphos walk on only four legs. The front pair are too small to be used for walking.

Morpho

Family: Nymphalidae
Size: wingspan 2.5–11 cm (1–4¼ in) long
Number of species: 3,500

Cairns birdwing

Cairns birdwings, like all birdwings, are found only in Southeast Asia and northern Australia. Females are bigger than males, but males are more colourful. Birdwings, which are the biggest butterflies in the world, are highly prized by collectors and many are now rare. Adults feed on flower nectar, but caterpillars eat the leaves of plants that are poisonous to most creatures.

Swallowtail

Boldly patterned swallowtail butterflies get their name from the tail-like extensions on the back wings. These may help to distract enemies away from the vulnerable head area. Adult swallowtails feed on flower nectar, and their caterpillars usually eat the leaves of trees such as ash and bay.

Family: Papilionidae
Size: wingspan 5–28 cm (2–11 in)
Number of species: 700

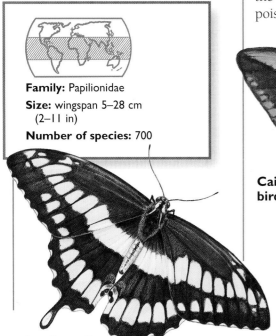

Swallowtail

Cairns birdwing

Male

Family: Papilionidae
Size: wingspan 5–28 cm (2–11 in)
Number of species: 700

226

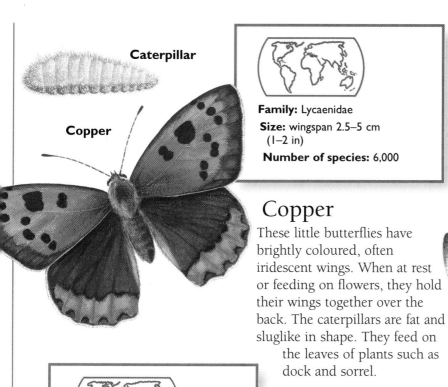

Caterpillar

Copper

Family: Lycaenidae
Size: wingspan 2.5–5 cm
(1–2 in)
Number of species: 6,000

Cabbage white

The cabbage white, like others in its family, is a very common butterfly. Unlike many butterflies, cabbage whites have well-developed front legs, which are used for walking. Adults feed on nectar. Their caterpillars eat cabbage and other leafy crops and can do great damage.

Copper

These little butterflies have brightly coloured, often iridescent wings. When at rest or feeding on flowers, they hold their wings together over the back. The caterpillars are fat and sluglike in shape. They feed on the leaves of plants such as dock and sorrel.

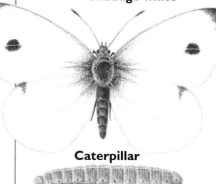

Cabbage white

Caterpillar

Family: Nymphalidae
Size: wingspan 2.5–11 cm
(1–4¼ in)
Number of species: 3,500

Monarch

Every autumn, millions of monarch butterflies fly south from Canada to Mexico – a distance of about 3,200 km (2,000 miles). The following spring, the butterflies lay their eggs as they return north. The new monarch butterflies then fly north to Canada before autumn comes again.

Family: Pieridae
Size: wingspan 0.9–7 cm
(¾–2¾ in) long
Number of species: 1,300

Monarch

Queen Alexandra's birdwing

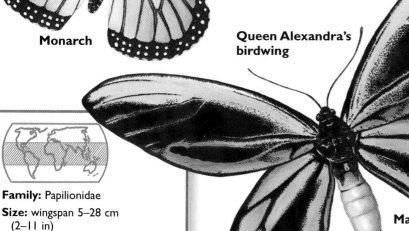

Male

Queen Alexandra's birdwing

The female of this giant butterfly is the biggest in the world, with a wingspan of up to 28 cm (11 in). It is very valuable, so local people catch it to sell to traders. It is hoped that if some of the forest in which the butterflies live can be saved in reserves, local people might be able to make money from tourism instead.

Family: Papilionidae
Size: wingspan 5–28 cm
(2–11 in)
Number of species: 700

Bees, wasps, ants and termites

Bees, wasps and ants belong to a large group of insects known as the Hymenoptera. Although they vary greatly in appearance, most have a definite "waist" at the front of the abdomen. They have chewing mouthparts and tonguelike structures for sucking liquids such as nectar from flowers. Hymenopterans that do have wings have two pairs, but many worker ants are wingless. Ants and some bees and wasps live in social colonies in elaborate nests. Termites are not related to ants, bees and wasps, but they do live in huge colonies. They make nests in soil, trees or specially built mounds.

Leafcutter bee

Family: Megachilidae
Size: 0.9–2 cm (³⁄₈–¾ in) long
Number of species: 3,000

Leafcutter bee

This bee gets its name from its habit of cutting circular pieces of leaves and flowers with its jaws. It uses these pieces to line larval cells in its tunnel nest, made in soil or rotting wood. Stores of nectar and pollen are put into the cells and an egg is then laid in each one.

Bees

There are about 22,000 species of bees. They have two pairs of wings and their bodies are covered with tiny hairs. Some kinds, such as leafcutter bees, live alone and make their own nests for their young. Others, such as honeybees and bumblebees, live in huge colonies that may contain thousands of bees. They are the only kinds of bees that produce honey.

Bumblebee

Bumblebee

Bumblebees are large hairy insects, usually black in colour with some yellow markings. In spring, queens, which are the only bumblebees to live through the winter, look for underground nest sites. Each queen collects pollen and nectar and makes food called beebread. Later, she lays eggs, and when the larvae hatch they feed on the beebread. These larvae become adult worker bees and they take over the work of the colony while the queen continues to lay eggs.

Family: Apidae
Size: 0.3–2.5 cm (¹⁄₈–1 in) long
Number of species: 1,000

Plasterer bee

Orchid bee

Most orchid bees live in tropical areas and are brightly coloured. Males are attracted to orchid flowers for their nectar. They pollinate the flowers and collect scent, which may play a part in their mating rituals.

Orchid bee

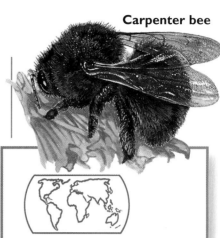

Carpenter bee

Family: Colletidae
Size: 0.3–2 cm (⅛–¾ in) long
Number of species: 6,000

Family: Apidae
Size: 0.3–2.5 cm (⅛–1 in) long
Number of species: 1,000

Plasterer bee

Plasterer bees nest in the ground in burrows with branching tunnels. They line the tunnels with a secretion from glands in the abdomen, which dries to a clear waterproof substance. Cells for larvae are made in the tunnels.

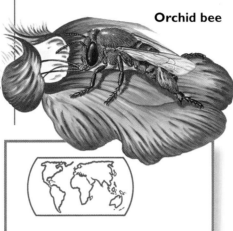

Family: Apidae
Size: 0.3–2.5 cm (⅛–1 in) long
Number of species: 1,000

Carpenter bee

The female carpenter bee chews a tunnel-like nest in wood. She makes a line of separate cells inside the tunnel, fills them with pollen and nectar food stores and lays one egg in each cell. She stays nearby and guards the nest against any enemies.

Cuckoo bee

Like its namesake the cuckoo bird, this wasplike bee lays its eggs in the nests of other bees, which have prepared food stores for their eggs. The cuckoo bee's eggs hatch first and the larvae eat up all the food intended for the host's larvae.

Family: Andrenidae
Size: 0.3–2 cm (⅛–¾ in) long
Number of species: 4,000

Stingless bee

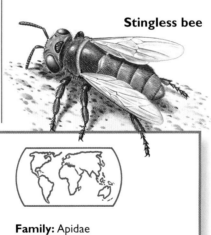

Mining bee

Family: Apidae
Size: 0.3–2.5 cm (⅛–1 in) long
Number of species: 1,000

Cuckoo bee

Family: Anthophoridae
Size: 0.9–1.2 cm (⅜–½ in) long
Number of species: 4,200

Mining bee

Mining bees nest in long branching tunnels which they dig in the ground. Cells in the tunnels are stocked with nectar and pollen and an egg is laid in each one. Each bee digs its own nest but large numbers may live close together.

Stingless bee

As their name suggests, these bees cannot sting, but they have strong jaws that they use to bite any intruders. They live in colonies and make nests under the ground in a tree trunk or even in part of a nest of a termite colony.

Wasps

Wasps are more useful than they seem. They feed their young on other insects, such as caterpillars and aphids, which harm garden and food plants. Without wasps there would be many more of these pests. Adult wasps feed mainly on nectar and the juice of ripe fruit. Many kinds of wasp, including mud daubers and spider wasps, live alone and make their own nests for their eggs. Others, such as common wasps and hornets, live in large colonies and make communal nests. Wasp colonies do not store food like honeybees and all the colony, except the queen, dies in winter.

Giant hornet

Family: Vespidae
Size: 1–3 cm (⅜–1¼ in) long
Number of species: 3,800

Giant hornet

Adult hornets feed on insects and nectar and grow up to 3 cm (1¼ in) long. They live in colonies in nests built of a papery material that is made from chewed up plants. The nest is usually in a tree or an old building. Larvae feed on insects caught by the adults

Gall wasp

These tiny wasps lay their eggs on particular species of plants. For reasons that are not fully understood the host plant forms a growth, called a gall, around the egg. When the larva hatches it feeds on the gall tissue.

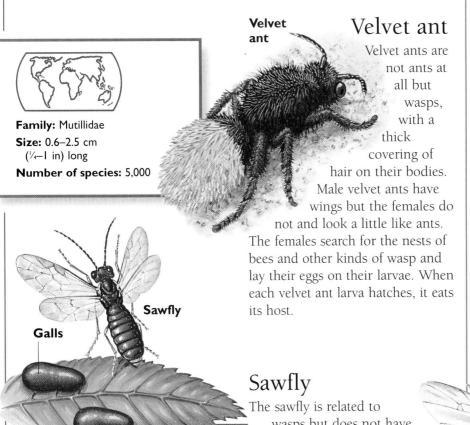

Velvet ant

Velvet ant

Velvet ants are not ants at all but wasps, with a thick covering of hair on their bodies. Male velvet ants have wings but the females do not and look a little like ants. The females search for the nests of bees and other kinds of wasp and lay their eggs on their larvae. When each velvet ant larva hatches, it eats its host.

Family: Mutillidae
Size: 0.6–2.5 cm (¼–1 in) long
Number of species: 5,000

Sawfly

Galls

Sawfly

The sawfly is related to wasps but does not have the "waist" between the abdomen and thorax. The female sawfly lays her eggs on willow leaves. Little red galls start to form on the leaf as soon as the eggs are laid. When the larvae hatch they eat the contents of the galls.

Family: Tenthredinidae
Size: 0.3–2 cm (⅛–¾ in) long
Number of species: 4,000

Family: Cynipidae
Size: 0.15–0.9 cm (1/16–⅜ in) long
Number of species: 1,250

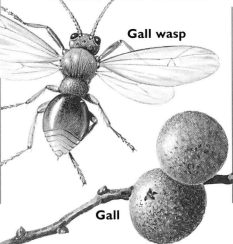

Gall wasp

Gall

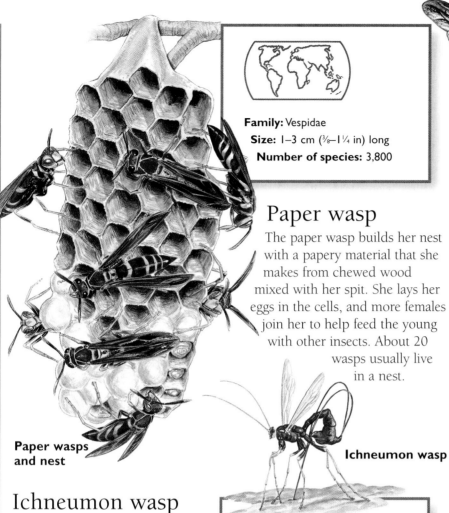

Blue-black spider wasp

Family: Vespidae
Size: 1–3 cm (⅜–1¼ in) long
Number of species: 3,800

Paper wasp

The paper wasp builds her nest with a papery material that she makes from chewed wood mixed with her spit. She lays her eggs in the cells, and more females join her to help feed the young with other insects. About 20 wasps usually live in a nest.

Paper wasps and nest

Family: Pompilidae
Size: 0.9–5 cm (⅜–2 in) long
Number of species: 4,000

Blue-black spider wasp

Adult spider wasps feed on nectar but the female catches spiders to feed her young. She paralyses the spider with her sting and then places it in a nest cell with an egg and seals the top with mud. When the wasp larva hatches, it eats the spider.

Ichneumon wasp

The female ichneumon wasp can bore through wood to lay her eggs near the larvae of other insects such as wood wasps. She has a special long egg-laying tube, called an ovipositor. When the egg hatches, the ichneumon larva feeds on the host larva.

Ichneumon wasp

Family: Ichneumonidae
Size: 0.3–5 cm (⅛–2 in) long
Number of species: 20,000

Mud dauber

Mud daubers are solitary wasps, which feed on other insects and nectar. The female mud dauber wasp makes a nest of damp mud. Into each cell she puts an egg and some paralysed insects for her young to eat when it hatches.

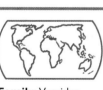

Family: Vespidae
Size: 1–3 cm (⅜–1¼ in) long
Number of species: 3,800

Common wasp

Common wasps, or yellow jackets, feed on nectar and other sweet things such as ripe fruit. They also catch other insects to feed their young. Wasps are well known for their sting. The pointed sting is at the end of the body and is linked to a bag of poison. The wasp uses its sting to kill prey and to defend itself against enemies – including humans.

Common wasp on an apple

Family: Sphecidae
Size: 0.9–5 cm (⅜–2 in) long
Number of species: 8,000

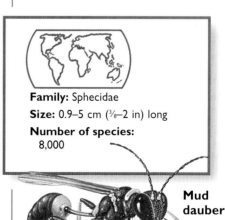

Mud dauber

231

Honeybees

Of all the many types of bees, honeybees are probably the best known. They pollinate countless food crops and produce millions of pounds' worth of honey and wax every year.

Many bees lead solitary lives, but honeybees live in huge colonies of thousands of bees, with a complex social organisation. Each colony has a queen. The queen bee is larger than the other bees and lays all the eggs of the colony. Most of the members of the colony are female workers. They care for the young, build and repair the nest and gather food, but they do not lay eggs.

There are male bees in the colony only at certain times of the year. They do not work and are there only to mate with new queens. The nest is made in a hollow tree or in a hive provided by a beekeeper and consists of sheets of hexagonal – six-sided – cells. These cells contain eggs and young as well as food stores of pollen and honey.

Workers

A worker honeybee lives only about six weeks. For the first week of her adult life she cares for the eggs and larvae of the colony. Then she helps to build cells and maintain the nest. Finally, she becomes a food gatherer, bringing nectar and pollen back to the nest.

The royal cell

Special cells for future queens hang from the edge of the comb. The larvae in queen cells are fed on royal jelly – a protein-rich substance from glands on the heads of workers. Worker larvae are fed royal jelly for a few days and then given pollen and nectar.

Busy bees

Worker bees always have plenty to do in the nest. When a bee returns from a foraging trip laden with pollen and nectar, the other bees gather around to collect the food stores. Workers also make the nest cells, building them from wax produced in glands on the underside of their abdomen. The bees pull out thin flakes of wax and knead them with their mouthparts until it is soft enough to use for building.

232

Equipped for work

All the tools needed by a worker bee are on her own body. On each front leg there are long hairs used to remove pollen from the body and a special notch for cleaning the antennae. On the middle legs there are fringes of hair for removing pollen from the forelegs and a spike for taking wax from glands in the abdomen. On each hind leg there is a pollen basket – a special area lined with hairs, where pollen is carried.

A worker **honeybee** has just returned from a foraging trip, with her pollen baskets full of golden-yellow pollen. Other workers gather round to help her unload the pollen and pack it into cells.

Ants and termites

Ants live in huge well-organised groups of thousands of individuals, called colonies. Most colonies make a nest of interconnecting tunnels in rotting wood or under the ground. Each colony includes at least one queen ant and she lays all of the eggs. The workers are also female but they cannot lay eggs. They do all the work of the colony, gathering food and looking after eggs and young. Termites are not related to ants, although their habits are similar. They build large nests with special chambers for eggs and young and for food storage.

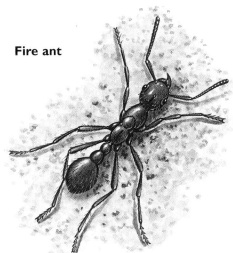

Fire ant

Fire ant

As its name suggests, the fire ant has a powerful bite and sting, which is extremely painful even to humans. It hunts other insects, which it stings to death, but also eats seeds, fruit and flowers. These ants make nests in the ground or under logs or stones.

Family: Formicidae
Size: 0.15–2.5 cm (¹⁄₁₆–1 in) long
Number of species: 8,800

Army ant

Unlike other ants, army ants do not build permanent nests. They march in search of prey, overpowering insects or other small creatures in their way. Periodically they stop to produce eggs and remain in one place until the young have developed. The worker ants link their bodies together, making a temporary nest called a bivouac to protect the queen and young.

Family: Formicidae
Size: 0.15–2.5 cm (¹⁄₁₆–1 in) long
Number of species: 8,800

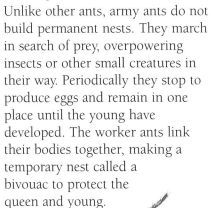

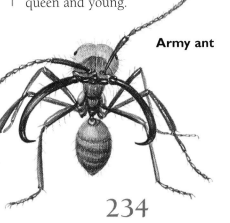

Army ant

Family: Formicidae
Size: 0.15–2.5 cm (¹⁄₁₆–1 in) long
Number of species: 8,800

Red ant

Red ant

The main food of red ants is aphid honeydew, a sweet liquid that is a by-product of the digestive system of these tiny bugs. The ant strokes the aphid to encourage it to release the sugary liquid from its body. Red ants also feed on flower nectar.

Family: Formicidae
Size: 0.15–2.5 cm (¹⁄₁₆–1 in) long
Number of species: 8,800

Harvester ant

Harvester ant

These ants get their name from their habit of feeding on seeds and grain crops. When the ants find a plentiful supply of seeds near their nest they leave scent trails to lead others in their colony to the food. In times of plenty, the ants collect more seeds than they can eat and store them in special granary areas in the nest.

Carpenter ant

Carpenter ant

Colonies of carpenter ants make their nests in wooden buildings or poles or in rotting tree trunks and often cause a great deal of damage. As with all ants, the queen lays all the eggs for the colony. As she lays, worker ants remove the eggs and take them to special brood chambers where they are cared for.

Leafcutter ant

These ants grow their own food. They cut pieces of leaves with their strong scissorlike jaws and carry them back to their underground nest. Here, the leaves are chewed up and mixed with droppings to make compost heaps. The ants eat the special fungus that grows on the compost.

Family: Formicidae
Size: 0.15–2.5 cm (¹⁄₁₆–1 in) long
Number of species: 8,800

Family: Formicidae
Size: 0.15–2.5 cm (¹⁄₁₆–1 in) long
Number of species: 8,800

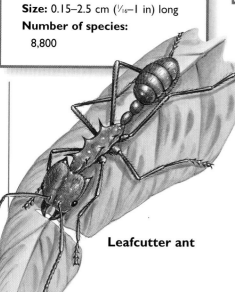

Leafcutter ant

Snouted termite

Most termite colonies have special soldier termites to defend them against enemies such as ants, which may attack their nests. The soldiers of this type of termite have long snouts, which they use to spray sticky bad-smelling fluid at ants and other enemies.

Snouted termite

Soldier

Family: Termitidae
Size: up to 6 cm (2¼ in) long
Number of species: 1,650

Drywood termite

These termites attack the wood of buildings, furniture and even stored timber. Special microscopic organisms in their gut help them digest their tough food. The special soldier termites have larger heads and jaws than the others and it is their job to defend the colony against enemies.

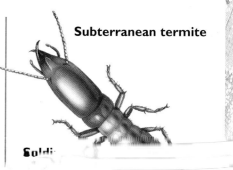

Family: Rhinotermitidae
Size: 0.6–0.9 cm (¼–⅜ in) long
Number of species: 200

Subterranean termite

As their name suggests, these termites live in underground nests. They live in warm wooded areas and eat the wood of rotting trees and roots.

Family: Kalotermitidae
Size: up to 2.5 cm (1 in) long
Number of species: 8,800

Drywood termite

Soldier

Spiders and scorpions

Arachnids, which include spiders, several types of scorpion, ticks and mites, are often confused with insects, but they are a separate group of invertebrates. They are very ancient creatures, which first lived on land at least 400 million years ago. Today, arachnids include a wide range of body forms, but generally they have four pairs of legs and do not have wings or antennae. Most live on land and hunt other creatures to eat.

Spiders

Most spiders are completely harmless. Only a few, such as the funnel-web spider, have a venomous bite that is dangerous to people. In fact, spiders do humans a service by keeping the insect population under control – all are hunters and they feed mostly on small insects. Some of the larger species, such as the bird-eating spider, even catch small animals and birds. All spiders can make silk with special glands at the end of the body, but not all build webs. Spiders use silk to line their burrows and some make silken traps that they hold between their legs to snare prey. Young spiders use long strands of silk as parachutes to help them fly away and find new territories.

Jumping spider

Unlike most spiders, the jumping spider has good eyesight, which helps it find prey. Once it has spotted something, the spider leaps on to its victim. Before jumping, it attaches a silk thread to the ground as a safety line along which it can return to its hideout.

Jumping spider

Family: Salticidae
Size: 0.3–1.5 cm (⅛–⅝ in) long
Number of species: 4,000

Black widow spider

The female black widow has comblike bristles on her back legs, which she uses to throw strands of silk over prey that gets caught in her web. She has a venomous bite. One drop is more deadly than the same amount of rattlesnake venom. Male black widows do not bite.

Family: Theridiidae
Size: up to 1.2 cm (½ in) long
Number of species: 2,500

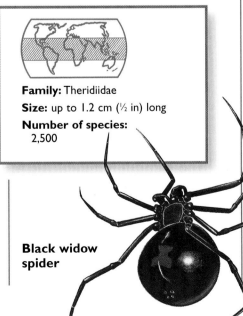

Black widow spider

Family: Lycosidae
Size: 0.3–4 cm (⅛–1½ in) long
Number of species: 2,500

Wolf spider

Fast-moving hunters like their namesake, wolf spiders creep up on prey and seize it after a final speedy dash. Most do not make webs. Wolf spiders have good eyesight, which helps them find prey.

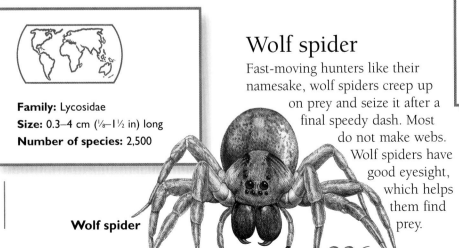

Wolf spider

Family: Ctenizidae
Size: 0.9–5 cm (⅜–2 in) long
Number of species: 700

Trapdoor spider

Trapdoor spider

The burrow of the trapdoor spider has a hinged lid at the top. The spider waits in its burrow until it senses the movement of prey overhead. It then pops out of the door, grabs the prey and takes it back into its burrow.

Crab spider

This spider moves by scuttling sideways like a crab. It does not make webs, but the smaller males sometimes use their silk to tie the females down before mating. Some crab spiders are dark brown or black, but those that usually sit on flowers to wait for prey are brightly coloured to match the petals.

Crab spider

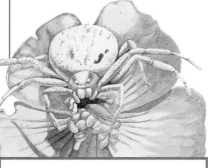

Family: Thomisidae
Size: 0.15–0.9 cm (¹⁄₁₆–⅜ in) long
Number of species: 3,000

Lichen spider

Mottled colours help keep this spider well hidden on lichen-covered tree bark. Tufts of tiny hairs on its legs break up any shadows which might otherwise reveal its presence. If the spider suspects an enemy is near, it flattens itself even more against the bark and becomes very difficult to see.

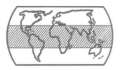

Family: Sparassidae
Size: 0.9–3 cm (⅜–1¼ in) long
Number of species: 1,000

Red-kneed tarantula

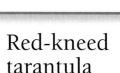

Family: Theraphosidae
Size: up to 9 cm (3½ in) long
Number of species: 300

Red-kneed tarantula

Tarantulas are some of the largest of all spiders, with legs spanning more than 20 cm (7¾ in). Most hide during the day and come out at night to hunt insects and small creatures which they kill with a venomous bite. Harmless to people, they are becoming popular pets. Local people are collecting so many for export that the spiders could soon become scarce in the wild.

Spitting spider

This unusual hunter approaches its victim and spits out two lines of a sticky substance from glands near its mouth. These fall in zigzags over the prey, pinning it down. The spider then kills its prey with a bite.

Family: Scytodidae
Size: 0.9 cm (⅜ in) long
Number of species: 200

Lichen spider

Spitting spider

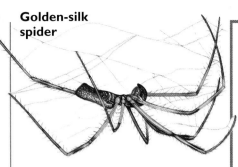

Golden-silk spider

Golden-silk spider

The female golden-silk spider is eight or nine times the length of the male and may weigh a hundred times as much. The male's size is, in fact, an advantage when he approaches the female to try to mate with her. Like any tiny insects that fly into her web, the male is too small to bother attacking so is left alone.

Family: Araneidae
Size: 0.15–3 cm (¹⁄₁₆–1¼ in) long
Number of species: 2,500

Common house spider

The house spider has long legs covered with strong bristles. It builds its large flat web in any quiet corner of a house, garage or shed. It stays beneath the web, waiting for prey to get tangled up in its sticky strands and then removes and eats the prey.

Purse-web spider

This spider builds a silken tube in a sloping burrow in the ground. The top of the tube extends above ground and is camouflaged with leaves. When an insect lands on the tube, the spider grabs it through the walls of the tube with her sharp fangs and drags it inside.

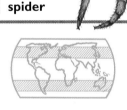

Purse-web spider

Family: Atypidae
Size: 0.9–3 cm (⅜–1¼ in) long
Number of species: 1

Common house spider

Family: Agelenidae
Size: 0.15–2 cm (¹⁄₁₆–¾ in) long
Number of species: 1,000

Funnel-web spider

This spider makes a funnel-shaped web that leads into an underground burrow. If a creature walks across the web, the spider senses the vibrations and rushes out for the kill. Funnel-webs prey on frogs and lizards as well as insects and have an extremely poisonous bite.

Family: Dipluridae
Size: about 3 cm (1¼ in) long
Number of species: about 100

Funnel-web spider

Dysdera crocata

These spiders have only six eyes – most spiders have eight. They spend the day hiding under stones and come out at night to hunt woodlice. Woodlice have strong external skeletons but this spider can pierce the body armour with its huge sharp fangs.

Family: Dysderidae
Size: 2 cm (¾ in) long
Number of species: 1

Dysdera crocata

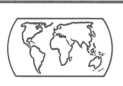

Family: Araeneidae
Size: 0.15–3 cm (¹⁄₁₆–1¼ in) long
Number of species: 2,500

Orchard spider

Family: Pisauridae
Size: 0.6–2.5 cm (¼–1 in) long
Number of species: 400

Orchard spider

Although a member of the orb weaver family, the orchard spider does not make a web. She simply sits on the branch of a tree and grabs any moth that comes near with her strong front legs. She may release a scent that attracts the moths to her.

Water spider

The water spider is the only spider that lives its whole life in water. It makes a special underwater home in which it can breathe air. Having spun a bell-shaped home of silk attached to water plants, the spider supplies it with bubbles of air collected at the water surface. It then sits inside its bell waiting for prey to come near. It pounces on the prey and takes it back to the bell to eat.

Nursery-web spider

These spiders do not build a web to catch prey but to protect their young. The female carries her egg sac with her until the eggs are almost ready to hatch. Then she spins a web over the eggs to protect them while they hatch. She stands guard nearby.

Nursery-web spider

Green lynx spider

Family: Agelenidae
Size: 0.15–2 cm (¹⁄₁₆–¾ in) long
Number of species: 1,000

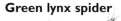

Family: Oxyopidae
Size: 0.3–1.5 cm (⅛–⅝ in) long
Number of species: 500

Water spider

Green lynx spider

The lynx spider is a fast-moving, active hunter. It does not build webs but chases its prey over plants, jumping from leaf to leaf. It has good eyesight, which helps it spot its prey and its green colour helps to keep it hidden when it rests on leaves. The female spins a silken egg sac that she attaches to plants.

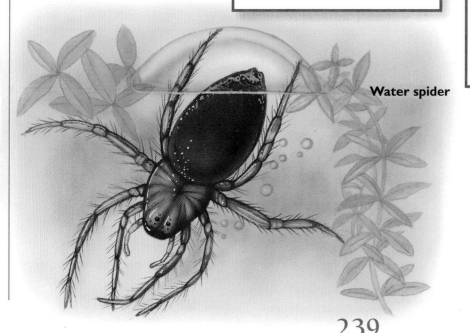

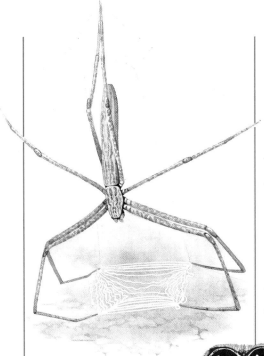

Orb weavers

Very few creatures build traps to catch their prey. Among the best known are the orb weaver spiders that build the webs most often seen in our houses and gardens. There are more than 2,500 different species of these spiders living all over the world.

Spiders build their webs with two types of silk, which comes from glands at the end of the body. The silk is liquid when it comes out of the nozzlelike openings of small structures, called spinnerets, at the end of the abdomen. One type hardens into extremely tough non-sticky thread; the other type is sticky and used for the centre of the web. Once the web is built, the spider waits near the centre or hides nearby, linked to the web by a signal thread. Through this, the spider can sense any movement or disturbance in the web. Once prey is caught in the sticky part of the web, the spider rushes over, bites it and wraps it in strands of silk to prevent it from escaping.

Ogre-faced spider

This spider takes its web to the prey. It makes a small but strong net of very sticky threads in a framework of dry silk. Once the trap is made, the spider hangs from a twig on silken lines, holding the net in its four front legs. When an insect comes near, the spider stretches the net wide so the prey flies into it and becomes entangled. The catch is then bundled up in the net and taken away to eat.

Building a web

First, the orb weaver spider makes a framework of strong non-sticky threads which are firmly attached to surrounding plants or other supports. Spokes are added and the spider spins a widely spaced temporary spiral. With everything locked in place, the spider then moves inwards, spinning the sticky spiral that will trap the prey and removing the temporary spiral. The whole process takes less than an hour and the spider may build a new web every night.

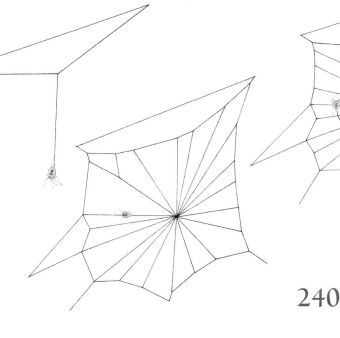

Sheet-web spider

Yet another kind of trap is woven by this spider. It makes a flat sheetlike web, which may measure as much as 30 cm (11¾ in) across, and lies in wait beneath it. Above the web there are many threads holding it in place. When prey hits these threads, it falls down on to the sheet web, where it is grabbed from below by the spider.

This orb weaver spider has caught a butterfly in her web and is wrapping the prey in threads of silk so that it cannot escape. She will then carry it off to eat in her hiding place near the web.

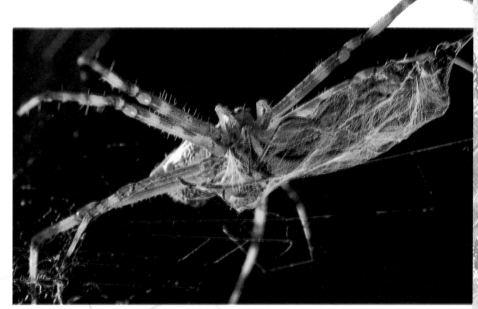

Waiting on the web

This garden spider is lying in wait for an insect to blunder into its web and get caught on its sticky threads. The spider has extra clawlike structures on each foot, which help it grip on to the dry lines of the web while avoiding the sticky threads. If the spider touches the sticky part, a special oily covering on its legs prevents it getting trapped.

Scorpions and other arachnids

Pseudoscorpion

There are about 1,500 kinds of scorpion living everywhere from deserts to rainforests in warm parts of the world. They use the venomous sting at the end of the body to kill prey and to defend themselves. A few kinds of scorpion have venom so strong that it can kill a human, but the sting of most is no worse than that of a bee or wasp. Also in the arachnid group are tiny mites and ticks. Mites eat aphid eggs and prey on other small insects. Some also live as parasites on other animals. Ticks feed on the blood of birds, mammals and reptiles.

Family: Chernetidae
Size: up to 0.6 cm (¼ in) long
Number of species: 1,000

Pseudoscorpion

These tiny soil-dwelling relatives of the scorpion have venom glands in their pedipalps, which they use when attacking prey. They do not have a sting. Pseudoscorpions have silk glands and they spin cocoons in which to spend the winter.

Centruroides scorpion

This scorpion hides under stones on the ground during the day and comes out at night to seize insects and spiders in its powerful pincers. The female carries her newborn young around on her back for a few weeks until they are big enough to fend for themselves.

Wind scorpion

Wind scorpion

Wind scorpions, also known as sunspiders, are related to true scorpions. Common in desert areas, these fast-running hunters come out at night to prey on insects and even small lizards. They use their large leglike pedipalps to catch prey and their front legs as feelers.

Family: Eremobatidae
Size: 1.5–4.5 cm (⅝–1¾ in) long
Number of species: 900

Whip scorpion

Not a true scorpion, the whip scorpion has a long thin tail and no sting. It has four pairs of legs but uses the first pair as feelers. The whip scorpion's other common name is vinegaroon because it can spray an acidic vinegary liquid from glands near the base of its tail when threatened.

Family: Buthidae
Size: 5–7 cm (2–2¾ in) long
Number of species: 700

Whip scorpion

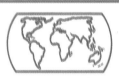

Centruroides scorpion

Family: Thelyphonidae
Size: 14.5 cm (5¾ in) long, including tail
Number of species: 100

Velvet mite

Family: Trombiculidae
Size: up to 0.5 cm (³⁄₁₆ in) long
Number of species: 200

Family: Pyroglyphidae
Size: 0.25–0.5 mm (¹⁄₁₀₀–³⁄₁₀₀ in) long
Number of species: 20

Velvet mite

This mite gets its common name from the thick soft hair that covers its rounded body. Adult velvet mites are free-living and feed mostly on insect eggs. They lay their eggs on the ground. When the larvae hatch they live as parasites on insects and spiders, feeding on their body fluids.

House dust mite

These mites are common in houses throughout the world. They feed on scales of skin found in house dust. Their droppings contain materials that can cause an allergic reaction or asthma (difficulty in breathing) in some sensitive people.

House dust mite

Scorpion

The scorpion finds prey mostly by its sense of touch, using fine hairs attached to nerves on the body, legs and claws to sense movements. It grabs the prey in its huge claws and then swings its sting forwards over its body to inject poison into its victim to paralyse or kill it before eating.

Family: Phalangiidae
Size: 0.3–2 cm (¹⁄₈–¾ in) long
Number of species: 3,400

Harvestman

Harvestman

Also known as the daddy-long-legs, this relative of spiders has a rounded body without the narrow waist typical of spiders. All its legs are very long and thin but the second pair are the longest. Usually active at night, the harvestman hunts insects. The female lays her eggs in the ground, where they stay through the winter until they hatch in the spring.

Scorpion

Family: Buthidae
Size: 5–7 cm (2–2¾ in) long
Number of species: 700

Family: Ixodidae
Size: 0.15–0.3 cm (¹⁄₁₆–¹⁄₈ in) long
Number of species: 650

Tick

Tick

Ticks are parasites – they live by feeding on the blood of birds, mammals and reptiles. They stay on the host for several days while feeding, attached by their strong mouthparts. Some species may pass on diseases as they feed.

Snails, slugs and other land invertebrates

As well as insects and spiders, there are many other kinds of invertebrate creature that spend their lives on land. Most molluscs live in the sea, but there are land species of slugs and snails. Woodlice are related to crustaceans such as the sea-living crabs and shrimps. Earthworms are relatives of the segmented worms in the sea, but they spend their lives burrowing through the soil in fields, woodlands and gardens. All of these animals are common worldwide.

Like insects and spiders, millipedes and centipedes are kinds of arthropod. Extremely successful creatures, they live everywhere from tropical rainforests to tundra. They may be mistaken for insects, but they have many more legs and do not have wings. Their bodies are sensitive to drying out in the sun, so these creatures usually come out only at night.

Earthworm

Earthworms are common in soil all over the world. They spend most of their lives underground and only come to the surface at night or in wet weather. Dead leaves and other plant material are their main food, but they also eat soil, digesting what they can and excreting the rest.

Size: up to 30 cm (11¾ in) long
Range: worldwide
Scientific name:
Lumbricus terrestris

Earthworm

Great black slug

The slug is a mollusc, like a snail, but has no external shell. All land molluscs make mucus. This slime helps stop the slug's body drying out and allows the creature to move more easily. The slug leaves trails of slime wherever it goes and these help it find its way. It feeds mostly on living and rotting plant and animal material, which it finds by smell.

Size: 15 cm (6 in) long
Range: Europe and North America
Scientific name:
Arion ater

Woodlouse

The woodlouse is related to the crustaceans, like the crab or shrimp, but it has become adapted to live on land. Its body is made up of 13 segments and it has 7 pairs of legs. It hides in moist dark places during the day and comes out at night to feed on decaying plants and tiny dead creatures.

Size: 1 cm (⅜ in) long
Range: worldwide
Scientific name:
Armadillidium vulgare

Great black slug   **Woodlouse**

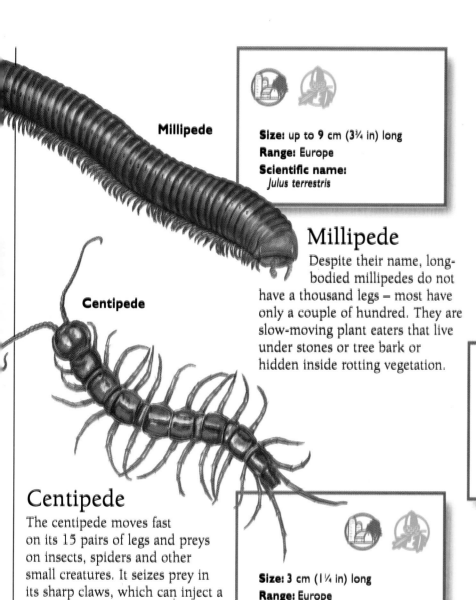

Millipede

Centipede

Millipede

Despite their name, long-bodied millipedes do not have a thousand legs – most have only a couple of hundred. They are slow-moving plant eaters that live under stones or tree bark or hidden inside rotting vegetation.

Size: up to 9 cm (3¾ in) long
Range: Europe
Scientific name:
   Julus terrestris

Centipede

The centipede moves fast on its 15 pairs of legs and preys on insects, spiders and other small creatures. It seizes prey in its sharp claws, which can inject a powerful poison to paralyse the victim.

Size: 3 cm (1¼ in) long
Range: Europe
Scientific name:
   Lithobius forficatus

Armoured millipede

Armoured millipedes have a hard outer shell. They live in forests, where they feed on leaves and other rotting plants on the forest floor. They have poison glands and some can actually spray poison to defend themselves against enemies.

Armoured millipede

Size: up to 13 cm (5 in) long
Range: worldwide
Scientific name:
   Polydesmus spp.

Garden snail

Different types of land snail live all over the world. All have a soft sluglike body and a hard shell that is carried on the back. Most snails spend the day inside their shell and come out at night to find food such as leafy plants. They move along by making rippling movements of the fleshy "foot" in a layer of slime which makes up the underside of the body.

Garden snail

Size: body: 9 cm (3½ in) long
Range: Europe
Scientific name:
   Helix aspersa

Sea creatures

As well as the thousands of kinds of fish that live in the oceans there is also a huge range of invertebrates. At least 160,000 species of invertebrate animals, including clams, crabs and jellyfish, live in every part of the ocean from the surface waters to the deepest sea. The most highly populated waters are those near the surface. Here, plenty of light penetrates to about 100 m (330 ft) and plant plankton thrive. These microscopic plants are eaten by animal plankton – tiny animals that drift in surface waters and are themselves eaten by larger sea creatures.

Sponges, jellyfish and relatives

Sponges have such simple bodies that they look more like plants than animals. Their larvae are free-swimming, but adult sponges remain in one place on a rock or on the seabed. Sea anemones, too, are plantlike. They belong to a large group of creatures called cnidarians, as do coral and jellyfish. Most have a simple tubelike body and tentacles armed with stinging cells. Comb jellies are a separate group. They are small translucent animals which float in surface waters. Lampshells are shelled creatures which can anchor themselves to rocks or the seabed by a fleshy stalk.

Lampshell

The lampshell belongs to a group of animals called brachiopods, members of which have lived on Earth for about 550 million years. It has two shells and a short stalk on which it can move around. When the shells open they expose folded tentacles lined with tiny hairs. These hairs drive water over the tentacles, which trap tiny particles of food.

Size: 3 cm (1¼ in) long
Range: Atlantic Ocean
Scientific name:
   Terebratulina septentrionalis

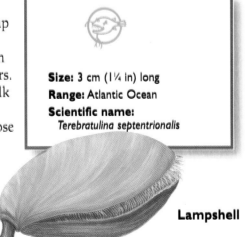

Lampshell

Common comb jelly

The comb jelly moves with the help of tiny hairs arranged in lines down its baglike body. These hairs are called comb plates and they beat together to push the comb jelly through the water. It catches prey such as shrimp and other small creatures.

Common comb jelly

Size: 15 cm (6 in) tall
Range: Arctic and Atlantic oceans
Scientific name:
   Bolinopsis infundibulum

Sponge

Sponges are among the simplest of animals. To feed, they draw water into the chambers of the body, where tiny particles of food are trapped and digested. The water also brings oxygen to the creatures and removes carbon dioxide.

Sponge

Size: up to 50 cm (19¾ in) long
Range: Caribbean Sea
Scientific name:
   Callyspongia spp.

Portuguese man-of-war

The Portuguese man-of-war is not a true jellyfish but a colony of hundreds of individual animals called polyps. They live together under the sail-like, gas-filled float that lies on the water's surface. Each type of polyp performs different tasks for the colony, such as capturing food or producing eggs.

Portuguese man-of-war

Size: float: 30 cm (11¾ in) long; tentacles: 18 m (60 ft)

Range: warm and tropical waters in Atlantic, Indian and Pacific oceans

Scientific name: *Physalia physalis*

Size: colony up to 2 m (6½ ft) wide

Range: tropical Indian and Pacific oceans and Caribbean Sea

Scientific name: *Meandrina* spp.

Brain coral

Brain coral is most common in water 6–12 m (19½–39½ ft) deep. It lives in dome-shaped colonies of tiny anemonelike creatures called polyps. Each of the polyps has a hard skeleton. These make up the rocky base of the colony.

Sea pen

The featherlike sea pen is not one animal but a group of many individuals called polyps. One large stemlike polyp stands in the seabed and supports the whole group. On the side branches there are many small feeding polyps. If touched, the sea pen glows with phosphorescence.

Size: up to 38 cm (15 in) tall

Range: north Atlantic Ocean

Scientific name: *Pennatula phosphorea*

Sea anemone

The sea anemone may look like a flower, but it is actually an animal that catches other creatures to eat. At one end of its body is a sucking disc that keeps it attached to a rock. At the other end is the mouth, surrounded by tentacles.

Sea anemone

Purple jellyfish

Like most jellyfish, this creature has many stinging cells on its long tentacles. These cells protect it from enemies and help it to catch plankton to eat. Although known as the purple jellyfish, it may be yellow, red or even brown in colour.

Purple jellyfish

Size: bell: 3 cm (1¼ in) wide; tentacles: 90 cm (35½ in) long

Range: Atlantic, Indian and Pacific oceans

Scientific name: *Pelagia noctiluca*

Size: up to 25 cm (9¾ in) tall

Range: Atlantic and Pacific coasts

Scientific name: *Tealia* spp.

Crustaceans

There are about 31,000 species of crustaceans, including creatures such as barnacles, crabs, lobsters and shrimps. Woodlice live on land and there are some shrimps and other species in fresh water, but most crustaceans live in the sea. Typically, they have a tough outer skeleton, which protects the soft body within. The head is made up of six segments, on which there are two pairs of antennae and several different sets of mouthparts. The rest of the body carries the walking legs, which may be divided into a thorax and abdomen.

Deep-sea shrimp

The deep-sea shrimp's antennae are longer than its body. It spreads the antennae out in the water to help it find food in the darkness of the deep sea. It eats any dead and decaying matter that it comes across.

Deep-sea shrimp

Size: 10 cm (4 in) long
Range: Atlantic Ocean
Scientific name:
  Pasiphaea spp.

Goose barnacles

Goose barnacles live fixed by their stalk to any object floating in the open sea, including logs, buoys and boats. The barnacle's body is enclosed by a shell made of five plates. These open at the top so that the barnacle can extend its six pairs of feathery arms and collect tiny particles of food from the water.

Goose barnacles

Size: 15 cm (6 in) including stalk
Range: Atlantic and Pacific oceans
Scientific name:
  Lepas anatifera

Giant isopod

A sea-living relative of the wood louse, the giant isopod lives in the Antarctic, where it catches any food it can find. It also scavenges on the seabed for dead and dying creatures. Antarctic isopods are much bigger than those elsewhere in the world.

Giant isopod

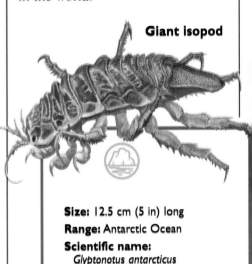

Size: 12.5 cm (5 in) long
Range: Antarctic Ocean
Scientific name:
  Glyptonotus antarcticus

Size: 30 cm (11¾ in)
Range: north Atlantic coasts
Scientific name:
  Homarus americanus

Lobster

During the day this large crustacean hides in rock crevices, but at night it comes out to hunt. It uses its huge pincers to crack and tear apart prey such as molluscs and crabs. In the summer, the female lobster lays thousands of eggs, which she carries around with her on the underside of her body. The eggs hatch into shrimplike larvae which float in surface waters for a few weeks. They then settle on the seabed and start to develop into adults.

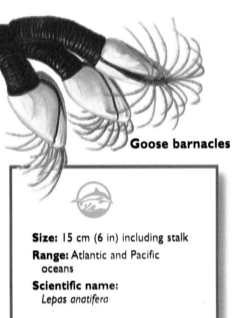

Lobster

Hermit crab

Unlike other crabs, the hermit crab has no hard shell of its own. It protects its soft body by living in the discarded shell of another creature, such as a snail. The crab has large pincers on its first pair of legs which it uses to grab its prey.

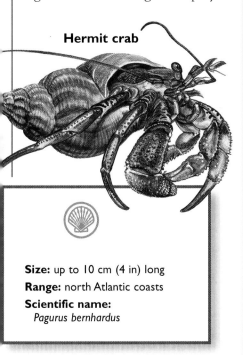

Hermit crab

Size: up to 10 cm (4 in) long
Range: north Atlantic coasts
Scientific name:
  Pagurus bernhardus

Montague's shrimp

Shrimps have much lighter shells than crabs or lobsters. The limbs on the abdomen are used for swimming, while some of those on the thorax are for walking and others are used as mouthparts.

Size: up to 12.5 cm (5 in) long
Range: north Atlantic coasts
Scientific name:
  Pandalus montagui

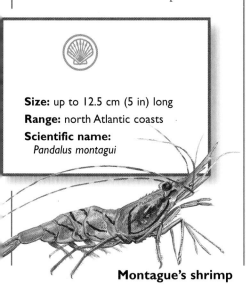

Montague's shrimp

Antarctic krill

Antarctic krill

Shrimplike krill feed on plant plankton and tiny creatures that they sieve from the water. In turn, they are the main food of many fish, penguins and even whales. A blue whale can eat as many as four million krill in a day. Krill are extremely common and sometimes occur in such large numbers that the sea looks red.

Size: up to 5 cm (2 in) long
Range: southern oceans
Scientific name:
  Euphausia superba

Amphipod

This small crustacean lives on the lower shore under rocks or among seaweed, and feeds on tiny pieces of plant and animal matter. On its abdomen are three pairs of jumping legs. The female amphipod holds her developing young in a pouch on the underside of her body.

Amphipod

Size: up to 2.5 cm (1 in) long
Range: Atlantic and Pacific coasts
Scientific name:
  Gammarus locusta

Edible crab

Size: 30 cm (11¾ in) wide
Range: north Atlantic coasts
Scientific name:
  Cancer spp.

Edible crab

Most crabs have a strong shell, which protects the body, and five pairs of legs. On the first pair are powerful pincers used to break open the shells of prey, such as molluscs. The other legs are smaller. Crabs live among rocks on the lower shore.

Molluscs

There are at least 100,000 living species of molluscs. They are divided into three main groups: gastropods, such as limpets and snails; bivalves, which include clams, mussels and scallops; and cephalopods, such as squid, cuttlefish, octopus and nautilus. Slugs and some kinds of snail live on land and there are freshwater snails and clams, but the greatest range of molluscs is found in the sea. In most molluscs, the body is divided into three parts – the head, which contains the mouth and sense organs, the body, and the foot, a fleshy part of the body on which the animal moves along. Most, but not all, molluscs have a tough shell that protects the soft body.

Scallop

Size: 10 cm (4 in) long
Range: Atlantic and Pacific oceans
Scientific name:
Chlamys islandicus

Atlantic deer cowrie

The cowrie is a type of sea snail with a beautiful shiny shell. Unlike most snails, the cowrie's mantle can be extended to cover the outside of the shell and camouflage the animal. (The mantle is a thin fold of tissue, part of which makes the shell.) The opening of the cowrie's shell is edged with 35 teeth.

Scallop

The scallop has a soft body protected by two shells. A row of well-developed eyes can be seen when the shells are slightly parted. The scallop moves by flapping its shells together, forcing out jets of water which push it forwards.

Size: up to 12.5 cm (5 in) long
Range: Atlantic Ocean and Caribbean Sea
Scientific name: *Cypraea cervus*

Clam

The usual home of the clam is a burrow deep in a sandy or muddy seabed. It digs the burrow with its foot, a fleshy part of its body. Two long tubes extend from the shell. Water and food (tiny living particles) go in through one tube. The water then goes out the other tube.

Clam

Size: 15 cm (6 in) long
Range: north Pacific Ocean
Scientific name:
Saxidomus nuttalli

Oyster

The oyster is a type of bivalve. It has a soft body protected by two hard shells, which are held together by strong muscles. It eats tiny pieces of plant and animal food, which it filters from the water. The water is drawn into the partly opened shell and any food is caught on tiny sticky hairs on the oyster's gills.

Size: up to 10 cm (4 in) long
Range: Atlantic and Pacific coasts
Scientific name:
Ostrea spp.

Atlantic deer cowrie

250

Oyster

Lightning whelk

Octopus

The octopus has a pouchlike body and eight long arms lined with two rows of suckers. It pulls itself along with its strong arms and can also swim quickly by shooting jets of water out of its body. It spends much of its time hiding in crevices or under rocks, watching out for prey, such as crabs, clams and shrimps. The octopus holds its prey in its tentacles and may kill or paralyse it with a poisonous bite.

Size: up to 100 cm (39½ in) long
Range: Atlantic coasts
Scientific name:
Octopus vulgaris

Size: 40 cm (15¾ in) long
Range: Atlantic Ocean
Scientific name:
Busycon contrarium

Lightning whelk

This large whelk has a very beautiful spiral shell with brown markings. It lives on sandy or muddy seabeds in shallow water and feeds mostly on other molluscs, such as clams, which it digs out of the mud.

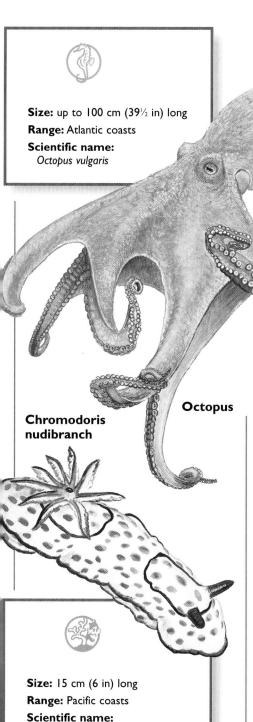
Chromodoris nudibranch

Octopus

Purple sea snail

This little snail cannot swim, but it drifts in the surface waters of the sea clinging to a raft of bubbles. These are made from mucus the snail secretes, which hardens when it enters the water.

Purple sea snail

Size: 2.5 cm (1 in) long, including tentacles
Range: Atlantic, Indian and Pacific oceans
Scientific name:
Janthina janthina

Size: 15 cm (6 in) long
Range: Pacific coasts
Scientific name:
Chromodoris elisabethina

Chromodoris nudibranch

Nudibranches, or sea slugs, are related to snails, but they have no shells and are often brightly coloured. This species has a pair of hornlike projections and a clump of feathery gills on its back. Sponges are its main food.

Squid

The squid has a long torpedo-shaped body, four pairs of arms and one pair of much longer tentacles. Suckers on the arms and the tips of the tentacles help the squid grasp its prey – mostly fish and crustaceans. A fast swimmer, the squid moves by a type of jet propulsion, shooting water out of its body to force itself backwards through the water.

Size: up to 76 cm (30 in) long, including tentacles
Range: Atlantic Ocean and Mediterranean Sea
Scientific name: *Loligo pealii*

Squid

Rock clingers

Rough periwinkle

There are many types of periwinkle, each adapted for life in different parts of the shore. The rough periwinkle lives on stones and rocks higher up the shore than most other species.

Chiton

Unlike other molluscs, the chiton has a shell made up of eight sections held together by muscles. If in danger, the chiton can roll itself up like an armadillo.

While most marine creatures swim or float freely in the water, some live firmly attached to rocks or other surfaces. This helps protect them from the waves that sweep over them twice a day as the tide comes in. Barnacles, one kind of rock clinger, are among the most common creatures on the shore. Huge colonies of them cover rocks and shore debris, and even attach themselves to other creatures such as mussels. Barnacles begin life as free-swimming larvae and spend a month or more floating in coastal waters, feeding on plankton. During its final larval stage, each barnacle finds somewhere to settle. It fixes itself to the surface with a cementlike substance that it makes in glands in its body. Once settled, it does not move again.

Limpets, periwinkles and chitons can all cling to rocks by means of a suckerlike foot, which is so strong that they are almost impossible to move. But all these creatures can also move around on their own to graze on algae.

Common limpet

As a limpet moves over rocks feeding on algae, it leaves a sticky trail of mucus behind it. This helps the limpet make its way back to the exact same place on the rock after each feeding trip.

Acorn barnacle

When covered by water at high tide, the barnacle opens its shell at the top and puts out its feathery arms to gather plankton to eat. When the tide is out, the barnacle keeps its trapdoor top firmly closed.

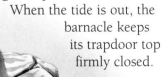

Common mussel

The threads that hold the mussel on to rocks are made as a sticky fluid inside a gland in the mussel's body. This fluid hardens to keep the mussel firmly in place. The shell is in two halves. These are normally held tight together, but they can be partly opened so that the mussel can filter tiny pieces of food from the water.

Blue-rayed limpet

Not all limpets cling to rocks. The blue-rayed limpet lives attached to seaweed, which is anchored to rock or the seabed near the shore. The limpet grazes on the seaweed fronds, feeding on the seaweed itself and small plants growing there such as algae.

A colourful **painted topshell** clings to rocks on the seashore, surrounded by sea anemones and other creatures. The topshell, which is a kind of snail, feeds on tiny plants called algae growing on the rocks.

Worms and echinoderms

There are about 11,500 species of segmented, or annelid, worms. They include earthworms, which live on land, as well as some freshwater worms, such as leeches, but most live in the sea. All have a body that is divided into a number of segments. All echinoderms live in the sea. There are four main groups – brittle stars, starfish, sea cucumbers, and sea urchins and sand dollars. Many have a body that is divided into five radiating parts with a mouth at one end and an anus at the other. Most echinoderms move around using tiny stilts called tube feet, each tipped with a sucking disc.

Sea mouse

Despite its plump shape, the sea mouse is actually a kind of worm. Its upper side is covered with lots of greyish-brown bristles which give it a furry look and inspire its common name. The sea mouse spends much of its life under mud or sand in shallow water.

Sea mouse

Size: 18 cm (7 in) long
Range: Atlantic and Mediterranean coasts
Scientific name: *Aphrodita aculeata*

Sea lily

Sea lily

This relative of the starfish lives attached to a rock by a stalk. Its branching arms are lined with tiny suckerlike tube feet. When feeding, the sea lily spreads its arms wide and traps plankton and other tiny particles with its tube feet. The food is then passed down grooves lined with hairs to the mouth, at the centre of the body.

Size: up to 60 cm (23½ in)
Range: Atlantic Ocean
Scientific name: *Ptilocrinus pinnatus*

Long-spined urchin

Sharp spines protect the urchin's rounded body from enemies. The urchin's mouth is on the underside of the body and has five teeth arranged in a circle for chewing food. By day these urchins stay hidden on the reef, but at night they come out to feed on algae.

Size: body: 10 cm (4 in) wide; spines: 10–40 cm (4–15¾ in) long
Range: Atlantic Ocean and Caribbean Sea
Scientific name: *Diadema antillarum*

Long-spined urchin

Brittle star

The brittle star has a central disclike body and five long spiny arms, each separate from the other. The animal's mouth is on the underside of the disc. The brittle star uses its long arms to catch small crustaceans and other creatures.

Brittle star

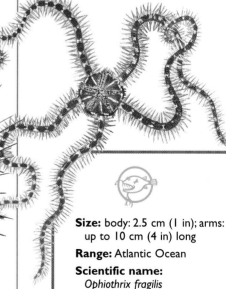

Size: body: 2.5 cm (1 in); arms: up to 10 cm (4 in) long
Range: Atlantic Ocean
Scientific name: *Ophiothrix fragilis*

Feather duster worm

The body of this spectacular worm usually stays hidden in a flexible tube attached to a reef or the seabed. The tube is made of fine sand stuck together with a gluey substance made in the worm's body. The worm catches food with its crown of feathery gills.

Feather duster worm

Size: 12.5 cm (5 in) long
Range: Atlantic Ocean and Caribbean Sea
Scientific name:
Sabellastarte magnifica

Common sand dollar

The sand dollar has a flattened disclike body and a shell that is covered with short spines. On its underside are rows of tiny tubelike feet, which help the sand dollar gather tiny pieces of food from the water.

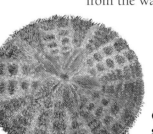

Common sand dollar

Size: 7.5 cm (3 in) wide
Range: north Atlantic and Pacific coasts
Scientific name:
Echinarachnius parma

Size: up to 25 cm (9¾ in) long
Range: north Atlantic Ocean
Scientific name:
Holothuria forskali

Sea cucumber

Sea cucumber

Sea cucumbers are related to starfish, but they have long simple bodies. At one end is the anus and at the other the mouth, which is surrounded by food-gathering tentacles. Rows of tiny tube feet run the length of the body. When disturbed, the sea cucumber ejects sticky white threads from its anus. These confuse predators.

Paddle worm

This worm lives under rocks among seaweed, both on the shore and in deeper water. It has four pairs of tentacles on its head and lots of tiny leaflike paddles down each side of its long body. It feeds mainly on other worms.

Size: up to 45 cm (17¾ in) long
Range: Atlantic and Pacific coasts
Scientific name:
Phyllodoce spp.

Thorny starfish

Thorny starfish

Large spines cover the body and five arms of this starfish. Two rows of special feet, called "tube feet", extend down each arm. The tube feet work together, extending and contracting, to move the starfish around as it searches for prey.

Size: 12 cm (4¾ in) across
Range: west Atlantic Ocean and Caribbean Sea
Scientific name:
Echinastur sentus

Paddle worm

Why do animals build nests?

Although many animals manage without a nest or home of any kind, others build structures which they use for shelter and for rearing their young in safety. This home may be specially built, like a bird's nest, or simply a natural hole or a sheltered spot. Homes may be made in trees, on the ground or in burrows under the ground. Birds generally only use their nests when breeding. They lay and incubate their eggs in nests and care for their young. The nest is usually left once the baby birds have gone. Some mammals, such as beavers and prairie dogs, spend much of their time in the homes they make. These may contain chambers for sleeping, caring for young and storing food. Insects such as bees, wasps, ants and termites also build elaborate homes.

The nest of the **penduline tit** hangs from the end of a slender twig, where it is hard for predators to reach it. The nest is woven from plant fibres and has an entrance near the top.

Beavers dam a stream with branches and mud to create a lake in which to store a winter food supply. A shelter, or lodge, is then made of branches by the dam.

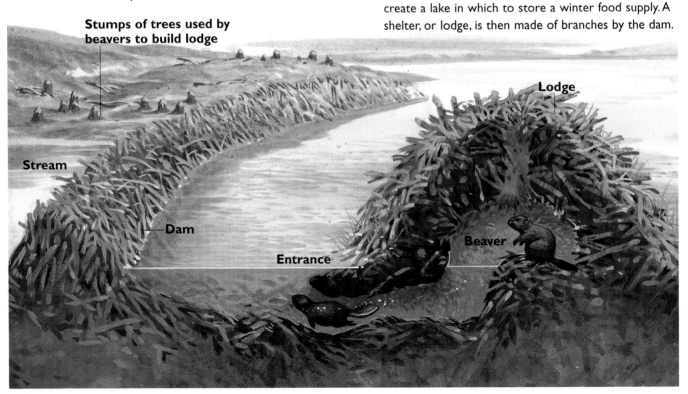

Stumps of trees used by beavers to build lodge

Lodge

Stream

Dam

Entrance

Beaver

The female **harvest mouse** builds a nest as a shelter for her young. She finds some sturdy cereal stems and starts by winding the leaves of one stem around another to make a platform about 50 cm (19¾ in) above the ground. She then takes lengths of grass or leaves and uses these to weave a ball-like structure, which measures about 10 cm (4 in) across.

This large mound is made by small soft-bodied insects called **termites**. The mound is made of soil mixed with the termites' faeces and inside is a complex nest. A maze of chambers and tunnels contains special areas for food storage and for eggs and young. Chimneys inside the mounds let air in and out and help keep the temperature in the nest comfortable.

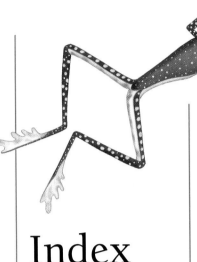

Index

aardvark 15
adalah 194
addax 55
adder, saw-scaled 137
agamid, Arabian toad-headed
   129
albatross 70, 84, 88
   wandering 88
alewife 166
alligator 118, 120
   American 120
amberjack, greater 176
amphibians 138–53
amphipod 249
anaconda 134
anemonefish, clown 178, 199
angelfish 158, 176, 178
   emperor 158
   queen 178
angler fish 67, 157, 159, 174,
   175
annelid worms 203
anole, green 130
ant 198, 228, 234–35, 256
   army 234
   black 198
   carpenter 235
   fire 234
   harvester 234
   leafcutter 235
   red 234
   velvet 230
anteater 14
   giant 14
antelope 50, 53, 54
antlion 208, 209
ape family 27
aphid 198, 212, 230
arachnids 201, 236–43
armadillo 14, 15
   giant 14
   nine-banded 15
arthropods 202–3, 244
auk, little see dovekie

avocet 78
axolotl 145
aye aye 22, 23

baboon, olive 25
badger 34, 198
   Eurasian 34
   honey 198
ballyhoo 186
bandicoot, brown 12
barbet, double-toothed 99
barnacle 248, 252
   acorn 252
   goose 248
barracuda 159, 176, 185
   great 185
bass, sea 176, 177
   giant 177
bat 14, 18–21
   common long-eared 19
   false vampire 18, 21
   fruit 19
   ghost 18
   greater false vampire 18
   greater horseshoe 19
   spear-nosed 18
   vampire 20–21
batagur see terrapin, river
bear 32, 33
   brown 33
   polar 6–7, 33
   spectacled 33
   sun 33
beardfish 190, 191
   stout 191
beaver 59, 60, 256
   American 60
bedbug 213
bee 228–29, 256
   carpenter 229
   cuckoo 229
   leafcutter 228
   mining 229
   orchid 229
   plasterer 229
   stingless 229
   see also bumblebee
      honeybee
bee-eater, European 99
beetle 201, 202, 212, 215–19
   carrion 218
   click 219
   darkling 219
   diving 218
   goliath 215
   jewel 218

mint leaf 200–201
longhorn 218
rove 215
stag 216–17
tiger 215
whirligig 215
bichir 164
biddy 210
bigmouth buffalo (fish) 168,
   169
bird, secretary 92
bird of paradise 108–9
   blue 108
   greater 109
   King of Saxony's 108
   raggiana 109
   ribbon-tailed 108
   Wilson's 109
birds 68–109, 114
   game 72–74
   ground 72, 75–77
   nests 256
   perching see song below
   sea 78, 84–89
   song 104–7, 109–13
   tree 96–103
   waders 78–79
   water 78, 80–83
birds of prey 90–95
birdwing 226, 227
   Cairns 226
   Queen Alexandra's 227
bison 54
   American 54
   European 54
bivalves 250
blenny, redlip 183
bluebird, eastern 105
bluefish 177
boa 117, 134
   constrictor 134
   emerald tree 116–17
boar, wild 9, 46
boll weevil 219
Bombay duck see bummalow
bongo 53
boomslang 135
bowerbird, satin 75
bowfin 164
boxfish 196
   blue-spotted 196
brachiopods 246
bream 168, 169, 179
   red sea 179
bristletail 204

brittle star 254
budgerigar 103
buffalo 53, 199
   Asian water 53
bug 212–14
   assassin 214
   plant 213
bulbul, red-whiskered 104
bullrout 192, 193
bumblebee 228
bummalow 186, 187
bunting, snow 106
burbot 174
bushbaby 22, 23
   greater 23
bustard, great 75, 76
butterfly 155, 202, 220, 222,
   226–27
   cabbage white 227
   copper 227
   monarch 155, 227
   morpho 226
   swallowtail 226
   fluminense 226
   see also caterpillar
butterfly fish, copperband 178
buzzard 90, 91, 93
   rough-legged 93

caddis fly 222, 223
large 223
caecilian 139, 140, 145
   South American 145
caiman 120, 121
   spectacled 121
camel 50, 66
   bactrian 50, 66
candirú 170
capercaillie, western 74
capuchin, white-fronted 26
capybara 64, 65
cardinal 106
caribou 51
carp 168
cascarudo 170
cassowary 75, 76
   common 76
cat 36–37, 114
   wild 36
caterpillar 154, 230
   butterfly 155, 222, 226, 227
   moth 222, 223, 224, 225
catfish 170–71
   Australian freshwater 170

blue 171
  glass 171
  sea 171
  walking 171
cattle 50
cavy see guinea pig
centipede 201, 202, 244, 245
cephalopods 250
chameleon 132–33
  dwarf 133
  flap-necked 133
  Jackson's 133
  Meller's 133
chamois 55
charr, Arctic 173
cheetah 37
chickadee, black-capped 105
chicken, greater prairie 74
chimpanzee 27
chinchilla 64
chipmunk 59, 60
  eastern 60
chiton 252
chuckwalla 128
cicada 212
cichlid 176
civet 34, 35
  African palm 35
clam 201, 246, 250
cleaner fish 198
clingfish, northern 183
clown anemonefish 199
cnidarians 203, 246
coati 32
cobra 137, 154
  Indian 137
cockatoo, sulphur-crested 103
cock of the rock 111
cockroach 204, 205
  American 205
  German 205
  Madagascan hissing 205
cod 174, 175, 182
  Atlantic 175
  Antarctic 182
coelacanth 196, 197
colobus, red 25
colugo 17
comb jellies 203, 246
  beroe 203
  common 246
condor 90
congo eel 142
  two-toed 142

coral 246, 247
  brain 247
cormorant, great 70, 84
cowrie, Atlantic deer 250
coyote 114
crab 115, 201, 202, 244, 246,
  248, 249
  edible 249
  fiddler 115
  hermit 249
crane 80, 81, 83
  common 81
  whooping 83
cricket 204, 206, 207
  mole 207
  true 207
crocodile 117, 118–19, 120,
  121, 122–23
  estuarine 121
  mugger 121
  Nile 118–19, 122–23
  West African dwarf 121
crow 70, 112
  American 112
  carrion 70
crustaceans 202, 244, 248–49
cuckoo 96, 102
  common 102
curassow 75
  great 75
curlew 78, 79
  eskimo 79
cusk-eel 174
  New Providence 174
cuttlefish 250

daddy-long-legs see
  harvestman
damselfly 210
  narrow-winged 210
darner see dragonfly, darner
darter 176, 211
  orange throat 176
dauber, mud 230, 231
deer 50–52
  forest musk 51
  pampas 52
  red 51
dinosaurs 118, 119
dipper, American 107
diver 80, 82
  red-throated 82
dog 28–29, 114
  bush 28
  hunting 28

dogfish, sandy 160
dolphin 38, 42, 43
  Atlantic bottle-nosed 7, 43
  common 43
  Ganges 43
dolphinfish 177
dormouse 64
  desert 64
dove, collared 99
dovekie 84
dragonet 183
dragonfly 208, 210, 211
  clubtail 210
  darner 211
dromedary 50
drum, black 179
duck 71, 78, 80, 81
  eider, common 82
  mallard 71, 80
  mandarin 81
dugong 45

eagle 70–71, 90, 91, 92, 93,
  94–95
  bald 93, 95
  crested serpent 94
  golden 71, 92
  harpy 70–71, 94
  Madagascar fish 93
  sea 94, 95
  Steller's 95
earthworm 244, 254
earwig 204, 205
  common 204
  long-horned 205
echidna 8, 10
  long-beaked 10
  short-beaked 8
echinoderms 203, 254, 255
eel 142, 166, 167, 172
  conger 167
  congo 142
  cusk 174
  electric 172
  European 167
  moray 167
  snipe 167
  spiny 167
egret 80, 82, 198
  cattle 198
  great 82
eider, common 82
electric eel 172

elephant 46, 48–49, 198
  African 48, 49
  Asian/Indian 8, 48
elephant snout fish 164, 165
elk see moose
emperor, sweetlip 179
emu 72, 75, 76

falcon 90, 92
  peregrine 92
fightingfish, Siamese 176, 184
filefish, scrawled 196
finch 71, 107
  zebra 107
firebrat 204
firefly 115, 219
fish 156–97
  bony 158–9, 164–97
  cartilaginous 158, 159, 160–63
  freshwater 157, 164–65,
    168–71, 172, 173, 188–89
  primitive 158, 160, 161, 196,
    197
  sea 157, 160–3, 166–7, 171,
    172, 173, 174–87, 190–97
flamingo 78, 80, 83
  greater 83
flatfish 157, 194–95
flea 212, 214
  cat 214
  chigoe 214
flounder, summer 195
fly 202, 220–1
  blow 221
  crane 221
  fruit 221
  horse 220
  house 202, 221
  hover 221
  robber 220
flycatcher, royal 69, 110
flyingfish 186
football fish 175
four-eyed fish 188, 189
fox 28, 29
  Arctic 29
  Fennec 29
  red 29
frigatebird, great 89
frog 139, 140, 141, 146, 148–53
  arrow-poison 150–51
  flaming 151
  golden 150
  arum lily 149
  bullfrog 153

common 140, 153
corroboree 148
Darwin's 149
eastern narrow-mouthed 152
European green tree 149
glass 146
gold 148
horned 148
marsh 153
marsupial 148
mottled burrowing 153
Natal ghost 146
northern leopard 153
South African rain 152
South American false-eyed 141
termite 152
Wallace's flying 152
froghopper 213

gannet 84, 89
northern 89
gar 164
longnose 164
garfish 186, 187
gastropods 250
gavial 120
gecko 128
leaf-tailed 128
web-footed 128
gerbil 62, 63
great 63
gibbon 9, 27
lar 27
pileated 9
gila monster 130
giraffe 50, 52
glider, greater 13
glow-worm 115, 219
goat 50
goby 157, 176, 183
pygmy 157
rock 183
goldeye 164, 165
goldfish 168
gopher, pocket 59, 60
plains 60
goose 80
Canada 80
gorilla 9, 27
goshawk 91
northern 91
grasshopper 204, 206
long-horned 206
short-horned 206

grayling 173
grebe 80, 81
great crested 81
grenadier, rough-head 174
grosbeak, pine 106
ground hornbill, southern 77
grouper, black 176
grouse 72, 74
black 74
grunion 188
California 188
guinea pig 64, 65
gull 68–69, 84
great black-backed 84
herring 85
guppy 188, 189
gurnard, flying 192, 193

haddock 174, 175
hagfish 158, 160, 161
hake 174
halfbeak 186
wrestling 186
halibut, California 194
hamster 61
common 61
hare 58
snowshoe 58
harvestman 243
hatchetfish 172
hawk 70, 90, 91
goshawk 91
red-tailed 91
sparrowhawk 91
hawksbill 126
hedgehog 16
Western European 16
hellbender 145
heron 78
herring 159, 166
Atlantic 166
hippopotamus 46–47
pygmy 47
hoatzin 102
honeybee 228, 232–33
honeycreeper, purple 106
honeyeater, cardinal 113
honeyguide 198
hoopoe 98
hornbill 77, 102
great Indian 102
southern ground 77
hornero, rufous 110

hornet 230
giant 230
horse 56–57
Przewalski's 57
howler, red 26
hummingbird 70, 71, 96, 97, 100–101
bee 100
crimson topaz 100
giant 71
ruby-throated 97
sword-billed 100
violet sabrewing 101
hutia 64, 65
hyena 36
striped 36

ibis 80, 83
glossy 80
hermit 83
icefish see cod, Antarctic
iguana 129
common 129
marine 128, 129
rhinoceros 129
impala 55
insects 200–255
invertebrates 4, 200–255
isopod, giant 248

jacamar, rufous-tailed 98
jacana 78, 79
jaguar 37
jay, blue 113
jellies, comb see comb jellies
jellyfish 201, 203, 246, 247
purple 203, 247
jerboa 64
great 64
John Dory 190, 191
junglefowl 73
jungle runner 130

kangaroo 13
Lumholtz's tree 13
musky rat 13
red 13
kangaroo rat, desert 60
katydid 206, 207
kestrel, common 92
kingbird, eastern 110
kingfisher, belted 99
kite, red 91
kiwi 75
brown 75
koala 12

Komodo dragon 128, 131
kowari 11
krill, Antarctic 249

lacewing 208
green 209
ladybird 219
lamprey 158, 160, 161
river 158
sea 161
lampshell 203, 246
lanternfish 186
lapwing 79
lark, shore 112
leaf insect 66, 206, 207
leatherback 126
lechwe 54
leech 203, 254
medical 203
lemming 62
Norway 62
lemur 22
ring-tailed 22
leopard 37
snow 37
limpet 250, 252, 253
blue-rayed 253
common 252
limpkin 83
ling 174, 175
lion 36, 37
mountain 36
lionfish 157, 192, 193
lizard 114, 117, 118, 128–33
desert night 130
frilled 131
snake 128, 131
Transvaal 131
lizardfish 186, 187
red 187
lobster 248
locust 206
longclaw, yellow-throated 113
loon see diver
lorikeet, rainbow 103
loris 22
slender 22
louse 212, 213, 214
bark 214
chewing 212
feather 214
head 213
sucking 212
lungfish 196, 197
South American 197

lynx 36
lyrebird, superb 110
lyretail 188, 189
  Cape Lopez 189

macaque, Japanese 24
macaw, scarlet 102
mackerel 158, 185
magpie, black-billed 112
mallard 71, 80
mamba, eastern green 136
mammals 6–65
manakin, wire-tailed 111
manatee, American 45
mandrill 24
man o' war fish 184
manta, Atlantic 161
mantidflies 208
mantids 208
mantis 208
  Angola 208
  flower 208
  praying 208
mantisfly 208, 209
marlin, blue 184
marmoset 22
  pygmy 22
marsupials 8–9, 10, 11–13
martin, sand 97
matamata 126
mayfly 210
meerkat 35
merganser, red-breasted 71
midge 220
millipede 201, 202, 244, 245
  armoured 245
minnow, sheepshead 188, 189
mite 236, 243
  house dust 243
  velvet 243
mockingbird, northern 105
mole 16
  European 16
  giant golden 16
mole-rat 61, 62
  naked 62
molluscs 203, 244, 250–53
mongoose 34, 35
  Indian 35
monkey 24–26, 114
  Allen's swamp 25
  Diana 24
  New World 26
  Old World 24–25

proboscis 25
  woolly spider 26
monotremes 8, 10–11
mooneye see goldeye
moorhen 81
Moorish idol 182
moose 51
mosquito 202, 220
moth 114, 220, 222–23
  atlas 223
  clothes 222
  cotton boll 223
  geometrid 222
  hawk see sphinx below
  hummingbird 222
  luna 223
  silk 114
  sphinx 224–25
  bee 224
  oleander 225
  poplar 224
  privet 225
  white-lined 225
  tiger 223
  see also caterpillar
motmot, blue-crowned 98
mouflon 56
mouse 59, 60, 61, 63
  deer 61
  harvest 257
  New World 61
  Old World 63
  pocket 59, 60
  wood 63
mudpuppy 139, 142, 143
mullet, red 179
mummichog 188, 189
mussel 201, 250, 253
  common 253
mustelids 34–35

narwhal 44
nautilus 203
needlefish 186, 187
newt 139, 142, 145
  eastern 145
  warty 145
nightingale 104
nightjar 96
nudibranch, chromodoris 251

oarfish 190
octopus 250, 251
okapi 52
olingo 32
olm 142

opah 190
opossum 11
  Virginia 11
  water 11
orang-utan 27
oriole, golden 107
oryx, Arabian 55
osprey 92
ostrich 70, 72, 75, 77
otter 34–35
  Eurasian 34
  sea 35
owl 90
  barn 90
  long-eared 90
  snowy 90
ox, musk 56
oxpecker 199
oyster 250
oystercatcher, common 79

pacu 168
paddlefish 165
panda 32, 33
  giant 32, 33
  red 32
pangolin, giant 15
paradise, bird of see bird of
  paradise
parrot 71, 96, 103
  eclectus 103
parrotfish, blue 178
parula, northern 106
peafowl 72–73
  Congo 72
  Indian 72–73
peccary 46, 47
  collared 47
peeper, spring 149
pee-wit see lapwing
pelican 85
  brown 85
penguin 84, 86–88
  Adélie 87
  chinstrap 86
  emperor 86
  fairy see little below
  Galápagos 88
  gentoo 86
  jackass 88
  king 86
  little 86, 88
perch 176
periwinkle 252
  rough 252

petrel, storm 89
pheasant 70, 72, 73
pig 46, 47
  bearded 47
pigeon 96, 98
  Victoria crowned 98
pika 58
  northern 58
pike 172
  northern 172
pinecone fish 190, 191
pipefish 192
pipit, water 112
piranha 168
  red 168
pirarucu 164, 165
pitta, garnet 111
plaice 195
platypus 10–11
plover 78
  American golden 78
pollock 175
pompano 177
poorwill 97
porcupine 64, 65
  crested 65
  tree 65
porcupinefish 196
porgy, northern see scup
porpoise 42
  Dall's 42
  harbour 42
Portuguese man-of-war 247
possum, brush-tailed 12
potoo 96
prairie dog, black-tailed 59, 256
primates 22–27
pronghorn 50, 52
pseudoscorpion 242
ptarmigan 72
pufferfish 159, 196
  common 197
puffin, Atlantic 89
python 119, 134
  Indian 134

quail, California 73
quelea, red-billed 107
quetzal 98

rabbit 8, 58
  European 58
raccoon 32
rainbow fish, crimson-spotted
  188

rat 58, 60, 61, 62, 63
  Arizona cotton 61
  bamboo 62
  brown 63
  desert kangaroo 60
  mole see mole-rats
  New World 61
  Old World 63
  swamp 62
ratel see badger, honey
rattlesnake, eastern
  diamondback 137
ray 158, 160, 162, 163
  eagle 163
  sting 163
redshank, common 71, 78
reindeer see caribou
reptiles 116–37
rhea 72, 75, 77
  greater 77
rhebok 54
rhinoceros 56, 57
  black 57
  Sumatran 57
roach 168, 169
roadrunner, greater 77
robin 104, 105
  European 105
rodents 58, 59–65
roughie 190, 191

saiga 55
sailfish 185
saki, monk 26
salamander 139, 140, 141,
  142, 143, 144
  California slender 142
  dusky 140
  fire 144
  Pacific giant 144
  red 143
  spotted 138–39, 141, 143
  Texas blind 143
  tiger 144
salmon 172, 173
  Atlantic 173
  sockeye 173
sand dollar 254, 255
  common 255
sandgrouse, Pallas's 75, 76
sandpiper 78, 79
sand smelt 188
sardine 166
saury 186, 187

sawfish, greater 160
sawfly 230
scallop 250
scorpion 155, 236, 242, 243
  centruroides 242
  pseudo 242
  whip 242
  wind 242
scorpionfish 192
scorpionfly 211
screamer, northern 82
scup 179
sea anemone 199, 246, 247
sea bass 176, 177
  giant 177
sea cucumber 254,
  255
seadragon, weedy 192
seagull see gull
seahorse 192, 192
  dwarf 192
seal 38, 39–41
  Antarctic 40–41
  crabeater 40
  elephant 40
  harbour 39
  harp 39
  leopard 39
  Ross 41
  South American fur 38
  Weddell 41
sea lily 254
sea lion 38, 39
  California 38
  Steller 39
sea mouse 254
sea pen 247
sea robin, northern 192, 193
seriema, red-legged 77
shark 157, 158, 159, 160–63
  blue 159
  carpet 162, 163
  hammerhead 160
  horn 162, 163
  mako 160
  nurse 162
  seabed 162–63
  whale 157, 160, 161
  white 161
sheathbill 84
shrew 16, 17
  armoured 17
  common tree 17
  short-eared elephant 17
shrike, northern 112

shrimp 244, 248, 249
  deep sea 248
  Montague's 249
sicklebill, white-tipped 100
sidewinder 136
silverfish 204
silverside, hardhead 188
siren 142, 143
  greater 143
skate 162
skimmer 211
skink 128, 130
  great plains 131
  western blue-tongued 130
skua, great 85
skunk 34, 35
  striped 35
slider, pond 124
sloth, three-toed 14
slug 244, 250
  great black 244
smalltooth see sawfish, greater
smelt 172
  sand 188
snail 201, 244, 245, 250
  garden 201, 245, 251
  purple 251
snake 117, 118, 128, 134–37
  banded sea 136
  eastern coral 136
  gopher 135
  grass 135
  paradise tree 136
  poisonous 117
  spotted water 135
  western blind 134
  whip, dark green 118
snakefly 208, 209
snakehead 184
snapper 157, 177
  bluestripe 156–57
  yellowtail 177
sole 195
  naked 195
solenodon, Cuban 17
spadefish, Atlantic 182
sparrow 104, 106
  house 106
  song 104
sparrowhawk 91
spatuletail, marvellous 101
spider 201, 202–3, 236–41
  bird-eating 236
  black widow 236
  common house 238

crab 237
Dysdera crocata 238
funnel-web 236, 238
garden 241
golden silk 238
green lynx 239
house, common 238
jumping 236
lichen 237
nursery-web 239
ogre-faced 240
orb weaver 240–41
orchard 239
purse-web 238
sheet-web 241
spitting 237
trapdoor 237
water 239
wolf 236
spiny eel 167
sponge 201, 203, 246
  glass 203
springhare 59, 60
squid 250, 251
squirrel 58, 59
  European red 59
  Indian striped palm 59
squirrelfish 190
starfish 254, 255
  thorny 255
stargazer, northern 183
starling 105
stick insect 206, 207
stickleback 192, 192
  three-spined 192
stinkbug 212, 213
stoat 34
stonefish 192, 193
stonefly, common 209
stork 80
sturgeon 164, 165
  common 165
sucker, white 168, 169
sunbird 112, 113
  red-tufted malachite 113
  yellow-backed 112
sunbittern 81
sunfish, ocean 197
sunspider see scorpion, wind
surubim 170
swallow 70, 97
  bank see martin, sand
  barn 97
swan 80
  tundra 80

swift 70, 96, 97
  crested tree 96
  white-throated 97
swordfish 176, 185

tamandua, northern 15
tamarin 22, 23
  emperor 23
  golden lion 23
tanager, scarlet 107
tang, blue 182
tapir 56, 57
  Malayan 57
tarantula, red-kneed 237
tarpon 166
tarsier 22, 23
  western 23
Tasmanian devil 12
tench 169
tenrec, streaked 16
termite 228, 234, 235, 256, 257
  drywood 235
  snouted 235
  subterranean 235
tern 84, 85
  common 85
terrapin, river 124
tick 236, 243
tiger 30–31, 36
tinamou 75
  great 75
tit, penduline 256
toad 139, 140, 146, 147, 149,
  154
  African clawed 146
  giant 147
  midwife 147
  natterjack 149
  Oriental fire-bellied 139,
    147, 154
  western spadefoot 147
tonguefish, blackcheek 195
topshell, painted 253
tortoise 118, 120, 124, 125
  Galápagos giant 125
  pancake 125
  Schweigger's hingeback 125
  spur-thighed 125
toucan 71, 103
  toco 103
tragopan, Temminck's 73
treehopper 212
triggerfish 196
  queen 196
tropicbird, red-tailed 88

trout, rainbow 173
tuatara 118, 129
tubesnout 192
tuna 180–81
  albacore 180
  bigeye 180
  bluefin 180
  skipjack 180
  yellowfin 180
turaco, red-crested 102
turbot 194
turkey 74
turtle 117, 118, 119, 120, 124,
  126–27
  alligator snapping 127
  Arrau river 124
  common musk 127
  European pond 118
  green 127
  loggerhead 117, 127
  Murray river 126
  softshell, spiny 127
  wood 124
tyrannulet, torrent 111

urchin 203, 254
  flower 203
  long-spined 254

vertebrates 4, 118, 140, 158
vicuña 50
viper, Gaboon 137
vole 62, 63
  meadow 63
vulture 70, 91, 93
  king 93
  lappet-faced 91

wahoo 185
wallaby 8–9, 13
  bridled nail-tail 13
  ring-tailed 8–9
walrus 38
warbler 71, 105, 115
  willow 105
  zitting cisticola 115
warthog 46

wasp 228, 230–31, 256
  common 231
  gall 230
  ichneumon 231
  paper 231
  spider 230, 231
  blue black 231
water chevrotain 50
weevil, boll 219
wels 171
whale 9, 38, 42–45, 114
  beluga see white below
  blue 9, 42–43
  Cuvier's beaked 44
  grey 44
  humpback 45
  killer 42
  minke 45
  sperm 44–45
  white 44
whalefish 190, 191
whelk, lightning 251
whipsnake, dark green 118
wildebeest, blue 53
wolverine 34
wolf 28
  grey 29
  maned 28
wombat 12
woodchuck 59
woodcock, American 79

woodcreeper, long-billed 111
woodlouse 244, 248
woodpecker 96, 99
  pileated 99
worm 131, 201, 202, 254, 255
  annelid 203, 254
  earth see earthworm
  feather duster 255
  paddle 255
  slow 131
wrasse 176
wren, northern 104

yak, wild 53

Zander 159
zebra 56, 66, 67
  Grevy's 56
zitting cisticola 115

List of abbreviations
Metric
cm = centimetres
m = metres
km = kilometres
km/h = kilometres per hour
km^2 = square kilometres
kg = kilogrammes

Imperial
in = inches
ft = feet
miles = miles
mph = miles per hour
sq miles = square miles
lb = pounds

Rainbow lorikeet

Acknowledgements

Photographic credits

t = top; b = bottom; l = left; r = right

6–7 Norbert Rosing/Oxford Scientific Films; 20 Haroldo Palo Jr./NHPA; 31 Frank Schneidermeyer/Oxford Scientific Films; 41 Rick Price/Oxford Scientific Films; 49 Martyn Colbeck/Oxford Scientific Films; 66t Alastair Shay/Oxford Scientific Films, 66b Eyal Bartov/Oxford Scientific Films, 66–67 Stan Osolinski/Oxford Scientific Films; 87 Colin Monteath/Oxford Scientific Films; 95 Lon E. Lauber/Oxford Scientific Films; 101 Michael Fogden/Oxford Scientific Films; 109 Hans Reinhard/Oxford Scientific Films; 114l Jeff Lepore/Oxford Scientific Films, 114r Alastair Shay/Oxford Scientific Films; 115 Jorge Sierra/Oxford Scientific Films; 116–117 Zig Leszczynski/Oxford Scientific Films; 123 David Cayless/Oxford Scientific Films; 133 David Haring/Oxford Scientific Films; 138–139 Zig Leszczynski/Oxford Scientific Films; 151 John Netherton/Oxford Scientific Films; 154 Alastair Shay/Oxford Scientific Films, 154–155 Michael Fogden/Oxford Scientific Films, 155 Marty Cordano/Oxford Scientific Films; 156–157 David B. Fleetham/Oxford Scientific Films; 163 Gary Bell/Planet Earth Pictures; 181 Richard Herrmann/Oxford Scientific Films; 198 Anthony Bannister/Oxford Scientific Films, 198–199 Andrew Plumptre/Oxford Scientific Films, 199t David B. Fleetham/Oxford Scientific Films, 199b Steve Turner/Oxford Scientific Films; 200–201 P.K. Sharpe/Oxford Scientific Films; 217 Stephen Dalton/NHPA; 225 Bob Fredrick/Oxford Scientific Films; 233 David Thompson/Oxford Scientific Films; 241 Oxford Scientific Films; 253 Paul Kay/Oxford Scientific Films; 256 Roland Mayr/Oxford Scientific Films; 257t Roger Hosking/NHPA, 257b Stan Osolinski/Oxford Scientific Films

Artwork credits

Artists:

Mammals: Graham Allen, John Francis, Elizabeth Gray, Bernard Robinson, Eric Robson, Simon Turvey, Dick Twinney, Michael Woods

Birds: Keith Brewer, Hilary Burn, Malcolm Ellis, Steve Kirk, Colin Newman, Denys Ovenden, Peter D. Scott, Ken Wood, Michael Woods

Reptiles and amphibans: John Francis, Elizabeth Gray, Steve Kirk, Alan Male, Colin Newman, Eric Robson, Peter D. Scott

Fish: Robin Boutell, John Francis, Elizabeth Gray, Elizabeth Kay, Colin Newman, Guy Smith, Michael Woods

Insects, spiders and other invertebrates: Robin Boutell, Joanne Cowne, Sandra Doyle, Bridget James, Steve Kirk, Adrian Lascom, Alan Male, Colin Newman, Steve Roberts, Bernard Robinson, Roger Stewart, Colin Woolf

Habitat symbols: Roy Flooks

Chapter panels: Michael Woods

Habitat map: Eugene Fleury

Cover design: Andy Smith

COMMERCIAL PROPERTY

COMMERCIAL PROPERTY

Paul Butt LLB (Manchester), Solicitor

Philip Rogers BSc, Solicitor (Hons)

JORDANS

2004

Published by
Jordan Publishing Limited
21 St Thomas Street
Bristol BS1 6JS

British Library Cataloguing-in-Publication Data
A catalogue record for this book is available from the British Library.

ISSN 1353–3584
ISBN 0 85308 908 6

Printed in Great Britain by Hobbs The Printers Ltd of Southampton

PREFACE

The aim of this book is to provide law students with a comprehensive introduction to three important areas of property law:

- town and country planning;
- commercial leases; and
- residential tenancies.

At first sight, the inclusion of residential tenancies in a book on Commercial Property might seem a little unusual. However, many sites bought for commercial development are subject to existing residential tenancies and it is thus important for all commercial property lawyers to know the protection they may enjoy and the chances of securing vacant possession.

Although it is hoped that the book will provide a useful guide to trainee solicitors and others involved in this type of work, it is primarily intended to complement the Commercial Property Elective on The College of Law's Legal Practice Course. These electives are only undertaken once the compulsory Conveyancing and Property course has been completed and this book, therefore, contains a few references to the book accompanying that course.

The authors would like to acknowledge the many valuable contributions made by Alan Riley of Halliwell Landau to previous editions of this book.

In the interests of brevity, the masculine pronoun has been used throughout to include the feminine.

The law is stated as at 31 July 2003.

PAUL BUTT
PHILIP ROGERS

The College of Law
Chester

CONTENTS

PREFACE   v

TABLE OF CASES   xiii

TABLE OF STATUTES   xix

TABLE OF STATUTORY INSTRUMENTS   xxv

TABLE OF ABBREVIATIONS   xxvii

PART I   **SITE ACQUISITIONS**   1

Chapter 1   THE NEED FOR PLANNING PERMISSION   3
                1.1   Introduction   3
                1.2   Sources of planning law   3
                1.3   The Office of the Deputy Prime Minister   4
                1.4   Local planning authorities   5
                1.5   Development plans   6

Chapter 2   WHAT IS DEVELOPMENT?   9
                2.1   The basic rule   9
                2.2   Permitted development   13
                2.3   Problem cases   16

Chapter 3   APPLYING FOR PLANNING PERMISSION   17
                3.1   Introduction   17
                3.2   Preliminary steps   17
                3.3   Full or outline permission?   18
                3.4   The procedure   19
                3.5   The decision   20
                3.6   Planning permissions subject to conditions   24
                3.7   Appeals against adverse planning determinations   27
                3.8   Types of appeal   28
                3.9   Costs in appeals   30
                3.10   Challenging the appeal decision   31

Chapter 4   PLANNING OBLIGATIONS   33
                4.1   Introduction   33
                4.2   Planning obligations   33
                4.3   'Planning gain'   34
                4.4   Practical points   36
                4.5   Modification and discharge of planning obligations   38
                4.6   Unilateral undertakings   38

Chapter 5   ENFORCEMENT OF PLANNING LAW   41
                5.1   Introduction   41
                5.2   Definitions and time-limits   41
                5.3   Certificates of lawful use or development (CLEUD)   42

	5.4	Right of entry for enforcement purposes	43
	5.5	Planning contravention notice	44
	5.6	Breach of condition notice	45
	5.7	Injunctions	46
	5.8	Enforcement notice	46
	5.9	Stop notice	51
	5.10	Appeals against enforcement notices	53

Chapter 6		THE PROBLEM OF CONTAMINATED LAND	57
	6.1	Introduction	57
	6.2	The consequences of contamination	57
	6.3	Steps to take to reduce the risks	59
	6.4	Contractual terms	60

Chapter 7		MATTERS OF CONTRACT	61
	7.1	The contract of sale	61
	7.2	Different types of contract	62
	7.3	Searches and enquiries	67

Chapter 8		CONSTRUCTION PROJECTS	71
	8.1	Introduction	71
	8.2	Who will be involved?	71
	8.3	Duties owed to third parties	73
	8.4	Protecting other parties	76

| **PART II** | | **COMMERCIAL LEASES** | 81 |

Chapter 9		LANDLORD AND TENANT LAW AND COMMERCIAL LEASES	83
	9.1	Introduction	83
	9.2	Liability of the parties on the covenants in the lease	83
	9.3	Security of tenure	84
	9.4	Lease/licence distinction	84

Chapter 10		AN OUTLINE OF TAXATION OF COMMERCIAL PROPERTIES	87
	10.1	Value added tax	87
	10.2	Stamp duty on leases	94

Chapter 11		LEASE DRAFTING	97
	11.1	Principles of drafting	97
	11.2	Rules of construction	97
	11.3	The structure of the lease	98

Chapter 12		THE PARTIES TO THE LEASE	105
	12.1	Introduction	105
	12.2	The landlord	105
	12.3	The tenant	107
	12.4	The guarantor	111
	12.5	Rent deposits	116

Chapter 13		THE PARCELS CLAUSE	119
	13.1	Purpose	119
	13.2	Airspace and underground	119
	13.3	Fixtures	119

| | 13.4 | Rights to be granted and reserved | 120 |

Chapter 14	**TERM**		121
	14.1	Introduction	121
	14.2	Break clauses	121
	14.3	Options to renew	123

Chapter 15	**RENT**		125
	15.1	Introduction	125
	15.2	Amount	125
	15.3	Time for payment	126
	15.4	Other payments reserved as rent	126
	15.5	Suspension of rent	126
	15.6	Interest	127
	15.7	VAT	127

Chapter 16	**THE RENT REVIEW CLAUSE**		129
	16.1	The need for review	129
	16.2	Regularity	129
	16.3	Types of rent review clauses	130
	16.4	Open market revaluations	131
	16.5	The hypothetical letting	132
	16.6	The mechanics of the review	141
	16.7	Ancillary provisions	144

Chapter 17	**REPAIRING COVENANTS**		147
	17.1	Introduction	147
	17.2	Tenant's covenant to repair	147
	17.3	Landlord's covenant to repair	151
	17.4	Covenant to yield up in repair	152
	17.5	Decorating	152
	17.6	Statutory curtailment	152

Chapter 18	**ALIENATION**		153
	18.1	Introduction	153
	18.2	Restrictions on alienation	154
	18.3	Notice of assignment or sub-letting	160

Chapter 19	**USER COVENANTS**		161
	19.1	The need for a user covenant	161
	19.2	The permitted use	162
	19.3	The extent of the landlord's control	164
	19.4	Ancillary clauses	166

Chapter 20	**ALTERATIONS**		167
	20.1	Existing restrictions	167
	20.2	The need for an alterations covenant	167
	20.3	The extent of the landlord's control	169
	20.4	Other lease clauses	172
	20.5	Compensation for improvements	173

Chapter 21	**THE LANDLORD'S COVENANT FOR QUIET ENJOYMENT**		175
	21.1	Nature of the covenant	175
	21.2	Acts constituting a breach	175

Chapter 22	INSURANCE	177
	22.1 Introduction	177
	22.2 Who is to insure?	177
	22.3 Who is to pay?	177
	22.4 In whose name?	178
	22.5 Risks covered	178
	22.6 The sum insured	178
	22.7 What if the premises are damaged?	179
	22.8 Additional provisions	181
	22.9 Insurance by the tenant	182
Chapter 23	PROVISO FOR RE-ENTRY	183
Chapter 24	LEASE OF PART	185
	24.1 Introduction	185
	24.2 Boundaries and easements	185
	24.3 Responsibility for repairs	185
	24.4 Service charges	187
	24.5 Sinking and reserve funds	191
	24.6 Insurance	192
Chapter 25	UNDERLEASES	193
	25.1 Liability of sub-tenants	193
	25.2 Reasons for sub-letting	193
	25.3 Drafting points	193
	25.4 The sub-tenant's concerns	196
Chapter 26	AGREEMENTS FOR LEASE	199
	26.1 Introduction	199
	26.2 When are they used?	199
	26.3 A typical agreement	200
Chapter 27	SELLING THE LEASE	207
	27.1 Applications for consent to assign	207
	27.2 The landlord's licence	209
	27.3 Additional rules for leases granted on or after 1 January 1996	209
Chapter 28	REMEDIES FOR BREACH OF COVENANT	211
	28.1 Landlord's remedies	211
	28.2 Tenant's remedies	216
Chapter 29	THE EFFECT OF INSOLVENCY	221
	29.1 Bankruptcy of the tenant	221
	29.2 Liquidation of the tenant	223
	29.3 The tenant in administration	223
	29.4 The tenant in receivership	224
	29.5 Insolvency and forfeiture	224
	29.6 Insolvency and claims for rent or damages	226
	29.7 Landlord's insolvency	227
Chapter 30	METHODS OF TERMINATION	229
	30.1 Introduction	229
	30.2 Expiry	229
	30.3 Notice to quit	229

30.4	Operation of break clause	230
30.5	Forfeiture	230
30.6	Surrender	234
30.7	Merger	235

Chapter 31 THE LANDLORD AND TENANT ACT 1954, PART II — 237
31.1	Introductory matters	237
31.2	Termination under the Act	241
31.3	The tenant's application to court	246
31.4	Interim rents	247
31.5	Grounds of opposition	248
31.6	Compensation for failure to obtain a new tenancy	253
31.7	The renewal lease	255
31.8	The order for the new lease	258
31.9	Proposals for reform of the 1954 Act	258

PART III   **RESIDENTIAL TENANCIES** — 261

Chapter 32 INTRODUCTION TO RESIDENTIAL TENANCIES — 263
32.1	Residential occupiers	263
32.2	The common law	263
32.3	The statutes	264
32.4	Public sector lettings	264
32.5	Private sector lettings	264
32.6	The next step	265

Chapter 33 ASSURED TENANCIES — 267
33.1	Introduction	267
33.2	What is an assured tenancy?	267
33.3	Tenancies which cannot be assured	269
33.4	Transitional provisions	270
33.5	Rents under assured tenancies	270
33.6	Succession on death	271
33.7	Sub-lettings	271
33.8	Security of tenure	271

Chapter 34 ASSURED SHORTHOLD TENANCIES — 277
34.1	Introduction	277
34.2	Old shortholds	277
34.3	New shortholds	279
34.4	Rent control	280
34.5	What happens when a shorthold expires?	281
34.6	How does the landlord obtain possession?	281
34.7	Are there any other grounds for possession?	281

Chapter 35 THE RENT ACT 1977 — 283
35.1	Introduction	283
35.2	Protected tenancies	283
35.3	Statutory tenancies	283
35.4	The fair rent system	284
35.5	Succession to Rent Act tenancies	284

Chapter 36 PROTECTION FROM EVICTION — 287
36.1	Introduction	287

36.2   Criminal sanctions: the Protection from Eviction Act 1977   287
36.3   Criminal sanctions: the Criminal Law Act 1977   288
36.4   Civil proceedings   288

Chapter 37   REPAIRS TO RESIDENTIAL PROPERTIES   291
37.1   Introduction   291
37.2   Who is liable for repair?   291
37.3   Landlord and Tenant Act 1985, s 11   292

Chapter 38   ENFRANCHISEMENT: LONG LEASES OF HOUSES   295
38.1   Introduction   295
38.2   The qualifying conditions in outline   295
38.3   Enfranchisement or extended lease   296
38.4   Terms of the conveyance of the freehold   297
38.5   The price of the freehold   297

Chapter 39   LANDLORD AND TENANT ACT 1987   299
39.1   Introduction   299
39.2   The tenant's right of first refusal   299
39.3   Compulsory acquisition of the reversion   301

Chapter 40   LEASEHOLD REFORM, HOUSING AND URBAN DEVELOPMENT
                ACT 1993   303
40.1   Introduction   303
40.2   Collective enfranchisement   303
40.3   Individual acquisition of a long lease   307

Chapter 41   COMMONHOLD   311
41.1   What is it?   311
41.2   Why is it needed?   311
41.3   History   311
41.4   How will it work?   311
41.5   The commonhold association (CA)   312
41.6   The commonhold community statement (CCS)   313
41.7   How is a commonhold created?   313
41.8   Ombudsman scheme   314
41.9   Termination of commonhold   314
41.10 Commonhold in practice   314

INDEX   317

TABLE OF CASES

References in the right-hand column are to paragraph numbers.

Addiscombe Garden Estates v Crabbe [1958] 1 QB 513, CA   31.1.2

Allen v Corporation of the City of London [1981] JPL 685   3.5.1

Allied Dunbar Assurance plc v Homebase Ltd [2002] EWCA Civ 666, [2002] 27 EG 144, CA   25.3.2

Allied London Property Investment Ltd v Secretary of State for the Environment
(1996) 72 P&CR 327, QBD   3.6.4

Allnatt London Properties Ltd v Newton [1984] 1 All ER 423, CA   18.2.5, 30.6, 31.1.5

Amalgamated Estates Ltd v Joystretch Manufacturing Ltd (1980) 257 EG 489, CA   16.6.3

Anglia Building Society v Secretary of State for the Environment and Another [1984] JPL 175,
QBD   3.5.1

Anstruther-Gough-Calthorpe v McOscar and Another [1924] 1 KB 716, CA   17.2.4

Arundel Corporation v The Financial Training Co Ltd [2000] 3 All ER 456, QBD   30.6, 31.2

Ashworth Frazer Ltd v Gloucester City Council [2000] 12 EG 149, CA   18.2.5

BHP Petroleum Ltd v Chesterfield Properties Ltd [2001] 50 EG 88 (CS), CA   12.2.2

Bairstow Eves (Securities) Ltd v Ripley [1992] 2 EGLR 47, CA   14.2.2, 30.4

Bacchiocci v Academic Agency Ltd [1998] 1 WLR 1313, CA   31.2

Barclays Bank plc v Daejan Investments (Grove Hall) Ltd [1995] 18 EG 117, ChD   19.3.2

Barclays Bank plc v Savile Estates Ltd [2002] EWCA Civ 589, [2002] 24 EG 152, CA   16.6.1

Barnes v City of London Real Property Co; Webster v City of London Real Property Co; Sollas v
City of London Real Property Co; Oakley, Sollas & Co v City of London Real Property Co
[1918] 2 Ch 18, ChD   24.4.2

Barrett v Lounova (1982) Ltd [1990] QB 348, CA   17.1, 24.3.2

Barrett v Morgan [2000] 2 AC 264, HL   30.4

Barth v Pritchard [1990] 1 EGLR 109   31.5.6

Betty's Cafes Ltd v Phillips Furnishing Stores Ltd [1959] AC 20, HL   31.5.6

Billson v Residential Apartments [1992] 1 AC 494, HL   30.5.3

Bolton (HL) Engineering Co Ltd v Graham (TJ) & Sons Ltd [1957] 1 QB 159, CA   31.5.7

Booth v Thomas [1926] Ch 397   21.2

British Telecom plc v Sun Life Assurance Society plc [1995] 45 EG 133, CA   17.3

Broadgate Square plc v Lehman Brothers Ltd [1995] 01 EG 111, CA   11.2, 16.5.2

Brown v Liverpool Corporation [1969] 3 All ER 1345, CA   37.3.3

Brown & Root Technology v Sun Alliance [1997] 18 EG 123, CA   14.2.1

Burdle and Another v Secretary of State for the Environment and Another [1972] 3 All ER 240,
DC   2.1.2

Burt v British Transport Commission (1955) 166 EG 4, QBD   28.1.3

Bylander Waddell Partnership v Secretary of State for the Environment and Harrow London
Borough Council [1994] JPL 440, QBD   3.5.1

C&A Pensions Trustees Ltd v British Vita Investments Ltd [1984] 2 EGLR 75, ChD   16.5.2, 19.1.1

Cambridge Water Co v Eastern Counties Leather Ltd [1994] 2 AC 264, HL   6.2.2

Campden Hill Towers v Gardner [1977] QB 823, CA   37.3.3

Caparo Industries v Dickman [1990] 2 AC 605, HL   8.3.4

Central Estates Ltd v Secretary of State for the Environment [1997] 1 EGLR 239   16.6.1

Chartered Trust plc v Davies [1997] 49 EG 135, CA   28.2.2

Cheryl Investments Ltd v Saldhana; Royal Life Saving Society v Page [1978] 1 WLR 1329, CA   31.1.2

Cheverell Estate Ltd v Harris [1998] 02 EG 127, QBD   28.1

Church Commissioners for England v Secretary of State for the Environment (1995) 7 P&CR 73,
QBD   2.1.2

City of Edinburgh Council v Secretary of State for Scotland; Revival Properties Ltd v City of
Edinburgh Council; Secretary of State for Scotland v Revival Properties Ltd [1997] 1 WLR
1446, HL   1.5.2

City of London Corporation v Fell [1993] 49 EG 113, HL   12.3.1, 31.1.6

Claire's Accessories UK Ltd v Kensington High Street Associates [2001] PLSCS 112 — 14.2.2
Commercial Union Life Assurance Co Ltd v Label Ink Ltd [2001] EG 20 January 129 — 14.2.2
Connaught Restaurants Ltd v Indoor Leisure Ltd [1993] 46 EG 184, CA — 15.1
Cook v Shoesmith [1951] 1 KB 752, CA — 18.1.2
Co-operative Insurance Society Ltd v Argyll Stores (Holdings) Ltd [1997] 23 EG 137, HL — 28.1.3
Coppin v Bruce-Smith [1998] EGCS 45 — 31.5.6
Credit Suisse v Beegas Nominees Ltd [1994] 11 EG 151, ChD — 17.2.7
Creska Ltd v Hammersmith and Fulham London Borough Council (No 2) (1999) 78 P&CR D46 — 28.1.2
Cricket Ltd v Shaftesbury plc [1999] 3 All ER 283, ChD — 31.1.3
Crown Estate Commissioners v Town Investments Ltd (National Investment Bank, Third Party) [1992] 08 EG 111, QBD — 31.7.3
Croydon London Borough Council v Gladden [1994] JPL 723, CA — 5.7
Cunliffe v Goodman [1950] 2 KB 237, CA — 31.5.6

D & F Estates Ltd v Church Commissioners for England [1989] AC 177, HL — 8.3.3
Daiches v Bluelake Investments Ltd [1985] 2 EGLR 67, ChD — 28.2.1
Dayani v Bromley London Borough Council [1999] 3 EGLR 144, QBD — 17.1
Dennis & Robinson Ltd v Kiossos Establishment [1987] 1 EGLR 133, CA — 16.5.2
Department of the Environment v Allied Freehold Property Trust Ltd [1992] 45 EG 156, Mayor's and City of London Ct — 31.4.2
Dong Bang Minerva (UK) Ltd v Davina [1996] 31 EG 87, CA — 27.1
Donovan v Secretary of State for the Environment [1988] JPL 118, QBD — 5.8.2
Dukeminster (Ebbgate House One) Ltd v Somerfield Properties Co Ltd [1997] 40 EG 157, CA — 16.5.2

Elite Investments Ltd v TI Bainbridge Silencers Ltd [1986] 2 EGLR 43, ChD — 17.2.5
Elitestone Ltd v Morris [1997] 2 All ER 513, HL — 13.3
English Exporters (London) Ltd v Eldonwall Ltd [1973] Ch 415, ChD — 31.4.2
Envirocor Waste Holdings v Secretary of State for the Environment [1995] EGCS 60, QBD — 3.5.1
Esselte AB v Pearl Assurance plc [1997] 1 WLR 891, CA — 31.1.6, 31.2
Essexcrest Ltd v Evenlex Ltd [1988] 1 EGLR 69, CA — 31.1.5
Esso Petroleum Co Ltd v Fumegrange Ltd [1994] 46 EG 199, CA — 9.4
Expert Clothing Service & Sales Ltd v Hillgate House Ltd [1986] Ch 340, CA — 30.5.3
Ezekiel v Orakpo [1976] 3 WLR 693, CA — 29.5.1

FR Evans (Leeds) Ltd v English Electric Co Ltd (1977) 245 EG 657, QBD — 16.5.2
Family Management v Grey (1979) 253 EG 369, CA — 16.5.3
Fawke v Viscount Chelsea [1980] QB 441, CA — 31.7.3
Finchbourne v Rodrigues [1976] 3 All ER 581, CA — 24.4.2, 24.4.4
First Property Growth Partnership v Royal & Sun Alliance Services Ltd [[2002] EWHC 305 (Ch), [2002] 22 EG 140, ChD — 16.6.1
Flairline Properties Ltd v Hassan [1999] 1 EGLR 138, QBD — 31.1.2
Fluor Daniel Properties Ltd v Shortlands Investments Ltd [2001] PLCS 10, ChD — 24.4.2
Footwear Corporation Ltd v Amplight Properties Ltd [1999] 1 WLR 551, ChD — 18.2.4
Forbuoys plc v Newport Borough Council [1994] 24 EG 156, Cty Ct — 31.7.3
Friends' Provident Life Office v British Railways Board [1996] 1 All ER 336, CA — 12.3.1, 12.4.3
Fuller v Happy Shopper Markets Ltd [2001] 1 WLR 1681, ChD — 28.1.1

G & K Ladenbau (UK) Ltd v Crawley and de Reya (A Firm) [1978] 1 All ER 682, QBD — 7.3.4
Gateshead Metropolitan Borough Council v Secretary of State for the Environment [1995] JPL 432, CA — 3.5.1
Go West Ltd v Spigarolo [2003] EWCA Civ 17, [2003] 07 EG 136, CA — 27.1
Goldmile Properties Ltd v Lechouritis [2003] EWCA Civ 49, [2003] 15 EG 143, CA — 21.2
Good and Another v Epping Forest District Council [1994] 1 WLR 376, CA — 4.3.3
Good's Lease, Re; Good v Trustee of the Property of W, A Bankrupt, and W [1954] 1 All ER 275, ChD — 18.1.2
Graysim Holdings Ltd v P&O Property Holdings Ltd [1995] 3 WLR 854 — 31.1.2
Great Portland Estates plc v Westminster City Council [1985] AC 661, HL — 3.5.1

Greater Nottingham Co-operative Society v Cementation Piling [1989] QB 71, CA   8.4.1
Greenwich London Borough Council v Discreet Selling Estates Ltd [1990] 48 EG 113, CA   30.5.1
Gurton v Parrot [1991] 1 EGLR 98, CA   31.1.2

Hadley v Baxendale (1854) 9 Exch 341   8.3, 28.1.3
Hambleton District Council v Bird [1995] 3 PLR 8, CA   5.7
Hancock & Willis v GMS Syndicate Ltd (1982) 265 EG 473, CA   31.1.2
Harborough District Council v Wheatcroft & Son Ltd [1996] JPL B128, QBD   5.7
Harmer v Jumbil (Nigeria) Tin Areas Ltd [1921] 1 Ch 200, CA   28.2.2
Havant International Holdings Ltd v Lionsgate (H) Investments Ltd [1999] EGCS 144, ChD   14.2.2
Havenridge Ltd v Boston Dyers Ltd [1994] 49 EG 111, CA   22.3, 24.4.2
Hazel v Akhtar [2002] EWCA Civ 1883, [2002] 07 EG 124, CA   31.5.2
Hedley Byrne & Co Ltd v Heller & Partners Ltd [1964] AC 465, HL   8.3.2, 8.3.3, 8.3.4
Henderson v Merrett Syndicates Ltd [1994] 3 All ER 506, HL   8.4.1
Herbert Duncan Ltd v Cluttons [1992] 1 EGLR 101, QBD   12.3.1, 15.1, 31.1.6
Hills (Patents) Ltd v University College Hospital Board of Governors [1956] 1 QB 90, CA   31.1.2
Hindcastle Ltd v Barbara Attenborough Associates Ltd [1996] 15 EG 103   29.1.3
Historic Houses Hotels Ltd v Cadogan Estates [1997] AC 70, HL   16.5.4
Holland and Another v Hodgson and Another (1872) LR 7 CP 328, Exch   13.3
Holme v Brunskill (1877) 3 QBD 495, CA   12.4.3
Hopwood v Cannock Chase District Council [1975] 1 WLR 373, CA   37.3.3
Hua Chiao Commercial Bank Ltd v Chiaphua Industries Ltd [1987] 1 AC 99, PC   12.5

International Drilling Fluids Ltd v Louisville Investments (Uxbridge) Ltd [1986] 1 All ER 321,
    CA   18.2.5

JT Developments v Quinn [1991] 2 EGLR 257, CA   31.2.3
Janmohamed v Hassam (1976) 241 EG 609, ChD   7.2.1
Javad v Aqil [1991] 1 WLR 1007, CA   31.1.3
Jervis v Harris [1996] Ch 195, CA   28.1.2
Jolley v Carmel [2000] 43 EG 185, CA   7.2.1
Junction Estates Ltd v Cope (1974) 27 P&CR 482, QBD   12.4.2
Junior Books v Veitchi Co [1983] 1 AC 520, HL   8.3.4

Kalford Ltd v Peterborough City Council [2001] EGCS 42   20.3.2
Kalra v Secretary of State for the Environment [1996] JPL 850, CA   2.1.3
Kammins Ballrooms Ltd v Zenith Investments (Torquay) Ltd [1971] AC 850, HL   31.2.3, 31.3.2
Kataria v Safeland plc [1998] 05 EG 155, CA   30.5.2
Killick v Second Covent Garden Property Co Ltd [1973] 2 All ER 337, CA   18.2.5
King v South Northamptonshire District Council [1992] 06 EG 152, CA   37.3.3
Kissel v Secretary of State for the Environment and Another [1994] JPL 819, QBD   3.5.1

Lambert v Keymood Ltd [1997] 43 EG 131, QBD   22.4
Lambert v F W Woolworth & Co Ltd (No 2) [1938] 2 All ER 664, CA   20.3.2
Laurence v Lexcourt Holdings Ltd [1978] 2 All ER 810, ChD   11.3.5
Law Land Co Ltd v Consumers Association Ltd (1980) 255 EG 617, CA   19.2.2
Lee-Parker v Izzet [1971] 1 WLR 1688, ChD   28.2.1
Lee-Parker and Another v Izzet and Others (No 2) [1972] 2 All ER 800, ChD   7.2.1
Lemmerbell Ltd v Britannia LAS Direct Ltd [1998] 48 EG 188, CA   14.2.2
Linden Garden Trust Ltd v Lenesta Sludge Disposals Ltd; St Martins Property Corporation Ltd v
    Sir Robert McAlpine & Sons Ltd [1993] 3 WLR 408, HL   8.4.2
Lister v Lane & Nesham [1893] 2 QB 212, CA   17.2.5
Liverpool City Council v Irwin [1971] AC 239, HL   17.1, 37.2.1
London Baggage Co (Charing Cross) Ltd v Railtrack plc [2000] EGCS 57, ChD   31.1.3
London Hilton Jewellers Ltd v Hilton International Hotels Ltd [1990] 1 EGLR 112, CA   31.5.7
London Residuary Body v Lambeth Borough Council [1990] 2 All ER 309, HL   3.5.1
Lurcott v Wakeley & Wheeler [1911] 1 KB 905, CA   17.2.5

M&P Enterprises (London) Ltd v Norfolk Square Hotels Ltd [1994] 1 EGLR 129, ChD   31.2.1
M'Alister (or Donoghue) (Pauper) v Stevenson [1932] AC 562, HL   8.3.2, 8.3.3
McCausland v Duncan Lawrie Ltd [1996] 4 All ER 995, CA   26.3.2
McDonald's Property Co Ltd v HSBC Bank plc [2001] 36 EG 181, ChD   16.6.1
Mannai Investment Co Ltd v Eagle Star Life Assurance Co Ltd [1997] AC 749, HL   14.2.2, 30.4
Meadfield Properties Ltd v Secretary of State for the Environment [1995] 03 EG 128, ChD   14.1
Metropolitan Properties Co (Regis) Ltd v Bartholomew [1995] 14 EG 143, QBD   12.4.2
Ministerial Decision [1977] JPL 116   2.1.2
Ministerial Decision [1991] JPL 184   3.6.2
Mira v Aylmer Square Investments Ltd [1990] 1 EGLR 45, CA   21.2
Moat v Martin [1950] 1 KB 175, CA   18.2.5
Morcom v Campbell-Johnson [1955] 3 All ER 264, CA   17.2.5
Morgan Sindall plc v Sawston Farms (Cambs) Ltd [1999] 1 EGLR 90, CA   24.4.4
Moss Bros Group plc v CSC Properties Ltd [1999] EGCS 47, ChD   18.2.5
Moule v Garrett and Others (1872) LR 7 Exch 101, Exch   12.3.1
Mullaney v Maybourne Grange (Croydon) Ltd [1986] 1 EGLR 70, ChD   24.4.1
Mumford Hotels Ltd v Wheler and Another [1964] Ch 117, ChD   22.7.3
Murphy v Brentwood District Council [1990] 2 All ER 908, HL   8.3.3

National Car Parks Ltd v Paternoster Consortium Ltd [1990] 15 EG 53, ChD   31.7.2
National Car Parks Ltd v Trinity Development Co (Banbury) Ltd [2001] EWCA Civ 1686, [2001]
      28 EG 144, CA   9.4
National Carriers Ltd v Panalpina (Northern) Ltd [1981] AC 675, HL   15.5, 22.7
National Grid Co plc v M25 Group Ltd [1999] 08 EG 169, CA   24.4.4
National Westminster Bank plc v Arthur Young McClelland Moores & Co [1985] 1 WLR 1123,
      CA   16.5.2
New England Properties plc v Portsmouth News Shops Ltd; Sterling Surveys v New England
      Properties; New England Properties v Ex-Eltronics [1993] 23 EG 130, ChD   17.2.5
Newbury District Council v Secretary of State for the Environment; Newbury District Council v
      International Synthetic Rubber Co [1981] AC 578, HL   3.6.2, 4.3.3
Newham London Borough Council v Secretary of State for the Environment [1995] EGCS 6, QBD   3.5.1
Next plc v National Farmers Union Mutual Insurance Co Ltd [1997] EGCS 181, ChD   27.1
Nicholas v Kinsey [1994] 16 EG 145, CA   31.1.5
North Yorkshire County Council v Secretary of State for the Environment and Griffin [1996] JPL
      32, CA   3.5.1
Northways Flats Management Co (Camden) v Wimpey Pension Trustees [1992] 31 EG 65, CA   24.4.1
Norwich Union Life Insurance Society v Low Profile Fashions Ltd [1992] 21 EG 104, CA   27.1
Norwich Union Life Insurance Society v Shopmoor Ltd [1999] 1 WLR 531, ChD   18.2.5
Nynehead Developments Ltd v RH Fibreboard Containers Ltd and Others [1999] 9 EG 174   28.2.2

O'Brien v Robinson [1973] AC 912, HL   17.3, 37.3.6
O'May v City of London Real Property Co Ltd [1983] AC 726, HL   31.7.4
Oceanic Village Ltd v Shirayama Shokusan Co Ltd [2001] All ER (D) 62 (Feb), ChD   28.2.2
Orlando Investments v Grosvenor Estate Belgravia [1989] 2 EGLR 74   18.2.5
Owen v Gadd [1956] 2 QB 99, CA   21.2

P&A Swift Investments v Combined English Stores Group plc [1988] 3 WLR 313, HL   12.2.1, 12.2.2
P&O Property Holdings v International Computers Ltd [2000] 2 All ER 1015, ChD   11.3.2
Palisade Investments Ltd v Secretary of State for the Environment [1995] 69 P & CR 638, CA   2.1.3
Pearson v Alyo [1990] 1 EGLR 114, CA   31.2.1
Pennycook v Shaws Ltd [2002] EWHC 2769 (Ch), [2002] 50 EG 113, ChD   31.2.3
Perry v Stanborough (Developments) Ltd [1978] JPL 36, ChD   5.8.2
Petra Investments Ltd v Jeffrey Rogers plc [2000] 3 EGLR 120, ChD   28.2.2
Plinth Property Investments Ltd v Mott, Hay & Anderson [1979] 1 EGLR 17, CA   16.5.2, 19.1.1
Pontsarn Investments Ltd v Kansallis-Osake-Pankki [1992] 22 EG 103, ChD   16.5.3
Port v Griffith [1938] 1 All ER 295, ChD   28.2.2
Post Office Counters Ltd v Harlow District Council [1991] 2 EGLR 121, ChD   19.2.2

Post Office v Aquarius Properties Ltd [1987] 1 All ER 1055, CA 17.2.3
Price v West London Investment Building Society [1964] 2 All ER 318, CA 31.2.4
Proudfoot v Hart (1890) 25 QBD 42, CA 17.2.4
Prudential Assurance Co Ltd v Grand Metropolitan Estate Ltd [1993] 32 EG 74, ChD 16.5.4
Prudential Assurance Co Ltd v London Residuary Body [1992] 3 All ER 504, HL 14.1

R v Canterbury City Council, Robert Brett & Sons ex parte Springimage Ltd [1994] JPL 427,
    QBD 3.5.1
R v Greenwich London Borough Council ex parte Patel [1985] JPL 851, CA 5.8.5
R v Hillingdon London Borough Council ex parte Royco Homes Ltd [1974] 1 QB 720, QBD 3.6.2
R v Kuxhaus [1988] 2 WLR 1005, [1988] 2 All ER 705, CA 5.10.4, 32.11.4
R v Plymouth City Council and Others ex parte Plymouth and South Devon Co-operative Society
    Ltd [1993] JPL B81, CA 4.3.3
R v West Oxfordshire District Council ex parte C. H. Pearce Homes [1986] JPL 523, QBD 3.5.1, 3.5.3
Railtrack plc v Gojra [1998] 08 EG 158, CA 31.2.4
Rainbow Estates Ltd v Tokenhold Ltd [1999] Ch 64, ChD 28.1.2
Ravenseft Properties Ltd v Davstone (Holdings) Ltd [1980] QB 12, DC 17.2.6
Razzaq v Pala [1997] 38 EG 157, ChD 29.5.1
Receiver for Metropolitan Police District v Palacegate Properties Ltd [2001] 2 Ch 131, CA 31.1.5
Rogan v Woodfield Building Services Ltd [1994] EGCS 145, CA 33.8.3
Romulus Trading Co Ltd v Comet Properties Ltd [1996] 2 EGLR 70, QBD 28.2.2
Romulus Trading Co Ltd v Henry Smith's Charity Trustees [1990] 2 EGLR 75, CA 31.5.6
Rowlands (Mark) Ltd v Berni Inns Ltd [1986] 1 QB 211, CA 22.4
Royal Bank of Scotland plc v Jennings and Others [1997] 19 EG 152, CA 11.2, 16.6.2, 16.7.1
Royal Borough of Windsor and Maidenhead v Brandrose Investments [1983] 1 WLR 509, CA 4.4.1

Sabella Ltd v Montgomery [1998] 09 EG 153, CA 31.2.1
St Albans District Council v Secretary of State for the Environment and Allied Breweries Ltd
    [1993] JPL 374, QBD 3.5.1
St George Developments Ltd and Kew Riverside Developments v Secretary of State for the
    Environment and Richmond upon Thames London Borough Council [1996] JPL 35, QBD 3.5.1
Saloman v Akiens [1993] 14 EG 97, CA 31.2.3
Scala House & District Property Co Ltd v Forbes [1974] QB 575, CA 30.5.3
Scholl Manufacturing Ltd v Clifton (Slim-Line) Ltd [1967] Ch 41, CA 31.2.1
Secretary of State for Employment v Pivot Properties Ltd (1980) 256 EG 1176, CA 16.5.2
Secretary of State for the Environment v Possfund (North West) Ltd [1997] 39 EG 179, ChD 24.5
Shanklin Pier Co Ltd v Detel Products Ltd [1951] 2 KB 854, KBD 8.2.2
Shanley v Ward (1913) 29 TLR 714 18.2.5
Sight and Sound Education Ltd v Books etc Ltd [1999] 43 EG 161, ChD 31.2
Skilleter v Charles [1992] 13 EG 113, CA 24.4.1
Smiley v Townshend [1950] 2 KB 311, CA 28.1.2
Smith v Draper [1990] 2 EGLR 69, CA 31.2.1
Smith v Marrable [1843] 11 M & W 5 37.2.1
Southport Old Links Ltd v Naylor [1985] 1 EGLR 66, CA 31.2.1
Southwark London Borough Council v Mills and Others; Baxter v Camden London Borough
    Council [1999] 3 WLR 939, HL 21.2
Sovmots v Secretary of State for the Environment; Brompton Securities Ltd v Secretary of State
    for the Environment [1977] 1 QB 411, QBD 3.5.1
Spelthorne Borough Council v Secretary of State for the Environment and Lawlor Land plc
    [1995] JPL 412, QB 3.5.1
Spiro v Glencrown Properties Ltd [1991] Ch 537, ChD 7.2.2
Starmark Enterprises Ltd v CPL Distribution Ltd [2001] 32 EG 89 (CS), CA 16.6.1
Sterling Land Office Developments Ltd v Lloyds Bank plc (1984) 271 EG 894, ChD 16.5.2, 19.2.1
Stevens v Bromley London Borough Council [1972] 2 WLR 605, CA 5.8.5
Stevens & Cutting Ltd v Anderson [1990] 11 EG 70, CA 31.2.3
Stile Hall Properties Ltd v Gooch [1979] 3 All ER 848, CA 31.2.2
Street v Mountford [1985] AC 809, [1985] 2 All ER 289, HL 9.4, 18.1.3, 28.1.3

Stringer v Minister of Housing and Local Government [1971] 1 All ER 65, QBD   3.5.1
Surrey County Council v Single Horse Properties Ltd [2002] EWCA Civ 367, [2002] 1 WLR
    2106, CA   31.1.6
Sykes v Harry [2001] EWCA Civ 167, [2001] 3 WLR 62, CA   17.3

Tandon v Trustees of Spurgeons Homes [1982] AC 755, HL   38.2.1
Tesco Stores Ltd v Secretary of State for the Environment and West Oxfordshire District Council
    [1995] 2 All ER 636, HL   4.3.3
Thatcher v CH Pearce & Sons (Contractors) Ltd [1968] 1 WLR 748   30.5.2
Thomas Heliport plc v Tower Hamlets LBC [1997] 2 PLR 72   2.1.2
Thrasyvoulou v Secretary of State for the Environment [1990] 2 WLR 1, HL   5.8.2
Tidswell v Secretary of State for the Environment [1977] JPL 104   5.8.2
Transworld Land Co Ltd v J Sainsbury plc [1990] 2 EGLR 255, ChD   28.1.3
Trustees of the Viscount Folkestone 1963 Settlement and Camden Homes Ltd v Secretary of State
    for the Environment and Salisbury District Council [1995] JPL 502, QB   3.5.1

Ultraworth Ltd v General Accident Fire and Life Assurance Corporation [2000] 2 EGLR 115,
    QBD   28.1.2
United Dominion Trust Ltd v Shellpoint Trustees [1993] 4 All ER 310, [1993] EGCS 57, CA   30.5.4
United Scientific Holdings v Burnley Borough Council [1978] AC 904, [1977] 2 All ER 62, HL   14.2.2, 16.6.1

Vaux Group plc v Lilley [1991] 1 EGLR 60, ChD   18.2.5

Wallington v Secretary of State for the Environment [1991] JPL 942, CA   2.1.2
Wallis Fashion Group Ltd v General Accident Life Assurance Ltd [2000] EGCS 45   31.7.4
Warren v Marketing Exchange for Africa [1988] 2 EGLR 247, ChD   18.2.5
Welsh v Greenwich London Borough Council [2000] PLSCS 149, CA   17.2.7
Willison v Cheverell Estates Ltd [1996] 26 EG 133, CA   31.4.3
Wood v Secretary of State for the Environment [1993] 1 WLR 707, HL   2.1.2

Zarvos v Pradhan [2003] EWCA Civ 208, [2003] 13 EG 114, CA   31.5.7

TABLE OF STATUTES

References in the right-hand column are to paragraph numbers.

Agricultural Holdings Act 1986	31.1.3
Arbitration Act 1996	16.6.4
Bankruptcy Act 1914	29.5.1
Common Law Procedure Act 1852	
s 210	30.5.2
Commonhold and Leasehold Reform	
Act 2002	32.3, 38.1,
	40.1, 40.2.3, 41.3
ss 1–10	41.7
s 16	41.6.3
ss 31–33	41.6
ss 34–36	41.5
s 37(2)	41.5.2
s 42	41.8
ss 43–56	41.9
Companies Act 1985	
s 395	12.5
s 725	31.2.4
Contracts (Rights of Third Parties) Act	
1999	8.3.1, 25.4
s 2	8.3.1
Criminal Law Act 1977	
s 6	30.5
(1)	36.3
Defective Premises Act 1972	17.2.8, 17.3
Disability Discrimination Act 1995	18.2.1, 18.2.5
Enterprise Act 2002	29.3, 29.4
Environment Act 1995	6.1, 6.2.3,
	6.3, 7.3.3, 11.3.2
Environmental Protection Act 1990	
s 34	6.2
ss 78A–78Y	6.2.3
s 78B	6.2.3
s 78R	6.3
ss 157, 158	6.2
Finance Act 1984	
s 111	26.1
Finance Act 1989	10.1
Finance Act 1994	
s 240(1)	10.2, 26.1
(2)	10.2
Finance Act 1997	10.1.3
Fire Precautions Act 1971	20.3.1

Fires (Prevention) Metropolis Act 1774	22.7.3
Highways Act 1980	4.4.1
Housing Act 1985	32.3, 32.4, 36.2.1
Housing Act 1988	32.3, 32.5, 33.1, 33.2, 33.3.1,
	33.4, 33.6, 35.2, 36.2.1,
	36.4.2, 37.3.3, 37.3.6, 39.2.3,
	40.1, 40.2.1, 40.3.6
Pt IV	33.8.3
s 1	33.2
s 3	33.2.3
s 6	33.8.1
s 8	33.8.2–33.8.4, 34.7
s 13	34.4
s 14	34.4
s 15	33.6
s 17	33.6
s 18	33.7
s 19A	34.3.1
s 20	34.2.1, 34.3.2
s 21	34.6, 34.7
(1)	34.5
s 27	36.4.2
Sch 1, para 8	33.8.3
Sch 2	33.8.2, 33.8.3
Pt I	33.8.3
Ground 1	33.8.3, 34.3.2
Ground 2	33.8.2, 33.8.3, 34.2.1
Grounds 3, 4	33.8.3
Ground 5	33.8.3
Ground 6	33.8.3, 33.8.4
Ground 7	33.8.3
Ground 8	33.8.2, 33.8.3,
	34.2.1, 34.7
Ground 9	33.8.4
Grounds 10, 11	33.8.2, 33.8.4, 34.2.1, 34.7
Grounds 12, 13	33.8.2, 33.8.4, 34.2.1
Ground 14	33.8.2, 33.8.4,
	34.2.1, 34.3.1
Ground 14A	33.8.2, 33.8.4, 34.2.1
Ground 15	33.8.2, 33.8.4, 34.2.1
Ground 16	33.8.4, 35.3.1
Ground 17	33.8.4
Sch 2A	34.3.2
Sch 4, Pt I	33.8.3
Pt II	33.8.3
Housing Act 1996	32.3, 33.1, 33.8.3,
	34.1, 34.3.1, 34.3.2,
	39.1, 39.2.5
Human Rights Act 1998	28.1.1, 30.5
Income and Corporation Taxes Act 1988	22.5

Insolvency Act 1986	12.4.4, 28.1.1, 29.1.3
s 145	12.4.3, 29.2
s 178(2)	29.2
(5)	29.2
s 179	29.2
s 181	29.2
s 285(1)	29.5.1
(3)	29.5.1
s 315	29.1.2
(3)	29.1.3
s 316	29.1.2
s 320	29.1.3
Land Charges Act 1972	31.3.2, 38.3.1
Land Registration Act 1925	
s 24(1)(a)	12.3.1, 12.3.2
s 70(1)(g)	31.3.2
Landlord and Tenant Act 1927	17.2.8, 20.3.1,
	20.5, 20.5.2,
	28.1.2, 31.2.4
Pt I	20.5
s 18	28.1.1, 28.1.2, 28.2.1
s 19	33.6
(1)	18.2.4
(a)	18.2.4, 18.2.5, 25.3, 27.1, 27.3
(1A)	18.2.4, 18.2.5, 25.3, 27.1
(1C)	18.2.5
(2)	20.3.2, 20.3.3, 20.4
(3)	19.3.2, 19.3.3
s 23(1)	31.2.4
Landlord and Tenant Act 1954	9.3, 9.4, 11.3.5,
	12.3.1, 14.2.4, 22.7.4, 25.3.1, 30.1,
	31.1.1, 31.1.3, 31.1.4, 31.1.6, 31.2,
	31.2.1, 31.2.4, 31.4.1, 31.5.1, 31.5.7
	31.7, 31.9, 33.3.4
Pt I	40.1, 40.2.5, 40.3.6
Pt II	9.3, 11.3.5, 12.3.1,
	14.1, 14.2.4, 14.3, 18.1.2,
	18.2.5, 22.7.4, 25.3.1, 30.1,
	30.4, 30.6, 31.1.1, 33.3.4,
	39.2.3, 40.2.6, 40.3.6
Pt III	20.5
s 23	31.1.2, 31.1.3
(1)	31.1.2
(3)	31.1.4
s 24	9.3, 12.3.1, 12.4.2, 15.1,
	31.1.1, 31.1.6, 31.2.2
(1)	16.2
(3)	31.1.2
s 24A	11.3.2, 12.3.1, 15.1, 16.2, 31.1.6,
	31.4.1, 31.4.2, 31.4.3
s 25	20.5.4, 31.2, 31.2.1, 31.2.2, 31.2.3, 31.3.1,
	31.3.2, 31.4.1, 31.5, 31.5.6, 31.5.7,
	31.6.1, 31.9
s 26	20.5.4, 31.2, 31.2.2, 31.2.3, 31.3.1, 31.3.2,
	31.4.1, 31.5, 31.5.6, 31.5.7, 31.6.1, 31.9
s 27	31.1.6, 31.2
s 30	31.2.1, 31.5, 31.7
(1)	31.5
s 30(1)(a)	31.5, 31.5.1
(b)	31.5, 31.5.2
(c)	31.5, 31.5.3
(d)	31.5, 31.5.4
(e)	31.5, 31.5.5, 31.6, 31.6.1
(f)	14.2.4, 31.5, 31.5.6,
	31.5.7, 31.6, 31.6.1
(g)	14.2.4, 31.5, 31.5.7, 31.6, 31.6.1
(2)	31.5.7
(3)	31.5.7
s 31	31.5
s 31A	31.5.6, 31.7.1
s 34(3)	31.7.3
s 37	11.3.5
s 38	30.6
(1)	31.1.5
(2)	31.6.4
(4)	31.1.5
s 40	31.1.4
s 41	31.1.2, 31.5.7
s 41A	31.1.2
s 42	31.1.2, 31.5.7
s 44	31.1.4
s 64	31.4.1
Landlord and Tenant Act 1985	32.3, 37.2.3
s 11	37.3.1, 37.3.3, 37.3.5, 37.3.6, 37.6.3
(2)	37.3.6
(3)	37.3.5
Landlord and Tenant Act 1987	32.3, 39.1, 39.2,
	39.2.2, 39.2.4, 39.2.5
Pt I	39.1, 39.2, 39.3
Pt III	39.3
s 10A	39.2.5
s 48	33.8.3
Landlord and Tenant Act 1988	18.2.4, 19.3.3, 27.1
s 1	22.3.3, 25.3, 27.1
(3)(b)	18.2.4
s 3	27.1
Landlord and Tenant (Covenants) Act 1995	
	9.2.2, 12.1, 12.2.2, 12.3.1,
	12.3.2, 12.4.3, 12.4.5, 12.5,
	14.2.1, 18.2.7, 18.3, 26.3.15,
	27.1, 27.3, 28.1, 28.1.4,
	31.7.3, 31.7.4
s 6	12.2.2
s 8	12.2.2
s 18	12.3.1, 12.4.3
s 22	18.2.4
s 24(2)	12.4.2
s 25	12.4.2
s 28(1)	26.3.15
Late Payment of Commercial Debts (Interest) Act 1998	15.6
Latent Damage Act 1986	8.4.1
Law of Distress Amendment Act 1908	28.1.1
s 6	28.1.1

Law of Property Act 1925   11.3.3, 12.2.2
   s 44   25.1
   s 61   11.3.3
   s 77   12.3.1, 12.3.2
   s 99   33.8.3
   s 101   33.8.3
   s 141   12.2.2
     (1)   12.2.1
   s 142   12.2.2
     (1)   12.2.1
     (2)   12.2.1
   s 144   18.2.6, 27.1
   s 146   11.3.2, 15.4, 25.4,
     28.1.2, 29.5.2, 30.5.3
     (2)   30.5.3
     (4)   30.5.4
   s 147   17.6, 30.5.3
   s 150   30.6.1
   s 192   2.3.1, 2.2.3
   s 196   7.2.2, 11.3.5
   s 205   13.3
Law of Property Act 1969   31.4.1
Law of Property (Miscellaneous
   Provisions) Act 1989
   s 2   7.2.2, 26.3.2
Leasehold Property (Repairs) Act 1938
   17.2.8, 17.6, 28.1.2, 30.5.3
Leasehold Reform Act 1967   32.3, 38.1,
     38.2.1, 38.2.3,
     38.3, 38.3.1, 38.5, 40.2.5
   s 1(1)(a)(i)   38.5
   s 2(1)   38.2.1
   s 3   38.2.2
   s 5   38.3.1
   s 7(7)   38.2.3
   s 9(1)   38.5
     (1A)   38.5
Leasehold Reform, Housing and Urban
   Development Act 1993   32.3, 32.4,
     40.1, 40.2.1, 40.2.2,
     40.2.14, 40.3.1, 40.3.5
   Sch 5   40.2.13
   Sch 8   40.2.12
Limitation Act 1980   8.3, 28.1.1
Local Government Act 1972
   s 250(5)   3.9
Local Government and Housing Act
   1989
   s 10   33.8.3

Mental Health Act 1983
   s 99   12.4.4
Misrepresentation Act 1967
   s 3   11.3.5

Perpetuities and Accumulations Act 1964
   s 1(1)   11.3.5
Planning and Compensation Act 1991
     1.2.1, 1.5.2, 11.3.2
Protection from Eviction Act 1977   30.5, 32.3,
     36.2.2,
   s 1   36.2.1
     (1)   36.2.1, 36.2.2
     (3)   36.2.2
     (3A)   36.2.2
   s 3   36.4.2

Race Relations Act 1976   18.2.1, 18.2.5
   s 19A   3.5.1
Recorded Delivery Service Act 1962   11.3.5
Rent (Agriculture) Act 1976
   s 4   33.8.3
Rent Act 1977   32.3, 32.5, 33.1, 33.3.1,
     33.4, 33.5, 34.2.1, 34.4, 35.1,
     35.2, 35.3, 35.4.1, 36.2.1,
     36.2.2, 36.4.2, 39.2.3, 40.3.6
   s 1   35.2
   Sch 15   35.3

Sex Discrimination Act 1975   18.2.1, 18.2.5
Stamp Act 1891
   s 75(1)   26.1
Supply of Goods and Services Act 1982   24.4.2
   s 4   8.2.2
   s 13   8.2.2
Supreme Court Act 1981
   s 37   28.2.1

Town and Country Planning Act 1990   1.1, 1.2.1,
     2.1.1, 2.1.2, 3.5.3,
     3.10, 5.7, 5.9.1, 11.3.2
   Pt III (ss 55–106)   5.1
   Pt VII (ss 171A–196)   5.1
   ss 1–9   1.4
   s 1   1.4.1
     (2)   1.4.2
   s 2   7.2.2
   ss 10–54   1.5
   ss 12–16   1.5.1
   ss 31–35C   1.5.1
   ss 36–45   1.5.1
   s 54A   1.5.2, 3.2, 3.5.1
   s 55   11.3.2, 20.1
     (1)   2.1
     (1A)   2.1.1
     (2)   2.1.1, 2.1.2
      (a)   2.1.1
      (d)   2.1.2
      (e)   2.1.2
      (f)   2.1.2, 2.1.3

Town and Country Planning Act 1990

cont	
s 55(2)(g)	2.1.1, 2.2.2
(3)	2.1.2
(5)	2.1.2
s 56	3.5.3
s 57	3.5.2
(1)	2.1
(2)–(6)	2.2.1
(2)	2.2.2, 3.5.2
ss 59–61	2.2.2
ss 62–69	3.4
s 65(8)	3.4.4
s 69	3.4.5, 5.3.4
s 70(1)	3.5.1, 3.5.4, 3.6.1, 3.6.2, 4.3.3
s 72(1)	3.6.1
s 73	3.6.4, 3.7, 4.4.2
s 73A	3.6.4, 3.7, 4.4.2, 5.8.7
s 75(1)	3.5.2
s 78	3.7
ss 91–93	3.5.3
s 94	3.5.3
s 95	3.5.3
s 97	3.5.2
s 106	4.2, 4.2.2, 4.2.4, 4.3.3
(1)	4.2.1, 4.3.3, 4.6.1
(2)	4.2.1
(3)	4.2.3
(4)	4.2.1, 4.2.3
(5)	4.2.4
(6)	4.2.4
(12)	4.2.4
s 106A	4.5
(3)–(4)	4.5.2
s 106B	4.5.4
s 171A	5.2.1
(1)	5.8.4
s 171B	5.2.2, 5.8.3
(4)	5.2.2
(b)	5.2.2, 5.8.3
s 171C	5.5, 5.5.1, 5.9.6
(1)	5.5.2
(2)–(6)	5.5.2
(5)	5.5.1
s 171D	5.5
(2)–(4)	5.5.2
(5), (6)	5.5.2
ss 172–177	5.8.4
ss 172–182	5.8
s 172	5.10.1
(1)	5.8.2
(2), (3)	5.8.5
s 173	5.8.4
(1)–(9)	5.8.4
(2)	5.8.9
(11), (12)	5.8.7
s 173A	5.8.8
ss 174–177	5.10

s 174	5.8.6
(1)	5.10.3
(2)	5.10.1
(a)	5.9.6
(3)	5.10.2
(b)	5.10.2
(4)	5.10.4
(6)	5.10.3
s 175(5)	5.10.1
s 176(1)	5.10.1
(2)	5.8.6
s 177(5)	5.10.1
s 178	5.8.9
(1)	5.8.9
s 179	5.8.9
(1)–(5), (7)–(9)	5.8.9
ss 183–187	5.9
s 183(1)–(3)	5.9.2
(6)	5.9.2
(7)	5.9.5
s 184(1)–(3)	5.9.2
(7)	5.9.5
s 186	5.9.6
s 187	5.9.4
s 187A	5.6
s 187B	5.7, 5.8.9
s 188	5.8.9, 5.9.2
s 191	5.3, 5.3.2
(1)	5.3.2
(2), (3)	5.3.1
(4)	5.3.2, 5.3.4
(6), (7)	5.3.2
s 192	2.3.1, 2.3.2, 5.3, 5.3.3
(4)	5.3.3
s 193(4)	5.3.4
(6)	5.3.4
s 194	5.3.4
s 195	5.3.4
s 196	5.3.4
ss 196A–C	5.4
s 196A	5.4.1
s 196B	5.4.2
s 196C	5.4.3
s 284	3.10
s 285	5.8.6
(1)	5.8.5
s 288	3.10, 5.3.4
s 289	5.10.4, 5.10.6
(4A)	5.10.4
s 320	5.10.5
(2)	3.9
s 322	3.9, 5.10.5
s 336(1)	2.1.1, 5.8.5
Sch 1	1.4
para 1	1.4.1
Sch 2	1.5

Unfair Contract Terms Act 1977   11.3.5
s 8   11.3.5

Value Added Tax Act 1994
s 89   10.1.4

TABLE OF STATUTORY INSTRUMENTS

References in the right-hand column are to paragraph numbers.

High Court and County Courts Jurisdiction Order 1991, SI 1991/724 — 31.3.2

Landlord and Tenant Act 1954, Part II (Notices) Regulations 1983, SI 1983/133 — 31.2.1, 31.2.2
Landlord and Tenant Act 1954, Part II (Notices) (Amendment) Regulations 1989, SI 1989/1548 — 31.2.1

Town and Country Planning (Applications) Regulations 1988, SI 1988/1812 — 3.3.2, 3.4
  reg 3 — 3.6.4
Town and Country Planning (Determination by Inspectors) (Inquiries Procedure) (England) Rules
  2000, SI 2000/1625 — 3.8.2, 3.8.5
Town and Country Planning (Enforcement Notices and Appeals) Regulations 1991, SI 1991/2804
  regs 3, 4 — 5.8.4
  reg 5 — 5.10.4
Town and Country Planning (General Development Procedure) Order 1995, SI 1995/419 — 1.1, 1.3.1, 3.4
  art 1(2) — 3.3.2
  arts 3, 4 — 3.3.1
  art 6 — 3.4.3, 3.4.4
    (6) — 3.4.4
  art 7 — 3.4.1, 3.4.3
  art 8 — 3.4.5
  art 20 — 3.5.1, 3.7
  art 22 — 3.5.1
  art 23 — 3.7, 3.7.2
    (1)(b) — 3.7.2
  art 24 — 5.3.4
  art 25(2) — 3.5.1
  Sch 2, Pt I — 3.4.4
Town and Country Planning (General Permitted Development) Order 1995, SI 1995/418 — 1.1, 1.3.1,
  2.2.2, 3.6.4, 6.2.2
  art 1(5) — 2.2.2
  art 3(5) — 2.2.2
  art 4 — 2.2.2
  Sch 2 — 2.2.2
    Pt 1, classes A–H — 2.2.2
    Pt 2, classes A–C — 2.2.2
    Pt 3 — 2.2.2
    Pt 4, classes A, B — 2.2.2
    Pt 6 — 2.2.2
    Pt 31 — 2.1.1, 2.2.2
Town and Country Planning (Hearings Procedure) (England) Rules 2000, SI 2000/1626 — 3.8.3
Town and Country Planning (Inquiries Procedure) (England) Rules 2000, SI 2000/1624 — 3.8.2, 3.8.5
Town and Country Planning (Use Classes) Order 1987, SI 1987/764 — 1.3.1, 2.1.2, 2.1.3, 3.6.4, 19.2
  art 3(6) — 2.1.3
  Class A — 2.2.2
  Class A1 — 2.1.3, 2.2.2, 19.2.1
  Class A2 — 2.1.3, 2.2.2
  Class A3 — 2.1.3, 2.2.2
  Class B — 2.2.2
  Class B1 — 2.1.3, 2.2.2, 19.2.1
  Class B2 — 2.1.3, 2.2.2
  Class B8 — 2.1.3, 2.2.2

Town and Country Planning (Use Classes) Order 1987, SI 1987/764 *cont*
    Class C3   2.1.3

Value Added Tax (Buildings and Land) Order 1995, SI 1995/279   10.1.3
Value Added Tax (Land) Order 1995, SI 1995/282   10.1.5

TABLE OF ABBREVIATIONS

The following abbreviations are used throughout this book.

AGA	authorised guarantee agreement
BCN	breach of condition notice
CA	commonhold association
CCS	commonhold community statement
CGT	capital gains tax
CLEUD	certificate of lawful use or development
DCPNs	development control policy notes
DETR	Department of the Environment, Transport and the Regions
DoE	Department of the Environment
DTLR	Department of Transport, Local Government and the Regions
EA 1995	Environment Act 1995
EPA 1990	Environmental Protection Act 1990
GDPO	Town and Country Planning (General Development Procedure) Order 1995
GPDO	Town and Country Planning (General Permitted Development) Order 1995
HA 1985	Housing Act 1985
HA 1988	Housing Act 1988
HA 1996	Housing Act 1996
IA 1986	Insolvency Act 1986
LPA	local planning authority
LPA 1925	Law of Property Act 1925
LP(MP)A 1989	Law of Property (Miscellaneous Provisions) Act 1989
LRA 1925	Land Registration Act 1925
LRA 1967	Leasehold Reform Act 1967
LRHUDA 1993	Leasehold Reform, Housing and Urban Development Act 1993
LTA 1927	Landlord and Tenant Act 1927
LTA 1954	Landlord and Tenant Act 1954
LTA 1985	Landlord and Tenant Act 1985
LTA 1987	Landlord and Tenant Act 1987
LTA 1988	Landlord and Tenant Act 1988
LTCA 1995	Landlord and Tenant (Covenants) Act 1995
ODPM	Office of the Deputy Prime Minister
OMRV	open market retail value
PCA 1991	Planning and Compensation Act 1991
PCN	planning contravention notice
PEA 1977	Protection from Eviction Act 1977
PPGs	planning policy guidance notes
RA 1977	Rent Act 1977
RICS	Royal Institution of Chartered Surveyors
RTE	right to enfranchise
SDO	special development order
TCPA 1990	Town and Country Planning Act 1990
UCO	Town and Country Planning (Use Classes) Order 1987
VATA 1994	Value Added Tax Act 1994
WO	Welsh Office

PART I

SITE ACQUISITIONS

Parts I and II of this Resource Book take the reader through the various stages of a commercial property transaction, from initial acquisition of a green field site through the grant of a commercial lease, the assignment of that lease and its termination. Part III of the book deals with the law relating to residential tenancies.

In this first part of the book, matters relevant to property development are considered. These include the acquisition of the site, the requirement for planning permission, environmental implications, the inter-relation of developers and members of the construction industry, and the funding of commercial development.

The procedure to be followed on the sale and purchase of a plot of vacant land for development purposes is essentially the same as that adopted in residential conveyancing. Apart from the matters specifically mentioned in this part of the book, the law and practice relating to the drafting of the contract of sale, the making of pre-contract enquiries and searches, deducing and investigating title, exchanging contracts, preparing and executing the purchase deed, pre-completion searches, completion and post-completion steps do not differ from the law and practice in relation to residential conveyancing. The Law Society's National Conveyancing Protocol does not apply to commercial transactions.

Chapter 1

THE NEED FOR PLANNING PERMISSION

1.1 INTRODUCTION

Chapter 1 contents
Introduction
Sources of planning law
The Office of the Deputy Prime Minister
Local planning authorities
Development plans

The principal purpose of planning law is to control the development or use of land in order to improve amenity. This control is mainly exercised by local planning authorities by reference to development plans which they prepare. It is important to bear in mind from the outset that the basic rule is that planning permission is required from the relevant local planning authority for any operational development or material change of use of land.

For the sake of brevity, the following abbreviations have been used:

GDPO   Town and Country Planning (General Development Procedure) Order 1995

GPDO   Town and Country Planning (General Permitted Development) Order 1995

JPL   Journal of Planning and Environmental Law

LPA   local planning authority (which the Town and Country Planning Act 1990, and therefore the text, refers to throughout as a plural entity)

PPGs   planning policy guidance notes

Over recent years, planning matters have been the responsibility of various Government departments. Until May 1997, the Department of the Environment (DoE) had responsibility. From then until May 2002 responsibility passed to the Department of Transport, Local Government and the Regions (DTLR). Currently planning matters are dealt with by the Office of the Deputy Prime Minister (ODPM).

1.2 SOURCES OF PLANNING LAW

1.2.1 Statutory provisions

The principal Act is the Town and Country Planning Act 1990 (TCPA 1990) as substantially amended by the Planning and Compensation Act 1991 (PCA 1991). All references in Chapters 1–5 of this book to section numbers or 'the Act' are to the 1990 Act as amended unless the contrary is stated.

Although the Act is very large, running to 337 sections and 17 Schedules, it sets out only the main framework of the planning system. The majority of the detail (including procedural rules and regulations, prescribed forms and many more substantive matters) is provided by a vast body of delegated legislation.

1.2.2 Government policy

The policies of the government can be found in various publications and are nearly always of considerable importance as many planning matters are concerned with questions of policy.

There are two main sources which set out ODPM policy, namely circulars and policy guidance notes.

ODPM circulars

ODPM circulars are usually issued in conjunction with a new Act, commencement order or statutory instrument. They are primarily meant for LPAs and their principal purpose is to explain the new provisions being introduced and give guidance on how the provisions should be applied in practice. Notwithstanding that they are written for LPAs, ODPM circulars are a valuable source of guidance for practitioners in that they reveal how the LPA will, should or is likely to, deal with a particular matter. If an LPA fails to follow relevant advice in a circular, it will significantly increase the chances of success of any appeal against the LPA's decision.

Policy guidance notes

The guidance and policy statements contained in ODPM circulars are gradually being replaced by guidance in policy guidance notes. Until the process is complete, however, circulars remain an important source.

1.2.3 Case-law

The primary importance of case-law in the context of planning is in defining the meaning or extent of statutory provisions, defining the limits of the many discretionary powers that are given to LPAs and the ODPM, clarifying the status of policy guidance contained in circulars and PPGs, etc, and establishing which matters are questions of law and which are questions of fact or degree.

It is important to remember that, where a matter is a question of fact or degree, case-law will be of little help in deciding the matter in a particular case in practice because cases cannot be precedents on questions of fact. Further, the courts will not interfere with the decision of an LPA or the ODPM on an appeal as regards a question of fact or degree unless the LPA or the ODPM have misdirected themselves on the law or reached a totally unreasonable decision on the facts.

1.3 THE OFFICE OF THE DEPUTY PRIME MINISTER

The ODPM has three broad classes of function under the Planning Acts, namely legislative, administrative and quasi-judicial.

1.3.1 Legislative powers

The Acts contain many powers for the ODPM to make orders, rules and regulations, usually by statutory instrument. Examples include the Town and Country Planning (Use Classes) Order, the Town and Country Planning (General Permitted

Development) Order, the Town and Country Planning (General Development Procedure) Order and special development orders.

1.3.2 Administrative powers

These powers include the dissemination of policy guidance through the medium of circulars. He also has powers to 'call in' a wide variety of matters for his own consideration (such as development plans and applications for planning permission).

1.3.3 Quasi-judicial powers

The Principal Secretary of State in the ODPM is the person to whom one appeals in the first instance against most decisions of a planning authority; in particular, appeals lie to him in respect of a refusal of, or conditions imposed on, a planning permission or the service of an enforcement notice.

1.3.4 The position in Wales

Until recently, the powers of the ODPM were exercised in Wales by the Secretary of State for Wales. However, with the establishment of the Welsh Assembly, the legislative powers of the Secretary of State have been transferred to the Assembly. Although, at the present time, there are no fundamental differences between England and Wales as regards planning matters, it may well be that over a period of time the Assembly will exercise its powers differently to the ODPM in London and thus create differences between the two countries.

1.4 LOCAL PLANNING AUTHORITIES (ss 1–9 and Sch 1)

1.4.1 The general rule (s 1)

Subject to any express provision to the contrary (see **1.4.2**), all references in the Planning Acts to an LPA should be construed as a reference to both the relevant county planning authority and district planning authority. The county council is the county planning authority and the district council is the district planning authority.

The county planning authority

The county planning authority normally has exclusive jurisdiction over preparing the structure plan (see **1.5.1**), mineral planning, and development control and enforcement which relate to 'county matters'. 'County matters' are defined in Sch 1, para 1, as being concerned with minerals and operational development falling partly within and partly outside a national park.

The district planning authority

Subject to the exceptions mentioned below, the district planning authority has exclusive jurisdiction over preparation of the local plan, development control and enforcement which does not concern a county matter and hazardous substances.

1.4.2 Exceptions to the general rule

Unitary councils

Where unitary councils have been established, those councils will normally be the LPAs for all purposes.

Greater London and the metropolitan areas (s 1(2))

In these areas there is only one planning authority, namely the appropriate London borough council (the Common Council in the City of London) or metropolitan district council.

1.5 DEVELOPMENT PLANS (ss 10–54 and Sch 2)

1.5.1 What are they?

Outside Greater London and the metropolitan areas

In the majority of the country the development plan consists of the structure plan and any local plan(s) in force.

STRUCTURE PLAN (ss 31–35C)

The structure plan is prepared normally by the county planning authority for the whole of their area. It basically consists of a broad statement of the county planning authority's strategic planning policies for the area illustrated by such diagrams and other illustrations as are necessary to explain the proposals. It must deal in particular with conservation of beauty and amenity, improvement of the physical environment, management of traffic, and social and economic conditions. It must also take into account regional planning guidance from the ODPM, national policies, resources and any other matters which the ODPM may prescribe (by regulations) or direct.

LOCAL PLAN (ss 36–45)

The local plan is prepared normally by the district planning authority in general conformity with the structure plan. Each district planning authority was due to prepare a local plan for the whole of their area within 5 years from 10 February 1992. Although the date for implementation has now passed, many LPAs have not yet completed the adoption of their area-wide local plan. Until the new local plans have been made and adopted, the local plans which were in force on that date will remain in force.

Local plans are much more detailed. They must deal with the same type of matters as structure plans and take into account the same guidance, but in greater depth. In addition, they must contain a reasoned justification of the policies formulated by the plan.

In Greater London and the metropolitan areas

In these areas the development plan consists of a 'unitary development plan' (ss 12–16).

The responsibility for making and altering a unitary development plan is that of the relevant London borough or metropolitan district council. Despite its name, a unitary development plan is in two parts where Part I is the broad equivalent of a structure plan, and Part II is the equivalent of a local plan. These two parts have to deal with and take into account very similar matters to their ordinary development plan counterparts and must be illustrated and justified in a similar way.

1.5.2 The importance of the development plan

In various parts of the Planning Acts, regard is required to be had to the development plan and any other material considerations. By s 54A (introduced by the PCA 1991):

> 'where, in making any determination under the Planning Acts, regard is to be had to the development plan, the determination shall be made in accordance with the plan unless material considerations indicate otherwise.'

The House of Lords confirmed in *City of Edinburgh Council v Secretary of State for Scotland and Others* [1997] 3 PLR 71 that there is now a statutory presumption that the development plan is to govern the decision on an application for planning permission.

The practical consequences of s 54A are that because there is now, in effect, largely a plan-led development system, developers will need to look very carefully at the development plan to see if it contains any policy on the development proposed; if it does so and the proposal is not in accordance with the plan, any planning application is unlikely to succeed in most cases.

1.5.3 Planning and Compulsory Purchase Bill 2003

At the time of writing, the Planning and Compulsory Purchase Bill 2003 was proceeding through Parliament. It is likely to be 2004 at the earliest before its provisions, if enacted, are brought into force. The object of the Bill is to speed up the planning system. The provisions introduce powers which allow for the reform and speeding up of the plans system and an increase in the predictability of planning decisions, and the speeding up of the handling of major infrastructure projects.

The Bill also provides for a number of reforms to make the handling of planning applications, both by central government and local authorities, quicker and more efficient. Old county structure plans will be replaced by a regional spatial strategy, setting out the Secretary of State's policies in relation to the use of land within the region. Structure, local and unitary development plans will be replaced by 'Local Development Documents'.

The Bill originally provided for the replacement of outline planning consents (see **3.3.5**) by a 'statement of development principle'. This would not amount to planning consent but would be a material consideration to take into account in determining any planning application. Due to opposition, it is not clear when, or if, this will now take place.

Chapter 2

WHAT IS DEVELOPMENT?

2.1 THE BASIC RULE

The basic rule is to be found in s 57(1) which states that planning permission is required for the carrying out of any development of land. The term 'development' is defined in s 55(1) as: 'the carrying out of building, engineering, mining or other operations in, on, over or under land, or the making of any material change in the use of any buildings or other land'. It is important to realise at the outset that the term 'development' thus has two mutually exclusive parts to it, namely the carrying out of operations and the making of a material change of use.

2.1.1 Operations

Relevant definitions (ss 55(1A) and 336(1))

'Building operations' include demolition of buildings (see further below), rebuilding, structural alterations of, or additions to buildings, and other operations normally undertaken by a person carrying on business as a builder.

'Engineering operations' includes the formation or laying out of means of access to highways.

'Mining operations' and 'other operations' are not defined in the Act.

Operations not constituting development (s 55(2))

Works for the maintenance, improvement or other alteration of a building which affect only the interior of the building or which do not materially affect its external appearance and which do not provide additional space underground do not constitute development (s 55(2)(a)).

Demolition

The position as regards demolition is governed by the provisions of s 55(1A) and (2)(g) which state that the demolition of any description of building specified in a direction given by the ODPM does not constitute development. The direction exempts demolition of the following:

(1) listed buildings;
(2) buildings in a conservation area;
(3) scheduled monuments;
(4) buildings other than dwelling houses or buildings adjoining dwelling houses;
(5) buildings not exceeding 50m³ in volume.

(Note as regards the first three categories in the above list that, although planning permission is not required for demolition, consents under the legislation dealing with these types of buildings and structures will be needed, eg listed buildings consent.)

Thus, the control of demolition will apply mainly to that of dwelling houses and buildings adjoining dwelling houses. However, demolition of these buildings may be permitted development under the GPDO, Sch 2, Part 31 (see **2.2.2**).

2.1.2 Change of use

In order to constitute development, a change of use must be material. The Act does not define what is meant by 'material'.

Case-law

Case-law makes it clear that the question as to whether a change of use is material is one of fact and degree in each case. It follows, therefore, that the courts will not normally interfere with a planning decision on the question of the materiality of a particular change of use unless the decision is totally unreasonable on the facts, or the deciding body has misdirected itself as to the relevant law.

Note, however, the following general points decided by case-law.

(1) It is necessary to look at the change in the use of the relevant 'planning unit'. In many cases this will be the whole of the land concerned, ie the land in the same ownership and occupation. Occasionally, particularly with larger sites, a single unit of occupation may comprise two or more physically distinct and separate areas which are occupied for substantially different and unrelated purposes, in which case each area (with its own main or primary use) should be considered as a separate planning unit (see *Burdle and Another v Secretary of State for the Environment and Another* [1972] 3 All ER 240 and *Thames Heliport plc v Tower Hamlets LBC* [1997] 2 PLR 72). In a mall-type development, it now seems that each shop unit will be a separate planning unit (*Church Commissioners for England v Secretary of State for the Environment* (1995) 7 P&CR 73).

(2) The use of a planning unit may involve various (and possibly fluctuating) ancillary uses which do not need planning permission provided that they remain ancillary to, and retain their connection with, the primary use. For instance, where produce grown on an agricultural unit is sold on a limited scale from the farmhouse, this retail use is ancillary to the primary agricultural use; however, the ancillary status is lost if, for example, produce is subsequently bought in for the purposes of resale (see *Wood v Secretary of State for the Environment* [1973] 1 WLR 707, HL).

Non-statutory guidance

As the courts will not normally interfere with decisions on questions of fact and degree, it will therefore be the ODPM or one of his inspectors who will generally be the final arbiter of the question as to whether a particular change of use is material. Thus, their views in similar cases will be important and guidance can be found, in particular, in relevant ODPM circulars, PPGs and in Ministerial Decisions such as those reported in the JPL.

Statutory provisions

CHANGES OF USE DECLARED TO BE MATERIAL

For the avoidance of doubt, s 55(3) and (5) declare the following to be material changes of use:

(1) the use as two or more separate dwelling houses of any building previously used as a single dwelling house;

(2) (generally) the deposit of refuse or waste materials.

Building previously used as a single dwelling hse

CHANGES OF USE NOT CONSTITUTING DEVELOPMENT

These are set out in s 55(2) and include the following.

(1) The use of any building or other land within the curtilage of a dwelling house for any purpose incidental to the enjoyment of the dwelling house as such (s 55(2)(d)).

Factors to be considered in deciding whether the use is 'incidental to the enjoyment of the dwelling house as such' include the nature and scale of the use and whether it is one which could reasonably be expected to be carried out in or around the house for domestic needs or incidental to the personal enjoyment of the house by its occupants: see *Ministerial Decision* [1977] JPL 116. Thus, for example, in *Wallington v Secretary of State for the Environment* [1991] JPL 942, CA, the keeping of 44 dogs as pets was held not to be an incidental use. Note that enjoyment of the dwelling house must be distinguished from the enjoyment of the occupier (ie the test for enjoyment is objective, not subjective).

(2) The use of any land or buildings occupied with it for the purposes of agriculture or forestry (s 55(2)(e)).

(3) In the case of buildings or other land which are used for a purpose of any class specified in the Town and Country Planning (Use Classes) Order 1987, the use of the buildings or other land for any other purpose of the same class (s 55(2)(f)). This very important exemption is dealt with in more detail at **2.1.3**.

2.1.3 The Town and Country Planning (Use Classes) Order 1987

This order specifies 16 use classes for the purposes of s 55(2)(f). Thus, a change of use within any such class does not, prima facie, amount to development (but see 'UCO checklist' below).

Change of use w/in of same class does not amount 2 devt.

The classes are divided into four main groups as follows:

(1) Group A: shopping area uses;
(2) Group B: other business and industrial uses;
(3) Group C: residential uses;
(4) Group D: non-residential uses.

Note in particular the following seven use classes.

Class A1: shops

Use for all or any of the following purposes: retail sale of goods other than hot food; post office; ticket or travel agency; sale of cold food for consumption off the premises; hairdressing; direction of funerals; display of goods for sale. In all cases, however, the sale, display or service must be to visiting members of the public.

NOT INCLUDED

Class A2: financial and professional services

Use for the provision of financial services, professional services (other than health or medical services) or any other services (including use as a betting office) which it is appropriate to provide in a shopping area, where the services are provided principally to visiting members of the public.

Class A3: food and drink

Use for the sale of food or drink for consumption on the premises or of hot food for consumption off the premises.

[handwritten: Hot Food 4 consumptn off d Premises]

Class B1: business

Use for all or any of the following purposes, namely as an office other than a use within Class A2, for research and development of products or processes, or for any industrial process, being a use which can be carried out in any residential area without detriment to the amenity of that area.

Class B2: general industrial

Use for the carrying out of an industrial process other than one falling within Class B1.

Class B8: storage or distribution

Use for storage or as a distribution centre.

Class C3: dwelling houses

Use as a dwelling house by a single person or by people living together as a family or by not more than six residents living together as a single household (including a household where care is provided for residents).

Exclusions

Nothing in the Use Classes Order permits use as a theatre, amusement arcade, launderette, garage or motor showroom, taxi or hire-car business, hostel, or scrapyard (art 3(6) of Use Classes Order).

Note also that not all uses come within the Use Classes Order. The courts have consistently held that there is no justification for stretching the meaning of the wording of the classes and that other uses will therefore be outside the terms of the Order.

Problems

Many of the above use classes are not without their problems. For example, is a sandwich bar which sells tea and coffee and a few hot pies, within Class A1 or Class A3? (For guidance, see Circular 13/87.)

Is a high street solicitor's office within Class A2 or Class B1? The crucial question here is whether the firm principally serves visiting members of the public. (In *Kalra v Secretary of State for the Environment* [1996] JPL 850, CA, the Court of Appeal held that the introduction of an appointment system did not of itself prevent a solicitor's office falling within Class A2.)

UCO checklist

Although a change of use within a class does not amount to development, it does not necessarily follow that a change of use from one class to another will constitute development. Whether it will depends on the basic rule, ie is that change of use 'material'? However, *Palisade Investments Ltd v Secretary of State for the Environment* [1995] 69 P&CR 638, CA, suggests that it will be extremely rare for this not to be the case.

A change of use within a class may be accompanied by building operations which could amount to development in their own right (remember that development has two parts to it).

A change of use within a class may have been validly restricted by a condition attached to a previous planning permission, in which case permission will be needed to change to a use restricted by that condition.

[margin handwritten note: If a condition restricted a ∆ of use on d planning permiss a devt cld well ∆ a ∆ of use]

2.2 PERMITTED DEVELOPMENT

Once it has been established that development is involved, then the basic rule is that planning permission will be required. However, it is not always necessary to make an express application for planning permission for the reasons given below.

2.2.1 Resumption of previous use

By s 57(2)–(6), certain changes of use do not require planning permission even though they may amount to development, for example, the resumption of a previous lawful use after service of an enforcement notice.

2.2.2 The Town and Country Planning (General Permitted Development) Order 1995 (as amended) *GPDO*

By ss 59–61, the ODPM may provide by statutory instrument for the automatic grant of planning permission by means of development orders. The most important of these orders is the GPDO. This lists, in Sch 2, 31 broad categories of development for which planning permission is automatically granted, ie there is not normally any need to make an application for planning permission in these cases (but see 'GPDO checklist' below).

Note in particular the following six categories.

Part 1: development within the curtilage of a dwelling house

Part 1 is divided into classes as follows:

(1) Class A: the enlargement, improvement or other alteration of the dwelling house;
(2) Classes B and C: additions or alterations to its roof;
(3) Class D: the erection of a porch;
(4) Class E: the provision within the curtilage of the dwelling house of any building, enclosure or pool for a purpose incidental to the enjoyment of the dwelling house as such, or the maintenance, improvement or alteration of such a building or enclosure;

(5) Classes F and G: the provision of a hard surface or a container for the storage of domestic heating oil;

(6) Class H: the installation, alteration or replacement of a satellite antenna.

All of these classes of permitted development (except for Class F) are, however, subject to certain restrictions, limitations or conditions (see below).

There may occasionally be problems in determining the extent of the curtilage of the dwelling house. It is the small area of land forming part of the land on which the house stands and used for the purposes of the enjoyment of the house. Its extent is a question of fact and degree in each case. It is not necessarily synonymous with 'garden'.

Restrictions on Class A development (enlargement, improvement, etc) include:

(1) a limit on the increase in the cubic content of the dwelling house;

(2) height;

(3) distance from highway;

(4) the area covered by all the buildings (other than the original dwelling house) within the curtilage must not exceed one half of the area of the curtilage excluding the area of the original dwelling house.

Restrictions on Class E development (the provision of buildings within the curtilage, etc) include the latter two restrictions above (ie distance from highway and area covered by buildings within the curtilage). Additional restrictions include:

(1) a height limit; and

(2) a volume and nearness to house restriction.

Note that for a dwelling house on 'article 1(5) land' (ie within a National Park, an area of outstanding natural beauty or conservation area) there are further restrictions.

Restrictions on Class H development (satellite antennae) include dish size, height and siting.

Part 2: minor operations

Part 2 permits:

(1) the erection, construction, maintenance, improvement or alteration of a gate, fence, wall or other means of enclosure (Class A);

(2) the construction of a means of access to a highway which is not a trunk or classified road (Class B);

(3) the painting of the exterior of a building (Class C).

In Class A, any gates, fences, etc must be for the purpose of enclosure. They must not exceed 1 metre in height if they adjoin a highway, or 2 metres in any other case.

In Class C, painting of the exterior is not permitted if it is for the purpose of advertisement, announcement or direction.

Part 3: changes of use

Part 3 permits certain changes of use within Classes A and B of the Use Classes Order as follows:

(1) from A3 (food and drink) to A2 (financial and professional services);

(2) from A2 to A1 (shops) provided the premises have a display window at ground level;

(3) from A3 directly to A1;

(4) from B8 (storage and distribution) to B1 (business) and vice versa;

(5) from B2 (general industrial) to B8 or B1.

Part 4: temporary buildings and uses

Part 4 permits:

(1) the provision of buildings, structures, plant, etc required temporarily in connection with authorised operations (Class A);

(2) the use of open land for any purpose for not more than 28 days in any calendar year of which not more than 14 days may be used for holding a market or motor racing/trials (Class B).

Class A rights are subject to conditions requiring removal of the buildings, etc or reinstatement of land at the end of the operations.

The right to revert to the previous use of the land after the expiry of the temporary use is permitted by s 57(2) (see **2.2.1**).

Part 6: agricultural buildings and operations

Part 6 permits, inter alia, the carrying out on agricultural land of certain operations (in particular the erection, extension or alteration of buildings or excavation or engineering operations) which are reasonably necessary for the purposes of agriculture on that unit. These are subject to many exceptions and conditions.

Part 31: demolition of buildings

Part 31 permits any building operation consisting of the demolition of a building except where the building has been made unsafe or uninhabitable by the fault of anyone who owns the relevant land or where it is practicable to secure health or safety by works of repair or temporary support. Because of the provisions of s 55(2)(g) (see **2.1.1**), this provision will need to be applied only in the case of demolition of a dwelling house or a building (exceeding 50m^3) adjoining a dwelling house.

GPDO checklist — *IMPORTANT*

If the proposed development is permitted by the GPDO there should, prima facie, be no need to make an application for planning permission. However, before deciding, the following other matters should also be checked.

LIMITATIONS, ETC

Confirm that all the limitations, restrictions and conditions imposed by the GPDO will be complied with. There are two categories of these. First, there is a general one in art 3(5) which applies to all the Parts in Sch 2 and which states that (subject to limited exceptions) the making or altering of an access to a trunk or classified road, or any development which obstructs the view of road users so as to cause them danger, is not permitted. Secondly, there are specific limitations, conditions, etc in almost all of the Parts of Sch 2 which must be observed (see above).

If the limitations, etc are not complied with then, as a general rule, the whole development will be unauthorised and not merely the excess. This, though, is subject to the LPA's power to under-enforce if they think fit (see **5.8.7** for details of this). If the excess is de minimis it can be ignored.

CONDITIONS ON EXISTING PLANNING PERMISSION

Check any existing planning permission to see whether it contains a condition excluding or restricting relevant permitted development rights. Such conditions can be imposed in appropriate cases (see further **3.6**).

ARTICLE 4 DIRECTION

Ascertain by means of an appropriate enquiry of the local authority whether an art 4 direction is in force which may affect the proposed development.

GPDO, art 4, empowers the ODPM or an LPA (usually with the ODPM's approval) to make a direction removing from the classes of permitted development under the GPDO any development specified in the direction as regards the area of land specified in it.

The making of an art 4 direction will not affect the lawfulness of any permitted development commenced before the direction was made.

SPECIAL DEVELOPMENT ORDERS

Check whether the land is in an area covered by a special development order (SDO).

Some SDOs restrict the provisions of the GPDO which would otherwise apply in the relevant area; others (especially those made for urban development areas) confer wider permitted development rights. It is therefore important to be aware of what SDOs exist and, where relevant, their provisions.

2.3 PROBLEM CASES

2.3.1 General considerations

It will be seen from the above that there are many matters to be considered before one can properly decide whether a particular proposal amounts to development and, if so, whether it is permitted development or whether it needs an express grant of planning permission. Although, in practice, it will be obvious in many cases whether or not planning permission will be needed, in quite a few cases (especially those involving small-scale development proposals) there may be some considerable uncertainty as to whether a particular proposal amounts to development or whether it is permitted development. In such a case there are two main options, namely either to go ahead without permission (thereby risking enforcement action if it did need an express grant of permission) or to apply under s 192 to the LPA for a determination of the question.

2.3.2 Certificate of lawful use or development

Under s 192, any person who wishes to ascertain the lawfulness of any proposed use or development, can apply to the LPA for a Certificate of Lawful Use or Development (see **5.3**).

If a certificate is granted, it will be conclusive as to the lawfulness of the use or operations described in it unless there was a material change, before the use was instituted, or the operations were begun, in any of the matters relevant to the determination.

Chapter 3

APPLYING FOR PLANNING PERMISSION

3.1 INTRODUCTION

Chapter 3 contents
Introduction
Preliminary steps
Full or outline
  permission?
The procedure
The decision
Planning permissions
  subject to conditions
Appeals against adverse
  planning
  determinations
Types of appeal
Costs in appeals
Challenging the appeal
  decision

Solicitors are not often involved in the completing and submission of an application for planning permission as this is usually done by the client's architect or planning consultant. However, it is very important to know what the statutory requirements are as this may be crucial in later negotiations with the LPA or on an appeal in case the action previously taken was flawed.

3.2 PRELIMINARY STEPS

(1) Consider whether planning permission is required at all: ie do the proposals amount to development and, if so, are they permitted development (see **2.1** and **2.2**)?

(2) Assuming planning permission is needed, the next step is to visit the site if possible. A site visit can be very valuable as it may:

    (a) clarify the client's maps, diagrams and plans;

    (b) provide information about the immediate environment;

    (c) alert the solicitor to potential problems with the application.

(3) Obtain copies of the relevant parts of the development plan and any non-statutory plans which may affect the proposed development. This could be vital in many cases as, for the application to stand a chance of succeeding, the development proposed will usually have to be in accordance with the development plan (see s 54A at **3.5.1**).

(4) Investigate the title to the land concerned. This is necessary for two main reasons, namely to check whether the proposed development is in breach of an enforceable covenant affecting the land concerned and to identify any other 'owners' who will need to be given notice of the application (see further **3.4.4**).

(5) Obtain the relevant application form from the LPA. Note that each LPA produces its own form which can be obtained free of charge.

(6) Consider whether a pre-application discussion with the appropriate case officer might be beneficial. This is encouraged by the ODPM in order to reduce uncertainty and delay in processing applications. Such discussions can be particularly helpful in the case of large-scale or potentially controversial development proposals to enable the developer to find out in what respects the proposals may not be acceptable and in what ways chances of success can be improved; it also enables the LPA to advise the developer of probable objections to the development which, if remedied, should lead to a quicker determination. Note that LPAs have no statutory duty to enter into such discussions (although recent research has shown that 93% of LPAs do so regularly). It follows therefore that any advice, etc given in such discussions is merely informal and advisory and cannot bind the LPA ultimately. Note also

that LPAs may not charge a fee for the time taken in such pre-application discussions.

3.3 FULL OR OUTLINE PERMISSION?

One final matter to consider before completing and submitting the application form is whether to apply in full for planning permission or whether to apply for outline permission.

3.3.1 General

By the GDPO, arts 3 and 4, where the application is for permission to erect a building, the applicant may, if he wishes, apply for outline permission. In such a case, the application merely has to contain a description of the proposed development sufficient to indicate its major features (eg for residential developments, the number and type of dwellings). A plan is also required of sufficient detail to identify the boundaries of the site and the nearest classified public highway. However, the application need not contain the considerable amount of detail that is required for a full application for permission.

[handwritten left margin: Application 4 an outline PP mere description of major features Plan also required]

3.3.2 The 'reserved matters'

If outline planning permission is granted, it will be subject to a condition setting out certain matters for which the subsequent approval of the LPA is required. The only matters which can be so specified ('reserved matters') are defined in the GDPO, art 1(2), and the Town and Country Planning (Applications) Regulations 1988 as those concerned with siting, design, external appearance, means of access and landscaping of the development.

3.3.3 The effect of outline permission

[handwritten left margin: Allows devt in principle subj 2 approval]

The effect of outline planning permission is that the LPA are committed to allowing the development in principle subject to approval of any reserved matters. This is because it is the grant of the outline permission which constitutes the grant of planning permission for the proposed development, ie no further planning permission is required. *[handwritten: outline]*

Accordingly, the LPA cannot revoke the outline permission except on payment of compensation (see revocation of planning permissions at **3.5.2**) nor can they impose additional conditions subsequently except as regards the reserved matters.

3.3.4 Approval of reserved matters

When an applicant comes to apply for approval of the reserved matters he is equally bound by the outline permission. If the application for approval of reserved matters includes additional development, it will normally be invalid.

3.3.5 Planning and Compulsory Purchase Bill 2003

This Bill contains proposals which may see the replacement of outline planning consent with 'statements of development principles', which will not amount to planning permission but would be a material consideration in determining any future planning application.

3.4 THE PROCEDURE

Procedure is governed mainly by ss 62 to 69, the GDPO and the Town and Country Planning (Applications) Regulations 1988.

3.4.1 What is submitted to whom?

The application form and such other documents, plans, drawings, etc as are needed to describe the proposed development should be submitted (usually in triplicate) to the district planning authority, London borough or metropolitan district council or unitary council (as the case may be).

The application must be accompanied by the appropriate fee and a GDPO article 7 Certificate (see **3.4.2** and **3.4.3**).

3.4.2 The fee

The fees vary according to the type of application and the scale of development involved.

3.4.3 Article 7 certificate

The application must be accompanied by an article 7 Certificate and an Agricultural Holdings Certificate.

The certificates have to be given to certify compliance with the GDPO, art 6, which requires the applicant, where he is not the sole owner of the land concerned, to notify or try to notify the owners of the land and any relevant agricultural tenant of the fact of the application for planning permission (see **3.4.4**).

3.4.4 Notification of persons by the applicant

By the GDPO, art 6, where the applicant is not the sole owner of the application site, he must give notice (in the form prescribed in the GDPO, Sch 2, Part I) to all persons who are 'owners' or 'tenants' of the land.

where applicant is not a sole owner he must notify all persons owners of d land.

'Owner' is defined by s 65(8) as meaning any person who owns the fee simple or a tenancy granted or extended for a term certain of which not less than 7 years remain unexpired.

'Tenant' is defined by the GDPO, art 6(6), as meaning the tenant of an agricultural holding any part of which is comprised in the application site.

3.4.5 Action by the LPA

Entry in the planning register

By s 69, the LPA must enter certain particulars of the application in the register that they are required to keep by that section. The register is open to public inspection.

— searches reveal entries

Notification

By the GDPO, art 8, the LPA must publicise the application. This publicity may consist of a site notice, notifying neighbours, or a local advertisement, depending upon the type of development proposed.

3.5 THE DECISION

3.5.1 General points

By s 70(1), the LPA may grant planning permission either unconditionally or subject to such conditions as they think fit or they may refuse planning permission.

In reaching their decision they must have regard to the provisions of the development plan if it is relevant to the application and to any other material considerations (see further, below). They must also take into account any representations received in response to the publicity of the application (see **3.4.5**) and certain other matters if the development affects a listed building or a conservation area.

'... *have regard to ... the development plan* ...'

This must be read in conjunction with s 54A which states that where regard is to be had to the development plan, any determination must be made in accordance with the plan unless material considerations indicate otherwise. Thus, if the proposed development is covered by the plan, the LPA's decision should be made in accordance with the plan unless there are material considerations to the contrary.

Policy guidance on s 54A can be found in PPG 1 where, in para 40, the ODPM advises that: 'Applications which are not in accordance with relevant policies in the plan should not be allowed unless material considerations justify granting planning permission ... In all cases where the plan is relevant, it will be necessary to decide if the proposal is in accordance with the plan and then to take into account other material considerations'. The section does not, however, create a legitimate expectation that a particular application will or must be determined solely by reference to the development plan (see *Trustees of the Viscount Folkestone 1963 Settlement and Camden Homes Ltd v Secretary of State for the Environment and Salisbury District Council* [1995] JPL 502).

Recently, however, there has been a spate of cases (see, eg, *St Albans District Council v Secretary of State for the Environment and Allied Breweries Ltd* [1993] JPL 374; *R v Canterbury City Council, Robert Brett & Sons ex parte Springimage Ltd* [1994] JPL 427; *Bylander Waddell Partnership v Secretary of State for the Environment and Harrow London Borough Council* [1994] JPL 440) which have suggested that 'material considerations to the contrary' can include advice in ODPM circulars and PPGs.

The LPA, or the inspector or ODPM on an appeal, do not have to refer expressly to s 54A in their decision. It is sufficient that the decision was reached in accordance with the section: see, for example, *Newham London Borough Council v Secretary of State for the Environment* [1995] EGCS 6, *Spelthorne Borough Council v Secretary of State for the Environment and Lawlor Land plc* [1995] JPL 412, and *North Yorkshire County Council v Secretary of State for the Environment and Griffin* [1996] JPL 32, CA.

Note that it seems that s 54A applies also to the determination of an application for approval of reserved matters pursuant to an outline planning permission (see *St George Developments Ltd and Kew Riverside Developments v Secretary of State for the Environment and Richmond upon Thames London Borough Council* [1996] JPL 35).

'... *other material considerations*'

For other considerations to be 'material', they must be relevant to the application and be planning considerations, ie relate to the use and development of land: see *Stringer v Minister of Housing and Local Government* [1971] 1 All ER 65. Note the following examples (which are not exhaustive) of matters which the courts have held to be capable of being 'material considerations':

(1) a development plan which is in the course of preparation (see, eg, *Allen v Corporation of the City of London* [1981] JPL 685 and *Kissel v Secretary of State for the Environment and Another* [1994] JPL 819). The closer the new plan gets to adoption, the greater the weight that should be given to it;

(2) the protection of private interests in a proper case and, in exceptional circumstances, personal hardship (see, eg, *Great Portland Estates plc v Westminster City Council* [1985] AC 661, HL);

(3) financial considerations involved in the proposed development (see, eg, *Sovmots v Secretary of State for the Environment; Brompton Securities Ltd v Secretary of State for the Environment* [1977] 1 QB 411);

(4) planning obligations (as to which, see **4.2**);

(5) retention of an existing use (see, eg, *London Residuary Body v Lambeth Borough Council* [1990] 2 All ER 309, HL);

(6) the previous planning history of the site;

(7) a real danger of setting an undesirable precedent (see, eg, *Anglia Building Society v Secretary of State for the Environment and Another* [1984] JPL 175);

(8) planning policies of the ODPM (as evidenced in circulars and PPGs), of other government departments where relevant (eg transport, energy, etc) and the LPA concerned (as evidenced in their own policy statements and non-statutory plans);

(9) racial discrimination (by s 19A of the Race Relations Act 1976 it is unlawful for an LPA to discriminate on racial grounds when exercising any of their planning functions);

(10) environmental considerations: likely environmental pollution from a proposed development is a material consideration. However, it is not the function of the planning system to duplicate statutory pollution controls (see *Gateshead Metropolitan Borough Council v Secretary of State for the Environment* [1995] JPL 432, CA; *Envirocor Waste Holdings v Secretary of State for the Environment* [1995] EGCS 60, QB).

The making of the decision

The decision should be made within 8 weeks of the submission of the application or such longer period as may have been agreed in writing with the applicant (GDPO, art 20). If no decision has been made in time the applicant can appeal to the ODPM.

Procedure after the decision

After making the decision, the LPA must register it in their planning register (which they are required to keep by virtue of s 69: see **3.4.5** and also the GDPO, art 25(2)). In addition, the applicant must be given written notification of the decision and, where the decision is a planning permission subject to conditions or a refusal, written reasons (see the GDPO, art 22, and **3.5.4**).

It is the written notification which constitutes the grant of planning permission (see *R v West Oxfordshire District Council ex parte C.H. Pearce Homes* [1986] JPL 523).

3.5.2 Effect of planning permission

By s 75(1), without prejudice to the provisions of the Act on duration, revocation or modification (for all of which, see below), planning permission shall (except insofar as the permission otherwise provides) enure for the benefit of the land and of all persons for the time being interested in it.

Therefore, the benefit of planning permission runs with the land concerned and, prima facie, lasts forever, but see **3.5.3**. Note, however, that any conditions attached to the planning permission will also run, ie will burden the relevant land.

A grant of planning permission is effective for planning purposes only; it does not confer, for example, listed building consent, building regulation consent or any consent required under any other enactment, nor does it confer the right to break any enforceable covenant affecting the land.

Note also that planning permission is merely permissive; it does not have to be implemented and the LPA cannot compel implementation, but see **3.5.3** as to the service of a completion notice.

'... the permission otherwise provides'

Planning permission may be expressly granted for a limited period or be made personal to the applicant.

Once such a permission lapses, the right to revert to the previous use of the land is permitted by s 57(2) (see **2.2.1**).

Revocation and modification of planning permissions

By s 97, the LPA may, if they think it expedient to do so, revoke or modify (to the extent they consider necessary) any planning permission provided they do so before the development authorised by the permission is completed.

Abandonment of planning permission

It follows from the provisions in s 75(1) that the doctrine of abandonment cannot apply to planning permissions. Note, however, that once a permission has been fully implemented its effect is spent, ie it does not authorise the re-carrying out of that development.

3.5.3 Duration

General

Although, prima facie, the benefit of a planning permission lasts forever, there are some important statutory time-limits governing the implementation of the permission which, if not observed, may terminate it. These are set out in ss 91 to 93 which provide that with ordinary permissions, development must be commenced within 5 years of the grant of permission.

With outline permissions, there are two time-limits. Application for approval of the reserved matters must be made within 3 years of the grant of the outline permission, and the development must be commenced within 5 years of the grant of the outline permission or 2 years of the approval of the reserved matters, whichever is the later.

Note also that with all permissions, the LPA may substitute longer or shorter time-limits if they think it appropriate on planning grounds; if they do this, however, they must give their reasons for doing so in case the applicant should wish to appeal against this (see further paras 53–58 of ODPM Circular 11/95).

The start and end of the period

If the time-limit expires without the development having been started, then the permission effectively lapses. Any further development will be unauthorised and subject to possible enforcement proceedings. Because of this, it is important to know two things, namely what is the effective date of the permission and when does development commence?

As regards the effective date of the permission, the Act provides no guidance; however, the case of *R v West Oxfordshire District Council ex parte C.H. Pearce Homes* [1986] JPL 523, established that this is the date which appears on the written notification to the applicant (ie it is not the date on which the decision was made by the LPA). This is, therefore, the starting date for the time-limit.

As regards the date when development commences, the Act defines this very carefully in s 56 which provides that development is taken to be begun on the earliest date on which any of the following operations begin to be carried out:

(1) any work of construction in the course of erection of a building;
(2) any work of demolition of a building;
(3) the digging of a trench for the foundations of a building;
(4) the laying of an underground main or pipe to the foundations;
(5) any operation in the course of laying out or constructing a road;
(6) any material change in the use of any land.

Renewal of a planning permission

What if a developer cannot start the development within the time-limit because of, for instance, financial problems? In such a case, the developer can apply for a renewal of the permission using a simplified procedure, but should do so before the original permission expires, otherwise the whole permission will lapse and a fresh application for planning permission will therefore have to be made.

Completion notice (ss 94–95)

What happens if a developer starts the development within the time-limit but the time-limit subsequently expires without the development having been completed? In such a case, if the LPA is of the opinion that the development will not be completed within a reasonable period, it may serve a completion notice on the owner and any occupier of the land stating that the permission will cease to have effect at the expiration of a further period specified in the notice (being not less than 12 months after the notice takes effect). The notice is subject to confirmation by the ODPM. Any part of the development carried out before a confirmed completion notice takes effect is not affected.

3.5.4 Refusals and planning permissions subject to conditions

As stated at **3.5.1**, by s 70(1), an LPA may grant planning permission unconditionally or subject to such conditions as they think fit or they may refuse permission (permissions subject to conditions are dealt with in detail at **3.6**). In the latter two cases, the written notification of the decision must state clearly and precisely the full reasons for the conditions imposed or the refusal as the case may be. If full reasons are not given this will probably not invalidate the decision itself although the decision could be challenged by judicial review or dealt with by way of appeal.

There is also a general right of appeal to the ODPM against a permission subject to conditions, a refusal and a 'deemed refusal' (ie where no decision is reached within the relevant period, as to which see **3.5.1**).

3.6 PLANNING PERMISSIONS SUBJECT TO CONDITIONS

3.6.1 General points

The power in s 70(1) for an LPA to impose such conditions as they think fit (see **3.5.1**) is supplemented by s 72(1) which provides that, without prejudice to the generality of s 70(1), conditions may be imposed on the grant of planning permission for the purpose of:

(1) regulating the development or use of any land under the control of the applicant (whether or not it is land in respect of which the application was made) or requiring the carrying out of works on any such land, so far as appears to the LPA to be expedient for the purposes of or in connection with the development authorised by the permission; or

(2) requiring the removal of any buildings or works authorised by the permission, or the discontinuance of any use of land so authorised, at the end of a specified period, and the carrying out of any works required for the reinstatement of land at the end of that period.

Whether an applicant has 'control' of the relevant land is a question of fact and degree in each case.

3.6.2 Judicial restrictions on the power

The general power to impose conditions in s 70(1) is not as wide or unfettered as it appears because over the years the courts have imposed restraints on it.

The leading case on the judicial control of the power is *Newbury District Council v Secretary of State for the Environment; Newbury District Council v International Synthetic Rubber Co* [1981] AC 578, where Viscount Dilhorne (at p 599) said:

> 'The conditions imposed must be for a planning purpose and not for any ulterior one and ... they must fairly and reasonably relate to the development permitted. Also they must not be so unreasonable that no reasonable planning authority could have imposed them.'

'Planning purpose'

There are many cases illustrating the first element of the above test (ie that conditions must be imposed for a planning purpose). For example, in *R v Hillingdon London Borough Council ex parte Royco Homes Ltd* [1974] 1 QB 720, outline permission for a residential development was granted subject to a condition that the dwellings should first be occupied by persons on the local authority's housing waiting list with security of tenure for 10 years. The court held that the principal purpose of the condition was to require the applicants to assume at their expense a significant part of the authority's statutory duties as a housing authority. The condition was therefore ultra vires.

'Fairly and reasonably related to the development permitted'

The second part of the test in *Newbury* is probably the most difficult one to understand and apply. In *Newbury* the facts were that planning permission was granted for a change of use of aircraft hangers to warehouses subject to a condition requiring removal of the hangers at the end of 10 years. The House of Lords held that, although this condition satisfied the first test in that the removal of unsightly old buildings was a proper planning purpose, the condition was not sufficiently related to the change of use permitted by the permission and was therefore void.

'Manifestly unreasonable'

The final part of the test in *Newbury* is that the condition must not be manifestly unreasonable in the sense that no reasonable LPA would have imposed the condition in question.

Under this element, a condition may not require the applicant to pay money or provide other consideration for the granting of planning permission (but see Chapter 4 where a similar practical result can be achieved by means of a planning obligation). Nor may a condition require the ceding of land owned by the applicant for public purposes (eg a highway) even if the applicant consents.

General note on Newbury

It is important to bear in mind that the majority of conditions imposed by LPAs on planning permissions do not fall foul of the test in *Newbury*.

In the very few cases where a condition does fail, it will normally breach more than one of the elements in the test. This is because there are potentially considerable areas of overlap between the three elements in the test. This is illustrated by the *Ministerial Decision* noted at [1991] JPL 184 where a condition attached to a planning permission restricting car parking spaces on the land to residents of a specified London borough was held to be void on the grounds that it did not fulfil a proper planning purpose and that it was manifestly unreasonable. In reality, despite the three elements, there is just one basic test.

Severability of void conditions

If the condition in question is fundamental to the permission (ie if the permission would not have been granted without the condition) the court will not sever the offending condition. (Most conditions are considered to be fundamental to their permissions.) Thus, if the condition is quashed, the whole permission will fail, ie the applicant will be left with no permission at all. This is, therefore, an important point to bear in mind in deciding how to challenge a particular condition's validity (ie by way of application to the High Court for judicial review, or by appeal to the ODPM). In most cases, it will be better to appeal to the ODPM as, unlike the courts, he has power to grant the permission free from the offending condition or conditions if he thinks fit (see **3.6.3**). In addition, an application for judicial review must be made promptly, and in any event within 3 months of the decision, whereas an appeal to the SSTLR must be made within 6 months (see **3.7**).

3.6.3 The Secretary of State's guidance

General points

The Annex to ODPM Circular 11/95 gives detailed guidance to planning authorities on the imposition of conditions. It is, therefore, essential reading when considering whether or not to appeal against a permission subject to conditions.

The main starting point is para 14 of the Annex to the Circular, which sets out six criteria that conditions must satisfy, namely that they should be imposed only where they are:

(1) necessary (see further paras 15–17 of the Annex);
(2) relevant to planning (see paras 20–23);
(3) relevant to the development to be permitted (see paras 24 and 25);
(4) enforceable (see paras 26–29);
(5) precise (see paras 30–33); and
(6) reasonable in all other respects (see paras 34–42).

These basic principles (which are clearly based on the courts' criteria, see **3.6.2**) are expanded in paras 15 to 42, following which there are a further 78 paragraphs dealing with particular problem areas.

3.6.4 Section 73 and section 73A applications

Section 73

Section 73 entitles a person to apply for planning permission to develop land without complying with conditions subject to which a previous planning permission was granted. Such an application must, though, be made before the previous permission expires.

The application merely has to be made in writing and give sufficient information to enable the LPA to identify the previous grant of planning permission and the condition or conditions in question (Town and Country Planning (Applications) Regulations 1988, reg 3).

The important feature of a s 73 application is that in determining the application, the planning authority may consider only the question of the conditions subject to which the permission should be granted and thus may only:

(1) grant unconditional permission;

(2) grant permission subject to different conditions; or

(3) refuse the application.

In the first two cases above, the applicant will then have the benefit of two permissions (ie the original one and the one obtained on the s 73 application). In cases (2) and (3), the applicant can appeal to the ODPM in the usual way. Thus, whatever happens on the s 73 application, the applicant will retain the benefit of the original planning permission.

This procedure may be particularly useful in securing the removal of a condition restricting freedom of change of use within a class of the Use Classes Order 1987 or a condition restricting permitted development rights under the GPDO. Further, this is the only procedure available for challenging a condition where the time-limit for appealing has passed.

In *Allied London Property Investment Ltd v Secretary of State for the Environment* (1996) 72 P & CR 327, it was held that there is no distinction to be drawn between time and other conditions. Therefore, s 73 could be used to apply for, for example, an extension of time for applying for approval of reserved matters under an outline permission (instead of applying for a renewal of the outline permission – see **3.5.3**).

Section 73A

Section 73 applies only to applications for the removal, etc of a condition before it is breached. However, under s 73A an application may be made for planning permission for, inter alia, development carried out before the date of the application in breach of a condition subject to which planning permission was previously granted.

Permission for such development may be granted to have effect from the date on which the development was carried out thereby rendering it retrospectively lawful.

3.7 APPEALS AGAINST ADVERSE PLANNING DETERMINATIONS

Where an LPA has:

(1) refused to grant planning permission, or

(2) granted planning permission subject to conditions to which the applicant objects, or

(3) refused approval of reserved matters on an outline permission, or

(4) refused an application or granted a permission subject to conditions under s 73 or s 73A, or

(5) failed to notify their decision within the prescribed period (normally 8 weeks),

the applicant may appeal to the ODPM within 6 months of the notice of the decision or failure to determine as the case may be (s 78, and the GDPO, arts 20 and 23).

3.7.1 Who may appeal?

Only the applicant may appeal; this is so even though the applicant may not be the owner of an interest in the land. Third parties have no right of appeal and neither does the owner of the freehold have an independent right of appeal.

3.7.2 Initial procedure (GDPO, art 23)

An appeal must be made on the form supplied by the ODPM.

As well as setting out the grounds of appeal (see **3.9**), the appellant must also indicate whether he would like the appeal to be determined by the written representations procedure, or whether he wishes it to be heard by an inspector (see **3.8**).

The completed form together with all relevant documents must be sent to the Planning Inspectorate to reach them within the time-limit. Copies of the form must also be sent to the LPA together with copies of any documents sent to the Inspectorate which the LPA have not yet seen (GDPO, art 23(1)(b)).

3.8 TYPES OF APPEAL

As mentioned above, when filling in the appeal form the appellant must notify the ODPM whether he wishes to proceed by way of written representations or to be heard by an inspector.

3.8.1 Written representations *Both side argue in writing*

quick & cheap

Under the written representations procedure the appeal is decided, as its name suggests, almost entirely on the basis of written representations submitted to the Inspectorate by the appellant, the LPA and any other interested parties. No oral evidence is permitted and that includes evidence by way of video or audio tape; maps, plans and photographs are, however, acceptable and in many cases will be necessary. At some point before a decision is made, the inspector will visit the site either unaccompanied, if the site can be seen sufficiently well from a public road or place, or accompanied by the appellant or his representative and a representative from the LPA.

The procedure is governed by the Town and Country Planning (Appeals) (Written Representations Procedure) Regulations 2000. It is speedy and cost-effective and is recommended by the ODPM for simpler or non-controversial cases. It is by far the most common appeal procedure accounting for about 80% of current appeals. Because of its nature, it also offers less scope for third parties to influence the eventual decision. Note, however, that the written representations procedure can be used only if the applicant requests it and the LPA agree.

Statement of case

The appellant's statement of case must be set out in the appeal form. If this is not given or is considered to be inadequate, the appeal will be returned for full details to be given.

As a general guide, the statement should:

(1) start with quotations from planning policy guidance notes and ODPM circulars which support the appellant's case;
(2) consider each of the reasons given (where relevant) for the refusal, etc and analyse and refute them, by logical argument. In this part, any precedent (ie

showing that the LPA have granted a similar application) should be mentioned as should any policies of the LPA which contradict the LPA's reasons;

(3) justify the appellant's case. Here there should be a brief description of the development proposed together with additional plans, photographs, etc if desired. The local environment may be described (although the inspector will visit the site). Any policies from the structure or local plans which support the appellant's case should be quoted. Any special circumstances should be set out and any objections from third parties should be addressed;

(4) conclude (optionally) with a general policy statement in support of the appellant's case.

3.8.2 Inquiry →7

The appellant and the LPA have the right to be heard by an inspector appointed by the ODPM. If either requests an inquiry then, subject to the Inspectorate suggesting and both sides agreeing to a less formal hearing instead (see below), the Inspectorate will appoint a suitable inspector, arrange a date and notify interested parties.

The procedure is more formal and is governed by the Town and Country Planning (Inquiries Procedure) Rules (England) 2000 or the Town and Country Planning (Determination by Inspectors) (Inquiries Procedure) Rules (England) 2000 (as appropriate) and is explained in ODPM Circular 5/2000. The purpose of the Rules is to try to be as fair as possible to all parties, in particular by ensuring that the parties are in possession of all relevant information before the inquiry begins. Because it involves a public hearing for all interested parties and because the appellant will normally wish to be represented at the inquiry, it is therefore a slower and much more costly procedure.

The appeal form

In the appeal form, it is not necessary or desirable to give a full statement of case. Full grounds of appeal must, however, be included. Thus, the appellant must, as before, consider each of the LPA's reasons and analyse and refute them briefly. The entire case should be summarised by describing the development proposed, the environment and any special needs or circumstances, and by referring to any appropriate parts of the structure and local plans and government policies. Any relevant previous decisions (whether by the LPA or on appeal) should be set out as being 'material considerations' and potential planning gain to the LPA should also be outlined.

It is important that the full grounds of appeal are stated and that nothing is omitted, as the appellant or his representative at the appeal will largely be bound by the grounds, and any omissions may cause adjournments and may have financial consequences (see **3.9**).

3.8.3 Hearing   *Informal*

Where the appellant has not opted for the written representations procedure the Inspectorate may, in an appropriate case, offer a hearing instead of a full inquiry; either side may also suggest a hearing. Both sides must agree to this more informal procedure before it can be used.

The procedure is governed by the Town and Country Planning (Hearings Procedure) (England) Rules 2000. The procedure is intended to save time and money for the parties. In essence, it will be an informal hearing before an inspector who will try to stimulate a discussion on the main issues between the parties. It is not appropriate for complex or controversial appeals but where it is appropriate it is quicker and more cost-effective than an inquiry.

3.8.4 Factors influencing choice of forum

It is not possible to set out specific criteria upon which a decision can be reached as to the most appropriate forum for any given case in practice. As a general rule, however, the more important or larger the development and the more controversial it is, the more likely it is that an inquiry is the correct forum. In the 'Planning Appeals' booklet sent to appellants, the Inspectorate suggest the following considerations:

(1) that where the outcome of the appeal will depend on the planning merits of the appeal, the written representations procedure will normally be appropriate;
(2) that written representations are quicker and cheaper;
(3) that an inquiry will be necessary if there is considerable local interest or if the issues are likely to be complex;
(4) that at an inquiry the appellant can address the inspector personally and can challenge the evidence put forward by the LPA and any third parties;
(5) whether the decision is of sufficient importance to justify the additional costs and time involved in an inquiry;
(6) the possibility of costs being awarded (see **3.9**).

In addition, consideration should be given to the appellant's contractual obligations and the potential for third party influence at an inquiry.

3.8.5 Inquiry

The procedure is governed by the Town and Country Planning (Inquiries Procedure) (England) Rules 2000 (which only apply where the ODPM causes the inquiry to be held before he determines the appeal) or the Town and Country Planning (Determination by Inspectors) (Inquiries Procedure) (England) Rules 2000. These Rules are explained in ODPM Circular 5/2000.

3.9 COSTS IN APPEALS

By ss 320(2) and 322, the ODPM is given the powers of s 250(5) of the Local Government Act 1972 to award costs in planning appeals. Inspectors may now exercise the ODPM's powers. There is power to make an award in all cases, although at the moment the power is not yet in force for written representations cases.

Detailed guidance on the exercise of power to award costs is contained in Circular 8/93. The basic principle is that, unlike in civil cases, costs do not 'follow the event', ie normally, each party will bear their own costs. Costs may, however, be awarded against one party in favour of another where:

(a) a party has sought an award at the appropriate stage of the proceedings; and
(b) the party against whom costs are sought has behaved unreasonably; and

(c) this has caused the party seeking costs to incur or waste expense unnecessarily.

3.10 CHALLENGING THE APPEAL DECISION

By s 284, the validity of an appeal decision may not be challenged in any legal proceedings. However, by s 288, a 'person aggrieved' may question the decision by appeal to the High Court if the decision was not within the powers of the Act or if any relevant procedural requirements have not been complied with.

In certain limited cases, a challenge may alternatively be mounted by way of judicial review.

Chapter 4

PLANNING OBLIGATIONS

4.1 INTRODUCTION

A planning obligation (formerly a planning agreement) is a negotiating tool available to an LPA and a developer who is seeking planning permission. It is a legal instrument which offers a degree of flexibility to both parties which might not otherwise be available through the medium of a planning permission subject to conditions (see **3.6**).

Chapter 4 contents
Introduction
Planning obligations
'Planning gain'
Practical points
**Modification and
    discharge of planning
    obligations**
Unilateral undertakings

4.2 PLANNING OBLIGATIONS (s 106)

4.2.1 The basic provision

Any person interested in land in the area of an LPA may, by agreement or otherwise, enter into a planning obligation which may:

(1) restrict the development or use of the land in a specified way; or
(2) may require specified operations or activities to be carried out in, on, over or under the land; or
(3) require the land to be used in a specified way; or
(4) require money to be paid to the LPA on a specified date or dates, or periodically (s 106(1)).

Note the following points:

(1) 'Person interested in land' means a person with a legal estate or interest in the land concerned and not, for example, a developer who merely has an option to purchase the land at the time the obligation is entered into.
(2) 'Agreement or otherwise' indicates that a planning obligation may be created either by agreement between the LPA and the developer or by means of a unilateral undertaking offered by the developer or a combination of both (as to the potential use of unilateral undertakings, see **4.6**).
(3) A planning obligation may impose both restrictive covenants (eg restricting the development or use of the land) and positive ones (eg requiring works to be done or money to be paid). These covenants will then be enforceable against successors in title of the developer (see **4.2.3**).
(4) A planning obligation may be unconditional or subject to conditions and may impose its restrictions and requirements either indefinitely or for a specified period. It may also provide that a person will only be bound by the obligation whilst he has an interest in the land (s 106(2) and (4)).

4.2.2 Formalities

A planning obligation must be made by a deed which states that it is a planning obligation for the purposes of s 106 and identifies the land and the parties concerned (including the interest of the developer). It is registrable by the LPA as a local land charge.

4.2.3 Enforceability

By s 106(3) and (4), a planning obligation is enforceable by the LPA against the original person interested ('developer') and any person deriving title from him but subject to the terms of the obligation (see **4.2.1**).

Note the following points:

(1) The obligation will bind only the interest or estate of the developer and those deriving title from him. It cannot bind a superior title. Thus, for example, if a tenant enters into a planning obligation, it cannot bind the landlord of that tenant.
(2) A planning obligation cannot bind parties who have rights in the land existing at the time the obligation is entered into unless they consent to be bound by it. Thus, for example, existing mortgagees of the land will not be bound (unless they consent) so that if they subsequently sell under their statutory power, the purchaser will take the land free from the obligation which will only be enforceable against the original covenantor.

4.2.4 Enforcement by the LPA

Section 106 provides three main methods of enforcement as follows.

(1) Injunction to restrain a breach of any restrictive covenant in the obligation (s 106(5)).
(2) By s 106(6), where there is a failure to carry out any operations required by a planning obligation, the LPA may enter upon the land, carry out the operations and recover their expenses from the person or persons against whom the obligation is enforceable (see **4.2.3**).
(3) Any sums due under the planning obligation (including any expenses recoverable under s 106(6) above) may be charged on the land in accordance with regulations yet to be made (s 106(12)). Until regulations have been made, it is unclear whether such a charge will be registrable as a local land charge or as a private charge (and therefore registrable as a land charge or by notice, etc on the register of title).

4.3 'PLANNING GAIN'

4.3.1 Introduction

The main function of planning obligations is to allow the LPA and the developer to deal with issues that are necessary to be dealt with in order for a proposal to be acceptable, but which cannot be dealt with by condition, given the limitations (imposed by case-law etc) on the purposes for which conditions can be used. Planning obligations are not subject to such strict limitations and so can be used as a flexible means of solving any problems that a development proposal may cause.

The danger with this flexibility is that the use of planning obligations could be open to abuse. The fear was that developers would be tempted to offer inappropriate inducements to LPAs in order to obtain, or effectively 'buy', planning permission, and equally that LPAs would be tempted to draw up 'shopping lists', which they would expect developers to agree to pay for, in return for planning permission. This is sometimes referred to as planning gain and is clearly not in the public interest.

It is not surprising, therefore, that there is detailed policy and case-law guidance setting out what it is legitimate to include in a planning obligation. What follows is a summary of the key policy and case-law principles that govern this area.

4.3.2 ODPM's advice – Circular 1/97

General policy

As a matter of policy, Circular 1/97 states that the use of planning obligations will be acceptable if they are:

'(i)   necessary to make a proposal acceptable in land use terms;
(ii)   relevant to planning;
(iii)   directly related to the proposed development;
(iv)   fairly and reasonably related in scale and kind to the proposed development;
(v)   reasonable in all other respects.'

Specific guidance

Paragraph B3 of Circular 1/97 states:

'Acceptable development should never be refused because an applicant is unwilling or unable to offer benefits. Unacceptable development should never be permitted because of unnecessary or unrelated benefits offered by the applicant. Those benefits that go beyond what is necessary should not affect the outcome of a planning decision.'

Paragraph B4 of Circular 1/97 states:

'... local planning authorities and developers should place more emphasis on the overall quality of a development proposal than the number (or value) of planning benefits they can obtain or offer. Planning obligations ... may provide a means of ensuring high quality development. But good quality is an integral part of development and should be at the heart of all planning; the provision of add-on benefits should not be regarded as an acceptable alternative to such an integrated approach.'

Paragraph B9 states:

'In general it will be reasonable to seek ... a planning obligation if what is sought or offered:

(i)   is needed from a practical point of view to enable the development to go ahead and, in the case of financial payment, will meet or contribute towards the cost of providing such necessary facilities in the future;

(ii)   or is necessary from a planning point of view and is so directly related to the proposed development and to the use of the land after its completion that the development ought not to be permitted without it.'

Paragraph B12 states:

'... a reasonable obligation would seek to restore facilities, resources and amenities equivalent to that existing before the development. Developers may reasonably be expected to pay for or contribute to the cost of infrastructure which would not have been necessary but for their development ... Developers should not be expected to pay for facilities which are needed solely in order to resolve existing deficiencies ...'

Paragraph B20 states:

> '... if there is a choice between imposing conditions and entering into a planning obligation, the imposition of a condition which satisfies the policy tests in DoE Circular 11/95 is preferable because it enables a developer to appeal to the Secretary of State.'

4.3.3 Case-law

There have recently been several cases concerned with the reasonableness of benefits contained in planning obligations and what weight should be given to them in deciding whether planning permission should be granted. The principal cases are *R v Plymouth City Council and Others ex parte Plymouth and South Devon Co-operative Society Ltd* [1993] JPL B81, CA; *Tesco Stores Ltd v Secretary of State for the Environment and Others* [1995] 2 All ER 636, HL; and *Good and Another v Epping Forest District Council* [1994] 1 WLR 376, CA. These cases are authority for the following propositions.

(1) The tests in *Newbury District Council v Secretary of State for the Environment; Newbury District Council v International Synthetic Rubber Co* [1981] AC 578 (see **3.6.2**) apply in determining whether the benefits offered in a planning obligation are material considerations to be taken into account when the LPA are deciding whether to grant planning permission. There is no requirement that the benefits offered also have to be necessary in the sense that they overcome what would otherwise be a planning objection to the development.

(2) If a benefit is a material consideration because it passes the tests in *Newbury*, the weight to be given to it is a matter of discretion (governed by policy considerations) for the LPA or ODPM.

(3) The powers of LPAs under s 106 are not controlled by the nature and extent of the power to impose conditions under s 70(1). Thus, provided a benefit in a planning obligation satisfies s 106(1) (see above) and is not manifestly unreasonable, it is valid.

4.4 PRACTICAL POINTS

In view of the law and guidance above, the following points should be borne in mind when drafting and negotiating a planning obligation.

4.4.1 By the LPA

(1) It is important that the title to the land is thoroughly investigated before the LPA enters into the planning obligation. All parties with a legal interest in the land should be made parties to it including any persons with existing interests (such as a prior mortgagee); otherwise the obligation may not be enforceable against a successor in title to that interest.

(2) The future exercise of any of the LPA's statutory powers should not be fettered by the obligation. If this does occur and the obligation is later challenged in court, it could invalidate the planning obligation (see *Royal Borough of Windsor and Maidenhead v Brandrose Investments* [1983] 1 WLR 509, CA).

(3) The planning obligation should be executed either before, or simultaneously with, the grant of the planning permission otherwise the developer may have the benefit of the permission without being bound by the obligation.

(4) The timing of related infrastructure agreements should be carefully considered. It will normally be preferable, where possible, to have all related agreements (eg agreements under the Highways Act 1980) executed at the same time as the planning obligation.

(5) Consideration should be given as to whether the obligation ought, in the circumstances of the case, to provide that liability under the obligation will cease once the owner of the interest parts with it. In the absence of such a provision, liability will continue against not only the original covenantor(s) but also against all subsequent successors in title to him (them).

(6) If there is a disagreement about the inclusion of a particular term in the planning obligation, the LPA should consider whether it is within the guidance contained in Circular 1/97. If it is doubtful, or may be considered excessive, the LPA may find that the developer will appeal and offer a unilateral undertaking on the appeal (see further **4.6**).

(7) Consideration should also be given as to whether a clause should be included providing for payment of the LPA's costs in connection with the negotiation, drafting and execution of the planning obligation. If there is no such clause the LPA will have to bear their own costs.

4.4.2 By the developer

(1) The draft planning permission should be included in one of the schedules to the obligation so that it is clear from the terms of the obligation what conditions, etc will be attached to the planning permission.

(2) The developer should try to ensure that the terms of the obligation do not continue to bind after he has sold his interest to a successor. This is particularly important where positive covenants in the obligation are likely to continue well into the future.

(3) For the same reasons as for the LPA, it is important for the developer that the LPA do not fetter their statutory powers in the obligation. If there is such a fetter, the planning obligation may be challenged later by a third party.

(4) The developer should attempt to have a clause inserted to the effect that the planning obligation will be discharged or cease to have effect if the planning permission expires or is revoked or if planning permission is later granted for some other development which is incompatible with that originally granted.

(5) The obligation should not contain a covenant to comply with the conditions attached to the related planning permission (see para B20 of Circular 1/97 quoted at **4.3**). If there is such a covenant and the conditions on the planning permission are subsequently varied (under s 73 or s 73A, see **3.6.4**) or the permission lapses or is revoked, the conditions will continue to bind the land by virtue of the covenant in the planning obligation. (As an alternative, the obligation could contain a covenant to comply with the conditions originally imposed or as subsequently varied or removed and only insofar as the planning permission remains in effect.)

(6) Covenants should be avoided which impose obligations (in particular, positive ones) which take effect as soon as the planning obligation is executed (as opposed to when the planning permission is implemented). There may be a gap

of quite a few months, if not a few years, between the developer obtaining the permission and being in a position to implement it.

4.5 MODIFICATION AND DISCHARGE OF PLANNING OBLIGATIONS (s 106A)

4.5.1 The power to modify or discharge

A planning obligation may be modified or discharged by either agreement between the LPA and the person(s) against whom it is then enforceable, or by application by such person to the LPA, or by appeal to the ODPM.

4.5.2 Application for modification or discharge

A person against whom a planning obligation is enforceable may, at any time after the expiry of 5 years from the date of the planning obligation, apply to the LPA for the obligation to have effect subject to such modifications as may be specified in the application, or to be discharged (s 106A(3)–(4)).

4.5.3 Determination of application by the LPA

The LPA must notify the applicant of their decision within 8 weeks or such longer period as may be agreed in writing between the parties. Where the application is refused, the notification must state clearly and precisely the LPA's full reasons for their decision and tell the applicant of his rights of appeal (see below).

4.5.4 Appeal against determination (s 106B)

Where the LPA fail to reach a decision in the 8-week period or determine that the planning obligation shall continue to have effect without modification, the applicant may appeal to the ODPM within 6 months of the date of the notice or deemed refusal, or such longer period as the ODPM may allow.

The appeal procedure is closely modelled on that for ordinary planning appeals (see Chapter 3).

4.6 UNILATERAL UNDERTAKINGS

4.6.1 Introduction

By s 106(1), planning obligations may be entered into 'by agreement or otherwise'; 'or otherwise' indicates that a fully enforceable obligation may be offered unilaterally by the developer. The rules as to the contents and formalities of unilateral undertakings are the same as those that apply to ordinary planning obligations entered into by agreement except that the agreement of the LPA is not needed.

The reason for the introduction of the unilateral undertaking was 'to enable developers to break the stalemate when local planning authorities play for time or hold out for excessive gain ... They should be particularly useful in clarifying the position at appeal' (Baroness Blatch quoted in *Hansard*, House of Lords, 27 November, 1990, col 907).

4.6.2 ODPM guidance

The ODPM's guidance to LPAs on the use of unilateral undertakings is contained in paras B5 and B6 of Circular 1/97 which state that:

> 'It is reasonable to expect developers and LPAs to try to resolve any planning objections the authority may have to the development proposal by agreement, in accordance with this guidance. Where a developer considers that negotiations are being unneccessarily protracted or that unreasonable demands are being made, he may wish to enter into a planning obligation by making a unilateral undertaking ... The use of unilateral obligations is therefore expected to be principally, but not solely, at appeals, where there are planning objections which only a planning obligation can resolve, but the parties cannot reach agreement ... Such an undertaking should be in accordance with this guidance ... Undertakings should be relevant to planning and directly related to the needs created by the development proposal concerned.'

4.6.3 Practical effect

Thus, the normal course of events will be to attempt to reach an agreement first. If there is deadlock on this, the developer will then appeal to the ODPM against the refusal or deemed refusal of planning permission. At the appeal the developer will offer a unilateral undertaking which, if it is considered appropriate by the inspector, may result in the developer obtaining planning permission. The unilateral undertaking will then become enforceable by the LPA.

Chapter 5

ENFORCEMENT OF PLANNING LAW

5.1 INTRODUCTION

In order to ensure that the planning controls set out in Part III of the Act (ss 55–106) are observed, LPAs are given wide powers of enforcement in Part VII (ss 171A–196). These powers are:

(1) a right of entry for certain enforcement purposes;
(2) service of a planning contravention notice to obtain information about a breach or suspected breach;
(3) service of a breach of condition notice to require compliance with a condition or limitation attached to a planning permission;
(4) the right to apply for an injunction to restrain any breach or threatened breach of planning control;
(5) service of an enforcement notice (sometimes followed by a stop notice) to secure compliance with planning controls.

Before looking at these powers in more detail, though, it is necessary to set out some basic definitions and time-limits which apply to enforcement generally and to consider certificates of lawful use or development which can provide immunity from enforcement action.

Chapter 5 contents
Introduction
Definitions and time-limits
Certificates of lawful use or development (CLEUD)
Right of entry for enforcement purposes
Planning contravention notice
Breach of condition notice
Injunctions
Enforcement notice
Stop notice
Appeals against enforcement notices

5.2 DEFINITIONS AND TIME-LIMITS

5.2.1 Definitions (s 171A)

For the purposes of the Act:

(1) A 'breach of planning control' occurs when development is carried out without the requisite planning permission or when any condition or limitation attached to a permission is not complied with.
(2) 'Taking enforcement action' means the issue of an enforcement notice or the service of a breach of condition notice.

5.2.2 Time-limits (s 171B)

The LPA can take enforcement action only if they do so within the appropriate time-limits. There are two of these:

(1) Where the breach of planning control consists of:

(a) operational development carried out without planning permission; or
(b) a change of use of any building to use as a single dwelling house;

the LPA must take enforcement action within 4 years from the date on which the operations were substantially completed or the change of use occurred (as the case may be).

(2) With all other breaches (ie any material change of use other than to use as a single dwelling house and any breach of condition or limitation attached to a planning permission) no enforcement action may be brought after the expiry of 10 years from the date of the breach.

Note as regards both of the above time-limits, the provisions of s 171B(4)(b) at **5.8.3**.

Once the relevant time-limit has passed, immunity is in effect given to the breach. It is therefore vital to check whether the relevant time-limit has passed and this in turn depends on the nature of the breach committed.

5.3 CERTIFICATES OF LAWFUL USE OR DEVELOPMENT (CLEUD) (ss 191–192)

5.3.1 Preliminary definitions (s 191(2) and (3))

Uses and operations are 'lawful' if no enforcement action can be taken for any reason, including the expiry of the relevant time-limit (see **5.2.2**), and they are not in contravention of a current enforcement notice.

Breach of a condition or limitation attached to a permission is 'lawful' if the 10-year time-limit for taking enforcement action has expired and the breach is not in contravention of a current enforcement notice.

5.3.2 Existing development (s 191)

Any person who wishes to ascertain the lawfulness of any existing use or any operations which have been carried out or any other matter constituting a breach of condition or limitation may apply to the LPA specifying the land and describing the use, operations or other matter (s 191(1)). The certificate is often referred to as a CLEUD. (Note that 'any person' may apply; so, for instance, a prospective purchaser of land could apply for such a certificate.)

Onus of proof

The onus of proof is on the applicant who must prove the lawfulness on a balance of probabilities. The planning merits of the case (ie whether or not the development is desirable) are irrelevant; the sole question in issue is whether or not the matters described in the application are lawful.

Issue of CLEUD (s 191(4))

If the LPA is satisfied of the lawfulness at the time of the application of the use, etc, they must issue a certificate. In any other case they must refuse one; note, though, that a refusal merely indicates that the matter has not been proved on a balance of probabilities.

Effect of CLEUD (s 191(6) and (7))

The lawfulness of any use, operations, etc for which a certificate is in force shall be conclusively presumed. Thus, no enforcement action may be brought in respect of the matters stated as lawful in the certificate.

5.3.3 Proposed development (s 192)

Any person who wishes to ascertain the lawfulness of any proposed use or operational development of land can apply to the LPA specifying the land and describing the use or operations in question.

Effect of certificate (s 192(4))

The lawfulness of any use or operations stated in the certificate shall be conclusively presumed unless there is a material change, before the proposed use or operations are started, in any of the matters relevant to the determination.

5.3.4 General provisions applying to certificates of lawful use or development

A certificate may be issued in respect of part only of the land or just some of the matters specified in the application (s 193(4)) or, with existing development, may be issued in terms which differ from those specified in the application (s 191(4)).

The LPA must enter prescribed details of any applications and decisions in its s 69 register (s 193(6)) and must notify the applicant of its decision within 8 weeks or such longer period as may be agreed in writing between the parties (GDPO, art 24).

Appeals (ss 195, 196 and 288)

The applicant can appeal to the ODPM against a refusal, a refusal in part or a deemed refusal (ie where the LPA fails to determine the application within the relevant time). The time-limit is 6 months from the date of notification of the decision or the deemed refusal.

Further appeal lies to the High Court within 6 weeks of the decision of the ODPM.

Offences (s 194)

It is an offence for any person to procure a particular decision on an application by knowingly or recklessly making a statement which is misleading or false in a material particular, or (with intent to deceive) using a document which is false or misleading in a material particular or withholding any material information.

If a statement was made or a document was used which was false or misleading in a material particular, or if any material information was withheld (whether or not this was done knowingly or recklessly or with intent to deceive), the LPA may revoke the certificate.

5.4 RIGHT OF ENTRY FOR ENFORCEMENT PURPOSES (ss 196A–196C)

5.4.1 Right of entry without a warrant (s 196A)

Any person duly authorised in writing by the LPA may enter any land at any reasonable hour without a warrant to:

(1) ascertain whether there is or has been any breach of planning control on that or any other land; or

(2) determine whether any enforcement power should be exercised and, if so, how; or

(3) ascertain whether there has been compliance with any enforcement power that has been exercised.

There must, however, be 'reasonable grounds' for doing so, ie entry must be the logical means of obtaining the information in question.

In the case of a dwelling house (which includes any residential accommodation in, eg, a commercial building), 24 hours' notice of the intended entry must be given to the occupier. This requirement does not apply, however, to land or outbuildings in the curtilage of the house.

5.4.2 Power to enter under a warrant (s 196B)

A justice of the peace may issue a warrant to any person duly authorised as above for any of the purposes listed above if he is satisfied on sworn information in writing that:

(1) there are reasonable grounds for entering for the purpose in question; and

(2) admission has been refused, or it is reasonably apprehended that it will be refused, or it is an urgent case.

Entry is deemed to be refused if no reply is received within a reasonable time to a request for admission.

Entry under a warrant must be at a reasonable hour (except in cases of urgency) and must be within one month from the date of issue of the warrant. Each warrant authorises one entry only.

5.4.3 Restrictions and offences (s 196C)

The person entering the land must produce his authority and state the purpose of his entry, if requested, and may take with him such other persons as may be necessary (eg policeman, expert, etc). On leaving the land, if the owner or occupier is not then present, he must ensure that the land is as secured against trespassers as when he entered.

Anyone who wilfully obstructs a person exercising a lawful right of entry is guilty of an offence.

5.5 PLANNING CONTRAVENTION NOTICE (ss 171C–171D)

A planning contravention notice (PCN) (rather than the power of entry) is the principal power available to an LPA for obtaining information needed for enforcement purposes.

5.5.1 Contents of a PCN

There is no prescribed form of PCN although a model is suggested in the Appendix to Annex 1 of ODPM Circular 21/91.

Section 171C states that a PCN may require the person on whom it is served to give any information specified in the notice in respect of any operations, use or activities being carried out on the land and any matter relating to conditions or limitations attached to an existing permission. In particular, it may require the person served, so far as he is able, to:

(1) state whether the land is being used as alleged in the notice or whether alleged operations or activities are or have been carried out;
(2) state when any use, operation or activity began;
(3) give particulars of any person known to use or have used the land for any purpose or to be carrying out or have carried out any operations or activities;
(4) give any information he holds about any relevant planning permission or to state why planning permission is not required;
(5) state his interest (if any) in the land and the name and address of any person he knows to have an interest in the land.

A PCN may also give notice of a time and place at which the LPA will consider:

(1) any offer from the person served to apply for planning permission or to refrain from operations or activities or to undertake remedial work; and
(2) any representations he may wish to make about the notice.

If the notice states this, the LPA must give him the opportunity to make the offer or representations at that time and place.

By s 171C(5), a PCN must warn the person served that if he fails to reply enforcement action may be taken and he may be deprived of compensation if a stop notice is served (see **5.10**).

5.5.2 The person served

A PCN may be served on anyone who is the owner or occupier of the land to which the notice relates or who has any other interest in it, or on anyone who is carrying out operations on the land or using it for any purpose (s 171C(1)).

It is an offence for any person served with a PCN to fail to reply to it within 21 days unless he has a reasonable excuse. The offence is a continuing one, even after conviction (s 171D(2)–(4)).

It is also an offence knowingly or recklessly to make a statement in a purported reply which is false or misleading in a material particular (s 171D(5)–(6)).

5.5.3 Effect of a PCN

Apart from the consequences mentioned above, service of a PCN does not affect the exercise of any other enforcement power available to the LPA.

5.6 BREACH OF CONDITION NOTICE (s 187A)

A breach of condition notice (BCN) is primarily intended as an alternative remedy to an enforcement notice where the LPA desires to secure compliance with conditions or limitations attached to an existing planning permission.

5.6.1 When and on whom a BCN may be served

Where there has been a breach of condition or limitation attached to an existing permission, the LPA may serve a BCN on any person who is carrying out or has carried out the development or on any person having control of the land.

5.6.2 Contents of a BCN

The notice must specify the steps which the LPA considers ought to be taken or the activities which ought to cease in order to secure compliance with the conditions, etc specified in the notice. Where, however, a notice is served on a person who has control of the land but who is not carrying (or has not carried) out the development, it can only require compliance with any conditions regulating the use of the land.

The notice must also specify a period for compliance which must not be less than 28 days from the date of service of the notice.

5.6.3 Effect of a BCN

If the person served has not remedied the breach by the time specified in the notice (or by the time specified in any further notice served by the LPA), he is guilty of an offence: the offence is a continuing one. It is a defence, however, for the person served to prove that he took all reasonable measures to secure compliance with the notice or, if he was served as the person having control of the land, that he did not have control at the time he was served.

5.7 INJUNCTIONS (s 187B)

An LPA may apply to the High Court or county court for an injunction if it considers it necessary or expedient to restrain an actual or apprehended breach of planning control. It may do this whether or not it has used, or proposes to use, any of its other enforcement powers under the Act.

Whether an injunction is granted and, if so, its terms, are entirely a matter for the discretion of the court as the remedy is an equitable one. Thus, an LPA will need to show not only that the remedy is expedient and necessary but also that it has taken into account all relevant considerations in coming to that decision, that there is a clear breach or a clear likelihood of a breach, and that the remedy is the most appropriate one in the circumstances of the case. (For good illustrations, see *Croydon London Borough Council v Gladden* [1994] JPL 723, CA, at p 729ff, *Harborough District Council v Wheatcroft & Son Ltd* [1996] JPL B128 and *Hambleton District Council v Bird* [1995] 3 PLR 8.)

5.8 ENFORCEMENT NOTICE (ss 172–182)

5.8.1 Introduction

As a general rule, there is no criminal liability for breaches of planning control. There are exceptions to this rule, for instance, where unauthorised works are done to a listed building, or where there is a breach of a tree preservation order or the display of an advertisement without consent. Subject to this, however, there is no criminal liability for a breach until a valid enforcement notice has been served, become effective and not complied with.

5.8.2 Issue of enforcement notice

By s 172(1), an LPA may issue an enforcement notice where it appears to it that there has been a breach of planning control and that it is expedient to issue the notice having regard to the provisions of their development plan and any other material considerations. Issue of an enforcement notice is the most commonly used method of enforcement.

Pre-requisites to issue

There must be an apparent breach of planning control and it must be expedient to issue an enforcement notice.

APPARENT BREACH OF PLANNING CONTROL

There is no duty on the LPA to satisfy themselves that there is a breach (see, eg, *Tidswell v Secretary of State for the Environment* [1977] JPL 104) although with the powers now available to them, in particular the right to serve a PCN, it may be required to do some preliminary research before issuing an enforcement notice.

IT MUST BE EXPEDIENT TO ISSUE AN ENFORCEMENT NOTICE

The LPA should not automatically issue an enforcement notice whenever there appears to be a breach of planning control. They must consider their development plan and any other material considerations (which will include advice in circulars and PPGs).

In PPG 18 the ODPM gives detailed guidance on this matter to LPAs. For example, in para 5 it states that enforcement action should always be commensurate with the breach to which it relates; thus, it will usually be inappropriate to take enforcement action against a trivial or technical breach which causes no harm to amenity in the locality. Another factor to consider is whether planning permission, if applied for, would be granted for the unauthorised development in question.

The decisive issue, therefore, is whether the breach would unacceptably affect public amenity or the existing use of the land which merits protection in the public interest.

Challenging the issue or failure to issue

A decision to issue an enforcement notice cannot be challenged unless the decision was arbitrary or capricious (see, eg, *Donovan v Secretary of State for the Environment* [1988] JPL 118).

Equally, a decision not to issue an enforcement notice is not challengeable unless the decision is arbitrary or capricious (see *Perry v Stanborough (Developments) Ltd* [1978] JPL 36).

5.8.3 Time-limits

An enforcement notice must be issued (though not necessarily served) within the relevant time-limit as defined in s 171B (see **5.2.2**). Failure to do so will render the breach lawful.

However, by s 171B(4)(b), an LPA is not prevented from taking further enforcement action in respect of a breach of planning control if, during the 4 years prior to the new action being taken, the LPA has taken or purported to take enforcement action in respect of that breach. This would enable an LPA, for example, to serve another enforcement notice within 4 years of one which had been set aside on an appeal or one which had been withdrawn (see **5.8.8** and **5.10**).

5.8.4 Contents of an enforcement notice (s 173)

No statutory form is prescribed but the notice must comply with the following.

(1) It must state the matters alleged to constitute the breach of planning control in such a way as to enable the person served to know what those matters are, and must state the paragraph of s 171A(1) (development without permission or breach of condition/limitation: see **5.2.1**) within which, in the opinion of the LPA, the breach falls (s 173(1) and (2)).

(2) It must specify the steps to be taken or the activities to be discontinued in order to achieve wholly or partly the remedying of the breach or of any injury to amenity caused by the breach (s 173(3) and (4)). Examples of requirements that may be included are given in s 173(5)–(7) and include:

   (a) alteration or removal of buildings or works;
   (b) carrying out of any building or other operations;
   (c) cessation of any activity except to the extent permitted by the notice;
   (d) modification of the contour of any deposit of refuse or waste;
   (e) construction of a replacement building after unauthorised demolition.

(3) It must state the calendar date on which the notice is to take effect which must be at least 28 days from service of the notice (s 173(8)).

(4) It must state the period within which any steps specified in the notice are to be taken and may specify different periods for different steps (s 173(9)).

(5) It must state such additional matters as may be prescribed. These are set out in the Town and Country Planning (Enforcement Notices and Appeals) Regulations 1991, regs 3 and 4, which require that the notice:

   (a) states the reasons why the LPA considered it expedient to issue the enforcement notice. This is intended to enable appellants to direct their minds to relevant issues (see ODPM Circular 21/91, Annex 2, para 12);
   (b) defines the precise boundaries of the site by reference to a plan or otherwise (ibid, para 13);
   (c) is accompanied by a copy or summary of ss 172–177, the booklet *Enforcement Notice Appeals – A Guide to Procedure* and a copy of the recommended appeal form.

5.8.5 Service (s 172(2) and (3))

Persons to be served

The enforcement notice must be served on:

(1) the owner: this term is defined in s 336(1) as being the person (other than a mortgagee not in possession) who is entitled to receive a rack (ie full) rent or who would be so entitled if the land were let; and

(2) the occupier: this includes any person occupying by virtue of a lease or tenancy but may also extend to licensees if their occupation resembles that of a tenant (see *Stevens v Bromley London Borough Council* [1972] 2 WLR 605, CA); and

(3) any other person having an interest in the land, being an interest which, in the opinion of the LPA, is likely to be materially affected by the notice; this would include, in particular, known mortgagees.

Time for service

The notice must be served not more than 28 days after its issue and not less than 28 days before the date specified in the notice as the date on which it is to take effect. Failure to comply with these provisions is a ground for appeal to the ODPM and, in general, is only challengeable in that way (s 285(1) and see *R v Greenwich London Borough Council ex parte Patel* [1985] JPL 851, CA; see also **5.10**).

5.8.6 Validity of notice

An error or defect in an enforcement notice may render it either a nullity or invalid.

Nullity

The notice will only be a nullity where there is a major defect on the face of it, for example, where it does not state what the alleged breach is, what must be done to put it right or on what date the notice takes effect. The notice will also be a nullity if it does not fairly and reasonably tell the recipient what he must do to remedy the breach.

If the notice is a nullity it is of no effect. This is therefore a complete defence to any prosecution brought for non-compliance with it. In addition, there is technically no right of appeal to the ODPM under s 174 although, in practice, an appeal will normally be made at which the ODPM may find as a preliminary issue that the notice is a nullity and that he therefore has no jurisdiction to hear the appeal. Any such finding may be challenged by the LPA by way of judicial review.

Invalidity

Other defects, errors or misdescriptions in an enforcement notice do not render it a nullity. In such a case, it can only be challenged by way of appeal under s 174 (see s 285 and **5.10**).

On a s 174 appeal, the ODPM may correct such defects, etc, or vary the terms of the notice if he is satisfied that this will not cause injustice to either the appellant or the LPA (s 176(2)).

5.8.7 Effect of enforcement notice

An enforcement notice does not have to require restoration of the status quo, ie under-enforcement is possible. Where a notice could have required buildings or works to be removed or an activity to cease but does not do so and the notice is complied with, then planning permission is deemed to have been given under s 73A (see **3.6.4**) for those buildings, works or activities (s 173(11)).

Similarly, where an enforcement notice requires construction of a replacement building and is complied with, planning permission is deemed to have been given (s 173(12)).

Where a notice has become effective and has not been complied with, the then owner is guilty of an offence. In addition, the LPA may enter the land and take the steps required by the notice and recover their expenses of so doing (see **5.8.9**).

5.8.8 Variation and withdrawal (s 173A)

The LPA may withdraw or waive or relax any requirement of an enforcement notice whether or not it has become effective. If they do so they must immediately notify everyone who was served with the enforcement notice or who would have been served if it had been re-issued.

Note that the withdrawal of the notice (but not the waiver or relaxation of any requirement in it) does not affect the power of the LPA to issue a further enforcement notice in respect of the same breach.

5.8.9 Non-compliance with notice (ss 178–179)

Offences

Where the notice has become effective and any step required by the notice has not been taken or any activity required to cease is being carried on, the then owner is in breach and is liable on summary conviction to a fine of up to £20,000 or, on indictment, an unlimited amount. The court in assessing any fine must take into account any financial benefit or potential benefit accruing or likely to accrue as a result of the offence (s 179(1), (2), (8) and (9)). Note that the burden of proving ownership is on the prosecutor.

Any person (other than the owner) who has control of, or an interest in, the land must not carry on, or permit to be carried on, any activity required by the notice to cease. If he does so, he is guilty of an offence (s 179(4) and (5)).

Defences

It is a defence for the owner to show that he did everything he could be expected to do to secure compliance (s 179(3)).

It is also a defence for the person charged to show that he was not served with the enforcement notice, and that it was not entered in the s 188 register (in which LPAs are required to note all enforcement and stop notices), and that he did not know of the existence of the notice (s 179(7)).

It is no defence to show that the notice was defective because it failed to comply with s 173(2) (see **5.8.4**), although it would be a defence to show that the notice was a nullity (see **5.8.6**) or that the LPA exceeded their powers.

Action by the LPA

After any period for compliance with an enforcement notice has passed and the notice has not been fully complied with, the LPA, in addition to prosecuting, may enter the land and take any steps required by the notice. They may then recover any reasonable expenses incurred from the owner of the land at that time (s 178(1)).

Where the breach is a continuing one, the LPA may seek an injunction whether or not after any conviction (s 187B, see **5.7**).

5.9 STOP NOTICE (ss 183–187)

5.9.1 Introduction

As an enforcement notice cannot become effective earlier than 28 days after service and as its effect is suspended until final determination of any appeal (but subject to any court order to the contrary), it may be many months before the LPA can take steps to enforce it other than by way of an injunction. In the meantime, local amenity may suffer detriment because of the continuing breach. Accordingly, the Act provides for the possibility of a stop notice to be served to bring activities in breach of planning control to an end before the enforcement notice takes effect.

5.9.2 Procedure

General

Where an LPA consider it expedient to prevent, before the expiry of the period for compliance, any activity specified in the enforcement notice they may serve a stop notice (s 183(1) and (2)). Details of this should be entered in the register of enforcement and stop notices kept under s 188.

Contents of the notice

The stop notice must refer to the enforcement notice and must have a copy of it annexed. It must also state the date on which it will take effect being at least 3 days and not more than 28 days after service of the notice; an earlier date may be specified if the LPA consider that there are special reasons and a statement of those reasons is served with the notice (s 184(1)–(3)).

Service

A stop notice may be served with the enforcement notice or subsequently but must be served before the enforcement notice takes effect (s 183(1) and (3)).

It must be served on any person who appears to have an interest in the land or to be engaged in any activity prohibited by the enforcement notice (s 183(6)).

Where a stop notice has been served, the LPA may also display a 'site notice' on the land concerned stating that a stop notice has been served, giving its details, and stating that any person contravening it may be prosecuted (see **5.9.4**).

5.9.3 Restrictions

A stop notice cannot prohibit the use of any building as a dwelling house or the carrying out of any activity which has been carried on for more than 4 years (whether continuously or not) unless, in the latter case, the activities consist of, or are incidental to, building, etc operations or the deposit of waste or refuse.

There is no appeal against the service of a stop notice.

5.9.4 Offences (s 187)

Any person who contravenes a stop notice (or causes or permits its contravention) after a site notice has been displayed or after he has been served with the stop notice is guilty of an offence which is punishable in the same way as for enforcement notices (including the taking into account of any financial benefit, see **5.8.9**).

It is a defence to prove that the stop notice was not served on him and that he did not know, and could not reasonably be expected to know, of its existence.

5.9.5 Withdrawal

By ss 183(7) and 184(7), the LPA may at any time withdraw a stop notice without prejudice to their power to serve another one. If they do withdraw a stop notice they must serve notice of this on everyone who was served with the original stop notice and, if a site notice was displayed, display a notice of withdrawal in place of the site notice. Compensation may then become payable (see **5.9.6**).

5.9.6 Compensation (s 186)

When payable

The LPA is liable to pay compensation in respect of any prohibition in a stop notice if:

(1) the enforcement notice is quashed on any ground other than that in s 174(2)(a) (see **5.10.1**); or

(2) the enforcement notice is varied other than under s 174(2)(a) so that the activity would no longer have fallen within the stop notice; or

(3) the enforcement notice is withdrawn otherwise than in consequence of a grant of planning permission or of permission to retain or continue the development without complying with a condition or limitation attached to a previous permission; or

(4) the stop notice is withdrawn.

No compensation is payable:

(1) if the enforcement notice is quashed or varied on the ground in s 174(2)(a); or

(2) in respect of any activity which, when the stop notice was in effect, constituted or contributed to a breach of planning control; or

(3) in respect of any loss or damage which could have been avoided if the claimant had provided the information when required to do so under s 171C (ie a PCN, see **5.5**).

Amount and to whom payable

Compensation is payable to the person who, when the stop notice was first served, had an interest in or occupied the relevant land. The amount payable is that loss or damage which is directly attributable to the prohibition in the notice and can include any sum payable for breach of contract caused by compliance with the stop notice.

Any claim must be made within 12 months of the date compensation became payable (ie the date on which the enforcement notice was quashed, varied, etc). In the event of a dispute as to the amount, the matter must be referred to the Lands Tribunal.

5.10 APPEALS AGAINST ENFORCEMENT NOTICES (ss 174–177)

5.10.1 Grounds of appeal

Section 174(2) lists seven grounds of appeal as follows.

(a) Planning permission ought to be granted or any condition or limitation attached to an existing permission ought to be discharged (as the case may be) in respect of the matters alleged to be a breach of planning control in the enforcement notice.
(b) The matters alleged have not occurred.
(c) The matters, if they occurred, do not amount to a breach of planning control.
(d) No enforcement action could be taken at the date the notice was issued as regards the matters alleged in it (ie the LPA were out of time, see **5.2.2**).
(e) Copies of the enforcement notice were not served as required by s 172 (see **5.8.5**).
(f) The steps required by the notice or the activities required to cease exceed what is necessary to remedy any breach of planning control or injury to amenity (as the case may be).
(g) The period specified in the notice for the taking of steps, etc falls short of what should reasonably be allowed.

Note also the following points.

(1) Whether or not ground (a) is expressly made a ground of appeal, there is a deemed application for planning permission when a notice of appeal is lodged (s 177(5)).
(2) As regards ground (e), the ODPM may disregard failure to serve any person if that failure has not caused substantial prejudice to that person or to the appellant (s 175(5)).
(3) Grounds (f) and (g) do not go to the validity of the enforcement notice and the ODPM may vary the requirements of the original notice (s 176(1)).

5.10.2 Time-limit (s 174(3))

Written notice of appeal (which can be by letter, although the standard form supplied by the ODPM is normally used) must be given to the ODPM before the date on which the enforcement notice takes effect.

There is no power for the ODPM or the court to extend the time-limit for appealing.

Note that if the notice is sent to the proper address by pre-paid post at such time that, in the ordinary course of post (2 working days in the case of first-class post), it would have been delivered before the enforcement notice takes effect, the appeal will be in time even if it is delayed in the post (s 174(3)(b)).

5.10.3 Who may appeal? (s 174(1) and (6))

Any person having an interest in the land (whether served with the enforcement notice or not) may appeal as may any person who was occupying the land under a licence at the time the notice was issued and continues to occupy the land when the appeal is brought.

5.10.4 Procedure

Documentation and fees to be submitted

By s 174(4), and reg 5 of the Town and Country Planning (Enforcement Notices and Appeals) Regulations 1991, the applicant may submit with the notice of appeal a statement in writing specifying the grounds on which he is appealing and stating briefly the facts in support of those grounds. If he does not submit this with the appeal he must do so within 14 days of being required to do so by notice from the SSE. It is important for the appellant to specify all the grounds on which he wishes to rely as amendments adding additional grounds are unlikely to be allowed subsequently.

As there is a deemed application for planning permission, whether or not the applicant also specifies ground (a), a fee is payable.

The fee is refundable in certain circumstances (eg if the appeal is allowed on grounds (b) to (e) or the enforcement notice is quashed or found to be invalid).

Appeal forum

The two main options are to proceed either by way of written representations or by public local inquiry. There is a right to a public local inquiry and, in practice, half of enforcement notice appeals are disposed of in this way. Written representations may be used if the appellant and the LPA agree; the ODPM will suggest written representations where it thinks the circumstances of the case are appropriate.

Where the dispute is entirely concerned with the planning merits of the notice and the appeal, or the requirements and time for compliance in the notice, the matter may proceed by way of an informal hearing rather than a full public inquiry. An informal hearing is not appropriate where there is a dispute as to the evidence or a challenge on legal grounds.

Effect of appeal

Until the final determination or withdrawal of the appeal, the enforcement notice is of no effect. According to the Court of Appeal in *R v Kuxhaus* [1988] 2 WLR 1005, [1988] 2 All ER 705, CA, 'final determination' means when all rights of appeal have been exhausted, including appeals to the High Court under s 289. However, under s 289(4A) the High Court or Court of Appeal have power to order, if they think fit, that the notice shall have effect in whole or in part pending the final determination. Such an order may also require the LPA to give an undertaking as to damages.

Written representations and informal hearings

As mentioned above, the ODPM may suggest these alternatives in appropriate cases but they can be used only with the consent of both parties.

5.10.5 Costs

The ODPM or his inspector has power to award costs in all cases, even where the appeal was by way of written representations or even where the inquiry was not held (ss 320 and 322).

5.10.6 Further appeals (s 289)

Further appeal to the High Court, but on a point of law only, lies against any decision made by the ODPM in proceedings on an enforcement appeal. No such appeal lies, though, under s 289 if the ODPM declined to entertain the appeal or set the enforcement notice aside as being a nullity; in these cases the appropriate way to proceed is by way of judicial review.

Chapter 6

THE PROBLEM OF CONTAMINATED LAND

6.1 INTRODUCTION

Chapter 6 contents
Introduction
The consequences of contamination
Steps to take to reduce the risks
Contractual terms

The definition of 'contaminated land' found in the Environment Act 1995 is:

'Any land which appears to [a] local authority to be in such a condition by reason of substances in, on or under the land that:

(a) significant harm is being caused or there is a significant possibility of such harm being caused; or

(b) pollution of controlled waters is being, or is likely to be caused ...'

'Harm' is defined as 'harm to the health of living organisms or other interference with the ecological systems of which they form part and, in the case of man, includes harm to his property'.

In determining whether any land is contaminated the local authority must act in accordance with guidance to be issued by the ODPM.

Most contaminated land is located in industrialised urban areas and conurbations.

6.2 THE CONSEQUENCES OF CONTAMINATION

6.2.1 The problem of contaminated land

The presence of contaminants in land can have very serious consequences; the site may be 'blighted', making it difficult to sell or mortgage; the use of the land for certain purposes may be impossible, or only possible if extensive (and expensive) clean up works are undertaken. Potential buyers and lenders should be aware of the legal and financial consequences of buying land which is already contaminated or of contaminating land which they already own.

6.2.2 The legal risks

The legal risks associated with contaminated land are:

(1) potential civil liability for damage caused by migrating pollution. In *Cambridge Water Co v Eastern Counties Leather Ltd* [1994] 2 WLR 53, the House of Lords decided that a defendant can be liable in nuisance if he brings onto his land any substance which may cause damage if it escaped. He will be liable for any damage caused without proof of fault or negligence, the only precondition to liability being that he must have been able reasonably to foresee the consequences of any escape, when he brought the substance onto his land. This means that a landowner could be liable for pollution damage following an escape even where he uses state-of-the art technology, and was not negligent in causing the escape;

[handwritten margin note: defendant can be liable even if he was not negligent in causing of escape.]

(2)   potential criminal liability for offences resulting from migrating pollution. For example, s 34 of the Environmental Protection Act 1990 (EPA 1990) imposes a duty of care to prevent the escape of waste from your control. Accordingly, any waste must be stored safely and securely;

(3)   statutory liability for clean-up costs (see below);

(4)   after-care and restoration provisions imposed by LPAs. PPG 23, issued in 1994, sets out guidance to LPAs in relation to contaminated land. As well as encouraging the recycling of 'brownfield sites', it also states that 'such recycling can also provide an opportunity to deal with the threats posed by contamination'. So, a grant of planning permission in relation to contaminated land is likely to include conditions requiring the remediation of the contamination;

(5)   planning constraints restricting the scope of development of contaminated land. For example, the GPDO requires the LPA to consult with the relevant waste disposal authority in respect of any application for planning permission within 250 metres of existing or past waste disposal sites; and

(6)   s 157 of the EPA 1990 provides that where an offence is committed by a company and it can be proved that a director, manager, secretary or similar officer of the company either consented, connived or was negligent, he as well as the company is guilty of an offence (see also s 158 of the EPA 1990).

These risks may mean heavy financial liabilities on the owner or occupier of the land.

6.2.3 Statutory liability for clean-up costs

EPA 1990, ss 78A–78Y (inserted by the EA 1995), place the prime responsibility for securing the clean-up of contaminated sites on the local authority. These provisions came into force on 1 April 2000 and require local authorities to identify contaminated sites within their area. Having identified the contaminated land, the local authority (or sometimes the Environment Agency) must serve a remediation notice on the 'appropriate person' requiring such clean-up works as they consider reasonable. The cost of this is likely to be considerable. In one case, a developer bought a site for residential development only to discover that the site had at one time been used as a gas mantle factory and was mildly radioactive; the clean-up costs exceeded £11 million.

6.2.4 The 'appropriate person'

The 'appropriate person' to be served with a remediation notice will be either a Class A person or a Class B person. A Class A person is someone who caused or knowingly permitted the pollutant to be in the land; where no Class A person can be found after reasonable enquiry, then the Class B person will be liable (ie the owner or occupier of the land for the time being). A buyer of contaminated land can thus be liable for clean-up costs as a Class B person, if no Class A person can be found (eg the original polluter is dead or has been wound up) but also as a Class A person. A buyer who discovers that the land is contaminated, but does nothing to remediate the situation, could eventually be seen as having 'knowingly permitted' the pollutant to remain in the land. Where there are two or more persons within a particular 'Class', then there are complex rules for deciding which of those persons will be primarily liable.

6.2.5 Sold with information

On a sale by one Class A person to another, liability will be transferred to the buyer if, before the sale became binding, the buyer had information that would reasonably allow him to be aware of the presence on his land of the pollutant in question, and the broad measure of that presence. Further, in transactions since the beginning of 1990 where the buyer is a large commercial organisation or public body, permission from the seller for the buyer to carry out his own investigations of the condition of the land will normally be taken as sufficient indication that the buyer had information about the presence of the pollutant.

6.2.6 Payments for remediation

Further, on a sale by one Class A person to another, liability will be transferred to the buyer if the seller makes a payment to the buyer which would be sufficient to pay for remediation. This payment can take the form of a reduction in the purchase price specifically stated to be for the purpose of remediation.

6.2.7 Landlord and tenant issues

Failure to comply with a remediation notice, without reasonable excuse, is a criminal offence. Moreover, in default of compliance with a remediation notice, the local authority have power to carry out the required works at the expense of the 'appropriate person'.

From a landlord's point of view, he will be anxious to ensure that if pollution is discovered during the term of the lease, he can require the tenant to carry out any necessary clean-up works under the provisions of the lease. Most modern commercial leases deal with environmental issues expressly but in the absence of express provisions are there any other lease terms upon which the landlord could rely to require the tenant to clean-up the site? It is doubtful whether clean-up works would fall within the tenant's repairing covenant unless the pollution caused some physical damage to the building. However, the tenant's covenant to comply with the requirements of all statutory obligations may, depending on the exact form of wording used, be broad enough to extend to requirements under environmental law. Furthermore, if there is a service charge in the lease one of the items of expenditure recoverable from the tenant may include sums spent by the landlord on any necessary clean-up works. Even if this is not expressly mentioned in the list of services to be provided, the 'sweeping up' clause may be wide enough to embrace such work. It will be seen why such matters should be dealt with expressly in the lease.

6.3 STEPS TO TAKE TO REDUCE THE RISKS

There is no public list or register of sites which may be contaminated. However, s 78R of the EPA 1990 requires local authorities to maintain a register containing particulars of remediation notices served by them. The standard form, Enquiries of the Local Authority (Con 29) has been amended to include questions with regard to the service of remediation notices. Furthermore, from time to time, the Environment Agency, on the basis of the information provided by the authorities, is required to publish a report on the state of contaminated land in its area. Notwithstanding these provisions, there is a very real danger of buying, in ignorance, a contaminated site at a price which does not reflect the cost of necessary clean-up works. Those involved in commercial property, therefore, must make their own careful enquiries to discover whether contamination may be a problem on the site they are buying, leasing or accepting as security for a loan. This may be done in a number of ways:

(1) a desk-top (or documentary) study. This involves:

-   making specific enquiries of the various regulatory bodies such as local authorities and the Environment Agency to see if any pollution incidents have occurred on the site;
-   making specific enquiries of the occupier;
-   researching the previous planning history of the site;
-   checking through the title deeds, including pre-registration documents. Such a check might indicate high risk property. For example, there may be information in old deeds and search certificates relating to previous uses of the land. While a long history of agricultural use may not raise much concern, a history of heavy industrial use will give greater cause for concern. Also, old plans attached to deeds can prove a useful source of information. For example, an old plan may indicate that the land has previously been used as (or is close to) an old quarry. In the same way old Ordnance Survey Maps may reveal useful information.

There are now several commercial organisations specialising in providing environmental searches in relation to both residential and commercial properties;

(2) undertaking a detailed physical survey of potentially contaminated sites. The desk-top study should establish the likelihood of contamination being present in which case a physical survey should be considered. This will be very expensive but the risks involved are great and the cost may, therefore, be justified.

6.4 CONTRACTUAL TERMS

In some cases, it may be possible to make the contract conditional on, for example, satisfactory site investigations; or on clean-up by the seller prior to completion; or on the buyer securing insurance cover against the risks of liability resulting from past contamination or pollution. Insurance will usually only be granted following an environmental risk assessment by consultants appointed by the insurer and may only cover third-party damage or injury rather than clean-up costs.

It may be possible to negotiate an indemnity from the seller against any future clean-up costs incurred or against damages which become payable as a result of past contamination or pollution. However, a seller will be unwilling to give such an indemnity unless he is convinced that the possibility of contamination is remote and the state of the market requires such an indemnity to be given. As an alternative, the buyer may seek a warranty from the seller that he has no knowledge of any pollution being present on site and that he has made full disclosure to the buyer of all relevant information. Alternatively, the buyer could seek a reduction in the purchase price to cover the likely clean-up costs. As always, much will depend on the relative bargaining power of the parties.

If the buyer considers the risk too high, he should withdraw from the transaction.

Chapter 7

MATTERS OF CONTRACT

7.1 THE CONTRACT OF SALE

Chapter 7 contents
The contract of sale
Different types of contract
Searches and enquiries

As in residential conveyancing, it is the seller's solicitor who will draft the contract of sale, in duplicate, for submission to the buyer's solicitor for approval. The seller's solicitor may use the *Standard Commercial Property Conditions* form of contract and will draft the contract adopting the same drafting principles applicable in residential conveyancing. Further, on the sale of a green field site, where the seller's main interest is in the receipt of money, and the buyer's in obtaining vacant possession, he will include clauses similar to those used in residential conveyancing. It is only where matters are complicated (eg by the need to obtain planning permission before completion) that drafting techniques will differ from residential conveyancing. Many solicitors will use their own word-processed form of contract which will incorporate the *Standard Commercial Property Conditions* (or some other comparable conditions of sale).

The following points may be noted in connection with a contract to sell a commercial site.

(1) The seller will insist upon the payment of a full 10% deposit on exchange of contracts and is very unlikely to agree to accept a reduced deposit. The buyer, being in business, should be able to meet the demand of the usual contractual deposit. However, he is likely to insist that the deposit is to be held by the seller's solicitor as stakeholder and he may insist that the interest on the deposit (which may itself amount to a sizeable sum) is to be paid to the buyer at completion. Some larger organisations may try to dispense with the payment of a deposit when buying a commercial site on the basis that the size and reputation of the organisation is a sufficient guarantee that completion will take place.

(2) It will be very important to the commercial buyer to ensure that the contract provides for vacant possession of the whole of the site at completion so that the buyer's development plans are not frustrated. In most cases there is an implied term for vacant possession, but for the avoidance of doubt an express term should be included.

(3) VAT must be clearly dealt with in the agreement. The danger for the buyer is that if the contract is silent as to VAT, and after exchange of contracts, the seller (being a person registered for VAT) elects to charge VAT on the purchase price, the buyer will have to add 17.5% VAT to the purchase price. The buyer may want to ensure that the contract contains an express warranty by the seller that he has not, before exchange, elected to charge VAT on the purchase price, and that he will not do so thereafter, or that the purchase price is paid inclusive of VAT. In any case, the buyer will want to make enquiries of the seller to ascertain his intentions regarding VAT on the purchase price. VAT on property is dealt with more fully at **10.1**.

(4) The seller, having entered into a bargain with a chosen buyer, will usually want to deal with the chosen buyer alone and will, therefore, want to ensure there is a

clause in the contract which prevents the buyer from assigning the benefit of the contract to a third party. Further, the seller will often attempt to prevent the buyer from entering into a sub-sale of the property by stipulating that the seller cannot be required by the buyer to execute a conveyance or transfer of the property to anyone other than the buyer. (This latter clause does not prevent a sub-sale but makes it less attractive to the buyers since stamp duty will be payable both on the conveyance to the buyer, and on the buyer's conveyance to the sub-buyer.)

(5) Frequently, the seller will deal with the possibility of the buyer becoming bankrupt, or going into liquidation, or becoming subject to other insolvency proceedings before completion of the sale by giving himself the right to rescind the contract upon the happening of any such event. This frees the seller to arrange a sale to another buyer without the delay of having to await completion, and the expiry of a notice to complete.

(6) If the buyer has agreed to pay all or part of the seller's legal and other expenses in connection with the sale, the contract should so provide.

(7) Express provision should be made, where appropriate, for the grant and reservation of easements and the imposition of covenants. If the seller is retaining some adjoining or neighbouring land, he will be anxious to retain some control over the future development of the property.

(8) Where the property already has the benefit of planning permission obtained by the seller, the benefit of that permission will automatically pass to the buyer, since planning permission enures for the benefit of the land concerned (unless it states otherwise). The buyer will no doubt want to develop in accordance with the plans and specifications upon which the application for permission was based, but copyright in those plans and specifications will be retained by the architect who drew them up in the first place. The buyer should, therefore, ensure that the contract provides for the seller to assign to him, or procure the grant to him, of a valid licence to use the plans and specifications.

7.2 DIFFERENT TYPES OF CONTRACT

Sometimes the sale will be by simple private treaty; sometimes it will be by way of auction or tender; and sometimes the nature of the transaction may justify a departure altogether from the straightforward kind of sale and purchase contract. There are many types of commercial contracts which can be entered into by a seller and buyer of a commercial site, catering for widely differing circumstances, and the agreement between the seller and buyer will need to reflect the bargain they have struck. This part of the book considers two alternative forms of agreement, although in practice, the reader will meet many other forms drafted for use in the particular circumstances of the case at hand.

7.2.1 Conditional agreements

There will be occasions when one of the parties to the contract will be either unable, or unwilling immediately to enter into an unconditional agreement for the sale or purchase of the property, and so arrangements may be made to effect a conditional exchange of contracts. The seller is usually reluctant to agree to a conditional exchange, since what the seller ordinarily seeks is the security of knowing that his buyer is firmly committed to paying over money on a specified date for completion.

A conditional contract rarely serves a useful purpose for the seller. It is normally the buyer who suggests a conditional exchange of contracts, in a situation where the buyer is anxious to avoid losing the property to another buyer, but is not yet in a position to commit himself irrevocably to the purchase.

Types of conditional agreements

A conditional agreement may be contemplated in the following situations:

(1) where planning permission in respect of the development of the site has not yet been obtained;

(2) where the results of the buyer's local search and enquiries of the local authority have not yet been received;

(3) where vacant possession of the site is not yet available owing to the existence of a tenancy agreement in respect of all or part of the site, which the buyer requires to be terminated;

(4) where the property is leasehold, and the consent of the landlord is required (and has not yet been obtained) in respect of the proposed assignment to the buyer (see also Standard Commercial Property Condition 8.3), or in respect of alterations to the property, or a change in the use of the property proposed by the buyer.

Great care must be taken to distinguish between a contract which contains a condition precedent to the formation of the contract itself (in which case no contract exists unless and until the condition is performed), and a contract which contains a condition precedent to performance (in which case a binding contract is immediately created, but if the condition is not fulfilled, the contract becomes unenforceable). In drafting the contract, the seller's solicitor should make it expressly clear which type of agreement is intended.

If the former type of contract is used, then, despite the fact that the parties have entered into a written agreement, effectively they will still be in the same position as if negotiations were continuing since, until the condition has been satisfied, no binding contract exists, and either party is free to back out. The condition must be fulfilled if the contract is to come into effect. If the latter type of contract is used (and in order to obtain a degree of certainty and commitment, both of the parties are likely to favour this type), a binding contract immediately comes into effect so that neither party can back out without the other's consent whilst the condition still remains to be performed. If the condition is not fulfilled, the contract becomes unenforceable, unless the party for whose sole benefit the condition was inserted, waives the benefit of the condition and elects to proceed.

The condition

Certainty is required with conditional agreements. If the court cannot judge with certainty whether the conditionality of the contract has been removed, the court will reluctantly declare the entire contract void. Hence, in *Lee-Parker and Another v Izzet and Others (No 2)* [1972] 2 All ER 800, a contract which was stated to be conditional upon the buyer obtaining a satisfactory mortgage was held to be void since the concept of a satisfactory mortgage was too vague and indefinite. By way of contrast, in *Janmohamed v Hassam* (1976) 241 EG 609, a contract which was conditional upon the receipt of a mortgage offer satisfactory to the buyer was held to be valid, since the court was prepared to imply an obligation upon the buyer to act reasonably in deciding whether the mortgage offer was satisfactory to him.

In drafting the conditional clause, the seller's solicitor should clearly set out what is required to be done, by whom, and by when, in order for the contract to become unconditional. Consider the following situations by way of example.

(1) If the buyer has not yet received the results of his local search and replies to enquiries of the local authority, the contract can be made conditional upon the buyer receiving what he considers to be satisfactory results and replies, by a stipulated date. The contract should contain an obligation upon the buyer to submit the correct forms to the local authority and to pay the fees (in case he has not already done so). Upon receipt of the search certificate and replies, the buyer should be obliged to notify the seller of receipt, indicating one of three things:

(a) that the buyer considers the results and replies to be satisfactory, in which case the contract proceeds to completion; or

(b) that the buyer considers them to be unsatisfactory, in which case the contract becomes unenforceable, and the contract should provide for the return of the deposit to the buyer, and of the evidence of title to the seller; or

(c) that the buyer is prepared to waive the benefit of the condition.

Such a contract is heavily weighted in favour of the buyer, since it is up to him to determine whether or not the condition has been satisfied. A more neutral and objectively based conditional clause could make the contract conditional upon the receipt by the buyer of a set of results and replies to the local search and enquiries which disclose no adverse matters of a kind which would materially affect the value or beneficial use or occupation of the property by the buyer. This type of clause may not be favoured by the buyer since it leaves some scope for argument.

(2) If the buyer is not prepared to complete without the benefit of planning permission for the type of development he proposes to carry out on the property, the contract could be made conditional upon the receipt of an 'acceptable' planning permission by a stipulated date. Again, the buyer should be obliged by the contract to submit a valid planning application without delay, to serve the correct statutory notices, and to pay the fees for the application. Consideration ought to be given as to whether provision should be made so that, upon refusal of permission (which ordinarily would render the contract unenforceable), the buyer may be allowed or, perhaps, obliged to pursue an appeal. Particular consideration must be given to the definition of an 'acceptable' planning permission. It ought to be one which is granted pursuant to an application, precise details of which are set out in the contract, and which is subject only to the usual planning conditions imposed by statute (eg conditions imposing time-limits for the commencement of development), or which relate simply to the materials to be used or the provision of works of landscaping, or which are conditions which the buyer should reasonably accept. If this clause appears to be too objectively based for a developer's liking, he can be given control over the conditionality of the contract (in the same way as above) by having a clause which allows him to accept or reject the suitability of the permission, or to waive the benefit of the clause.

Time for performance

The condition must be satisfied either by a stipulated date, or if none is stated, by the contractual completion date, or if neither, within a reasonable time. It is good practice to stipulate in the contract a long-stop date by which the condition must be satisfied. The contract can then provide that if the condition is fulfilled by that date, completion is to take place within 14 or 21 days of the contract becoming unconditional. The contract should be drafted to oblige one party to notify the other that the contract has become unconditional (eg if the buyer receives the outstanding local search, then unless the seller is notified, the seller will not know that the contract has become unconditional, and that a completion date has been triggered).

If fulfilment of the condition depends upon action by one of the parties (eg the submission of a local search, or the making of an application for planning permission by the buyer) that party will not be able to rely upon his own inaction to argue that the contract has become unenforceable due to the non-fulfilment of the condition. To avoid this situation arising, the contract should place a contractual obligation upon the party of whom action is required to act with all reasonable speed and endeavour, and to pay the costs of the action required (eg search fees, planning application fees).

However, in *Jolley v Carmel* [2000] 43 EG 185, the Court of Appeal was prepared to adopt a construction of a conditional contract that was commercially realistic and practical, and to imply terms into it to that end. In particular, terms were implied that the buyer would use reasonable efforts to obtain planning permission within a reasonable time. What was reasonable would depend upon the circumstances that actually existed and would not be judged by an objective test. It was also implied that the seller would do nothing to hinder the grant of the planning permission. It was held that the buyer would not be in breach of the implied term to obtain planning permission so long as any delay in obtaining the permission was attributable to causes beyond its control and so long as it had not acted negligently or unreasonably.

7.2.2 Option agreements

Whilst a conditional agreement is useful to a developer who is trying to commit a landowner to a sale of land at a time when the developer is not able unconditionally to commit himself, option agreements have many more varying uses for the developer, and are particularly useful in his attempts to piece together a development site. The usual form of option agreement entered into with a landowner gives the grantee of the option the right, within a specified time, to serve notice upon the grantor requiring the latter to convey the property either at an agreed price, or at the market value of the property at the time the option notice is served. Under a conditional contract, unless the contract is drafted in a manner which favours the developer, the developer is usually obliged to complete the purchase at the contract price once the condition has been fulfilled, even though in the meantime market conditions have caused him to rethink the development. With option agreements, the buyer can exercise the option if he wants to, or he can let it lapse if market conditions are no longer in his favour.

Nature of an option

At one time, there was considerable academic debate (for good practical reasons) as to whether an option agreement was in the nature of a conditional contract, containing a condition precedent to performance which needed to be satisfied by the grantee by his serving a notice to exercise the option, or whether the agreement was simply an irrevocable offer (ie one not capable of being withdrawn), which the grantee could accept by service of an option notice, but until such time, no binding contract for the sale of the property had been entered into. The importance of the debate was that, if the latter view prevailed, the contract created by the service of the option notice would fall foul of the strict requirements of s 2 of the Law of Property (Miscellaneous Provisions) Act 1989, since, although the option notice might well incorporate, by reference to the option agreement, all of the agreed terms, it would not be signed by or on behalf of both parties.

These problems appear to have been resolved by the case of *Spiro v Glencrown Properties Ltd* [1991] Ch 537 where Hoffmann J conveniently described an option contract as a relationship 'sui generis ... not strictly speaking either an offer or a conditional contract' which had some of the characteristics of each, but not all of either. Whilst not declaring an option to be a conditional contract for every purpose, he was content to view an option for the purposes of s 2 in the light of its characteristics as a conditional contract, which therefore meant that the provisions of s 2 were satisfied.

Once the option agreement has been entered into, the grantee acquires an immediate equitable interest in the land which the grantee must protect by registration of a C(iv) land charge, or notice or caution.

Uses of options

An option agreement may be contemplated in the following situations.

(1) Where planning permission for development proposed by the developer has not yet been applied for, the developer may consider securing an option over the land before investing resources into making an application for permission. Once the application succeeds, the option can be exercised by the developer. This is very similar to a conditional agreement, but with an option, the developer may be able to delay the exercise of the option until he is prepared to part with his money and commence development, whereas under a conditional agreement, as soon as the condition has been satisfied, the developer will have to complete.

(2) Where the land proposed as the site for development is sub-divided amongst landowners, and there is no guarantee that all of them will sell. The developer can assemble the development site gradually, by acquiring options over each parcel of land. Once the entire site is under option, the developer can then apply for planning permission (it would not make financial sense to do so beforehand), and then once permission has been obtained, he could exercise each option.

(3) Where a developer developing a site feels that there is some prospect of his being able to expand the development at some future date, he may attempt to acquire an option over adjacent land which can be exercised when the prospect becomes a reality.

(4) Where a speculator attempts to acquire options over land where there is little immediate prospect of obtaining planning permission (eg because the land forms part of the green belt, or is land not allocated for any particular purpose in the local planning authority development plan). The developer may either adopt a wait-and-see approach in the hope that planning policy in the area changes, or (as is more likely to be the case) he may invest time and resources in seeking to influence planning policy to get the land released for development purposes

when the next draft development plan is being prepared. In this way, developers build up considerable land banks to be drawn upon when conditions are right.

Terms of an option

The option will grant the developer the right to acquire the property by serving a written notice on the grantor within a specified period. In an option agreement, time-limits are construed by the courts to be of the essence of the agreement. The option agreement should set out the correct method of serving the option notice, or alternatively incorporate the provisions of s 196 of the Law of Property Act 1925 (LPA 1925) into the agreement. In specifying a time for the service of the notice, care should be taken to ensure that the rule against perpetuities is not infringed, and that the grantor has sufficient powers vested in him to grant an option capable of being exercised within the time period proposed. *fee payable*

The option will be granted in consideration of an option fee, which can be nominal, but is more likely to be a considerable sum, depending upon the development potential of the land. A landowner, realising the intentions of the grantee, is not likely to grant a valuable interest to him except for adequate consideration. When the option is exercised, the agreement will usually require the land to be conveyed to the grantee for a further consideration (credit usually being given for the option fee already paid) which may be fixed by the agreement at the outset, or may be determined at the time of the exercise of the option either by reference to the market value of the land at that time or by reference to the development value of the land as ascertained by a valuation formula set out in the agreement. It should be noted that both the option agreement, and the subsequent conveyance of the land are subject to ad valorem stamp duty (at the normal rate, with appropriate certificates of value). Further, because of the VAT implications of the transaction, the developer should ensure that the agreement clearly states that the option fee and purchase price is inclusive of VAT. There are also CGT implications for the landowner, since an option is treated as an asset for CGT purposes, separate from the land itself, which is disposed of in consideration of the option fee.

Provision should be made in the agreement for the deduction of title and the raising of requisitions on title after the option notice is served, and for the other usual conveyancing steps which need to be taken before completion. It is usual for the option agreement to incorporate a set of conditions of sale (eg the Standard Commercial Property Conditions current at the time of the option agreement).

In many cases, the developer will want title to be deduced before the option agreement is entered into (requisitions on title then being barred), and he will require the seller to enter into a condition in the agreement not to incumber the land any further without the developer's consent.

7.3 SEARCHES AND ENQUIRIES

A buyer of development land (or other commercial property) will make the same pre-contract searches, and raise broadly similar pre-contract enquiries as a buyer of residential property. This part of the book does not intend to repeat sections of the LPC Resource Book *Property Law and Practice* (Jordans), rather it focuses upon the particular concerns of a buyer of a development site at the pre-contract stage.

7.3.1 Local search and enquiries

The usual form of application for a search and enquiries should be submitted to the local authority in duplicate together with the fee. A plan should be attached so that the local authority can identify the land concerned.

In commercial transactions, consideration ought to be given to the possibility of raising the optional enquiries which are set out in Part II of the local authority enquiry form, in addition to the usual Part I enquiries. To make an optional enquiry, the buyer's solicitor should place a tick in the appropriate box at section G on the front page of the enquiry form. An additional fee is payable in respect of each optional enquiry. These enquiries are designed to cover matters which are only relevant in particular kinds of transactions. By way of example, on the acquisition of a development site, the buyer's solicitor ought to consider raising the optional enquiry relating to the location of public footpaths or bridleways which may cross the development site (since consent of the local authority would be required in order to divert them), and the optional enquiry relating to the location of gas pipelines, to see if any run under or near the property (since this may affect development of the land). Prudent purchasers will opt for safety by paying for replies to all of the optional enquiries.

In perusing replies to Part I enquiries, particular attention should be given to information relating to planning matters affecting the property, the location of foul and surface water main drains, and access to the site over adopted highways.

Planning matters

The developer will want to know whether planning permission currently exists in respect of all or part of the site, or whether there have been any past applications for permission which have been unsuccessful. (The fact that an application for development was recently refused will be an important consideration for a developer.) He will also need to know what type of land use is currently indicated by the local planning authority in the development plans for the area in which the site is situated. Any existing or proposed tree preservation orders must be clearly pointed out to the developer.

Drainage

It will be important for the developer to establish how foul and surface water currently drains away from the property to the public sewers (ie through main drains, private drains, or watercourses) so that he can estimate whether the current drainage system will be able to cope with foul and surface drainage from the developed site, or whether new drains will have to be constructed. If the site is vacant land, there are unlikely to be any drains serving it and, therefore, he will need to know the location of the nearest public sewer where connection of newly constructed drains may be made.

Highways

The developer will need to know that immediate access to the site can be obtained from a public highway, and that there are no new highways proposed in the vicinity of the site which would adversely affect his development.

Some of the information to be gleaned from the enquiries may simply confirm matters already known to the developer through site inspections, surveys, and through discussions between the developer and the local authority regarding the possibility of obtaining planning permission to develop the site.

Contaminated land

There is a danger that a buyer of land will become liable to pay excessive clean-up costs in relation to contaminated land. See Chapter 6 as to this and the suggested ways of reducing the risk.

7.3.2 Enquiries of the seller

Pre-contract enquiries of the seller will be raised on one of the standard printed forms of enquiry or on the buyer's solicitors' own word-processed form of enquiry. Additional enquiries may be raised as the buyer's solicitor considers appropriate. These may focus upon discovering further information about the planning status of the site, the location of public drains and highways, and the suitability of the land for building purposes, and possible past contamination of the land. Again, information regarding these matters is often discoverable from other sources, but that alone should not be a sufficient reason for the seller to refuse to provide answers.

7.3.3 Survey and inspection

Even though the land may be vacant, the developer–client should be advised to commission a survey of the land. Primarily, his surveyor will be checking on the suitability of the land for building purposes, both in terms of land stability, and means of access and drainage. However, regard must also be had to the provisions of the Environment Act 1995 (EA 1995), and a thorough environmental survey of the land should be conducted to ensure that the developer does not acquire land which could have a potential clean-up liability under that Act.

For a number of reasons, an inspection of the property must always be conducted before exchange of contracts in order to:

(1) assist in establishing ownership of, or responsibility for boundary walls, hedges and fences;

(2) discover the existence of public or private rights of way which may be evidenced by worn footpaths, stiles, or breaks in the hedgerows;

(3) spot the presence of overhead electricity power lines which would prevent or impede development. If there are power lines, the land is likely to be subject to a written wayleave agreement between the landowner and the electricity company giving the company the right to maintain its supply across the land. A copy of the agreement should be requested from the seller;

(4) discover the rights of persons in occupation of the land. Solicitors are accustomed to thinking only in terms of a contributing spouse as the type of person who has occupiers' rights. However, with a development site, it is not unknown for a solicitor to overlook the presence of several cows in the corner of a field, which is unremarkable if the seller is a farmer, but could be serious if the cows are grazing by virtue of rights of common, or under an agricultural or farm business tenancy;

(5) ensure that adjoining landowners do not enjoy the benefit of easements of light or air which would impede the buyer's proposed development.

7.3.4 Special searches

The need to make a search of the commons register maintained by the county council will depend upon the type and location of the land being acquired, but the case of *G. & K. Ladenbau (UK) Ltd v Crawley and de Reya* [1978] 1 All ER 682 serves as a warning to all solicitors of the dangers of overlooking the necessity for conducting such a search in appropriate cases. In that case, solicitors were held to be negligent for not having carried out a search in respect of a site being acquired for a new factory development. If a rural site is being acquired, a search of the commons register should always be made. If an inner city industrial site is being acquired for redevelopment, such a search would appear to be inappropriate. However, between these two extremes there will be other cases where the buyer's solicitor is unsure as to whether or not such a search is necessary, and in those cases it would, therefore, be prudent to conduct a search.

Other special searches may be appropriate depending on the circumstances of the acquisition.

7.3.5 Investigation of title

Title is almost invariably deduced and investigated at pre-contract stage of the transaction.

A thorough investigation of title is required in the same way as in the case of residential property. The developer–client will be particularly concerned to ensure that the property enjoys the benefit of all necessary easements and rights of access (both for the purpose of developing, and for future occupiers of the completed development) and drainage (for foul and surface water). He will also need to be satisfied that there are no covenants restricting the proposed development or use of the land, or if there are, that they will be released, removed or modified, or that appropriate insurance will be available, and that any easements which burden the property will not prevent or restrict the proposed development or use.

Chapter 8

CONSTRUCTION PROJECTS

8.1 INTRODUCTION

Chapter 8 contents
Introduction
Who will be involved?
Duties owed to third
parties
Protecting other parties

Having completed the acquisition of a site which is physically capable of being developed, and which is not incumbered in a way which would impede development, and having obtained satisfactory planning permission and sufficient funds, the client will now want to obtain a building which will be completed within a satisfactory time scale, within budget, and in accordance with his specified requirements.

8.2 WHO WILL BE INVOLVED?

8.2.1 The employer

The employer is the owner of the site who will employ various professionals to design and construct a building upon his land. For the purposes of this book, the employer is a client who has acquired a site with the aim of developing it, and who will grant leases of the completed development. This part of the book assumes that the client, whilst involved in commercial property, is not a member of the construction industry, and will, therefore, need to employ other persons in connection with design and construction.

8.2.2 The building contractor

In a traditional building contract the building contractor is engaged by the employer to construct a building in accordance with plans and specifications prepared by the employer's architect. The contractor (sometimes called the 'main contractor') will enter into a building contract with the employer, although he may not necessarily carry out all, or indeed any, of the building works. Instead, the contractor may enter into sub-contracts with other builders who will carry out the work. The sub-contractors are likely to be specialists in particular areas of the construction industry, so that, in a large project, there may be several different sub-contractors who execute works on different parts of the development. In some building contracts, the employer chooses who will be the sub-contractors, in which case they are called 'nominated sub-contractors'. In other building contracts, it will be the main contractor's responsibility to select the sub-contractors, in which case they are termed 'domestic sub-contractors'. Most traditional forms of building contract only permit sub-contracting with the prior written consent of the employer (to be given through the agency of his architect).

There are many different standard forms of building contract used in the construction industry and this book does not intend a detailed analysis of the obligations of employer and main contractor. The basic obligations of the employer under most traditional forms of contract are to give up possession of the site to the contractor (to enable uninterrupted building to commence), not to interfere with the execution of building works, to appoint an architect for the purposes of the contract (ie to supervise the execution of the works, and to certify when the building has reached the stage of 'practical completion'), to nominate sub-contractors to carry out the works (unless the contractor is to select his own), and to pay the price payable to the contractor as and when the contract requires.

In return, the contractor agrees to complete the work set out in the contract in the form of the architect's plans and specifications. Whether the works have been satisfactorily completed is a matter to be judged by the architect who, if satisfied, will issue a certificate of practical completion which will entitle the contractor to receive full payment of the contract price, and the employer to resume possession of the site for the purpose of granting leases to his tenants. Obligations as to quality and fitness of the building materials are implied under s 4 of the Supply of Goods and Services Act 1982, and s 13 of that Act implies a term that the contractor will exercise reasonable care and skill in the performance of building services. However, notwithstanding his implied obligations, the contractor is likely to have entered into a building contract which contains an express obligation to execute the works in accordance with a standard prescribed by the contract.

It should be noted that there is no privity of contract between the employer and the sub-contractors (whether they are nominated or domestic) since it is the main contractor who engages their services. However, it may be possible to establish an implied collateral contract between them, as in *Shanklin Pier Co Ltd v Detel Products Ltd* [1951] 2 KB 854, and further the main contractor may also be liable under the terms of the main contract in respect of the acts or omissions of the sub-contractors.

Some more modern forms of building contract operate quite differently from the traditional form. Design-and-build contracts are increasingly being used in new developments. In simple terms, all of the design work is carried out by the main contractor's architect and, therefore, the employer does not engage an architect. The employer will enter into a single contract with the main contractor under which the contractor agrees both to design (or cause to be designed), and to build. This means that having indicated his requirements to the main contractor, all the employer has to do is wait for the building to be finished, whereupon he can grant a lease of the completed building to a tenant.

8.2.3 The architect

In a traditional form of contract the architect is engaged by the employer to carry out various tasks in relation to the design of the building. Broadly speaking, the architect prepares plans and specifications of the works required by the employer from which the builders will take their instructions, and he will supervise the execution of those works by the building contractor (or sub-contractors) in accordance with the plans and specifications. When the architect is satisfied that the works required by the building contract have been completed, he will issue a certificate of practical completion.

8.2.4 The quantity surveyor

The quantity surveyor is engaged by the employer (or by the architect on behalf of the employer) to estimate the quantities of the materials to be used, and to set them into bills of quantities. What the quantity surveyor does is to measure the amount of work and materials which will be necessary to complete construction in accordance with the architect's plans and specifications. On the basis of his bills of quantities, building contractors will be able to work out the amount of their tenders.

8.2.5 The engineers

In large construction projects, there may be a team of consulting engineers, including a structural engineer, engaged by the employer to give advice on structural design, and mechanical, electrical, heating and ventilating engineers, who give advice to the employer on matters within their areas of competence.

The architect, quantity surveyor and consulting engineers, as professional people, owe the employer a duty by contract to carry out the work required of them with proper care. The standard of care expected is the standard of the ordinary skilled man exercising and professing to have that special skill. If any one of them falls below that standard, or below any higher standard of care set by the contract of engagement under which he is engaged, he will be liable in damages for breach of contract.

8.3 DUTIES OWED TO THIRD PARTIES

If the project results in the employer obtaining a completed building which turns out to be defective by reason of its design, or the materials used, or by reason of the manner in which it was constructed, the employer is likely to have an action for breach of contract against those members of the design and construction team who caused the defect. Contractual damages are assessed under the rule in *Hadley v Baxendale* (1854) 9 Exch 341 and are likely to enable the employer to recover any costs incurred in carrying out remedial repairs, subject to the normal limitation rules under the Limitation Act 1980.

However, consider the position of a buyer from the employer who discovers a defect after completion of his purchase of the freehold; or that of a mortgagee of the freehold who discovers that the value of his security is seriously impaired because of a hidden design or construction defect; or that of a tenant of the building who enters into a lease on the basis of a full repairing covenant, which therefore obliges him to repair damage caused by such inherent defects. Traditionally, such third parties were unable to bring an action for breach of contract as they did not have a contractual relationship with the employer's development team. Because of the rules of privity of contract, the practice arose of members of the development team giving a collateral warranty with such parties in order to enable them to bring a claim; as to collateral warranties, see **8.4.1**. In the absence of such a collateral warranty, the only other potential remedy for a third party lay in tort. There are, however, problems in bringing such a claim, as to which, see **8.3.2** below.

8.3.1 Contracts (Rights of Third Parties) Act 1999

This Act came into force on 11 May 2000, and applies to contracts entered into on or after that date. It allows the parties to a contract to confer rights on third parties. A third party, such as a future tenant or mortgage lender, may enforce the contract as if he were a party to it, provided that the contract expressly provides that he may or that it purports to confer a benefit on him. The third party must be expressly identified in the contract by name, as a member of a class or as answering a particular description, but need not be in existence when the contract is entered into.

In theory, therefore, this Act provides a mechanism whereby third parties would be able to enforce the contractual obligations of the employer's development team, if, for example, the contract was stated to be for the benefit of 'all future tenants' of the building. However, at the time of writing, it seems that virtually all contracts with builders and professionals involved in the development process are expressly excluding this Act. One of the reasons for this is that, under s 2 of the Act, where a third party has been given rights under the Act, the contract cannot be amended or rescinded so as to vary those rights without the third party's consent. This prospect of having to obtain the consent of all relevant mortgage lenders, tenants or purchasers before the employer and the contractor or professionals are able to vary the terms of their original agreements, would be a major obstacle in practice to the efficient management of a development project. It seems likely, therefore, that for the time being at least, traditional forms of protection (eg tort or collateral warranties) will still need to be relied upon.

8.3.2 Liability in tort

In seeking to bring an action in tort, the problem that the buyer, lender or tenant will encounter is that any loss they sustain as a result of faulty design, materials or workmanship is likely to be classified as pure economic loss and, therefore, generally irrecoverable in tort. For example, in the case of the freehold buyer, if he discovers after completion of his purchase that the foundations of the building have been laid in a negligent fashion, so that the building cannot be used without remedial works first being carried out, he can either execute the repairs himself (thereby incurring repair costs), or dispose of the defective building to someone else (probably at less than the purchase price), or simply abandon the property (thereby wasting the money paid for the building in the first place); but whichever course of action the buyer takes, the loss he incurs is purely economic, and only in limited circumstances will the courts allow the plaintiff to recover such loss in tort.

To establish a claim in negligence the plaintiff will have to show that the defendant owed him a duty of care, that the defendant breached that duty, and that the plaintiff suffered an actionable form of damage as a result. Following a series of House of Lords' decisions in the late 1980s and early 1990s, it is safe to say that liability in the tort of negligence will only arise if there is a breach of one of two categories of duty. The first duty is based upon the decision in *M'Alister (or Donoghue) (Pauper) v Stevenson* [1932] AC 562 where liability will arise out of a lack of care which results in reasonably foreseeable damage to persons or to property (other than to the property which causes the damage). The second duty is founded upon the case of *Hedley Byrne & Co Ltd v Heller & Partners Ltd* [1964] AC 465 and is concerned with a lack of care which causes non-physical economic loss.

8.3.3 Liability for physical damage

The duty of care under *M'Alister (or Donoghue) (Pauper) v Stevenson* [1932] AC 562 is a duty to avoid physical injury to person or property. It imposes a duty upon the manufacturer of a product (eg a builder constructing a building) to take reasonable care to avoid damage to person or property through defects in the product. However, it does not impose a duty upon the manufacturer to ensure that the product itself is free from defects. Simply because the design or construction of the building is defective does not necessarily render the person who was responsible for the defect liable in damages, even if a duty was owed, and the damage was foreseeable. The case would turn upon whether the plaintiff suffered a type of loss recognised by the courts as legally recoverable. Pure economic loss (eg the cost of repairing the defect, and the loss of profits while repairs are carried out) is not recoverable under *Donoghue v Stevenson* principles.

In *D&F Estates Ltd v Church Commissioners for England* [1989] AC 177, the House of Lords held that liability in tort arises only where there is some physical damage to person, or to some other property, and that damage to the building itself which merely reduced its value, is pure economic loss, and thus irrecoverable in tort, (except under *Hedley Byrne v Heller* principles). In *Murphy v Brentwood District Council* [1990] 2 All ER 908, the House of Lords reaffirmed its earlier decision, and stated that the idea that component parts of the same building could amount to separate species of property, (the 'complex structure' theory) so that, for example, negligently laid foundations could be said to have damaged 'other' property when they led to cracks appearing in the walls, was not correct.

To give an example of what may be recoverable, consider the position where, after completion of his purchase of the freehold, a defectively constructed roof collapses and causes personal injury to a buyer. The buyer may be able to recover damages in respect of his personal injuries, and any economic loss arising out of those injuries (eg loss of earnings), but he will not be able to recover the cost of repairing the roof itself since that loss is pure economic loss.

8.3.4 Liability for economic loss

Economic loss is a term which can be used to describe any monetary loss. Pure economic loss is monetary loss which is not connected to physical injury to person or property. With one or two isolated and doubtful exceptions (see eg *Junior Books v Veitchi* [1983] 1 AC 520), pure economic loss is only recoverable in tort where, in a special relationship of close proximity, a duty of care is owed to avoid loss arising from a negligent misstatement. In *Hedley Byrne & Co Ltd v Heller & Partners Ltd* [1964] AC 465, the House of Lords decided that, in a relationship of close proximity, where a person was seeking information from one who was possessed of certain skills, a duty was owed by the latter to exercise reasonable care if he knew, or ought to have known that reliance was being placed upon his skill and judgment. Put simply, the duty amounts to a duty to prevent pure economic loss arising from the making of a statement, or the giving of advice. In the context of a building project, many statements are made, and much advice is given, but proximity of the parties, and reliance are the fundamental factors.

The extent of this duty has recently been restated and redefined by the House of Lords in *Caparo Industries plc v Dickman* [1990] 2 AC 605. It is now the case that, in order for there to be the requisite degree of proximity between the parties for the duty to arise, the defendant (ie the person who made the statement, or gave the advice) must have known (both in the preparation of what was said, and in the delivery) that the statement would be communicated to an identified person or group of persons in connection with a transaction of a particular type, and that the recipient would be very likely to rely upon it.

Whilst the employer, by reason of his contractual relationship with his professional advisers (eg the architect, or structural engineer) might easily establish the requisite degree of proximity, and show reliance upon the advice given, his tenant, buyer, or the buyer's lender are unlikely to be able to show the requisite proximity. In other words, the pure economic loss that a successor in title to the employer suffers remains irrecoverable.

As a result of this inability to recover the cost of repairing damage to the building outside a contractual relationship, various devices have been utilised by buyers, their lenders, tenants, and the employer's own financiers.

8.4 PROTECTING OTHER PARTIES

8.4.1 Collateral warranties

A collateral warranty is an agreement (under hand or by deed) entered into by someone engaged in the construction or design of a building by virtue of which that person assumes a contractual duty of care for the benefit of someone who has an interest in seeing that the building is free from defects, but who does not otherwise have a contractual relationship with the warrantor. Collateral warranties are commonly required to be given by the consultants, the main contractor and the sub-contractors to the freehold buyer, his lender, the developer's financiers, and possibly (if negotiated) the tenant. With one exception, the employer does not need warranties, as he is in a contractual relationship with his design and construction team. However, he will require warranties from the sub-contractors with whom the employer has no direct contractual relationship.

The advantages of warranties are twofold. First, they create the certainty of a contractual relationship, as opposed to the uncertainty that exists in tort. All the plaintiff would need to show in order to establish a claim is that the contractual duty contained in the warranty had been breached, and that damage had ensued. Secondly, the beneficiary of the warranty is likely to be able to recover in contract loss that can be described as purely economic. All the plaintiff has to show in this regard is that the loss suffered as a result of the breach of warranty could reasonably be said to have been in the contemplation of the parties at the time the warranty was entered into.

The main disadvantage of collateral warranties appears to be that the Latent Damage Act 1986 which, in certain situations, extends the limitation period for bringing civil actions, does not apply to claims for breach of contract and, therefore, if defects do not manifest themselves until more than 6 years after the warranty was entered into (or 12 years if by deed), no action can then be brought.

Many firms of solicitors have their own preferred form of collateral warranty and, although attempts have been made to standardise the type of warranty to be used in the construction industry, those attempts have not always been enthusiastically received. In practice, the terms of collateral warranties are being dictated increasingly by the warrantor's professional indemnity insurers, who are concerned to limit their potential liability. Most warranties will contain a basic warranty by the warrantor that he has exercised and will continue to exercise reasonable skill and care in the performance of his duties under the contract of engagement with the employer, and that the warrantor will maintain professional indemnity insurance with cover up to a stated amount. There is usually a clause preventing or restricting the assignment of the benefit of the warranty. It is extremely unlikely that warranties will be given after the professional has been engaged. It is therefore essential that the professional is contractually committed to give warranties by the contract of engagement.

It seems that an action in contract arising out of a breach of a collateral warranty will not exclude an alternative action in tort (if a cause of action exists). In *Henderson v Merrett Syndicates Ltd* [1994] 3 All ER 506, Lord Goff said that 'an assumption of responsibility, coupled with the concomitant reliance, may give rise to a tortious duty of care irrespective of whether there is a contractual relationship between the parties, and in consequence, unless the contract precludes him from doing so, the plaintiff, who has available to him concurrent remedies in contract and tort, may choose that remedy which appears to him to be the most advantageous'.

8.4.2 Other methods

Assignment of rights

The employer may consider attempting to satisfy the demands of his financier, buyer or tenant for protection against latent defects by assigning whatever rights the employer may have (primarily under contract law) against the contractor and the consultants. An assignment is probably only appropriate if made in favour of a financier, a buyer or a tenant of the whole of the development site. However, even where a tenant takes a lease of the whole of a development site, a landlord will be reluctant to part with his contractual rights in case the tenant's lease is forfeited or disclaimed.

Building contracts and contracts for the engagement of consultants may contain prohibitions on the assignment of the benefit of the contract without consent and it now seems that, following the House of Lords' decision in *Linden Garden Trust Ltd v Lenesta Sludge Disposals Ltd*, and *St Martins Property Corporation Ltd v Sir Robert McAlpine & Sons Ltd* [1993] 3 WLR 408, most prohibitions will be effective, although each clause will have to be interpreted to discover its exact meaning.

Declaring a trust of rights

Declaring a trust of rights may be considered as an alternative to an outright assignment where the employer is retaining an interest in the property and, therefore, does not wish to part with valuable contractual rights. In this way the employer can retain the benefit of the rights he has against the contractor and consultants, but declares that he holds them upon trust for the benefit of himself and his tenants.

Latent defects insurances

With residential properties, buyers are anxious to ensure that a newly constructed property is covered by the NHBC scheme, or other equivalent insurance. In the commercial field, there are no such standard schemes. However, following the BUILD report (Building Users Insurance against Latent Defects) published in 1988 by the National Economic Development Office, several of the leading insurance companies in the UK have introduced latent defects insurance in respect of commercial properties.

Policies will vary from company to company (and, indeed, from development to development), but the essential elements are likely to be similar across the board.

Latent defect insurance commonly provides cover against damage caused by defective design or construction works for a period of 10 years after practical completion of the development (or such longer period as may be agreed with the insurer). The beneficiary of the policy is covered against the cost of making good most (but not necessarily all) damage caused by a design or construction defect (although not other risks), and the policy may cover other items of economic loss such as loss of rent, or loss of use of the building whilst repairs are being carried out. The policy can be taken out to cover the employer (as initial owner of the building) and his financiers. Most policies will also automatically insure subsequent owners and occupiers, which will obviously be the desired aim from the employer's point of view. The premium is likely to be substantial (perhaps 1.5% of development costs).

The advantages of such a policy is that there is no need for the claimant under the policy to establish legal liability for the damage incurred, and there ought to be easy access to funds to finance repairing costs and, possibly, to cover other economic loss. The disadvantages are that, as with other policies, the insurance may be subject to excesses (meaning that the claimant might have to fund, say, the first £50,000 of a claim), and that the insurer will invariably require some element of supervision over the execution of the works, since the risk he is taking on will be considerable. Such insurance is not something which can be obtained economically after the construction process is complete.

Proposals have been put to the European Commission regarding compulsory insurance of all new residential, commercial and civil engineering construction projects (see the Mathurin Report 1990) and legislation in this area may eventually materialise.

Limiting repair covenants

In a landlord and tenant relationship, the tenant should consider limiting the scope of his repairing covenant. The main problem for a tenant is that the landlord is likely to insist upon the tenant entering into a lease which contains a covenant by the tenant to repair the demised premises. Provided the damage amounts to disrepair (see **17.2.6**), the usual repair covenant imposed by the landlord will oblige the tenant to repair damage which is caused by a defect in the design or construction of the building. Whilst the tenant can commission a full structural survey of the premises prior to the grant of the lease in an effort to discover defects, the very nature of a design or construction defect makes it unlikely that it will exhibit itself until some time after the building has been completed and the lease granted.

It is, therefore, suggested that, on the grant of a lease of a relatively new building, the tenant should attempt to limit the scope of his repairing covenant by excluding (either totally, or for a limited period of, say, 3 or 6 years after the grant of the lease) liability to repair damage caused by an inherent, or latent, design or construction defect. Not only should the tenant seek to exclude such liability from his own covenant, but he should make sure that no vacuum is left in the repairing obligations under the lease by insisting that the landlord assumes this liability. If this is not done, there is a risk that the property may remain in disrepair. The landlord will be anxious to avoid having to bear any repair costs in respect of the building, and so the limitation of the tenant's repairing obligations is a matter to be negotiated and will depend upon the relative bargaining strengths of the parties. It is most unlikely that the tenant would succeed in his negotiations if, in the agreement for lease, the tenant had insisted upon a degree of control and supervision over the execution of the landlord's works (see **26.3.4**). The landlord would probably argue that the tenant had had every opportunity before the lease was granted to discover defects, and that he should, therefore, consider taking action against his professional advisers.

On the grant of a lease of part of a building, where the tenant would not ordinarily undertake repairing responsibilities in respect of the structure and external parts, but would instead be expected to contribute by way of service charge to the landlord's costs incurred in maintaining those parts, the tenant would seek to ensure that he was not obliged to contribute to the landlord's costs of repairing damage caused by design or construction defects (either throughout the term, or for a limited period). Again, whilst the tenant could commission a full structural survey, design defects may not be apparent at the time of the survey, or may be hidden in some other part of the building to which the surveyor was unable to gain access.

Defect liability periods

In a landlord and tenant relationship, the tenant may seek the benefit of a defect liability period. If the landlord will not agree to exclude the tenant's liability for inherent defects in the lease, the tenant ought to press for the inclusion of a clause in the agreement for lease obliging the landlord to remedy any defects which appear within a short period of time following practical completion of the building. If the landlord agrees to the inclusion of a defects liability period, it is likely to mirror a similar clause in the building contract entered into with the contractor. Quite often, building contracts provide for the contractor to remedy any defects which manifest themselves within, say, the first 6 or 12 months after practical completion. By including a similar clause in the agreement for lease, the landlord is indirectly passing on the benefit of the clause to the tenant.

Forced enforcement of remedies

A tenant may seek a side letter, or supplemental deed from his landlord whereby the landlord agrees to enforce any rights he may have against the contractor or the consultants, by way of civil proceedings, in respect of defects which would otherwise render the tenant liable to repair under the repairing covenant. However, whether the landlord suffers any loss upon which an action could be based is doubtful where the tenant has entered into a full repairing lease.

A buyer, financier or tenant may seek the inclusion of a provision whereby the employer agrees to enforce his rights as original contracting party against the contractor or the consultants in respect of defects where loss or liability to repair would otherwise fall upon the former. Difficulties have arisen in this area in that, if the employer has received full market value on a sale of the property to a buyer, or has secured the inclusion of a full repairing covenant on the grant of a lease of the property to a tenant, he cannot be said to have suffered any loss upon which an action could be maintained.

However, the House of Lords' decision in the *Linden Garden* case has shown that in a commercial contract where it was in the contemplation of the contracting parties that title to the property which formed the subject matter of the contract might be transferred to a third party before a breach had occurred, the original contracting party is taken to have entered into the contract for the benefit of himself and all persons who may acquire an interest in the property before the breach occurs. What this means is that, in certain circumstances, the employer may be able to recover damages for breach of contract in respect of loss incurred by his buyer, financier or tenant. This area is not without its complications, and the full ramifications of recent developments in this area have not yet been explored.

PART II

COMMERCIAL LEASES

Chapter 9

LANDLORD AND TENANT LAW AND COMMERCIAL LEASES

9.1 INTRODUCTION

A thorough knowledge and understanding of landlord and tenant law is essential for all commercial conveyancers; without such an understanding it would be impossible to properly advise clients on their rights and liabilities under the lease. Consequently, this part of the book starts with a consideration of the more important principles governing the relationship between landlords and tenants of business premises.

Chapter 9 contents
Introduction
Liability of the parties on the covenants in the lease
Security of tenure
Lease/licence distinction

9.2 LIABILITY OF THE PARTIES ON THE COVENANTS IN THE LEASE

The detailed rules relating to the enforceability of covenants are considered in Chapter 12. The following is intended only as an outline of the main issues involved.

9.2.1 Leases granted before 1 January 1996

Position of the original parties

Unless the lease provides to the contrary, the original parties will remain liable on their express covenants in the lease by privity of contract throughout the whole term, despite any disposition of their interests. Thus, the original tenant must appreciate that he will be liable not just for breaches committed whilst he is the tenant but also for any breach of covenant committed by his successors. This continuing liability may have serious consequences for the original tenant and means, for example, that he will be liable for any arrears of rent occurring throughout the whole term.

In the same way, through privity of contract, the original landlord will remain liable on his covenants to the original tenant for the whole term, despite any assignment by him of the reversion, ie he will be liable to the original tenant if a buyer of the reversion breaks a covenant.

Position of landlord and tenant for the time being

The relationship between an assignee of the lease and the landlord for the time being and between a buyer of the reversion and the tenant for the time being rests on the doctrine of privity of estate. Liability under this doctrine extends only to those covenants which touch and concern the land.

Further, a party is only liable for breaches committed during his period of ownership of the lease or reversion, as the case may be. Thus, for example, an assignee of the lease, for the period while he has the lease, has the benefit of the landlord's covenants and is liable on the tenant's covenants provided, in both cases, the covenants touch and concern the land.

9.2.2 Leases granted on or after 1 January 1996

The Landlord and Tenant (Covenants) Act 1995 (LTCA 1995) abolished the concept of privity of contract for leases entered into on or after 1 January 1996. Thus once the original tenant has assigned the lease he is not liable for any future breaches (although he may be required to guarantee his immediate assignee: see **18.2.7**). On a sale of the reversion, the landlord may apply to the tenant for release from the landlord's covenants in the lease (see **12.2.2**).

9.3 SECURITY OF TENURE

The majority of business tenants will enjoy security of tenure under Part II of the Landlord and Tenant Act 1954 (LTA 1954) and the importance of this Act in its effect on termination of the lease cannot be overstated. The protection given to tenants covered by the Act is two-fold. First, a business tenancy will not come to an end at the expiration of a fixed term, nor can a periodic tenancy be terminated by the landlord serving an ordinary notice to quit. Instead, notwithstanding the ending of the contractual term, the tenancy will be automatically continued under s 24 until such time as it is terminated in one of the ways specified in the Act. Secondly, upon the expiration of a business tenancy in accordance with the Act, business tenants normally have a statutory right to apply to court for a new tenancy and the landlord may only oppose that application on certain statutory grounds (some of which involve the payment of compensation by the landlord if the tenant has to leave). Any new tenancy granted will also enjoy the protection of the Act.

It is possible, in certain circumstances, for the landlord and tenant to apply to court to contract out of the Act, but certain formalities must be observed.

Further consideration of this Act is dealt with in Chapter 31.

9.4 LEASE/LICENCE DISTINCTION

The security of tenure provisions in the LTA 1954 and other statutory provisions dealt with later do not apply to licences. It therefore becomes necessary to examine the distinction between a lease and a licence. A lease is an interest in land. A licence, on the other hand, confers no interest in land; it merely authorises that which would otherwise be a trespass. One of the leading cases in this area is *Street v Mountford* [1985] 2 All ER 289. Whilst this case concerned a residential tenancy, similar principles have subsequently been applied to business tenancies. Subject to certain exceptions, for example, lack of intention to create legal relations or occupation pending the grant of a lease, the House of Lords held that as a general rule:

(1) the grant of exclusive possession,
(2) for a term,
(3) at a rent,

will create a tenancy rather than a licence; and the court will ignore any shams or pretences aimed at misleading the court.

In the context of business premises, some arrangements will clearly not confer exclusive possession and will thus remain licences, for example, the 'shop within a

Licence

Licence

'shop' sometimes found in department stores, or the kiosks often found in theatres or hotel foyers. Moreover, there seems to be a greater readiness by the courts to find that exclusive possession was not granted than is the case with residential premises (see, eg, *Esso Petroleum Co Ltd v Fumegrange Ltd* [1994] 46 EG 199 and *National Car Parks Ltd v Trinity Development Co (Banbury) Ltd* [2001] EWCA Civ 1686, [2001] 28 EG 144).

To avoid the risk inadvertently of creating a lease, the use of licences needs very careful consideration. As an alternative, the parties should consider the 'contracting out' provisions in the LTA 1954.

Chapter 10

AN OUTLINE OF TAXATION OF COMMERCIAL PROPERTIES

10.1 VALUE ADDED TAX

Chapter 10 contents
Value added tax
Stamp duty on leases

At the outset of any property transaction, it is essential to consider the impact of VAT legislation, and to advise the client accordingly. One of the aims of the Finance Act 1989 was to bring UK law into line with EC Law by bringing many property transactions and the provision of construction and other services within the scope of VAT. The reader will already be aware of the basic principles of VAT, which dictate that VAT may be payable in respect of a supply of goods or services made in the course of a business. Whether VAT is payable depends upon a number of things including whether the supplies in question are exempt, zero-rated or standard-rated. The reader will also be aware of the effects of such supplies, the payment and receipt of input and output tax, and the recovery of VAT incurred.

Supplies of goods and services made in relation to a property transaction can be grouped as follows.

(1) Residential properties:

    (a) sale of a green field site: exempt (but subject to the option to tax, as to which, see **10.1.3**);

    (b) construction services: zero-rated;

    (c) civil engineering works: zero-rated;

    (d) professional services (eg legal and other professional fees): standard-rated;

    (e) sale of a new house: zero-rated;

    (f) grant of a lease of a new house (for a term exceeding 21 years): zero-rated.

(2) Commercial properties:

    (a) sale of a green field site: exempt (but subject to the option to tax);

    (b) construction services: standard-rated;

    (c) civil engineering works: standard-rated;

    (d) professional services: standard-rated;

    (e) sale of a new freehold building or the grant of an option to purchase such a building: standard-rated;

    (f) sale of an old freehold building: exempt (but subject to the option to tax);

    (g) the grant of a lease (for any length of term): exempt (but subject to the option to tax);

    (h) the assignment of a lease: exempt (but subject to the option to tax);

    (i) the surrender of a lease: exempt (but subject to the option to tax by the person who receives the consideration);

    (j) repair, alteration and demolition works: standard-rated.

Rules relating to work carried out on listed buildings are not considered in this book, and the particular problems associated with premises of mixed use are also outside the scope of this book.

Some of the supplies listed above are exempt supplies, but are subject to what is called the 'option to tax' (also known as the 'option to waive exemption'). This is dealt with more comprehensively at **10.1.3**. What the option means is that the person who makes the supply can voluntarily convert the supply from one which is exempt and, therefore, gives rise to no VAT liability into a standard-rated supply.

The VAT consequences arising in residential and commercial developments are now considered.

10.1.1 Residential developments

In a typical new residential development, the VAT consequences will not be too complicated. If, for example, a property company, ABC Limited, buys a green field site, the seller is making an exempt supply to ABC Limited which will not be subject to VAT unless the seller, being a taxable person, has elected to waive the exemption. In any event if, as is often the case, the seller is a private individual, he is not likely to be selling the land in the course of a business, and the supply will, therefore, be outside the scope of VAT. Any construction services (such as work provided by builders and the provision of materials) and civil engineering works (such as the construction of the roads and sewers serving the development) supplied to ABC Limited will be supplied at a zero-rate of VAT. It is, therefore, probable that the only significant VAT incurred by the property company in constructing the residential development will be in respect of professional fees paid to surveyors, solicitors, architects and selling agents for services supplied.

On completion of construction, ABC Limited will dispose of the houses. The purchase price payable on the freehold sale of a newly built house, or the premium (or rent) payable in respect of a lease of the house granted for a term exceeding 21 years does not attract VAT. These supplies are zero-rated. However, when zero-rated supplies are made, whilst no VAT is paid for the supply, tax is deemed to be charged at a nil rate on the output (so that they are still technically regarded as taxable supplies) and therefore related input tax incurred can be recovered. What this means is that ABC Limited will account to HM Customs & Excise for output tax on supplies made (which will be nil), less input tax on related supplies received (ie the VAT paid on professional fees). This clearly leads to a deficit which means that a refund of VAT will be due from HM Customs & Excise.

A subsequent sale of a dwelling (either freehold or leasehold) will be made by a private individual and will not, therefore, be made in the course of a business. In the event that the sale is made in the course of a business (eg by a relocation company), the supply would be exempt.

10.1.2 Commercial developments

In a typical new commercial development, the same process can be followed, with different VAT consequences. The sale of a green field site to a developer is again an exempt supply, subject to the option to tax. However, the provision of construction services and civil engineering works to a commercial developer are standard-rated supplies, which means that considerable VAT will be incurred in addition to VAT on the standard-rated supply of professional services.

Once the building has been completed, the developer may either sell the freehold, or grant a lease of it to a tenant. The sale of a 'new' or partially completed building is a standard-rated supply. VAT must be charged in respect of the purchase price. In this context, a 'new' building is one which was completed within the 3 years preceding the sale, and 'completion' of a building takes place on the earlier of either the day upon which the certificate of practical completion was issued by the architect or the day upon which the building was completely occupied. The grant of a lease of all or part of commercial premises (whether new or old) is an exempt supply, subject to the right of the landlord to opt to tax the rents, premium and other sums payable under the lease. In both cases, whether the freehold sale or the grant of a commercial lease, the developer is able to charge VAT, either because it is a standard-rated supply, or because the exemption has been waived. This means that output tax will be received to facilitate recovery of related input tax incurred.

Take, by way of example, a commercial development where the construction costs paid by the developer amount to £2 million (with VAT on a standard-rated supply of £350,000), the cost of roads and sewers amounts to £500,000 (with £87,500 VAT) and professional fees total £100,000 (with £17,500 VAT). The total input tax paid by the developer adds up to £455,000.

If the developer, being a taxable person, is able to sell the 'new' freehold building for £4 million, he will have to charge VAT amounting to £700,000. This output tax can be set against related input tax incurred, resulting in only the difference (£245,000) having to be accounted for to HM Customs & Excise. The developer suffers from cash flow difficulties in that he is likely to incur the input tax some time in advance of receiving the output tax, but he is not left out of pocket. The same result will be achieved if, instead of selling the freehold, the developer chooses to grant a lease of the building and elects to charge VAT on the sums payable under the lease. The making of the election facilitates immediate recovery of related input tax.

10.1.3 The option to charge VAT

The election to waive exemption or, as it is more commonly called, the option to tax was introduced on 1 August 1989 in order to lessen the impact of the VAT changes on commercial developers. The purpose of the option to tax is to enable the commercial owner to convert what would otherwise be exempt supplies in respect of a particular property into supplies chargeable to VAT at the standard rate, so that the developer will be able to recover the input tax which he incurred when acquiring or developing the property.

The consequence of making the election is that all future grants in the property by the person who makes the election will be subject to VAT at the standard rate.

How is the election made?

As a preliminary to waiving the exemption, the owner must check that he is registered for VAT, or else the election will be meaningless. There is no prescribed form or procedure for electing, nor is there any requirement to consult with or notify anyone who might be affected by the election. However, from a practical point of view, it is advisable that a landlord notifies his tenants, since it is the tenants who will bear the VAT. The one procedural requirement that must be followed when making the election is that written notice of the election must be given to HM Customs & Excise within 30 days of the election.

If an exempt supply (eg the grant of a lease) has been made by the elector in respect of the relevant property since 1 August 1989, consent of HM Customs & Excise will be required before the election can be made, and consent will only be granted if HM Customs & Excise are satisfied that the input tax which the elector will be able to recover as a consequence of his making the election is fair and reasonable. It is therefore advisable for a landlord intending to make an election to do so before he grants a lease of his property.

In all other cases, consent of HM Customs & Excise is not required.

Since the purpose of making the election is to charge VAT, the elector should ensure that he is registered for VAT.

Who or what is affected?

The election is personal, done on a property-by-property basis and, once made, it may only be revoked within 3 months of the election, or after 20 years (see the Value Added Tax (Buildings and Land) Order 1995). The fact that the election is personal means that whilst a landlord who elects to waive the exemption would have to charge VAT on the rents payable by its tenants, its tenants would not, unless they too elected, have to charge VAT to their sub-tenants, and the same applies to a buyer of the landlord's interest. As an exception to the general rule, an election made by a company in respect of a property will bind other companies (in respect of that property) if they are in the same VAT group of companies at the time of the election, or joined the group later, when the property affected was still owned by a group company.

The fact that the election is made on a property-by-property basis means that a commercial owner can pick and choose which of its properties should be voluntarily standard-rated. Once made, the election affects the whole of the property or, if the elector owns an interest in only part of the property, it will affect the entirety of that part. Hence, the elector cannot choose to waive the exemption in respect of the ground floor and not the upper two floors if he owns the entire building. What may appear to be separate buildings, but which are linked together internally or by covered walkways are to be treated as one building. Therefore, if a shopping precinct is owned by one landlord (as is usually the case) an election by that landlord will affect all of the shops in the precinct.

Should the election be made?

The reason for making the election is to facilitate the recovery of related input tax incurred on the acquisition or development of the property. If no related input tax has been or is likely to be incurred, there is no reason why the election should be made. If considerable input tax has been or will be incurred, consideration must be given to whether or not the election should be made, but the elector must have regard to the effect that the election will have on the persons to whom supplies are being made.

If a developer-landlord, having incurred VAT on acquisition or development costs, wants to waive the exemption and charge VAT on the rents it will receive from its tenants, and those tenants make mainly standard-rated or zero-rated supplies in the course of their businesses (eg tenants of retail foodstores, solicitors or surveyors offices), the tenants would not be adversely affected by a charge to VAT on rent, since there will be output tax (actual or deemed) to offset against the input tax. The tenants will not end up out of pocket.

Tenants who make only exempt supplies in the course of their businesses (eg banks, building societies, insurance companies) will be hard hit by the election. The VAT that these tenants have to pay on the rent will be irrecoverable, and will have to be borne as an overhead of the business. This could have the effect of frightening off a class of tenants whom the developer might have been hoping to attract to the development or lead to their reducing the amount of rent that they would be prepared to pay.

The Finance Act 1997 makes provision for a limited disapplication of the election where the ultimate end-user of the property occupies wholly or mainly for exempt purposes and was involved in some way in the acquisition, construction or financing of the property. The provision is an anti-avoidance device and the circumstances in which the disapplication will apply will be few and far between.

10.1.4 Drafting points

Is the election on its own sufficient to render VAT payable by the person who receives the supply? It is necessary to look at two principal relationships: seller and buyer, and landlord and tenant.

Seller and buyer

If a seller sells a 'new' commercial building (whether it is the first sale or a subsequent sale of the still 'new' building) the seller is making a standard-rated supply, and so there will be mandatory VAT on the purchase price. The basic rule is that, unless the contrary appears, the purchase price stated in the contract is deemed to include VAT. It is, therefore, important that the seller includes a clause in the contract obliging the buyer to pay VAT in addition to the purchase price. Failure to do so will result in the seller having to account to HM Customs & Excise for the VAT out of the purchase price received which, at current rates, will mean that the seller will be left with seven forty-sevenths less than he anticipated. This can result in the seller incurring a huge loss, for which his solicitor would no doubt be liable in negligence. Consider a sale at a price of £1 million. If an express provision is included in the contract, the buyer will have to pay £1.175 million to complete, HM Customs & Excise will get the VAT on the purchase price, and the seller will be left with £1 million. If the express clause is left out, the buyer need only pay £1,000,000 to complete, out of which HM Customs & Excise will get £148,936 leaving the seller with only £851,064.

If the seller sells an old commercial building (ie one which is now more than 3 years old) then the supply which is being made is an exempt supply and the position is different. If the seller waives the exemption before exchange then he converts the supply into a standard-rated supply and the above paragraph would then be applicable. The seller would have to make an express provision in the contract. If the exemption is waived after exchanging contracts then, under s 89 of the Value Added Tax Act 1994 (VATA 1994), the option to tax would operate as a change in the rate of tax from 0% to 17.5% (ie from an exempt to a standard-rated supply) and accordingly the seller could add VAT to the purchase price, without the need for an express clause in the contract enabling him to do so. In this case, it is important that the buyer's solicitor ensures that the contract makes it clear that the purchase price is inclusive of VAT so that no hardship is felt by the buyer if the seller chooses to elect after exchange. Only if the contract expressly excludes s 89, or the purchase price is expressly stated to be payable inclusive of VAT, will the seller be unable to add VAT to the purchase price.

Landlord and tenant

The grant of a commercial lease (of either an old or new building) is an exempt supply, unless the landlord has opted to tax. In respect of existing leases, s 89 of the VATA 1994 again operates so that an election by the landlord after the grant of the lease effects a change in the rate of VAT from 0% to 17.5%. The landlord does not need the benefit of an express clause in the lease, and can simply add VAT to the rent (and other sums payable under the lease) unless there is a clause in the lease (which would not usually be the case) expressly exonerating the tenant from liability to VAT on such payments, or excluding s 89.

If the election is made before the grant of the lease, so that the supply is converted to a standard-rated supply from the outset, s 89 will not operate, and the rent will be deemed to be payable inclusive of VAT. It is, therefore, essential that the landlord's solicitor ensures that the lease contains a covenant by the tenant to pay VAT on the rent (and the other sums payable under the lease). Whenever a lease is drafted, irrespective of whether advantage can be taken of s 89, there ought to be a covenant by the tenant to pay VAT in addition to the sums payable under the lease. This avoids problems for the landlord.

10.1.5 Other areas of concern

VAT is a far-reaching tax in the property world which can impact on other aspects of property transactions.

Reverse premiums and rent-free periods

A reverse premium is a payment made by the landlord to a prospective tenant as an inducement to him to enter the lease. Money is passing from landlord to tenant, and is the consideration for a supply being made by the tenant. This payment will be subject to VAT and the tenant should ensure that the terms of the contract allow this to be added to the payment. The landlord will not, however, be able to recover this VAT as input tax if, when granting the lease, he is making an exempt supply. So the cost to the landlord will be increased by 17½%. The landlord could recover this VAT if he elected to tax in respect of the property, but this would also mean that he would have to charge VAT on the rent. This would then be a particular problem for exempt tenants, such as banks or insurance companies, as the VAT on the rent will not be recoverable and they may wish to try and negotiate a lower rent to compensate for this.

Rent-free periods give rise to difficult VAT problems. It appears that if the rent-free period is being given because the tenant is carrying out work to the premises which will benefit the landlord, or simply because the landlord is trying to induce the tenant to enter into the lease (as an alternative to a reverse premium), then VAT at the standard rate will be payable on the amount of rent forgone. The tenant is making a supply to the landlord (ie is positively doing something) in consideration of a rent-free period. However, if the rent-free period is given simply because the state of the market means that it is part of the bargain negotiated between landlord and tenant (eg where it is given to allow the tenant some time in which to fit out the premises for his own benefit, or arrange sub-lettings), there will be no VAT on the rent-free period, since nothing is being done in return for it.

Surrenders

When a tenant surrenders his lease to the landlord, consideration may move in either direction, either because the tenant is desperate to rid himself of the liability to pay rent and perform the covenants, or because the landlord is anxious to obtain vacant possession. By virtue of the Value Added Tax (Land) Order 1995, the supply made in either case is an exempt supply, subject to the option to tax by the person who receives the consideration.

Where a surrender is effected by operation of law, it is unclear whether any VAT can be claimed by HM Customs & Excise. Indeed, it may be difficult to establish the value of the supply being made. If such a surrender is to arise, it may be advisable to ensure that liability for VAT is clearly documented by the parties before surrender occurs.

Transfers of going concerns

There are complicated rules regarding the transfer of a going concern, which can include the sale of a tenanted building. However, these rules are outside the scope of this book.

VAT on costs

Sometimes, a lease will oblige the tenant to pay the landlord's legal costs incurred on the grant of the lease. Often, a lease will oblige the tenant to pay the landlord's legal costs on an application for licence to assign, or alter, or change use. The position as regards VAT on those costs is complicated by the approach of HM Customs & Excise, which treats the payment of the landlord's legal costs, in either case, as part of the overall consideration for the grant of the lease. Hence, the VAT position depends upon whether the landlord has opted to waive the exemption.

If the landlord's solicitor charges his client £1,000 plus VAT for legal services provided on the grant of the lease, he will issue his client with a VAT invoice requiring payment of £1,000 plus VAT of £175. The landlord, having waived the exemption in respect of this property, and making use of his VAT invoice, will be able to recover the input tax (£175) from the output tax which he will receive on the rents. If the lease contains a clause obliging the tenant to pay those legal costs, the landlord will look to the tenant for a reimbursement of the outstanding £1,000. However, since HM Customs & Excise treats such a payment as part of the consideration for the grant of the lease, and since the landlord has waived the exemption, the tenant must pay £1,000 plus VAT, the landlord must issue the tenant with a VAT invoice, and the landlord must account to HM Customs & Excise for the VAT element received. The tenant may be able to recover the VAT which he has paid, depending on the nature of his business.

If the landlord has not waived the exemption, the position is different. First, he will not be able to recover the VAT charged by his solicitor, since that VAT was incurred in relation to an exempt supply. Secondly, therefore, he will require the tenant to reimburse the full amount of costs and VAT (ie £1,175), but because this reimbursement is treated as part of the consideration for the grant of the lease, and because the supply made by the landlord is an exempt supply, no VAT invoice can be issued to the tenant (as, in fact, there is no charge to VAT being made to the tenant), and the tenant will be unable to recover any part of the reimbursement.

The same principles are adopted where, during the term, the tenant exercises a right given to him under the lease and pays the landlord's legal costs (eg on an application for licence to assign pursuant to a qualified covenant (see **18.2.2**)).

10.2 STAMP DUTY ON LEASES

Ad valorem stamp duty will be assessed on any premium paid and also on the rent. Fixed duty of £5.00 is payable on the counterpart lease. Stamp duty must be paid within 30 days of the execution of the instrument.

The amount of duty payable on the premium is assessed in the same way as on purchases of land. The normal reduced rates of duty are available on giving the appropriate certificate of value. However, for the nil rate to apply (ie on certifying that the premium does not exceed £60,000), the rent must not exceed £600 per annum. The rates of duty payable on the rent differ according to the length of the term and the amount of the rent, and are outside the scope of a book of this nature. If no single rent is payable under the lease (eg because of fixed increases), duty is payable on the average rent throughout the term. Where rent is wholly or partly unascertainable, duty will be assessed on the basis of the market rent at the time the lease is executed. As from 10 April 2003, no duty is payable if the property is an a 'disadvantaged area'.

An agreement for lease is required to be stamped as if it were the lease itself, although when the tenant eventually attends to the stamping of the lease, credit will be given for any duty paid on the agreement. However, by virtue of s 240(1) of the Finance Act 1994, if the agreement for lease and the lease are presented for stamping at the same time (ie after completion of the lease), no penalty will be charged for what is likely to be a late presentation of the agreement. This provision is particularly useful with regard to conditional agreements for lease. Duty might otherwise be paid on an agreement which, because the condition is not satisfied, does not complete.

The lease itself must, by virtue of s 240(2), contain either a certificate that there is no agreement for lease to which the lease gives effect, or a denoting stamp which denotes that the agreement was not chargeable with any duty, or denotes the amount of duty paid on the agreement.

Where VAT is or may, at the election of the landlord, become payable on the rent under the lease, the Inland Revenue will assess stamp duty on the VAT element in addition to the rent, whether or not the landlord has actually elected to charge VAT. It seems that the only occasion when the Inland Revenue will not assess stamp duty upon actual or potential VAT payable by the tenant is when the lease makes it clear that no VAT will be payable in addition to the rent. This is done either by stating that the rent payable is inclusive of any VAT that may become chargeable, or by including a covenant by the landlord not to elect to charge VAT at any time during the term (although whether this covenant will bind the landlord's successor as a covenant which has reference to the subject matter of the lease is uncertain). Where a premium is being paid, however, stamp duty will only be payable on the VAT on the premium if the landlord has actually elected to tax at the date of the lease.

Particulars delivered

A tenant under a lease which is granted for a term of 7 years or more must deliver particulars of the transaction to the Inland Revenue and obtain a 'Particulars Delivered' stamp within 30 days of the execution of the instrument.

At the time of writing, the Finance Bill 2003 proposed wide-ranging reforms to the stamp duty regime and these were due to come into force on 1 December 2003. These included:

- a change of name to stamp duty land tax (SDLT);
- raising the threshold for the payment of duty from £60,000 to £150,000 for non-residential properties;
- introducing the new regime for the rental element of leases. Duty would be payable at a flat rate of 1% on the 'net present value' (NPV) of the total rent payable over the term of the lease. The NPV is calculated by discounting rent payable in future years by 3.5% per annum;
- where the NPV of the total rent does not exceed £150,000, no duty will be payable;
- duty will not be chargeable on the VAT element of consideration provided the landlord has not opted to charge tax by the time the lease is granted;
- changes are also proposed as to the methods of payment of duty. In particular, there will no longer be a need for a 'stamp' to appear on a document as proof of payment.

Chapter 11

LEASE DRAFTING

11.1 PRINCIPLES OF DRAFTING

Chapter 11 contents
Principles of drafting
Rules of construction
The structure of the lease

A commercial property lawyer will encounter many different types of commercial lease, since every firm of solicitors engaged in property matters is likely to have its own commercial lease precedent which it will adapt for use in each commercial letting in respect of which the firm is instructed. Most firms restrict their office precedent to a document of manageable length. However, it is not uncommon when acting for a tenant to receive a draft lease which runs to 60 or more pages of relatively small print, all of which has to be carefully examined by the tenant's solicitor. Brevity and concise language must always be encouraged in the drafting (and the amending) of a lease. If the draft lease is kept short, less time will be taken in the subsequent negotiation of the terms and, therefore, in the transaction generally. It will also be easier to read for both clients and solicitors, and will result in legal fees being kept to a minimum. However, the draftsman cannot always restrict the length of the document where complex and extensive legal obligations are being entered into. Clauses cannot be left out of the lease simply to reduce its length, and even though the possibility of a clause being relied upon during the term might appear slight, if a reason exists for the inclusion of the clause, it should be retained. There are many matters to be contemplated in a landlord and tenant relationship, all of which require regulation in the lease.

If, following the grant of the lease, the reversion is to be sold to an investment fund (which is the case with many commercial developments, both new and old), the draftsman should always have regard to the requirements of institutional investors who will require the form of lease to be as close to their standard 'institutional' form as possible. If an institutionally preferred form of lease has not been granted, the landlord will have greater difficulty in disposing of the freehold. All leading commercial practices ensure that their office precedent is in an institutional form. An 'institutional' lease is one which places all the costs of repairing and insuring upon the tenant, thereby ensuring that the income derived by the landlord from the rent is subject to as little fluctuation (in terms of outgoings) as possible. It is often granted for a term of 15 years with a 5-yearly rent review pattern although in recessionary times, shorter leases are common.

The techniques to be adopted in the drafting of the lease are outlined in the drafting section of the LPC Resource Book *Skills for Lawyers* (Jordans) and are not repeated here.

11.2 RULES OF CONSTRUCTION

The purpose of interpreting any legal contract is to discover the real intention of the parties, but that intention can only be ascertained from the wording of the contract itself, and not from extrinsic evidence.

In construing a lease, the court is always reluctant to hold a clause void for uncertainty and thus, if the court can find a way to interpret the clause, some sense will be given to it. Equally, however, the court is generally unwilling to imply terms into a document which has been entered into after extensive negotiations between legally represented parties (although see the approach of the Court of Appeal in *Royal Bank of Scotland plc v Jennings and Others* [1997] 19 EG 152). Faced with an ambiguity, the court will usually adopt the literal approach to interpretation, unless this would lead to a result so absurd that, in the commercial reality of the situation the parties find themselves in, they could not reasonably have intended it (see *Broadgate Square plc v Lehman Brothers Ltd* [1995] 01 EG 111). The court will not examine the offending clause in isolation, but will construe the lease as a whole, to see if some assistance can be gained from other parts of the deed, where similar words and phrases may have been used in other contexts. Ordinary and technical words of the English language will be given the meanings usually attributed to them by the lay person unless the lease clearly directs some other meaning (eg by use of a definitions or interpretation clause).

If, owing to a common mistake between the parties, the lease, as executed, does not embody the common intentions of the parties, the remedy of rectification may be available. This is, however, an equitable and discretionary remedy, and there is a heavy burden upon the plaintiff in an action for rectification to show the existence of a common mistake. Rectification will not be awarded so as to prejudice a bona fide purchaser of the interest of either landlord or tenant who did not have notice of the right to rectify.

If there is a discrepancy between the executed original lease and counterpart, the former prevails over the latter, unless the original is clearly ambiguous.

11.3 THE STRUCTURE OF THE LEASE

11.3.1 Commencement, date and parties

It is customary to commence the drafting of a document by describing the document according to the nature of the transaction to be effected; for example, a lease will commence with the words 'This Lease'. The date of the lease will be left blank until it is manually filled on completion with the date of actual completion. The draft lease should then set out the names and addresses of each party to the lease (eg landlord, tenant and any guarantors).

11.3.2 Definitions

Every well-drafted document should contain a definitions section. If a word is to bear a specific meaning in a document, that meaning ought to be clearly defined at the start of the document. If certain phrases or words are likely to recur in the document, those phrases or words ought to be given a defined meaning at the start of the document. The use of a definitions clause in a legal document avoids needless repetition of recurring words and phrases, and permits a more concise style of drafting. If a word or phrase is to be defined in the definitions clause, the first letter of the defined term should be given a capital letter, and every use of that word or phrase thereafter should appear in the same form.

The following words and phrases are commonly used as defined terms in commercial leases.

'Development'

The lease is likely to regulate the carrying on of building, mining, engineering or other operations at the premises, and the making of a material change in the use of the premises. Rather than having to repeat the statutory definition of development at each reference, it is simpler just to refer to 'Development', which can be defined in the definitions clause as having the meaning given to it by s 55 of the TCPA 1990.

'Insured Risks'

There are many risks against which the lease will require the premises to be insured, and there will be several references to those risks in the insurance and repairing provisions of the lease. A full list of risks can be set out in the definitions clause, and then referred to elsewhere as the 'Insured Risks'.

'Interest'

If the tenant delays paying rent or any other sums due to the landlord under the lease, the landlord will want to charge the tenant interest on the unpaid sums. The rate of interest can be set out in the definitions clause. It is usually agreed to be a rate which is between 3 and 5% above the base lending rate of a nominated bank. The landlord usually stipulates that if the base rate of that bank should cease to exist, the interest rate under the lease will be a reasonably equivalent rate of interest.

'Pipes' or 'Conduits'

The tenant may be granted rights to use pipes in other parts of the landlord's building in order to run services to and from the premises. The landlord may reserve the right to use pipes passing through the tenant's premises. The lease should make it clear that 'Pipes' includes all pipes, sewers, drains, watercourses, wires, cables and other conducting media. In this sense the defined term is not so much a definition, as an expansion of the meaning of the word.

'Planning Acts'

The lease will contain several references to the TCPA 1990, the EA 1995, the PCA 1991, and other statutes relating to planning and environmental law, and the tenant will have obligations to comply with them. Those statutes can be grouped together and called 'the Planning Acts'.

'Premises'

There will be many references in the lease to the premises demised to the tenant. The draftsman will not want to repeat anything other than 'the Premises' at each reference. Hence, the definitions clause should define the premises demised by the lease, and a full verbal and legal description should be set out either here, or in the parcels clause, or in one of the schedules to the lease.

'Term'

The term of the lease is one of the phrases most commonly referred to in the lease. Thought should be given to whether the definition should relate just to the contractual term, or whether it should include any extension, holding over or continuation of the term.

'VAT'

In defining value added tax, it should be made clear that 'VAT' also includes any tax replacing VAT, or becoming payable in addition to it, in case the fundamental principles of the tax are changed.

'Rent'

Rent will also be a commonly recurring word. Careful thought should be given as to what 'Rent' is to mean, and in the light of its definition, whether it is appropriate to use the term at every reference to rent in the lease. If the landlord wants to reserve service charge payments, insurance premiums and VAT as rent, so that he enjoys the same remedies for recovery of those sums as he enjoys in respect of rent (eg distress, and forfeiture without the need to serve a s 146 notice), 'Rent' should be defined to include those items. It should also be made clear that 'Rent' means not only the original contractual rent, but also any revised rent which becomes payable by virtue of the rent review clause, and any interim rent which becomes payable under s 24A of the LTA 1954 during a statutory continuation tenancy. In this manner, it is made clear that, in a case where a tenant's liability continues after assignment, the liability relates to the payment of a rent which may be increased after the date he assigns his interest in the premises. The term 'Rent' is not an appropriate term in every case under the lease. For instance, in the rent review clause, it is the annual rent which is to be reviewed from time to time during the term, not necessarily the 'Rent' as defined. Also, the landlord might be prepared to allow payment of the annual rent to be suspended for a period of time if there is damage to the premises by an insured risk, but he may not wish to have suspended the payment of other sums (eg service charge) which have been reserved as 'Rent'. This was the point in issue in the case of *P&O Property Holdings Ltd v International Computers Ltd* [2000] 2 All ER 1015, ChD.

'Building'

If the lease is of part only of the landlord's building, the building itself should be identified, as the landlord will probably be entering into covenants in the lease to repair the structure and exterior of the building. There may be other references to the 'Building' with regard to the provision of services and the grant and reservation of easements.

'Common Parts'

Where a lease of part of a building is intended, the tenant will be granted rights to use the 'Common Parts' of the 'Building'. The extent of the 'Common Parts' should be clearly expressed.

11.3.3 The interpretation clause

Certain words or phrases do not require a fixed definition for the purposes of the lease, rather their meaning needs to be expanded or clarified to assist the reader in his interpretation and construction of the lease. Common examples of matters of interpretation are the following.

Joint and several liability

The lease should make it clear that, if the landlord or tenant is more than one person, the obligations placed upon those persons by the lease will be enforceable against either or both of them.

One gender to mean all genders

Section 61 of the LPA 1925 applies in respect of all deeds executed after LPA 1925 came into force so that any reference in a deed to the masculine will include the feminine, and vice versa. However, s 61 does not deal with the neuter (ie 'it'), and it is therefore common to state, for the avoidance of doubt, that a reference to one gender includes all others.

References to statutes

Leases usually provide that, unless a particular clause expressly provides to the contrary, a reference in the lease to a statute or to a statutory instrument is to be taken as a reference to the Act or instrument as amended, re-enacted or modified from time to time, and not restricted to the legislation as it was in force at the date of the lease.

Expanding the meaning of words or phrases

If one of the tenant's covenants states that the tenant is prohibited from doing a certain act, the tenant will not be in breach of covenant if the act is done by a third party. It is, therefore, usual to state that if the tenant is required by the lease not to do a certain act, neither may he permit nor suffer the act to be done by someone else. If one of the tenant's covenants prohibits the carrying out of a certain act without the landlord's prior consent, and it is stipulated that the landlord's consent cannot be unreasonably withheld, it is usual to stipulate that his consent may not also be unreasonably delayed. Rather than dealing with these matters of drafting as and when the need arises in the lease, both of these points can be concisely dealt with by using an appropriate form of wording in the interpretation clause at the beginning of the lease.

11.3.4 The letting

The letting is the operative part of the lease which will create the tenant's interest, define the size of that interest, reserve rent, impose covenants, and deal with the grant and reservation of rights and easements. The clauses will be set out in the following logical sequence.

The operative words

Sufficient words of grant should be used to show the intention of the landlord to grant an interest in favour of the tenant. The landlord usually either 'demises' or 'lets' the premises to the tenant.

The parcels clause

A full description of the premises, including the rights to be granted to the tenant should be contained in the parcels clause. Often, the description is removed to one of the schedules (see below) so that the parcels clause simply refers to 'the Premises' (which will be a defined term).

Exceptions and reservations

Usually, the rights to be reserved for the benefit of the landlord are only briefly referred to in this part of the lease, and are set out extensively in one of the schedules.

The habendum

The habendum deals with the length of term to be vested in the tenant, and its commencement date.

The reddendum

The reddendum deals with the reservation of rent (which may be varied from time to time by a rent review clause), the dates for payment, and the manner of payment (ie whether in advance or in arrear).

The covenants

Although the covenants on the part of landlord, tenant and surety are often set out in separate schedules, the parties expressly enter into them in the operative part of the lease.

11.3.5 The provisos

(handwritten margin note: For Landlords benefit)

Grouped together under the heading of provisos is a wide variety of clauses which cannot easily be dealt with elsewhere in the lease, being clauses which are neither in the nature of covenants nor easements, and do not impose obligations upon one or other of the parties to the lease. They are clauses which have no common thread except that most of them are inserted into the lease for the landlord's benefit alone.

The provisos usually include the following clauses.

(1) The proviso for re-entry, (ie the forfeiture clause). This is dealt with in greater detail in Chapter 23.

(2) An option to determine the lease where the premises are damaged by an insured risk so that they are no longer fit for use or occupation, and the landlord either cannot or, after a period of time, has not reinstated the premises (see **22.7**).

(3) A rent abatement clause, which provides that the rent (and, possibly, other sums payable by the tenant under the lease) should cease to be payable if the premises are rendered unusable by damage caused by an insured risk (see **22.7.2**).

(4) A provision which states that the landlord does not, by reason of anything contained in the lease, imply or represent that the tenant's proposed use of the premises is a permitted use under planning legislation. In *Laurence v Lexcourt Holdings Ltd* [1978] 2 All ER 810 (a case at first instance), the landlord had let premises to the tenant as 'offices'. After completion of the lease, the tenant discovered that only part of the premises enjoyed the benefit of planning permission for office use, and that the local planning authority was only prepared to grant planning permission in respect of all of the premises on a temporary basis. The court held that the tenant was entitled to rescind on account of the landlord's misrepresentation, since it was implicit in what was said in the lease that the premises could lawfully be used by the tenant for the intended purpose throughout the term. The landlord should therefore make it clear in the lease that, simply because the lease (or any licence granted

subsequently) permits a certain type of business activity at the premises, the landlord does not warrant that permission is available for that use.

(5) A provision whereby the tenant acknowledges that he has not entered into the lease in reliance upon any statement made by or on behalf of the landlord. This provision seeks to prevent the tenant from pursuing a remedy against the landlord in respect of a misrepresentation, but it will be subject to s 3 of the Misrepresentation Act 1967 (as amended by s 8 of the Unfair Contract Terms Act 1977) and will have to satisfy the test of reasonableness set out in the 1977 Act.

(6) A provision regulating the method of service of notices under the lease. On occasions during the lease, one party will want or need to serve a notice on the other under one of the provisions in the lease (eg to implement a rent review clause, or to give notice of an assignment of the lease, or as a preliminary step to the exercise of a right of re-entry). Whether or not a notice has been validly served will be an important issue and should, therefore, be a matter which is capable of conclusive determination. Accordingly, the lease should specify the method of service of notices, either by incorporating the provisions of s 196 of the LPA 1925 (as amended by the Recorded Delivery Service Act 1962) into the lease, or by expressly setting out the methods of service to be permitted by the lease.

(7) Excluding compensation under the LTA 1954. If the parties agree that the tenant should not be entitled to compensation under s 37 of the LTA 1954 at the end of his lease (see **31.6**), this part of the lease should include a clause whereby the tenant's right to compensation is excluded.

(8) Fixing a perpetuity period. The landlord commonly reserves rights in the lease to use service pipes which currently pass through the tenant's premises, or which may at some future date be laid through them. The grant of a future right may be void if it infringes the rule against perpetuities. To avoid any possibility of this, the lease may specify a perpetuity period not exceeding 80 years (Perpetuities and Accumulations Act 1964, s 1(1)).

(9) Excluding the tenant's security of tenure. Occasionally, the parties agree that the security of tenure provisions contained in the LTA 1954, Part II should not apply to the lease (see **31.1.5**). If this is to be the case, the contracting-out provision should appear in this part of the lease. Consent of the court would be required in respect of such an agreement.

(10) Options to break. If either party is to enjoy the right to terminate the lease early by the exercise of an option to break (see **14.2**), the option is usually contained in this part of the lease.

11.3.6 Schedules

Most of the detail of the lease can be omitted from the main body of the document and placed in separate schedules. This will make the lease easier to read, and from the client's point of view, it makes it easier for him to refer to the various provisions of the lease.

Most leases contain schedules dealing with the following matters.

The premises

The first schedule to the lease often contains a description of the premises, which should be complete and accurate and, where appropriate, refer to plans to be incorporated in the lease.

Rights

If rights are to be granted to the tenant (eg on a lease of part), they are usually referred to briefly in the body of the lease and set out in detail in a schedule.

Exceptions

Where the landlord is reserving rights (which will usually be the case) those matters will briefly be referred to in the body of the lease, and set out in detail in a schedule.

Rent review

Provisions relating to revisions of the annual rent during the term will either be contained in a separate clause in the body of the lease, or removed to a schedule.

Covenants

There will be separate schedules detailing the tenant's covenants, the landlord's covenants and the covenants to be entered into by the tenant's guarantor on the grant of the lease, the assignee's guarantor on the assignment of the lease, and an outgoing tenant as an authorised guarantor (as to which, see **18.2.8**).

Service charge provisions

If there is to be a service charge, it is usual to group all the service charge provisions in one schedule to the lease.

11.3.7 Execution

The lease and its counterpart are deeds and, therefore, the usual rules relating to the execution of deeds are applicable. A testimonium clause is not an essential part of a lease but, if one is included, it ought to appear immediately before the first schedule. Attestation clauses will, of course, be essential.

Chapter 12

THE PARTIES TO THE LEASE

12.1 INTRODUCTION

Chapter 12 contents
Introduction
The landlord
The tenant
The guarantor
Rent deposits

Following the date and commencement, the lease will set out details of the parties to the lease, namely the landlord, the tenant and any guarantor (who is also often referred to as a surety).

In respect of a corporate party, the lease should give the company's full name and either its registered office or its main administrative office, and the company's registration number. In respect of an individual party, the full name and postal address of the individual will suffice.

The purpose of this chapter is to examine the extent and duration of liability of the parties to a lease, the Landlord and Tenant (Covenants) Act 1995 (LTCA 1995) (which came into force on 1 January 1996) brought about considerable changes in this area. In particular, it abolished the concept of privity of contract in relation to leases which are defined as new leases for the purposes of the Act (see **12.2.2**). Accordingly, this chapter examines the law and practice both in relation to leases already in existence at the date when the Act came into force (the old regime), and those which are new leases (the new regime).

12.2 THE LANDLORD

The landlord's primary purpose as a party to the lease is to grant to the tenant the leasehold interest that both parties intend, upon the terms agreed between them. These terms may require the landlord to enter into covenants with the tenant in order to ensure that the tenant peaceably enjoys occupation of the premises, and a certain quality of accommodation (see, more specifically, Chapter 21).

12.2.1 The old regime

The original landlord

By virtue of the principle of privity of contract, the original landlord, as an original contracting party, remains liable in respect of any covenants entered into in the lease, even after he has sold the reversion. The landlord protects himself against the possibility of being sued for a breach of covenant committed by his successor by obtaining from him an express indemnity covenant in the transfer of the reversion. Such a covenant is not implied at law.

If the landlord has granted a lease of an entire building, it is unlikely that he entered into many covenants with the tenant. If the landlord has granted a lease of part of a building, or of premises forming part of a larger commercial site, the landlord may have entered into covenants to provide services to the tenants. If this is the case, the landlord may have limited expressly the duration of his liability under the covenants to the time the reversion is vested in him, rather than relied upon obtaining an indemnity covenant.

A successor to the reversion

The landlord's successor in title is bound during his period of ownership by all covenants imposed upon the landlord which have reference to the subject matter of the lease (see s 142(1) of the LPA 1925). At the same time, he takes the benefit of the tenant's covenants which have reference to the subject matter of the lease under s 141(1) of the LPA 1925. There was some doubt as to whether the benefit of surety covenants contained in the lease would pass to a buyer of the reversion without an express assignment, but it now appears in the light of *P&A Swift Investments v Combined English Stores Group plc* [1988] 3 WLR 313 that it will, provided the lease made it clear that a reference in the lease to the landlord includes his successors in title.

12.2.2 The new regime

The original landlord

Under a lease affected by the LTCA 1995 (as a general rule, those granted on or after 1 January 1996), on an assignment of the reversion by the original landlord, while there is no automatic release from his obligations under the lease, ss 6 and 8 of the Act provide a procedure whereby the assigning landlord can apply to the tenant to be released from his obligations under the lease. The outgoing landlord may serve a notice (in a prescribed form) on the tenant (either before or within 4 weeks after the assignment) requesting his release. If, within 4 weeks of service, the tenant objects by serving a written notice on the landlord, the landlord may apply to the county court for a declaration that it is reasonable for the covenant to be released. If the tenant does not object within that time-limit, the release becomes automatic. Any release from a covenant under these provisions is regarded as occurring at the time when the assignment in question takes place. However, in the case of *BHP Great Britain Petroleum Ltd v Chesterfield Properties Ltd* [2001] EWCA Civ 1797, [2002] 2 WLR 672, the Court of Appeal held that the statutory release mechanism did not operate to release the landlord from those covenants which were expressed to be personal. In respect of such covenants, the original landlord would continue to be liable even after the assignment of the reversion had taken place. This decision may have significant implications for landlords.

Once a landlord is released under these provisions, he ceases to be entitled to the benefit of the tenant covenants in the lease as from the date of the assignment of the reversion.

A successor to the reversion

The landlord's successor becomes bound, as from the date of the assignment, by all of the landlord covenants in the lease, except to the extent that immediately before the assignment they did not bind the assignor (eg covenants expressed to be personal). Similarly, the new landlord becomes entitled to the benefit of the tenant covenants in the lease. Sections 141 and 142 of the LPA 1925 do not apply in relation to new leases, so there is no need to enquire whether the relevant covenant is one which 'has reference to the subject matter of the lease'. The benefit of surety covenants (not being tenant covenants for the purposes of the Act) will pass to an assignee of the reversion in accordance with *P&A Swift Investments* on the basis that the assignee has acquired the legal estate, and the surety covenants touch and concern that estate. In the same manner, the benefit of a former tenant's authorised guarantee agreement (see **18.2.7**) will pass to the assignee.

A successor can apply to be released from his obligations under the lease when, at some future time, he assigns the reversion. If at that time a former landlord is still liable on the lease covenants (because he did not obtain a release from the tenant when he assigned the reversion), he can make another application to the tenant to be released.

12.3 THE TENANT

The person to whom the lease is granted is known as the original tenant. The person to whom the tenant later assigns his lease is known as the assignee. The original tenant will be required to enter into many covenants in the lease regulating what can be done in, on or at the premises.

12.3.1 The old regime

The original tenant – privity of contract

Prior to the LTCA 1995, basic principles of privity of contract dictated that the original tenant, as an original contracting party, remained liable in respect of all of the covenants in the lease for the entire duration of the term, even after he assigned the lease. The original tenant under the existing regime is in the undesirable position of being liable for a breach of covenant committed after he has parted with his interest in the premises. If, for example, the tenant was granted a 25-year term which he assigned at the end of the 5th year to an assignee who then failed to pay rent and allowed the premises to fall into disrepair, the landlord could choose to sue, not the assignee, but the original tenant for non-payment of rent and breach of the repairing covenant. It does not matter that since the assignment the rent has been increased under the rent review clause (unless the increase is referrable to a variation of the lease terms agreed between the landlord and assignee – see s 18 of the LTCA 1995 and the case of *Friends' Provident Life Office v British Railways Board* [1995] 1 All ER 336).

The effect of privity of contract becomes increasingly significant in recessionary times. If the reason why the assignee has defaulted in his obligations under the lease is that the assignee has become insolvent, instead of pursuing a worthless action against the assignee, the landlord would look to the original tenant for payment of rent.

For how long is the original tenant liable?

The original tenant's liability lasts for the entire duration of the contractual term. Once he has assigned his interest in the lease, his liability will not extend into any continuation of that term that may arise under s 24 of the LTA 1954, unless there is an express provision in the lease to the contrary. As will be seen later (at **31.1.6**), a tenancy which is protected by Part II of that Act will not come to an end on the expiration of the contractual term. Instead, s 24 continues the tenancy on exactly the same terms, and at the same rent, until the tenancy is terminated in one of the methods prescribed by the Act. Hence, the contractual rent remains payable beyond the expiry date of the lease, but the effect of the House of Lords' decision in *City of London Corporation v Fell* [1993] 49 EG 113 is that, where the original tenant has already assigned his lease before the contractual expiry date of the lease, his liability will cease at that date, and will not be continued.

However, even before *City of London Corporation v Fell*, landlords were drafting leases to include a provision to ensure that the original tenant (and any assignees who entered into a direct covenant with the landlord) would remain liable to perform the covenants during a statutory continuation. This would be done by defining 'the Term' in the lease to include 'the period of any holding over or any extension or continuance whether by agreement or operation of law'. The tenant is then required to pay the rent and perform his covenants during 'the Term'. The one consolation for a tenant who has assigned the lease but remains liable because of the definition of 'the Term' is provided by *Herbert Duncan Limited v Cluttons* [1992] 1 EGLR 101, which held that the continuing liability to pay rent relates only to the contractual rent under the lease, and not to any interim rent fixed by the court under s 24A of the LTA 1954 unless the lease states otherwise.

The need for an indemnity

As a result of the continuing nature of the original tenant's liability under the old regime, it is essential that, on an assignment, the original tenant obtains an indemnity from the assignee against all future breaches of covenant (whether committed by the assignee or a successor in title). An express indemnity may be taken, but this is not strictly necessary since s 77 of the LPA 1925 automatically implies into every assignment for value a covenant to indemnify the assignor against all future breaches of covenant. If the lease is registered at HM Land Registry, s 24(1)(a) of the Land Registration Act 1925 (LRA 1925) implies a similar covenant for indemnity into a transfer of the lease, whether or not value is given.

From a practical point of view, it should be noted that an indemnity from an assignee (whether express or implied) is worthless if the assignee is insolvent, and this may be the very reason why the landlord is pursuing the original tenant in the first place.

Where there has been a succession of assignments, and the original tenant finds that he is unable to obtain a full indemnity against his immediate assignee, the assignee in possession may be liable at common law to indemnify the original tenant who has been sued for breach of covenant (see *Moule v Garrett and Others* (1872) LR 7 Exch 101), but again the indemnity may be worthless owing to the insolvency of the defaulting assignee.

The assignee – privity of estate

By virtue of the doctrine of privity of estate, an assignee under the old regime is liable in respect of all of the covenants in the lease which 'touch and concern' the demised premises, for as long as the lease remains vested in him.

An assignee cannot be sued for a breach of covenant committed prior to the lease being vested in him, save to the extent that the breach in question is a continuing breach (eg breach of a covenant to repair) which effectively becomes the assignee's breach from the date of the assignment. If, at the time of the assignment there are arrears of rent, the landlord's action to recover the arrears would be against the assignor, not the assignee. However, from a practical point of view, the landlord is unlikely to give his consent to an assignment (assuming the lease requires his consent) unless the arrears are cleared. Further, the assignee is unlikely to take the assignment while rent is in arrear because of the risk of forfeiture of the lease on account of the outstanding breach.

An assignee is not liable for breaches of covenant committed after he has parted with his interest in the premises, (although he may still be sued in respect of breaches committed while he was the tenant) and he is not liable in respect of covenants which do not touch and concern the premises (but see below).

Covenants which touch and concern

Under the old regime, an assignee is liable only in respect of those covenants which touch and concern the demised premises. These are covenants which are not in the nature of personal covenants, but have direct reference to the premises in question by laying down something which is to be done or not to be done at the premises, and which affect the landlord in his normal capacity as landlord, or the tenant in his normal capacity as tenant. If the purpose of the covenant is to achieve something which is collateral to the relationship of landlord and tenant, then the covenant does not touch and concern.

Nearly all of the covenants in a typical commercial lease touch and concern the demised premises. For example, the covenants:

(1) to pay rent;
(2) to repair;
(3) to use the premises for a particular purpose;
(4) not to make alterations without consent;
(5) not to assign or sublet without consent;

are all covenants which relate to the premises and have reference to the landlord and tenant relationship in respect of those premises.

By contrast, the following covenants do not touch and concern:

(1) to pay a periodic sum to a third party;
(2) to build premises for the landlord upon some other land;
(3) to repair or renew chattels (as distinct from fixtures, which would form part of the premises).

These covenants do not have any reference to the relationship of landlord and tenant in respect of the land in question and, therefore, would not bind an assignee.

Direct covenants

Landlords have never liked the limited duration of an assignee's liability under the doctrine of privity of estate. In practice, therefore, it is common for the landlord to try to extend the liability of an assignee under the old regime by requiring him, as a condition of the landlord's licence to assign, to enter into a direct covenant to observe the covenants in the lease for the entire duration of the term, thereby creating privity of contract between landlord and assignee. This covenant is usually contained in the formal licence to assign (see **27.2**). The landlord will always then have a choice between original tenant and present assignee as to whom to sue for a breach of covenant committed by the latter. Where intermediate assignees have entered into direct covenants in this manner, the landlord's options are increased.

If an assignee has given a direct covenant to the landlord, the extent of his continuing liability is governed by the *Fell* case, and the definition of 'the Term' in the lease in the same way as applies to the original tenant.

The need for an indemnity

The assignee from the original tenant will have covenanted, either expressly or impliedly, with the original tenant to indemnify him against liability for loss arising out of any future breach of covenant (whether committed by the assignee or a successor in title). Irrespective of whether the assignee is affected by privity of estate or contract, because he gave an indemnity covenant to his assignor, he needs to obtain one from his assignee. An express indemnity may be taken, but s 77 of the LPA 1925 and s 24(1)(a) of the LRA 1925 will operate in the same way as before.

12.3.2 The new regime

As stated above, the main purpose of the LTCA 1995 was to abolish privity of contract in leases, and it is therefore in the area of tenant liability that the Act has the most significant impact.

The original tenant – privity of contract release

The basic rule is that a tenant under a lease which is a new lease for the purposes of the LTCA 1995 is only liable for breaches of covenant committed while the lease is vested in him. Thus, on assignment of the lease, the assignor is automatically released from all the tenant covenants of the tenancy (and he ceases to be entitled to the benefit of the landlord covenants). This means that while the outgoing tenant can be sued for breaches of covenant committed at a time when the lease was vested in him, he cannot be sued for any subsequent breaches.

The assignee – liability on covenants

The basic rule applies equally to assignees. As from the date of assignment, an assignee becomes bound by the tenant covenants in the lease except to the extent that immediately before the assignment they did not bind the assignor (eg they were expressed to be personal to the original tenant), but when he assigns the lease, he is automatically released from all of the tenant covenants. One slight change for leases under the new regime is that an assignee will be liable on all the tenant covenants in the lease whether or not they 'touch and concern' the land. The combination of this slight change, and the statutorily imposed limitation on the duration of an assignee's liability, makes the practice under the old regime of obtaining direct covenants from assignees inapplicable to leases granted under the new regime.

In the same way that the assignee becomes bound by the tenant covenants, so too does the assignee become entitled, as from the date of the assignment, to the benefit of the landlord covenants in the lease.

Excluded assignments

Assignments in breach of covenant (eg where the tenant has not complied with a requirement in the lease to obtain his landlord's consent before assigning) or by operation of law (eg on the death or bankruptcy of a tenant) are excluded assignments for the purposes of the LTCA 1995. On an excluded assignment, the assignor will not be released from the tenant covenants of the lease, and will remain liable to the landlord, jointly and severally with the assignee, until the next assignment, which is not an excluded assignment, takes place.

Authorised guarantee agreements

To counterbalance the loss to the landlord of the benefits of the old privity regime, the LTCA 1995 allows the landlord to require an outgoing tenant, who will be released from liability under the Act, to enter into a form of guarantee whereby the outgoing tenant guarantees the performance of the tenant covenants by the incoming tenant (see **18.2.8**).

Indemnity covenants?

As an assigning tenant is not liable for the breaches of covenant committed by his successor, the LTCA 1995 has repealed s 77 and s 24(1)(a) in relation to leases granted under the new regime. However, it should be noted that an outgoing tenant may remain liable to the landlord for an assignee's breaches of covenant under the terms of an authorised guarantee agreement and, in such circumstances, an express indemnity from the assignee should be obtained.

12.4 THE GUARANTOR

Much attention in practice is given to the financial status of the proposed tenant, and a consideration of what is called 'the strength of the tenant's covenant'. A tenant is said to give 'a good covenant' if it can be expected that the tenant will pay the rent on time throughout the term, and diligently perform his other obligations under the lease. An established, high performing and renowned public limited company (such as one of the large retail food companies) will be regarded as a good covenant in the commercial letting market, whereas newly formed public limited companies and many private companies, whose reputation, reliability and financial standing are unknown in the property market, will not be perceived as giving a good covenant. If the covenant is so bad that the landlord has reservations about the proposed tenant's ability to maintain rental payments throughout the term without financial difficulties, the landlord will consider not granting a lease to that tenant in the first place. However, in situations which fall between these two extremes, the landlord often requires a third party, known as a guarantor, to join in the lease to guarantee the tenant's obligations.

12.4.1 Practical points

The landlord's aim is to ensure that he receives the rent due under the lease on time throughout the term, either from the tenant, or if the tenant defaults, from the guarantor. Therefore, just as the landlord ought to investigate the financial status of his proposed tenant, so too should he investigate the status of the guarantor nominated by the tenant.

With private limited companies or newly formed public limited companies (who, even with plc status, may be just as likely to be in breach as any other tenant) many landlords will ask for one or more of the company's directors to guarantee the tenant's performance of its obligations. However, the landlord should not necessarily be so blinkered in his approach, since other options may prove to be more fruitful.

Does a subsidiary company have a parent or sister company which can stand as guarantor? If the directors are not of sufficient financial standing, are the shareholders of the company in any better position to give the landlord the element of reliability he requires? Will the tenant's bank guarantee the obligation of its client?

The guarantor should be advised to seek independent advice, since there is a clear conflict of interests between tenant and guarantor. The conflict arises in that, on the one hand the advice to be given to the tenant is that, without a guarantor, the tenant will not get a lease, whilst on the other hand, the advice to give to the guarantor would be to avoid giving the guarantee. Further, in seeking to make amendments to the surety covenants in the lease on behalf of the guarantor, the solicitor may be prejudicing the negotiation of the lease terms between the landlord and his tenant–client, causing delay or disruption.

12.4.2 The extent of the guarantee

The old regime

The purpose of the guarantee is to ensure that the guarantor will pay the rent if the tenant does not, and will remedy or indemnify the landlord against any breaches of covenant committed by the tenant. Two points should be noted. First, it is usual for the landlord in drafting the lease to define 'the Tenant' to include the tenant's successors in title. This means that in guaranteeing the obligations of 'the Tenant', the guarantor has guaranteed the performance of future (and as yet unknown) assignees of the lease. His liability would, therefore, extend throughout the duration of the lease (even after the original tenant had assigned the lease). Secondly, even if the guarantee was limited to a guarantee of the original tenant's obligations, an original tenant remains liable by virtue of privity of contract under the existing regime to perform the covenants in the lease for its entire duration. Should, therefore, the landlord choose to sue, not the assignee in possession, but the original tenant, the guarantee would remain active.

Ideally, the guarantor should seek to limit the extent of his liability so that the guarantee applies only for so long as the lease remains vested in the tenant in respect of whom the guarantee was originally sought. This is a matter for negotiation with the landlord.

The new regime

Abolition of the concept of privity of contract in leases applies equally to guarantors. Section 24(2) of the LTCA 1995 provides that where a tenant is released under the LTCA 1995 from the tenant covenants of the lease, any person (ie the guarantor) who was bound, before the release, by a covenant imposing liability upon that person in the event of default by the tenant, is released to the same extent as the tenant. Any attempt to extend the liability of a guarantor beyond the duration of the liability of the tenant whose performance was guaranteed is likely to fall foul of the anti-avoidance provisions of s 25 of the LTCA 1995. However, it is arguable that a guarantor can be required to undertake a separate obligation to guarantee the tenant's performance under any authorised guarantee agreement he may enter into.

There is some comfort for the guarantor in either regime in that, unless there is an express provision in the lease to the contrary, the liability of the guarantor will cease upon the contractual term date and will not continue during a statutory continuation tenancy under s 24 of the LTA 1954 (see *Junction Estates Ltd v Cope* (1974) 27 P&CR 482). However, it is common practice to define the lease term to include 'the period of any holding over or any extension or continuance whether by agreement or operation of law', and to prolong the guarantor's liability by requiring him to covenant with the landlord throughout 'the term' as so defined.

12.4.3 Discharge or release

The guarantor cannot unilaterally revoke his guarantee, but in certain cases, usually where the landlord acts to the prejudice of the guarantor, the conduct of the landlord might operate as a release.

Variations

If the landlord, without obtaining the consent of the guarantor, agrees with the tenant to vary the terms of the lease (eg by substituting more onerous repairing obligations), the variation of the lease will operate to discharge the guarantor. A guarantor cannot stand as surety and be made liable for the tenant's default in the performance of terms different to those guaranteed to be performed, unless the guarantor has agreed to the variation. However, an immaterial variation of the lease which would not prejudice the guarantor (eg by substituting less onerous repairing obligations) is not likely to discharge the guarantor, although authority appears to suggest that it is for the guarantor to decide whether or not he would be prejudiced by the proposed variation. In *Holme v Brunskill* (1877) 3 QBD 495, a surrender of part of the premises comprised in the lease (which might not appear in any way to prejudice the guarantor, particularly if the rent is reduced as a result), which was agreed without the consent of the guarantor, operated to discharge the guarantee. However, a variation which does not affect the terms of the (tenant's) principal contract will not affect the guarantor's secondary contract (see *Metropolitan Properties Co (Regis) Ltd v Bartholomew* [1995] 14 EG 143).

A surrender of the whole of the premises comprised in the lease will operate to end the liability of the guarantor as from the date of surrender, but not in respect of any breaches of covenant outstanding at that time.

Increasing the rent by exercising a rent review clause does not amount to a variation and so will not release the guarantor. This means that a guarantor may be guaranteeing the payment in future of an unknown level of rent (although see the protection given to guarantors of former tenants by s 18 of the LTCA 1995 and the *Friends' Provident* case).

'Giving time'

'Giving time' to the tenant may operate to discharge the guarantee. A landlord 'gives time' to a tenant if, in a binding way, he agrees to allow the tenant to pay rent late, or not at all. It does not seem that a mere omission to press for payment (eg due to an oversight, or perhaps to avoid a waiver of the right to forfeit the lease) will amount to the giving of time.

Release of co-guarantor

According to general principles of suretyship, if there is more than one guarantor, the release by the landlord of one of them operates as a release of all of them.

Death

The death of the tenant is not likely to bring an end to the guarantee, since the lease will vest in the tenant's personal representatives who, as the tenant's successors in title, will become 'the Tenant' under the lease, whose obligations are guaranteed by the guarantor. Under the new regime, such a vesting would be an excluded assignment, and so the guarantor would not be released. Further, the death of the guarantor will not necessarily bring an end to the guarantee since the guarantor's own personal representatives will remain liable under the guarantee to the extent of the deceased's assets passing through their hands. However, it is more common for the landlord to make provision for the possible death of the guarantor by obtaining a covenant from the tenant obliging him to find a suitable replacement.

Bankruptcy or liquidation

The bankruptcy or liquidation of the tenant will not operate to release the guarantor. On the bankruptcy of an individual tenant, the lease will vest in the trustee-in-bankruptcy who will become 'the Tenant' for the purposes of the lease (and such a vesting is an excluded assignment under the new regime), whilst on the liquidation of a corporate tenant the lease will remain vested in the company (unless the liquidator obtains an order under s 145 of the Insolvency Act 1986 (IA 1986)).

Even if the trustee or liquidator chooses to disclaim the lease, the disclaimer will not operate to end the guarantor's liability (see **29.1.2**).

12.4.4 Drafting points for the landlord

The landlord should ensure that the guarantor joins in the lease to give the covenants the landlord requires.

The two basic obligations of a guarantor are to pay the rent (and any other sums payable by the tenant under the lease) if the tenant does not pay, and to remedy, or to indemnify the landlord against loss caused by, any breaches of covenant committed by the tenant. The landlord will ensure that the guarantor is liable for the period in respect of which the tenant is liable under the lease (and, possibly, under any authorised guarantee agreement that the tenant may enter into).

Several other provisions are usually required by the landlord:

(1) a covenant from the tenant to provide a replacement guarantor should one of several unfortunate or undesirable events happen. For instance, if the guarantor is an individual who dies, or becomes mentally incapable (ie a receiver is appointed under s 99 of the Mental Health Act 1983) or has a petition in bankruptcy presented against him (or is affected by other proceedings under the IA 1986 which the landlord considers serious enough to warrant substitution) the landlord will require the tenant to find a replacement of equivalent financial standing. If the guarantor is a company and a winding-up commences (or, as above, it is affected by other adverse insolvency proceedings), again the tenant will be required to find a reasonably acceptable replacement;

(2) a provision protecting the landlord against the tenant's trustee-in-bankruptcy or liquidator disclaiming the lease to bring the tenant's liability to an end. The effect of a disclaimer is dealt with at **29.1.3**. For present purposes it can be said that, whilst disclaimer does not end the liability of a guarantor, most landlords will nevertheless want the ability to require the guarantor to take a lease from

the landlord in the event of disclaimer, for the full unexpired residue of the term then remaining;

(3) a provision to deal with situations which might otherwise operate to release the guarantor. As part of the guarantor's covenants, the landlord will include a declaration that a release will not be effected by the giving of time to the tenant, or by a variation in the terms of the lease (although as a concession, the landlord might accept that a variation prejudicial to the guarantor will still operate as a release unless the guarantor has consented to it). The effect of stating in the lease that the guarantor will not be released 'by any other event which, but for this provision, would operate to release the Surety' is doubtful.

12.4.5 Drafting points for the guarantor

If the guarantor has accepted the principle of giving a guarantee, he should make all efforts to minimise his liability. There are several provisions a guarantor can seek to negotiate:

(1) a limit on the length of his liability; whilst the LTCA 1995 releases a guarantor to the same extent as it releases the tenant, the guarantor should try to ensure that he is not contractually bound to guarantee the tenant under any authorised guarantee agreement (as to which, see **18.2.7**);

(2) an obligation on the landlord's part to notify the guarantor of any default by the tenant; one would expect the tenant to tell his guarantor if the tenant was experiencing difficulties in meeting his obligations under the lease. However, this might not always be the case, and in order to alert the guarantor to possible claims under the guarantee and, perhaps, to enable him to put pressure on the tenant, he could seek to include a covenant by the landlord to notify him in writing whenever the tenant falls into arrears with the rent, or otherwise breaches a covenant in the lease;

(3) participation in rent reviews; as the guarantor guarantees payment of future unascertained rents he may try to persuade the landlord to allow him to play a part in the rent review process. This would necessitate amendments to the usual rent review clause, and would not be attractive to the landlord. Further, the tenant would not be keen either to hand over the review negotiations to the guarantor or to have him involved as a third party in the review process, and an assignee of the lease would certainly see it as an unattractive proposition;

(4) an ability to demand an assignment of the lease from the tenant where the tenant is in default under the lease. This would enable the guarantor to minimise his liability by being able to call for an assignment and then assign the lease to a more stable assignee.

12.4.6 An assignee's guarantor

The above paragraphs have concentrated on the guarantee to be provided by the original tenant on the grant of the lease. However, as a condition of granting licence to assign the lease, the landlord may require the assignee to provide a suitable guarantor in respect of his obligations (see **18.2.3**). Under the old regime, it will be the landlord's intention to fix the new guarantor with liability for the duration of the contractual term and beyond, in the same way that he tries to fix the liability of the original tenant's guarantor. Under the new regime, liability should not exceed the liability of the assignee.

12.5 RENT DEPOSITS

As an alternative (or in addition) to a guarantee, the landlord may require the tenant to enter into a rent deposit deed whereby the tenant is required to deposit with the landlord, on the grant of the lease, a sum of money equivalent to, say, 12 months' rent, which the landlord is allowed to call upon in the event of tenant default. At the end of the lease (or, perhaps, on lawful assignment), the deposit should be returned to the tenant.

Careful thought must be given to the setting up of this arrangement and to the drafting of the rent deposit deed. The following factors should be kept in mind.

(1) The deed should specify what default by the tenant will trigger access to the deposit (eg non-payment of rent, VAT or interest, or other breaches of covenant).

(2) If the deposited money is to be viewed as belonging to the landlord, it will be at risk if the landlord becomes insolvent. For instance, it would fall under the control of the landlord company's liquidator if the company went into liquidation. Equally, if the money is to be viewed as belonging to the tenant, it will be at risk at the precise moment when the tenant is likely to be in default in the performance of the lease terms (ie the occasion of his insolvency). It is, therefore, usual to place the money in a separate deposit account (managed in such a way that only the landlord and his nominees may draw money out of the account) which is then charged to the landlord in order that the landlord has first call on the money in a liquidation or bankruptcy. If the tenant is a company, the charge it creates will have to be registered at Companies House pursuant to s 395 of the Companies Act 1985.

(3) Under the old regime, the obligations under the rent deposit deed are personal obligations between the original landlord and the original tenant, and the obligation to repay the deposit at the end of the term will not bind an assignee of the reversion: see *Hua Chiao Commercial Bank Ltd v Chiaphua Industries Ltd* [1987] 1 AC 99. Further, the benefit of the obligation to repay does not pass to an assignee of the lease and thus, if the landlord inadvertently repaid the deposit to an assignee, the obligation to pay to the original tenant would still exist. The deed should deal with the personal nature of the obligations by providing that the landlord should not assign his interest in the reversion other than to a buyer who, by supplemental deed executed in favour of the tenant, expressly takes over the obligations of the landlord contained in the rent deposit deed. It should further provide that, on assignment of the lease, the deposit should be repaid to the tenant if the landlord has consented to the assignment in the usual manner under the alienation covenant. The assignee will be required to enter into a fresh rent deposit agreement.

Under the new regime, unless expressed to be personal, the obligation to repay the deposit will pass to an assignee of the reversion as one of the landlord covenants of the tenancy. Similarly, the benefit of repayment will pass to an assignee of the lease. The original tenant should, therefore, ensure either that the benefit of repayment is expressed to be personal to him, or that the assignee pays to him a sum equivalent to the deposit at the time of the assignment. An assignee of the reversion should ensure that, as he will have the burden of the covenant to repay the deposit, he has control of the deposit itself. An original landlord may be reluctant to part with the deposit unless he is able to secure a release from the covenant to repay the deposit under the LTCA 1995. If he is unable to secure a release, he may prefer to retain the deposit (various schemes have been suggested which enable the landlord to keep the deposit under his control but, at the same time, allow the assignee access to it in the event of tenant default).

(4)   The parties should consider to whom the interest earned on the money belongs (usually the tenant), whether the interest can be drawn out of the account, and at what stage the tenant will be required to make up any shortfall in the deposit (if, eg, the level of the account drops below an agreed figure due to the tenant's default). The deed will also have to make clear the situations in which the landlord will be entitled to draw upon the deposit.

One overriding factor that remains is that the tenant may not have sufficient money to put up a deposit in the first place.

Chapter 13

THE PARCELS CLAUSE

13.1 PURPOSE

The purpose of the parcels clause is to accurately and unambiguously describe the property being let to the tenant so that it is clear what is included and what is excluded. Where the whole of a building is being let, the parcels clause will contain the same sort of description as in the case of the sale of freehold land. Moreover, provided the boundaries are clearly identifiable it may be possible to adequately describe the premises in words alone. However, where a lease of part only of a building is intended, the parcels clause needs more care and attention and a plan will be essential (see **24.2**).

13.2 AIRSPACE AND UNDERGROUND

A lease of land includes the buildings on it and everything above and below the land. Thus, a lease of a building includes the airspace above it to such a height as is necessary for the ordinary use and enjoyment of the land and buildings. However, the parties may limit the extent of the parcels clause by excluding the airspace above the roof. If there is such a limitation, this will prevent the tenant from adding extra floors by extending upwards since to do so would be a trespass. The tenant should also appreciate that problems may be caused if he had to erect scaffolding above roof height to comply with his obligation to repair the roof; that would also amount to a trespass. The tenant should, therefore, ensure that he has any necessary right to enter the airspace above his building to the extent necessary to comply with his obligations under the lease. Without any limitation on the airspace the tenant will be free to extend upwards subject only to obtaining any necessary planning permission and consent under the alterations covenant.

13.3 FIXTURES

The point about a fixture is that it is part of the demised premises and prima facie belongs to the landlord. If an article is not a fixture, it will be a chattel. Yet, despite the apparent simplicity of the matter, it is not always easy to distinguish between the two, and over the years the courts have developed a test based on the degree of annexation of the item to the land and the purpose of annexation (see, eg, *Holland and Another v Hodgson and Another* (1872) LR 7 CP 328). However, the application of this test to a given set of facts is notoriously difficult and the reader is referred to one of the standard works on land law for further consideration of this issue (and in particular the House of Lords judgment in *Elitestone v Morris* [1997] 2 All ER 513).

For the avoidance of doubt, a prospective tenant should always compile a full inventory of the fixtures which are present at the commencement of the lease.

Chapter 13 contents
Purpose
Airspace and underground
Fixtures
Rights to be granted and reserved

13.3.1 Repair of fixtures

If an article is a fixture, it is treated as part of the demised premises and the tenant will become responsible for its repair under his obligation to repair 'the demised premises'. This can have a significant impact on the tenant bearing in mind that many business premises include expensive fixtures such as central heating and air conditioning plant. For this reason the tenant should always inspect the condition of the fixtures before completion of the lease and if any defects are discovered, the tenant must make sure that he does not become liable to remedy those defects under his repairing obligation. This can be achieved by getting the landlord to do any necessary repairs before the lease commences or by agreeing the state and condition with the landlord and ensuring that the covenant to repair does not require any higher standard than that existing at the date of commencement.

13.3.2 Removal of fixtures

The tenant may have the right to remove fixtures at the end of the lease depending upon whether they are 'landlord's fixtures', which cannot be removed, or 'tenant's fixtures', which the tenant is entitled to remove unless the lease provides to the contrary. Tenant's fixtures are those articles:

(1) affixed by the tenant;
(2) for the purpose of his trade; and
(3) which are capable of removal without substantially damaging the building and without destroying the usefulness of the article.

The terms of the lease may require the tenant to yield up the premises at the end of the term together with all fixtures. Whether this excludes the tenant's right to remove tenant's fixtures depends on the form of wording used; very clear words will be required before the right is excluded. However, it has been held that an obligation to yield up the premises 'with all and singular the fixtures and articles belonging thereto', is sufficient to exclude the right but the tenant should resist such a clause. Where the tenant is entitled to remove fixtures, he must make good any damage he causes by their removal and, as a general rule, the right only exists during the term.

13.4 RIGHTS TO BE GRANTED AND RESERVED

The tenant may need to be granted rights to enable him to use the demised premises to their full extent. For example, he may need the right to enter upon the landlord's adjoining property to comply with his obligation to repair; this can be particularly important where the walls of the demised premises are flush against the boundary. The tenant may also need the right to connect into services on the landlord's adjoining property.

From the landlord's point of view, he may need to reserve rights such as a right to enter the demised premises to view the state and condition or to repair. The service pipes and cables for the landlord's adjoining property may pass under or through the demised premises and the landlord will thus need to reserve rights in respect of them.

Chapter 14

TERM

14.1 INTRODUCTION

Chapter 14 contents
Introduction
Break clauses
Options to renew

The duration of a lease for a term of years must be fixed and certain before the lease takes effect. Thus, for example, a tenancy 'until the landlord requires the land for road widening', is void for uncertainty (*Prudential Assurance Co Ltd v London Residuary Body* [1992] 3 All ER 504). This principle applies to all leases, including periodic tenancies. A provision that one party is unable to determine a periodic tenancy, or for it only to be determined in certain circumstances, is inconsistent with the concept of a periodic tenancy. If termination on the happening of an uncertain event is required by either party, this can be achieved by granting a long fixed term with a break clause exercisable only on the happening of the event in question (see **14.2**).

Most business tenancies will be for a fixed term in which case the lease must specify the date of commencement of the term and its duration (eg 'for a term of ten years from and including the 29 September 1994'). There is no need for the commencement of the term to be the same date as the date of completion of the lease. It may be more convenient for the landlord, particularly when he is granting several leases in the same block, to choose one specific date from which the term of each will run. If this is an earlier date than completion then, unless the lease provides to the contrary, the tenant's rights and obligations will only arise on completion, not the earlier date. However, for the avoidance of doubt, the lease should expressly state the precise date from which the rent is to be payable.

In specifying the date of commencement, it is important to avoid any ambiguity so that it is clear beyond doubt when the term expires (but note the effect of the lease being protected under Part II of the LTA 1954). The presumption is that if the term is stated to run 'from' a particular date, the term begins on the next day. If, however, the term is expressed to begin 'on' a particular date, that day is the first day of the term. To avoid any possible argument, it is always best to use clear words such as 'beginning on', 'beginning with' or 'from and including' (see *Meadfield Properties Ltd v Secretary of State for the Environment* [1995] 03 EG 128).

14.2 BREAK CLAUSES

14.2.1 Who may operate them and when?

Either or both parties may be given an option to determine the lease at specified times during the term, or on the happening of certain specified events. For example, the tenant may be given the option to determine a 21-year lease at the end of the seventh and fourteenth years, or if he is prevented from trading due to the withdrawal of any necessary statutory licences. The landlord may be given an option to determine if he, at some future date, wishes to redevelop the premises or to occupy them for his own business purposes. The tenant should try to stipulate that the landlord cannot exercise the option until after a specified number of years as otherwise from the tenant's point of view the venture will be too uncertain in its duration.

Some options to break are expressed to be personal to the original tenant in order to prevent them being exercised by successors in title following an assignment. However, in *Brown & Root Technology v Sun Alliance* [1997] 18 EG 123, the court held that following the assignment of a registered lease to the tenant's parent company, the option was still exercisable by the original tenant until the assignment was completed by registration. It was only on registration of title that the legal estate vested in the assignee; until then the assignor remained the tenant and thus retained the ability to exercise the option. However, the position may be different for those leases granted on or after 1 January 1996, the date the Landlord and Tenant (Covenants) Act 1995 came into force. That Act defines 'assignment' to include an equitable assignment, and thus liability on the lease covenants is not dependent on registration of the title.

14.2.2 How are they exercised?

The break clause must be exercised in accordance with its terms. Thus, it must be exercised at the correct time and in the correct manner (see, eg, *Claire's Accessories UK Ltd v Kensington High Street Associates* [2001] PLSCS 112, as to the correct place of service). If there are any pre-conditions for the exercise of the option, they must be strictly complied with. Consequently, the tenant should be wary of any provision in the lease making compliance of tenant covenants a pre-condition for the exercise of the option. In such a case, even a trivial, immaterial breach of covenant on the part of the tenant may prevent him from validly exercising the option. The tenant should modify such a pre-condition so that it requires 'substantial' or 'material' compliance (see, eg, *Bairstow Eves (Securities) Ltd v Ripley* [1992] 2 EGLR 47 and *Commercial Union Life Assurance Co Ltd v Label Ink Ltd* [2001] EG 20 January 129). Similarly, any notice requirements for the exercise of the option must be strictly complied with because, unless the lease states to the contrary, time is of the essence of a break clause (*United Scientific Holdings v Burnley Borough Council* [1978] AC 904). If an incorrect date is specified in the break notice, the court may be prepared to correct it if the mistake would not have misled a reasonable recipient (*Mannai Investment Co Ltd v Eagle Star Life Assurance Co Ltd* [1997] AC 749). Subsequent cases have shown that the courts will adopt a similar approach when dealing with other errors in break notices, but it must always be borne in mind that each case will turn on its own facts (see, eg, the contrasting cases of *Lemmerbell Ltd v Britannia LAS Direct Ltd* [1998] 3 EGLR 67 and *Havant International Holdings Ltd v Lionsgate (H) Investments Ltd* [1999] EGCS 144).

14.2.3 Effect of exercise on sub-tenants

The effect of the exercise of an option in a head-lease may be to terminate any sub-lease granted. This is dealt with further at **30.4**.

14.2.4 Relationship with the LTA 1954, Part II

The landlord must be aware of the inter-relationship with Part II of the LTA 1954 and may wish to give thought to drafting the circumstances giving rise to the exercise of the option in line with the requirements of s 30(1)(f) or (g) of that Act (see **31.5**). This is desirable because the exercise of the option may not necessarily entitle the landlord to recover possession as he must also, where necessary, comply with the provisions of the 1954 Act (see **31.2**). Further, where necessary, regard should be had to the relationship between the notice required under the break clause and the notice provisions of the 1954 Act.

14.3 OPTIONS TO RENEW

Options to renew are not often found in business leases because most tenants are protected under Part II of the LTA 1954 and will, therefore, have a statutory right to a new tenancy which the landlord may only oppose on certain grounds (see Chapter 31).

Chapter 15

RENT

15.1 INTRODUCTION

Chapter 15 contents
Introduction
Amount
Time for payment
Other payments reserved
 as rent
Suspension of rent
Interest
VAT

One of the primary purposes in granting the lease is to enable the landlord to receive income in the form of rent. However, the payment of rent by the tenant is not essential to the landlord and tenant relationship and it is not uncommon, when property is difficult to let, for landlords to grant rent-free periods to tenants as an inducement for them to take the lease or to allow the tenant to fit out the premises.

The lease must contain a covenant by the tenant to pay the rent. In certain rare situations the tenant may have the right to deduct sums from the rent payable. For example, the tenant has the right to deduct those sums allowed by statute and, where the landlord is in breach of his repairing obligation, the tenant seemingly has an ancient right to undertake the repairs himself and deduct the expense from future payments of rent (see **28.2**). In addition, the tenant may be able to exercise a right of set-off and deduct an unliquidated sum for damages where the landlord is in breach of covenant and the tenant has thereby suffered a loss. Landlords often seek to counter the tenant's right to make deductions by stating in the covenant to pay rent that rent is to be paid 'without deduction'. However, this will not prevent a tenant from making a deduction authorised by statute, nor from exercising his right of set-off (see *Connaught Restaurants Ltd v Indoor Leisure Ltd* [1993] 46 EG 184). To exclude the tenant's right of set-off, very clear words must be used.

The covenant to pay rent is usually followed by a covenant by the tenant to pay all taxes, rates, assessments and outgoings imposed on the demised premises; this will include rates and water rates. For the avoidance of doubt, the tenant should make it clear that this obligation does not extend to any taxes payable by the landlord arising out of the receipt of the rent or due to any dealing by the landlord with the reversion.

In the definitions clause of the lease the landlord should seek to define 'Rent' as also including any 'interim rent' which may become payable under s 24A of the LTA 1954 (see **31.4**). If this were not done and the original tenant's continuing liability was stated by the lease to extend into the statutory continuation (under s 24), he would remain liable only for the contractual rent during that period and not for any interim rent which an assignee may be ordered to pay as part of any future renewal proceedings under the 1954 Act (*Herbert Duncan Ltd v Cluttons* [1992] 1 EGLR 101).

15.2 AMOUNT

The amount of rent must be certain. However, the actual amount need not be stated as long as some means are provided by which the exact amount can be ascertained. For example, the rent may be fixed at £25,000 per annum for the first 5 years of a 10-year lease and then at 'such revised rent as may be ascertained'. Provided the means of ascertaining the new rent are clearly stated, this is a valid method of dealing with the rent. Such clauses are dealt with in Chapter 16 where consideration is also given to the different methods of assessing the revised rent.

15.3 TIME FOR PAYMENT

The lease should set out:

(1) the date from which the rent is payable and the date of the first payment. It is usual to state that the first payment, or an apportioned part of it, is payable on the date of the lease unless a rent-free period is to be given;
(2) the payment dates, otherwise, in the case of a tenancy for a fixed term of years, there is authority for the proposition that the rent will be payable yearly. It is common practice in business leases to make the rent payable on the usual quarter days, ie 25 March, 24 June, 29 September and 25 December;
(3) whether rent is to be payable in advance or arrear. Unless the lease provides to the contrary, as is usual, the general law provides that rent is payable in arrears.

In modern commercial leases, provision is often made for the payment of rent by way of direct debit or standing order to minimise the risk of delay.

15.4 OTHER PAYMENTS RESERVED AS RENT

It is common for leases to provide for the tenant to make other payments to the landlord such as a service charge, or reimbursement of insurance premiums paid by the landlord. Landlords will often require the lease to state that such sums are payable as additional rent. The advantage to the landlord is that if the tenant defaults, the remedy of distress will be available; a remedy which can only be used for non-payment of rent and not for breaches of other covenants. Further, the landlord will be able to forfeit the lease for non-payment of sums defined as rent without the need to serve a notice under s 146 of the LPA 1925, see **30.5**.

It would also be possible for any VAT payable on the rent to be reserved as additional rent.

15.5 SUSPENSION OF RENT

In the absence of any contrary provision in the lease, the rent will continue to be payable even if the premises are damaged or destroyed and so cannot be used by the tenant. The contractual doctrine of frustration will only apply to leases in exceptional circumstances (see *National Carriers Ltd v Panalpina (Northern) Ltd* [1981] AC 675). From the tenant's point of view, therefore, he should insist on a proviso that the rent is suspended if the premises become unfit for use. If the lease contains a service charge, provision should also be made for this to be suspended as otherwise it too would continue to be payable. This issue is considered further at **22.7**.

15.6 INTEREST

Unless there is provision to the contrary, interest cannot be charged by the landlord on any late payment by the tenant of rent or other sums due under the lease (unless judgment is obtained against the tenant for such amounts). The Late Payment of Commercial Debts (Interest) Act 1998 does not apply to leases. It is, therefore, usual for a lease to provide that interest is payable by the tenant on any late payment of money due under the lease (from the due date to the date of actual payment). If, as usual, the rate of interest is geared to the base rate of a named bank (eg 4% above), a problem may arise if that bank no longer fixes a base rate. It is, therefore, sensible to provide for an alternative rate should this situation arise. For the tenant's protection, this should be stated to be 'some other reasonable rate as the landlord may specify'. Without the addition of the word 'reasonable' the tenant would have no right to dispute any new rate he thought excessive.

From the landlord's point of view, it is preferable for the lease to state that the interest rate is to apply 'both before and after any judgment'.

15.7 VAT

The implications of VAT on business leases has been discussed in Chapter 10. The landlord should include an appropriate clause entitling him to add VAT to the rent and other payments due from the tenant by providing that the rent and other sums are payable exclusive of VAT.

Chapter 16

THE RENT REVIEW CLAUSE

16.1 THE NEED FOR REVIEW

If the lease is granted for anything longer than about 5 years, the parties will have to address their minds to the question of whether provision should be made in the lease for varying the annual rent at intervals during the term. Traditionally, rent review clauses are included in commercial leases in order to give the landlord the ability to increase the rent, and this chapter generally proceeds on the basis that only upward revisions of rent are contemplated by the parties. However, the government's Code of Practice for Commercial Leases published in 2002 envisages upwards and downwards rent reviews becoming much more commonplace. It is too early to say what impact this voluntary Code will have on the commercial letting market.

Chapter 16 contents
The need for review
Regularity
Types of rent review
  clauses
Open market
  revaluations
The hypothetical letting
The mechanics of the
  review
Ancillary provisions

16.2 REGULARITY

Reviews are commonly programmed to occur at 3- or 5-year intervals during the term. In a modern 15-year 'institutional' letting (so called because a 15-year lease, where the tenant is obliged to repair and pay for the insurance of the premises is the type of letting favoured by those institutions which frequently invest in the commercial property market), reviews will be programmed to occur at every fifth anniversary of the term.

It is suggested that computation of the review dates in the lease is best achieved by reference to anniversaries of the term commencement date. However, if this method is adopted, the tenant should check that the term commencement date has not been significantly backdated by the landlord, as this would have the effect of advancing the first review date (eg if the term runs from 29 September 2001, but the lease is only completed on 1 November 2002, the fifth anniversary of the term is now less than 4 years away). Instead of calculating the dates as anniversaries of the start of the term, some leases set out the exact review dates in the lease. This, however, ought to be avoided since it can create valuation problems at review if the rent review clause in the lease (with its specific review dates) is incorporated as a term of the hypothetical letting (as to which, see **16.5**).

Landlords may attempt to insert a rent review date on the penultimate day of the term. At first sight this might seem illogical since the term is about to end, but of course the tenant is likely to enjoy a statutory continuation of his tenancy under LTA 1954, s 24(1) whereby his tenancy will continue beyond the expiry date at the rent then payable. Where the tenant enjoys the benefit of a statutory continuation, the landlord may be able to apply to the court under LTA 1954, s 24A for an interim rent to be fixed (see **31.4**) in order to increase the rent payable by the tenant during the continuation. However, many landlords are not content to rely on the provisions of s 24A, preferring instead to achieve a rental uplift by implementing a contractual rent review clause on the penultimate day of the contractual term (ie just before the

[handwritten margin note: Example wra L can back date review.]

statutory continuation is due to begin). In practice, because the contractual method of assessment in the rent review clause is likely to differ from the statutory basis of assessment adopted by the court, a penultimate day rent review usually secures a greater increase in rent and therefore ensures that the rent payable during the statutory continuation is greater than would be the case under the interim rent provisions. An interim rent is often assessed at some 10% to 15% below a full market rent (see **31.4.2**).

The tenant ought to resist a penultimate day rent review for the obvious reason that s 24A is likely to give him a better deal, and that a penultimate day review takes away the 'cushion effect' of s 24A (see **31.4.3**).

16.3 TYPES OF RENT REVIEW CLAUSES

There are various ways in which rent can be varied during the term.

16.3.1 Fixed increases

The lease could provide, for example, that in a lease for a 10-year term, the rent is set at £10,000 for the first 3 years of the term, £15,000 for the next 3 years, and £20,000 for the remainder of the term. This sort of clause would be very rare since the parties to the lease would be placing their faith in the fixed increases proving to be realistic.

16.3.2 Index-linked clauses

Some of the early forms of rent review clauses required the rent to be periodically re-assessed by linking the rent to an index recording supposed changes in the value of money. Indexes such as the General Index of Retail Prices and the Producer Price Index can be used in order to revise the rent either at the review dates, or at every rent payment date. Reference should be made to one of the standard works on landlord and tenant law for information as to how such clauses work in practice.

16.3.3 Turnover and sub-lease rents

A turnover rent is one which is geared to the turnover of the tenant's business, and can only therefore be considered by the landlord where turnover is generated at the premises. A turnover rent would be impractical in the case of office or warehouse premises. The tenant's rent (or at least a proportion of it) is worked out as a percentage of the turnover. If a turnover rent clause is to be used, thought will have to be given in the lease to the definition of the turnover of the business (eg whether credit sales are to be included with cash sales as part of the turnover or whether internet sales are to be included). Other considerations include whether access will be given to the landlord to inspect the tenant's books, how turnover is to be apportioned if it is generated at the demised premises and other premises and whether the tenant is to be obliged in the lease to continue trading from the premises in order to generate turnover. Reference should be made to one of the standard works on landlord and tenant law for further details of the operation of turnover rent clauses.

16.3.4 Open market revaluation

An open market revaluation review clause requires the rent to be revised in accordance with changes in the property market.

The most common form of rent review clause will provide that at every rent review date (eg every fifth anniversary of the term) the parties should seek to agree upon a figure that equates to what is then the current open market rent for a letting of the tenant's premises. The aim of the exercise is to find out how much a tenant in the open market would be prepared to pay, in terms of rent per annum, if the tenant's premises were available to let in the open market on the relevant review date. This agreement is achieved either by some form of informal negotiated process between the landlord and the tenant, or by the service of notices and counter-notices which specify proposals and counter-proposals as to the revised rent. If agreement cannot be reached, the clause should provide for the appointment of an independent valuer who will determine the revised rent. The valuer will be directed by the review clause to take certain matters into account in conducting his valuation, and to disregard others, and he will call upon evidence of rental valuations of other comparable leasehold interests in the locality.

A clause which provides for an open market revaluation is the type of review clause most frequently encountered in practice, and is the one upon which the rest of this chapter will concentrate.

16.4 OPEN MARKET REVALUATIONS

First and foremost it should be understood that a valuer of commercial leasehold premises cannot find the rental value of 'the premises' since 'the premises' as such are not capable of rental valuation. It is a leasehold interest in the premises, a lease granted for a particular length of time, for a particular purpose, and upon certain terms and conditions which is capable of rental valuation, and which must fall to be valued.

Having established that it is not the premises, but an interest in the premises which has to be valued at each review date, it must be clearly understood that it is not the tenant's own interest that will be valued but a hypothetical interest in the premises. The reason for this is that valuing the tenant's interest gives rise to many problems, uncertainties and injustices. For example, consider the position of the tenant who, in breach of his obligations under the lease, has allowed the premises to fall into disrepair, which has had the effect of reducing the open market rental valuation (OMRV) of the premises. Is it fair that the landlord should suffer at rent review by having the rent depressed on account of the tenant's breach of covenant? From a tenant's perspective consider the position of a tenant who, in the fourth year of the term, at his own expense, voluntarily made improvements to the premises which had the effect of increasing the OMRV of his interest in the premises. Is it fair that the tenant should suffer at rent review by having to pay an increased rent which reflects in part the rental value attributable to his improvements?

These are just two of the many problems inherent in a valuation of the tenant's actual lease. As a result of these difficulties and injustices connected with such a valuation, it is accepted that the valuer should be instructed by the rent review clause to ascertain the OMRV of a hypothetical interest in the premises. He should be directed by the clause to calculate how much rent per annum a hypothetical willing tenant would be prepared to pay for a letting of the premises, with vacant possession, for a hypothetical term. He is directed by the lease to make certain assumptions about the terms of the letting, and to disregard certain matters which might otherwise distort the OMRV, in order to overcome the difficulties and eradicate the injustices referred to above.

16.5 THE HYPOTHETICAL LETTING

It is important that the parties ensure that the terms and circumstances of the hypothetical letting (which will form the basis of valuation at review) are clearly stated in the lease, and achieve a fair balance between the parties without departing too far from the reality of the tenant's existing letting.

The lease should make it clear that the date of valuation, when the OMRV is assessed, is the review date itself. A negotiated agreement as to the revised rent between the landlord and the tenant, or a determination by an independent valuer, may occur several months before or after the relevant review date, although the new rent is usually stated to be payable from the review date itself. Irrespective of the date of assessment, the tenant should not allow the valuation date to be capable of variation; it should be fixed at the relevant review date. Any clause which purports to allow the valuation date to be fixed by the service of a notice by the landlord is to be resisted for the simple reason that in a falling market, the landlord would serve his notice early to secure a higher rent, whilst in a rising market he would serve his notice late at a time when the market was at its peak, safe in the knowledge that the revised rent would be backdated and payable from the review date. In a similar way, any clause which defines the valuation date as the day upon which agreement is reached, or the third party determination is to be made is to be resisted, as it might encourage the landlord to protract the review process to get the benefit of a later valuation date.

16.5.1 The aim of the exercise

The valuer will be directed by the lease to ascertain the open market rental value of a hypothetical letting of the premises at each review date. Different phrases are used by different clauses to define the rent to be ascertained. Some leases will require the valuer to find a 'reasonable rent' for a letting of the premises, or a 'fair rent', or a 'market rent', or a 'rack rent' or 'the open market rent'. It is submitted that the latter clause is the preferred phrase to adopt, as it is the one most commonly used in practice, and is therefore a phrase with which professional valuers are familiar. Other phrases are less common, and are open to adverse interpretations by valuers and the court.

Most tenants would want to avoid the use of the expression 'the best rent at which the premises might be let' since this might allow the valuer to consider the possibility of what is known as a special purchaser's bid. If, by chance, the market for a hypothetical letting of the premises contains a potential bidder who would be prepared to bid in excess of what would ordinarily be considered to be the market rent, the 'best' rent would be the rent which the special bidder would be prepared to pay. For example if the premises which are the subject matter of the hypothetical letting are situated next to premises occupied by a business which is desperate to expand, the 'best' rent might be the rent which that business would be willing to pay.

16.5.2 The circumstances of the letting

To enable the valuer to do his job, the rent review clause must clearly indicate the circumstances in which a hypothetical letting of the premises is to be contemplated. For example, he must be able to establish which premises are to be the subject matter of the letting, whether there is a market for such a letting, whether the premises would be available with or without vacant possession, and what the terms of the letting would be. It is common for the clause to require the valuer to find the open market rent of a letting of the tenant's vacant premises, for a specified duration, on the assumption that there is a market for the letting which will be granted without the payment or receipt of a premium, and subject only to the terms of the actual lease (except as to the amount of the annual rent).

The premises

Usually, the valuer is required to ascertain the rental value of a hypothetical letting of the premises actually demised by the tenant's lease. The draftsman should therefore ensure that the demised premises are clearly defined by the parcels clause in the lease, and that they enjoy the benefit of all necessary rights and easements to enable them to be used for their permitted purpose.

A valuer uses comparables as evidence in his valuation of a letting of the premises. He draws upon evidence of rents currently being paid by tenants of comparable buildings, let in comparable circumstances, on comparable terms. If the actual premises demised to the tenant are unique or exceptional (eg an over-sized warehouse) there may be no comparables in the area for the valuer to use. In that case, the lease ought to require the valuer to adopt a different approach to his valuation, perhaps by directing him to take account of rental values of other premises which would not ordinarily count as comparables. This in itself may lead to valuation problems as, for example, in *Dukeminster (Ebbgate House One) Ltd v Somerfield Properties Co Ltd* [1997] 40 EG 157.

The market

As the hypothetical letting is an artificial creation, and since leasehold valuations cannot be carried out in the abstract, an artificial market has to be created. If the rent review clause does not create a well balanced hypothetical market in which the letting can be contemplated, it would be open for the tenant (in appropriate cases) to argue at review that no market exists for a letting of the tenant's premises, and that therefore an 'open market' rent for the premises would be merely nominal, or a peppercorn. An example of this could occur if the tenant was occupying premises which were now outdated to such an extent that they were impractical for modern use, or that the premises were so exceptional that only the tenant himself would contemplate occupying them. Only the actual tenant would be in the hypothetical market for such premises, and even he might not be in the market if he can show that he has actively been trying to dispose of his lease. The market might truly be dead.

To create a market, the rent review clause usually requires the valuer to assume that the hypothetical letting is taking place in the open market and being granted by a 'willing landlord' to a 'willing tenant'. In *FR Evans (Leeds) Ltd v English Electric*

Co Ltd (1977) 245 EG 657 it was held that where such phrases are used, it means that the valuer must assume that there are two hypothetical people who are prepared to enter into the arrangement, neither of whom is being forced to do so, and neither of whom is affected by any personal difficulties (eg a landlord with cash-flow problems, or a tenant who has just lost his old premises) which would prejudice their position in open market negotiations. A willing landlord is an abstract person, but is someone who has the right to grant a lease of the premises, and a willing tenant, again an abstraction, is someone who is actively seeking premises to fulfil a need that these premises would fulfil. It is implicit in the use of these phrases that there is at least one willing tenant in the market, and that there is a rent upon which they will agree.

Even if the lease is silent as to whether there is assumed to be a willing tenant, the Court of Appeal has held in *Dennis & Robinson Ltd v Kiossos Establishment* [1987] 1 EGLR 133 that such a creature is in any case to be assumed, since a rent review clause which asks for an open market valuation by its nature requires there to be at least one willing tenant in the market. This means that for rent review purposes, where an open market valuation is required, there will always be someone in the hypothetical market who would be prepared to take a letting of the premises, and therefore the tenant cannot argue that the market is completely dead. However quite how much a willing tenant would be willing to pay is for the valuer to decide.

If the market is well and truly dead, the landlord's only protection is an upwards-only rent review clause.

The consideration

Any consideration moving between the parties at the time of the grant is likely to have a bearing on the amount of rent to be paid by the tenant. Such movements are not uncommon in the open market. For example, a landlord may seek to induce a tenant to take the lease at a certain level of rent by offering him a reverse premium without which the tenant might only be prepared to pay rent at a lower level. A rent-free period may be offered by a landlord, either as a straightforward inducement as above, or to compensate a tenant for the costs that he will incur in fitting out the premises at the start of the term. Without the rent-free period, the tenant might only be prepared to pay a lower rent. If the tenant pays a premium to the landlord at the outset, this may be reflected in the tenant paying a rent lower than he would otherwise pay.

As far as the hypothetical letting is concerned, it is common for the rent review clause to assume that no consideration (in the form of a premium) will be moving between the parties on the grant of the hypothetical letting. As seen above, such payments can distort the amount of initial rent payable by a tenant. Therefore to get the clearest indication of what the market rent for the letting would be, it ought to be assumed that no premium is to be paid on the grant of the hypothetical letting.

Furthermore, the landlord may seek to include a provision which states that no inducement in the form of a rent-free period will be given to the hypothetical tenant on the grant of the hypothetical lease. This is an attempt by the landlord to deprive the tenant of the effect of such concessions granted in the market place (thereby keeping the level of rent, on review, artificially high). The landlord is trying to achieve a headline rent rather than an effective rent. For example, if the tenant agrees to take a lease at £100,000 per annum for a term of 5 years, but is to receive a 12-month rent-free period, whilst the headline rent (the rent stated to be payable under the lease) remains at £100,000 per annum, the annual rent effectively payable (the 'effective' rent) is only £80,000. At review, therefore, the landlord would argue that the effect of disregarding any rent-free period which might be available in the open market, is that the new rent payable from review should be a headline rent not an effective rent. The tenant would argue that, since the hypothetical tenant is not getting the benefit of a rent-free period, therefore, the revised rent should be discounted to compensate the hypothetical tenant for a benefit he has not received.

There have been several cases on the effect of these types of provisions. The Court of Appeal in *Broadgate Square plc v Lehman Brothers Ltd* [1995] 01 EG 111, applying the purposive approach to the interpretation of the relevant clause said that '... the court will lean against a construction which would require payment of rent upon an assumption that the tenant has received the benefit of a rent-free period, which he has not in fact received ...' (per Leggatt LJ). However, such an approach cannot be adopted in the face of clear, unambiguous language. According to Hoffmann LJ, '... if upon its true construction the clause deems the market rent to be whatever is the headline rent after a rent-free period granted ... the tenant cannot complain because in changed market conditions it is more onerous than anyone would have foreseen'. The presence of such a clause in the hypothetical letting may itself be an onerous provision which justifies a reduction in the OMRV (possibly to the extent that it negates the effect of the landlord's clever drafting).

Possession

As the valuer is assessing the rental value of the tenant's existing premises, is he to assume that the tenant is still there (in which case rent to be paid by a hypothetical bidder would be very low), or is he to assume that the tenant has vacated? Naturally, he must assume that the tenant has moved out, and therefore most rent review clauses of this type include an assumption that vacant possession is available for the hypothetical letting.

Care must be taken in making this assumption, because in certain cases it can give rise to problems:

(1) If the tenant has sub-let all or part of the premises, an assumption that vacant possession is to be available will mean that the effect on rent of the presence of the sub-tenant will have to be disregarded. If the sub-tenant occupies for valuable business purposes (eg the premises in question are high street offices where the ground floor has been sub-let as a high class shop), the presence of the sub-tenancy would ordinarily increase the rental value of the head leasehold interest since the head tenant would expect to receive lucrative sub-lease rents. The assumption of vacant possession would deny the landlord the opportunity to bring a valuable sub-letting into account at review. If the sub-tenancy was for residential purposes yielding precious little in terms of sub-lease rents, the assumption of vacant possession would allow the landlord to have the sub-letting disregarded and, depending on the other terms of the hypothetical letting, enable the premises to be valued as a whole for the permitted business purpose.

(2) The assumption of vacant possession means that the tenant is deemed to have moved out of the premises and, as all vacating tenants would do, he is deemed to have removed and taken his fixtures with him. In respect of shop premises, this might mean that all of the shop fittings must be assumed to have been removed, leaving nothing remaining but a shell. (Of course, in reality, the premises are still fully fitted out, but for hypothetical valuation purposes, the

tenant's fixtures are assumed to have gone.) If a hypothetical tenant were to bid in the open market for these premises then, depending upon market forces prevalent at the time, he might demand a rent-free period in order to compensate him for the time it will take for him to carry out a notional fitting out of the premises (ie to restore the fittings that have notionally been removed). Since the revised rent has to be a consistent figure payable throughout the period until the next review date, this notional rent-free period would have to be spread out during the review period, or possibly over the rest of the term, thereby reducing the general level of rent; (eg the valuer finds that the rent for the next 5 years should be £10,000 per annum, but that an incoming tenant would obtain a rent-free period of 12 months. By spreading the notional rent-free period over the 5-year review period the rent would be £8,000 per annum). The landlord can counter this problem by including an assumption that, notwithstanding vacant possession, the premises are fully fitted out for occupation and use. (See **16.5.3**.)

The terms

The valuer, in ascertaining the OMRV of a leasehold interest, must look at all of the proposed terms of the lease. The more onerous the lease terms, the less attractive the lease becomes from a tenant's point of view, and therefore the lower the OMRV of the interest. If the rent review clause is silent, the hypothetical letting will be assumed to be granted upon the terms of the tenant's existing lease, since the court does not like to stray too far away from reality, and there is a general preference by the court to construe rent review clauses in such a way as to ensure that the tenant does not end up paying in terms of rent for something that he is not actually getting. Usually, however, the clause directs the valuer to assume that the letting is to be made upon the terms of the tenant's actual letting, as varied from time to time. (The fact that the valuer must take account of variations means that it is imperative that, when conducting the review, the valuer checks the terms of all deeds of variation entered into, and all licences granted since the date of the lease to see if the terms of the actual lease have been changed.)

Each of the terms of the lease will be analysed by the valuer at review to see if they will have any effect on the rental value. If either party, with sufficient foresight, feels that a particular term will have a detrimental effect on the rental value (because the term is too wide, or too narrow, or too onerous) that party may seek to have the term excluded from the hypothetical letting, by use of an assumption or a disregard (see **16.5.3**).

The valuer will look closely at all of the terms of the lease, but in particular at the following.

THE ALIENATION COVENANT

If the alienation covenant in the actual lease is too restrictive (eg by prohibiting all forms of alienation), its incorporation as a term of the hypothetical letting will lead to a decrease in the OMRV of that interest. Similarly, if the actual lease allows only the named tenant to occupy the premises (or only companies within the same group of companies as the tenant), this will have a negative impact on the OMRV. In these cases it will be advisable for the landlord to exclude the excessive restrictions on alienation from the terms of the hypothetical letting. The tenant might consider this to be unfair and, perhaps, a compromise would be to widen the alienation covenant in the actual lease.

THE USER COVENANT

If the actual lease narrowly defines the permitted use of the premises and allows little or no scope for the tenant to alter that use, a tenant bidding for the lease in the open market is likely to reduce his rental bid to reflect the fact that he would be severely hindered should he wish to dispose of the premises during the term, or change the nature of his business. It became clear in *Plinth Property Investments Ltd v Mott, Hay & Anderson* (1979) 1 EGLR 17 (a Court of Appeal decision) that the possibility of the landlord agreeing to waive a breach of covenant (eg by allowing a wider use of the premises than the covenant already permits) has to be ignored. This principle is not just applicable to user covenants (although the *Plinth* case specifically concerned a user covenant) but to all covenants where the landlord is freely able to withhold his consent to a change. It is not open to the landlord at review to disregard the detrimental effect on rent of a restrictive clause which has been incorporated into the hypothetical letting by saying that he is or might be prepared to waive the restriction. Further, a landlord cannot unilaterally vary the terms of the lease (see *C & A Pensions Trustees Ltd v British Vita Investments Ltd* (1984) 272 EG 63). If the landlord is intent on tightly restricting the tenant in the user clause in the actual lease, but wants to maximise the rental value of the hypothetical letting at review and is concerned that the incorporation of the restrictive clause into the hypothetical letting will harm the OMRV, he should draft the review clause so that the actual user covenant is to be disregarded, and an alternative permitted use is to be assumed. Obviously, the tenant should strongly resist such an approach, since he would find himself paying a rent from review assessed on the basis of a freedom that he does not in fact possess. Again, a compromise might be to widen the user covenant in the actual lease.

If the lease allows only the named tenant to use the premises for a named business (ie a very restrictive user covenant), the landlord should try to have the user covenant disregarded at review. If he fails to do so, the court might be prepared to step in to assist the landlord as in *Sterling Land Office Developments Ltd v Lloyds Bank plc* (1984) 271 EG 894 where a covenant not to use the premises other than as a branch of Lloyds Bank plc was incorporated into the hypothetical letting, but with the name and business left blank, to be completed when the name and business of the hypothetical tenant were known.

RENT AND RENT REVIEW

The review clause will state that the hypothetical letting is to be granted upon the same terms as the actual lease save as to the amount of rent. As the aim of the review exercise is to vary the amount of rent, it is clear that the rent initially reserved by the lease must not be incorporated into the hypothetical letting. However, the tenant must be alert to guard against any form of wording which has the effect of excluding from the hypothetical letting not only the amount of rent reserved, but also the rent review clause itself. It is a commonly held view that a tenant bidding for a medium or long term letting of premises in the open market, where the annual rent cannot be increased during the term, is likely to pay more than if the letting contained a rent review clause. The tenant would pay a rent in excess of the current market rent in return for a guarantee that the rent will not rise but would be fixed at the initial rent for the entire duration of the term. A long series of cases followed the decision in *National Westminster Bank plc v Arthur Young McClelland Moores & Co* [1985] 1 WLR 1123 where the provisions of a rent review clause were interpreted in such a way as to exclude from the hypothetical letting the rent review provisions. This alone led to the annual rent being increased from £800,000 to £1.209 million, instead of £1.003 million if the rent review clause had been incorporated. Courts today tend to shy away from interpreting a rent review clause in such a way as to exclude a provision for review from the hypothetical letting. In the absence of clear words directing the rent review clause to be disregarded, the court will give effect to the underlying purpose of the clause and will assume that the hypothetical letting contains provisions for the review of rent. However, the tenant must always check carefully that the review clause is not expressly excluded from the hypothetical letting, since the court would be bound to give effect to such clear words. Ideally, the hypothetical letting should be '... upon the terms of this lease, other than the amount of rent'.

THE LENGTH OF TERM

Whether the lease is for a short term or a long term will affect how much rent a tenant is prepared to pay. Whilst a landlord often needs to guarantee rental income by granting a long-term lease, in times of uncertain trading tenants often prefer short-term lettings in order to retain a degree of flexibility, and to avoid long-term liability in the event of business failure. If a short-term letting is more attractive to tenants in the current market, it follows that a tenant would be prepared to bid more in terms of rent per annum for such a letting than if a longer term was proposed. On the other hand, other tenants with long-term business plans and a desire for stability and security would be prepared to increase their rental bid in return for a longer letting.

The rent review clause must define the length of the hypothetical letting. The landlord will want to maximise the rental value of the hypothetical letting by specifying as the hypothetical term a length which is currently preferred in the market by prospective tenants of premises of the type in question. The landlord will have to ask his surveyor for advice in this regard, since the term to be adopted is purely a matter of valuation, which will differ from lease to lease.

When the valuer makes his valuation, he is allowed to take into account the prospect of the term being renewed under the LTA 1954 (see *Secretary of State for Employment v Pivot Properties Limited* (1980) 256 EG 1176). Obviously, the rent will turn out to be higher if there is a strong possibility of renewal. In the *Pivot* case, that possibility led to an uplift in the rent of £850,000 per annum.

16.5.3 Assumptions to be made

Several assumptions have already been considered in respect of the circumstances of the hypothetical letting. Certain other assumptions are also commonly made.

(1) An assumption that the premises are fully fitted out and ready for immediate occupation and use by the incoming tenant. An assumption of vacant possession necessarily leads to an assumption that the tenant has moved out and taken all his fixtures with him. The assumption that the premises are fully fitted out attempts to counter the deemed removal of fixtures by assuming that the hypothetical tenant would be able to move straight into the premises without asking for a rent-free period in which he could carry out his notional fitting out works. Hence the assumption removes any discount the tenant would claim at review in respect of the rent-free period that the hypothetical tenant might have claimed. The phrase 'fit for occupation' does not appear to go as far as 'fully fitted out' since the former assumption anticipates a stage where the premises

are simply ready to be occupied for fitting out purposes, in which case the hypothetical tenant might still demand a rent-free period (see *Pontsarn Investments Ltd v Kansallis-Osake-Pankki* [1992] 22 EG 103). Some solicitors prefer to deal with this problem in a different way by including an assumption that '... no reduction is to be made to take account of any rental concession which on a new letting with vacant possession might be granted to the incoming tenant for a period within which its fitting out works would take place'.

(2) An assumption that the covenants have been performed. Most rent review clauses include an assumption that the tenant has complied with his covenants under the lease. In the absence of such a provision, a court is willing to imply one in any case, since it is a general principle that a party to a transaction should not be allowed to profit from its own wrongdoing (see *Family Management v Grey* (1979) 253 EG 369). This is particularly important when considering the tenant's repairing obligation. Clearly the hypothetical tenant can be expected to pay more in terms of rent if the premises are in good repair and, conversely, less if they are in a poor condition (for whatever reason). A tenant should not be allowed to argue in reduction of the rent at review that the premises are in a poor condition, if it is through his own default that the disrepair has come about and hence the reason for the assumption under consideration.

The landlord may try to include an assumption in respect of his own covenants (ie that the landlord has performed his covenants). The tenant ought to resist this, especially where the landlord will be taking on significant obligations in the actual lease. For example, in a lease of part of the landlord's premises, the landlord may be entering into covenants to perform services, and to repair and maintain the structure, exterior and common parts of the building. If the landlord fails to perform his covenants, the likely result is that the rental value of an interest in the building will decrease, since the building will be less attractive to tenants in the market. Accordingly, the rent at review would be adjusted to reflect this. However, an assumption that the landlord has performed his covenants enables the landlord to have the review conducted on the basis that the building is fully in repair (without regard to his own default), which means that the tenant would be paying for something at review (ie a lease of premises in a building which is in first-rate condition) that he does not in fact have. Such an assumption should be resisted by the tenant.

However, the landlord will not concede the tenant's argument easily. Landlords will argue that, without it, the valuer will assess the new rent at a lower level, even though immediately afterwards the tenant might bring proceedings against the landlord in respect of the landlord's breach of covenant, forcing the landlord to put the building into repair. They argue that it is unfair that the rent will be set at a low level for the entire review period on the basis of a temporary breach of covenant, which the landlord might soon be required to remedy. The tenant's counter-argument is that an action for breach of covenant is no substitute for a dilapidated building.

(3) If the landlord has waived the VAT exemption in respect of the premises, so that VAT is payable in addition to the rent, this will negatively affect a tenant who has an adverse VAT status. Organisations such as banks, building societies and insurance companies make exempt supplies in the course of their business and therefore do not receive any output tax which can be set off against the input tax to be paid on the rent. These organisations have to bear the VAT on

the rent as an overhead of the business. Arguably, such tenants in the market would reduce their bids in order to compensate for the VAT overhead that they will have to absorb. Some landlords counter this by including an assumption that the hypothetical tenant will be able to recover its VAT in full (thereby removing the need for the hypothetical tenant to ask for a discount on rent to cover his VAT overhead), or by ensuring that the hypothetical letting includes a covenant by the landlord not to waive the exemption for VAT purposes. Tenants ought to try to resist such a provision, leaving the valuer to value the lease on the basis of the reality of the actual letting.

16.5.4 Matters to be disregarded

In order to be fair to the tenant, the landlord usually drafts the review clause so that certain matters which would otherwise increase the OMRV of a letting of the premises are disregarded.

Goodwill

A letting of premises will be more attractive in the open market if there is existing goodwill at the premises, in the shape of a regular flow of clients or customers, or the benefit of a good reputation. The letting would command a higher rent than could otherwise be expected, as tenants will be eager to obtain possession of the premises in order to take advantage of the goodwill. However, it is the tenant who generates such goodwill and so it is only fair that any effect on rent of that goodwill ought to be disregarded at review.

Occupation

The fact that the tenant, his predecessors or his sub-tenants have been in occupation of the premises is usually disregarded. It is accepted that, if the tenant was bidding for a letting of his own premises, he would bid more than most others in the market in order to avoid the expense of having to move to other premises. The rental effect of occupation should therefore be disregarded. In appropriate cases, where the tenant also occupies adjoining premises, his occupation of those premises should also be disregarded, to avoid the argument that the tenant would increase his bid for the demised premises to secure a letting of premises which are adjacent to his other premises.

If the rent review clause requires occupation by the tenant to be disregarded, but makes no similar requirement as regards his goodwill (see above), the valuer should nevertheless disregard the rental effect of the tenant's goodwill, since goodwill must necessarily be the product of the tenant's occupation (see *Prudential Assurance Co Ltd v Grand Metropolitan Estate Ltd* [1993] 32 EG 74).

Improvements

If the tenant improves the premises, then he usually does so at his own expense, but the result will inevitably be that the rental value of an interest in the premises will increase. It is unfair for the landlord to ask that the rent be increased at review to reflect the increase in rental value brought about by the tenant's improvements. If improvements were to be taken into account, the tenant would be paying for his improvements twice over (once on making them, and once again when the revised rent becomes payable). The landlord usually drafts the rent review clause so that the effect on rent of most of the tenant's improvements are disregarded.

Which improvements are to be disregarded? The tenant will want to make sure that the effect on rent of all improvements that have been carried out either by him or his sub-tenants or his predecessors in title are disregarded, whether they were carried out during the term, during some earlier lease or during a period of occupation before the grant of the lease (eg during a pre-letting fitting out period). He will also want to have disregarded the effect on rent of improvements executed by the landlord, but which were carried out at the tenant's expense. The landlord will want to make sure that any improvements that the tenant was obliged to make are taken into account. These will include improvements made under the lease granted in consideration of the tenant carrying out works to the premises, or improvements the tenant was obliged to carry out under some other document, such as an agreement for lease, or by virtue of a statutory provision requiring the tenant to carry out work (eg the installation of a fire escape and doors). An obligation in a licence to alter to execute permitted works in accordance with agreed drawings, or by a stipulated time, is not on obligation in itself to do the works in a particular way (see *Historic Houses Hotels Ltd v Cadogan Estates* [1997] AC 70).

User, alienation and improvements

It is possible that for his own benefit the landlord might try to have disregarded some of the more restrictive covenants contained in the actual lease such as user, alienation and improvements. This is unfair to the tenant who ought to be advised to resist such a disregard.

16.6 THE MECHANICS OF THE REVIEW

There are two principal ways in which the review process can be conducted:

(1) by negotiations between the parties, but in default of agreement, by reference to an independent third party for determination (see **16.6.2**);

(2) by the service of trigger notices and counter-notices in an attempt to agree the revised rent, but in default, by reference to a third party (see **16.6.3**).

Whichever method is to be adopted, the first consideration to be dealt with is whether time is to be of the essence in respect of any time-limits contained in the clause, or in respect of the rent review dates.

16.6.1 Is time of the essence?

As a general rule, if time is of the essence of a particular clause, a party who fails to act by the time-limit specified loses the right given by that clause. If time is of the essence of the whole rent review clause, the slightest delay will mean that the landlord will be denied the opportunity to increase the rent until the next review date, (or, indeed, the tenant will be denied the opportunity to decrease the rent until the next review date if the clause permits downward reviews).

The House of Lords in *United Scientific Holdings Ltd v Burnley Borough Council* [1977] 2 All ER 62 held that, in the absence of any contrary indications in the express wording of the clause, or in the interrelation of the rent review clause with other clauses in the lease, there is a presumption that time is not of the essence of the clause and that the review can still be implemented and pursued, even though specific dates have passed (see, eg, *McDonald's Property Co Ltd v HSBC Bank plc* [2001] 36 EG 181). It follows from this decision that there are three situations where time will be of the essence, either of the whole clause, or in respect of certain steps in the review procedure.

An express stipulation

Time will be of the essence in respect of all or any of the time-limits in the review clause if the lease expressly says so.

Any other contrary indication

The phrase 'time is of the essence' may not have been used in the lease, but there are cases where other forms of wording used by the draftsman have been sufficient to indicate an intention to rebut the usual presumption. In *First Property Growth Partnership v Royal & Sun Alliance Services Ltd* [2002] EWHC 305 (Ch), [2002] 22 EG 140, the clause required the landlord to serve notice of intention to review upon the tenant 12 months before the relevant review date 'but not at any other time'. This was held to make time of the essence and thus the landlord's notice served after the relevant review date was invalid. In *Starmark Enterprises Ltd v CPL Distribution Ltd* [2001] 32 EG 89 (CS), the lease provided for service of a trigger notice by the landlord specifying the amount of rent payable for the following period but went on to provide that if the tenant failed to serve a counter-notice within one month the tenant would be 'deemed to have agreed to pay the increased rent specified in that notice'. The Court of Appeal held that time was of the essence; the 'deeming' provision was a sufficient contra-indication to rebut the usual presumption. Reference should be made to one of the standard works on landlord and tenant law for further consideration of the many cases dealing with this issue.

The interrelation of the review clause with other clauses in the lease

The usual way in which a clause might interrelate with the review clause in such a way as to make time of the essence is if the tenant is given an option to break the term on or shortly after each review date. The inference in such an interrelation is that, if the tenant cannot afford to pay the revised rent or, where the level of rent is not yet known, he does not envy the prospect of an increase, he is given an opportunity to terminate the lease by exercising the break clause. Since time is usually of the essence in respect of the exercise of a break clause, time may also be construed to be of the essence of the rent review clause. It does not matter that the review clause and the option are separate clauses in the lease; the court simply has to be able to infer a sufficient interrelation. Nor, apparently, does it matter that the option to break is mutual and linked to only one of several rent review dates (*Central Estates Ltd v Secretary of State for the Environment* [1997] 1 EGLR 239).

Unless a rigid timetable for conducting the review is required by either party, it is not often that time will be made of the essence, because of the fatal consequences arising from a delay. It might be advisable to state expressly that time is not of the essence. However, in most leases the timetable is so flexibly drafted that the parties do not feel the need to make express declaration that time is not of the essence, preferring instead to rely upon the usual presumption (but see *Barclays Bank plc v Savile*

Estates Ltd [2002] EWCA Civ 589, [2002] 24 EG 152). If any time clauses are intended to be mandatory, the lease should clearly say so.

16.6.2 The negotiated revision

The informal approach to arriving at a revised rent usually provides for the new rent to be agreed between the parties at any time (whether before or after the relevant review date), but if agreement has not been reached by the review date, either or both of the parties will be allowed by the clause to refer the matter to an independent third party for him to make a determination as to the new rent. If such an approach is adopted, the tenant should ensure that the rent review clause does not reserve the right to make the reference to the third party exclusively to the landlord. The tenant must ensure that he also has the ability to make the reference. Even though the rent review clause may permit only upward revisions, it may be in the tenant's interests to have a quick resolution of the review, particularly if he is anxious to assign his lease or sell his business. In exceptional cases (eg *Royal Bank of Scotland plc v Jennings and Others* [1997] 19 EG 152), the court might be prepared to imply an obligation upon the landlord to refer a review to the third party to give business efficacy to the clause.

16.6.3 Trigger notices

The service of a trigger notice is the more formal approach, which usually requires the parties to follow a rigid timetable for the service of notices. One party sets the review in motion by the service of a trigger notice, specifying his proposal for the revised rent, and the other party responds by the service of a counter-notice. A typical clause might provide for the landlord to implement the review by the service on the tenant of a trigger notice, between 12 and 6 months before the relevant review date, in which the landlord specifies a rent that he considers to be the current market rent for the premises. The tenant should be given the right to dispute the landlord's proposal by serving a counter-notice within, say, 3 months of the service of the trigger notice. The parties would then be required to negotiate, but in default of agreement within, say, 3 months of the service of the counter-notice, either or both parties may be given the right to make a reference to a third party for a determination. Time may be stated to be of the essence in respect of all or part of the timetable.

Great care must be taken with this more rigid style of approach, particularly if time is of the essence (see **16.6.1**). Problems can easily arise as follows.

(1) There is no requirement for the landlord to be reasonable when he specifies his proposal for the revised rent in his trigger notice (see *Amalgamated Estates Ltd v Joystretch Manufacturing Ltd* (1980) 257 EG 489). This is very dangerous for the tenant where time is of the essence in respect of the service of the tenant's counter-notice. If the tenant fails to respond within the time-limit required by the lease, he will be bound by the rent specified in the landlord's notice. A well-advised tenant should avoid such a clause.

(2) There has been much litigation surrounding the question of whether a particular form of communication, often in the form of a letter between the parties' advisers, suffices as a notice for the purposes of the review clause. If a communication is to take effect as a notice it ought to be clear and unequivocal, and must be worded in such a way as to make it clear to the recipient that the

sender is purporting to take a formal step, or exercise some right under the review clause. Phrases such as 'subject to contract' and 'without prejudice', although not necessarily fatal to the notice, are to be avoided.

(3) For the same reasons stated in connection with informally negotiated reviews, the tenant must ensure that the review timetable allows him to implement the review and to refer the rent revision for determination by the third party. These rights must not be left exclusively with the landlord.

Unless there is some compelling reason to the contrary, the informal approach is to be preferred.

16.6.4 The third party

A surveyor usually acts as the independent third party. The lease will provide for the parties to agree upon a surveyor, failing which one or both of the parties will be allowed to make an application to the President of the Royal Institution of Chartered Surveyors (RICS) for the appointment of a surveyor to determine the revised rent. The RICS operates a procedure to deal efficiently with such applications, and will appoint a surveyor with knowledge and experience of similar lettings in the area. It is important that the lease makes it clear in which capacity the surveyor is to act; as an arbitrator between the parties, or as an expert. There are considerable differences between the two.

(1) An arbitrator seeks to resolve a dispute by some quasi-judicial process, whereas an expert imposes his own expert valuation on the parties.

(2) The arbitrator is bound by the procedure under the Arbitration Act 1996, which deals with hearings, submission of evidence and the calling of witnesses. An expert is not subject to such external controls, and is not bound to hear the evidence of the parties. Whilst an arbitrator decides on the basis of the evidence put before him, an expert simply uses his own skill and judgement.

(3) There is a limited right of appeal to the High Court on a point of law against an arbitrator's award, whereas an expert's decision is final and binding unless it appears that he failed to perform the task required of him.

(4) An arbitrator is immune from suit in negligence, whereas an expert is not.

Using an expert tends to be quicker and cheaper and is, therefore, often provided for in lettings of conventional properties at modest rents. Where there is something unorthodox about the property, which might make it difficult to value, or where there is a good deal of money at stake in the outcome of the review, an arbitrator is to be preferred so that a fully argued case can be put. Alternatively, the review clause could leave the capacity of the third party open, to be determined by the party who makes the reference at the time the reference is made.

16.7 ANCILLARY PROVISIONS

The landlord invariably includes additional provisions to deal with:

(1) payment of the revised rent where the review is implemented after the review date;

(2) recording a note of the revised rent.

16.7.1 The late review

If time has not been made of the essence of the rent review date, the landlord can attempt to increase the rent by implementing the clause after the date for review has passed. To deal with this possibility, the review clause is usually drafted to include the following types of provisions:

(1) that the existing rent (the old rent) continues to be payable on account of the new rent until the new rent has been ascertained;

(2) that the new rent, once ascertained, becomes payable from, and is backdated to the rent review date;

(3) that as soon as the new rent has been ascertained, the tenant is to pay to the landlord the amount by which the old rent paid on account of the new rent since the review date actually falls short of the new rent, and because the landlord has been denied the benefit of this shortfall pending the outcome of the review, the tenant is to pay it with interest calculated from the rent review date until the date of payment.

The tenant should check the operation of these provisions. If the rent review clause permits both upward and downward reviews, he should ensure that there is some equivalent provision for the landlord to pay any shortfall (with interest) to the tenant if the new rent turns out to be lower than the old rent (although in *Royal Bank of Scotland v Jennings* (above) the court was prepared to imply such a term in any case). He should also check that the rate of interest at which the shortfall is to be paid is not set at the usual interest rate under the lease (4% or 5% above base rate, see **15.6**). The usual rate is intended to operate on the occasion of tenant default, whereas in the case of a late rent review, the fault may lie with a delaying landlord as much as a delaying tenant. The interest rate should be set at base rate itself or, perhaps, 1% or 2% above base rate. Finally, the tenant should check that the review clause allows the tenant to instigate the review process, and to force negotiations or the third party reference, since the tenant might prefer a speedy settlement of the review as an alternative to facing a future lump sum payment of a shortfall with interest.

16.7.2 Recording the review

It is good practice to attach memoranda of the revised rent to the lease and counterpart as evidence for all persons concerned with the lease of the agreement or determination. The rent review clause usually obliges both parties to sign and attach identical memoranda to their respective parts of the lease. It is usual for both parties to bear their own costs in this regard.

Chapter 17

REPAIRING COVENANTS

17.1 INTRODUCTION

Chapter 17 contents
Introduction
**Tenant's covenant to
 repair**
**Landlord's covenant to
 repair**
**Covenant to yield up in
 repair**
Decorating
Statutory curtailment

Responsibility for repairs is one of the most common sources of dispute between landlord and tenant and unless the matter is dealt with expressly in the lease there is a danger that neither party will be liable to repair. Whilst it is true that certain obligations will be implied, these are of relatively little practical importance; they include the following:

(1) the tenant is under a duty to use the premises in a tenant-like manner (and see *Dayani v Bromley London Borough Council* [1999] 3 EGLR 144);
(2) the landlord may be liable if he fails to take care of the common parts of the building, for example, the neglect of a lift or staircase in a high rise block, but much will depend on the surrounding circumstances (see *Liverpool City Council v Irwin* [1971] AC 239, a case concerning a block of residential flats);
(3) in rare situations the landlord may be under an implied obligation to repair so as to give business efficacy to the agreement between the parties (see *Barrett v Lounova (1982) Ltd* [1990] QB 348).

Thus, in the absence of a comprehensive code of implied obligations, it is imperative that the responsibility for repairs is dealt with expressly in the lease. The landlord's objective on granting anything more than a short-term letting will be to obtain a 'clear' lease, under which the rent always represents the landlord's clear income so that the tenant ends up paying the cost of any repairs, regardless of who carries them out. If the lease is of the whole of a building, the landlord will usually impose a full repairing covenant on the tenant. If, however, the lease is of only part of a building, the responsibility for repairs will usually be divided between the parties. For example, the tenant may be made liable for internal non-structural repairs whilst the landlord covenants to repair the remainder of the building. However, any expense incurred by the landlord in complying with his obligation will be recovered from the tenant under the service charge provisions. The special problems associated with a lease of part of a building and service charges are dealt with in Chapter 24.

17.2 TENANT'S COVENANT TO REPAIR

17.2.1 Subject matter of the covenant

In the lease the tenant will invariably covenant to repair the demised premises and, therefore, it must be made clear what the subject-matter of the covenant is, ie what is the covenantor liable to repair? Thus, it will be necessary to read the repairing covenant in conjunction with the definition of the 'demised premises' in the parcels clause. On the grant of a lease of the whole of a building there should not be any difficulty as the responsibility for repairs will doubtless extend to the whole of the demised premises. On the grant of a lease of part of a building where the responsibility for repairs is to be divided between the parties it must be made clear who is to be responsible for repairing each part of the building. This will require very careful drafting of both the parcels clause and the repairing covenant (see **24.4** where this matter is dealt with in more detail).

As general rule, a covenant to repair the demised premises will also extend to:

(1) any landlord's fixtures attached to them;
(2) any buildings erected after the date of the lease. If, however, the covenant is to repair 'the buildings demised', it will only extend to the buildings existing at the date of the lease.

One further issue which requires clarification is the question of responsibility for site contamination. If the site is subsequently discovered to be contaminated, can the tenant be required to remove the contamination under a simple repairing covenant? As yet there is a lack of judicial authority but it is submitted that there may be a problem for the landlord in persuading the court that a simple repairing covenant can be extended to the soil as well as the buildings. In the absence of judicial guidance the matter should be dealt with expressly in the lease; perhaps by defining the term 'repair' to include the remediation of site contamination.

17.2.2 Extent of liability

In examining the extent of the tenant's liability, a number of important matters need to be considered. For example, are the premises in disrepair? What is the standard of repair? Does the covenant require the tenant to renew or improve the premises? Is the tenant liable for inherent defects? Each of these is considered in turn.

17.2.3 Are the premises in disrepair?

If the tenant is under an obligation to repair the premises, he will only be liable if it can be shown that there is damage or disrepair to them. In other words, before the tenant incurs any liability, the landlord will need to show that the premises have deteriorated from their previous physical condition so that they are in a worse condition now, than when they were let. This requirement led to the downfall of the landlord in *Post Office v Aquarius Properties Ltd* [1987] 1 All ER 1055, where the basement of a building flooded due to a defect in the structure. The landlord's problem in fixing the tenant with responsibility for repair was the fact that the defect had caused no damage to the building itself. This being so, the court held that the tenant was not liable to remedy the defect under his covenant to repair.

17.2.4 The standard of repair

Sometimes the word 'repair' is qualified by the addition of the word(s), 'good', 'tenantable', or 'sufficient', but it would appear that these additions add little to the word 'repair' itself (*Anstruther-Gough-Calthorpe v McOscar and Another* [1924] 1 KB 716). The standard of repair required is 'such repair as having regard to the age, character and locality would make it reasonably fit for the occupation of a reasonably minded tenant of the class likely to take it' (per Lopes LJ in *Proudfoot v Hart* (1890) 25 QBD 42). Further, the standard will be determined by reference to the age, character and condition of the premises at the time the lease was granted. It makes no difference that the neighbourhood now attracts a superior or inferior class of tenant; the tenant need only keep them in the same condition as they were when let to him. If, however, the premises are in disrepair at the date of the lease, a covenant to keep in repair will require the tenant to first put the premises into repair (according to their age, character and locality), and then to keep them in repair.

17.2.5 Is the tenant liable to renew or improve the premises?

If the tenant is just under an obligation to 'repair', difficult questions can arise as to the meaning of that word. Do the works contemplated fall within the obligation, or are they more properly classified as works of renewal or improvement, for which the tenant is not responsible under a simple covenant to repair. It was said in *Lurcott v Wakeley & Wheeler* [1911] 1 KB 905 [1911] 1 KB 905, that 'Repair is restoration by renewal or replacement of subsidiary parts of a whole. Renewal, as distinguished from repair, is the reconstruction of the entirety, meaning by the entirety not necessarily the whole but substantially the whole ...'. Thus, the fundamental question is whether the work done can properly be described as repair, involving no more than renewal or replacement of defective parts, or whether it amounts to renewal or replacement of substantially the whole. This will be a question of degree in each case. In *Lurcott v Wakeley*, the rebuilding of a defective wall of a building was held to be within the tenant's covenant because it was the replacement of a defective part rather than the replacement of the whole. However, the tenant may be required to replace part after part until the whole is replaced. On the other hand, in *Lister v Lane & Nesham* [1893] 2 QB 212, the tenant was held not to be liable for the cost of rebuilding a house which had become unsafe due to poor foundations: 'a covenant to repair ... is not a covenant to give a different thing from that which the tenant took when he entered into the covenant. He has to repair that thing which he took; he is not obliged to make a new and different thing ...', per Lord Esher MR. In deciding whether the tenant is being asked to give back to the landlord a wholly different thing from that demised, guidance may sometimes be found by considering the proportion which the cost of the disputed work bears to the value or cost of the whole premises (see also *Elite Investments Ltd v TI Bainbridge Silencers Ltd* [1986] 2 EGLR 43). It must be stressed, however, that decided cases can do no more than lay down general guidelines and each case will turn on its own facts.

In the same way that the tenant need not renew the premises, a covenant to repair does not impose any obligation on the tenant to improve them. A tenant may sometimes be concerned that his landlord is trying to get him to upgrade or improve the premises under the guise of carrying out repairs. The distinction is not always easy to make but Lord Denning stated in *Morcom v Campbell-Johnson* [1955] 3 All ER 264 that 'if the work which is done is the provision of something new for the benefit of the occupier, that is, properly speaking, an improvement; but if it is only the replacement of something already there, which has become dilapidated or worn out, then, albeit that is a replacement by its modern equivalent, it comes within the category of repairs and not improvements' (see also *New England Properties plc v Portsmouth News Shops Ltd; Sterling Surveys v New England Properties; New England Properties v Ex-Eltronics (UK) Ltd* [1993] 23 EG 130).

17.2.6 Inherent defects

At one time it was thought that a covenant to repair did not require the tenant to repair damage caused by 'inherent defects' (ie defects in design or construction of the building). However, it now seems that this approach was wrong and that there are no special rules relating to damage caused by inherent defects. As with all kinds of disrepair it will, therefore, be a question of degree as to whether what the tenant is being asked to do can properly be described as repair or whether it would involve giving back to the landlord something wholly different from that which he demised (*Ravenseft Properties Ltd v Davstone (Holdings) Ltd* [1980] QB 12). Even the possibility of the tenant being liable for damage caused by such defects will alarm the tenant as it may require, not only repair of the damage, but also eradication of the defect itself if this is the only realistic way of carrying out the repairs (see **17.2.7**).

If the inherent defect has not caused any damage to the premises, they are not in disrepair and thus the tenant is not liable on his covenant.

17.2.7 Varying the obligation

In drafting the repairing obligation, it is possible to restrict or widen its scope from that imposed by a simple covenant to repair. Looked at from the landlord's point of view, it is possible to extend the liability of the tenant by the use of clear words which make the tenant liable to renew or improve the demised premises (see, eg, *Credit Suisse v Beegas Nominees Ltd* [1994] 11 EG 151). In *Welsh v Greenwich London Borough Council* [2000] PLSCS 149, the Court of Appeal held that a reference to keeping the premises in 'good condition' in the repairing obligation was a significant addition and would extend the obligation to defects which had not caused any damage to the structure of the premises (on the facts, damage caused by condensation).

From the tenant's point of view, there are a number of ways in which he may seek to reduce his liability.

(1) The tenant may be alarmed at the prospect of having to repair inherent defects. For that reason, tenants of new buildings will often seek to limit their liability by excluding from their obligation liability for defects caused by design or construction faults, at least for a specified period of time. From the tenant's point of view, the landlord should covenant to repair damage caused by these defects (see **8.4.2**).

(2) In most leases the landlord will insure the premises against a number of stated risks. The tenant should always insist that his repairing covenant does not render him liable to repair damage caused by a risk against which the landlord has or should have insured. The landlord should not object since he will be able to claim on the insurance policy. However, the landlord will insist that the tenant remains liable if the insurance is avoided because of an act or omission of the tenant or someone at the premises with the tenant's consent (see **22.7.1**).

(3) If the premises are in disrepair at the commencement of the lease but it has been agreed between the parties that the tenant need not repair the premises to a higher standard, this should be expressly stated in the covenant. Further, for the avoidance of future disputes, a detailed schedule of condition, with appropriate photographic evidence, should be prepared by a surveyor, agreed by the parties and annexed to the lease.

(4) The covenant to repair may be qualified by a proviso 'fair wear and tear excepted'. This will exclude from the obligation to repair damage attributable to the normal effects of time and weather and of normal and reasonable use of the premises but it will not exclude liability for consequential damage.

17.2.8 Access by landlord to execute works in default

A covenant to repair given by the tenant is often followed by a covenant to permit the landlord to enter the demised premises, upon reasonable notice, to ascertain their state and condition. This covenant should make two further provisions. First, a provision for the landlord to serve a notice of disrepair on the tenant if he is found to be in breach of his repairing obligation. Secondly, a covenant to repair by the tenant upon receipt of the notice followed by a right for the landlord to enter upon the premises to carry out the repairs, at the tenant's expense, if the tenant fails to do so within a specified time. The expense incurred by the landlord acting under such a power should be expressed to be recoverable 'as a debt'. This is an attempt to avoid the restrictions imposed by the Landlord and Tenant Act 1927 (LTA 1927) and the Leasehold Property (Repairs) Act 1938 on the recovery of damages, as opposed to a debt, for disrepair (see **28.1.2**).

The landlord should be aware, however, that if he reserves the right to enter the demised premises to carry out repairs in default, he will, in certain circumstances, become liable under the Defective Premises Act 1972 (see **17.3**).

17.3 LANDLORD'S COVENANT TO REPAIR

The only common situation in which a landlord will covenant to repair is on the grant of a lease of part of a building, where the landlord will be able to recover his expenditure under the service charge provisions. A landlord's covenant to repair will be subject to the same rules of construction as a tenant's covenant and thus, for example, the landlord need not carry out works so as provide the tenant with something wholly different from that originally demised.

Where the covenant is to repair the demised premises, it is implied that the landlord is not liable until he has had notice of the disrepair (see, eg, *O'Brien v Robinson* [1973] AC 912). This requirement of notice is not affected by the fact that the landlord has a right of entry onto the premises. Once the landlord has notice, he must take steps to carry out the necessary repairs. If immediate permanent repairs are not possible, the landlord must take immediate steps to render the premises temporarily safe. If, on the other hand, the landlord's obligation is to keep in repair some part of the building not comprised in the demise (eg the common parts), the landlord's liability runs from the moment the disrepair occurs, regardless of the question of notice (*British Telecommunications plc v Sun Life Assurance Society plc* [1995] 45 EG 133).

Where the landlord is under an obligation to repair, there is an implied right for him to enter upon the demised premises to carry out those repairs (but this should always be dealt with expressly).

Under the Defective Premises Act 1972, a landlord who is under an express or implied obligation for the repair of the demised premises owes to all persons who might reasonably be expected to be affected by defects in the state of the premises a duty to take such care as is reasonable in all the circumstances to see that they are reasonably safe from personal injury or damage to their property. This duty arises as soon as the landlord knows or ought to have known of the defect (see *Sykes v Harry* [2001] EWCA Civ 167, [2001] 3 WLR 62). Further, even where the landlord is under no obligation to repair but merely has a right to do so, he is made subject to the same duty, although he will not be liable to the tenant if the defect arose from the tenant's failure to comply with an express covenant to repair.

17.4 COVENANT TO YIELD UP IN REPAIR

The tenant will often enter into a covenant to yield up the premises in repair at the end of the term. This covenant, which requires the tenant to leave the premises in repair, is entirely independent of the covenant to repair by the tenant. Thus, if the landlord had previously obtained judgment against the tenant for breach of the repairing covenant, yet the premises remain in disrepair, he will still be able to bring an action at the end of the term on the covenant to yield up in repair (but obviously the amount of damages will be affected).

17.5 DECORATING

Because some doubt exists as to the amount of decoration required by a covenant to repair, the matter is best dealt with expressly in the lease. The usual form of covenant requires the tenant to decorate the exterior and interior of the demised premises at specified intervals during the term, and during the last year of the term. The obligation to decorate in the last year could require the tenant to decorate in two consecutive years depending on when the lease is terminated (eg in a 10-year lease with a decorating obligation every 3 years). The tenant may, therefore, wish to provide that the obligation to decorate in the last year shall not apply if he has decorated in the previous, say, 18 months. The landlord may wish to retain some control by requiring the tenant to obtain consent (not to be unreasonably withheld) before any change in the colour scheme is made.

Some covenants specify the materials to be used, for example 'with two coats of good quality oil paint'. Care should be taken to ensure that the materials specified are appropriate to the type of building concerned as it is not uncommon to find that the specified materials are wholly inappropriate to the nature of the building and its method of construction. More modern covenants simply require the tenant to carry out his obligation 'in a good and workmanlike manner with good quality materials'.

On the grant of a lease of part of a building the exterior decoration would normally be undertaken by the landlord who would recover his expenses under the service charge.

17.6 STATUTORY CURTAILMENT

Oppressive enforcement of a tenant's repairing obligations may be curtailed as follows.

(1) A landlord's right to bring an action for damages in respect of the tenant's breach of a repairing covenant may be limited by the operation of the Leasehold Property (Repairs) Act 1938 (see **28.1.2**).

(2) Under s 147 of the LPA 1925, the court may, in certain circumstances, relieve a tenant of his obligations in respect of a covenant relating to internal decorative repairs (see **30.5.3**).

Chapter 18

ALIENATION

18.1 INTRODUCTION

Unless the lease contains some restriction, the tenant will be free to deal with his interest in any way he wishes. He will be able to assign the lease, grant sub-leases of the whole or part, charge the lease and part with possession of the premises, without obtaining his landlord's consent. Complete freedom like this is unlikely to prove acceptable to the landlord for a number of reasons and thus a fair balance between the competing concerns and aims of both parties will have to be reached.

18.1.1 Assignment

From the tenant's point of view, the lease may become a burden if he is unable to dispose of it freely when he no longer has any use for the premises. This situation may arise, for example, where the premises have become surplus to his requirements or because they are no longer suitable for his needs. The tenant would also be in difficulty if his business venture failed and he could no longer afford the rent. However, from the landlord's point of view, close control over assignment is essential, because without it the landlord may find his premises occupied by an unsatisfactory tenant, and the value of his reversionary interest may be reduced. The assignee will become responsible for the rent and the performance of the other covenants in the lease, and the landlord will want to ensure that he is of good financial standing. The identity and status of any potential assignee is, therefore, important to the landlord for financial reasons. Further, there may be estate management reasons why the landlord will wish to exercise some control over assignees, for example, where the landlord owns the adjoining premises.

A covenant against assignment is not broken by an involuntary assignment such as occurs on the death or bankruptcy of the tenant. Nor is a restriction on assignment broken by a sub-letting of the premises.

18.1.2 Sub-letting

In some situations the tenant may wish to grant a sub-lease of the demised premises (see 25.2). The landlord will want the ability to control sub-letting because in certain circumstances the head tenancy may cease to exist and the sub-tenant will become the immediate tenant of the landlord. This could happen, for example, on the surrender of the head-lease or on the forfeiture of the head-lease followed by the sub-tenant's successful application for relief. A similar situation could arise at the end of the contractual term if the head tenant does not apply (or is unable to apply) for a new tenancy under Part II of the LTA 1954 but the sub-tenant does; the sub-tenant may be granted a new tenancy of his part against the head landlord. In all these situations the landlord would want to be sure that the sub-tenant was able to pay the rent and perform the covenants and will, therefore, wish to have some control over the identity and status of any proposed sub-tenant. Where a tenant mortgages his

Chapter 18 contents
Introduction
Restrictions on alienation
Notice of assignment or
sub-letting

lease by way of sub-lease, this has been held to be a breach of the covenant, though possibly not where the mortgage is by way of legal charge (see *Re Good's Lease* [1954] 1 All ER 275). However, a covenant against sub-letting will not prevent the tenant from granting licences. Similarly, a covenant against sub-letting 'the demised premises' will not be broken by a sub-lease of part only (*Cook v Shoesmith* [1951] 1 KB 752). If such a restriction is intended, it must be dealt with expressly.

18.1.3 Parting with/sharing possession

A covenant preventing the tenant from parting with possession of the premises is wider in its effect than the two provisions mentioned above but it will not prevent the tenant from allowing another person to use the premises provided the tenant retains legal possession. It will not, therefore, prohibit a tenant from granting a licence of the premises to another unless the licence confers exclusive possession on the licensee (see *Street v Mountford* [1985] AC 809).

Arrangements under which a business tenant shares his premises with someone else are not uncommon with 'shops within shops' being frequently encountered. However, such an arrangement would not be possible if there was a covenant against sharing possession in the lease, forbidding, as it does, the granting of licences by the tenant. The tenant should try to resist the imposition of such a wide restriction, particularly where the tenant is a member of a group of companies and intends to share the premises with other members of the group.

18.1.4 The landlord's concerns on a dealing of part of the demised premises

Landlords often impose much stricter control on a dealing with part only of the demised premises because of the estate management problems which dealings of part can create. A sub-tenant can in certain circumstances become the immediate tenant of the head landlord. If a number of sub-leases have been granted, a landlord who had let a building as a whole to a single tenant could, at some future date, be faced with the estate management problems associated with having a number of different tenants each with a lease of a different part of the building.

Further, if the tenant was allowed to grant a sub-lease of part only of the premises, this could lead to the division of the demised premises into commercially unattractive units. If, in the future, the head-lease was forfeited and the sub-tenant successfully applied for relief in respect of his part, the head landlord might have difficulty in re-letting the vacant part if that part is no longer attractive to the market because of the way in which the premises have been sub-divided.

18.2 RESTRICTIONS ON ALIENATION

For the reasons mentioned above, it is common for the landlord to impose restrictions on dealing, such restrictions being either absolute in effect, ie an unqualified (absolute) covenant by the tenant not to assign, underlet, part with possession, etc or alternatively, in the form of a qualified covenant: not to deal with the premises without the landlord's consent.

18.2.1 Absolute covenants against dealings

If the covenant is absolute, the tenant cannot assign or underlet without being in breach of covenant. Whilst the landlord may be prepared to waive the covenant in a given case, the tenant will be entirely at the mercy of his landlord who may refuse consent quite unreasonably subject only to the restrictions imposed by the Sex Discrimination Act 1975, Race Relations Act 1976 and Disability Discrimination Act 1995. Also, if the covenant is absolute, the landlord is not obliged to give any reason for his refusal. An absolute covenant against dealings is unusual in business leases, except in very short-term leases, or to the extent that it prohibits dealings with part of the premises (see **18.2.3**). Any wider form of absolute restriction should be resisted by the tenant and if, exceptionally, there is such a restriction, the tenant should make sure its presence is reflected in the rent he has to pay.

18.2.2 Qualified covenants against dealings

A qualified covenant prohibits alienation by the tenant without the landlord's consent. Sometimes, the covenant will state that the landlord's consent is not to be unreasonably withheld; this is known as a fully qualified covenant.

18.2.3 A common form of covenant

The form of covenant encountered in practice will contain elements of both the absolute and qualified restrictions by prohibiting absolutely dealings in relation to part only of the premises, and dealings which stop short of an assignment or sub-letting of the whole (eg parting with possession or sharing occupation of the premises), and then prohibiting without the landlord's prior written consent assignments or sub-lettings of the whole.

Such a clause attempts to strike a fair balance between both landlord and tenant as it will allow the tenant to assign or sub-let the whole of the premises subject to obtaining the landlord's prior consent (and the landlord will not be able to unreasonably withhold his consent). This should meet the tenant's main concern of being unable to divest himself of the lease should his circumstances change. At the same time, it will allay the landlord's fears by imposing an absolute prohibition on dealings with part only of the premises.

Other provisions will be found in a common form of alienation covenant. For example:

(1) *Assignments.* In relation to leases granted before 1 January 1996, the lease will invariably require the assignee to enter into a direct covenant with the landlord to perform the covenants in the lease. This will make the assignee liable on the covenants in the lease during the whole term, rather than just during the currency of his ownership. Further, on an assignment to a limited company, the alienation clause may require the assignee company to provide sureties.

(2) *Sub-leases.* If the landlord is prepared to permit sub-letting, the terms of the sub-lease will often be dictated by the alienation clause. In particular, the landlord will wish to ensure that any sub-lease is at a rent no less than that in the head-lease and with similar review provisions; that the sub-tenants enter into direct covenants with the head landlord; and that no further sub-letting is allowed. Sometimes, the prohibition against sub-letting part will be absolute only insofar as it applies to sub-leases of less than a certain area; for example, in

an office block to sub-leases of less than one floor (sub-leases are dealt with in more detail in Chapter 25).

(3) *Conditions on assignment.* In relation to commercial leases granted on or after 1 January 1996, the lease will usually stipulate conditions which must be satisfied, or circumstances which must exist before the landlord will give his consent to the assignment (see below).

18.2.4 Consent not to be unreasonably withheld

Section 19(1)(a) of the LTA 1927 provides that, notwithstanding any contrary provision, a covenant not to assign, underlet, charge or part with possession of the demised premises or any part thereof without the landlord's licence or consent, is subject to a proviso that such licence or consent is not to be unreasonably withheld. In other words, a qualified covenant can be converted into a fully qualified covenant by the operation of s 19(1). The section has no application to the operation of an absolute covenant, where the landlord remains free to refuse his consent to an assignment quite unreasonably. Furthermore, the section has to be read in the light of s 19(1A) of the LTA 1927 (introduced by s 22 of LTCA 1995) as regards covenants against assigning.

The Landlord and Tenant Act 1988 (LTA 1988) further strengthens the position of a tenant seeking consent to assign or sub-let. The Act applies where the lease contains a fully qualified covenant against alienation (whether or not the proviso that the landlord's consent is not to be unreasonably withheld is express or implied by statute). When the tenant has made written application for consent, the landlord owes a duty, within a reasonable time:

(1) to give consent, unless it is reasonable not to do so (see below). Giving consent subject to an unreasonable condition will be a breach of this duty; and

(2) to serve on the tenant written notice of his decision whether or not to give consent (see LTA 1988, s 1(3)(b), and *Footwear Corporation Ltd v Amplight Properties Ltd* [1999] 1 WLR 551), specifying in addition:

    (a) if the consent is given subject to conditions, the conditions; or

    (b) if the consent is withheld, the reasons for withholding it.

The burden of proving the reasonableness of any refusal or any conditions imposed is on the landlord. The sanction for breach of this statutory duty is liability in tort for damages. The LTA 1988 does not specify what is to be regarded as a reasonable time nor when refusal of consent is to be deemed reasonable. Again, this Act has to be read in the light of s 19(1A) of the LTA 1927. The operation of the LTA 1988 is further considered in Chapter 27.

18.2.5 Can the landlord refuse consent?

Whether the landlord can refuse consent will depend upon whether the landlord has made use of s 19(1A) of the LTA 1927 or, if not, his reasonableness in the circumstances of the case.

Making use of s 19(1A)

Section 19(1A) of the 1927 Act (which operates only in relation to qualified covenants against assigning) allows the landlord, in commercial leases granted on or after 1 January 1996, to stipulate in the lease (or in a written agreement entered into with the tenant at any time before he applies for licence to assign) conditions which need to be satisfied, or circumstances which must exist, before the landlord will give his consent to the assignment. It is provided by s 19(1A) that if the landlord withholds his consent on the grounds that the specified circumstances do not exist, or that the specified conditions have not been satisfied, then the landlord will not be unreasonably withholding his consent. If the landlord withholds his consent on grounds other than those specified, s 19(1)(a) of the LTA 1927 will apply in the usual way (see **18.2.4** and below). However, it can be seen that the effect of s 19(1A) is to reduce the protection afforded to tenants by s 19(1)(a).

The nature and type of condition to be satisfied (or circumstances which must exist) is left to the parties to decide, but s 19(1C) of the LTA 1927 envisages their falling in two categories: those which can be factually or objectively verified; and those where the landlord has a discretion.

Factual conditions or circumstances might include a requirement that the proposed assignee is a publicly quoted company on the London Stock Exchange, or has pre-tax net profits equal to three times the rent, or a requirement that the assignor enter into an authorised guarantee agreement (see **18.2.7**), or that the assignee procure guarantors.

Discretionary circumstances or conditions are those which cannot be verified objectively, and a judgment or determination will have to be made as to whether they have been satisfied. This type of condition will be valid only if either it provides for an independent third party reference (in the event of the tenant disagreeing with the landlord's determination), or the landlord commits himself to making a reasonable determination. Typical examples of discretionary circumstances or conditions may include a provision that the proposed assignee must, in the opinion of the landlord, be of equivalent financial standing to the assignor, and should the tenant not agree, the matter is to be referred to an independent third party; or a provision that the assignee must not, in the reasonable opinion of the landlord, be in competition with other tenants in the same development.

Where s 19(1A) does not apply

Section 19(1A) has no application to covenants against sub-letting, charging or mortgaging, and does not apply in relation to leases granted before 1 January 1996. In such cases, s 19(1)(a) of the LTA 1927 applies in the usual way, meaning that, notwithstanding any express provision to the contrary, the landlord cannot unreasonably withhold his consent where the covenant is a qualified one. Whether the landlord is acting reasonably in such cases has to be judged from the circumstances existing at the time of the landlord's decision. Here, the parties to the lease cannot lay down in advance that refusal of consent for a particular reason shall be deemed to be reasonable since that is for the court to decide. However, it is open to the landlord to agree that he will not refuse his consent to an assignment or sub-letting in favour of, for example, 'a respectable and responsible person'. If the proposed assignee or sub-tenant is respectable and responsible, the landlord will be unable to refuse his consent, even on other reasonable grounds (*Moat v Martin* [1950] 1 KB 175). Further, it has been held that a lease may validly provide that, before applying for consent to assign or sub-let, the tenant shall first offer to surrender the lease. Such a requirement does not contravene s 19(1)(a), since if the landlord accepts the offer to surrender, no question of consent to assign arises. However, if the lease is protected under Part II of the LTA 1954, the landlord's acceptance of the tenant's offer may be void. Even so, the tenant may still have to make his offer if he is not to be found in breach of covenant (see *Allnatt London Properties Ltd v Newton* [1984] 1 All ER 423, and **31.1.5**).

The Court of Appeal laid down a number of guidelines on the issue of the landlord's reasonableness under s 19(1)(a) in *International Drilling Fluids Ltd v Louisville Investments (Uxbridge) Ltd* [1986] 1 All ER 321:

(1) the purpose of a fully qualified covenant against assignment is to protect the landlord from having his premises used or occupied in an undesirable way, or by an undesirable tenant or assignee;

(2) a landlord is not entitled to refuse his consent to an assignment on grounds which have nothing whatever to do with the relationship of landlord and tenant in regard to the subject matter of the lease;

(3) it is unnecessary for the landlord to prove that the conclusions which led him to refuse to consent were justified, if they were conclusions which might be reached by a reasonable man in the circumstances;

(4) it may be reasonable for the landlord to refuse his consent to an assignment on the ground of the purpose for which the proposed assignee intends to use the premises, even though that purpose is not forbidden by the lease;

(5) while a landlord need usually only consider his own relevant interests, there may be cases where there is such a disproportion between the benefit to the landlord and the detriment to the tenant if the landlord withholds his consent to an assignment, that it is unreasonable for the landlord to refuse consent;

(6) subject to the above propositions, it is, in each case, a question of fact, depending on all the circumstances, whether the landlord's consent to an assignment is being unreasonably withheld.

The following are examples of situations where consent has been held to have been reasonably withheld:

(1) where the proposed assignee's references were unsatisfactory (*Shanley v Ward* (1913) 29 TLR 714). A landlord is rightly concerned that any assignee should be in a position to pay the rent and perform the covenants in the lease. Can the landlord, therefore, require the provision of a surety by the assignee as a condition of consent? If the lease does not require the provision of sureties, the reasonableness of the landlord's request for one will depend to a large extent on the financial strength of the assignee. The landlord will wish to see a bank reference and, usually, 3 years' audited accounts, but if he still entertains reasonable doubts, it may not be unreasonable for him to require a surety in which case the landlord will wish to be satisfied that their combined strength is sufficient to secure compliance with the lease terms. However, it has been held that the provision of a surety is not always a substitute for a satisfactory and responsible tenant in possession (*Warren v Marketing Exchange for Africa* [1988] 2 EGLR 247). In cases where s 19(1A) of the LTA 1927 has not been used, if the alienation covenant in the lease expressly required the production of sureties, the question arises as to whether the landlord can insist on a surety, however unreasonable that may be. There are conflicting views on the issue but the case of *Vaux Group plc v Lilley* [1991] 1 EGLR 60, contains obiter remarks suggesting that this may be possible, at least if the requirement was appropriately drafted;

(2) where there was a long-standing and extensive breach of the repairing covenant by the assignor and the landlord could not be reasonably satisfied that the

assignee would be in a position to remedy the breach (*Orlando Investments v Grosvenor Estate Belgravia* [1989] 2 EGLR 74);

(3) where the assignee would be in a position to compete with the landlord's business;

(4) where the assignment would reduce the value of the landlord's reversion (but see *International Drilling Fluids Ltd v Louisville Investments (Uxbridge) Ltd* above);

(5) where the proposed assignee intends to carry on a use detrimental to the premises or a use inconsistent with the landlord's 'tenant mix' policy (see *Moss Bros Group plc v CSC Properties Ltd* [1999] EGCS 47);

(6) where the assignee would, unlike the assignor, acquire protection under Part II of the LTA 1954.

The following are examples of situations where consent has been held to have been unreasonably withheld:

(1) where the landlord has refused consent in an attempt to obtain some advantage for himself, for example, the surrender of the lease by the tenant;

(2) where there are minor breaches of the repairing covenant;

(3) where, on an application to sub-let the premises, the landlord refused consent because the underlease rent was to be less than the market value (something which was not prohibited by the terms of the lease). The landlord argued that a sub-letting below market value, whilst not affecting the value of the reversion of the demised premises, would adversely affect the reversionary value of neighbouring properties it owned. The court held this to be a case of the landlord seeking a collateral advantage unconnected with the demised premises (*Norwich Union Life Insurance Society v Shopmoor Ltd* [1999] 1 WLR 531).

An issue which has been before the court on more than one occasion is whether the landlord would be acting unreasonably in refusing consent where he anticipated a breach of the user covenant by the assignee. In *Ashworth Frazer Ltd v Gloucester City Council* [2002] 05 EG 133, the landlord refused consent in these circumstances. The earlier Court of Appeal case of *Killick v Second Covent Garden Property Co Ltd* [1973] 1 WLR 658 had seemed to suggest that refusal of consent because of an anticipated breach of covenant would be unreasonable because the landlord would retain his remedies for breach of covenant and thus be in no worse position than if the current tenant breached the clause. The House of Lords in *Ashworth Frazer* rejected this approach saying:

> '... it could not be said, as a matter of law, that a refusal of consent was necessarily unreasonable where it was founded on the landlord's belief, reasonable or otherwise, that the proposed assignee intended to use the demised premises for a purpose which would give rise to a breach of the user covenant.' (per Lord Rodger)

In other words, each case will be looked at on its own merits in light of what a reasonable landlord would do.

Under the provisions of the Race Relations Act 1976, the Sex Discrimination Act 1975 and the Disability Discrimination Act 1995, any discrimination in withholding consent for the disposal of the demised premises on grounds of race, sex or disability is generally unlawful.

What if consent is refused?

If, having applied for consent to assign or sub-let, the tenant thinks his landlord is being unreasonable in his refusal to give such consent, the tenant has a number of options open to him. These are dealt with at **27.1**.

18.2.6 Restrictions on charging for consent to assign or sub-let

In the case of a qualified covenant against dealings, s 144 of the LPA 1925 implies a proviso that no fine or like sum of money shall be charged for giving such consent to assignment or sub-letting, unless the lease expressly provides for this. However, this does not prevent a landlord from requiring his tenant to pay a reasonable sum for legal and other expenses incurred in connection with the grant of consent.

18.2.7 Authorised guarantee agreements

Although the LTCA 1995 has abolished privity of contract in relation to leases caught by the Act, an outgoing tenant may sometimes be required to guarantee his immediate assignee's performance of the obligations contained in the lease. This is achieved by the outgoing tenant entering into an authorised guarantee agreement (AGA) with the landlord. The landlord may require an AGA from an outgoing tenant in the following circumstances, where:

(1) the lease provides that the consent of the landlord (or some other person) is required to the assignment;

(2) such consent is given subject to a condition (lawfully imposed) that the tenant is to enter into the AGA. For example, the requirement of an AGA may be one of the conditions which the parties had previously agreed had to be satisfied before the landlord was prepared to give his consent to an assignment (see **18.2.5**);

(3) the assignment is entered into by the tenant pursuant to that condition.

The terms of the guarantee are left to the parties (provided that the purpose of the LTCA 1995 is not frustrated) but the Act specifically permits the guarantee to require the outgoing tenant to enter into a new lease should the current lease be disclaimed following the assignee's insolvency (as to which, see **29.1.2**).

18.3 NOTICE OF ASSIGNMENT OR SUB-LETTING

There is no common law obligation for a tenant to give his landlord notice of any dealing with the lease, but a well-drafted lease will provide for this so that the landlord knows at any given time in whom the lease is vested and whether any sub-lease has been granted. The clause should specify the occasions on which the covenant is to operate (eg assignment, sub-letting, mortgage). The tenant is usually required to pay a registration fee to the landlord with each notice served.

In the case of assignment, it will fall to the assignee to give notice (and pay any registration fee prescribed by the lease), since it will be his interest which will be jeopardised by the breach of covenant involved in failing to give notice.

For a more detailed consideration of the practical implications of the LTCA 1995, see Fogel et al *Leasehold Liability* (Jordans, 2000).

Chapter 19

USER COVENANTS

19.1 THE NEED FOR A USER COVENANT

Chapter 19 contents
**The need for a user
  covenant**
The permitted use
**The extent of the
  landlord's control**
Ancillary clauses

There are several ways outside the terms of the lease in which the tenant's use of the premises may be restricted:

(1) *Planning legislation.* The tenant may not be able to carry out any building or other operations at the premises, and he will not be able to make a material change in the use of the premises without obtaining planning permission from the local planning authority. Generally, there is no implied warranty by the landlord that the tenant's use of the property is an authorised use under the planning legislation. It is, therefore, for the tenant to satisfy himself that planning permission is available for the use intended.

(2) *Covenants affecting a superior title.* There may be restrictive covenants affecting the landlord's reversionary title (or if the landlord is himself a tenant, affecting a superior title) which bind the tenant and prevent him from carrying out certain activities at the premises. Despite being restricted by statute as to the evidence of title he can call for, the tenant should always press the landlord for evidence of all superior titles.

(3) *Common law restraints.* The law of nuisance may prevent the tenant from using the premises in a such a way as to cause disturbance to a neighbour.

Whilst these restraints operate to exert some degree of control over the tenant, they do not provide the landlord with any remedy should the tenant act in breach. A user covenant (together with several ancillary clauses) will, therefore, be required to give the landlord the desired level of control.

19.1.1 The landlord's concerns

There are various financial and estate management reasons why a landlord will wish to control use of the premises by the tenant:

(1) to maintain the value of the landlord's interest in the premises;
(2) to maintain the rental value of the premises;
(3) to avoid damaging the reputation of the premises by immoral or undesirable uses;
(4) to maintain the value of adjoining premises owned by the landlord;
(5) to avoid the tenant competing with other premises of the landlord in the vicinity;
(6) to maintain a good mix of different retail uses in a shopping precinct owned by the landlord.

The landlord has to be careful when drafting the user covenant to ensure that he does not restrain the tenant's use of the premises any more than is strictly necessary for the landlord's purposes, since a tight user covenant may have an adverse impact from the landlord's point of view on rental values both initially and at rent review. The wider the scope of the user covenant, the more attractive would be a letting of the premises on the open market and, therefore, the higher the rental value may be, both initially and at review. The tighter the covenant, the less attractive would be a letting of the premises on the open market (since the number of potential bidders for this letting would be restricted by the narrowness of the user covenant) and, therefore, the lower the rental value would be. The landlord is not able to argue at rent review that the valuer should assess the revised rent on the basis that the landlord might be prepared to waive a breach of the user covenant in order to permit a more profitable use (thereby increasing the rental value of the tenant's interest), nor is he allowed to vary the lease unilaterally in order to gain a benefit at review (see *Plinth Properties Ltd v Mott, Hay & Anderson* [1979] 1 EGLR 17 and *C&A Pension Trustees Ltd v British Vita Investments Ltd* [1984] 2 EGLR 75 and the comments made at **16.5.2**).

The landlord will, therefore, need to perform a balancing act between control of the tenant and good estate management on the one hand, and maximisation of rental values on the other. Valuation advice may be necessary here.

19.1.2 Tenant's concerns

From the tenant's point of view, a narrow user covenant ought to be avoided since, although the clause would work favourably for the tenant on rent review, his ability to dispose of the premises at some stage in the future will be hampered in that he will only be able to assign or sub-let to someone who is capable of complying with the covenant and who does not require any greater flexibility.

Additionally, the tenant must have regard to his own future use of the premises. There is a risk that the nature of the tenant's business may change to such a degree that he is taken outside the scope of the user covenant and, therefore, finds himself in breach. The tenant must ensure that sufficient flexibility is built into the covenant to permit future diversification of the tenant's business. However, he should not allow the landlord to insert a covenant that is wider than is strictly necessary for his purposes, since this may penalise the tenant at rent review by increasing the rental value of the tenant's interest. Once again a balancing act is required.

The user clause usually contains a principal covenant by the tenant governing the permitted use of the premises, followed by a range of ancillary clauses prohibiting or controlling a range of other activities.

19.2 THE PERMITTED USE

There are several ways in which the permitted use can be defined in the lease. First, the landlord may be prepared to permit a wide range of uses by broadly stipulating the type of use to be permitted on the premises, for example, use as offices, or as a retail shop, or for light industrial purposes. This would give the tenant a large degree of flexibility and enable him to diversify his business operations within the broad range permitted.

Alternatively, the landlord may choose to restrict the tenant to a very narrow range of uses by defining the permitted use by reference to the nature of the business to be carried on at the premises, for example, use as offices for the business of an estate agency, or as a retail shop for the sale of children's footwear, or as a factory for the manufacture of computer software. This would give the tenant no flexibility to diversify and would hamper the tenant in any efforts to assign his lease, or sub-let the premises to someone who was not in the same line of business.

As a third possibility, the landlord may adopt an approach which is mid-way between the first two by restricting the tenant's use of the premises to a class of similar uses by, for example, defining the permitted use as offices for the business of a solicitor, accountant, architect or other professional person. If the landlord intends permitting the tenant to use the premises for one of a number of similar uses, he may consider defining the use by reference to the Town and Country Planning (Use Classes) Order 1987 (as amended).

19.2.1 Making use of the Use Classes Order

It is often considered desirable that the permitted user is linked to available planning permission. For example, if planning permission is available for any office use within class B1 of the Use Classes Order 1987, then the landlord, being quite happy for the premises to be used for any such office purposes, may choose simply to prohibit any use other than B1 office use. However, if this approach is to be adopted, the landlord should check carefully to ensure that there are no uses which could conceivably fall within the definition of B1 office use which the landlord would consider to be unattractive. The same principle is more clearly demonstrated if the lease prohibits any use other than as a retail shop within class A1. This is a very wide-ranging class of uses and there are likely to be several types of shop uses within that class which the landlord would not be prepared to tolerate at the premises.

If the landlord is to make use of the Use Classes Order in the user covenant, he should ensure that the lease clearly states that any reference to the Use Classes Order 1987 is intended to refer to the Order as enacted at the time the lease was granted. The danger is that at some stage during the term the Use Classes Order could be amended to bring within the class of use permitted by the lease a use which the landlord considered to be undesirable, thereby converting that use into a permitted use under the lease.

19.2.2 A covenant that names the tenant

It is sometimes difficult to define the type of business to be carried on by the tenant at the premises because of its peculiar nature, and so the landlord feels inclined to restrict use of the premises to the tenant's particular business. This is a dangerous approach to adopt, and it can lead to problems for the tenant (in terms of his ability to dispose of the premises) and can give rise to complicated valuation problems at rent review (*Sterling Land Office Developments Ltd v Lloyds Bank plc* (1984) 271 EG 894 and *Post Office Counters Ltd v Harlow District Council* [1991] 2 EGLR 121).

If the user covenant restricts the use of the premises to, for example, the offices of a particular company which is named in the lease, this would effectively prevent an assignment or sub-letting by the original tenant, even if the lease otherwise anticipated alienation (*Law Land Co Ltd v Consumers Association Ltd* (1980) 255 EG 617).

If the user covenant, without specifically naming the tenant, restricts use of the premises to 'the tenant's business', problems of interpretation will arise. Does the clause refer to the original tenant, or the current tenant? Does it refer to the business being conducted at the outset or the business being conducted from time to time? The danger from the landlord's point of view is that if, as is usually the case, the lease defines 'the Tenant' to include his successors in title, such a clause is likely to be construed by the court as permitting whatever business is currently being carried on by whoever is then the tenant. In other words, the landlord will have lost control. If reference is made to 'the tenant's business as a solicitor', does that mean that only the original tenant can comply with the covenant, or can an assignee? Would sub-letting be impossible since a sub-tenant, not being a tenant under the lease, would inevitably be in breach?

In view of these complications, it is advisable to avoid the use of covenants which either name the tenant, or refer to the tenant's business without sufficient clarity.

19.2.3 A positive or negative covenant?

If the covenant is positive, it will require the tenant 'to use the premises for the purposes of [the named permitted use]'. The benefit from the landlord's point of is that non-user (eg because of a temporary shut-down during a recession) will amount to a breach of covenant entitling the landlord to damages should the landlord suffer loss. Loss can arise if the premises form part of a shopping precinct which is dependent upon the continued presence of the tenant's shop in order to generate a flow of shoppers into the precinct. If the tenant's shop is a large food store, its closure will reduce the number of shoppers in the precinct, thereby affecting the profitability of other shops in the precinct and resulting eventually in an adverse effect on the value of the landlord's reversion. The tenant ought to resist a positive covenant (see **28.1.3**).

Most user covenants are negative obliging the tenant 'not to use the premises other than for the purposes of ... [permitted purpose]' in which case a breach is committed by the tenant only if he uses the premises for a purpose not authorised by the landlord. A negative user covenant is not breached by non-user.

Neither form of covenant will be breached if the tenant uses the premises for a purpose ancillary to the permitted use. For example, use of some rooms in a shop for storage purposes where the user covenant permits the retail sale of books, magazines and periodicals would not amount to a breach.

19.3 THE EXTENT OF THE LANDLORD'S CONTROL

The principal covenant may be absolute, qualified or fully qualified.

19.3.1 Absolute covenants

An absolute covenant gives the landlord absolute control over any change in the use of the premises in that it permits the tenant to use the premises for the purpose of the permitted use and no other. The tenant will not be able to use the premises for a use falling outside the scope of the covenant without obtaining from the landlord a waiver of the tenant's breach, or getting the landlord to agree to a variation of the lease. If the permitted use is narrowly defined, the tenant should be advised to resist an absolute covenant, unless he is sure that he will not want to assign or sub-let the premises, or diversify his business. If the permitted use is sufficiently widely defined (eg use as offices only), then an absolute covenant should not unduly concern the tenant.

19.3.2 Qualified covenants

A qualified covenant allows the tenant to alter the use of the premises from a permitted use to some other use with the landlord's prior consent, which is usually required to be given in writing. However, such a covenant gives the tenant little extra comfort than is afforded by an absolute covenant since, unlike qualified covenants relating to alienation and improvements, there is no statutorily implied proviso that the landlord's consent is not to be unreasonably withheld. This means that, despite the additional wording added to the covenant, the tenant is still at the mercy of the landlord who may decline the request for a change of use for whatever reason he chooses. The only benefit from the tenant's point of view of a qualified covenant is derived from s 19(3) of the LTA 1927 which states that, provided the change of use will not entail any structural alterations to the premises (which would not often be the case), the landlord is not allowed to demand as a condition of his giving consent the payment of a lump sum or an increased rent (as to which, see *Barclays Bank Plc v Daejan Investments (Grove Hall) Ltd* [1995] 18 EG 117). However, s 19(3) does allow the landlord, as a condition of his consent, to insist upon the payment of reasonable compensation in respect of damage to or diminution in the value of the premises or any neighbouring premises belonging to the landlord (which might occur if a valuable use of the premises is abandoned), and the payment of expenses incurred in the giving of consent, such as legal and surveyor's fees.

Section 19(3) does not apply to agricultural or mining leases.

19.3.3 Fully qualified covenants

A fully qualified covenant allows the tenant to change the use of the premises from a permitted use to some other use with the prior consent (in writing) of the landlord, whose consent is not to be unreasonably withheld. Most covenants of this kind will also stipulate (either in the wording of the covenant, or in the interpretation section of the lease) that the landlord cannot unreasonably delay giving consent. Should the landlord, in the tenant's opinion, be guilty of an unreasonable refusal of consent, the tenant may, if he is certain of his ground, change the use of the premises without the landlord's consent. However, this course of action carries a risk and, therefore, most tenants would prefer to follow the safer course of action which is to apply to the court for a declaration that the landlord is acting unreasonably, and then proceed without the landlord's consent. The question of the landlord's reasonableness is ultimately left in the hands of the court. The only potential drawbacks of such a clause for the tenant are that, without an express provision in the lease, there is no obligation on the landlord to provide the tenant with reasons for refusing consent (making it difficult for the tenant to assess whether he has a good chance of success in his application for a declaration) and there is no positive duty upon the landlord to give consent along the lines of the statutory duty imposed by the LTA 1988 in respect of alienation covenants, which means that the tenant does not have a remedy in damages if he suffers loss as a result of an unreasonable refusal.

Section 19(3) of the LTA 1927 applies equally to fully qualified covenants.

19.4 ANCILLARY CLAUSES

It is usual for the landlord to impose many other covenants upon the tenant which also impact upon user, obliging the tenant:

(1) to comply in all respects with the Planning Acts (as defined in the definitions section of the lease). It is important for the landlord to have the benefit of this covenant since enforcement action for a breach of planning control committed by the tenant could be taken against the landlord, resulting in a possible fine;

(2) not to apply for planning permission, or to carry out acts of development at the premises. This covenant may be absolute, qualified or fully qualified. The landlord will not want the tenant to have freedom to change the authorised use of the premises as this may result in an existing profitable use being lost, thereby reducing the value of the premises. Although, as owner of the reversion, the landlord may be able to raise objections at the application stage, he would prefer to be able to veto the application under the terms of the lease in the first place. It should be noted that such a covenant may restrict the tenant's ability to alter or change the use of the premises even if elsewhere in the lease such action is more freely permitted;

(3) where the landlord has consented to an application for planning permission, and development has commenced, to fully implement all permissions obtained before the end of the term in accordance with any conditions attached to the permission;

(4) not to cause a nuisance, annoyance or inconvenience to the landlord or its tenants of adjoining premises. Whether an activity amounts to a nuisance is to be determined on the basis of ordinary tortious principles. An annoyance is anything which disturbs the reasonable peace of mind of the landlord or an adjoining occupier, and is a wider concept than nuisance. The concept of inconvenience is probably wider still;

(5) not to use the premises for any immoral or illegal use (since such uses may tarnish the reputation of the building and reduce its value);

(6) not to carry out any dangerous activities, or bring any noxious or inflammable substances onto the premises. The landlord's primary purpose behind this covenant is to preserve the premises. One consequence of a breach by the tenant might be an increase in the insurance premium for the premises, and although the tenant is likely to be obliged to pay the increased premium by virtue of the insurance covenant, the landlord would not want the level of insurance premiums to rise;

(7) not to overload the premises in any way. The landlord is simply trying to preserve the premises with this covenant;

(8) not to allow anyone to sleep or reside at the premises;

(9) not to allow any licence which benefits the premises to lapse (eg gaming licences, liquor licences). If the premises consist of a betting shop, the value of those premises will depend to a large extent on the continued existence of a betting office licence. The tenant will, therefore, be obliged by the landlord to maintain and where necessary renew the licence.

Chapter 20

ALTERATIONS

20.1 EXISTING RESTRICTIONS

Chapter 20 contents
Existing restrictions
The need for an
alterations covenant
The extent of the
landlord's control
Other lease clauses
Compensation for
improvements

As with user covenants, there are external restraints, outside the scope of the lease, which may prevent the tenant from altering the premises, or may at least regulate the way in which they are carried out, for example:

(1) *Planning legislation.* If the alterations proposed by the tenant amount to development within the meaning of s 55 of the TCPA 1990 then planning permission will be required.

(2) *The Building Regulations.* Any works to be carried out by the tenant will have to comply with the Building Regulations.

(3) *Covenants affecting a superior title.* The tenant's proposed works may be prohibited by the terms of a covenant affecting the landlord's reversion (which may either be the freehold title, or a leasehold title if the landlord is himself a tenant), or may require the consent of the person currently benefited by the covenant.

(4) *The common law.* The tenant will have to ensure that any works he carries out at the premises do not give rise to a cause of action in the tort of nuisance. He will also have to ensure that he will not, in executing his works, infringe an easement benefiting an adjoining property (eg a right to light or air over the tenant's premises).

(5) *Other legislation.* The tenant, in altering the premises, will have to bear in mind any requirements of the fire authority in regard to fire safety, and if his works are more than just minor works, the tenant must have regard to environmental legislation regarding noise and other kinds of pollution.

20.2 THE NEED FOR AN ALTERATIONS COVENANT

20.2.1 The landlord's concerns

There are various reasons why the landlord will want to control the ability of the tenant to make alterations to the premises:

(1) to ensure that the tenant does not breach the external restraints set out at **20.1**, which may well lead to action being taken against the landlord;

(2) to ensure that at the end of the lease the tenant would not be giving back to the landlord premises differing substantially from those demised;

(3) to maintain the character, appearance and reputation of the building and, therefore, the value of the landlord's interest in the building and any adjoining premises;

(4) to maintain the rental value of the premises;

(5) to preserve the physical state of the premises.

In a short-term letting the landlord will probably want to exercise tight control over the tenant's ability to make alterations to the premises. However, in a longer-term letting, where the tenant may need to adapt the premises during the term to suit his changing business needs, the landlord will be prepared to allow the tenant a greater degree of freedom. In the commercial letting market, a lease for a term of 15 years will not be an attractive prospect for a tenant if there are severe restrictions in the lease on his ability to make alterations. Such restrictions would give the landlord problems at the outset in securing a letting of the premises, and later on at rent review where the restrictive alterations covenant may be taken into account in reduction of the rental value of the premises.

20.2.2 The tenant's concerns

The tenant will be anxious to ensure that the lease gives him the right degree of flexibility. In considering the alterations covenant, the tenant must bear in mind four things.

(1) Will the tenant need to make any immediate alterations to the premises, before occupying them for the purposes of his business? For example, if the premises form the shell of a large shop, and the tenant has not been allowed access to the premises before completion of the lease, the tenant will need to fit out the premises before being able to trade. If the premises are open-plan offices, the tenant may need to install internal partition walls. If the premises in their present state are unsuited to the tenant's needs, the tenant may need to convert them. The tenant should ensure that the alterations covenant does not prohibit these works, or if the covenant permits them with the consent of the landlord, the tenant should ensure that such consent will be forthcoming.

(2) Does the tenant anticipate that his business needs may change during the term in such a way that he will need to alter the premises to accommodate these changes?

(3) Will the tenant's assignee be content with the restrictions on alterations in the lease? Even if the tenant does not anticipate the need to make any changes during the term, an assignee might need to make changes, and if the alterations covenant is too restrictive, an assignee might be dissuaded from taking an assignment of the lease.

(4) Will the tenant suffer at rent review? If the tenant secures a covenant that is too flexible, in that it gives the tenant extensive freedom to alter and improve the premises as he sees fit, the rental value of the letting may be increased at review as a result.

The tenant should ensure that, in the light of the above points, he has sufficient flexibility, but he should not let the landlord give him any more freedom than is strictly required, or else the tenant might suffer at review.

The covenant against alterations is usually drafted by the landlord to prohibit all alterations and additions to the premises save those expressly permitted by the terms of the lease, or those in respect of which written consent of the landlord has been obtained.

20.3 THE EXTENT OF THE LANDLORD'S CONTROL

As with other covenants, the covenant against alterations may be absolute, qualified or fully qualified.

In all cases, the landlord must first consider the type of premises involved, and the length of term proposed. In a short-term letting of, say, 3 years or less, an absolute prohibition against all alterations may be appropriate. In a letting of a large warehouse or factory or other industrial premises, the landlord may only require absolute control over alterations affecting the structure and exterior of the premises, leaving the tenant free to do more or less as he pleases on the inside. In a shopping parade, in order to maintain the general appearance of the parade and the quality of the development, the landlord may feel that he wants to have a very tight control over all alterations, inside and out.

On occasions, the landlord may allow the tenant unrestricted freedom to carry out certain types of alterations or additions. In office leases, where the initial design of the building is open-plan, the lease often allows the tenant to erect internal partitioning walls without having to obtain the landlord's prior consent. The lease would merely require the tenant to notify the landlord of the additions, and to remove them if required to do so by the landlord at the end of the term.

However flexible the landlord proposes to be, in many cases the landlord will consider imposing an absolute covenant against structural alterations for the simple reason that the structure, being such a fundamental part of the building, should not be tampered with by the tenant.

20.3.1 Absolute covenants

If the lease contains an absolute covenant against the making of any alterations, or against the making of a particular type of alteration, the landlord will have total control over the tenant in that regard. As was the case with user covenants, this does not necessarily mean that the tenant will be unable to carry out prohibited alterations, since, although the tenant is at the mercy of the landlord, at some later date the landlord may be prepared to agree to vary the lease, or grant a specific waiver in respect of the tenant's proposed breach of covenant.

Sometimes, the requirements of a particular statute permit the tenant to obtain a court order varying the terms of an absolute covenant where the tenant has been required to carry out works to the premises by a body acting under statutory authority (eg a fire authority ordering the tenant to install a fire escape, see the Fire Precautions Act 1971). Further, the provisions of the LTA 1927 can, in certain circumstances, enable the tenant to alter the premises notwithstanding an absolute covenant.

The tenant should be advised to avoid an absolute covenant except, perhaps, where the covenant only relates to structural or external alterations (in which case the tenant may agree that it is reasonable that he should not be allowed to tamper with the structural parts of the building) or where the letting is for a short term and the tenant is confident that he will not need to alter the premises in the future to accommodate changes in his business, and that he will not need or want to assign the lease during the term. However, the longer the term, the more the tenant should ensure that he has sufficient flexibility to alter the premises.

20.3.2 Qualified covenants

A qualified covenant against alterations prohibits alterations to the premises by the tenant without the landlord's prior consent (which is usually required to be given in writing). A typical lease of office premises might be drafted to contain an absolute covenant against all alterations to the premises 'except those expressly permitted by this clause'. This absolute covenant would then be followed by a qualified covenant obliging the tenant 'not to make any internal non-structural alterations without the prior written consent of the landlord'.

Section 19(2) of the LTA 1927 implies into a qualified covenant against making improvements a proviso that the landlord's consent is not to be unreasonably withheld. The proviso cannot be excluded by the landlord. However, under s 19(2), the landlord can, as a condition of his giving consent, require payment by the tenant of reasonable compensation in respect of damage to or diminution in the value of the premises or any adjoining premises belonging to the landlord, payment of any legal and other expenses (eg legal and surveyor's fees) properly incurred in the giving of consent and, where it is reasonable to do so, an undertaking from the tenant to reinstate the premises at the end of the term to the condition they were in prior to the execution of the improvement.

Section 19(2) leaves the tenant with three questions as set out below.

(1) When does an alteration amount to an improvement?

In deciding whether the tenant's proposed works amount to improvements to the premises, the matter is to be viewed through the eyes of the tenant, not the landlord (see *Lambert v F.W. Woolworth & Co Ltd (No 2)* [1938] 2 All ER 664). Provided the alteration has the effect of increasing the value or usefulness of the premises from the tenant's point of view, it is irrelevant that the alterations will inevitably lead to a decrease in the value of the landlord's reversionary interest. The tenant may propose knocking through a party wall to an adjacent building which is also in the occupation of the tenant, but which is not owned by the landlord. If such alterations increase the usefulness of the premises to the tenant (which they surely will), they will amount to improvements, and the landlord will not be able to withhold his consent unreasonably. As a consequence of the judicial interpretation of 'improvements', most disputes arising under s 19(2) revolve around the amount of compensation payable to the landlord rather than the classification of the tenant's works, since the tenant should always to be able to show that his alterations will improve the premises from his point of view.

(2) When will the landlord be acting unreasonably in withholding his consent?

First of all, the tenant must have supplied the landlord with all the information necessary for the landlord to reach an informed decision (*Kalford Ltd v Peterborough City Council* [2001] EGCS 42. Assuming this has been done, a landlord will only be acting reasonably in refusing consent where his reasons relate to the relationship of landlord and tenant in regard to the premises in question. Withholding consent on the grounds that the premises, if improved, would be more attractive and, therefore, likely to take trade away from the landlord's own premises in the neighbourhood would appear to be unreasonable on the grounds that the landlord is seeking to gain some collateral advantage outside the landlord and tenant relationship.

Since s 19(2) allows the landlord to be compensated for a reduction in the value of the reversion, a landlord would be acting unreasonably if he withheld consent to improvements on the ground of the reduction. The correct approach for the landlord would be to seek reasonable compensation under s 19(2). However, should the tenant refuse to pay a reasonable sum in compensation, or should he refuse to give an undertaking to reinstate the premises at the end of the term where it is reasonable for the landlord to ask for one (eg in the example above, where the tenant is uniting the premises with other premises not owned by the landlord), the landlord would be acting reasonably in withholding consent.

If the landlord gives his consent, but subject to an unreasonable condition (eg that the tenant pays an excessive amount of compensation to the landlord, or that the tenant agrees to surrender his lease one year earlier than the end of the term), the landlord will be unreasonably withholding his consent.

(3) What remedies does the tenant have?

If the landlord, in the tenant's opinion, unreasonably withholds consent to improvements, the tenant may seek a declaration from the court that the landlord is acting unreasonably and that the tenant may, therefore, proceed without the landlord's consent. Alternatively, confident in the belief that the landlord is acting unreasonably the tenant may decide to take a risk by proceeding to execute his proposed works without waiting for the landlord's consent. If subsequently sued for a breach of covenant for altering the premises without the landlord's consent, the tenant can use the landlord's alleged unreasonable withholding of consent as a defence to the action. However, unless there is an express provision in the lease, there is no obligation on the landlord to give any reasons for refusing consent, and so it may be difficult for the tenant to assess his chances of succeeding either in his application for a declaration, or in the defence of the landlord's action for breach if the tenant proceeds without waiting for the landlord's consent.

The tenant does not have an action in damages against the landlord if the refusal of consent results in loss to the tenant (eg where the tenant's well-advanced business plans are thwarted by the landlord's refusal) since, unlike alienation covenants, there is no positive duty on the landlord to give consent.

Section 19(2) does not apply to mining or agricultural leases.

20.3.3 Fully qualified covenants

Section 19(2) converts a qualified covenant against alterations into a fully qualified covenant insofar as improvements are intended by the tenant. However, to avoid the argument that the tenant's works are not improvements, most tenants will insist on converting a qualified covenant into a fully qualified covenant expressly by adding to the qualified covenant drafted by the landlord the words 'such consent not to be unreasonably withheld or delayed'. That having been done, the landlord may not now unreasonably withhold, nor delay giving his consent in respect of an application by the tenant to carry out any alterations of a kind permitted by the clause.

20.4 OTHER LEASE CLAUSES

The landlord is likely to include many other covenants in the lease which have a bearing on what the tenant will be allowed to do to the premises.

(1) If the terms of the lease permit certain alterations (either with or without the landlord's consent), the landlord may include a provision requiring all alterations and additions to be removed and the premises reinstated at the landlord's request at the end of the term. Section 19(2) of the LTA 1927 allows the landlord to impose this requirement as a condition of the licence to alter where it is reasonable to do so. By including the requirement in the lease, the landlord is trying to avoid the argument that he is attaching an unreasonable condition to his consent. Further, by obliging the tenant to reinstate the premises at the end of the term, the landlord may be able to avoid paying compensation to the tenant on account of his improvements (see **20.5**) on the basis that, if the improvements have been removed, there will be nothing in respect of which compensation can be paid at the end of the term.

(2) In the same way that the licence to alter may impose a requirement to reinstate, the landlord may also impose a condition obliging the tenant to allow the landlord access to the premises to view the tenant's works. To avoid the argument that such a condition is an unreasonable one to impose, many landlords prefer to insert an express right of entry for inspection in the lease itself.

(3) The doctrine of waste may operate to prevent the tenant from altering the premises. Waste is any act which changes the nature of the premises, and can be voluntary, permissive, ameliorating or equitable. Reference should be made to text books on land law for a more detailed consideration of the doctrine of waste. It is common to find a prohibition on waste (save to the extent that it might otherwise be permitted in the lease) in the alterations covenant.

(4) Many landlords impose a covenant on the tenant not to tamper with the electrical supply or installations, especially in a lease of part of a building.

(5) The landlord will want to control the tenant's ability to make applications for planning permission. This covenant may be absolute, qualified or fully qualified. If the tenant is allowed to obtain planning permission, the landlord is likely to require the tenant to fully implement all permissions obtained before the end of the term where development has been commenced by the tenant.

(6) The landlord will usually require a covenant by the tenant not to display any signs or advertisements at the premises without the landlord's prior written consent, since a proliferation of signs or advertising hoardings can give the premises an unsightly appearance, thereby reducing the value of the landlord's interest in the building. In a shopping precinct, some landlords want to prevent tenants emblazoning 'sale' signs in shop front windows, as they feel that a 'sale' can sometimes imply that the business of the shop is suffering, which might be interpreted by some people as an indication that the shop is badly situated in the precinct. This can in turn lead to a reduction in the rental value of the premises, and a possible reduction in the value of the landlord's reversion. The tenant will normally ask, and is usually able to negotiate that the covenant is fully qualified.

(7) The decorating covenant can be said to control the manner in which the tenant may alter the premises since it may dictate that the tenant is not to change the colour of the premises (either inside, outside or both) without the landlord's prior consent.

20.5 COMPENSATION FOR IMPROVEMENTS

Part I of the LTA 1927 (as amended by Part III of the LTA 1954) makes provision for the tenant to claim compensation from the landlord upon the termination of the lease in respect of improvements which the tenant (or his predecessor) has carried out to the premises. The concept is fair in that the tenant will be returning to the landlord an asset that has increased in value as a result of the tenant's expenditure.

In addition, the LTA 1927 provides a mechanism whereby the tenant may obtain permission for improvements he would like to carry out to the premises even in the face of an absolute covenant.

The LTA 1927 provides that a tenant of business premises (defined under the LTA 1927 as any premises held under a lease and used wholly or partly for the carrying on upon them of a trade or business) is entitled to compensation upon quitting the premises at the end of his lease (no matter how it is terminated) in respect of certain improvements.

20.5.1 Qualifying improvements

To qualify as an improvement for the purposes of the compensation provisions:

(1) it must be one which, at the termination of the lease, adds to the letting value of the premises;
(2) it must not consist of trade or other fixtures which the tenant is entitled to remove at the end of the lease;
(3) it must be reasonable and suitable to the character of the premises;
(4) it must not diminish the value of any adjoining premises belonging to the landlord; and
(5) it must not be made in pursuance of a contract made for valuable consideration (where, eg, the lease obliged the tenant to make the improvement, or the improvement was made under some statutory obligation and the tenant was bound by the lease to perform all statutory obligations affecting the premises, or the landlord paid for the tenant to improve the premises, or reduced his rent).

In order to be entitled to compensation on quitting, the tenant must have obtained prior authorisation for his improvements by using the statutory procedure, and he must claim within the statutory time-limits.

20.5.2 Authorisation

To obtain authorisation, the tenant must serve upon the landlord notice of intention to make improvements. It does not matter that the covenant in the lease is absolute, or is qualified and the landlord has reasonable grounds to withhold consent. There is no prescribed form for the tenant's notice and, therefore, a letter would suffice, but the tenant should submit with his notice plans and specifications of his proposed works. The landlord has 3 months from receipt to serve written notice of objection upon the tenant. If the landlord fails to object, the improvements are treated as automatically authorised and will, therefore, attract compensation under the LTA 1927. If the landlord does object in time, the tenant may apply to the court for a certificate that the improvement is a proper one to make. The court will grant the certificate if satisfied that the improvement qualifies as an improvement for the purposes of the LTA 1927 (see **20.5.1**). The tenant is then authorised to make the improvements in accordance with his plans and specifications. Again, it does not matter that the improvements are prohibited by the lease, since it is provided that if the tenant has received no objection from the landlord, or has obtained the certificate of the court, he can carry out the improvements notwithstanding 'anything in any lease of the premises to the contrary'.

20.5.3 Amount of compensation

The amount which the tenant is to receive must not exceed either the net addition to the value of the premises directly resulting from the improvements or the reasonable cost (as at the date of termination of the tenancy) of carrying out the improvement. It follows, therefore, that if the improvement does not add to the value of the premises, no compensation will be payable.

20.5.4 Time-limits

If the landlord does not voluntarily pay compensation to the tenant, the tenant must apply to the court for compensation within 3 months of the service of the landlord's s 25 notice, or counter-notice to the tenant's s 26 request (see **31.2**) or within 3 months of the forfeiture of the lease (either by re-entry, or court order). If the lease is to expire by effluxion of time, application must be made between 3 and 6 months before the expiry date of the lease.

The parties cannot contract out of the provisions relating to compensation for improvements.

The Law Commission has recommended abolition of compensation for improvements.

Chapter 21

THE LANDLORD'S COVENANT FOR QUIET ENJOYMENT

21.1 NATURE OF THE COVENANT

Chapter 21 contents
Nature of the covenant
Acts constituting a breach

Most leases will contain an express covenant for quiet enjoyment by the landlord (and, even in the absence of an express covenant, one will be implied). The usual form of express covenant provides that if the tenant pays the rent and performs his covenants, he may quietly hold and enjoy the demised premises without interruption by the landlord or anyone lawfully claiming under him. This usual form of covenant is restricted in that it only extends to interruption of or interference with the tenant's enjoyment of the demised premises by the landlord or any person lawfully claiming under him; it does not extend to the acts of anyone with a title superior to that of the landlord. However, the parties are free to negotiate a more extensive covenant for quiet enjoyment which does extend to the acts of those with a superior title, thereby providing the tenant with a greater degree of protection.

The covenant only extends to the lawful acts of those claiming under the landlord since, if they are unlawful (eg trespass) the tenant will have his own remedies against the person committing the act. This means that there is no breach of the covenant in the event of an interruption by an adjoining tenant which is unauthorised by the landlord.

21.2 ACTS CONSTITUTING A BREACH

The covenant will provide the tenant with a remedy in the case of unlawful eviction or where there is substantial interference with the tenant's use or enjoyment of the demised premises. Whilst this is a question of fact in each case the following situations have given rise to a breach:

(1) where the landlord erected scaffolding on the pavement in front of a shop which blocked the access to the shop (*Owen v Gadd* [1956] 2 QB 99). This illustrates that it is not necessary for there to be any physical intrusion into the demised premises provided (it would seem) that there is physical interference with the enjoyment of the premises;

(2) where the demised premises were flooded due to the landlord's failure to repair a culvert on his adjoining land (*Booth v Thomas* [1926] Ch 397);

(3) where the landlord carried out work to the building in a manner which caused prolonged and substantial interference to the tenant by reason of 'dust, noise, dirt ... deterioration of common parts ... general inconvenience ... and water penetration' (see *Mira v Aylmer Square Investments Ltd* [1990] 1 EGLR 45). If the landlord is under an obligation to repair the premises, he must take all reasonable precautions to prevent disturbance (*Goldmile Properties Ltd v Lechouritis* [2003] EWCA Civ 49, [2003] 15 EG 143).

Until recently, it had been thought that the word 'quiet' in the covenant did not refer to the absence of noise and that some direct and physical interference was required before the landlord incurred liability under it. However, in the case of *Southwark London Borough Council v Mills and Others; Baxter v Camden London Borough Council* [1999] 3 WLR 939, the House of Lords held that no such limitation exists. The fact that the tenant was complaining of noise from adjoining premises in the block due to poor sound insulation did not in itself preclude an action for breach of the covenant for quiet enjoyment. However, it was also held that the covenant applies only to the subject matter of the lease at the date of the grant. If, at that date, the premises already suffer from poor soundproofing qualities, the covenant is one not to interfere with the tenant's use or enjoyment of premises with that feature.

The covenant for quiet enjoyment is closely linked with the landlord's implied obligation not to derogate from his grant; which is dealt with at **28.2.2**.

Chapter 22

INSURANCE

22.1 INTRODUCTION

There is no implied obligation on either party to insure the demised premises. However, it is very important to both parties, and their lenders, that their respective interests are fully protected and it is, therefore, essential for the lease to make express provision for insurance. There are a number of important issues which will need to be addressed by the draftsman.

22.2 WHO IS TO INSURE?

In a lease of business premises, it is common practice for the landlord to effect the insurance cover. On a lease of part of a building (eg one unit in a shopping centre, or a suite of offices in a block) it is more appropriate for the landlord to arrange insurance for the whole building including any car parks, pedestrian areas etc, as in this way only one policy is needed. Further, all the common parts of the building will be covered under the same policy and there is no danger of any parts of the building being left uninsured. On the grant of a lease of the whole of a building, either party could be made to insure but the landlord will usually wish to assume the responsibility, rather than face the risk of the tenant failing to comply with his covenant to insure. Whilst the landlord would be able to sue the tenant for breach of covenant, the tenant may have insufficient funds to satisfy the judgment.

If the landlord effects the insurance, before completion the tenant should ask to see a copy of the policy so that he can satisfy himself as to the amount and terms of cover. As the tenant has a continuing interest in the insurance of the demised premises he should also require the landlord to produce evidence of the terms of the policy and of payment of the premiums, at any time during the term of the lease.

22.3 WHO IS TO PAY?

Where the landlord has insured the demised premises, there will be a covenant in the lease requiring the tenant to reimburse the cost of insurance to the landlord. This sum is likely to be reserved as rent in order to give the landlord better remedies for recovery. If the demised premises are part of a larger building which the landlord has insured, recovery can either be through the service charge provisions or, alternatively, there may be a separate covenant by the tenant to reimburse an apportioned part of the premium. The tenant must ensure that the apportionment of the premium between the tenants is fair, particularly if the business of some of the tenants involves hazardous activities which lead to an increase in the premium.

It should be noted that a covenant by the tenant to reimburse premiums that the landlord 'shall from time to time properly expend' does not impose an obligation on

Chapter 22 contents
Introduction
Who is to insure?
Who is to pay?
In whose name?
Risks covered
The sum insured
What if the premises are damaged?
Additional provisions
Insurance by the tenant

the landlord to shop around for a reasonable level of premium (see *Havenridge Ltd v Boston Dyers Ltd* [1994] 49 EG 111).

22.4 IN WHOSE NAME?

Where the landlord is to insure, the tenant should press for it to be effected in the joint names of the landlord and tenant. This will be to the tenant's advantage because the insurance company will not allow the policy to lapse unless both parties have been given notice. It will also ensure that the proceeds of the policy will be paid out to both parties jointly, and thus give the tenant some control over how they are laid out.

Another advantage to the tenant is that insurance in joint names will prevent subrogation. This is the right of the insurer to step into the shoes of the insured and pursue any claims that the insured has against third parties to recover the loss. This means that if the landlord had a cause of action against the tenant arising out of some default on the tenant's part which caused the damage, the insurers would be able to pursue that claim. If, however, the insurance is in the joint names of the landlord and tenant, subrogation will not be possible. Even in those cases where the insurance is in the landlord's name alone, the tenant may still be able to prevent subrogation occurring where it can be shown that the insurance has been taken out for the mutual benefit of both parties (eg, see *Mark Rowlands Ltd v Berni Inns Ltd* [1986] 1 QB 211, where the tenant agreed to reimburse the landlord the premiums paid; see also *Lambert v Keymood Ltd* [1997] 43 EG 131).

If the landlord objects to insurance in joint names, or if it is not a realistic possibility, for example, where the demised premises consist of one shop in a large shopping centre, the tenant should seek to have his interest 'noted' on the landlord's policy so that he will be notified before the policy lapses.

22.5 RISKS COVERED

The lease should contain a comprehensive definition of the insured risks listing, for example, fire, lightning, explosion, impact, storm, tempest, flood, overflowing and bursting of water tanks or pipes, riot, civil commotion, and many other risks commonly included in a buildings insurance policy. To give the landlord flexibility, at the end of the definition there should be a 'sweeping up' provision along the lines 'and such other risks as the landlord may from time to time reasonably consider to be necessary'.

Consideration also needs to be given to the issue of insurance cover against terrorist acts and reference should be made to one of the specialist texts on drafting leases for further information on this topic.

22.6 THE SUM INSURED

Whilst the demised premises could be insured for their market value, the better approach for the tenant is to require cover for the full reinstatement cost. This will allow the landlord to replace the building should it be totally destroyed. Care must be taken to ensure that site-clearance costs, professional fees and fees for any necessary planning applications, and any VAT are also recoverable. As to the actual amount of cover, specialist advice will be needed and the insuring party should consult experienced insurance brokers.

22.7 WHAT IF THE PREMISES ARE DAMAGED?

Although the doctrine of frustration is capable of applying to leases (*National Carriers Ltd v Panalpina (Northern) Ltd* [1981] AC 675), it will only do so in exceptional circumstances. Accordingly, unless the doctrine applies, the lease will continue notwithstanding any accidental damage to the demised premises, and the loss will fall on the party obliged to repair.

22.7.1 Will the tenant have to repair?

Since the tenant will be paying for the insurance taken out by the landlord, he should ensure that he is not obliged to repair the premises if they are damaged by one of the insured risks. It is common practice to exclude from the tenant's repairing covenant liability for damage caused by an insured risk, unless the insurance policy had been invalidated, or the insurance proceeds are not fully paid out by reason of the act or omission of the tenant (or some other person who was at the premises with the tenants' authority).

It is important that the tenant carefully checks the definition of insured risks, since, if there were significant omissions from the definition, the benefit of the limitation of the tenant's repair covenant would be seriously eroded. To take an extreme example, if fire was not an insured risk, the tenant would remain liable to repair damage caused by fire under the basic obligation to repair. The tenant must, therefore, make sure that the definition of insured risks includes all risks normally covered by a comprehensive buildings insurance policy.

22.7.2 Will the rent be suspended?

Unless the lease is frustrated, rent continues to be payable where the premises are damaged, even if the damage is extensive. It is, therefore, common to include a provision in the lease that if the demised premises are damaged by an insured risk, and become unfit for occupation or use by the tenant, the rent (or a fair proportion of it, depending on the extent of the damage) should cease to be payable.

The landlord will agree to a rent suspension only if the damage results from an insured risk, so that the tenant will remain liable for rent where the demised premises become unusable as a result of damage for which the tenant is ordinarily liable under his repair covenant. Again, it is important that the tenant examines the defined list of insured risks to ensure that the rent abatement clause operates on the occasion of damage by all usual insurable risks. The landlord will want to further qualify the suspension by stipulating that rent continues to be payable where the landlord's insurance policy has been invalidated by the act or omission of the tenant (or someone at the premises with the tenant's consent). If this were not the case, the landlord might lose both the rent, and the insurance proceeds.

The suspension will continue for such period as is specified in the lease. The landlord usually seeks to limit it to a period of 2 (or perhaps 3) years, or, if earlier, until the premises have been reinstated and are again fit for use and occupation, for the purpose permitted by the lease. It should be noted that there is a subtle difference between premises being fit for occupation and use, and the premises being fit for occupation or use.

The tenant should press for a similar suspension in respect of other payments under the lease, such as the service charge, because if the premises are damaged, and the tenant is unable to occupy them, he will not be able to take advantage of the services provided by the landlord. However, the landlord will not give way to the tenant easily. If damage is occasioned to the tenant's premises alone, this is not likely to reduce significantly the level of services provided to the rest of the tenants, and the landlord will, therefore, argue that he is not prepared to suffer any reduction in the amount of service charge income.

If the demised premises are damaged, and the rent abatement clause operates, the landlord will lose rental income. The landlord will, therefore, require insurance against loss of rent during the period of suspension, and since the tenant is getting the benefit of the rent abatement clause, he will require the tenant to pay the premiums. If a rent review is possible during the period of suspension, the review clause will almost certainly require the rent to be revised on the assumption that the demised premises have been fully restored. This being so, the insurance against loss of rent should be for a sum which anticipates an increased rent on review. Valuation advice will be needed in this regard.

22.7.3 Who will reinstate?

If the insurance is in the joint names of landlord and tenant, the proceeds of the policy will be paid to both of the insured who have equal control over the application of the proceeds and, therefore, the reinstatement of the premises. However, where the policy is in the sole name of the landlord, unless the lease provides to the contrary, there is no obligation on the landlord to use the proceeds of the policy to reinstate the demised premises. Whilst the Fires (Prevention) Metropolis Act 1774 (which applies throughout England and Wales) entitles any person interested in a building (whether as landlord or tenant) to require the insurers to apply the proceeds of a fire policy for that building towards its repair or replacement, the Act has no application to damage other than by fire, and the requirement must be made clear before the moneys are paid out. In those cases where the tenant is under an obligation to pay the cost of the insurance, it has been held that the landlord may be presumed to have insured on behalf of the tenant as well as himself, and thus the tenant can require the proceeds to be laid out on reinstatement (*Mumford Hotels Ltd v Wheler and Another* [1964] Ch 117). Notwithstanding this, where the landlord insures in his sole name, the tenant should always insist on an express covenant from the landlord to apply the proceeds of the policy in reinstating the demised premises.

A covenant by the landlord to reinstate often provides that in the event of damage to or destruction of the premises by an insured risk, the landlord will use the insurance proceeds in reinstating the premises. The landlord should make it clear that any insurance money in respect of loss of rent is not to be applied in the reinstatement of the premises. From the tenant's point of view, he should pay particular attention to the wording of the covenant which is often an obligation just to lay out the insurance moneys received in respect of damage to the premises in the reinstatement. This does not deal with the situation where the insurance proceeds are insufficient to cover the entire cost of reinstatement. Although the landlord might be in breach of covenant for underinsuring the premises, the tenant should nevertheless press for a covenant by the landlord to make up the difference, or, more effectively, an unqualified covenant to reinstate. Where this latter form of covenant is chosen, the landlord should qualify the absolute nature of his obligation by providing that he is not liable in the event that the policy is invalidated, or the proceeds irrecoverable by reason of the act or omission of the tenant (or anyone at the premises with the tenant's consent).

In any event, the landlord would not want to be liable to reinstate the premises if circumstances beyond the landlord's control contrive to prevent him from doing so (eg strikes, lock-outs, shortages of materials).

22.7.4 What if reinstatement is impossible?

The tenant should try to specify a reasonable period (eg 2 or 3 years) within which reinstatement must take place. If reinstatement has not been completed within that period, so that the premises are still incapable of use, or if reinstatement simply proves to be impossible, for example, because the landlord is unable to obtain the necessary planning and other consents required for reinstatement, the lease may provide for either party to serve notice to terminate the lease. Indeed, the tenant may consider it appropriate to negotiate a provision allowing him to terminate the lease immediately the premises are rendered unfit for occupation or use by an insured risk, so that he may relocate his business without delay. The landlord should always bear in mind that the tenancy may be protected by Part II of the LTA 1954, and consequently the lease would need to be terminated in accordance with the provisions of that Act (see Chapter 31).

If reinstatement is not possible (or the parties do not desire it), in the absence of an express provision in the lease, it is unclear as to whom the insurance proceeds will belong, and it will be left to the court to ascertain the intention of the parties by looking at the lease as a whole.

22.8 ADDITIONAL PROVISIONS

Certain other covenants on the part of the tenant are commonly included in relation to the insurance of the premises:

(1) not to cause the insurance to be invalidated;
(2) to pay any increased or additional premiums that become payable by reason of the tenant's activities at the premises;
(3) to pay the cost of annual valuations for insurance purposes. The tenant should beware the cost of such regular valuations;
(4) not to bring dangerous or explosive items onto the premises;
(5) to comply with the requirements and recommendations of the landlord's insurers and the fire authority;
(6) to insure and reinstate any plate glass at the premises;
(7) to bear the responsibility of any excess liability under the landlord's insurance policy.

22.9 INSURANCE BY THE TENANT

If, exceptionally, the tenant covenants to insure the demised premises, the landlord must make sure his interest as landlord is fully protected. The landlord will have similar concerns to those expressed above on behalf of the tenant and so will wish to ensure:

(1) that insurance be effected in the joint names of the landlord and tenant, with insurers to be approved by the landlord;

(2) that the insurance is effected upon terms to be approved by the landlord (eg as to the basis of cover, the risks insured and amount);

(3) that in the event of damage or destruction the tenant covenants to reinstate the demised premises.

There will not be a rent abatement clause.

Chapter 23

PROVISO FOR RE-ENTRY

IMPORTANT

The lease should always contain a proviso enabling the landlord to re-enter the demised premises and prematurely end the lease on breach by the tenant of any of his covenants, or upon the happening of certain specified events. The right to forfeit the lease is a valuable remedy for the landlord but the right is not automatic; it only exists where the lease expressly includes such a right (or where, rarely, the lease is made conditional upon the performance by the tenant of his covenants; or where the tenant denies his landlord's title).

Forfeiture is not automatic, L cant exercise unless it expressly stated so of lease

The proviso for re-entry should specify the events giving rise to the right. These are commonly:

(1) where the rent reserved by the lease is in arrear for 21 days after becoming payable (whether formally demanded or not);

(2) where there is a breach by the tenant of any of the covenants, agreements and conditions contained in the lease;

(3) where the tenant has execution levied on his goods at the demised premises;

(4) upon the bankruptcy or liquidation of the tenant, or the happening of other insolvency events such as:

    (a) the presentation of a petition in bankruptcy;

    (b) the presentation of a petition for a winding-up order, or the passing of a resolution for a voluntary winding up;

    (c) the presentation of a petition for an administration order, or the making of such an order;

    (d) the creation of a voluntary arrangement; or

    (e) the appointment of a receiver or an administrative receiver.

The landlord's intention is to give himself as many opportunities as possible to forfeit the lease where the tenant is in financial difficulty. In some insolvency proceedings, the landlord will want to give himself two attempts at forfeiting the tenant's lease (eg once on the presentation of the petition in bankruptcy, and once on the making of the bankruptcy order) in case the landlord inadvertently waives his right to forfeit on the first occasion.

Forfeiture in Bankruptcy

A tenant should resist the inclusion of some of the less serious events (eg the mere presentation of the petition) or those insolvency events which are designed to cure insolvency (eg administration proceedings, voluntary arrangements, liquidations for the purpose of restructuring). Further, if the tenant's lease is likely to possess sufficient capital value to provide security for a loan (though this may be unlikely), the tenant should try to restrict the landlord's right to forfeit in these circumstances.

T shld refuse to have clause for forfeiture coz of mere presentation of petition & those designed to cure insolvency

Despite the existence of a right of forfeiture and the happening of one of the above events, the lease does not end automatically; but the landlord will have the right to end the lease. The way in which that right is exercised, and the complex formalities surrounding its exercise, are dealt with at **30.5**.

Chapter 24

LEASE OF PART

24.1 INTRODUCTION

Chapter 24 contents
Introduction
**Boundaries and
 easements**
Responsibility for repairs
Service charges
Sinking and reserve funds
Insurance

The purpose of this chapter is not to deal with every single issue of relevance on the lease of part of a building; some can only be dealt with in the context of particular clauses. The reader will, therefore, find references to leases of parts elsewhere in this book. However, there are some important issues which can be dealt with separately and by drawing these together in this chapter, particularly the service charge provisions, the reader will become aware of the special considerations which apply whenever a lease of part of a building is contemplated.

24.2 BOUNDARIES AND EASEMENTS

It is important that the parcels clause fully and accurately identifies the boundaries of the property to be let. This is particularly important bearing in mind that the tenant's liability to repair is often co-extensive with the demise; if he has to repair the 'demised premises' it must be clear where they start and finish.

As far as easements are concerned, the tenant will usually need to be granted rights over the parts of the building retained by the landlord or let to other tenants. The case of *B&Q plc v Liverpool and Lancashire Properties Ltd* [2000] EGCS 101, illustrated the way in which rights granted to tenants may hinder the landlord's future development proposals. In the same way, the landlord will wish to reserve certain rights over the property being let.

These matters are more fully considered in the LPC Resource Book *Property Law and Practice* (Jordans).

24.3 RESPONSIBILITY FOR REPAIRS

On the grant of a lease of part of a building, for example, one floor in an office block or one unit in a shopping precinct, it would be unusual to impose the responsibility for repairing the demised premises on one party alone. It is more practical for the responsibility to be shared between the parties. Whilst every lease and building is different, a common division of the repairing obligation in a large multi-occupied building is to make the tenant responsible for the internal non-structural parts of the demised premises whilst the landlord covenants to repair the remainder of the building. Any expense incurred by the landlord in complying with this obligation will usually be recoverable under the service charge provisions, see **24.4**.

Great care must be exercised in drafting the appropriate obligations.

24.3.1 Drafting considerations

(1) The whole building must be covered; there must be no doubt over who is responsible for the repair of each part of the building. If the tenant's covenant is limited, as it often is, to repairing the internal non-structural parts of the demise, he must make sure that the landlord assumes responsibility for the structure (including the roof, main loadbearing walls and foundations), the common parts, the conducting media, and the exterior (including any landscaped areas, forecourts, roadways and fences). To guard against the inadvertent omission of a part of the building from the landlord's repairing obligation, many repairing covenants begin by obliging the landlord generally to repair the 'Building and Grounds' (as defined in the lease) and then go on to list the items intended to be covered, adding 'without prejudice to the generality of the foregoing'. The following are some of the matters which will need consideration:

   (a) Walls. It must be made clear who is responsible for each wall in the building. Often the landlord will assume responsibility for the structural walls and possibly the outer half of the internal non-structural walls dividing the demised premises from the other parts of the building. The obligation to repair should be attributed as regards each physical layer of the wallcovering, plaster, brick etc.

   (b) The same meticulous approach is required for floors, ceilings and the joists and girders, etc, which lie between them.

   (c) Windows. There are conflicting authorities on the responsibility for the repair of windows and thus the matter should be dealt with expressly in the lease, usually by making the tenant responsible.

   (d) Roofs and roof spaces. Again, this is a notoriously grey area and the matter must be dealt with expressly in the lease.

   (e) Conducting media. Often the landlord will be made responsible (unless perhaps the conduits exclusively serve the demised premises), but the lease must put the matter beyond doubt.

   (f) The plant, including all heating and cooling systems, generators, boilers etc.

   (g) Decorative repairs. The landlord will usually assume responsibility for the exterior decoration and recover his costs under the service charge (see **24.4**).

(2) The obligation to repair is often co-extensive with ownership, and care must be taken to link together the repairing obligations with the definition of the demised premises in the parcels clause.

(3) The draftsman must also appreciate the precise meaning of certain words and phrases which have been judicially defined in a plethora of case-law. Thus, for example, 'structural repairs', 'main walls', 'external walls' and 'exterior' have all been judicially considered; and reference should be made to one of the standard works on landlord and tenant law for a more detailed analysis of such technicalities.

24.3.2 Other considerations

The lease should attribute responsibility for repair of every part of the building. If, however, the lease is silent on a particular point the question arises as to whether the courts will imply a repairing obligation on behalf of either the landlord or tenant? In this regard there are a number of cases in which the landlord of residential properties have been held impliedly liable to carry out various repairs. For example, in *Barrett v Lounova (1982) Ltd* [1990] QB 348, it was held that a covenant by a periodic tenant of an old house to keep the interior in repair would lack business efficacy unless there were implied a corresponding obligation on the landlord to maintain the structure and exterior. It remains to be seen to what extent cases like this will be applied to business leases. See Chapter 19 for a discussion of repairing covenants in general.

24.4 SERVICE CHARGES

In a letting of the whole of a property the landlord will normally wish to impose all responsibility for the repair and maintenance of the property on the tenant. This will not usually be possible in the case of lettings of part of a building, but the landlord will seek to achieve the same economic effect by the use of a service charge. The landlord will be responsible for repair and maintenance and the provision of services but will require the costs he incurs on these matters to be reimbursed by the tenants. The landlord could charge a higher inclusive rent to cover his anticipated costs, but he then runs the risk of inflation or unexpected outgoings proving his estimate incorrect. The inclusive rent method is unpopular with institutional landlords and lenders who prefer a 'clear lease', where the rent will always represent the landlord's clear income from the property and the landlord is reimbursed for the expenditure on the provision of services by means of a service charge which fluctuates annually according to the actual costs incurred.

From the landlord's point of view, it is necessary to decide whether the service charge should be reserved as additional rent. The advantages of reserving it as rent have already been considered (see **15.4**).

24.4.1 Services to be provided

Tenants need only pay for the provision of those services specified in the lease. If there is no provision for the tenant to pay, the landlord cannot recover his expenditure. Therefore, when drafting the service charge provisions, the landlord's solicitor needs to be careful to include all the expenditure to be laid out on the building (excluding those parts for which the tenant is made responsible). This will require a thorough examination of all the lease terms. The following is not a comprehensive list of items to be included in a service charge as each lease needs individual consideration. However, some common items of expenditure are set out below.

Repairs and decoration

The clause should allow the landlord to recover all his expenses in performing his repairing obligation. Thus it may need to allow him to recover his expenses in inspecting, cleaning, maintaining, repairing and decorating the common parts and any other parts of the building for which he is responsible, for example, the conducting media, roof, structural parts, plant, etc. Whether the landlord can go beyond 'repair', and rebuild or carry out improvements is a question of construction of the relevant clause but the tenant must be aware of the danger of having to contribute to work which would be outside a simple covenant to 'repair', for example, the replacement of defective wooden window frames with modern double glazed units. In such a case the landlord would be unduly profiting at the tenant's expense. Another concern of the tenant is that the clause may require his contribution to expenditure incurred by the landlord in remedying inherent defects in the building, for example, those caused by a design defect or through the use of defective materials. The tenant should resist such an onerous obligation.

The landlord should pay particular attention to the wording of the service charge provision. In *Northways Flats Management Co v Wimpey Pension Trustees* [1992] 31 EG 65, the clause required the landlord, before carrying out the work, to submit details and estimates to the tenants. The court held that this was a pre-condition to the recovery of the service charge and since it had not been complied with, the landlord was unable to recover his expenditure.

Heating, air-conditioning etc

The landlord will wish to recover his costs in supplying heating, air-conditioning and hot and cold water to the common parts of the building and possibly the demised premises as well. Sometimes, the landlord will restrict the provision of heating to the winter months. The tenant may want some minimum temperature to be specified but the landlord may be unwise to agree to this, preferring to provide heating to a temperature which the landlord considers adequate. The landlord should also ensure that he is not liable to the tenant for any temporary interruption in supply due to a breakdown.

Staff

The landlord will wish to recover his costs in employing staff in connection with the management of the building such as receptionist, maintenance staff, caretakers and security personnel. The clause should also extend to any staff employed by the managing agents for the purpose of providing services at the building. From the tenant's point of view he should guard against having to pay the full-time wages of staff who are not wholly engaged in providing the services.

Managing agents

If the landlord employs managing agents to provide the services, he should ensure that the service charge allows him to recover their fees since in the absence of an express provision it is unlikely that the landlord would be able to recover those fees. A company owned by the landlord can be employed as managing agents provided such an arrangement is not a sham (*Skilleter v Charles* [1992] 13 EG 113).

The tenant must make sure that the amount of fees recoverable is reasonable and may want some restriction placed on them in the lease.

If the landlord performs his own management services, the service charge should enable him to recover his reasonable costs for so doing.

Other common items of expenditure

Other common items of expenditure include:

(1)   maintaining the lifts, boilers and other plant and machinery;
(2)   lighting of the common parts;
(3)   refuse removal;
(4)   fire prevention equipment;

(5) window cleaning;

(6) legal and other professional fees;

(7) service staff accommodation;

(8) insurance (although sometimes this is dealt with outside the service charge provisions);

(9) interest on the cost of borrowing money to provide the services;

(10) maintenance of landscaped areas;

(11) outgoings payable by the landlord;

(12) advertising and promotion costs, in the case of a shopping centre.

'Sweeping up' clause

No matter how comprehensive the landlord thinks he has been in compiling the list of services to be provided, it is advisable to include a sweeping up clause to cover any omissions and to take account of any new services to be provided over the lifetime of the lease. However, careful drafting of such a clause is required as the courts construe them restrictively (see *Mullaney v Maybourne Grange (Croydon) Ltd* [1986] 1 EGLR 70). From the tenant's point of view he should guard against the clause being drafted too widely and insist on the service being of some benefit to him before having to pay for it.

24.4.2 Landlord's covenant to perform the services

The services to be provided often fall into two categories: essential services which the landlord should be obliged to provide (eg heating and lighting the common parts and repairing and maintaining the structure) and other non-essential services which he has a discretion to provide. From the tenant's point of view, he must make sure that, in return for paying the service charge, the landlord covenants to provide the essential services. Without such an express provision, it is by no means certain that one would be implied, leaving the tenant with no remedy if the services were not provided (see, however, *Barnes v City of London Real Property Co; Webster v City of London Real Property Co; Sollas v City of London Real Property Co; Oakley, Sollas & Co v City of London Real Property Co* [1918] 2 Ch 18).

In drafting the covenant the tenant should require the services to be provided in an efficient and economical manner; and to a reasonable standard, rather than a standard the landlord considers adequate. The Supply of Goods and Services Act 1982 provides that where a service is provided in the course of a business there is an implied term that the supplier will carry out the service with reasonable care and skill but it is obviously better for the tenant to deal with the matter expressly. In *Finchbourne v Rodrigues* [1976] 3 All ER 581, the view was expressed that the costs claimed should be fair and reasonable to be recoverable under the service charge. However, this view may no longer reflect current judicial thinking (see *Havenridge Ltd v Boston Dyers Ltd* [1994] 49 EG 111) and therefore, again, an express provision is preferable. From the landlord's point of view, he may wish to restrict the covenant so that he is liable to use only 'reasonable endeavours' or 'best endeavours' to provide the services, rather than be under an absolute obligation to do so. In any event, the covenant should be limited so that the landlord is not liable to the tenant for failure to provide the services due to circumstances outside his control such as industrial action.

Another consideration for tenants is the length of the unexpired residue of their lease as they will be understandably reluctant to pay for works which are calculated to benefit future interests in the property rather than tenants under the current lease. This was held to be a relevant factor in deciding what was recoverable by the landlord under the service charge provisions in the case of *Fluor Daniel Properties Ltd v Shortlands Investments Ltd* [2001] PLCS 10 (although much will, of course, depend on the exact form of wording used).

As a general rule, the obligation to provide the services is independent of the obligation to pay for them. Therefore, in the event of non-payment by the tenant, the landlord cannot withdraw services (and in any event it is unlikely that the landlord could withdraw services from one tenant alone).

24.4.3 The tenant's contribution: basis of apportionment

In addition to setting out the items which can be charged to the tenant, the clause must deal with how the total cost is to be apportioned between the tenants in the building. The following are some commonly used methods:

(1) by reference to rateable value. This can be arbitrary since rateable values can vary for reasons which bear no relationship to the amount of services consumed;
(2) according to floor areas. This can be a reasonable method, depending on the nature of the building, but some method of measurement will have to be agreed;
(3) according to anticipated use of services. This can be difficult to assess and depends on the nature of each tenant's business and its location within the building;
(4) as a fixed percentage. This provides certainty for both parties but is inflexible. Further, the landlord must make provision for any future enlargement of the building which would necessitate a recalculation of the percentages.

Each method has its own advantages and disadvantages and reference should be made to one of the standard works on the drafting of business leases for further consideration of the matter. Whatever method is adopted, the tenant will want to ensure that he does not become liable for any unlet units; the landlord should be required to pay the service charge for these.

24.4.4 Payment of the charge

Advance payments

Typical service charge provisions stipulate that the service charge is to be paid by the tenant periodically in advance (usually on rent days). Advance payments are necessary because otherwise the landlord would have to fund the provision of work and services out of his own resources and recoup his expenditure from the tenants later. The amount of the advance payments can give rise to disputes between the parties unless the tenant can be sure such payments are not excessive. There are different ways of calculating the payments, for example, it can be based on the previous year's actual expenditure or on an estimate of the likely expenditure in the current year. If the latter method is adopted, the tenant should insist on the amount payable being certified by, for example, the landlord's surveyor, and that the payment is only to be made upon receipt of such a certificate (see below).

The tenant may wish to consider a requirement that the landlord is to pay the advance payments into a separate account to be held on trust in order to avoid the problems which will arise if the landlord becomes insolvent.

Final payments and adjustments

At the end of the year the service charge provisions will, typically, require the landlord to prepare annual accounts showing his actual expenditure in the year: such accounts to be certified by the landlord's accountant (see below). Where advance payments have been made an adjustment will be necessary to correct any over or underpayment. In the case of underpayment the tenant will be required to pay this amount within a specified time. If there is an overpayment, the lease may provide for its refund to the tenant or, more usually, it will be credited to the following year's payments.

Certification of amounts due

It is common for the service charge provisions to stipulate that the landlord pro vides a certificate given by his surveyor or accountant, acting as an expert, in connection with the amount of both the advance and end of year payments. Unless the lease provides to the contrary, the expert must be independent from the landlord (*Finchbourne v Rodrigues* above), although the tenant may wish this to be expressly stated in the lease. If the certificate is said to be 'final and conclusive as to the facts stated', its finality is likely to be upheld by the courts. If the lease makes the expert's certificate conclusive on matters of law, for example, as to the construction of the lease, there are conflicting views on its validity but it may be that it will be upheld if the expert is given the exclusive right to determine the issue and the lease is clear on the party's intention to exclude the jurisdiction of the courts (see *National Grid Co plc v M25 Group Ltd* [1999] 08 EG 169 and *Morgan Sindall v Sawston Farms (Cambs) Ltd* [1999] 1 EGLR 90).

24.5 SINKING AND RESERVE FUNDS

The object of sinking and reserve funds is to make funds available when needed for major items of irregular expenditure. A sinking fund is a fund established for replacing major items such as boilers and lifts which may only be necessary once or twice during the lifetime of the building. A reserve fund is established to pay for recurring items of expenditure such as external decoration which may need attending to, not annually, but perhaps every 4 or 5 years. The estimated cost of such decoration will be collected over each 5-year period to avoid the tenants from being faced with a large bill every 5 years.

The advantage of such funds is that money is available to carry out these major works when needed without any dramatic fluctuations in the service charge payable from one year to another. However, the creation of such a fund needs careful thought and many difficult questions will need to be addressed at the drafting stage. Who is to own the fund? Is it to be held absolutely or on trust? What is to happen to the fund when the landlord sells the reversion? What will be the position upon termination of the lease? (See *Secretary of State for the Environment v Possfund (North West) Ltd* [1997] 39 EG 179.) Further, there may be considerable tax disadvantages. Such matters are beyond the scope of this book, but the parties will need specialist advice about these matters.

24.6 INSURANCE

On a lease of part of a building in multi-occupation the landlord will usually insure the whole building and recover the premium from the tenants under the service charge provisions or in a separate insurance clause. Insurance is dealt with in Chapter 22.

Chapter 25

UNDERLEASES

25.1 LIABILITY OF SUB-TENANTS

Chapter 25 contents
Liability of sub-tenants
Reasons for sub-letting
Drafting points
The sub-tenant's
   concerns

Ordinarily, there is neither privity of contract nor privity of estate between a head landlord and a sub-tenant and, therefore, the head landlord is unable to sue a sub-tenant in respect of any breaches of the terms of the head-lease. However, it is a common practice for the head landlord to require a sub-tenant as a condition of granting consent to the sub-letting, to enter into a direct covenant with the head landlord to observe and perform the covenants in the head-lease. This will make the sub-tenant liable to the head landlord in contract. Further, a sub-tenant may be bound by those restrictive covenants in the head-lease of which he had notice when he took his sub-lease. As the sub-tenant is entitled to call for production of the head-lease on the grant of his sub-lease (LPA 1925, s 44), he will be deemed to have notice of the contents of the head-lease even if he does not insist on his right to inspect it (see the LPC Resource Book *Property Law and Practice* (Jordans) for further consideration of this matter).

25.2 REASONS FOR SUB-LETTING

There are many reasons why a tenant may want to grant an underlease of all or part of the premises demised by the head-lease. It may be that the tenant finds that he has surplus accommodation which is not required for the purpose of his business and, therefore, instead of leaving that part vacant (thereby wasting money) the tenant may try and cut his losses by finding a sub-tenant. Indeed, the tenant may well seek to create space for a sub-letting in the knowledge that the current market would lead to the sub-tenant paying a rent per square foot in excess of what the tenant is paying to the head landlord.

On other occasions, the tenant may be sub-letting the premises as an alternative to assigning the lease. Where a tenant has a continuing liability (either under privity of contract or under an authorised guarantee agreement), despite his ability to call for an overriding lease in the event of later default by an assignee (see **28.1.4**), the tenant might prefer to retain control of the premises by sub-letting rather than assigning.

25.3 DRAFTING POINTS

Where the tenant proposes to grant an underlease of all or part of the premises, he must have regard to the terms of his own lease, and in particular to the terms of the alienation covenant which is likely to control or regulate in some way the content of the underlease. The head-lease will usually require the tenant to obtain the consent of the head landlord before granting the sub-lease. Section 19(1)(a) of the LTA 1927 and s 1 of the LTA 1988 apply to qualified covenants against sub-letting.

In drafting the sub-lease, the tenant should bear in mind the following matters.

25.3.1 The term

The tenant should ensure that the term of the sub-lease is at least one day shorter than the unexpired residue of his head-lease term, since a sub-lease for the whole residue of the head-lease term will take effect as an assignment of that term. Not only will this be contrary to the tenant's intention, it will also probably breach the alienation covenant in the head-lease, as the landlord will have given his consent to a sub-letting, but not an assignment.

In taking up possession, the sub-tenant will be in occupation for the purpose of a business and may, therefore, enjoy security of tenure under Part II of the LTA 1954 (see Chapter 31). The tenant may want to consider excluding the sub-letting from the protection of the Act so that he can be sure to resume occupation at the end of the sub-lease. Indeed, it may be a requirement of the alienation covenant in the head-lease that any sub-leases are to be contracted-out of the LTA 1954, so that if the tenant's interest is terminated in circumstances which result in the sub-tenant becoming the immediate tenant of the head landlord, the head landlord will be guaranteed possession at the end of the sub-lease.

25.3.2 The rent

The tenant will want to ensure that the rent to be paid by the sub-tenant is as high as the market will currently allow, and if the sub-lease is to be granted for anything longer than a short term, the tenant will want to review the rent from time to time. Careful attention must again be paid to the alienation covenant in the head-lease which might dictate the terms upon which any sub-lettings are to be granted.

It is common for the head landlord to attempt to include several requirements in the head-lease:

(1)   that any sub-letting by the tenant is granted at a rent which is the greater of the rent payable under the head-lease, and the full open market rent for the premises;
(2)   that any sub-letting is granted without the payment of a premium; and
(3)   that the sub-letting contains provisions for the review of rent (in an upwards direction only) which match the head-lease review provisions in terms of frequency, timing and basis of review.

The reason the landlord seeks to impose such conditions is that at some future date, the interest of the intermediate tenant might determine (eg by reason of surrender) leaving the sub-tenant as the landlord's immediate tenant upon the terms of the sub-lease. However, if the tenant, at the grant of his lease, had agreed to excessively restrictive conditions on sub-letting, he may now find it difficult to arrange a sub-letting, particularly at a time when the market is falling and potential sub-tenants are only prepared to pay a rent below the current rent payable under the head-lease. One popular way around this was for the tenant to enter into a side letter or collateral agreement with the proposed sub-tenant in which the tenant agreed to reimburse the sub-tenant the difference between the head lease rent and the current market rent. However, the case of *Allied Dunbar Assurance plc v Homebase Ltd* [2002] EWCA Civ 666, [2002] 27 EG 144 has ruled that this is not a valid way of avoiding restrictions in the head lease preventing subletting below the head lease rent.

The sub-tenant should be wary of an obligation in the sub-lease which simply requires him to pay the rents payable from time to time under the head-lease, since such a provision would give him no input into any negotiations for the review of rent during the term, and is likely to give little incentive to the tenant to argue with any vigour against the landlord at review, since he knows that whatever figure is agreed, it will be paid by the sub-tenant.

If the head landlord has elected to waive the exemption for VAT purposes, so that VAT is payable by the tenant, the election in no way affects the sub-lease rents. It would, therefore, be wise for the tenant to waive the exemption in respect of these premises so that VAT can be charged to the sub-tenant, although careful consideration must always be given to the effect of waiving the exemption.

25.3.3 The covenants

In drafting the sub-lease, the tenant will attempt to mirror the provisions of the head-lease. He should be careful not to allow the sub-tenant scope to do anything at the premises which is forbidden under the provisions of the head-lease.

Particular attention should be paid to:

(1) *Alienation.* It is unlikely that the head-lease will allow any further sub-letting of the premises. Care should, therefore, be taken to impose appropriate restrictions in the sub-lease. There ought to be an absolute covenant against sub-letting (or sharing or parting with possession of the premises), with a qualified covenant against assigning the sub-lease.

(2) *Repair.* The same repairing obligation as affects the tenant (or an even tighter one) ought to be imposed upon the sub-tenant. In interpreting a repair covenant, regard is to be had to the age, character and locality of the premises at the time the lease was granted. If there has been a considerable lapse of time between the grant of the head-lease, and the grant of the sub-lease, different standards of repair might be required by the respective repair covenants, leading to a possible residual repair liability on the part of the tenant. The sub-tenant's obligation will be to repair 'the premises'. The tenant must make sure that 'the premises' are defined in the sub-lease to include all of the premises demised by the head-lease, or if a sub-letting of part is contemplated, that the division of responsibility is clearly stated.

(3) *Insurance.* In all probability, the head landlord will be insuring the premises, with the tenant reimbursing the premium. The sub-lease should, therefore, provide that the sub-tenant reimburses the premiums paid by the tenant (or a proportionate part if a sub-lease of part is contemplated).

(4) *Decoration.* The tenant should ensure that the sub-lease obliges the sub-tenant to decorate the premises as frequently as, and at the times, and in the manner required by the head-lease.

25.3.4 Rights of access

The tenant is unlikely to extend the usual covenant in the sub-lease for quiet enjoyment to cover liability for the acts and omissions of someone with a title paramount (eg the head landlord). If he did so, he would be in breach of the covenant if the head landlord disturbed the sub-tenant's occupation by exercising a right of entry contained in the head-lease. However, in any case, to avoid a possible dispute, the tenant should ensure that in reserving rights of entry onto and access over the sub-let premises, those rights are reserved for the benefit of the tenant and any superior landlord.

25.3.5 An indemnity

Despite imposing broadly similar covenants in the sub-lease to those contained in the head-lease, the tenant will also want to include a sweeping-up provision obliging the sub-tenant to perform all of the covenants in the head-lease in so far as they affect the sub-let premises, and to indemnify the tenant against liability for breach. The sub-tenant might prefer, however, to enter into a negative obligation not to cause a breach of the head-lease covenants. Care must be taken on a sub-lease of part to ensure that a correct division of liability is made between tenant and sub-tenant in respect of the head-lease covenants.

25.4 THE SUB-TENANT'S CONCERNS

Before the sub-lease is granted, the sub-tenant must ensure that the consent of the head landlord (if required) has been obtained. The usual condition of granting consent is that the sub-tenant is to enter into a direct covenant with the head landlord to perform the covenants in the head-lease (at least insofar as they relate to the sub-let premises). Ordinarily, there is no privity of contract or estate between a head landlord and a sub-tenant, but the direct covenant creates a contractual relationship.

Unless entered into does ordinarily no Privity of cont or est btw L & ST

As he is likely to be giving a direct covenant, and as he is also likely to covenant with the tenant in the sub-lease to perform the head-lease covenants, it is essential that the sub-tenant inspects the head-lease (including all licences and supplemental deeds which may have effected a variation of its terms). The sub-tenant's liability under the direct covenant with the head landlord should not extend beyond his liability on the tenant covenants in the sub-lease.

As an alternative to requiring the sub-tenant to enter into a direct covenant with the head landlord, use could be made of the Contracts (Rights of Third Parties) Act 1999. Under the provisions of this Act, a non-contracting party has the right to enforce a contract term if the contract expressly provides that he may or, subject to contrary intention, the term purports to confer a benefit on him. In the context of sub-leases, the head lease could be drafted to require any permitted sub-lease to contain a covenant by the sub-tenant to observe and perform the head-lease covenants and conferring upon the head landlord the right to enforce that covenant. Such a covenant would be a tenant covenant of the sub-lease and thus the sub-tenant would be released from future liability following a lawful assignment (and, of course, the assignee would become bound by it). In the same way, the landlord's obligations in the head-lease may be expressed to be for the benefit of sub-tenants, thus giving sub-tenants the right to enforce, for example, the head landlord's obligation in the head lease to provide services.

With regard to the drafting of the sub-lease, the following points may be borne in mind.

(1) Where there is to be a direct covenant in the licence to sub-let, it is important for the sub-tenant to remember that it will not work both ways, and so the sub-tenant does not have any means of enforcing a breach of covenant by the head landlord. The sub-tenant should consider insisting upon a covenant by the tenant

in the sub-lease obliging the tenant to enforce a breach of covenant by the head landlord as and when required by the sub-tenant. The sub-tenant is likely to concede that he should bear the cost of any action.

(2) The usual covenant for quiet enjoyment exempts an intermediate landlord from liability in respect of the acts or omissions of a superior landlord. The sub-tenant may consider extending the usual covenant.

(3) The sub-tenant should ask the tenant to covenant with him to pass on to him any notices received from the head landlord (eg s 146 notices).

(4) The sub-tenant should explore the possibility of having his interest noted on the head-landlord's insurance policy. He should ask for details of the policy and ensure that provision is made to enable the policy to be produced to him from time to time. The provision referred to at (1) above should enable the sub-tenant to force the tenant to force the landlord to reinstate the premises if they are damaged by an insured risk.

Chapter 26

AGREEMENTS FOR LEASE

26.1 INTRODUCTION

Chapter 26 contents
Introduction
When are they used?
A typical agreement

The agreement for lease, if used, will be drafted by the landlord's solicitor in duplicate, and submitted to the tenant's solicitor for approval together with the draft lease in duplicate (attached to each part of the draft agreement). If the landlord requires the tenant to pay the landlord's costs of drafting, negotiating and executing the lease, he is also likely to require the tenant to pay his costs in connection with the agreement for lease. In recessionary times, the tenant is likely to resist such requirements.

If an agreement for lease is used, the agreement is liable to ad valorem stamp duty as if it were the lease itself (Stamp Act 1891, s 75(1), as amended by s 111 of the Finance Act 1984). When the lease is completed and is presented to the Inland Revenue for stamping, the amount of duty payable on the lease will be reduced by the amount of duty already paid on the agreement (which will, in most cases, reduce the amount of duty payable on the lease to nil).

The agreement for lease is an estate contract and can be protected by way of a C(iv) land charge against the landlord's name, or notice or caution against the landlord's registered title. The circumstances in which an agreement may be used will necessarily involve a delay between exchange and completion, in which case it might be considered advisable to protect the agreement against the possibility of the landlord selling the reversion and defeating the tenant's interest. In the light of s 240(1) of the Finance Act 1994 (see **10.2**), HM Land Registry will require the agreement to be stamped before entering a notice of it on the register. The tenant may, therefore, prefer to lodge a caution.

26.2 WHEN ARE THEY USED?

In most commercial letting transactions, the parties proceed straight to the completion of the lease without concerning themselves with the formality of entering into an agreement for lease. The reason for this is that the agreement would simply exist as a contractual commitment between the parties to enter into a lease, the form and content of which had already been agreed by negotiation. With the terms of the lease already agreed, why bother to embody them in an agreement for lease, when the parties could proceed immediately to the execution and exchange of the lease and counterpart? There is little risk in either party backing out of the arrangement in the time between the conclusion of negotiations and completion of the lease, especially since both parties will have invested considerable time and resources in the negotiation process.

The circumstances when an agreement for lease is used are usually limited to occasions where one (or both) of the parties is required to do something to the premises prior to the grant of the lease.

Typically, an agreement for lease is used where the landlord has commenced, or is about to commence constructing the premises. The landlord's aim is to secure an agreed letting of the premises to a prospective tenant as soon as possible so that, when construction has been completed, the tenant will be bound to complete the lease, and rent will become payable to the landlord to provide income to offset his building costs. On other occasions, an agreement may be used where the landlord, at the request of the tenant, is carrying out substantial works of repair or refurbishment to the premises prior to the grant of the lease. In this kind of situation the landlord would not want to go to the expense of executing works without a commitment from the tenant to enter into a lease once the works have been carried out. An agreement may also be used where it is proposed that the tenant carries out major works to the premises prior to the grant of the lease, in which case both parties would ideally like the security of a binding commitment to enter into a lease upon completion of the works.

The main aim of the agreement, apart from recording the agreed terms of the lease to be entered into, is to stipulate the nature of the works to be carried out to the premises, the time in which they are to be carried out, and the manner in which they will be executed. There is little point in the landlord agreeing to grant a lease of premises to the tenant upon the completion of the construction of a building if the agreement does not state, amongst other things, who will construct the building, and by when, and to what specifications.

26.3 A TYPICAL AGREEMENT

In order to consider the type of clauses commonly found in an agreement for lease where works are required to be carried out, this part of the book concentrates on an agreement in which the landlord will be obliged to construct a building prior to the grant of the lease. Many of the points raised will be equally applicable, or can be adapted to a situation where it will be the tenant who is carrying out works to the premises before completion.

The basic thrust of the agreement will be that the landlord, as the owner of the site, will construct (or, by engaging building contractors, cause to be constructed) premises for occupation by the tenant. Once the premises reach a stage of 'practical completion' (see **26.3.5**) the tenant will be obliged to enter into the form of lease attached to the agreement. Rent will then become payable under the terms of the lease, giving the developer/landlord a return on his investment. Naturally, the terms of the agreement are open for negotiation. In particular, negotiations will revolve around the extent of control, input or supervision the tenant will be allowed to have in respect of the execution of the works, and how much protection he will have if, after completion of the lease, the works turn out to be defective.

The following is a list of some of the problems to be addressed in the drafting and negotiation of the agreement.

26.3.1 What works will be carried out by the landlord?

In the type of agreement under consideration, the works will involve the construction of the entire building which will house the premises to be demised by the lease. The extent of works proposed by the landlord must be clearly indicated in the agreement.

It will, therefore, be necessary for detailed plans and specifications, recording exactly what is to be constructed, to be attached to the agreement for lease, and for the agreement to stipulate that the landlord is to develop in accordance with them.

26.3.2 Will the landlord be able to depart from the agreed plans and specifications?

The tenant will not want the agreement to permit the landlord's development to vary from the plans and specifications, since this might result in the tenant being obliged to take a lease of premises radically differing from those originally planned. On the other hand, the landlord would like to build into the agreement a degree of design and construction flexibility, so that if, as the development proceeds, it becomes apparent to the architect that a variation in design or construction is necessary or desirable (either on economic, architectural, or purely aesthetic grounds), the agreement will permit a variation to be made. This is a matter for negotiation between the parties. A possible compromise might be reached if the agreement allows certain 'permitted variations', which could be defined to mean those required by the local planning authority under the terms of any planning permission for the development of the site, or those which are insubstantial and are reasonably required by the landlord.

It should be noted that if a contract is varied in a material manner, outside the scope of existing contractual provisions, a new contract will come into being which will have to satisfy the requirements of s 2 of the Law of Property (Miscellaneous Provisions) Act 1989 (LP(MP)A 1989) (see *McCausland v Duncan Lawrie Ltd* [1996] 4 All ER 995).

26.3.3 What standard of works is required?

It is usual to include an obligation in the agreement on the landlord's part to ensure that the works described in the agreement are carried out with reasonable skill and care, and in accordance with all relevant statutory approvals (eg planning permission, Building Regulations).

26.3.4 Is there to be any degree of supervision?

The landlord will want complete freedom to enable his builders to progress the development of the site without any interference from the tenant, and may be able to insist upon this in his negotiations. However, the tenant may have sufficient bargaining strength to demand a degree of control and supervision over the execution of the landlord's works. He may require the agreement to make provision allowing a surveyor, appointed by the tenant, to inspect the works as they are being carried out, in order to make comments and representations to the landlord (or his architect), and to point out errors in the works, and variations not permitted by the agreement. The issue of whether the tenant is to have any involvement in the development and, if so, the degree of control to be allowed, is a matter which will depend heavily upon the relative bargaining strengths of the parties.

26.3.5 Who decides when the building is ready for occupation?

The determination of the date upon which the building is completed is important since it will trigger the commencement of the lease (and therefore liability for rent).

Completion

A landlord is interested in achieving completion as soon as possible in order to obtain rent, whereas the tenant may have an interest in delaying completion (unless he is especially keen to gain possession). The tenant will not want the agreement to force him to complete the lease until the premises have been fully completed to his satisfaction, and are ready for immediate occupation and use. However, the landlord will not want to give the tenant any scope for delaying the transaction beyond a date when the premises are sufficiently ready. The landlord will want to be able to force the tenant to complete the lease notwithstanding one or two imperfections. It is, therefore, a representative of the party who is carrying out the works who usually certifies that the building has reached the stage of 'practical completion' for the purposes of the agreement.

Practical completion occurs when the building works have been sufficiently completed to permit use and occupation for the intended purpose, even though there may be some minor matters outstanding.

The certificate of practical completion, in the type of agreement under consideration, will be given by the landlord's architect (as defined by the agreement). Care should be taken where the agreement is drafted 'back-to-back' with a design-and-build building contract, where the landlord will not have engaged the architect (see **8.2.3**). Issues which will concern the tenant are whether the tenant should have any control over who should act as the architect, whether the architect is to be independent (ie whether he may be someone who is in the employ of the landlord), and whether, at the final inspection of the works, the tenant can insist upon the attendance of his own representative to make representations to the landlord's architect, or to carry out a joint inspection for the purpose of issuing the certificate. The tenant's main aim in this regard is to be able to object to and delay the issue of the certificate of practical completion (which triggers completion) if in his opinion the works have not yet been satisfactorily completed. As ever, this is a matter upon which negotiations are required.

26.3.6 Will the agreement specify a completion date?

If the building is being built between exchange and completion, there will not be a fixed date for completion. The agreement will provide for the lease to be completed within a specified number of days after the issue of the certificate of practical completion. The landlord would seek to resist being obliged to complete his building works within a fixed time-scale, since there are any number of reasons why the execution of the works might be delayed. However, on the other hand, the tenant would like the agreement to impose some time restraints upon the landlord, as he will not want to be kept waiting indefinitely for the building to be completed. Presumably the tenant would be anxious to obtain possession of a completed building as soon as possible in order to satisfy his business needs. The tenant may press for the inclusion of a clause which requires the landlord to use his best (or reasonable) endeavours to ensure that the building is completed by a certain date. The landlord may be prepared to accept such a clause provided he is not liable for delays caused by matters outside his control.

26.3.7 Is the person carrying out the works to be liable for any delay?

It is usual for the agreement to include what is called a 'force majeure' clause to ensure that the person executing the works will not be in breach of the requirement to

tenant may require if done to by a clause in d agreement + d LL to use his best endeavours complete in a certain date

it is possible + LL 2 agree to such clause but subj) to him not been liable + delay caused by matters out of his control

complete the works by a certain date if the delay is caused by matters which are outside his control. A 'force majeure' clause covers delaying factors such as adverse weather conditions, strikes, lock-outs, or other industrial action, civil commotion, shortages of labour or materials and others.

26.3.8 Will there be any penalties for delay?

Usually, the tenant can only delay the transaction by failing to complete the lease within the stipulated number of days after the issue of the certificate of practical completion. To discourage the tenant from delaying completion, and to compensate the landlord, the agreement should stipulate a 'rent commencement date' from which rent will become payable under the lease, regardless of whether the tenant has completed the lease. If the tenant delays completion beyond the rent commencement date, he will still be bound to pay rent to the landlord on completion of the lease calculated from the earlier rent commencement date. In this way the tenant is penalised for his delay by having to pay rent in respect of a period when he was not in occupation of the premises, and the landlord is thus not left without income. The rent commencement date is usually stated to be the day upon which the lease is due to be completed (ie a certain number of days after the issue of the certificate of practical completion) or, if a rent-free period is being given to the tenant, a certain number of months after the day upon which completion is due.

If the landlord fails to complete the building by any long-stop date inserted in the agreement, and is unable to avail himself of the force majeure clause, the tenant could just sit tight and await completion, in the knowledge that rent will not become payable until then. However, most tenants will not want to be kept waiting indefinitely, since premises are usually required for immediate business needs. Therefore, as an incentive to the landlord to build within the timescale specified by the agreement, the tenant should insist upon a clause providing for liquidated damages to be payable by the landlord if he delays beyond the long-stop date. The agreement ought to state a daily rate of damages payable to the tenant in the event of a delay. The landlord should ensure that the building contract entered into with his building contractors runs 'back-to-back' with the agreement for lease so that he may claim liquidated damages from his contractors in the event of a delay. The tenant may want a further provision enabling him to terminate the agreement in the event of a protracted delay.

26.3.9 What if there are any defects in the works or materials?

If, after completion, the tenant discovers that there are defects in the design or construction of the premises, or in the materials used, then insofar as the defects amount to disrepair (see 17.2.6) the tenant will be bound to remedy them under the repairing covenant in the lease. A well-advised tenant will have instructed a surveyor to look for defects in the works prior to the grant of the lease. However, the nature of a design or construction defect is such that it rarely manifests itself until some time after the lease has been completed. The tenant should, therefore, ask for some protection in the agreement (or in the lease itself) against the prospect of such 'latent' or 'inherent' defects arising. There are several ways in which this can be done.

(1) In negotiating the terms of the repairing covenant, the tenant could seek to exclude liability (either absolutely, or during the first few years of the term) in respect of any disrepair which arises out of a defect in the design or construction

of the building, or in the materials used. Liability for repair necessitated by latent defects, if excluded from the tenant's covenant, ought to be transferred to the landlord under the lease.

(2) In the agreement for lease, the tenant could negotiate the inclusion of a clause which creates a 'defects liability period' to oblige the landlord to put right any defects which become apparent within, for example, the first 12 months after practical completion.

(3) In the agreement, the tenant could insist upon a provision obliging the landlord to enforce a clause in the building contract entered into by the landlord with his building contractor whereby the contractor had undertaken to remedy any defects becoming apparent within an initial defects liability period. Similarly, the agreement could oblige the landlord to pursue, for the tenant's benefit, any other contractual remedies the landlord may have against the other members of his design and construction team (eg architects, engineers, surveyors) under their contracts of engagement.

(4) The tenant could either take out, or require the landlord to take out insurance for the benefit of the tenant and his successors in title against damage caused by design of construction defects.

(5) In the agreement the tenant could insist that the landlord procures collateral warranties for the tenant from the landlord's design and construction team (eg builders, architects, engineers and surveyors) whereby those persons who have been involved in developing the site enter into a warranty with the tenant (and successors in title) that they have exercised reasonable skill and care in performing their duties under their respective contracts of engagement. The reason for this is that the tenant has no contractual relationship with the landlord's builders and designers, and so would be without a remedy in contract if their contractual obligations were not met.

26.3.10 Who is to be responsible if the premises are damaged after practical completion, but before completion of the lease?

If the premises are damaged before practical completion, then the certificate will not be issued, for the obvious reason that the premises will not have reached the stage of practical completion. The landlord will have to put right the damage before the certificate can be issued. If the premises are damaged after practical completion, but before actual completion, the agreement ought to stipulate that the premises remain at the landlord's risk since the tenant is not yet entitled to possession. The landlord ought to maintain insurance cover until the premises are handed over, and the agreement may make this a requirement.

26.3.11 What form will the lease take?

Before the agreement is entered into, the final form of the lease which the tenant will be required to enter into must have been agreed between landlord and tenant. Full negotiations must have taken place regarding the terms of the lease. The agreed form of draft should be appended to the agreement, with an obligation in the agreement upon the tenant to take a lease in that form on the date of actual completion. It is unwise to attach the travelling draft lease which, after amendments and counter-amendments, may now be untidy and difficult to interpret. A fair copy of the agreed draft should be prepared and attached to the agreement. There seems little point in the parties entering into an agreement for lease unless all negotiations regarding the lease terms have been concluded.

26.3.12 To which premises will the agreement relate?

The agreement will normally describe the premises by reference to the parcels clause in the draft lease, which in turn will refer to plans attached to the agreement showing the exact extent of the premises. Plans will be essential where a lease of part is intended.

26.3.13 Should any conditions of sale be incorporated?

The terms of the agreement for lease ought to set out extensively the rights and obligations of the landlord and tenant, in which case there may be no need to incorporate a set of conditions of sale. However, safety ought to dictate that they be incorporated in any case, with a provision that they apply except insofar as they are inconsistent with any other terms of the agreement.

26.3.14 Will the agreement require the landlord to deduce title, and will he disclose incumbrances in the agreement?

If title is deduced to the tenant, the agreement will usually prohibit requisitions after exchange.

26.3.15 Will the agreement merge with the lease?

The usual conveyancing doctrine of merger applies to an agreement to grant a lease, but it is common practice to include a clause excluding the doctrine since many of the contractual obligations are intended to continue in operation post-completion.

Insofar as they do continue in operation, they may be construed as landlord or tenant covenants of the tenancy, and therefore binding upon successors in title (see the definition of 'covenant' and 'collateral agreement' in s 28(1) of the LTCA 1995).

Chapter 27

SELLING THE LEASE

27.1 APPLICATIONS FOR CONSENT TO ASSIGN

It will nearly always be the case that the lease will restrict the tenant's right to assign the lease. There may be an absolute covenant against assignment, in which case the tenant is absolutely prohibited from assigning his lease. The landlord may (or may not) agree to waive the breach in a particular case but the tenant will be entirely at the mercy of his landlord. An assignment in breach of an absolute covenant will be effective, but the lease will be liable to forfeiture by the landlord because of the breach of covenant. More commonly, there will be a qualified covenant, ie not to assign without the landlord's prior written consent. In the case of a qualified covenant against assignment, s 19(1)(a) of the LTA 1927 implies a proviso that, notwithstanding any contrary provision, the landlord's licence or consent is not to be unreasonably withheld. The reasonableness of the landlord's refusal of consent has been dealt with earlier in this book (see **18.2.5**), and it will be recalled that if the parties have specified for the purposes of s 19(1A) of the LTA 1927 conditions to be satisfied, or circumstances to exist, before consent is to be given, a refusal of consent on the grounds that they are not satisfied, or they do not exist, is not an unreasonable withholding of consent.

Assuming the alienation covenant is qualified, the first step is for the tenant to make written application to his landlord for consent to assign. If the landlord consents, the tenant can proceed with the assignment. If the landlord unreasonably refuses consent, the tenant can proceed to assign and will not be deemed in breach of covenant. The danger for the tenant is in knowing whether the landlord's refusal is unreasonable or not, because if the landlord's refusal turns out to have been reasonable, the landlord will have the right to forfeit the lease. Further, for the purposes of the LTCA 1995, the assignment will be an excluded assignment, meaning that the assignor will not be released from the tenant covenants in the lease. Alternatively, the tenant may pursue the safer course of action of seeking a court declaration that the landlord is acting unreasonably in withholding consent, but this may prove costly and time-consuming. A further problem, prior to the passing of the LTA 1988, was that the tenant could not, in the absence of an express covenant by the landlord, obtain damages if the landlord withheld consent unreasonably.

Section 1 of the LTA 1988 (which only applies to qualified covenants) provides that where the tenant has made written application to assign, the landlord owes a duty, within a reasonable time:

(1) to give consent, unless it is reasonable not to do so. Giving consent subject to an unreasonable condition will be a breach of this duty; and
(2) to serve on the tenant written notice of his decision whether or not to give consent, specifying in addition:

   (a) if the consent is given subject to conditions, the conditions; or
   (b) if the consent is withheld, the reasons for withholding it.

Chapter 27 contents
Applications for consent to assign
The landlord's licence
Additional rules for leases granted on or after 1 January 1996

No doubt the landlord will wish to see a bank reference, audited accounts (eg for the last 3 years) and, if appropriate, trade references for the proposed assignee and these should accompany the tenant's application. If the landlord needs any further information to enable him to process the application, he should request this from the tenant.

The Act does not define what amounts to a reasonable time and each case will turn on its own facts. However, in *Go West Ltd v Spigarolo* [2003] EWCA Civ 17, [2003] 07 EG 136, the judge commented:

> 'I find it hard to imagine that a period of ... almost 4 months could ever be acceptable, save perhaps in the most unusual and complex situations ... it may be that the reasonable time ... will sometimes have to be measured in weeks rather than days; but, even in complicated cases, it should be measured in weeks rather than months.'

As to whether the landlord is unreasonably withholding his consent, this is left to the general law. The burden of proving the reasonableness of any refusal or any conditions imposed is on the landlord and the sanction for breach of the statutory duty is liability in tort for damages. As a result of the Act, landlords must give careful consideration to the financial consequences of having delayed or refused consent unreasonably and they should set up efficient procedures to ensure that each application for consent is dealt with expeditiously and in accordance with the Act.

If the landlord is himself a tenant and the applicant for consent is the sub-tenant, then if the head-lease requires the superior landlord's consent to the assignment, the Act imposes a duty on the immediate landlord to pass on a copy of the application to the superior landlord within a reasonable time.

Section 3 of the Act deals with the situation where a head-lease contains a covenant by the tenant not to consent to a disposition by a sub-tenant without the consent of the head landlord, such consent not to be unreasonably withheld. In such circumstances, a similar duty to that contained in s 1 is imposed on the head landlord towards the sub-tenant.

In considering whether or not to give consent, the landlord does not owe earlier tenants a duty of care to ensure that the assignee is of sufficient financial standing. If the assignee turns out to be unsatisfactory, the landlord will still be able to serve a default notice on those former tenants who may still be liable to the landlord (according to whether it is an 'old' or 'new' lease for the purposes of the LTCA 1995) (*Norwich Union Life Insurance Society v Low Profile Fashions Ltd* (1992) 21 EG 104). In such a situation, the earlier tenants may then be able to secure an overriding lease under the provisions of the LTCA 1995 (see **28.1.4**).

The landlord's solicitor, on receiving the tenant's application to assign, will often seek an undertaking from the tenant's solicitor to pay the landlord's legal and other costs of dealing with the application and preparing the licence (plus VAT) (see *Dong Bang Minerva (UK) Ltd v Davina Ltd* [1996] 31 EG 87). This does not infringe s 144 of the LPA 1925. Care should be taken in drafting the undertaking to make it clear whether the obligation to pay the landlord's costs applies in the event of the licence not being granted; this may be a requirement of the lease in any case.

To prevent the court from finding that consent has been given before the licence to assign is entered into, the landlord would be wise to head all correspondence with the tenant's advisers 'subject to contract' until completion of the licence (see *Next plc v National Farmers Union Mutual Insurance Co Ltd* [1997] EGCS 181).

27.2 THE LANDLORD'S LICENCE

If the landlord is prepared to give his consent to the assignment, a licence to assign will usually be prepared by the landlord's solicitor in which the landlord will formally grant his consent. If the tenant and assignee are to enter into covenants in the licence then all three (ie landlord, tenant and assignee) will be parties to the licence, which will be in the form of a deed. The licence will include various covenants and conditions such as:

(1) a direct covenant by the assignee with the landlord, to observe and perform the covenants in the lease for the entire duration of the term. The reason for this is that it makes the assignee liable to the landlord in contract for the full term of the lease and not just for breaches of covenant committed during the assignee's ownership. As the assignor is likely to have given a similar covenant to the landlord when he acquired the property, the assignor must appreciate that he will remain liable for future breaches even after the assignment has taken place. It is thus in the assignor's interest to make sure that the assignee is responsible and financially sound;

(2) a covenant by the tenant:

    (a) to pay the landlord's costs and expenses in dealing with the tenant's application;

    (b) not to allow the assignee to take up possession until the assignment has been completed;

(3) that the licence extends only to the transaction specifically authorised;

(4) that the licence is not to act as a waiver of any breach committed by the tenant prior to the date of the licence;

(5) that the licence shall cease to be valid unless the assignment is completed within, say, 2 months.

27.3 ADDITIONAL RULES FOR LEASES GRANTED ON OR AFTER 1 JANUARY 1996

If the lease was granted on or after 1 January 1996 the provisions of the LTCA 1995 will apply and the above rules may need to be modified to take account of that Act:

(1) the LTCA 1995 allows parties to leases containing a qualified covenant against assignment to agree in the lease, or at a later stage, to modify the controls of s 19(1)(a) of the LTA 1927 so that conditions of the parties' own choosing should instead govern assignment. This enables the landlord and tenant to set out in advance the conditions which must be satisfied before the landlord will consent to an assignment. If the parties do not lay down conditions for assignment in this way, or if the landlord seeks to withhold consent on grounds other than those agreed, then the provisions of s 19(1)(a) of the LTA 1927 will apply in the usual way (see **18.2.5**);

(2) the landlord may require an AGA from the assignor (see **18.2.7**);

(3) any licence to assign should not require the assignee to enter into a direct covenant with the landlord making the assignee liable on the lease covenants for the entire duration of the lease.

The detailed working of the LTCA 1995 in this regard is dealt with in Chapter 18.

Chapter 28

REMEDIES FOR BREACH OF COVENANT

28.1 LANDLORD'S REMEDIES

Chapter 28 contents
Landlord's remedies
Tenant's remedies

Before the landlord takes any steps against a defaulting tenant, he should first consider whether any other party is also liable. For example, are there any sureties or guarantors, is the original tenant under a continuing liability, or did any of the previous assignees give the landlord a direct covenant on assignment, upon which they may still be liable? The reader will recall that the ability of the landlord to proceed against some of these other parties is affected by the Landlord and Tenant (Covenants) Act 1995 (LTCA 1995). These issues have been dealt with earlier in the book.

Before proceeding against a former tenant or his guarantor for a 'fixed charge', ie:

- rent; or
- service charge; or
- any liquidated sum payable under the lease; or
- interest on such sums,

the LTCA 1995 requires the landlord to serve a notice of the claim (usually referred to as a 'Default Notice') upon the former tenant or his guarantor, as the case may be, within 6 months of the current tenant's default (there is no requirement to also serve a notice on a former tenant before serving a notice on that tenant's guarantor: *Cheverell Estates Ltd v Harris* [1998] 02 EG 127). Failure to serve a valid notice will mean that the landlord is unable to recover that sum from the person concerned. This requirement applies to all leases and not just those granted after the commencement of the LTCA 1995.

Where the landlord does proceed against a former tenant or his guarantor, that person may be able to regain some control over the property by calling for an overriding lease (see **28.1.4**).

28.1.1 For non-payment of rent

Only 6 years' arrears of rent are recoverable, whether by action or distress (Limitation Act 1980).

By action

If the tenant, or one of the parties mentioned above, is liable for the rent, the landlord may pursue his normal remedies for recovery through the High Court or county court. As to the choice of court and type of proceedings, see the LPC Resource Book *Civil Litigation* (Jordans).

Bankruptcy and winding up

If the sum owed exceeds £750, the landlord, as an alternative to action, may wish to consider the possibility of serving a statutory demand on the tenant with a view to commencing bankruptcy or winding-up proceedings, in the event of non-compliance with the demand (IA 1986). The landlord must bear in mind that the enforced bankruptcy of the tenant may reduce the chances of payment in full since he will become an ordinary unsecured creditor.

Distress

Distress is the landlord's ancient common law right, when the tenant is in arrears with his rent, to enter upon the demised premises and seize chattels to the value of the debt. The remedy is lost once the landlord has obtained judgment for the outstanding sum and the remedy should, therefore, be regarded as an alternative to proceeding by way of action. The distress can be carried out by the landlord personally, or as is more often the case, by a certificated bailiff acting on the landlord's behalf.

The rules concerning entry onto the demised premises are technical and easily broken, for example, entry can be gained through an open window but a closed window must not be opened. Such rules are beyond the scope of this book. Once on the demised premises, the landlord (or bailiff) may seize goods to satisfy the outstanding debt. The seized goods are then impounded either on or off the premises. If they are impounded on the premises, they may be left there and the tenant will be asked to sign a 'walking possession agreement' to avoid any argument that the landlord has abandoned the distress. This agreement will list the goods against which distress has been levied. If the tenant removes the goods, he commits 'pound-breach' and will become liable for treble damages. After the expiry of 5 days the landlord may remove the goods and sell them to pay off the arrears and the costs of distress. Whilst a public auction is not essential, the landlord must obtain the best price and for that reason most landlords will auction the goods.

Certain goods which are on the premises cannot be distrained against, for example, cash, perishable goods, tools of the tenant's trade up to £150 in value, things in actual use and goods delivered to the tenant pursuant to his trade. In addition, there are provisions to protect the goods of third parties contained in the Law of Distress Amendment Act 1908.

Special rules apply in the event of the bankruptcy or winding up of the tenant.

The Law Commission has recommended the abolition of the remedy and the above is only intended as an outline of the subject. Moreover, it may be the case that the remedy will not survive a challenge under the Human Rights Act 1998 (see *Fuller v Happy Shopper Markets Ltd* [2001] 1 WLR 1681, ChD). More detailed coverage is contained in the standard works on landlord and tenant law.

Collecting the rent from a sub-tenant

If the premises have been sub-let, the superior landlord can serve notice on the sub-tenant under s 6 of the Law of Distress Amendment Act 1908, requiring the sub-tenant to pay his rent to the superior landlord until the arrears are paid off.

Forfeiture

Forfeiture for non-payment of rent is dealt with at **30.5.2**.

28.1.2 Breach of tenant's repairing covenant

From a practical point of view, and as a first step, the landlord, exercising his right of entry in the lease, should enter onto the demised premises with his surveyor to draw up a schedule of dilapidations. This should be served on the tenant with a demand that the tenant comply with his repairing obligation. If the tenant remains in breach of his obligation to repair the demised premises, the landlord has various remedies available to him.

Action for damages

THE MEASURE OF DAMAGES

The landlord may bring an action for damages against the tenant either during the term or after its expiry. Section 18 of the LTA 1927 limits the maximum amount recoverable in all cases by providing that the damages cannot exceed the amount by which the value of the reversion has been diminished by the breach. It follows that the cost of repairs will be irrecoverable to the extent that they exceed this statutory ceiling.

Where proceedings are commenced during the term of the lease the reduction in the value of the reversion will be influenced by the length of the unexpired residue: the longer the unexpired term, the less the reduction should be.

In proceedings commenced at or after the end of the lease the court may be prepared, at least as a starting point, to accept the cost of repairs as evidence of the measure of damages, subject to the ceiling imposed by s 18, see *Smiley v Townshend* [1950] 2 KB 311 (see also *Ultraworth Ltd v General Accident Fire and Life Assurance Corporation* [2000] 2 EGLR 115, a case where the diminution in the value of the reversion was unaffected by the tenant's breach of the repairing obligation).

If a sub-tenant is in breach of a repairing covenant in the sub-lease, the measure of damages is the reduction in value of the intermediate landlord's reversion. If the sub-tenant knows of the terms of the superior tenancy, the intermediate landlord's liability to the superior landlord will be relevant in assessing these damages.

Section 18 further provides that no damages are recoverable for failure to put or leave the premises in repair at the termination of the lease, if the premises are to be pulled down shortly after termination or if intended structural alterations would render the repairs valueless. To benefit from this provision the tenant must show that the landlord had a firm intention (to pull down or alter) at the end of the lease.

It is important to appreciate that s 18 applies only to actions for damages by the landlord and has no application where the sum owed by the tenant is in the nature of a debt. If, therefore, the tenant covenants to spend £X per year on repairs, but fails to do so, the landlord may recover the deficiency as a debt without regard to the statutory ceiling in s 18.

THE NEED FOR LEAVE TO SUE

If the lease was granted for 7 years or more and still has at least 3 years left to run, the Leasehold Property (Repairs) Act 1938 lays down a special procedure which the landlord must follow before being able to sue for damages (or forfeit the lease) for breach of the tenant's repairing covenant. Where the Act applies, it requires the landlord to serve a notice on the tenant under s 146 of the LPA 1925. Apart from the normal requirements of such a notice (see **30.5.3**), it must in addition, contain a statement informing the tenant of his right to serve a counter-notice within 28 days claiming the benefit of the Act. If such a counter-notice is served, the landlord cannot proceed further without leave of the court, which will not be given unless the landlord proves (and not just shows an arguable case):

(1) that the value of the reversion has been substantially diminished; or
(2) that the immediate remedying of the breach is required for preventing substantial diminution, or for complying with any Act or bye-law, or for protecting the interests of occupiers other than the tenant, or for the avoidance of much heavier repair costs in the future; or
(3) that there are special circumstances which render it just and equitable that leave be given.

Even if the landlord makes out one of the grounds, the court still has a discretion to refuse leave but this should only be exercised where the court is clearly convinced that it would be wrong to allow the landlord to continue. The court may, in granting or refusing leave, impose such conditions on the landlord or tenant as it thinks fit.

The Act does not apply to breach of a tenant's covenant to put premises into repair when the tenant takes possession or within a reasonable time thereafter.

Self-help

If the tenant is in breach of his repairing obligations, can the landlord enter the demised premises, carry out the necessary works and recover the cost from the tenant? In the absence of a statutory right or an express provision in the lease, the landlord has no general right to enter the demised premises even where the tenant is in breach of his obligations. Indeed, the tenant may be able to obtain an injunction to restrain the landlord's trespass. For that reason most leases will contain an express right for the landlord to enter the demised premises and carry out any necessary repairs at the tenant's expense, in default of the tenant complying with a notice to repair. In the case of *Jervis v Harris* [1996] Ch 195, the court accepted the landlord's argument that his action against the tenant to recover this expenditure was in the nature of a debt action rather than one for damages. Thus, the landlord was able to evade the statutory restrictions in the 1927 and 1938 Acts, mentioned above. However, in exceptional circumstances the court may refuse the landlord an injunction to enforce his right of entry in the lease (see *Creska Ltd v Hammersmith and Fulham London Borough Council (No 2)* (1999) 78 P&CR D46).

Specific performance

In *Rainbow Estates Ltd v Tokenhold Ltd* [1999] Ch 64, the court held that, in principle, there is no reason why the equitable remedy of specific performance should not be available to enforce compliance by a tenant with his repairing obligation. However, other remedies are likely to be more appropriate and the court stressed that specific performance will only be awarded in exceptional circumstances.

Forfeiture

The landlord may be able to forfeit the lease for breach of the tenant's covenant to repair; forfeiture is dealt with at **30.5**.

28.1.3 Breaches of other covenants by the tenant: an outline

Damages

Damages for breach of covenant are assessed on a contractual basis, the aim being to put the landlord in the same position as if the covenant had been performed. The general principle is that the landlord may recover as damages all loss which may be fairly and reasonably considered as arising in the natural course of things from the breach, or such as may be reasonably supposed to have been in the contemplation of both parties, at the time of entering into the lease as the probable result of that breach (*Hadley v Baxendale* (1854) 9 Ex 341). In the majority of cases the damages will be equal to the diminution in the value of the reversion.

The breach of some particular covenants will now be considered.

COVENANT TO INSURE

The landlord usually assumes responsibility for insurance. If, however, the tenant has covenanted to insure, there will be a breach of covenant if the premises are uninsured or under-insured at any time during the term. If the premises are damaged during the period of default, the measure of damages will be the cost of rebuilding (*Burt v British Transport Commission* (1955) 166 EG 4).

COVENANT AGAINST DEALINGS

There is little authority on the measure of damages obtainable by a landlord where, for example, the tenant has assigned the lease without consent. However, the landlord will probably be entitled to compensation for the fact that his new tenant is less financially sound than the assignor and the value of his reversion is thus reduced.

USER COVENANT

Damages may be awarded for breach by the tenant of a positive covenant to keep the premises open. For example, if the anchor tenant, in breach of covenant, closes its shop premises in a shopping centre, it may have such an adverse effect on the profitability of the other shops in the centre that the landlord may be forced to offer rental consessions to the other tenants. The landlord should be compensated for this loss by an award of damages; but there may be difficult problems in quantifying the amount of the damages. If the landlord can prove that his financial loss arises wholly from the tenant's breach, there should be no difficulty for the landlord. However, it may be the case that the centre was already in decline long before the tenant ceased trading so that the defaulting tenant's breach merely contributed to the already falling profitability of the centre (see, generally, *Transworld Land Co Ltd v J Sainsbury plc* [1990] 2 EGLR 255).

Injunction

In certain circumstances, the landlord may be able to obtain an injunction against the tenant. An injunction is an equitable remedy and thus at the discretion of the court which may award damages instead. In an appropriate case the landlord may be able to obtain an interlocutory injunction pending the full hearing. There are two types of injunction:

(1) *Injunctions prohibiting a breach of covenant.* The landlord may consider the use of such an injunction to prevent, for example:

(a) an assignment in breach of covenant;

(b) the carrying out of unauthorised alterations;

(c) an unauthorised use.

(2) *Mandatory injunctions.* These injunctions compel the tenant to do something to ensure the performance of a covenant. The court is cautious in its grant of mandatory injunctions.

Other standard works on landlord and tenant law contain a more detailed consideration of the subject of injunctions.

Specific performance

Like the injunction, this is an equitable remedy and is therefore discretionary. The House of Lords has confirmed that specific performance is not available against a tenant who is in breach of his 'keep open' covenant (*Co-operative Insurance Society Ltd v Argyll Stores (Holdings) Ltd* [1997] 23 EG 137).

Forfeiture

Often the landlord's most effective remedy will be to commence (or threaten to commence) forfeiture proceedings against the tenant with a view to ending the lease. This remedy is dealt with at **30.5**.

28.1.4 Right of former tenant or his guarantor to an overriding lease

If a former tenant, or guarantor, is served with a notice by the landlord requiring payment of a fixed charge (see **28.1**), the LTCA 1995 allows him to call for an overriding lease within 12 months of payment. For example, L granted a lease to T in 1980. The lease is now owned by A who fell into arrears with his rent. L served notice on T requiring T to pay this sum. T duly made full payment and now claims an overriding lease from L. This will be a headlease 'slotted in' above the lease of the defaulting tenant. The lease of the defaulting tenant moves one step down the reversionary line and becomes a sub-lease. Thus, T will become the immediate landlord of A and in the event of continued default by A can decide what action to take against him, eg forfeiture of the occupational lease (sub-lease). Under the overriding lease, T now has some control over the premises for which he is being held liable. The same situation would arise in leases granted on or after 1 January 1996 where the former tenant had been required under an authorised guarantee agreement to guarantee the performance of his immediate assignee, and that assignee is now in default (see **18.2.8**).

The terms of the overriding lease will be on the terms of the defaulting tenant's lease (with consequential adjustments to add a small reversionary period).

Before deciding to call for an overriding lease, a former tenant (or guarantor) should be made aware that he may become liable for significant landlord's covenants.

28.2 TENANT'S REMEDIES

28.2.1 Breach of an express covenant

In general, a breach by the landlord of one of his covenants in the lease will entitle the tenant to bring an action for damages. The measure of damages will usually be the difference between the value of the tenant's interest in the premises with the covenant performed and the value with the covenant broken. In certain circumstances, the tenant may seek a more appropriate remedy, such as specific performance or an injunction.

Particular attention should be paid to the landlord's repairing covenant.

Breach of landlord's repairing covenant

Unless the lease is of part of a building, it is unusual for the landlord to enter into a covenant to repair. Even where the landlord has assumed the responsibility for repairs, he will generally only be liable if he has notice of disrepair. If the landlord fails to carry out the repairs for which he is liable, the tenant has various remedies available to him. These include the following.

ACTION FOR DAMAGES

The tenant's normal remedy will be to bring an action against his landlord for damages for breach of covenant. Section 18 of the LTA 1927, which restricts a landlord's claim for damages (see **28.1.2**), is not relevant to a tenant's claim. Here, damages will be assessed by comparing the value of the premises to the tenant at the date of assessment with their value if the landlord had complied with his obligation. The tenant will also be entitled to damages for consequential loss such as damage caused to the tenant's goods. If the disrepair was such that the tenant was forced to move into temporary accommodation, the cost of this should also be recoverable, provided the tenant had acted reasonably to mitigate his loss.

SELF-HELP

Subject to notifying the landlord and giving him a reasonable opportunity to perform his covenant, the tenant is entitled to carry out the repair himself and deduct the reasonable cost of so doing from future payments of rent (*Lee-Parker v Izzet* [1971] 1 WLR 1688). If the landlord sues the tenant for non-payment of rent, the tenant will have a defence (see **15.1**).

SPECIFIC PERFORMANCE

The tenant, unlike the landlord, may be able to obtain an order of specific performance. The granting of the order is entirely at the discretion of the court, and being an equitable remedy it will not be granted if damages are an adequate remedy. Further, there must be a clear breach of covenant and must be no doubt over what is required to be done to remedy the breach.

APPOINTMENT OF RECEIVER

In the tenant's action against the landlord for breach of covenant, the tenant may seek the appointment of a receiver to collect the rents and manage the property in accordance with the terms of the lease (including the performance of the landlord's covenants). The court has this power whenever it appears just and convenient to make such an appointment (Supreme Court Act 1981, s 37). The power has been exercised not only where the landlord had abandoned the property but also where he has failed to carry out urgently needed repairs in accordance with his covenant (see *Daiches v Bluelake Investments Ltd* [1985] 2 EGLR 67).

The tenant must nominate a suitably qualified person to act as receiver, for example, a surveyor and before agreeing to act, the potential appointee should ensure that the assets of which he will have control will be sufficient to meet his fees or that he obtains an indemnity in respect of them from the applicant.

A receiver may also be appointed where the landlord collects a service charge from the tenants but fails to provide the services he has promised.

28.2.2 Breach of an implied covenant

Covenant for quiet enjoyment

Most leases will contain an express covenant by the landlord for quiet enjoyment (see Chapter 21). In the absence of an express covenant one will be implied arising out of the relationship of landlord and tenant. The implied covenant extends only to interruption of or interference with the tenant's enjoyment of the demised premises by the landlord or any person lawfully claiming under him; it does not extend to acts done by anyone with a title superior to that of the landlord. Express covenants are often similarly restricted, in which case the only significant difference between the express and the implied covenant is that under an express covenant the landlord will remain liable throughout the term granted, whereas under an implied covenant the landlord's liability operates only during the currency of his ownership of the reversion.

The covenant will provide the tenant with a remedy in the case of unlawful eviction or where there is any substantial interference with the tenant's use and enjoyment of the premises either by the landlord or by the lawful (rightful) acts of anyone claiming under him. The acts likely to amount to a breach of the covenant are discussed at **21.2**. The normal remedy will be damages, assessed on a contractual basis, to compensate the tenant for the loss resulting from the breach.

Derogation from grant

A landlord is under an implied obligation not to derogate from his grant. This covenant complements the covenant for quiet enjoyment and sometimes the two overlap. The landlord will be in breach of his obligation if he does anything which substantially interferes with the use of the demised premises for the purpose for which they were let. Having given something with one hand the landlord cannot take away its enjoyment with the other. The principle is often used to prevent the landlord from using his retained land in a way which frustrates the purpose of the lease. Thus, it has been held to be a derogation from grant for a landlord to grant a lease for the purpose of storing explosives and then to use his retained land in such a way as to render the storage of explosives on the demised premises illegal (*Harmer v Jumbil (Nigeria) Tin Areas Ltd* [1921] 1 Ch 200; see also *Petra Investments Ltd v Jeffrey Rogers plc* [2000] 3 EGLR 120, a case concerning the landlord's ability to alter the original concept of a shopping centre). Similarly, if the landlord uses machinery on his retained land which by reason of vibration affects the stability of the demised premises there will be a breach of the implied covenant. However, there will be no derogation from grant where the landlord's use of the adjoining land merely makes the user of the demised premises more expensive, for example, by letting the adjoining premises to a business competitor of the tenant (*Port v Griffith* [1938] 1 All ER 295 and *Romulus Trading Co Ltd v Comet Properties Ltd* [1996] 2 EGLR 70; but see also *Oceanic Village Ltd v Shirayama Shokusan Co Ltd* [2001] All ER (D) 62 (Feb) in which the High Court was prepared, exceptionally, to find the landlord in breach of the obligation in such circumstances).

Until the decision in *Chartered Trust plc v Davies* [1997] 49 EG 135, it was generally believed that it was insufficient to amount to derogation from grant for a landlord to stand back while tenant A, in breach of covenant, committed acts of nuisance against tenant B thus driving tenant B out of business. Just because the landlord failed to take action against tenant A to prevent the nuisance did not, so it was thought, amount to a repudiation of B's lease. However, the Court of Appeal held that inaction by the landlord in these circumstances may amount to derogation from grant. The implications of this decision will be felt most where, as in the instant case, the landlord has retained management control of a shopping centre and is responsible for the common parts. If, in breach of covenant, one of the tenants does something in the common parts which adversely affects another tenant, the landlord will have to consider acting to enforce the lease obligations or else run the risk of being found to have derogated from grant (see also *Nynehead Developments Ltd v RH Fibreboard Containers Ltd and Others* [1999] 9 EG 174).

Chapter 29

THE EFFECT OF INSOLVENCY

29.1 BANKRUPTCY OF THE TENANT

29.1.1 The trustee-in-bankruptcy

Chapter 29 contents
Bankruptcy of the tenant
Liquidation of the tenant
The tenant in administration
The tenant in receivership
Insolvency and forfeiture
Insolvency and claims for rent or damages
Landlord's insolvency

On the making of a bankruptcy order, the Official Receiver assumes control of the bankrupt tenant's property pending the appointment of a trustee-in-bankruptcy at a meeting of the bankrupt's creditors. As soon as he is appointed, the estate of the bankrupt automatically vests in the trustee to enable the trustee to realise the bankrupt's assets and pay off the creditors. Since he becomes the owner at law of the bankrupt's property, the trustee incurs personal liability in respect of that property until he disposes of it, or unless he exercises his right of disclaimer (see **29.1.2**). The leasehold interest of a bankrupt tenant will vest in the trustee, but not, therefore, without the obligation to pay the rent and the liability to repair the premises and observe the other covenants in the lease. The automatic vesting of the lease in the trustee is an involuntary assignment and does not breach the covenant against assigning without consent.

If the lease has some value attached to it (ie a premium could be demanded on an assignment), the trustee will seek to sell the lease to raise some money for the benefit of the creditors. He will have to comply with the alienation covenant in the lease which will probably involve obtaining the consent of the landlord, and he will be liable to pay rent until the assignment is completed. More often than not the lease does not have any value and amounts to a burden on the bankrupt's estate owing to the continuing obligation to pay rent and perform the covenants. In this case the trustee would prefer to disclaim the lease.

29.1.2 Disclaimer

Section 315 of the Insolvency Act 1986 (IA 1986) gives the trustee power to disclaim onerous property. Onerous property is defined as including any property comprised in the bankrupt's estate which is such that might give rise to a liability to pay money or perform any other onerous act. This clearly covers the typical commercial lease, which by its nature contains onerous continuing obligations. The trustee disclaims the lease by giving to the landlord notice of disclaimer in the prescribed form.

Initially, the landlord will not know whether the trustee intends retaining the lease, with a view to selling it at a premium, or disclaiming it. However, under s 316, the landlord can force the hand of the trustee by requiring him to decide whether or not he is going to disclaim the lease. If the trustee does not give notice of disclaimer within 28 days of receiving a written application from the landlord under s 316, he cannot then disclaim. Section 316 is of no relevance to a landlord who has decided to forfeit the lease (see **29.5**).

29.1.3 The effect of disclaimer

The effect of disclaimer is that it operates to determine the rights, interests and liabilities of the bankrupt and his estate in respect of the disclaimed property, and it discharges the trustee from all personal liability in respect of that property as from the date of his appointment. The lease will no longer form part of the bankrupt's estate; the trustee will no longer be liable to pay the rent or perform the covenants; the bankrupt and his trustee will have washed their hands of the lease. Any claims the landlord may have in respect of unpaid rent up until the date of disclaimer, or other breaches of covenant, or any loss arising out of the disclaimer (including future rent) will have to be proved for in the bankruptcy.

If the bankrupt tenant was the original tenant (with no sub-tenancies having been created, and no guarantor backing up the original tenant's obligations), disclaimer ends the lease itself and the landlord is entitled to recover possession. If the bankrupt tenant was an assignee, whilst disclaimer ends the lease, it does not destroy the liability of any other persons still liable to the landlord (eg the original tenant, his guarantor, any intermediate assignees who have given direct covenants to the landlord and their respective guarantors, and any former tenant under an AGA). To this extent, there is a deemed continuing tenancy for the purpose of preserving the liability of others (see *Hindcastle Ltd v Barbara Attenborough Associates Ltd* [1996] 15 EG 103). This leaves the landlord in the position of being able to pursue those persons for payment of the rent for the remainder of the term, unless and until the landlord takes steps to bring the deemed continuing tenancy to an end.

One option available to a predecessor who finds himself in this invidious position is to make an application to court under s 320 of the IA 1986. Under that section, any person who claims an interest in, or who is under any liability in respect of the disclaimed property (such as the original tenant who is under a liability to pay the rent), may apply to the court for an order vesting the lease in him. Having to pay the rent is bad enough, but not having possession of the leasehold interest out of which that liability arises is unacceptable. Once the lease is vested in him, the predecessor can either resume possession or, as will more often be the case, try to curtail his continuing liability to meet the rent by assigning the lease, with the landlord's consent, to a more reliable assignee.

Whilst the effect of a disclaimer on the bankrupt tenant's guarantor (including an authorised guarantor under an AGA) is that it does not release the guarantor from the guarantee it is common to include a provision in the lease (or in the AGA) requiring the guarantor to take a lease from the landlord in the event of disclaimer.

The IA 1986 does not deal with the effect of a disclaimer on a sub-lease in an entirely satisfactory manner. Section 315(3) provides that disclaimer 'does not ... affect the rights or liabilities of any other person'. Arguably, if disclaimer results in the lease ceasing to exist, the sub-lease must also end. However, this is subject to the principle of the deemed continuing lease established by the House of Lords in the *Hindcastle* case. Furthermore, the sub-tenant can apply under s 320 for a vesting order, and indeed the landlord can require the sub-tenant to take a vesting order and if the sub-tenant declines to accept it, his right to remain will cease. The court will grant the order on such terms as it thinks fit and the effect of the order will be to make the sub-tenant the immediate tenant of the landlord.

29.2 LIQUIDATION OF THE TENANT

Liquidation (or 'winding up') is the process by which all the company's assets are collected, realised and distributed amongst those entitled to them. The company's existence is then terminated. This usually occurs because of the company's poor financial position. Winding up can either be accomplished voluntarily or compulsorily following a court order.

Unlike bankruptcy, title to the lease does not vest in the liquidator (unless the liquidator takes the unusual step of applying for an order under s 145 of the IA 1986 to vest title in him) and the liquidator does not, therefore, incur any personal liability under the lease. It is the company that remains liable to pay the rent, but it may have stopped doing so, owing to its insolvency. However, if the liquidator is making efforts to assign the lease at a premium, and in the meantime pays rent under the lease, the rent may be considered to be an expense of the liquidation and, therefore, recoverable by the liquidator in priority to other debts.

The liquidator has the same power of disclaimer as the trustee-in-bankruptcy (IA 1986, s 178(2)). There are similar provisions allowing the landlord to force the liquidator to decide whether or not he will disclaim (s 178(5)), providing for notice of disclaimer to be served on any sub-tenants (s 179), and enabling persons having an interest in or being subject to a liability in respect of the premises to apply to the court for a vesting order (s 181).

Disclaimer is a possibility in a compulsory liquidation and a creditors' voluntary liquidation, but is unlikely in a members' voluntary liquidation where it is thought that the directors would either have to assign the lease, or quantify the company's liability under the lease by negotiating a surrender of it before making the declaration of solvency required by such a liquidation. If the liquidator in a members' voluntary liquidation disclaimed the lease, the landlord would be able to claim for his loss arising out of the disclaimer. This unliquidated claim would upset the declaration of solvency.

29.3 THE TENANT IN ADMINISTRATION

Administration is a process available to assist ailing companies. It is a short-term intensive care operation supervised by the court aimed at putting an insolvent company back on its feet. Previously, an administrator could only be appointed at the discretion of the court, on an application by the company, its directors or its creditors. However, the Enterprise Act 2002 has introduced a faster and simpler administration procedure whereby an administrator can be appointed by the holder of a qualifying floating charge, the company, or its directors, as well as by the court. However, while a company is in administration, a general moratorium is placed on all proceedings against the company without the administrator's consent or leave of the court.

The administrator is appointed to do all such things as may be necessary for the management of the affairs, business and property of the company with a view to achieving the survival of the company. He has no power to disclaim the company's property, but ordinarily he should not want to, since his purpose is to revive the company, and this would be frustrated by the loss of the company's operating premises. If the company does have surplus leasehold premises which are a drain on the limited resources of the company, the administrator should seek licence to assign the lease, and dispose of the lease in the usual way.

An administrator incurs no personal liability under the lease. The lease does not vest in him; his status is merely as the agent of the company.

29.4 THE TENANT IN RECEIVERSHIP

Receivership is a state of affairs which exists when a person is appointed to enter onto another's property to seize and sell assets charged by a mortgage or debenture deed in order to secure repayment of a debt, interest and costs. Usually, the receiver will be either an administrative receiver or a Law of Property Act receiver. A Law of Property Act receiver is appointed to take possession of and receive the income of a specific asset charged by an individual or a company. However, landlords will not often be faced with a Law of Property Act receiver since lenders rarely accept rack-rent leases (having precious little capital value) as security for a loan. An administrative receiver is appointed to take possession of the whole (or substantially the whole) of a company's assets which have been charged to the lender under a floating charge. A company tenant's main charge to the bank will contain a floating charge over all the assets of the company, including the lease of the company's premises and, therefore, a landlord is likely to have to deal with this type of receiver. However, under the Enterprise Act 2002, the holder of a qualifying floating charge created on or after the commencement date of that Act may not appoint an administrative receiver of the company (see **29.3**). Holders of floating charges already in existence at the commencement date will continue to have the right to appoint a receiver without any time-limit.

Both types of receiver act as agent of the borrower-tenant and do not, therefore, incur any personal liability for rent. There is no question of the receiver disclaiming the lease and nor should there be. The principal task of the receiver is to sell the assets charged in order to realise cash and repay the borrowings. Licence to assign will be required in the usual way, provided the landlord has not already forfeited the lease. If the lease is particularly onerous, the receiver will either negotiate a surrender or advise his appointor to release the asset from the charge.

There are no restrictions on a landlord's remedies when his tenant is in receivership.

29.5 INSOLVENCY AND FORFEITURE

Earlier chapters have dealt with the drafting issues relating to forfeiture clauses. The landlord will probably have drafted the clause to enable forfeiture to be effected upon non-payment of rent, breach of covenant, or the happening of one of several insolvency events.

If the tenant is insolvent, all three elements of the clause may be operative in that the tenant may have stopped paying rent, allowed the premises to fall into disrepair and a winding up petition may have been presented to the court. A tenant in financial difficulties in a shopping precinct may close down its premises in breach of a covenant to keep open for trade, withhold rent, and suffer the appointment of a receiver.

With regard to the happening of insolvency events, the landlord will wish to ensure that the forfeiture clause gives him more than one attempt at forfeiting the lease in the event of insolvency proceedings being instigated, in case the landlord inadvertently waives one right to forfeit the lease, when, with knowledge of circumstances giving rise to his right to forfeit, he demands or accepts rent. Hence, the landlord will reserve the right to forfeit both on the occasion of the presentation of the petition (for a winding up, bankruptcy or administration order as the case may be), and on the making of the order itself. Not only does this protect the landlord against an inadvertent waiver, but it also allows him to act at the earliest opportunity, on the presentation of a petition, in order to recover the premises before the insolvency proceedings are brought fully into operation.

However, it must be established how each insolvency event affects the right of the landlord to forfeit the lease.

29.5.1 Individual insolvency

At any time after the presentation of a petition in bankruptcy (or a petition for an interim order in bankruptcy), the court may, on application, order a stay on any action, execution or other legal process against the property of the debtor (s 285(1) of the Insolvency Act 1986). Once a bankruptcy order (or an interim order) has been made, no creditor may have a remedy against the property of the bankrupt in respect of a debt provable in the bankruptcy without the leave of the court (s 285(3) of the IA 1986). There is, however, a suggestion in *Ezekiel v Orakpo* [1976] 3 WLR 693 (which was decided in relation to similar provisions contained in the Bankruptcy Act 1914) that forfeiture does not come within the scope of the latter provision. This case was followed in *Razzaq v Pala* [1997] 38 EG 157. If this proposition is correct, and leave is not required to obtain possession by forfeiture after the bankruptcy order has been made, it is difficult to see how the court could be justified in restraining a forfeiture before the order is made.

29.5.2 Corporate insolvency

After the presentation of a winding up petition, the court may, on application, order a stay on any existing forfeiture proceedings. Once the winding up order is made, forfeiture proceedings cannot be continued without leave of the court although peaceable re-entry is probably still possible. If the company is in voluntary liquidation, application can be made to the court for a stay on forfeiture proceedings at any time after the commencement of the winding up, as if the company were being wound up by the court.

Once a petition for an administration order has been lodged at court, and during the period of administration, whilst there are no restrictions on the landlord's ability to serve a s 146 notice, the landlord cannot forfeit the lease by court proceedings without leave of the court or peaceable re-entry.

The court will grant leave as a matter of course in liquidation cases (and presumably also in bankruptcy cases) since the landlord, in enforcing a forfeiture, is seeking to recover only his own property. In administration cases, leave should not be refused unless it would seriously impede the achievement of the purposes of the administration, or inflict a loss upon others which is substantially greater than the loss to be inflicted upon the landlord if leave were denied.

If the tenant company is in receivership, the landlord's ability to forfeit is unaffected.

29.6 INSOLVENCY AND CLAIMS FOR RENT OR DAMAGES

As an alternative to forfeiting the lease (or possibly in addition) the landlord may pursue other remedies. For instance, if the tenant fails to pay the rent, the landlord may bring a civil action for the arrears, exercise his right to distrain for the arrears, or, if the tenant has created a sub-tenancy, he may serve notice on the sub-tenant under s 6 of the Law of Distress Amendment Act 1908 requiring the sub-tenant to pay rent direct to the head landlord until rent arrears under the head-lease have been paid off. If the tenant is in breach of any of the other covenants under the lease, the landlord may bring an action for damages against the tenant.

If the tenant company is in receivership, the landlord's remedies for non-payment of rent or breach of covenant are unaffected, although he may find that the only time any judgment he obtains is met by the receiver is when the receiver applies to the landlord for licence to assign. The landlord would be likely to impose a condition on assignment that all arrears of rent, and any sums in respect of loss arising out of any other breaches of covenant are paid to the landlord before consent is given. The receiver incurs no personal liability for the company's debts, unless, being an administrative receiver, he specifically adopts any of the liabilities of the company.

When an administrator is appointed, the landlord may not exercise a right of forfeiture by way of peaceable re-entry without the consent of the administrator or the court. Further, no proceedings or execution or other legal process may be commenced or continued, nor can any distress be levied without the consent of the administrator or the court. It can thus be seen that a landlord's remedies are very restricted. The landlord cannot sue for arrears of rent or levy distress or forfeit without consent.

In a compulsory liquidation, on the making of the winding-up order, no actions may be commenced or proceeded with against the company without leave of the court. This general stay on proceedings prevents the landlord from distraining for rent, but would not, it appears, prevent him from serving a s 6 notice on any sub-tenants. In a voluntary liquidation, the court may stay any proceedings upon application by the liquidator. Insofar as the landlord is a creditor of the company, he must prove for his debt in the liquidation as an ordinary unsecured creditor. However, if the liquidator decided to retain possession of the premises for the purposes of the winding up, rent accrued since the commencement of the winding up will be payable in full by the liquidator as an expense of the liquidation.

In a bankruptcy, since the trustee-in-bankruptcy incurs personal liability, he is likely to disclaim the lease unless it has a capital value. Any actions the landlord may have against the individual tenant may be stayed on application by the trustee in those proceedings, although the landlord is still permitted to distrain for arrears of rent accrued due in the 6 months preceding the date of the bankruptcy order.

29.7 LANDLORD'S INSOLVENCY

In many cases the insolvency of the landlord will not greatly affect the tenant since the landlord's receiver, liquidator, administrator or trustee-in-bankruptcy will be keen to continue receiving the income generated by the lease. Problems will arise where the tenant wishes to take action for breach of covenant against an insolvent landlord, or where the landlord ceases to perform services in accordance with service charge provisions, or apply advance service charge payments made by the tenants. These problems are beyond the scope of this book.

Chapter 30

METHODS OF TERMINATION

30.1 INTRODUCTION

There are a number of ways at common law in which a lease may be ended. Before looking at these in detail, it is important to appreciate that if the tenant enjoys the protection of the security of tenure provisions under Part II of the LTA 1954, the lease may be ended only in one of the ways specified by that Act. For example, a protected fixed term will not come to an end on the expiry of that term; a protected periodic tenancy will not come to an end by the service of a landlord's common law notice to quit. Such tenancies can only be terminated in one of the ways specified in the Act. These restrictions on termination are dealt with in Chapter 31. The methods of termination to be considered here are:

(1) expiry;
(2) notice to quit;
(3) operation of break clause;
(4) forfeiture;
(5) surrender;
(6) merger.

Chapter 30 contents
Introduction
Expiry
Notice to quit
Operation of break clause
Forfeiture
Surrender
Merger

30.2 EXPIRY

A fixed-term tenancy will terminate at the end of that term; there is no need for either party to take any steps at all. If the tenant remains in possession beyond the expiry date with his landlord's consent, he holds over as a tenant at will, ie on terms that either party may end the tenancy at any time. A tenancy at will may be converted into an implied periodic tenancy by the payment and acceptance of rent.

30.3 NOTICE TO QUIT

A periodic tenancy may be determined by service of a notice to quit by either party. There are many technical rules surrounding the drafting and service of such notices and reference should be made to one of the standard works on landlord and tenant law for a consideration of these. What follows is only intended as a reminder of some of the more important rules.

In the absence of contrary agreement, the minimum length of notice required is as follows:

(1) yearly tenancy: half a year's notice (or two quarters if the tenancy expires on a quarter day);
(2) monthly tenancy: one month's notice;
(3) weekly tenancy: one week's notice.

Not only must the length of notice be correct, it must also expire at the end of a completed period of the tenancy. In the case of a yearly tenancy, this means that the notice must expire on the anniversary of the commencement of the tenancy or on the day before the anniversary. For example, with a yearly tenancy beginning on 1 January in one year, the notice should expire on 1 January or 31 December in any subsequent year. A similar rule applies to other periodic tenancies.

At common law, no particular form of notice is required but it must be unambiguous and, for the avoidance of doubt, in writing.

As a general rule, unless the lease provides to the contrary, a notice to quit must relate to all of the land in the lease and not just part.

30.4 OPERATION OF BREAK CLAUSE

The lease may contain an option by which one or both parties may determine the lease, at a particular time or on the happening of a specified event, before it has run its full term. This is known as a break clause. If there are any conditions precedent to the exercise of the option, these must be strictly observed (*Bairstow Eves (Securities) Ltd v Ripley* [1992] 2 EGLR 47). If, for example, the option is only exercisable provided the tenant has performed all of his obligations, he will not be able to exercise it whilst in arrears or in breach of his repairing covenant. However, the exact wording of the option should be examined to see whether such conditions have to be satisfied at the date the notice exercising the option is served, or at the date when it expires. Whilst great care should always be taken in drafting the break notice, minor errors which would not mislead a reasonable recipient may not render the notice invalid (see *Mannai Investment Co Ltd v Eagle Star Life Assurance Co Ltd* [1997] AC 749 and **14.2.2**).

The exercise of a break clause in a head-lease may operate to terminate any sub-lease which has been created (this is certainly the case in the event of exercise by the superior landlord; see *Barrett v Morgan* [2000] 2 AC 264). However, the sub-tenant may have the right to remain in possession if he is protected under Part II of the LTA 1954.

30.5 FORFEITURE

Forfeiture is the landlord's right to re-enter the premises and determine the lease on breach by the tenant of any of his covenants, or upon the happening of certain specified events. However, the right to forfeit is not automatic; it exists only where the lease expressly includes such a right (or if the lease is made conditional upon the performance of the covenants). The drafting of an appropriate provision is dealt with in Chapter 23.

Before the landlord proceeds to forfeit the lease, he should consider carefully the consequences of so doing. In a rising market the landlord should have no difficulty in subsequently re-letting the premises, possibly at a higher rent. If, however, the landlord is faced with a falling market, re-letting the premises may not be so easy. As a result of forfeiture the landlord may be left with an empty property on his hands for a long time. This will lead to a loss of income and may have a detrimental effect on any adjoining property of the landlord, for example, other shops in a parade.

The right of forfeiture is enforced by the landlord in one of two ways. First, the landlord may issue and serve proceedings for recovery of possession or, secondly, the landlord may peaceably re-enter the premises. Landlords are sometimes reluctant to adopt the second alternative because an offence will be committed if any violence is used or threatened and the landlord knew that there was someone on the premises opposed to the entry (Criminal Law Act 1977, s 6). Furthermore, there is a feeling that peaceable re-entry may be open to significant challenge under the Human Rights Act 1998. There are further statutory restrictions on the right of peaceable re-entry where the premises are let as a dwelling (Protection from Eviction Act 1977 (PEA 1977)).

30.5.1 Waiver of the right to forfeit

A landlord will be prevented from forfeiting a lease if he has expressly or impliedly waived the right to forfeit. The landlord will still be able to pursue his other remedies but will have lost his right to forfeit. Waiver will be implied where the landlord, knowing of the breach, does some unequivocal act which recognises the continued existence of the lease. It is not, however, a question of intention. So long as the act is inconsistent with an intention to determine the lease, the motive for the act is irrelevant. Thus, a demand for rent, or receipt of rent falling due *after* the right to forfeit has arisen, will amount to waiver notwithstanding a clerical error by the landlord's agent, receipt of rent paid under a standing order, or that the rent is demanded or received 'without prejudice to the landlord's right to forfeit'.

Waiver operates only in respect of past breaches of covenant. Where the landlord waives a 'once and for all' breach (eg breach of a covenant against sub-letting) his right to forfeit is lost for ever. If, however, the breach is of a continuing nature (eg breach of a repairing covenant) the right to forfeit, though waived on one occasion, will arise again, as the property continues to be in disrepair (see *Greenwich London Borough Council v Discreet Selling Estates Ltd* [1990] 48 EG 113; as to the need for a fresh s 146 notice).

30.5.2 Forfeiture for non-payment of rent

That the tenant owes rent to his landlord may seem a necessary pre-condition of the landlord's right to forfeit. Yet, exceptionally, this may not be the case. If, on an assignment of the reversion, the tenant is in arrears with payment of the rent, the 'old' and 'new' landlords often come to some arrangement as to who has the right to sue for the outstanding arrears. Such was the situation in *Kataria v Safeland plc* [1998] 05 EG 155, where it was agreed that, on completion, the right to receive the arrears of rent and all rights of action relating thereto were vested in the 'old' landlord. Notwithstanding this, it was held that the 'new' landlord, following completion, was entitled to forfeit the lease for non-payment of rent (even though the arrears were owed to the 'old' landlord). Hence it becomes important to distinguish the right to forfeit from the right of action in respect of the arrears.

The landlord must make a formal demand for the rent before forfeiting unless the lease exempts him from this obligation. To avoid the technicalities of a formal demand, most leases will provide for forfeiture if the tenant is, for example, 21 days or more in arrears 'whether the rent is formally demanded or not' (see also s 210 of the Common Law Procedure Act 1852). If the rent falls into arrears, the landlord may proceed to forfeit either by court proceedings, or by peaceable re-entry.

However, the tenant may have the right to apply to court for relief from forfeiture which, if granted, will mean that the tenant continues to hold under the existing lease. Where the landlord is proceeding by way of court action, those proceedings will be stayed if the tenant pays all the arrears plus the landlord's costs before the hearing. In certain cases, the tenant may also apply for relief within 6 months from the landlord's recovery of possession, although the rules differ between the High Court and county court. Where the landlord is proceeding by way of peaceable re-entry, the tenant may still apply to the court for relief. Again, the tenant will have to pay the arrears and must, as a general rule, apply within 6 months of re-entry by the landlord (although in exceptional circumstances the court may be prepared to grant relief outside this period: *Thatcher v CH Pearce & Sons (Contractors) Ltd* [1968] 1 WLR 748).

30.5.3 Forfeiture for breach of other covenants

Before a landlord is able to forfeit for a breach of covenant, other than for the payment of rent, the landlord must normally serve a notice on the tenant under s 146 of the LPA 1925. Where there has been an unlawful assignment, the notice should be served on the unlawful assignee.

A s 146 notice must:

(1) specify the breach;
(2) require it to be remedied within a reasonable time, if it is capable of being remedied; and
(3) require the tenant to pay compensation for the breach, if the landlord so requires.

As far as the second requirement is concerned, the notice will be invalid if the landlord wrongly takes the view that the breach is irremediable and, therefore, does not require the tenant to remedy it within a reasonable time. Whether a breach is remediable is a question of fact in each case. As a general rule, breach of a positive covenant is usually remediable by the tenant doing that which he has left undone. Thus, for example, it has been held that breach of a covenant requiring the tenant to reconstruct the premises by a stated date, was capable of being remedied by the tenant carrying out the work within a reasonable time (*Expert Clothing Service & Sales Ltd v Hillgate House Ltd* [1986] Ch 340). With negative covenants the issue is less clear. Views have been expressed in the past that breaches of negative covenants can never be remedied; once the forbidden act has been done it cannot be undone. However, current thinking is that the breach of some negative covenants can be remedied. Where, for example, the tenant has erected advertisement hoardings in breach of covenant, the removal of them would, it is submitted, remedy the breach. On the other hand, it has been held that certain breaches of negative covenants cannot be remedied. Thus, the breach of an alienation covenant, a covenant against immoral user and a covenant against trading without the appropriate licences have all been held to be irremediable (see, generally, *Expert Clothing Service & Sales Ltd v Hillgate House Ltd* above, and *Scala House & District Property Co Ltd v Forbes* [1974] QB 575). If the landlord is in any doubt about whether a particular breach can be remedied, the notice should require the tenant to remedy the breach 'if it is capable of remedy'.

If the tenant does not comply with the requirements of a valid s 146 notice, the landlord may proceed to forfeit the lease by court proceedings or peaceable re-entry. In either case the tenant may be able to seek relief from forfeiture but there is a vital difference between the two methods. If the landlord takes court proceedings, the tenant can seek relief at any time before the landlord actually re-enters the premises: no relief can be granted afterwards. However, if the landlord re-enters peaceably, the tenant can seek relief even after the landlord has re-entered, though the court will take into account all the circumstances including any delay by the tenant in seeking relief (*Billson v Residential Apartments Ltd* [1992] 1 AC 494).

In deciding whether or not to grant relief, the court will have regard to the conduct of the parties and all other relevant circumstances. If relief is granted, it will be granted on such terms as the court thinks fit (LPA 1925, s 146(2)). This gives the court a very wide discretion and the House of Lords has refused to lay down any rigid rules on its exercise. Relief is usually granted where the breach has been remedied and is unlikely to re-occur.

Where the s 146 notice relates to internal decorative repairs, the tenant has a special right to apply to the court for relief under s 147 of the LPA 1925. This is separate from the general right to apply for relief under s 146. Under s 147, the court may wholly or partially relieve the tenant from liability for internal decorative repairs if, having regard to all the circumstances of the case and in particular the length of the tenant's term still unexpired, it thinks the notice is unreasonable. However, s 147 does not apply:

(1) where the liability is under an express covenant to put the property in a decorative state of repair which has never been performed; or
(2) to any matter necessary or proper for keeping the property in a sanitary condition, or for the maintenance or preservation of the structure; or
(3) to any statutory liability to keep a house fit for human habitation; or
(4) to any covenant to yield up the premises in a specified state of repair at the end of the term.

Three special cases

(1) Where the breach by the tenant is of a repairing covenant, a special procedure may apply. If the lease was granted for 7 or more years and still has 3 or more to run, the s 146 notice must also contain a notice of the tenant's right to serve a counter-notice within 28 days. If this is served, the landlord cannot proceed to forfeit without leave of the court. Such leave is only granted on specified grounds (Leasehold Property (Repairs) Act 1938, see **28.1.2**).
(2) A lease will usually give the landlord the right to forfeit upon the tenant's bankruptcy (or liquidation) or having the lease taken in execution. If the landlord wishes to forfeit, he need only serve a s 146 notice and the tenant may only apply for relief during the first year following the bankruptcy or taking in execution. However, there is an important exception to this rule. If, during that first year, the trustee or liquidator sells the lease, the s 146 protection lasts indefinitely. Without such an exception, it would be difficult for the trustee or liquidator to find a buyer for the lease because of the risk of forfeiture taking place after the expiration of the first year without the service of a s 146 notice and with no right to seek relief.

(3) Exceptionally, there is no need for the landlord to serve a s 146 notice following bankruptcy, liquidation or taking in execution, and the tenant has no right to apply for relief if the lease is of:

(a) agricultural land;
(b) mines or minerals;
(c) a public house;
(d) a furnished house;
(e) any premises where the personal qualifications of the tenant are important for the preservation of the nature or character of the premises or on the ground of neighbourhood to the landlord or anyone holding under him.

30.5.4 Position of sub-tenants and mortgagees on forfeiture

If the head-lease is forfeited, this will automatically end any sub-lease. This is unfair to sub-tenants who stand to lose their interest through no fault of their own. In order to protect sub-tenants in this situation, s 146(4) enables them to apply for relief against forfeiture of the head-lease even in those cases where the head tenant is unable to do so. The granting of relief is entirely at the discretion of the court which can impose such conditions as it thinks fit and may, for example, require the sub-tenant to comply with the terms of the head-lease. If the court grants relief, the sub-tenant will become the immediate tenant of the landlord but cannot be granted a longer term than that remaining under the sub-lease. Difficult problems can arise where the sub-lease is of part only of the premises comprised in the head-lease. The view has sometimes been expressed that the sub-tenant may, as a condition of granting relief, have to take a new lease of all the property comprised in the head-lease or pay the arrears of rent relating to the whole.

An important example of the operation of s 146(4) arises in the case of a mortgagee of a lease. Lenders (whether by sub-demise or legal charge) are sub-tenants for the purposes of the sub-section and can thus apply for relief from forfeiture of the lease (see *United Dominion Trust Ltd v Shellpoint Trustees* [1993] EGCS 57, as to the time within which relief must be sought by lenders).

30.6 SURRENDER

Surrender occurs where a tenant relinquishes his lease to his immediate landlord, with his landlord's consent. The lease will merge in the reversion and be extinguished. Surrender can be express or by operation of law. An express surrender must generally be made by deed. Surrender by operation of law occurs where the parties act in a way which is inconsistent with the continuance of the lease. For example, a surrender will occur if the parties agree a new lease to commence during the currency of the existing lease. A similar situation occurs if the tenant gives up possession and returns the key to the landlord and the landlord accepts this as surrender. However, surrender requires the agreement of both parties. If the key is merely left with the landlord, this in itself will not amount to surrender unless the landlord accepts it as surrender, for example, by re-letting the premises (see *Arundel Corporation v The Financial Training Co Ltd* [2000] 3 All ER 456).

If a lease protected under Part II of the LTA 1954 requires the tenant to offer to surrender the lease before seeking consent to assign, the landlord's acceptance of that offer may be void under s 38 (*Allnatt London Properties Ltd v Newton* [1984] 1 All ER 423, and see **31.1.5**).

30.6.1 Effect of surrender

A surrender will release the tenant from any future liability under the lease but not in respect of past breaches. A well-advised tenant should, therefore, seek a release from all breaches.

The surrender of a head-lease will not affect any sub-lease. The sub-tenant will become the immediate tenant of the head landlord on the terms of the sub-lease. Sometimes, a head tenant will agree to surrender his head-lease with a view to taking a new fixed term from his landlord; this may happen where the head-lease is coming to the end of its fixed term. In this situation, any new head-lease granted following the surrender will be subject to the sub-lease (LPA 1925, s 150).

30.7 MERGER

Merger occurs where a tenant acquires his immediate landlord's reversion or a third party acquires both the lease and the immediate reversion. In such a case the lease will end. However, merger will only take place where the person acquiring both the lease and immediate reversion holds both estates in the same capacity and intends merger to take place.

As with surrender, merger of a lease will not affect the position of any sub-tenant.

Chapter 31

THE LANDLORD AND TENANT ACT 1954, PART II

31.1 INTRODUCTORY MATTERS

31.1.1 The protection of the Act

The principal Act conferring security of tenure on business tenants and regulating the manner in which business tenancies can be terminated is Part II of the LTA 1954 (statutory references in this chapter are to this Act, unless otherwise stated). The protection given to tenants covered by the Act is twofold. First, a business tenancy will not come to an end at the expiration of a fixed term, nor can a periodic tenancy be terminated by the landlord serving an ordinary notice to quit. Instead, notwithstanding the ending of the contractual term, the tenancy will be automatically continued under s 24 until such time as it is terminated in one of the ways specified in the Act. Secondly, upon the expiration of a business tenancy in accordance with the Act, business tenants normally have a statutory right to apply to court for a new tenancy and the landlord may only oppose that application on certain statutory grounds. Any new tenancy granted will also enjoy the protection of the Act.

At the time of writing (July 2003), the Government has proposed amendments to the Act and the reader is advised to check the current position.

31.1.2 The application of the Act

Section 23(1) provides that:

> 'this Act applies to any tenancy where the property comprised in the tenancy is or includes premises which are occupied by the tenant and are so occupied for the purposes of a business carried on by him or for those and other purposes.'

This involves a number of elements.

There must be a 'tenancy'

Tenancy includes an agreement for a lease and an underlease (even an unauthorised one). However, licences are not protected. The lease/licence distinction is further considered at **9.4**. In view of the danger for landlords in inadvertently creating a protected tenancy, the use of licences as a means of avoiding the Act needs very careful consideration. Certain tenancies are specifically excluded from the protection of the Act and these are dealt with at **31.1.3**.

The premises must be occupied by the tenant

Occupation need not be by the tenant personally. It has been held that occupation may be sufficient where it is conducted through the medium of a manager or agent provided that such representative occupation is genuine and not a sham arrangement. If, however, the premises are occupied by a company owned by the tenant, this will not be sufficient because it is the company, a separate legal entity, which is the

Chapter 31 contents
Introductory matters
Termination under the Act
The tenant's application to court
Interim rents
Grounds of opposition
Compensation for failure to obtain a new tenancy
The renewal lease
The order for the new lease
Proposals for reform of the 1954 Act

occupier rather than the tenant. Occupation need not be continuous provided that the 'thread of continuity' of business user is not broken (*Hancock & Willis v GMS Syndicate Ltd* (1982) 265 EG 473 and *Flairline Properties Ltd v Hassan* [1997] 1 EGLR 138).

Problems may arise where a business tenant sub-lets part of the property to a business sub-tenant. In such a situation, they cannot both qualify for protection in respect of the sub-let part; there can be no dual occupation for the purposes of the Act. In normal circumstances, it will be the sub-tenant who enjoys the protection of the Act although in an exceptional case the head tenant may reserve sufficiently extensive rights over the sub-let part that he remains the occupier (see *Graysim Holdings Ltd v P&O Property Holdings Ltd* [1995] 3 WLR 854).

Special rules on occupation apply where a tenancy is held on trust, vested in partners as trustees or held by a member of a group of companies (ss 41, 41A and 42).

The premises must be occupied for the purposes of a business carried on by the tenant

'Business' is widely defined in s 23 to include a 'trade, profession or employment and includes any activity carried on by a body of persons, whether corporate or unincorporate'. Where the business is carried on by an individual, it must amount to a trade, profession or employment; but where it is carried on by a body of persons (corporate or unincorporate) 'any activity' may suffice. Thus, it has been held that the organising of a tennis club and the activities of the governors in running a hospital, both amounted to a business use (*Addiscombe Garden Estates v Crabbe* [1958] 1 QB 513 and *Hills (Patents) Ltd v University College Hospital Board of Governors* [1956] 1 QB 90). This does not mean however that the Act will apply whenever the tenant is a body of persons; the 'activity' must be correlative to the conceptions involved in the words 'trade, profession or employment'.

Two problem areas may arise with this requirement.

(1)   The demised premises will sometimes be used for two purposes, only one of which is a business user. For example, the letting may consist of a shop on the ground floor with living accommodation above. Does the Act still apply? In cases of mixed user the Act will apply provided the business activity is a significant purpose of the occupation and not merely incidental to the occupation of the premises as a residence (*Cheryl Investments Ltd v Saldhana* [1978] 1 WLR 1329 and *Gurton v Parrot* [1991] 1 EGLR 98). In the example mentioned, the Act is likely to apply. If, however, a residential tenant occasionally brought work home with him this would not result in his tenancy being protected under the Act.

(2)   The business user may be in breach of a covenant of the lease. How does that affect the tenant's rights? If the lease merely forbids a specific business use (eg not to use the shop as a newsagents), or any use except the business use specified (eg not to use the premises for any purpose other than as a newsagents), a business use in breach of such a provision will not deprive the tenant of the protection of the Act. However, s 24(3) does exclude from protection any tenancy where the use of the premises for business purposes is in breach of a general prohibition preventing all business use (eg not to carry on any business, trade, profession or employment) although if the landlord had consented to or acquiesced in the breach, the Act would still apply.

31.1.3 Exclusions from the Act

Apart from those tenancies which fail to satisfy the requirements of s 23, there are other tenancies which are not protected by the Act. These include:

(1) tenancies at will. In *Javad v Aqil* [1991] 1 WLR 1007, a prospective tenant who was allowed into possession while negotiations proceeded for the grant of a new business lease was held, on the facts, to be a tenant at will, and thus excluded from protection. A similar decision was reached in *London Baggage Co (Charing Cross) Ltd v Railtrack plc* [2000] EGCS 57, where a tenant holding over after the expiry of its lease, pending the negotiation of a new lease, was held to be a tenant at will;

(2) tenancies of agricultural holdings: these have their own form of protection under the Agricultural Holdings Act 1986;

(3) a farm business tenancy;

(4) mining leases;

(5) service tenancies. These are tenancies granted to the holder of an office, appointment or employment from the landlord and which continue only so long as the tenant holds such office etc. For the exclusion to apply the tenancy must be in writing and express the purpose for which it was granted;

(6) fixed-term tenancies not exceeding 6 months. These tenancies are excluded unless the tenancy contains provisions for renewing the term or extending it beyond 6 months, or the tenant (including any predecessor in the same business) has already been in occupation for a period exceeding 12 months (see *Cricket Ltd v Shaftesbury plc* [1999] 3 All ER 283);

(7) 'contracted out' tenancies (see **31.1.5**).

31.1.4 Two important definitions

The competent landlord

It is between the tenant and the competent landlord that the procedure under the Act must be conducted. It is important, therefore, that the tenant identifies his competent landlord and deals with him. Where a freeholder grants a lease, there is no cause for concern as the tenant's competent landlord can be no other than the freeholder. However, where the tenant is a sub-tenant, the statutory definition of competent landlord means that the sub-tenant's immediate landlord may not be his competent landlord. Using s 44 of the Act, the sub-tenant must look up the chain of superior tenancies for the first person who either owns the freehold or who has a superior tenancy which will not come to an end within 14 months. The following examples may assist:

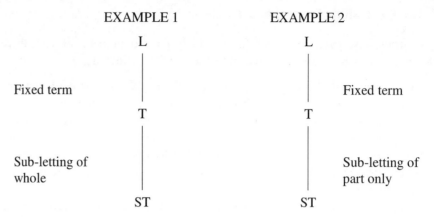

As the first example involves a sub-letting of the whole of the premises, T will not be in occupation, and will not, therefore, enjoy the protection of the Act. This means that the head-lease will come to an end on its contractual expiry date, with the result that as soon as the head-lease has entered the last 14 months of its contractual term, ST's competent landlord will be the freeholder. However, in the second example, because it is a sub-letting of part only, then provided T occupies the remaining part for business purposes, the head-lease will be protected. Therefore, it will not expire by effluxion of time. So even if the head-lease has entered the last 14 months of its contractual term, the sub-tenant's competent landlord will still be T (unless, eg, the freeholder has served an appropriate notice terminating the head-lease within 14 months, see **31.2.1**).

It is, therefore, very important for sub-tenants to identify their competent landlord and this can be done by serving a notice on their immediate landlord under s 40 of the Act seeking information about the landlord's interest. A s 40 notice should always be served by a sub-tenant before taking any other steps under the Act.

The 'holding'

The definition of the holding is important because the tenant's right to a new lease normally extends to only that part of the premises known as the 'holding'. Further, many of the landlord's grounds of opposition refer to the holding. This term is defined in s 23(3) of the Act as being the property comprised in the current tenancy excluding any part which is not occupied by the tenant or a person employed by the tenant for the purposes of the tenant's business. In practice, in the majority of cases, it is correct to describe the holding as comprising all the premises originally let except those parts which the tenant is currently sub-letting.

31.1.5 Contracting out

As a general rule, s 38(1) forbids any contracting out of the Act. This means that any agreement purporting to exclude or modify the tenant's security of tenure is void. However, under s 38(4) of the Act the court is empowered to make an order excluding the security of tenure provisions, provided certain conditions are satisfied:

(1) the proposed letting must be for a term of years certain (the definition of a term of years certain does not include a tenancy for 12 months and thereafter from year to year: *Nicholas v Kinsey* [1994] 16 EG 145); and

(2) there must be a joint application to court by both parties; and

(3) the lease entered into must be substantially the same as the draft lease attached to the court order (*Receiver for Metropolitan Police District v Palacegate Properties Ltd* [2001] 2 Ch 131).

Further, and most importantly, the court's approval must be obtained before the tenancy is granted (*Essexcrest Ltd v Evenlex Ltd* [1988] 1 EGLR 69).

Section 38(1) also renders void an agreement to surrender a business tenancy in the future, without the court's approval. Thus, where the terms of the lease require the tenant to offer to surrender the lease before seeking consent to assign, any resulting agreement to surrender will be void and unenforceable (*Allnatt London Properties Ltd v Newton* [1984] 1 All ER 423).

31.1.6 Continuation tenancies

A business tenancy protected by the Act will not come to an end on the expiry of the contractual term. Instead, s 24 continues the tenancy on exactly the same terms (except those relating to termination) and at exactly the same rent until it is terminated in accordance with the Act. However, the landlord may be able to obtain an increased rent by asking the court to fix an interim rent under s 24A (see **31.4**).

Section 24 continues the tenancy, but does it also continue the liability of the original tenant (or any previous assignees who have given direct covenants) for breaches committed by an assignee during the continuation tenancy? This was the question which arose in *City of London Corporation v Fell* and *Herbert Duncan Ltd v Cluttons* [1992] 1 EGLR 101. In both these cases the original tenant was sued by the landlord for arrears of rent that had accrued during the continuation tenancy due to non-payment by an assignee. The court decided that if the original tenant had covenanted to pay rent during the contractual term only, the landlord was unable to recover from him any rent accruing after that date. However, had the covenant been worded so that the original tenant was liable to pay rent during any statutory extension of the contractual term, the landlord would have been able to recover accordingly. Further, even if the lease had been drafted so that the tenant was bound to pay rent during the statutory continuation, this did not extend to any interim rent ordered by the court. Landlords must bear these points in mind when defining the term of the lease.

If the tenant ceases occupation of the premises on or before the contractual termination date then one of the qualifying conditions for the Act to apply is no longer fulfilled (see **31.1.2**). In these circumstances a fixed term tenancy will come to an end by effluxion of time and no continuation tenancy will arise (*Esselte AB v Pearl Assurance plc* [1997] 1WLR 891, and *Surrey County Council v Single Horse Properties Ltd* [2002] EWCA Civ 367, [2002] 1 WLR 2106). In this situation the tenant will not incur any further liability for rent (the tenant may also choose to serve a s 27 notice in these circumstances, see **31.2**).

31.2 TERMINATION UNDER THE ACT

A tenancy protected under the Act will not end automatically at the expiration of a lease for a fixed term nor, if it is a periodic tenancy, can it be ended by an ordinary notice to quit given by the landlord. Instead, such a tenancy can only be terminated in one of the ways prescribed by the Act:

(1) by the service of a landlord's statutory notice (a 's 25 notice');

(2) by the tenant's request in statutory form (a 's 26 request');

(3) forfeiture (or forfeiture of a superior tenancy);

(4) surrender. To be valid the surrender must take immediate effect;

(5) by the tenant giving the landlord a notice to quit, unless this was given before the tenant has been in occupation for a period of one month;

(6) where the lease is for a fixed term, by written notice under s 27 of the Act, served by the tenant upon the landlord at least 3 months before the contractual expiry date. If the time for serving this notice has already passed, then the tenant will have to give 3 months' written notice expiring on any quarter day. However, as noted above, the case of *Esselte AB v Pearl Assurance plc* [1997] 1 WLR 891 held that if a tenant ceases to occupy the premises for business purposes on or before the contractual expiry date, the lease will come to an end by effluxion of time and a s 27 notice is not needed. This decision must now be read in the light of subsequent cases (*Bacchiocci v Academic Agency Ltd* [1998] 1 WLR 1313, and *Sight and Sound Education Ltd v Books etc Ltd* [1999] 43 EG 61) which have created uncertainty over the period of absence required before it can be established that the tenant has ceased occupation for the purposes of the Act. In light of these cases it may be safer for a tenant to proceed by service of a s 27 notice (see also *Arundel Corporation v The Financial Training Co Ltd* [2000] 3 All ER 456 which, again, emphasises the desirability of a s 27 notice).

It is the first two of the above methods, the s 25 notice and s 26 request, which are the usual methods of terminating a protected business tenancy.

31.2.1 Section 25 notices

Form

If such a notice is to be effective, it must be in the prescribed form and be given to the tenant by the competent landlord not less than 6 months, nor more than 12 months, before the date of termination specified in it. The prescribed form is contained in the Landlord and Tenant Act 1954, Part II (Notices) Regulations 1983 as amended by the Landlord and Tenant Act 1954, Part II (Notices) (Amendment) Regulations 1989, although a form 'substantially to the like effect' can be used instead.

A tenant will often seek to attack the validity of his landlord's notice on the ground that it is not in the correct form. The task of the court in these circumstances is to ascertain whether the notice served is substantially the same as the prescribed form. In doing this, any omission from the notice of matters irrelevant to the tenant's rights or obligations may not affect the validity of the notice. However, if the court decides that the notice is not the same as, or substantially to the same effect as, the prescribed form, it is irrelevant that the recipient did not suffer any prejudice: the notice will be invalid (*Sabella Ltd v Montgomery* [1998] 09 EG 153).

In *Smith v Draper* [1990] 2 EGLR 69, it was held that a landlord who had served what turned out to be an invalid notice, could withdraw it and serve a second valid notice.

Content

The notice must comply with the following requirements.

(1) The notice must state the date upon which the landlord wants the tenancy to end. The specified termination date must not be earlier than the date on which the tenancy could have been terminated at common law (and, as mentioned above, the notice must be given not less than 6 months, nor more than 12 months, before this specified termination date).

For a periodic tenancy or a fixed term with a break clause, the specified termination date cannot be earlier than the date upon which the landlord could have ended the tenancy with an ordinary common law notice. If there is a break clause, it would appear that a separate contractual notice is unnecessary provided the s 25 notice states a date for termination no earlier than the date the break clause would operate (*Scholl Manufacturing Ltd v Clifton (Slim-Line) Ltd* [1967] Ch 41). If the tenancy is for a fixed term without a break clause, the specified termination date cannot be earlier than the last day of the contractual term. If, however, the contractual tenancy has already expired and the tenancy is being continued under the Act, the s 25 notice need only comply with the 6–12-month rule mentioned above.

(2) The notice must require the tenant within 2 months after the giving of the notice to notify his landlord, in writing, whether or not he is willing to give up possession of the premises on the specified termination date. Thus, the service of a s 25 notice always requires a response from the tenant. This is in the form of a tenant's 'counter-notice'.

(3) The notice must state whether or not the landlord will oppose an application to court by the tenant for the grant of a new tenancy and, if so, on which statutory ground(s). The tenant has the right to apply to court for a new tenancy but the landlord can oppose that application on one or more of the seven grounds of opposition set out in s 30 of the Act (see **31.5**). If this is the landlord's intention, he must state in his s 25 notice the ground(s) upon which he intends to rely. As there is no provision in the Act allowing the landlord to amend his notice, the choice of ground(s) is a matter which must be given very careful consideration.

It will not be in every case that the landlord states a ground of opposition. Often the landlord will be quite happy with the tenant's presence and is seeking to end the current tenancy simply with a view to negotiating a new tenancy upon different terms, for example, at an increased rent. In this type of situation the landlord should consult a valuer and obtain expert advice before proceeding further.

(4) The notice must relate to the whole of the premises contained in the lease. A s 25 notice cannot relate to part only of the demised premises (*Southport Old Links Ltd v Naylor* [1985] 1 EGLR 66, and see also *M&P Enterprises (London) Ltd v Norfolk Square Hotels Ltd* [1994] 1 EGLR 129).

(5) The notice must be given and signed by, or on behalf of, the landlord. If there are joint landlords, all their names must be given (*Pearson v Alyo* [1990] 1 EGLR 114).

31.2.2 Section 26 requests

Rather than wait for the landlord to serve a s 25 notice, the tenant can sometimes take the initiative and request a new tenancy from his landlord under s 26 of the Act. However, the tenant must remember that the sooner there is a new tenancy, the sooner the new rent will be payable, which may be higher than the rent payable under the old tenancy. Nevertheless, there are situations where the service of a request by the tenant has tactical advantages for him.

Not all tenants can request a new tenancy. A request cannot be served if the landlord has already served a s 25 notice. Further, a request is only possible where the tenant's current lease was granted for a term of years exceeding one year (or during its continuance under s 24). This will exclude both periodic tenants and those with fixed terms of one year or less; although these tenants still enjoy security of tenure.

Form

To be valid, the request must be in the prescribed form as laid down in the Landlord and Tenant Act 1954, Part II (Notices) Regulations 1983 and served on the competent landlord. As with the s 25 notice, a form 'substantially to the like effect' can be used instead.

Content

The request must comply with the following requirements:

(1) it must state the date on which the new tenancy is to begin. The current tenancy will terminate on that date. This date must not be more than 12 months nor less than 6 months after the making of the request, and cannot be earlier than the date on which the tenancy could have been terminated at common law;
(2) it must give the tenant's proposals as to:

    (a) the property to be comprised in the new tenancy, which must be either the whole or part of the property comprised in the current tenancy;
    (b) the proposed new rent. This issue requires the advice of a valuer;
    (c) the other terms of the tenancy (eg as to duration);

(3) the request must be signed by or on behalf of all the tenants.

A landlord who is unwilling to grant a new tenancy must, within 2 months of receipt of the request, give notice to the tenant that he will oppose any application to court for a new lease stating on which statutory ground(s) of opposition he intends to rely. This is effected by means of a landlord's counter-notice (see **31.2.3**).

As with a s 25 notice, the landlord must choose his ground(s) of opposition with care because he will be confined to those stated in his counter-notice.

If the tenant serves a valid s 26 request and then fails to apply to court for a new tenancy within time (see **31.3**), he will not be allowed to withdraw it and serve a new one with a view to complying with the time-limit the second time since the effect of the s 26 request was to fix the date of termination of the tenancy (*Stile Hall Properties Ltd v Gooch* [1979] 3 All ER 848).

Reasons for making a request

Usually a tenant is best advised not to make a request because it is not always in a tenant's interest to bring his current tenancy to an end. However, there are some situations in which it might be advisable. For example:

(1) if the rent payable under the current tenancy is more than that presently achievable in the open market. In a falling market like this the landlord is unlikely to serve a s 25 notice, as it is in his interests to let the existing tenancy

continue under the Act. Therefore, the tenant should give careful consideration to ending the current tenancy and obtaining a new one at a reduced rent;

(2) if, as is more often the case, the current rent is less than the present market rent, it is in the tenant's interest to prolong the tenancy for as long as possible. In this case the tenant may be able to make what is sometimes called a pre-emptive strike. Say the lease is contractually due to expire on 30 September. In the previous March the landlord is considering serving a s 25 notice with a view to bringing the tenancy to an end on 30 September and negotiating a new tenancy at an increased rent. If the tenant knows or suspects the landlord's plans, he can, before the landlord has acted, serve a request specifying sometime in the following March as the date for the new tenancy. The tenant has thus achieved an extra 6 months at the old rent;

(3) if the tenant has plans to improve the premises, he may prefer the certainty of a new fixed term as opposed to the uncertainty of a statutory continuation;

(4) if the tenant has plans to sell the lease, a buyer would prefer the security of a new fixed term rather than the uncertainty of a statutory continuation.

31.2.3 Counter-notices

The tenant's counter-notice

Within 2 months of receipt of the landlord's s 25 notice the tenant must notify the landlord in writing whether or not he is willing to give up possession by service of a counter-notice. There is no prescribed form: a letter will suffice. A tenant who has served a counter-notice, stating his willingness to give up possession, may not be bound by it if, within the 2 months, a second counter-notice is served indicating that the tenant is not willing to give up possession (*Pennycook v Shaws Ltd* [2002] EWHC 2769 (Ch), [2002] 50 EG 113).

If the tenant fails to serve a counter-notice within 2 months, he loses the right to apply to court for a new tenancy and, therefore, it must be served even where the landlord has stated that he would not oppose any application to court for a new tenancy. If no counter-notice is served, the tenant's occupation beyond the specified termination date would depend entirely on the willingness of the landlord to grant a new tenancy on such terms as the landlord pleases. However, cases like *Kammins Ballrooms Co Ltd v Zenith Investments (Torquay) Ltd* [1971] AC 850) and *JT Developments v Quinn* [1991] 2 EGLR 257 suggest that in appropriate circumstances it may be possible for a tenant to contend that the landlord's conduct has amounted to a waiver of strict adherence to the time-limit. Notwithstanding cases like this, it is of the utmost importance that tenants always serve a proper counter-notice. Failure to do so may lead to an action by the tenant against his solicitor in negligence.

The landlord's counter-notice

The service of a s 26 request by the tenant will require a counter-notice by the landlord if he wishes to oppose the tenant's application to court for a new tenancy. This must state any ground(s) of opposition that the landlord intends to rely on to oppose the tenant's application (see **31.5**). If the landlord fails to serve a counter-notice within 2 months of receipt of the tenant's request, he will lose his right to raise any ground of opposition to the tenant's application to court for a new tenancy although he will be allowed to raise issues relating to the terms of the new tenancy.

A landlord who has served a counter-notice stating that he will not oppose the tenant's application for a new tenancy will be bound by that decision. Similarly, the landlord cannot later amend his stated grounds of opposition.

There is no prescribed form of counter-notice but it should be unequivocal and in writing.

31.2.4 Service of notices and requests

Notices and requests given under the Act require service. Section 23(1) of the LTA 1927 provides for personal service or by leaving the notice at the last known place of abode (which includes the place of business of the person to be served, *Price v West London Investment Building Society* [1964] 2 All ER 318), or by sending it through the post by registered or (as now applies) recorded delivery. Service on a company may be effected at its registered office (s 725 of the Companies Act 1985). The effect of complying with one of the methods of service laid down in the LTA 1927 is that there is a presumption of service so that it does not matter that the recorded delivery letter may not have been received by the intended recipient because it went astray in the post. Other methods of service may be effective (eg the ordinary post) if in fact the notice is received by the person to whom it has been given. But the risk is that the letter may be lost in the post, in which case, notice will not have been given. The question also arises as to the date on which the notice is treated as having been served. In *Railtrack plc v Gojra* [1998] 08 EG 158, it was held that if the registered or recorded delivery method is used (both being methods laid down in the LTA 1927), the notice (or request) is served on the date on which it is posted. When, however, notice is sent through the ordinary post it is served on the date of receipt.

31.3 THE TENANT'S APPLICATION TO COURT

31.3.1 The need for an application

It will become apparent after service of a s 25 notice or counter-notice to a s 26 request, whether or not the landlord is willing to grant a new tenancy. Where a s 25 notice has been served, the contents will have told the tenant whether or not the landlord intends to oppose his application. If the tenant initiated the termination procedure with a s 26 request, the landlord will have responded with a counter-notice if he is not prepared to grant a new tenancy.

If the tenant wants a new tenancy, the next stage is for him to apply to court not less than 2 months, nor more than 4 months after the service of the landlord's s 25 notice or tenant's s 26 request, as the case may be. Where a s 25 notice has been served, the tenant will only be able to make an application if he has served a valid counter-notice stating that he is unwilling to give up possession. The need to make this application applies even where the landlord has indicated his willingness to grant a new tenancy and the parties are near to agreement. Unless the parties have already entered into a binding lease, the tenant must always apply to court at the appropriate time otherwise he will lose the right to a new tenancy.

31.3.2 The application

Applications may be commenced in either the High Court or, as is more usual, in the county court.

The application must be made not less than 2 months, nor more than 4 months after the service of the landlord's s 25 notice or tenant's s 26 request, as the case may be. Commencement in the first or second month is bad as being too early. Similarly, commencement in the fifth or sixth month is bad as being too late. The tenant must apply in either the third month or the fourth month after the notice or request was served. It is very important that the tenant complies strictly with these time-limits because the court has no power to extend them. However, it has been held that because the time-limits are procedural in nature the parties may themselves waive them (*Kammins Ballrooms Co Ltd v Zenith Investments (Torquay) Ltd* [1971] AC 850 and *Saloman v Akiens* [1993] 14 EG 97). If, therefore, the tenant fails to apply to court in time, his ability to make an out-of-time application will depend on him being able to show waiver on the landlord's part. An analysis of the relevant case-law shows that this will not always be easy for the tenant to establish and emphasises the importance of applying at the correct time (see, eg, *Stevens & Cutting Ltd v Anderson* [1990] 11 EG 70, where the issue of estoppel was also discussed).

Following the tenant's application to court it is advisable to protect the application by registration of a pending land action under the Land Charges Act 1972. This will make the tenant's application binding on a buyer of the reversion. Where the landlord's title is registered, the application may be an overriding interest under the LRA 1925, s 70(1)(g), but it would nevertheless be prudent to register a caution against the reversionary title.

31.4 INTERIM RENTS

31.4.1 The need for an interim rent

Where the tenant has validly applied to court for a new tenancy, his current tenancy will not terminate on the date specified in the s 25 notice or s 26 request. Instead, s 64 of the Act provides that the current tenancy will be continued at the old contractual rent until 3 months after the proceedings are concluded. As the Act was originally drafted there was thus an incentive for tenants to delay proceedings as much as possible, because the longer the current tenancy lasted the longer the old rent (which was usually below current market rents) remained payable. This was unfair to landlords particularly in those cases where, due to the effects of inflation, there was a substantial difference between the old contractual rent and the rent presently achievable in the open market. As a result of this unfairness, s 24A was inserted into the Act by the Law of Property Act 1969. This gives the court a discretion, on the application of the competent landlord, to determine an 'interim rent' to be substituted for the old contractual rent until such time as the current tenancy ceases. This interim rent is payable from the date on which the landlord applies for it or the termination date specified in the s 25 notice or s 26 request, whichever is the later.

31.4.2 Amount

The interim rent is an open market rent which is assessed by the court in the same way as the rent under the new tenancy. However, there are reasons why the interim rent is usually less than the open market rent:

(1) Section 24A requires the court to assess the interim rent on the basis of a yearly tenancy, whilst the rent payable under the new lease is usually assessed on the basis of a term of years. And market rents under yearly tenancies are usually less than under fixed terms, since the latter guarantee tenants a more substantial period of occupation.

(2) The court is obliged to have regard to the rent payable under the current tenancy. This is so that the court can exercise a discretion to 'cushion' the tenant from too harsh a blow in moving from the old out-of-date contractual rent to the new rent (see *English Exporters (London) Ltd v Eldonwall Ltd* [1973] Ch 415). However, a 'cushion' does not have to be provided in every case. The court has a discretion which it may use to specify the full market rent, especially in those cases where the tenant has already benefited from a low contractual rent for a long time (see, eg, *Department of the Environment v Allied Freehold Property Trust Ltd* [1992] 45 EG 156).

In a falling market, landlords should give careful consideration to the possibility of the interim rent being less than the contractual rent. In such a situation, landlords should seek specialist valuation advice before making the application.

31.4.3 Avoiding s 24A

Whilst the introduction of interim rents has been a step in the right direction for landlords, many still feel that the application of the 'cushion' can produce unfairness. Accordingly, the landlord may be able to avoid s 24A altogether by including a penultimate day rent review in the lease. This would revise the contractual rent just before the contractual term expired. In such a case the harshness of changing from the old rent to the new rent would be suffered during the contractual term without the imposition of any 'cushion'. Tenants, on the other hand, will wish to resist such a clause.

Another way of avoiding s 24A would be for the landlord, at the lease-drafting stage, to make it clear that the contractual rent review provisions are to continue to apply notwithstanding the ending of the contractual term. Careful drafting would be required to achieve this but the case of *Willison v Cheverell Estates Ltd* [1996] 26 EG 133 indicates that this is another possibility for the landlord.

31.5 GROUNDS OF OPPOSITION

When the landlord serves his s 25 notice or counter-notice in response to the tenant's s 26 request, he must, if he is intending to oppose the grant of a new tenancy, set out one or more of the seven grounds of opposition in s 30 of the Act. The landlord can only rely on the stated ground(s); no later amendment is allowed.

If the landlord has stated a ground of opposition and the tenant's application proceeds to a hearing, a 'split trial' will usually be ordered with the question of opposition being dealt with first as a preliminary issue. Only if the ground is not made out will the terms of the new tenancy be dealt with.

The statutory grounds of opposition are all contained in s 30(1) of the Act and, as will be seen, some of the grounds ((a), (b), (c) and (e)), confer a discretion on the court whether or not to order a new tenancy even if the ground is made out.

31.5.1 Ground (a): tenant's failure to repair

The landlord can oppose the tenant's application for a new tenancy on the ground of the tenant's failure to repair the holding. To succeed, the landlord will have to show that the tenant was under an obligation to repair or maintain them and that the tenant is in breach of that obligation. Problems can arise where the repairing obligation is divided between the landlord and tenant, for example, where the landlord is responsible for the exterior and the tenant for the interior of the premises. In such cases, an inspection will be necessary to determine the party in breach. The ground only applies to failure to repair the holding (see **31.1.4**), and not to the disrepair of another part of the demised premises not forming part of the tenant's holding (eg where the tenant has sub-let part and it is that part which is in disrepair).

This is one of the discretionary grounds and the landlord is only likely to succeed if the tenant's breaches are both serious and unremedied at the date of the hearing.

As an alternative, the landlord may be able to commence forfeiture proceedings to terminate the tenancy; this being one of the permitted methods of termination under the Act. This remedy may be available throughout the term and while the tenant may apply for relief, this will usually only be granted if the tenant rectifies the breach.

31.5.2 Ground (b): persistent delay in paying rent

The requirement of 'persistent delay' suggests that the tenant must have fallen into arrears on more than one occasion. However, the rent need not be substantially in arrears nor need the arrears last a long time. Indeed, there need not be any arrears at the date of the hearing; the court will look at the whole history of payment (see *Hazel v Akhtar* [2002] EWCA Civ 1883, [2002] 07 EG 124). Again, this is one of the discretionary grounds and the court is entitled to take into account the likelihood of future arrears arising should a new tenancy be ordered. The tenant should, therefore, consider offering to provide a surety for any new lease ordered.

31.5.3 Ground (c): substantial breaches of other obligations

Discretionary ground (c) requires other substantial breaches by the tenant of his obligations in the lease, or some other reason connected with the tenant's use or management of the holding. Any breach of an obligation may be relied upon by the landlord (eg breach of the user covenant) but the breach must be substantial and this will be a question of fact and degree. The ground also extends to reasons connected with the tenant's use or management of the holding and this has been held to include carrying on a use in breach of planning control.

31.5.4 Ground (d): alternative accommodation

The landlord must have offered and be willing to provide or secure alternative accommodation for the tenant. The accommodation must be offered on reasonable terms having regard to the terms of the current tenancy and all other relevant circumstances. Further, the accommodation must be suitable for the tenant's requirements, (including the requirement to preserve goodwill) bearing in mind the nature and type of his business and the location and size of his existing premises. It seems that offering the tenant part only of his existing premises may qualify as alternative accommodation.

This ground, unlike the three previously mentioned, is not discretionary. If the landlord proves the requirements of the ground, the court must refuse the tenant's application.

31.5.5 Ground (e): current tenancy created by sub-letting of part only of property in a superior tenancy

Ground (e) is the least used ground because the necessary requirements are seldom fulfilled. It only applies where the current tenancy was created by a sub-letting of part of the property in a superior tenancy, and the sub-tenant's competent landlord is the landlord under the superior tenancy. The competent landlord will succeed if he can show that the combined rents from the sub-divided parts of a building are substantially less than the rent to be obtained on a single letting of the whole building, and that he requires possession to let or dispose of the whole.

This is the last of the discretionary grounds.

31.5.6 Ground (f): demolition or reconstruction

Ground (f) is the most frequently used ground. The landlord must show that on termination of the tenancy:

(1) he has a firm intention;
(2) to demolish or reconstruct the premises in the holding (or a substantial part of them), or to carry out substantial work of construction on the holding (or part of it); and
(3) that he could not reasonably do so without obtaining possession of the holding.

Each of these elements is considered in turn.

The landlord's intention

The landlord must prove a firm and settled intention to carry out relevant work. It has been said that the project must have 'moved out of the zone of contemplation ... into the valley of decision' (per Asquith LJ in *Cunliffe v Goodman* [1950] 2 KB 237, approved in *Betty's Cafes Ltd v Phillips Furnishing Stores Ltd* [1959] AC 20). Not only must the landlord have made a genuine decision to carry out relevant work, he must also show that it is practicable for him to carry out his intention. This will be a question of fact in each case but the landlord's position will be strengthened if he has:

(1) obtained (or shown a reasonable prospect of obtaining) planning permission and building regulation approval (if necessary);
(2) instructed professional advisers;
(3) prepared the necessary drawings and contracts;
(4) obtained quotations and secured finance; and
(5) obtained the consent of any superior landlord (if necessary).

Where the landlord is a company, intention is normally evidenced by a resolution of the board of directors. Similarly, local authority landlords should pass an appropriate resolution and have it recorded in their minutes.

The landlord's intention must be established at the date of the hearing (*Betty's Cafes Ltd v Phillips Furnishing Stores Ltd*, above). It is thus irrelevant that the s 25 notice (or s 26 counter-notice) was served by the landlord's predecessor who did not have the necessary intention.

If the court is not satisfied that the landlord's intention is sufficiently firm and settled at the date of the hearing, a new tenancy will be ordered. In such cases, however, the court, in settling the terms of the new tenancy, may take into account the landlord's future intentions, and limit the duration of the new tenancy so as not to impede development later when the landlord is able to fully establish intention and the ability to carry it out (see **31.7.2**).

The nature of the works

The landlord must prove an intention to do one of six things:

(1) demolish the premises comprised in the holding (see *Coppin v Bruce-Smith* [1998] EGCS 45);

(2) reconstruct the premises comprised in the holding. For the works to qualify as works of reconstruction it has been held that they must entail rebuilding and involve a substantial interference with the structure of the building but need not necessarily be confined to the outside or loadbearing walls (*Romulus Trading Co Ltd v Henry Smith's Charity Trustees* [1990] 2 EGLR 75);

(3) demolish a substantial part of the premises comprised in the holding;

(4) reconstruct a substantial part of the premises comprised in the holding;

(5) carry out substantial work of construction on the holding. It has been held that such works must directly affect the structure of the building and must go beyond what could be more properly classified as works of refurbishment or improvement (*Barth v Pritchard* [1990] 1 EGLR 109);

(6) carry out substantial work of construction on part of the holding.

The need to obtain possession

The landlord must show that he could not reasonably execute the relevant work without obtaining possession of the holding. This means the landlord must show that he needs 'legal' (not just 'physical') possession of the holding. He has to show that it is necessary to put an end to the tenant's interest, and this may not always be the case. Accordingly, if the lease contains a right of entry for the landlord which is sufficiently wide to enable him to carry out the relevant work, his ground of opposition will fail. In such a situation, the tenant will be able to argue that the work can be carried out under the terms of the lease and there is thus no need to end it.

Even if the lease does not include a right of entry, the landlord may still fail in his opposition if the tenant is able to rely on s 31A of the Act. This provides that the court shall not find ground (f) to be established if the tenant will either:

(1) agree to a new lease which includes access and other rights for the landlord, which enable the landlord to reasonably carry out the relevant work without obtaining possession and without substantially interfering with the use of the holding for the tenant's business; or

(2) accept a new lease of an economically separable part of the holding with, if necessary, access rights for the landlord.

31.5.7 Ground (g): landlord's intention to occupy the holding

Ground (g) is another frequently used ground. The landlord must prove that on the termination of the current tenancy he intends to occupy the holding for the purposes, or partly for the purposes, of a business to be carried on by him, or as his residence. There are a number of elements to this ground which will be considered in turn.

The landlord's intention

As with ground (f), the landlord's intention must be firm and settled, and many of the matters discussed at **31.5.6** will be equally relevant here. Therefore, not only must the landlord be able to show a genuine intention to occupy the holding, he must also show that he has a reasonable prospect of being able to do so (see *Zarvos v Pradhan* [2003] EWCA Civ 208, [2003] 13 EG 114). It is, therefore, necessary for the court to take into account, for example, whether planning permission would be required to use the premises for the landlord's business and, if so, whether it would be likely to be granted. In some cases, the court has accepted as evidence of intention to occupy, an undertaking to do so given by the landlord. Such an undertaking is not conclusive but it is a relevant consideration when the court is determining the issue (see, eg, *London Hilton Jewellers Ltd v Hilton International Hotels Ltd* [1990] 1 EGLR 112). As with ground (f), the landlord's intention must be shown to exist at the date of the hearing.

The court will not assess the viability of the landlord's proposed business venture provided his intention to occupy is genuine. Thus, the court has held the ground to be established even where they thought the landlord's business plans to be ill thought out and likely to fail; his intention was nevertheless genuine.

The purpose of occupation

Occupation must be for the purpose of the landlord's business or as his residence. The landlord need not intend to occupy all the holding immediately, provided that within a reasonable time of termination he intends to occupy a substantial part of the holding for one of these purposes.

The wording of this ground refers to a business to be carried on by the landlord. However, the landlord need not physically occupy the premises and it will be sufficient if occupation is through a manager or agent provided that the arrangement is genuine. Further, the ground is still available where the landlord intends to carry on the business in partnership with others. Where the landlord has a controlling interest in a company, any business to be carried on by the company, is treated as a business carried on by the landlord. The landlord has a controlling interest for this purpose, either if he beneficially holds more than half of the company's equity share capital, or if he is a member and able, without consent, to appoint or remove at least half of the directors (s 30(3)). Where the landlord is a company in a group of companies, it may rely on ground (g) where another member of the group is to occupy the premises (s 42). If the landlord is a trustee, he may be able to rely on an intention to occupy by a beneficiary (s 41).

The 5-year rule

The most important limitation on the availability of this ground of opposition is the '5-year rule' in s 30(2) of the Act. A landlord cannot rely on ground (g) if his interest was purchased or created within 5 years before the end of the current tenancy, ie the termination date specified in the s 25 notice or s 26 request. However, the restriction only applies if, throughout those 5 years, the premises have been subject to a tenancy or series of tenancies within the protection of the Act.

The idea behind the provision is to stop a landlord buying a reversion within 5 years of the end of the lease, and then using this ground to obtain possession for himself at the end of the term. Thus, a landlord will not be able to rely on this ground if he purchased the premises subject to the tenancy within the last 5 years. However, the restriction does not apply where a landlord buys premises with vacant possession, grants a lease, and then seeks to end the lease within 5 years relying on this ground.

The wording of the provision refers to the landlord's interest being 'purchased' and this is used in its popular sense of buying for money (*Bolton (HL) Engineering Co Ltd v Graham & Sons Ltd* [1957] 1 QB 159). Thus, it will not cover a freeholder who has accepted the surrender of a head-lease without payment, and then seeks to use this ground against the sub-tenant.

Finally, a landlord who is unable to rely on ground (g) because of this restriction, may be able to rely on ground (f) if he intends to demolish or reconstruct the premises. This remains so even if the landlord then intends to use the reconstructed premises for his own occupation.

31.6 COMPENSATION FOR FAILURE TO OBTAIN A NEW TENANCY

On termination, a tenant may be entitled to compensation for any improvements he has made. Additionally, if the tenant is forced to leave the premises he may lose the goodwill which he has built up and he will be faced with all the costs of relocation. This is particularly unfair to those tenants who are forced to leave the premises through no fault of their own, ie if the landlord establishes one of the grounds of opposition (e), (f) or (g). In certain circumstances, therefore, the tenant may be entitled to compensation for failing to obtain a new tenancy where the landlord establishes one of these 'no fault' grounds.

31.6.1 Availability

Compensation is only available on quitting the premises in one of the following situations:

(1) where the landlord serves a s 25 notice or counter-notice to a s 26 request stating one or more of the grounds of opposition (e), (f) or (g) but no others, and the tenant either:

　　(a) does not apply to court for a new tenancy or does so but withdraws his application; or

　　(b) does apply to court for a new tenancy, but his application is refused because the landlord is able to establish his stated ground;

(2) where the landlord serves a s 25 notice or counter-notice to a s 26 request
specifying one or more of the grounds (e), (f) or (g) and others; the tenant
applies to court for a new tenancy but the court refuses to grant a new tenancy
solely on one or more of the grounds (e), (f) or (g). Here the tenant must apply
to court for a new tenancy and ask the court to certify that a new tenancy was
not ordered solely because one of these three 'no fault' grounds has been made
out.

31.6.2 Amount

The amount of compensation is the rateable value of the holding multiplied by the
'appropriate multiplier' which is a figure prescribed from time to time by the
Secretary of State, and is currently 1. In some cases, the tenant will be entitled to
double compensation.

31.6.3 Double compensation

Sometimes the appropriate multiplier is doubled. This happens when the tenant or his
predecessors in the same business have been in occupation for at least 14 years prior
to the termination of the current tenancy. These provisions are summarised in the
following illustration.

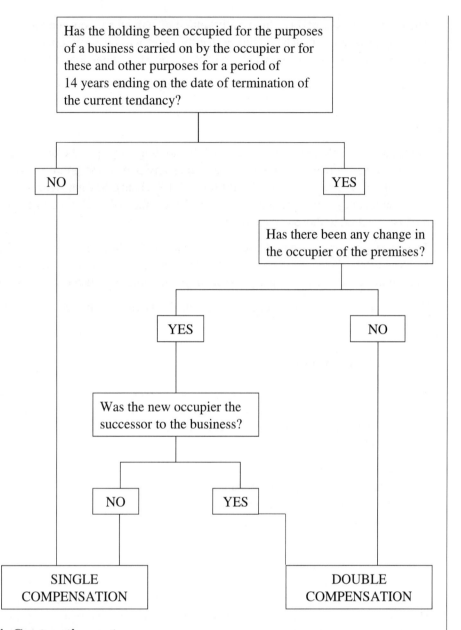

31.6.4 Contracting out

In some situations the tenant's right to compensation can be excluded by agreement between the parties. This agreement is often in the lease itself. However, s 38(2) of the Act provides that where the tenant or his predecessors in the same business have been in occupation for 5 years or more prior to the date of quitting, any agreement to exclude or reduce the tenant's right to compensation is void.

31.7 THE RENEWAL LEASE

If the tenant follows all the correct procedures and properly applies to court for a new tenancy, the court will make an order for a new lease in two situations:

(1) if the landlord fails to make out his s 30 ground of opposition; or

(2) if the landlord did not oppose the tenant's application for a new tenancy.

The terms of this new lease are usually settled by agreement between the parties and it is only in default of such agreement that the court will be called upon to decide the terms. In either event, any new lease will also enjoy the protection of the Act.

The court has jurisdiction over the premises, duration, rent and the other terms.

31.7.1 The premises

The tenant is entitled to a new tenancy of the holding only as at the date of the order. This term was defined in **31.1.4**, and excludes any part of the premises which have been sub-let. However, the landlord (but not the tenant), has the right to insist that any new tenancy to be granted shall be a new tenancy of the whole of the demised premises including those parts sub-let.

The court may grant a new lease of less than the holding under s 31A, where the landlord establishes ground (f), the redevelopment ground, but the tenant takes a new lease of an 'economically separable part' of the holding (see **31.5.6**).

The new lease may also include appurtenant rights enjoyed by the tenant under the current tenancy.

31.7.2 The duration

The length of any new lease ordered by the court will be such as is reasonable in all the circumstances but cannot exceed 14 years (often it is much less than this). In deciding this issue the court has a very wide discretion and will take into account matters such as:

(1) the length of the current tenancy;
(2) the length requested by the tenant;
(3) the hardship caused to either party;
(4) current open market practice;
(5) the landlord's future proposals.

It may be that the landlord was unable to rely on ground (f) because he could not prove that his intention to demolish or reconstruct was sufficiently firm and settled at the date of the hearing (see **31.5.6**). If, however, the court is satisfied that he will be able to do so in the near future, it may order a short tenancy so as not to impede development later. Similarly, if the premises are shown to be ripe for development, the new lease may be granted subject to a break clause (*National Car Parks Ltd v The Paternoster Consortium Ltd* (1990) 15 EG 53). In the same way, where the landlord has narrowly missed being able to rely on ground (g) because of the 5-year rule, the court may be prepared to grant a short tenancy.

31.7.3 The rent

The amount of rent to be paid is the greatest source of disagreement between the parties and specialist valuation advice will be essential. If the question of rent comes before the courts, they will assess an open market rent having regard to the other terms of the tenancy. However, in assessing the rent the court is obliged to disregard certain factors which may otherwise work to the detriment of the tenant, ie:

(1) any effect on rent of the fact that the tenant or his predecessors have been in occupation. The classic landlord's argument would be that the tenant, being a

sitting tenant, would pay more in the open market for these premises simply to avoid relocation. This would inflate an open market rent and is thus to be disregarded;

(2) any goodwill attached to the holding due to the carrying on of the tenant's business. The tenant should not have to pay a rent assessed partly on the basis of goodwill he generated;

(3) any effect on the rent of improvements voluntarily made by the tenant (certain conditions must also be satisfied);

(4) where the holding comprises licensed premises, any addition in value due to the tenant's licence.

Where the premises are in disrepair due to the tenant's failure to perform his repairing obligation, conflicting views have been expressed on whether the court should disregard this in setting the rent of the new tenancy. One view is that the premises should be valued in their actual condition. This will probably produce a lower rent but the landlord may be able to sue the tenant for breach of his repairing obligation.

The other view is that the premises should be valued on the basis that the tenant has complied with his obligation, thus preventing the tenant benefiting from his own breach. This view is supported by cases such as *Crown Estate Commissioners v Town Investments Ltd* (1992) 08 EG 111.

In *Fawke v Viscount Chelsea* [1980] QB 441, the premises were in disrepair because the landlord was in breach of his repairing obligation. The court decided that the premises should be valued in their actual condition and, therefore, fixed a new rent which was below open market value but which increased once the landlord had complied with his obligation.

Under s 34(3), the court has power to insert a rent review clause in the new lease whether or not the previous lease contained such a provision. The frequency and type of review is at the discretion of the court which may be persuaded by the tenant to make provision for downward revisions as well as upward (see *Forbuoys plc v Newport Borough Council* [1994] 24 EG 156).

As to the effect of the LTCA 1995, see **31.7.4**.

Finally, the court does have power to require the tenant to provide guarantors.

31.7.4 Other terms

It will only fall to the court to decide other terms in the absence of agreement between the parties. In fixing the other terms the court must have regard to the terms of the current tenancy and all other relevant circumstances. For that reason, the terms will be much the same as before. The leading case in this area is *O'May v City of London Real Property Co Ltd* [1983] AC 726 which held that if one of the parties seeks a change in the terms, it is for that party to justify the change. Further, the change must be fair and reasonable and 'take into account, amongst other things, the comparatively weak negotiating position of a sitting tenant requiring renewal, particularly in conditions of scarcity' (per Lord Hailsham in *O'May*). Therefore, the tenant should be on his guard against any attempt by the landlord to introduce more onerous obligations into the new lease (eg a more restrictive user covenant). In the *O'May* case the landlord was, in effect, trying to transfer the responsibility for the repair and maintenance of office premises to the tenant. This would have increased the value of the reversion by more than £1m but the House of Lords held that the landlord was not entitled to do this. Notwithstanding the effect of the *O'May* case, variations may be made in the renewal lease to reflect the changes introduced by the LTCA 1995. The renewal lease will, of course, be subject to the provisions of that Act. This will often mean that under the current lease (granted before 1 January 1996) the original tenant was liable for the entire duration of the term through privity of contract; whereas for the renewal lease, privity of contract will not apply. This change is one of the circumstances to which the court must have regard in fixing the rent and other terms of the new lease. For example, the landlord may wish to alter the terms of the alienation covenant to balance the effect of the loss of privity of contract (see *Wallis Fashion Group Ltd v General Accident Life Assurance Ltd* [2000] EGCS 45; and **18.2.5**).

31.8 THE ORDER FOR THE NEW LEASE

Any new lease ordered by the court will not commence until 3 months after the proceedings are 'finally disposed of'. This is when the time for appeal has elapsed, and for appeals to the Court of Appeal the time-limit is 4 weeks from the date of the order. The tenant continues to occupy under his old tenancy during this period. Either party may appeal.

If the court makes an order for a new tenancy upon terms which the tenant finds unacceptable (eg as to rent), the tenant may apply for revocation of the order within 14 days. In such a case, the existing tenancy will continue for such period as the parties agree or the court determines as necessary to enable the landlord to re-let the premises.

31.9 PROPOSALS FOR REFORM OF THE 1954 ACT

At the time of writing (July 2003) the Government has announced reforms to the Act. These include the following.

Contracting out (see 31.1.5)

This will no longer require the court's approval. Instead, the parties will be able to agree that the intended lease should not enjoy any security of tenure provided the tenant is given prior written notice of the consequences.

Occupation for business (see 31.1.2)

At present, to gain the protection of the Act, the tenant must be in occupation of the premises. Thus, occupation by a company controlled by the tenant is not sufficient. Under the proposals for reform, this would change so that the tenant will be deemed to be in occupation through a company controlled by the tenant.

Termination of fixed-term tenancies (see 31.2)

A tenant wishing to end a fixed-term tenancy will have a statutory right to do so by ceasing to occupy the premises on or before the contractual termination date. However, if the continuation tenancy has already commenced, the tenant will need to serve a 3-month s 27 notice ending on any date (not just a quarter day, as at present).

*Section 25 notices (see **31.2.1**)*

Where the landlord does not oppose renewal, the s 25 notice should set out the landlord's proposals for the new tenancy (if the tenant does not accept the terms, the court will settle them).

*Counter-notices (see **31.2.3**)*

The requirement for a tenant's counter-notice will be abolished (the landlord's counter-notice to a tenant's s 26 request will remain).

Applying to court for a new tenancy

Either party will be able to make application to court for renewal of a tenancy. If it is the landlord who makes such an application, the tenant may inform the court that he does not want a new tenancy. Neither party may apply for a new tenancy if the landlord has started proceedings to terminate a tenancy without the grant of a new lease (ie the landlord opposes a new tenancy). In the latter case, if the landlord is unsuccessful in proving his ground of opposition, the court will order a new lease and settle its terms.

*Time-limits (see **31.3.2**)*

An application to court for a new tenancy (by landlord or tenant) will have to be made before the end of the period specified in the s 25 notice or s 26 request, as the case may be. The parties will be able to agree in writing to extend the time-limit provided such agreement is made before the expiry of the specified period. Further agreements to extend will be possible provided they are made before the current agreement expires.

*Interim rents (see **31.4**)*

Tenants as well as landlords will be able to apply for an interim rent. The interim rent will be payable from the earliest date that could have been specified in the s 25 notice or s 26 request irrespective of which party served the notice or applied for the interim rent. The amount of the interim rent will normally be the rent for the new tenancy backdated to the date from which the interim rent becomes payable.

*Duration of new lease (see **31.7.2**)*

The maximum duration the court can order will be increased by one year to 15 years.

It is expected that these reforms will be introduced in the second half of 2004.

Part III

RESIDENTIAL TENANCIES

Chapter 32

INTRODUCTION TO RESIDENTIAL TENANCIES

32.1 RESIDENTIAL OCCUPIERS

This part of the book is concerned with both short-term and long-term lettings of residential property. It deals with the following potential problem areas:

- What happens at the end of a tenancy? Does the landlord have a right to possession?
- Who is responsible for repairs?
- Does the tenant have a right to compel the landlord to sell him the freehold or grant him a new lease?

Tenants with long leases (exceeding 21 years) are often given rights to compel the sale of the freehold; all residential tenants may have security of tenure, ie the right to stay on in possession even after the end of the contractual term.

All of these matters are significant, not only from the point of view of the tenant, but also from the point of view of the landlord or a potential purchaser of the freehold, who might have plans for redevelopment which may be affected by the tenant's rights.

In dealing with or advising upon a residential landlord and tenant matter, the question of the status of the residential occupier is of paramount importance in determining the relevant law.

It is necessary first of all to determine whether the occupier is a tenant or a licensee. The rights and obligations of the parties and the appropriate statutory provisions will, in many cases, hinge on this distinction. If a residential occupier is merely a licensee, he has no proprietary interest in the property that he occupies so that, in general terms, when the licence terminates or expires or when the owner dies or transfers ownership of the property, the occupier's right to occupy ceases. Further, there is very little statutory protection (or 'security of tenure') for residential licensees. Most legislation is aimed at the protection of tenants. Thus, the distinction between a tenancy/lease and a licence is of fundamental importance. This distinction is considered in detail at **9.4**.

Having dealt with the question of the status of the occupier as between tenant and licensee, it is then necessary to look at the relevant law affecting the tenancy or licence. It will normally be a mixture of common law and statute.

32.2 THE COMMON LAW

All licences, leases and tenancies are, to some extent, governed by common law. The law of contract, land law and the law of torts each play an important part, and must be the starting point when considering any problem that concerns leases, licences or

Chapter 32 contents
Residential occupiers
The common law
The statutes
Public sector lettings
Private sector lettings
The next step

tenancies. The relevant common law is dealt with where appropriate in later sections of the book. However, it must be appreciated that the common law is frequently modified or supplemented by statute.

32.3 THE STATUTES

The major statutory provisions are contained in the Leasehold Reform Act 1967 (LRA 1967), the Rent Act 1977 (RA 1977), the Protection from Eviction Act 1977 (PEA 1977), the Housing Act 1985 (HA 1985), the Landlord and Tenant Act 1985 (LTA 1985), the Landlord and Tenant Act 1987 (LTA 1987), the Housing Act 1988 (HA 1988), the Leasehold Reform, Housing and Urban Development Act 1993 (LRHUDA 1993) and the Housing Act 1996 (HA 1996). Most of these statutes will be further amended by the provisions of the Commonhold and Leasehold Reform Act 2002 when they are brought into force. This Act also introduces a new kind of land ownership known as commonhold. This is designed for use in the case of interdependent properties such as flats, shopping malls and the like. It is considered in Chapter 41.

These will be looked at in detail in later chapters. It should be appreciated at the outset, however, that most of this legislation was introduced on an ad hoc basis to deal with a particular problem and does not form part of an integrated consistent whole. So the qualifying conditions for each statute need to be looked at carefully to see whether any particular tenant is or is not protected.

32.4 PUBLIC SECTOR LETTINGS

Most tenants of local authorities (and certain others in the public sector) enjoy protection as secure tenants under the HA 1985. They have substantial security of tenure. If the landlord wishes to regain possession, it must usually comply with the procedure and the established grounds for possession laid down in that Act. However, there is no statutory control over the amounts of rent that local authorities can charge. In relation to repairs, harassment or unlawful eviction, there is generally no difference between public sector tenants and private sector tenants. Similarly, the rights given to long leaseholders under LRHUDA 1993 also apply to local authority tenants (see Chapter 40). However, the rights of secure tenants are otherwise outside the scope of this book.

32.5 PRIVATE SECTOR LETTINGS

The rights of short-term tenants of private landlords often depend upon when the tenancy was originally entered into. As regards security of tenure and rent control in the private sector, a clear distinction must be made between tenancies granted prior to 15 January 1989 and those granted on or after that date. The former are usually governed by the RA 1977 under which tenants enjoy substantial security of tenure and significant statutory control over the amount of rent that the landlord can charge. As regards tenancies granted on or after 15 January 1989 the rules are quite different and are contained in the HA 1988. This established the concept of the 'assured tenancy', with full security of tenure, and the 'assured shorthold tenancy', under which the landlord has an absolute right to possession at the end of the letting. However, in relation to tenancies under both the RA 1977 and the HA 1988, the rules relating to repairs, harassment and unlawful eviction are the same.

32.6 THE NEXT STEP

Having considered the question of residential status and, where appropriate, which statutory regime applies, it is then necessary to look at the detail of the relevant law and procedures and to apply them to the facts of the case and to the client's specific instructions.

Chapter 33

ASSURED TENANCIES

33.1 INTRODUCTION

The concept of assured tenancies and assured shorthold tenancies was introduced by the HA 1988. This came into force on 15 January 1989, and virtually all new lettings by private landlords after that date will be one or the other (but see **33.4**). Lettings entered into before that date will generally remain subject to the provisions of the RA 1977, see **33.3.1**.

An assured tenancy gives the tenant extensive security of tenure; at the end of the contractual term the tenant has a statutory right to remain in possession. If the landlord wishes to obtain possession, he must not only follow the prescribed procedure but also establish one of the prescribed grounds for possession. However, there is no statutory control over the amount of the rent which the landlord can charge; the rent is left to be decided by the ordinary operation of market forces. There is, however, some protection given to a tenant where the landlord wishes to increase the rent payable under an existing tenancy.

In the case of lettings entered into on or after 28 February 1997 (the commencement date of the HA 1996), most will be assured shorthold tenancies (see, generally, Chapter 39) and *not* assured tenancies. However, a shorthold is merely a type of assured tenancy and so must comply with the definition of an assured tenancy as well as the extra requirements which make it a shorthold (see **34.2.1**).

Tenancies which do *not* satisfy the definition of an assured tenancy (and so cannot be shortholds either) will not be subject to the provisions of the HA 1988 as set out in this chapter. Instead, ordinary common law rules as to termination etc will apply. They will, however, be subject to the protection from eviction protections set out in Chapter 36.

33.2 WHAT IS AN ASSURED TENANCY?

The definition of an assured tenancy is set out in s 1 of the HA 1988. A tenancy under which a dwelling house is let as a separate dwelling will be an assured tenancy, if and so long as all of the following requirements are met:

(1) the tenant or each of joint tenants is an individual; and
(2) the tenant or at least one of joint tenants occupies the dwelling house as his only or principal home; and
(3) the tenancy is not specifically excluded by other provisions of the Act.

Each of these requirements must be looked at in detail.

Chapter 33 contents
Introduction
What is an assured tenancy?
Tenancies which cannot be assured
Transitional provisions
Rents under assured tenancies
Succession on death
Sub-lettings
Security of tenure

33.2.1 Tenancy

There must be a 'tenancy'; licences to occupy dwelling houses are excluded from protection. See **9.4** as to the distinction between a licence and a tenancy.

33.2.2 Dwelling house

There is no statutory definition of 'dwelling house', and it will be a question of fact whether premises are a house or not, but any building designed or adapted for living in is capable of forming a dwelling house for these purposes. As well as including lettings of whole houses and self-contained flats, lettings of single rooms in a house will also be included, as will converted barns, windmills, etc.

33.2.3 Let as a separate dwelling

The premises, as well as being a dwelling house, must be let *as* a dwelling. So, if a building that would otherwise qualify as a dwelling house is let for business purposes, the tenant cannot claim that it is let on an assured tenancy merely because he decides to move in and live there.

There must be a *separate* dwelling. However, the House of Lords has held that even where the accommodation lacks one of the usual features of a dwelling, such as a kitchen, the property can still be the subject of an assured tenancy if the tenant does not actually live there. Further, s 3 of the HA 1988 makes special provision for the situation where the tenant shares some of the essential features of a dwelling with others. Such a letting is deemed to be an assured tenancy (assuming that all the other conditions are met). The tenant must, however, have the exclusive occupation of at least one room (otherwise it cannot be a tenancy), and if the other accommodation is shared with the landlord, the tenancy will be excluded from the definition of an assured tenancy for different reasons. However, the provisions of s 3 mean that arrangements whereby each tenant is given exclusive occupation of his own bed-sitting room, but shares bathroom and kitchen with other tenants, will be deemed to be capable of being assured tenancies. Such an arrangement must be contrasted, however, with the situation where each member of a group of people is given a right to share the occupation of the whole of the house with the others. No one has the right to exclusive possession of any part of the house, and the arrangement can only give rise to a licence.

33.2.4 'If and so long as'

The status of the tenancy is not to be determined once and for all at the commencement of the letting. Whether a tenancy is an assured tenancy can fluctuate according to changed circumstances. For example, one requirement of the definition is that the tenant must be occupying the house as his only or principal home. This may have been the case at the start of the tenancy, and so the tenancy would be assured, but if subsequently the tenant ceases to reside, the tenancy will no longer be assured. The tenant will thus lose his security of tenure.

33.2.5 The tenant must be an individual

Lettings to companies are excluded from the definition, even though an individual (eg a director or employee of the company) may be in occupation of the house.

33.2.6 The tenant must occupy as his 'only or principal home'

It is possible for a person to have more than one 'home'. If that is the case, then it is a question of fact as to which is the tenant's principal home. This could be a significant question, for example, for the person working in the City who has a flat nearby in which he lives during the week, and a house in the country in which he lives at weekends. Which is his principal home? Only a tenancy of the principal home can be an assured tenancy. Although the provision requires 'occupation', this does not mean continuous occupation. A mere temporary absence will not deprive a tenancy of its status as an assured tenancy.

33.3 TENANCIES WHICH CANNOT BE ASSURED

Various lettings which satisfy the basic definition of an assured tenancy will, in fact, not be protected if they fall within one of the following exceptions. Equally, as they cannot be assured tenancies, they cannot be assured shorthold tenancies either. The exceptions are as follows.

33.3.1 Tenancies entered into before the commencement of the HA 1988

The HA 1988 came into force on 15 January 1989; it is not retrospective. Only lettings entered into on or after that date can be assured tenancies. Any pre-existing tenancy will, if it has any protection at all, still remain subject to the provisions of the RA 1977 (see Chapter 40).

33.3.2 High value properties

Because of the abolition of domestic rates, a distinction has to be drawn between those tenancies granted before 1 April 1990 and those granted on or after that date. For tenancies granted before 1 April 1990, a tenancy of a dwelling house with a rateable value in excess of £750 (£1,500 in Greater London) cannot be an assured tenancy. If the tenancy was granted on or after 1 April 1990, it cannot be an assured tenancy if the rent payable is £25,000 or more per annum.

33.3.3 Tenancies at a low rent

This exclusion has also been affected by the abolition of domestic rates. Lettings made before 1 April 1990 cannot be assured if the annual rent is less than two-thirds of the rateable value of the property. For tenancies granted on or after 1 April 1990, the exclusion applies to tenancies in which the rent does not exceed £250 per annum (£1,000 per annum in Greater London).

33.3.4 Business tenancies

A tenancy to which Part II of the LTA 1954 applies cannot be an assured tenancy; see Chapter 31. This means that mixed-user lettings, ie lettings of property used partly for business and partly for residential purposes cannot be assured tenancies, despite being occupied by the tenant as his only or principal home, etc. Lettings contracted out, or otherwise outside the security of tenure provisions of the LTA 1954, will still not be within the definition of an assured tenancy.

33.3.5 Lettings to students

Lettings to students by specified educational bodies are outside the definition of an assured tenancy. This exception does not apply to lettings to students by landlords other than the specified universities and colleges; these are capable of being assured tenancies, subject to the normal requirements being fulfilled.

33.3.6 Holiday lettings

A letting for the purpose of a holiday cannot be an assured tenancy.

33.3.7 Lettings by resident landlords

A tenancy will have a resident landlord where the landlord lives in another part of the same building in which the accommodation let to the tenant is situated.

33.3.8 Crown, local authority and housing association lettings

Although Crown, local authority and housing association lettings are excluded from the definition of an assured tenancy, lettings by local authorities and housing associations may have other protections (see **32.4**).

33.4 TRANSITIONAL PROVISIONS

Provisions were inserted in the HA 1988 to ensure that any existing RA 1977 tenants were not deprived of their existing protections under that Act by landlords granting them new tenancies after the coming into force of the HA 1988. Thus, a tenancy granted to a person who was a protected or statutory tenant under the RA 1977 by that person's landlord (or one of joint landlords) will still be a protected tenancy even though it is granted on or after 15 January 1989. This will still be the case even if the new letting is of a different property to that comprised in the previous tenancy. Note also that it is the identity of the landlord at the time of the new letting that is relevant, not the landlord at the time of the original grant of the tenancy. So, if L grants a Rent Act tenancy to T on or after 15 January 1989, that new letting will still be protected by the Rent Act.

33.5 RENTS UNDER ASSURED TENANCIES

There is no restriction on the amount of rent which can initially be charged on the grant of an assured tenancy. This is so even if there is a subsisting registration of a fair rent for the purposes of the RA 1977 (see Chapter 35). However, if the landlord subsequently wishes to increase the rent, he may not be able to do so unless he follows the correct procedure. The details of this are outside the scope of this book.

33.6 SUCCESSION ON DEATH

On the death of a tenant, his tenancy does not die with him; it is a proprietary right and will pass in the same way as the deceased's other property. On the death of one of joint tenants, the tenancy will vest in the survivor(s). On the death of a sole tenant the tenancy will pass under his will or intestacy. The HA 1988, however, contains specific provisions (s 17) dealing with the succession to an assured periodic tenancy on the death of a sole tenant which will override these normal rules.

On the death of a sole periodic tenant the tenancy will vest in the tenant's spouse, notwithstanding the terms of the deceased's will, provided that immediately before the deceased tenant's death the spouse was occupying the dwelling house as his or her only or principal home. 'Spouse' is defined to include a person who was living with the tenant as his or her wife or husband as well as persons who were lawfully married. It also includes persons in an established same-sex relationship.

33.7 SUB-LETTINGS

As between the particular landlord and tenant, it is irrelevant whether the landlord owns the freehold interest in the property or merely a leasehold interest. If the conditions are complied with for the creation of an assured tenancy, then the tenant will have the benefit of security of tenure and the other assured tenancy provisions against his landlord, whether or not that landlord owns the freehold or is himself a tenant.

The question arises as to whether an assured sub-tenant has protection against the owner of the freehold reversion. The normal rule at common law is that if a head lease comes to an end then any sub-lease derived out of it will also determine. This, however, is varied by the provisions of s 18 of the HA 1988. This provides that in the case of a house lawfully sub-let on an assured tenancy, that on the ending of the head lease, the sub-tenancy will still continue. The assured sub-tenant will then become the direct tenant of the head landlord with full security of tenure.

33.8 SECURITY OF TENURE

33.8.1 Restriction on termination by landlord

An assured tenancy cannot be brought to an end by the landlord otherwise than by obtaining a court order for possession. Thus, in the case of a periodic assured tenancy, a notice to quit is of no effect. On the ending of a fixed-term assured tenancy (including a shorthold) otherwise than by an order of the court or by surrender, the tenant is entitled to remain in possession as a statutory periodic tenant. This statutory periodic tenancy will be on the same terms as the previous fixed-term tenancy (although there is a little used procedure for changing those terms: see s 6 of the HA 1988).

33.8.2 Obtaining a court order

The landlord will only obtain a court order for possession if he follows the correct procedure and can establish one or more of the grounds for possession set out in

Sch 2 to the HA 1988. Further, although some of these grounds are mandatory grounds, ie the court must order possession if the ground is established, many of them are discretionary grounds. With these, the court, on proof of the ground, may order possession only if it considers it reasonable to do so. The procedure for obtaining possession involves the landlord serving a notice on the tenant (a 's 8 notice'), in the prescribed form. The s 8 notice must specify the ground(s) upon which the landlord intends to rely and must give 2 weeks' notice of the landlord's intention to commence possession proceedings. (Sometimes 2 months' notice has to be given depending upon the ground used.) However, if Ground 14 is specified (whether or not with any other ground) then the proceedings can be commenced as soon as the s 8 notice has been served. The proceedings must then be commenced not earlier than the date specified and not later than 12 months from the date of service of the notice. It is possible for the court to dispense with the requirement for a s 8 notice (unless Ground 8 is being relied upon), but only if it considers it 'just and equitable' to do so.

In the case of a fixed-term assured tenancy, the landlord cannot normally obtain possession until after the end of the contractual fixed term (assuming that a ground for possession can then be established). However, as an exception to this, certain of the grounds for possession will be available to the landlord during the fixed term provided that the tenancy agreement contains a provision for it to be brought to an end on the ground in question. This provision can take any form at all, including a proviso for re-entry or a forfeiture clause. The grounds on which the landlord can obtain possession in this way during the fixed term are Grounds 2, 8 and 10 to 15.

33.8.3 The grounds for possession: mandatory grounds

The grounds are set out in Sch 2 to the HA 1988. Part I of the Schedule contains the mandatory grounds, ie those, on proof of which, the court must make an order for possession in the landlord's favour.

Ground 1 (owner-occupier etc)

> 'Not later than the beginning of the tenancy the landlord gave notice in writing to the tenant that possession might be recovered on this ground or the court is of the opinion that it is just and equitable to dispense with the requirement of notice and (in either case)—
>
> (a)   at some time before the beginning of the tenancy, the landlord who is seeking possession or, in the case of joint landlords seeking possession, at least one of them occupied the dwelling house as his only or principal home; or
>
> (b)   the landlord who is seeking possession or, in the case of joint landlords seeking possession, at least one of them requires the dwelling house as his or his spouse's only or principal home and neither the landlord (or, in the case of joint landlords, any one of them) nor any other person who, as landlord, derived title under the landlord who gave the notice mentioned above acquired the reversion on the tenancy for money or money's worth.'

This is one of the grounds for which s 8 requires 2 months' notice of impending proceedings being given.

Ground 2 (mortgagee exercising power of sale)

> 'The dwelling house is subject to a mortgage granted before the beginning of the tenancy; and

(a) the mortgagee is entitled to exercise a power of sale conferred on him by the mortgage or by section 101 of the Law of Property Act 1925; and

(b) the mortgagee requires possession of the dwelling house for the purpose of disposing of it with vacant possession in exercise of that power; and

(c) either notice was given as mentioned in Ground 1 above or the court is satisfied that it is just and equitable to dispense with the requirement of notice.'

As with Ground 1, 2 months' notice of proceedings must be served.

Ground 3 (out-of-season holiday accommodation)

'The tenancy is a fixed term tenancy for a term not exceeding eight months and—

(a) not later than the beginning of the tenancy the landlord gave notice in writing to the tenant that possession might be recovered on this ground; and

(b) at some time within the period of twelve months ending with the beginning of the tenancy, the dwelling house was occupied under a right to occupy it for a holiday.'

Ground 4 (out of term student accommodation)

'The tenancy is fixed-term tenancy for a term not exceeding twelve months and—

(a) not later than the beginning of the tenancy the landlord gave notice in writing to the tenant that possession might be recovered on this ground; and

(b) at some time within the period of twelve months ending with the beginning of the tenancy, the dwelling house was let on a tenancy falling within paragraph 8 of Schedule 1 to this Act.'

Paragraph 8 of Sch 1 applies to tenancies granted to students by a specified educational institution and which are outside the definition of an assured tenancy.

Ground 5 (minister of religion's house)

'The dwelling house is held for the purpose of being available for occupation by a minister of religion as a residence from which to perform the duties of his office and—

(a) not later than the beginning of the tenancy the landlord gave notice in writing to the tenant that possession might be recovered on this ground; and

(b) the court is satisfied that the dwelling house is required for occupation by a minister of religion as such a residence.'

Two months' notice of proceedings is required for this ground.

Ground 6 (demolition etc)

This is a long and complicated ground, but is quite simple in its basic intent. It allows a landlord to obtain possession if he intends to demolish or reconstruct the house (or a substantial part of it) and cannot reasonably do so without obtaining possession. However, if the landlord has acquired his interest in the property for money or money's worth since the date of the grant of the tenancy, then this ground is not available.

Two months' notice of proceedings must be served by the landlord for this ground to be available.

If this ground is established, the landlord must pay the tenant's reasonable removal costs.

Ground 7 (death)

'The tenancy is a periodic tenancy (including a statutory periodic tenancy) which has devolved under the will or intestacy of the former tenant and the proceedings for the recovery of possession are begun not later than twelve months after the death of the former tenant or, if the court so directs, after the date on which, in the opinion of the court, the landlord or, in the case of joint landlords, any one of them became aware of the former tenant's death.

Ground 8 (substantial rent arrears)

'Both at the date of the service of the notice under section 8 of this Act relating to the proceedings for possession and at the date of the hearing—

(a)   if rent is payable weekly or fortnightly, at least eight weeks' rent is unpaid;

(b)   if rent is payable monthly, at least two months' rent is unpaid;

(c)   if rent is payable quarterly, at least one quarter's rent is more than three months in arrears; and

(d)   if rent is payable yearly, at least three months' rent is more than three months in arrears;

and for the purpose of this ground "rent" means rent lawfully due from the tenant.'

Note that the rent must be 'lawfully due'. Under s 48 of the LTA 1987, no rent is lawfully due from a tenant unless and until the landlord has given to the tenant notice in writing of an address in England and Wales at which notices (including notices in proceedings) can be served upon him. In *Rogan v Woodfield Building Services Ltd* [1994] EGCS 145, the Court of Appeal decided that if the landlord's name and address in England and Wales was stated on the tenancy agreement without any qualification or limitation, then this would be sufficient to comply with s 48. Obviously, however, if the landlord's address changes during the currency of the tenancy, for example on a change of landlord, then a separate s 48 notice will be needed. This s 48 notice need not be in any prescribed form nor need the address be the landlord's home address (or registered office, in the case of a limited company); it could be, for example, the address of a solicitor or other agent.

It is not possible for the court to dispense with the requirement for the service of a notice under s 8 of the HA 1988 if this ground is being relied upon.

33.8.4   Grounds for possession: discretionary grounds

Proof of the following grounds for possession will not inevitably result in a possession order being made against a tenant. The court can only make such an order if it considers it 'reasonable to do so'. This will be a question of fact in each case, but this proviso will enable the court to consider the prospective hardship likely to be suffered by both the landlord and the tenant, depending upon whether it makes a possession order or not. The conduct of the parties during the tenancy will also be relevant to the question of 'reasonableness'.

Ground 9 (alternative accommodation)

'Suitable alternative accommodation is available for the tenant or will be available for him when the order for possession takes effect.'

To make use of this ground, 2 months' notice of proceedings is required. As with mandatory Ground 6, the landlord must pay the tenant's reasonable removal expenses if possession is ordered on this ground.

Ground 10 (rent arrears)

'Some rent lawfully due from the tenant—

(a) is unpaid on the date on which the proceedings for possession are begun; and

(b) ... was in arrears at the date of the service of the notice under that section relating to those proceedings.'

Ground 11 (persistent delay)

'Whether or not any rent is in arrears on the date on which proceedings for possession are begun, the tenant has persistently delayed paying rent which has become lawfully due.'

Ground 12 (breach of covenant etc)

'Any obligation of the tenancy (other than one related to the payment of rent) has been broken or not performed.'

Ground 13 (waste or neglect etc)

'The condition of the dwelling house or any of the common parts has deteriorated owing to acts of waste by, or the neglect or default of, the tenant or any other person residing in the dwelling house and, in the case of an act of waste by, or the neglect or default of, a person lodging with the tenant or a sub-tenant of his, the tenant has not taken such steps as he ought reasonably to have taken for the removal of the lodger or sub-tenant.'

Ground 14 (nuisance etc)

'The tenant or a person residing in or visiting the dwelling house—

(a) has been guilty of conduct causing or likely to cause a nuisance or annoyance to a person residing, visiting or otherwise engaging in a lawful activity in the locality, or

(b) has been convicted of—

(i) using the dwelling house or allowing it to be used for immoral or illegal purposes, or

(ii) an arrestable offence committed in, or in the locality of, the dwelling house.'

Normally, under s 8 of the HA 1988, 2 weeks' (or sometimes even 2 months') notice of the commencement of proceedings has to be given to a tenant; in the case of this ground, whether pleaded alone or with other grounds, proceedings can be commenced as soon as the s 8 notice has been served (see **33.8.2**).

Ground 14A (domestic violence)

'The dwelling house was occupied (whether alone or with others) by a married couple or a couple living together as husband and wife and—

(a) one of the partners is a tenant of the dwelling house,

(b) the landlord who is seeking possession is a registered social landlord or a charitable housing trust,

(c) one partner has left the dwelling house because of violence or threats of violence by the other towards —

(i) that partner, or

(ii) a member of the family of that partner who was residing with that partner immediately before the partner left, and

(d)   the court is satisfied that the partner who has left is unlikely to return.'

Ground 15 (damage to furniture etc)

'The condition of any furniture provided for use under the tenancy has, in the opinion of the court, deteriorated owing to ill-treatment by the tenant or any other person residing in the dwelling house and, in the case of ill-treatment by a person lodging with the tenant or by a sub-tenant of his, the tenant has not taken such steps as he ought reasonably to have taken for the removal of the lodger or sub-tenant.'

Ground 16 (former employee)

'The dwelling house was let to the tenant in consequence of his employment by the landlord seeking possession or a previous landlord under the tenancy and the tenant has ceased to be in that employment.'

Ground 17 (false statement by tenant)

'The tenant is the person, or one of the persons, to whom the tenancy was granted and the landlord was induced to grant the tenancy by a false statement made knowingly or recklessly by—

(a)   the tenant, or
(b)   a person acting at the tenant's instigation.'

Chapter 34

ASSURED SHORTHOLD TENANCIES

34.1 INTRODUCTION

Chapter 34 contents
Introduction
Old shortholds
New shortholds
Rent control
What happens when a
  shorthold expires?
How does the landlord
  obtain possession?
Are there any other
  grounds for possession?

A distinction must first of all be drawn between 'old' shortholds, ie those entered into before 28 February 1997, the commencement date of the HA 1996, and 'new' shortholds, ie those entered into on or after that date.

An old shorthold is a fixed-term tenancy of at least 6 months' duration with no security of tenure. Thus, once the fixed term has expired the landlord has an absolute right to recover possession, provided that he complies with the correct procedure. Prior to the grant of the tenancy, however, the landlord must have served a notice on the tenant, in the prescribed form, warning him of the lack of security of tenure. This notice cannot be dispensed with.

Because of the lack of security, shortholds became very popular with landlords and most lettings purported to be shortholds. However, sometimes a purported shorthold would fail due to non-compliance with the conditions, leading to an assured tenancy with full security of tenure (see Chapter 33). From 28 February 1997, however, all new lettings (with certain exceptions, see **34.3.2**) are deemed to be shortholds. The old conditions need no longer be complied with; the letting need not be for a fixed term, there is no need for a warning notice etc. However, the landlord still has the same absolute right to possession as in an old shorthold.

Note that 'old' shortholds continue as before and if one fails due to the conditions not have being complied with, for example, no warning notice was served, the tenancy will still become a fully protected assured tenancy. This means that the conditions for the grant of an old shorthold are still of considerable practical importance even after the introduction of new shortholds.

The only disadvantage of a shorthold (whether new or old) from a landlord's point of view is the right given to the tenant to refer the rent initially payable to the Rent Assessment Committee. However, the Committee can reduce the rent only if it is 'significantly higher' than the rents under other comparable assured tenancies.

34.2 OLD SHORTHOLDS

34.2.1 Definition

Section 20 of the HA 1988 sets out the qualifying conditions for shortholds entered into before 28 February 1997. It provides that an assured shorthold tenancy is an assured tenancy which:

(1) is a fixed-term tenancy granted for a term of not less than 6 months; and

(2) contains no power for the landlord to terminate it during the first 6 months; and

(3) was preceded by the giving to the tenant of the prescribed shorthold notice.

An assured tenancy

An assured shorthold tenancy is merely a type of assured tenancy. It must, therefore, comply with all the requirements of an assured tenancy (see Chapter 33).

A shorthold cannot be granted to an existing tenant under an ordinary assured tenancy (or to one of joint tenants), if it is granted by the landlord under that existing tenancy. This is so even if the lettings are not of the same premises. This is an anti-avoidance device to prevent landlords from depriving their existing tenants of security of tenure by purportedly granting them a shorthold. Similarly, as with all assured tenancies, a shorthold cannot be granted to an existing RA 1977 protected or statutory tenant (see **33.4**).

Minimum 6-month fixed term

The initial grant of a shorthold could not be for a periodic term. It had to be for a fixed term and for a minimum duration of 6 months.

No power for landlord to terminate during first 6 months

Even if a minimum period of 6 months is granted, any power, however expressed, which would or might allow the landlord to terminate the tenancy within the first 6 months of the tenancy will prevent the tenancy from amounting to a shorthold. Note, however, that a forfeiture clause or a clause allowing termination on assured tenancy Grounds 2, 8 and 10 to 15 will not breach this requirement even though it is exercisable during the first 6 months of the term.

Preceded by the giving of the prescribed shorthold notice

As the tenant under an assured shorthold has no security of tenure, he had to be served with a notice prior to the grant of the tenancy warning him of this fact. This notice must be in the prescribed form. The content of the necessary form changed twice since the introduction of assured shortholds on 15 January 1989 and care must be taken to ensure that the shorthold notice served was the correct one as at the date of service.

The notice must have been served before the tenancy agreement was entered into and not at the same time. Thus, it could not be included in the tenancy agreement itself.

Relevance of old shorthold rules

Although an old shorthold can no longer be created after 28 February 1997, it is still relevant to consider the application of these old shorthold rules in the case of shortholds granted before that date which are still subsisting or have been subsequently renewed. In the case, for example, of a purported old shorthold granted on 1 January 1997, if the old shorthold rules were not fully complied with, that tenancy would be a fully protected assured tenancy, as would any further letting on or after 28 February 1997 by the same landlord to the same tenant.

34.3 NEW SHORTHOLDS

34.3.1 Definition

Shortholds entered into on or after 28 February 1997 (otherwise than pursuant to a contract made before that date) are governed by s 19A of the HA 1988 (as inserted by the HA 1996). This provides that *any* assured tenancy entered into on or after the commencement date will be a shorthold *unless* it falls within one of the specified exceptions.

So there is no longer any need for a shorthold to be preceded by a prescribed form of notice. There is no need for a shorthold to be for a fixed term, it can be periodic; there is no need for a minimum period of 6 months; it can be for any period, no matter how short. However, although there is no prohibition on the landlord being able to terminate during the first 6 months, no order for possession using the shorthold ground can be made earlier than 6 months from the start of the tenancy, whether the tenancy is for a fixed term or it is a periodic tenancy (see **34.7**). However, this does not stop possession being obtained during the first 6 months using an assured tenancy ground, eg Ground 14; a new shorthold, like an old shorthold, is merely a type of assured tenancy, see **34.2.1**.

As a new shorthold is a type of assured tenancy, it must still comply with all the requirements of an assured tenancy (see Chapter 33). A tenancy which falls outside of the definition of an assured tenancy (eg due to the resident landlord rule) cannot be a shorthold either. Such a tenancy will be subject to ordinary common law rules as to termination.

34.3.2 Which lettings will not be new shortholds?

As previously stated (see **34.3.1**), all new assured tenancies granted on or after 28 February 1997 (other than those granted pursuant to a contract made before that date) will be shortholds subject to certain exceptions. These exceptions are set out in Sch 2A to the HA 1988 as inserted by the HA 1996. The following lettings will be excluded and will thus take effect as ordinary assured tenancies.

(1) Tenancies excluded by notice

The Schedule allows the landlord to serve a notice on the tenant either before or after the grant of the tenancy stating that the letting is not to be a shorthold. There is no prescribed form for this notice.

It is rather strange that a landlord can change the status of a tenancy *after* it has been entered into. In most cases this will be to the advantage of the tenant in that it will give him greater security of tenure than before; it will, however, take away from the tenant his right to refer the rent if he considers it excessive (see **34.4**).

(2) Tenancies containing a provision stating that the tenancy is not to be a shorthold

Similarly, if the tenancy agreement itself states that it is not to be a shorthold, it will then take effect as an ordinary assured tenancy.

(3) Lettings to existing assured tenants

A letting to an existing ASSURED (ie not shorthold) tenant (whether alone or with others) by a person who is the landlord (or one of the landlords) under the existing tenancy, will *not* be a shorthold *unless* the TENANT serves notice on the landlord, in the prescribed form, before the new tenancy is entered into that he wants it to be a shorthold.

The requirements that this notice must be served *before* the new tenancy is entered into will give rise to similar considerations as already exist with regard to the service of s 20 notices for old shortholds; see **34.2.1**.

Of course, this provision begs the question as to *why* should a tenant want to serve such a notice when it will result in him losing the security of tenure he had before? One possible advantage would be for a tenant who had no security as an assured tenant (eg because of Ground 1) and was unhappy about the rent under the new letting. By serving a notice stating that the tenancy was to be a shorthold, he would then have the right to refer the rent to the Rent Assessment Committee as being excessive. See **34.4** as to references of the rent to the Rent Assessment Committee.

The existence of this procedure, allowing a tenant to elect to have a shorthold, does give rise to worries as to whether there is a danger of undue pressure being placed on tenants by landlords anxious to take advantage of the provisions of the HA 1996.

34.4 RENT CONTROL

The protection given differs slightly depending upon whether the tenant has a new shorthold or an old shorthold, but the general principles are the same for both.

On the granting of the tenancy, the landlord can charge such rent for the premises as the market will bear. There is no statutory restriction on the amount of rent chargeable. Any existing registration of a 'fair rent' under the provisions of the RA 1977 (see Chapter 35) can be ignored, as can any rental figure previously determined by the Rent Assessment Committee under these provisions. However, an assured shorthold tenant can apply to the local Rent Assessment Committee for the determination of the rent which, in the Committee's opinion, the landlord might reasonably be expected to obtain under the shorthold tenancy.

If the tenant has an old shorthold, he can apply at any time during the first tenancy entered into between the parties; no application can be made during any subsequent letting.

If the tenant has a new shorthold, whether for a fixed term or a periodic letting, he cannot apply if more than 6 months have elapsed since the beginning of the tenancy.

In the case of old shortholds and fixed-term new shortholds, the rent as assessed will become the maximum rent chargeable for the property throughout the remainder of the fixed term.

In the case of a new shorthold which is a periodic tenancy, again the rent once fixed will, in theory, remain fixed throughout the tenancy. However, in practice, once 12 months have expired, the landlord will then be able to make an application under ss 13 and 14 of the HA 1988 to increase the rent. These provisions are, however, outside the scope of this book.

With both old and new shortholds, once the rent has been determined by the Committee no further application for the fixing of a different figure can be made by either landlord or tenant. However, the rent determined by the Committee only has relevance to the particular tenancy in question. It will not limit the amount of rent chargeable under any subsequent letting, even if this is between the same parties.

34.5 WHAT HAPPENS WHEN A SHORTHOLD EXPIRES?

On the ending of a fixed term, the tenant is allowed to remain in possession as a statutory periodic tenant. However, the tenant still has no security of tenure. Under s 21(1) of the HA 1988 the court must still make an order for possession if the landlord follows the correct procedure. This involves the service on the tenant of not less than 2 months' notice stating that the landlord requires possession (see **34.6**).

34.6 HOW DOES THE LANDLORD OBTAIN POSSESSION?

Unless the tenant leaves voluntarily, the landlord must apply to the court and obtain an order for possession. The court must order possession provided that the landlord follows the correct procedure. This involves the landlord serving a notice on the tenant (the 's 21 notice') giving the tenant at least 2 months' notice that he requires possession. Note, however, that possession cannot be obtained using this shorthold procedure during the continuance of a fixed term; possession is available only after its expiry (although the procedure can be set in motion during the fixed term so that possession can be obtained as soon as it has ended). Note also, that in the case of a new shorthold, possession cannot be obtained within 6 months of the commencement of the term using the shorthold procedure. This is so whether the tenancy is for a fixed term or is periodic.

34.7 ARE THERE ANY OTHER GROUNDS FOR POSSESSION?

A shorthold is a type of assured tenancy and so, during the term, the mandatory and discretionary grounds which apply to ordinary assured tenancies can also apply. For full details of these see **33.8.3** and **33.8.4**, but it does mean, for example, that mandatory Ground 8 and discretionary Grounds 10 and 11 (all of which relate to rent arrears) can be used during the subsistence of the shorthold should the landlord be faced with a defaulting tenant. However, in the case of a fixed-term letting, as with other assured tenancies, these grounds can be used during the fixed term only if the tenancy agreement so provides. In the case of a shorthold which is a periodic tenancy, these ordinary assured tenancy grounds will be available to a landlord without the need for any such provision in the tenancy agreement.

In the case of a fixed-term shorthold, however, it is always sensible to insert a provision allowing the landlord to terminate the tenancy on the specified grounds. In the case of an old shorthold, this is permissible despite the usual rule that there must be no power for the landlord to terminate within the first 6 months of the tenancy. This rule does not apply to termination because of a breach of the terms of the tenancy, for example non-payment of rent. Similarly, in the case of new shortholds, although possession cannot be obtained using the shorthold procedure within 6 months of the commencement (see **34.6**), possession can be obtained during that period using the ordinary assured grounds should they be satisfied.

When the landlord is seeking to obtain possession on one of the ordinary assured grounds, then the procedure relevant to an ordinary assured tenancy should be followed, and *not* the shorthold procedure. In particular, this will mean that a s 8 notice will have to be served on the tenant before proceedings can be commenced, and *not* a s 21 notice.

Chapter 35

THE RENT ACT 1977

35.1 INTRODUCTION

The RA 1977 applies to lettings entered into prior to 15 January 1989. There are still many thousands of such tenancies in existence today, although their numbers are likely to decline as the years go by and tenants leave. Further, it is also still possible for new RA 1977 tenancies to be created today, albeit in very limited circumstances (see **33.4**). Tenancies within the RA 1977 are given wide-ranging security of tenure, in many ways similar to that given to assured tenancies. The main difference from assured tenancies, though, is that they are also subject to rent control, the 'fair rent' system which tends to keep rents below those which would prevail in the open market. On the death of a tenant there are succession rights which tend to be more generous than those applying to assured tenancies.

35.2 PROTECTED TENANCIES

There will be a protected tenancy within the RA 1977 where a dwelling house is 'let as a separate dwelling' (RA 1977, s 1). See the discussion of the similarly worded requirement for an assured tenancy under the HA 1988 (at **33.2.3**). Unlike the HA 1988, there is no need for the letting to be to an individual, nor does the house need to be the tenant's only or principal home. There are various exceptions which are generally very similar to those for assured tenancies, for example, lettings by resident landlords, holiday lettings, tenancies at a low rent (see **33.3**). Protected tenancies will have rent control and succession rights, but not necessarily security of tenure.

35.3 STATUTORY TENANCIES

The statutory tenancy is the device by which security of tenure is given. At the end of the contractual protected tenancy, the tenant is given security of tenure and is allowed to remain in possession only 'if and so long as he occupies the dwelling house as his residence'. Only an individual can occupy as a residence, so a company tenant can be a protected tenant but not a statutory tenant. There is no requirement that the dwelling house should be occupied as the tenant's only or main residence; for RA 1977 purposes, it is accepted that a person can have two homes and that there can be a statutory tenancy of either or both of them. In order to obtain possession against a protected tenant, therefore, a landlord must first of all terminate that protected tenancy, for example, by serving notice to quit. If the tenant does not qualify as a statutory tenant, the landlord will be immediately entitled to a court order for possession. If a statutory tenancy does arise, the landlord will have to establish one (or more) of the grounds for possession laid down in the Act. As with assured tenancies, some of these grounds are mandatory and so the court must order

Chapter 35 contents
Introduction
Protected tenancies
Statutory tenancies
The fair rent system
Succession to Rent Act tenancies

possession on proof of the ground, but many are discretionary where the court can only order possession if it considers it reasonable to do so. The RA 1977 grounds are called 'cases' and are set out in Sch 15 to the RA 1977. Many are assured tenancy grounds.

35.4 THE FAIR RENT SYSTEM

35.4.1 The system

Both protected and statutory tenancies are subject to control as to the amount of the rent the landlord can charge for the property. The RA 1977 set up a register of 'fair rents' for dwelling houses. Once a rent has been registered in relation to a property then that becomes the maximum chargeable under any protected or statutory tenancy of that property. The rent is assessed by the rent officer, a local authority official, in accordance with criteria laid down by the Act. By requiring the rent officer to assume that there is no shortage of accommodation to let (even though there might be), the rent assessed is often considerably lower than it otherwise would be in the open market.

35.4.2 Applying for a fair rent

Assuming that no fair rent is registered in respect of the property, on the grant of a tenancy the landlord can charge whatever rent the market will bear. However, at any time during the continuance of the tenancy the tenant can apply for a fair rent to be assessed. Once assessed, this then becomes the maximum payable, despite the existence of a higher agreed figure in the tenancy agreement. The only way in which the landlord can increase the rent is by applying himself to the rent officer for the assessment of a higher fair rent. However, he normally cannot make such an application within 2 years of an earlier fair rent having been assessed.

35.5 SUCCESSION TO RENT ACT TENANCIES

On the death of a statutory or a protected tenant, that person's spouse (or a person living with the tenant as husband or wife) will become the statutory tenant of the house and thus entitled to the benefits of security of tenure and rent control. If there is no surviving spouse (or person who had lived with the tenant as husband or wife), then the succession rules differ depending upon the date of death of the tenant.

35.5.1 Deaths prior to 15 January 1989

In this case any member of the tenant's family who was living with him at the time of death and had lived with him for at least 6 months prior to the death would succeed as a statutory tenant.

35.5.2 Deaths on or after 15 January 1989

Now, for a family member to succeed, he needs to have resided for 2 years prior to the death. Further, in such cases the family member will only become entitled to an assured tenancy on the succession and *not* a statutory tenancy.

35.5.3 Second transmissions

On the death of the 'first successor', it is sometimes possible for a second 'transmission' to a 'second successor' to occur. In the situation where the first successor died before 15 January 1989, a second transmission was always possible in favour of the first successor's spouse or family member, using the same succession rules as applicable to the first succession. However, in the case of the death of a first successor after 15 January 1989, a second transmission is only possible in very limited circumstances.

Chapter 36

PROTECTION FROM EVICTION

36.1 INTRODUCTION

The most traumatic experience that residential tenants or licensees may have to face is the peremptory eviction from, or harassment in, their homes by their landlords. Landlords sometimes resort to threats and violence because they think it is a cheaper and quicker method of eviction than taking court proceedings for possession, which may not in any event be successful due to the security of tenure legislation. Tenants suffering such unacceptable actions on the part of their landlords may have civil remedies against them. There may also be criminal sanctions. The tenant's basic remedy will be damages, although an injunction will often be available to restrain future actions and to restore a dispossessed tenant to the property. The statutory protections apply not only to tenants but also to licensees.

Chapter 36 contents
Introduction
Criminal sanctions: the Protection from Eviction Act 1977
Criminal sanctions: the Criminal Law Act 1977
Civil proceedings

36.2 CRIMINAL SANCTIONS: THE PROTECTION FROM EVICTION ACT 1977

36.2.1 Protection from eviction

The offence

It is an offence unlawfully to evict a residential occupier unless it is reasonably believed that he no longer lives in the premises (PEA 1977, s 1).

Except in the case of an excluded licence or tenancy, eviction will be unlawful if a residential occupier is evicted otherwise than by means of a court order.

Residential occupier

Protection is given to residential occupiers as defined in s 1(1) of the PEA 1977. These are persons occupying the premises as a residence 'whether under a contract or by virtue of any enactment or rule of law giving him the right to remain in occupation or restricting the right of any other person to recover possession of the premises'. The definition thus includes all tenants, whether they are protected tenants under the RA 1977, assured or assured shorthold tenants under the HA 1988, secure tenants under HA 1985 or whether they have no statutory protection at all. The use of the term 'contract' will also include contractual licensees within these protections.

36.2.2 Protection from harassment

The offences

There are two offences of harassment laid down by PEA 1977: one requires intent on the part of the offender and is set out in s 1(3); the other is contained in s 1(3A) and requires only knowledge or belief. In both cases, protection is given to residential occupiers as defined in s 1(1) of the PEA 1977 (see **36.2.1**). The actions amounting to harassment would include, for example, removing doors and windows, disconnecting services, and acts and threats of violence.

Section 1(3) harassment

It is an offence to do acts likely to interfere with the peace or comfort of a residential occupier or to withhold services reasonably required for the occupation of the premises with intent to cause the residential occupier to give up the occupation of the premises. Problems are caused by the need to prove intent although it might be possible to infer intent if the particular result could be foreseen as the natural consequence of the actions in question.

Section 1(3A) harassment

It is an offence for a landlord to do acts likely to interfere with the peace and comfort of a residential occupier, or withhold services reasonably required for the occupation of the premises, if he knows or has reasonable cause to believe that the conduct is likely to cause the residential occupier to give up the occupation of the premises. As no specific intent is required for this offence, it may be easier to establish than s 1(3) harassment; this was certainly the intention of the legislature. It is a defence to the withholding of services if this can be justified on 'reasonable grounds'.

36.3 CRIMINAL SANCTIONS: THE CRIMINAL LAW ACT 1977

Under s 6(1) of the Criminal Law Act 1977, any person who 'without lawful authority' uses, or threatens to use, violence to secure entry to premises commits an offence if there is someone present on those premises at the time who is opposed to the entry.

36.4 CIVIL PROCEEDINGS

36.4.1 Why take civil proceedings?

Criminal sanctions will often not be an adequate remedy for a dispossessed or threatened occupier. The occupier may want an injunction to restrain future actions on the part of the landlord or to restore the tenant to possession of the property; compensation awarded in criminal proceedings is often not as much as would be ordered in civil proceedings. Damages and injunctions are available in civil proceedings in the county court and often provide a more effective and speedy remedy; if need be, emergency procedures can be followed in order to obtain immediate relief.

36.4.2 Causes of action

Alternative causes of action

Various causes of action are available to dispossessed or harassed tenants, some statutory, and some based upon the common law, depending upon the precise facts of the case in question. It is sensible to plead as many alternative causes of action as reasonably present themselves in the circumstances. Actions in both contract and tort may be possible.

Actions for breach of contract

BREACH OF THE COVENANT FOR QUIET ENJOYMENT

It is an implied term of every tenancy that the landlord will allow his tenant 'quiet enjoyment' of the premises. The obligation is for the landlord to allow the tenant peaceable, uninterrupted enjoyment of the property. Unlawful eviction and most actions of harassment will be a breach of this covenant. Thus, knocking on the tenant's door and shouting threats would be a breach of this implied term.

BREACH OF CONTRACT IN GENERAL

Any other breach of a term of the tenancy or licence agreement will be actionable by the occupier. So if a landlord evicts a tenant before the ending of the tenancy, he is in breach of contract. Similarly, if the landlord agrees to provide gas and electricity to a house and then withdraws these facilities, he is again liable for a breach of contract.

Actions in tort

TRESPASS TO LAND

A tenant has the right to the exclusive possession of the demised premises. If the landlord enters onto those premises without permission, he is liable as a trespasser. Licensees who do not have the right to exclusive possession probably cannot sue in trespass.

TRESPASS TO THE PERSON

Harassment and unlawful eviction are frequently accompanied by violence or threats of violence. These may well amount to the torts of assault and battery. A battery is the infliction of physical violence on another without lawful excuse; assault is any act which puts a person in immediate and reasonable fear of a battery. This cause of action will be available both to tenants and to licensees.

TRESPASS TO GOODS

In the process of harassing or evicting an occupier, a landlord frequently damages the occupier's furniture or other personal belongings. This would amount to trespass to goods. If the landlord detains or otherwise deprives the occupier of the use of the goods, this might amount to the tort of conversion. Both tenants and licensees can use this cause of action.

PEA 1977, s 3

Section 3 of the PEA 1977 provides that when a tenancy or licence which is not 'statutorily protected' comes to an end, but the former tenant continues to reside in the premises, he cannot be evicted without a court order. Any eviction of such a tenant will give rise to an action in tort for breach of statutory duty. The definition of 'statutorily protected tenancy' excludes from the protection of this section assured and assured shorthold tenancies under the HA 1988 and protected tenancies under the RA 1977.

Breach of the HA 1988, s 27

Section 27 of the HA 1988 creates a statutory tort if a landlord:

(1) attempts unlawfully to deprive a residential occupier of his occupation; or

(2) knowing or having reasonable cause to believe that the conduct is likely to cause a residential occupier to give up his occupation, does acts likely to interfere with the peace or comfort of the residential occupier or members of his household,

and (in either case) as a result the residential occupier gives up his occupation.

For definition of 'residential occupier' see **36.2.1**. Note, in particular, that it will include licensees. This tort is satisfied only if the residential occupier actually gives up occupation; this cause of action cannot be used for harassment that does not cause the occupier to leave. Further, there will be no liability under s 27 if the occupier is reinstated in the property either by the landlord or on an order of the court. It is a defence to this action if the landlord can prove that he believed and had reasonable cause to believe that the occupier had ceased to reside in the premises, or that he had reasonable grounds for doing the acts complained of.

Chapter 37

REPAIRS TO RESIDENTIAL PROPERTIES

37.1 INTRODUCTION

Chapter 37 contents
Introduction
Who is liable for repair?
**Landlord and Tenant Act
1985, s 11**

The issue of repairs may arise in various contexts. The most common is where the tenant complains that work needs doing to the house or flat, for example, that a leaking roof or defective gutter is causing dampness. The question may also arise in a rent arrears case where the tenant has refused to pay rent because of an alleged disrepair; or in a personal injury case where the tenant (or a visitor) has been injured by reason of defective premises.

The first question to be considered is the meaning of the word 'repair'. The basic definition of 'repair' is not affected by the nature of the property involved and so reference should be made to the chapter on repairs in the Commercial Leases part of the book (Chapter 17).

37.2 WHO IS LIABLE FOR REPAIR?

37.2.1 Position at common law

In the absence of any express provisions in the lease or tenancy agreement, the landlord gives no warranty that the premises will be fit for habitation or that he will repair them.

There are two exceptions.

(1) *Furnished lettings*: where there is a furnished letting, the landlord impliedly warrants that the premises are fit for habitation at the commencement of the term. This is a very limited exception based on the case of *Smith v Marrable* [1843] 11 M&W 5, where a furnished house was infested with bugs. It was held that the tenant could repudiate the tenancy and recover damages for loss suffered. However, there is no continuing obligation on the part of the landlord to keep the premises fit for habitation during the term.

(2) *Common parts*: in certain cases, the courts may imply a covenant to give business efficacy to a lease or tenancy. For example, if the premises consist of a tower block containing lifts, staircases, rubbish chutes and other common parts and the tenancy agreements of the individual flats do not impose obligations on either the tenant or landlord to maintain the common parts, the court may hold that, since the terms of the tenancy agreement are obviously incomplete, and that the premises cannot function without such common parts being maintained, the landlord must have impliedly taken responsibility to keep them in reasonable condition: see *Liverpool City Council v Irwin* [1977] AC 239. However, such implied term is not automatic and depends on the facts of each particular case and is based on the contractual principle that the courts may imply a term to make a contract function. If the lease or tenancy agreement expressly deals with these matters, there is clearly no room for an implied term.

As regards the tenant, there are no implied repairing obligations on his part at common law so that, in the absence of an express agreement, the tenant is not responsible for repair as such. However, a tenant must not commit waste. A tenant under a fixed-term lease is liable for both voluntary and permissive waste. This means that he must not carry out alterations or allow the property to fall into serious disrepair. A yearly periodic tenant is, however, only liable to keep the premises 'wind and water tight'. A weekly tenant on the other hand is not liable for permissive waste but must use the premises in 'a tenant-like manner'. This means that he must take proper care of them, for example, by unblocking drains, cleaning chimneys, mending fuses and doing the little jobs around the house that a reasonable tenant would do. The position at common law is not satisfactory from either the landlord's or the tenant's point of view. The question of repairing liability is, therefore, usually either dealt with expressly by the terms of the tenancy agreement or covered by some statutory provision. If a matter is covered both by an express obligation and also by a statutory provision, and the express obligation is in conflict with the statutory obligation, the statutory obligation prevails.

37.2.2 Express covenants

In many cases the lease or tenancy agreement will expressly set out the repairing obligations of the parties. Subject to the statutory provisions mentioned below, the parties are free to agree who should be liable for which repairs. For example, it may have been agreed that the landlord will be liable for exterior repairs and that the tenant will be liable for interior repairs and decoration. If the lease or tenancy agreement sets out these obligations expressly, those provisions will override the common law and will be enforceable, subject only to statutory intervention.

37.2.3 Modification by statute

Despite the presence or absence of express repairing obligations, the LTA 1985 implies certain repairing obligations on the part of the landlord which cannot be excluded except with leave of the court. These statutory implied terms are important and must now be considered.

37.3 LANDLORD AND TENANT ACT 1985, s 11

37.3.1 Leases to which s 11 applies

Section 11 of the LTA 1985 applies to any lease or agreement for lease of a dwelling house, granted on or after 24 October 1961, if the term is less than 7 years. This includes periodic tenancies even if the tenant has been in occupation for more than 7 years. It also applies to a fixed-term lease granted for more than 7 years if the landlord can determine the term within the first 7 years, ie there is a break clause in the landlord's favour. However, s 11 does not apply to a lease for less than 7 years if it contains an option for renewal by the tenant where the term can be extended to more than 7 years. No contracting out is allowed unless sanctioned by the county court. This includes indirect contracting out, for example, by placing an obligation on the tenant to pay money in lieu of repairs.

37.3.2 The implied terms

There is an implied covenant by the landlord:

(1) to keep in repair the structure and exterior of the dwelling house (including drains, gutters and external pipes); and

(2) to keep in repair and proper working order the installations in the dwelling house for the supply of water, gas and electricity and for sanitation (including basins, sinks, baths and sanitary conveniences but not other fixtures, fittings and appliances for making use of the supply of water, gas or electricity); and

(3) to keep in repair and proper working order the installations in the dwelling house for space heating and heating water.

37.3.3 'Structure and exterior'

The word 'structure' is not defined by the Act but would clearly include the main fabric of the building such as the main walls, roof, timbers and foundations as distinguished from decorations or fittings. The word 'exterior' is not defined either, but has been held to include paths or steps which form an essential means of access (*Brown v Liverpool Corporation* [1969] 3 All ER 1345) but not paving in the back yard (*Hopwood v Cannock Chase District Council* [1975] 1 WLR 373) nor a footpath at the rear of the house (*King v South Northamptonshire District Council* [1992] 06 EG 152). The words 'structure and exterior' can cause particular problems where a tenant in a block of flats is seeking to force the landlord to do repairs in respect of common parts or to the entire block rather than just the particular flat occupied by the complaining tenant.

It was held in *Campden Hill Towers v Gardner* [1977] QB 823 that the landlord's implied covenant extends only to the flat in question and not to the entire block; it extends to the outside of the inner party wall of the flat, the outer side of the horizontal division between the flat and the flats below and above but does not extend to the entire building. This problem has now been resolved by an amendment made by the HA 1988 but only in respect of leases or tenancies granted on or after 15 January 1989. The position now is that reference to 'dwelling house' in s 11 is extended to include any part of the building in which the landlord has an estate or interest and that any references to 'installations' in the dwelling house include installations directly or indirectly serving the house forming part of the same building or which are owned or under the control of the landlord. Thus, for leases granted on or after 15 January 1989 where the landlord owns the entire block, the landlord will be under an obligation to maintain the structure and exterior of the entire block including common parts and the stipulated facilities. However, it is expressly provided that the landlord is not liable unless the disrepair is such as to affect the tenant's enjoyment of the flat or common parts in question. As to the position with regard to common parts in the case of tenancies granted before 15 January 1989, see **37.2.1**.

37.3.4 'Installations in the dwelling house'

The landlord is also obliged to repair and keep in working order the installations for the supply of water, gas, electricity, sanitation, space heating and water heating. The section does not oblige the landlord to provide these facilities but simply to maintain such as exist at the commencement of the tenancy. Thus, if the house does not have these facilities to begin with there is no obligation on the part of the landlord to provide the necessary installations. Further, it applies only to installations that are actually within the house. If a fault occurs in a supply installation outside the house this is not within the section. However, in the case of flats, where the tenancy was granted on or after 15 January 1989, the obligation extends to installations within the entire building which the landlord owns or to installations within the building over which the landlord has control. Thus, if a flat is centrally heated by a communal boiler in the basement and the boiler breaks down, liability under the section will depend on when the tenancy commenced. If the tenancy commenced prior to 15 January 1989, the landlord will not be liable (under the section) whereas if the tenancy was granted on or after that date the landlord will be liable.

37.3.5 Standards of repair

The section provides that in determining the standards of repair regard must be had to the age, character and prospective life of the dwelling and the locality in which it is situated (LTA 1985, s 11(3)). Thus, a house in a poor condition at the commencement of the tenancy, in an area of poor quality housing, does not need to be comprehensively repaired under s 11. 'Patching' repairs may satisfy the section depending on the circumstances of each particular case.

37.3.6 Exceptions

There are some specific exceptions to liability under s 11.

Under s 11(2) the covenant does not extend to:

(1) repairs for which the tenant is liable by virtue of his duty to use the premises in a tenant-like manner;
(2) rebuilding or reinstating the premises in the case of destruction or damage by fire or by tempest or other accident;
(3) keeping in repair or maintaining anything that the tenant is entitled to remove from the dwelling house (tenant's fixtures).

Further, the landlord is not liable unless he has notice of the need for repair. Thus, in *O'Brien v Robinson* [1973] AC 912 the plaintiffs were injured when the ceiling of their flat fell on them. This was found to be the result of a latent defect. The landlords were not liable for the personal injuries caused to the plaintiffs since there had been no breach of the duty of repair under s 11 in that the landlord did not know of this latent defect at the material time. However, this requirement for notice applies only to those premises or parts of premises actually demised to the tenant. There is no need for notice in respect of those parts of the premises which remain in the possession or control of the landlord. This will be particularly relevant in relation to the extension of the landlord's liability to the whole of a building made by the HA 1988 (see **37.3.3**).

Chapter 38

ENFRANCHISEMENT: LONG LEASES OF HOUSES

38.1 INTRODUCTION

The LRA 1967 confers on certain tenants holding long leases of houses the right to acquire the freehold (and superior leasehold reversions) on their properties. Alternatively, they can acquire an extended lease. For these rights to apply, various conditions must be fulfilled. The qualifying conditions in the 1967 Act were amended by the Commonhold and Leasehold Reform Act 2002 in respect of applications received on or after 26 July 2002. This book sets out the conditions applicable as from that date. In particular, the former requirements that the lease must be at a low rent and that the tenant must have resided in the house for at least 3 years, have been removed.

Chapter 38 contents
Introduction
The qualifying conditions in outline
Enfranchisement or extended lease
Terms of the conveyance of the freehold
The price of the freehold

38.2 THE QUALIFYING CONDITIONS IN OUTLINE

There are three major requirements:

(1) there must be a 'house';
(2) let on a 'long lease';
(3) tenanted by a 'qualifying tenant'.

38.2.1 'A house'

The LRA 1967 applies only to houses and not to flats.

Section 2(1) of the LRA 1967 defines a house as:

> 'For the purposes of this Part of this Act, "house" includes any building designed or adapted for living in and reasonably so called, notwithstanding that the building is not structurally detached, or was not or is not solely designed or adapted for living in, or is divided horizontally into flats or maisonettes.'

This definition includes ordinary purpose-built houses, and it can include buildings which were not originally houses (eg barns, warehouses, stables, etc) later converted or adapted as houses.

The main problem area is deciding what is a house 'reasonably so called'. This definition can cause problems in relation to shops with living accommodation above and also with properties which have been converted into flats.

As regards shops with living accommodation, the leading authority is the House of Lords' decision in the case of *Tandon v Trustees of Spurgeons Homes* [1982] AC 755, which concerned a purpose-built shop with a flat above. Approximately 75% of the property was attributed to the shop and 25% to the living accommodation. By a majority decision, it was held that the premises were a house reasonably so called even though it was also reasonable to call them something else, ie a shop! It is a question of law whether it is reasonable to call a building a house, but if the building is designed or adapted for living in, in exceptional circumstances only will a judge be justified in holding that it is not reasonable to call it a house.

Another problem concerns buildings which are converted into flats. Many properties which were originally houses have been converted into flats. An individual flat cannot be a house but, nevertheless, the whole building may retain its characteristics as a house. For example, if a house is converted into two self-contained flats by the owner of a long lease who continues to occupy one of the flats, sub-letting the other, the long leaseholder may be in a position to enfranchise. The building looked at as a whole may still reasonably be called a house notwithstanding the internal sub-division.

38.2.2 'Long lease'

Section 3 of the LRA 1967 defines a long lease as a 'tenancy granted for a term of years certain exceeding 21 years'. It is the length of the original term that matters. The fact that less than 21 years remains unexpired when the rights are exercised is not relevant to this particular issue. Further, the fact that the lease may be terminated before it runs 21 years (eg by forfeiture, break clause, etc) is to be ignored. If the long lease has expired but the tenant holds over under another tenancy of the property, the new tenancy is deemed to be a long lease (subject to exceptions).

38.2.3 'Qualifying tenant'

The LRA 1967 does not use the expression 'qualifying tenant' but it does impose certain minimum requirements which must be satisfied before the tenant 'qualifies' for enfranchisement or an extended lease. The tenant must, at the date when he serves the appropriate notice (see **38.3.1**) exercising his rights, have had the lease vested in him for at least 2 years.

38.3 ENFRANCHISEMENT OR EXTENDED LEASE

The tenant who satisfies the above conditions will normally wish to enfranchise. This means that the landlord must convey the fee simple to the tenant at a price, and on the terms, referred to in the LRA 1967. Alternatively, the tenant may elect to take an extended lease. Here, the landlord must grant the tenant a new lease for the unexpired residue of the term of the existing lease plus a further 50 years. The new lease will be, broadly, on the same terms as the existing lease and the rent will be the same until the expiry date of the existing lease, but thereafter, the rent will be replaced by a modern ground rent (reviewed after 25 years of the extra 50 years).

38.3.1 Desire notice

The tenant must serve written notice of his desire ('the desire notice') in the prescribed form to have either the freehold or an extended lease. This desire notice is normally the first step in the procedure to obtain the rights granted by the Act. The desire notice is deemed to be an estate contract and it should, therefore, be protected by an appropriate registration under the Land Charges Act 1972 or the LRA 1925 as the case may be. The landlord must, within 2 months, serve a Notice in Reply admitting or objecting to the tenant's claim. For the detailed procedure, reference should be made to the Act and the regulations made under it.

Although the desire notice is deemed to create an estate contract, it is generally personal to the tenant and is not assignable to third parties. However, if the tenant assigns the lease, he can assign the benefit of the desire notice at the same time to the assignee of the lease. The assignee could then proceed with the acquisition of the freehold or an extended lease even though the assignee does not qualify under the Act (LRA 1967, s 5).

38.4 TERMS OF THE CONVEYANCE OF THE FREEHOLD

The conveyance (or transfer if the landlord's title is registered) will be subject to:

(1) the tenancy; and
(2) tenant's incumbrances but free from other incumbrances.

The broad effect of this is that the tenant will be bound by any mortgages or charges which have been created in respect of the leasehold interest, but will take free from mortgages or charges created by the landlord over the freehold interest.

The conveyance will grant and reserve, broadly, the same easements as existed under the lease.

Disputes about the terms of the conveyance (other than as to price) are resolved by the court.

38.5 THE PRICE OF THE FREEHOLD

The LRA 1967 lays down the principles and formulae for ascertaining the price and the appeals machinery if it cannot be agreed between the parties.

There are two methods of ascertaining the price depending on the value of the house and premises. They are dealt with by s 9(1) and s 9(1A) of the LRA 1967 respectively.

The valuation under s 9(1) is very favourable to the tenant. It must be assumed for valuation purposes that the landlord is selling the freehold subject to the lease and on the assumption that this had been extended for a further 50 years under the Act and assuming the tenant is not the buyer. It is thus looked at as if the freehold is being bought largely for its investment income (which, by definition, is likely to be fairly small). The fact that the tenant can, on acquisition, merge the freehold and leasehold interests is ignored. This 'marriage value', as it is sometimes called, is not taken into account under s 9(1).

The valuation under s 9(1) only applies to lower value properties. For higher value properties, a much less favourable formula has to be used. This not only requires marriage value to be taken into account, but also requires an assumption that the tenant has no right to extend the lease under LRA 1967. Both these assumptions will result in a considerably higher price being paid than if the lower value formula were to be used. The method of deciding whether a house falls into the lower or higher value bands depends upon whether the house had a rateable value on 31 March 1990. If it did (and most houses in existence at that date would have had a rateable value), then the rule is that houses with rateable values of £500 or less (£1,000 or less if the house is in Greater London) will be classed as lower value. Any other houses will be classed as higher value. Owing to the abolition of domestic rates, it is not possible to use rateable value as a deciding factor for houses not rated on 31 March 1990, ie basically houses built since that date. For these houses, a complex formula is applied based on the premium originally paid on the grant and the length of the term, for which, see s 1(1)(a)(i) of the LRA 1967 (as amended).

In addition to the purchase price, the tenant must pay all reasonable legal and valuation fees incurred by the landlord. Disputes as to price are dealt with by the Leasehold Valuation Tribunal.

Chapter 39

LANDLORD AND TENANT ACT 1987

39.1 INTRODUCTION

Under the LTA 1987, if a landlord of a building composed of flats wishes to dispose of his freehold reversion he is obliged, subject to the conditions specified in the Act, to offer it first to the relevant tenants.

Further, in the case of 'bad management' by the landlord the court can, in certain circumstances, compel the landlord to transfer his interest to the tenants.

However, the main impact of the Act is the so-called 'tenant's right of first refusal'. The relevant law is contained in Part I of the Act. This has been almost entirely substituted by the HA 1996, with the object of making it easier for tenants to enforce their rights. Criminal sanctions have also been imposed for landlords who evade the Act.

Chapter 39 contents
Introduction
The tenant's right of first refusal
Compulsory acquisition of the reversion

39.2 THE TENANT'S RIGHT OF FIRST REFUSAL

There are four major conditions before tenants can claim the pre-emption rights conferred by Part I of the Act:

(1) the premises must come within the Act;
(2) the landlord must not be an exempt landlord;
(3) the tenant must be a qualifying tenant; and
(4) there must be a proposed 'relevant disposal'.

39.2.1 The premises

The premises must consist of a building divided into at least two flats occupied by 'qualifying tenants' where not more than 50% of the floor area is used for non-residential purposes. Thus, if there are shops on the ground floor with flats above, the Act will not apply if the floor area of the shops exceeds the floor area of the flats.

39.2.2 The landlord

Certain landlords are excluded from the Act. These are mainly public sector landlords, for example, local authorities, the Housing Corporation and certain housing associations. In the private sector, resident landlords are excluded. A resident landlord is a landlord who lives in part of the building (not being a purpose-built block of flats) and who occupies a flat in the premises as his only or principal home and who has occupied it for at least 12 months.

Subject to the above, the landlord is the tenant's immediate landlord but if that landlord does not own the freehold or a reversion of at least 7 years then the superior landlord is also regarded as a landlord for the purposes of the Act.

39.2.3 Qualifying tenants

A tenant is a qualifying tenant unless his tenancy falls into one of the following categories:

(1) a protected shorthold tenancy;
(2) a business tenancy under Part II of the LTA 1954;
(3) a tenancy terminable on cessation of employment;
(4) an assured tenancy under the HA 1988.

So which tenancies will be qualifying? Although there is no requirement for a qualifying tenant to have a long lease, the exclusion of assured tenancies in practical terms dictates that most qualifying tenants will be long leaseholders at low rents. However, any surviving RA 1977 tenants will also qualify, as these are not excluded from the definition.

39.2.4 Relevant disposal

A relevant disposal is the disposal of any estate or interest in the premises which is not excluded from the Act. The exclusions consist of the following:

(1) the grant of a tenancy of a single flat;
(2) the grant of a mortgage, although a sale by a lender in exercise of his power of sale would be a relevant disposal;
(3) a disposal to a trustee in bankruptcy or liquidator;
(4) transfers ordered by the court in connection with matrimonial or succession proceedings;
(5) a disposal following a compulsory purchase order;
(6) a gift to a member of the landlord's family or to a charity;
(7) the surrender of a lease in pursuance of a provision in the lease to that effect;
(8) a disposal to the Crown;
(9) a disposal within a group of companies which have been associated for at least 2 years.

If the landlord proposes to make a relevant disposal (as defined above), he must serve notice on the qualifying tenants detailing the proposed terms, including the price, and stating that the notice constitutes an offer to dispose of the property to them on these terms and certain other particulars. If more than 50% of the qualifying tenants decide to accept the offer, they must do so within the period stated by the notice which must be not less than 2 months. The purchasing tenants are then given a further 2 months in which to nominate a person who will purchase the landlord's interest on the tenants' behalf, for example, a limited company formed for that purpose. If the tenants do not elect to purchase within the first 2 months or do not make a nomination within the second 2 months or if the tenants fail to complete within 3 months, the landlord is free to proceed with the disposal elsewhere.

If the landlord makes a disposal without complying with the Act, the tenants have a right of acquisition against the buyer. Thus, a buyer from a landlord falling within the Act should always ensure the requisite notices have been served and the time-limits complied with before the relevant disposal proceeds.

39.2.5 Anti-avoidance measures – HA 1996

As originally drafted, the LTA 1987 did not impose any real sanctions for landlords who failed to comply with its provisions and some freeholders sought to exploit ways round the legislation. The HA 1996 attempts to solve these omissions.

A new s 10A is inserted into the LTA 1987 which makes it a criminal offence not to notify the tenants of a proposal to make a relevant disposal. New provisions are also inserted making it clear that a contract to make a relevant disposal is itself a relevant disposal and making it easier for tenants to enforce their rights both against a disposing landlord and against a person who takes the property under a disposal not complying with the Act.

39.3 COMPULSORY ACQUISITION OF THE REVERSION

Part I of the Act applies where the landlord wishes to dispose of his reversion, but under Part III of the Act the landlord can, in certain circumstances, be forced to sell his interest to the tenants against his wishes. Part III applies where there has been a history of bad management by the landlord. The detailed rules are complex and are beyond the scope of this book.

Chapter 40

LEASEHOLD REFORM, HOUSING AND URBAN DEVELOPMENT ACT 1993

40.1 INTRODUCTION

Chapter 40 contents
Introduction
Collective
  enfranchisement
Individual acquisition of
  a long lease

Tenants of flats have traditionally been excluded from the benefits of enfranchisement afforded to other long leaseholders (see Chapter 38). One major problem has always been the need to ensure the proper management and repair of a block of flats. This might prove difficult between freehold flat-owners. There is also the question as to who would own the common parts of the block. The LRHUDA 1993 has now given to flat-owners a collective right to enfranchise, the freehold in the whole block being acquired by a nominee on behalf of the individual tenants. It also contains an alternative right for individual tenants to purchase a new lease running until 90 years after the term date of their original lease. Tenants under long leases of flats (and houses) do, in any event, have a right under the LTA 1954, Part I (as amended) to remain in possession following the ending of their leases, basically as assured tenants under the HA 1988. Although flat tenants do thus have security of tenure at the end of their long leases, this is only at a price. As an assured tenant, they will be required to pay the full open market rent for their flat. This will be fixed, without taking into account any premium which was paid on the acquisition of the lease.

The qualifying conditions under the 1993 Act were amended by the Commonhold and Leasehold Reform Act 2002 in respect of applications received on or after 26 July 2002. This book sets out the conditions applicable as from that date. When further provisions of the 2002 Act are brought into force (probably during 2003), it will then be mandatory for the enfranchisement to be effected by a 'right to enfranchise' (RTE) company. This will be a private company, limited by guarantee, with articles and memorandum in a form prescribed by the Secretary of State.

40.2 COLLECTIVE ENFRANCHISEMENT

40.2.1 The right

Collective enfranchisement consists of the tenants in a block of flats acquiring the freehold in the block, the freehold being conveyed into the name of a nominee on their behalf. This conveyance can take place without the landlord's consent, although there are limited grounds on which the landlord can resist a claim (see **40.2.4**). For the right to exist, various conditions must also be fulfilled. In particular, the tenants must be 'qualifying tenants' of 'flats' which are themselves in 'premises', all as defined by the Act.

For the right to be available, 'qualifying tenants' must hold at least two-thirds of the total number of flats in the premises. The premises in question, therefore, need not be let exclusively to tenants on long leases; some of the flats might be let to HA 1988 tenants, for example. Equally, the premises need not be let exclusively for residential purposes, but see **40.2.16**.

40.2.2 Nature of the collective right

The right to collective enfranchisement is the right to have the freehold in the premises acquired on behalf of the participating qualifying tenants by a person or persons appointed by them at a price to be determined in accordance with the Act.

40.2.3 Exercise of the collective right

As stated in **40.2.1**, at least two-thirds of the flats in a block must be held by 'qualifying tenants' before the collective right arises. However, it is not necessary for all of the qualifying tenants in the block to be involved in the enfranchisement. The right to enfranchise is exercised by the service of the appropriate notice on the reversioner and to be valid, the tenants serving the notice must occupy at least one half of the flats in the block. When further provisions of the Commonhold and Leasehold Reform Act 2002 are brought into force (probably during 2003), the right to enfranchise will only be exercisable by a 'right to enfranchise' company. This will be a company limited by guarantee with articles and memorandum in a prescribed form. Membership of the company is limited to the qualifying tenants, and at least half of the qualifying tenants in the block must be members of the company.

40.2.4 Landlord's grounds for opposition

A landlord can dispute the right to enfranchise if he can establish that one or more of the qualifying conditions have not been complied with by the applicants, for example, if two-thirds of the flats in the block are not held by qualifying tenants. Apart from this, his only ground of opposition will be if he can establish that he intends to redevelop the whole or a substantial part of the premises. Such a ground for opposition will only be possible, however, where not less than two-thirds of the long leases in the block are due to terminate within 5 years and the landlord cannot reasonably carry out his redevelopment without obtaining possession.

40.2.5 Qualifying tenants

A person will be a 'qualifying tenant' for collective enfranchisement if he is a 'tenant' of a 'flat' under a 'long lease'.

'Tenant' is defined to include a person holding a lease or tenancy or an agreement for a lease or tenancy; and lease and tenancy includes a sub-lease and a sub-tenancy. Joint leaseholders are treated together as a single tenant.

'Flat' means a separate set of premises, whether or not on the same floor, which forms part of a building, and is constructed or adapted for use as a dwelling, and either the whole or some material part lies above or below some other part of the building. The emphasis in the definition is to at least part of the flat being above or below some other part of the building. Thus, flats above shops etc will be included in this definition, but 'granny flats', or similar premises, which consist of an extension to an existing building, but are not above or below part of that building, will not be within the definition. This part of the definition ties in with the definition of a house for the purposes of the LRA 1967 (see Chapter 38).

'Long lease' is defined to mean, inter alia:

(1) a lease granted for a term of years certain exceeding 21 years. Any provisions for determination within that period, whether by landlord or by tenant, and whether by forfeiture or otherwise, will not prevent the lease from being a long lease;

(2) a new tenancy granted expressly or impliedly to a tenant on the expiry of a long lease at a low rent will itself be deemed to be a long lease irrespective of its length. Similarly, where a lease is being continued under the terms of Part I of the LTA 1954, it will be included in the definition of a long lease.

40.2.6 Qualifying tenants: exclusions

A person will not be a qualifying tenant if:

(1) his lease is within Part II of the LTA 1954 (business tenancies);

(2) his immediate landlord is a charitable housing trust and the flat forms part of the accommodation provided by it for its charitable purposes;

(3) the lease is an unlawful sub-lease out of a superior lease which is not itself a long lease at a low rent.

40.2.7 Premises: definition

The flats must be in premises, as defined. Premises are defined as a self-contained building or as a self-contained part of a building.

A building is a self-contained building if it is structurally detached; part of a building is a self-contained part if it consists of a vertical division of the building and its structure is such that that part could be redeveloped independently of the remainder. In addition, the services provided for the occupiers (by pipes, cables, etc) are or could be provided independently of the services provided for the rest of the building.

40.2.8 Premises: exclusions

The 'premises' need not be used exclusively for residential purposes, provided that any parts occupied or intended to be occupied for non-residential purposes do not exceed 25% of the internal floor area of the premises as a whole. In making this calculation, any common parts of the building are to be ignored.

Premises will not be included within the definition if they have a resident landlord. There will be a resident landlord if, at any time, the freeholder or an adult member of his family occupies a flat in the premises as his only or principal home and has done so for at least the previous 12 months. However, this exclusion does not apply if the premises contain more than four units or are a purpose-built block of flats. Nor, as from 26 July 2002, does it apply unless the same person has owned the freehold since before the conversion. In these cases, the Act will still apply even though there is a resident landlord.

40.2.9 Interests included in the collective right

The acquisition will cover not only the freehold of the premises in which the flats are situated, but also any garages, etc let with the flats and any surrounding grounds over which the flat owners have easements, for example for access or for parking.

40.2.10 Interests excluded from the collective right

The freeholder can retain the title to any underlying minerals, provided that proper provision is made for the support of the premises.

40.2.11 Interests to be leased back

The freeholder can also retain, by means of a lease-back arrangement, certain parts of the acquired premises. The following must be leased back:

(1) flats let by the freeholder on secure tenancies;
(2) flats let by housing associations on tenancies other than secure tenancies.

The following are to be leased back if the freeholder so requires:

(1) units which are not flats let to qualifying tenants. This could include any part of the premises which are let on a business tenancy, or on tenancies which are not long leases at a low rent; it will also include unlet flats;
(2) a flat occupied by a resident landlord.

40.2.12 Terms of the lease back

There are detailed provisions dealing with the terms of any lease to be granted back to the freeholder (see Sch 8 to the Act). Basically, unless the parties agree otherwise, or the Residential Property Tribunal otherwise directs, they are to be 999-year leases at a peppercorn rent with appropriate appurtenant rights, landlord's covenant for repair, rebuilding and insurance and service charge provisions.

40.2.13 Enfranchisement price (Sch 5)

The price to be paid for the freehold will be the total of three separate elements:

(1) market value;
(2) half of the marriage value;
(3) compensation.

Where the freehold and intermediate leases are being acquired, each interest is to be valued and paid for separately, so the market value, marriage value and any compensation for each individual interest being acquired will need to be calculated and paid over to the respective owner. In addition, the reasonable costs of each respective owner will be payable.

40.2.14 Market value

Market value is the price which might be expected to be realised if the property was sold on the open market by a willing seller, with neither the nominee buyer nor any participating tenant seeking to buy. Any defects in the landlord's title will thus serve to reduce the value of his interest as they would on any other sale. The following assumptions (inter alia) are also to be made in arriving at the market value of the interest:

(1) on the assumption that the seller is selling the fee simple:

    (a) subject to any leases subject to which the freeholder's interest is to be acquired by the buyer; but

(b) subject also to any intermediate or other leasehold interests in the premises which are to be acquired by the buyer;

(2) on the assumption that the Act confers no rights to acquire the premises or to acquire a new lease;

(3) on the assumption that any increase in value caused by improvements carried out by any participating tenant is to be disregarded.

40.2.15 Marriage value

Marriage value is a complex valuation principle and follows from the fact that when both leasehold and freehold interests in a property become vested in the same person then the value of those interests to that person will be more than the combined value of the interests when held by different persons. It is, of course, generally the case that a freehold subject to a tenancy will be worth a lot less than the same freehold when vacant possession is available. So, to give an example, if the freehold when held by X is worth £30,000 and the leasehold interest when held by Y £40,000, it may well be that when Y also acquires the freehold the value of the property may now be £110,000, ie £40,000 more than the sum total of freehold and leasehold interests when owned by different people. This £40,000 is the marriage value and the landlord is entitled to one half of it. However, the landlord is not entitled to any share of the marriage value in the case of leases having more than 80 years unexpired.

40.2.16 Compensation

The third element in assessing the price is compensation to the freeholder for any loss or damage he may suffer by result of the enfranchisement. This will include any diminution in the value of any other property owned by the landlord, including loss of development value. This is to cover the situation, for example, where the landlord is now unable to redevelop his adjoining property due to the fact that he no longer is the owner of the enfranchised premises.

40.3 INDIVIDUAL ACQUISITION OF A LONG LEASE

40.3.1 Nature of the right

The right given is the right to be granted a new lease to expire 90 years after the expiry date of the tenant's existing lease. This new lease is to be at a peppercorn rent, but the tenant must pay a premium to be calculated as laid down by the Act. The new lease is to take effect immediately in substitution for the tenant's existing lease. This right is available whether or not the right to collective enfranchisement is also available. The new lease will be binding upon the landlord's lenders even if the existing lease was granted in breach of the terms of the mortgage.

40.3.2 Entitlement to a new lease

Entitlement to a new lease is given to a tenant if:

(1) he is a qualifying tenant; and

(2) the lease has been vested in him for at least the previous 2 years.

The definition of qualifying tenant is the same as for the purposes of enfranchisement (see **40.2.5**).

40.3.3 Refusal of new lease

The landlord can obtain a court order declaring that the tenant's right to a new lease is not exercisable, where the court is satisfied that:

(1) the tenant's existing lease is due to terminate within 5 years from the date of the tenant requesting a new lease; and

(2) the landlord intends, once the existing lease has expired, to demolish or reconstruct the whole or a substantial part of the premises and he could not reasonably do so without obtaining possession of the flat.

40.3.4 Terms of the new lease

The new lease is to be on the same terms as the existing lease except as to:

(1) the rent, which will be a peppercorn;

(2) the term, which will be for a period to end 90 years after the term date of the existing lease;

(3) the omission of property comprised in the existing lease but not comprised in the flat. However, for these purposes, 'flat' includes any garage, outhouse, garden or yard let to the tenant with the flat;

(4) the inclusion, where the existing lease is inadequate, of provisions for variable service charges in respect of repairs, services, maintenance and insurance;

(5) the inclusion of a statement that the lease has been granted under these provisions;

(6) the omission of any options or pre-emptions contained in the existing lease;

(7) limitation of the landlord's liability under his covenants to breaches for which he is personally responsible;

(8) modifications to reflect defects in the existing lease or other provisions which it would be unreasonable to include without modification;

(9) the reservation of a right for the landlord to apply to the court for possession for redevelopment purposes during the last 12 months of the term of the original lease or during the last 5 years of the new lease, subject to compensation being payable.

40.3.5 The amount of the premium

Complex provisions are laid down for the calculation of the premium. Briefly, the premium is to be the aggregate of:

(1) the diminution in the market value of the landlord's interest, comparing the value before and after the grant of the new lease, and ignoring the tenants' rights under this Act; and

(2) 50% of the marriage value. However, the landlord has no entitlement to any share if the marriage value has more than 80 years left unexpired; and

(3) reasonable compensation to the landlord for loss or damage resulting from the grant of the new lease in respect of other property, including loss of development value.

In addition, the tenant will be responsible for the landlord's costs in granting the new lease.

40.3.6 The effect of the grant of a new lease

Once a new lease has been granted, this will not preclude a subsequent exercise of the right to collective enfranchisement. Equally, a further claim to another new lease under these provisions can be brought in relation to any new lease granted. However, that is the only security of tenure applicable to such lease; no other security of tenure provisions are to apply to the lease nor to any sub-tenancies granted out of it once the term date has passed. This means that neither the tenant nor any sub-tenant (whether lawful or otherwise) can claim protection after the end of the 90-year extended term, whether under the LTA 1954 (Part I or II), RA 1977, HA 1988 or any similar legislation.

Chapter 41

COMMONHOLD

41.1 WHAT IS IT?

Commonhold is a new system of freehold ownership designed for use in the case of interdependent properties (eg blocks of flats or offices, shopping malls and business parks, etc). Technically, it is not a new estate in land; it is the ordinary fee simple (or freehold) estate with special attributes to make it suitable for use in the case of such properties.

41.2 WHY IS IT NEEDED?

At the moment, such properties are usually disposed of as leaseholds. In the case of blocks of flats and the like, the stability of the whole building depends upon satisfactory arrangements for the proper maintenance and repair of the structure of the building. Positive obligations (eg repair, payment of service charges) can only be enforced satisfactorily by the grant of leases; the burden of a positive covenant does not pass on a sale of freehold land. But leases, by their very nature, are a depreciating asset. As the unexpired residue reduces they become less saleable (or mortgageable – see the *CML Lenders' Handbook* as to mortgage lenders often requiring a minimum unexpired residue of 50 years before they will accept a leasehold flat for mortgage purposes.)

41.3 HISTORY

Other jurisdictions (including Scotland!) have had similar schemes for many years. We have been thinking about it since the report of the Wilberforce Committee on positive covenants recommended the introduction of a similar scheme in 1965!

The Commonhold and Leasehold Reform Act 2002 received the Royal Assent on 1 May 2002, but the provisions introducing commonhold are not likely to be brought into force until March 2004.

41.4 HOW WILL IT WORK?

Commonhold can only be created out of registered land. Each separate property in the development (eg each flat) will be called a 'unit'. This is to emphasise that commonhold is not just designed for use in the context of residential flats; it will also be available for use in commercial developments.

Each 'unit-holder' will own the freehold in their respective unit; the unit-holder will be registered at HM Land Registry as 'the proprietor of the fee simple in a Commonhold unit'. So it will be clear to any buyer that the land is commonhold.

Chapter 41 contents
What is it?
Why is it needed?
History
How will it work?
The commonhold association (CA)
The commonhold community statement (CCS)
How is a commonhold created?
Ombudsman scheme
Termination of commonhold
Commonhold in practice

The freehold in the common parts will then be vested in a 'Commonhold Association' of which all the unit-holders will be members. There will also be a 'Commonhold Community Statement' which will set out the rights and liabilities of the unit-holders and the Commonhold Association.

It will be possible for a unit to consist of two or more physically separate areas of land (eg a flat and a garage in a separate block).

Units may be divided from one another vertically (eg terraced houses), horizontally (eg flats) or may be free-standing (eg detached houses).

Where the divisions are horizontal, no part of the commonhold may be over or under any part of the building which is not part of the commonhold development. So the whole of a building must be developed as commonhold; part cannot be sold off as commonhold and the remainder let leasehold.

41.5 THE COMMONHOLD ASSOCIATION (CA) (ss 34–36)

41.5.1 What is it?

This will be a private company limited by guarantee and will be registered at Companies House in the usual way.

Membership, however, will be limited to the unit-holders within the development.

The CA will have a standard set of Memorandum and Articles which will be prescribed by the Lord Chancellor from time to time.

41.5.2 Rights and duties

The CA will be under a duty to manage the development in such a way as to allow the unit-holders to exercise their rights and enjoy their occupation of their units. It is also charged, however, with ensuring that the unit-holders comply with their obligations. Regulations will be made dealing with the enforcement of rights and duties under the commonhold community statement (CCS). However, the CA is given discretion not to enforce these if that would be more conducive to maintaining harmonious relationships between all the unit-holders, provided that this will not cause any unit-holder significant loss or significant disadvantage.

It is not clear what these enforcement powers will be. However, s 37(2) states that the regulations may in particular make provision for:

(1) the payment of compensation;
(2) enabling recovery of costs where work is carried out for the purpose of enforcing a right or duty or because of failure to perform a duty
(3) requiring the use of arbitration before legal proceedings are commenced.

41.6 THE COMMONHOLD COMMUNITY STATEMENT (CCS) (ss 31–33)

41.6.1 What is it?

The CCS contains the rules and regulations of the development. It will set out the rights and duties of the commonhold association and of the individual unit-holders. In many respects it will take the place of the lease in a leasehold development and will contain many of the same provisions.

41.6.2 What will it contain?

It will contain many of the usual provisions found in a lease, for example:

(a) easements over the common parts (these can be granted in the CCS without any further formality, eg a deed which is usually required to grant an easement);
(b) obligation to pay the service charge;
(c) obligation to repair and maintain each;
(d) the permitted use for the development;
(e) obligation to insure;
(f) obligation to repair and maintain the common parts.

Regulations will be made prescribing the contents of the statement. However, it is intended that there will be a degree of flexibility to take into account the different nature of the various types of properties which might be subject to a commonhold, so the regulations may make different provision for different circumstances.

41.6.3 Effect of CCS (s 16)

The terms of the CCS will be binding on the commonhold association and all present and future unit-holders. However, former unit holders will not be liable in relation to matters arising after they have ceased to be unit holders; any existing liability will continue.

41.7 HOW IS A COMMONHOLD CREATED? (ss 1–10)

41.7.1 New developments

Creation will be voluntary, both for new and existing developments. A developer can choose to develop a new block of flats etc leasehold, should he wish to do so.

There need only be a minimum of two units in the development.

In the case of a new development, the freeholder will apply to the Land Registry for the registration of a commonhold in relation to the land in question. The application must be accompanied by the prescribed documentation. This is likely to include detailed plans of the development, the CCS and the articles and memorandum of the CA.

41.7.2 Conversions of existing developments

In the case of an existing leasehold development (eg a block of flats), it is again only the freeholder who can convert it into a commonhold. However, he will need the consent of *all* existing tenants with leases for terms of more than 21 years and their mortgagees. Because of the requirement for unanimity, it is thought likely that only a few existing blocks of flats will convert in the short term.

The application must again be accompanied by the prescribed documentation.

Regulations will be made dealing with the form which this consent must take. It is likely to include a detailed explanation of the effect of converting. The regulations may also make provision for consent to be deemed or dispensed with in certain circumstances. However, due to the emphasis on the need for unanimous consent, it is likely that this will only apply in cases where a person whose consent is needed cannot be traced or fails to reply to correspondence.

It will not be possible for long leaseholders to convert directly to commonhold; they will firstly have to enfranchise under the existing Leasehold Reform legislation (as amended) and then the company owning the freehold will apply to convert as above. Consent of all the leaseholders (etc) will still be required, as above.

41.8 OMBUDSMAN SCHEME (s 42)

The Act provides for an Ombudsman scheme to be set up and for a CA to be a member of it. The Ombudsman will deal with disputes between the CA and a unit holder. The CA will be required to comply with any decision of the Ombudsman and if it does not the matter may be referred to the High Court which may order the directors of the CA to ensure that it complies with the decision.

41.9 TERMINATION OF COMMONHOLD (ss 43–56)

There are detailed provisions dealing with the termination of a CA (eg if the block becomes life-expired). There are two basic methods:

(1) where a winding-up resolution has been passed with 100% of the members voting in favour, by application to HM Land Registry; *or*
(2) where 80% of the members have voted in favour, by an application to the court.

41.10 COMMONHOLD IN PRACTICE

Despite its availability for both residential and commercial developments, it is thought that, initially at least, the main use of commonhold will be for blocks of flats and other residential development. There may well be a commercial advantage in this as many lay clients regard leases with suspicion as being something inferior to freehold land and may, therefore, be prepared to pay a premium to obtain a freehold flat. It is likely, therefore, that most new flat developments after the Act comes into force will be as commonholds.

The position with regard to commercial developments is less clear. Office blocks, shopping centres, business parks are generally developed leasehold at the moment. This, however, is perhaps less driven by the legal need to make covenants enforceable, than by commercial realities. Many occupiers of commercial premises do not want to buy the freehold in their unit; they prefer the flexibility of a lease. Of course, it would be possible for a property company to purchase the freehold in a particular unit from a commonhold developer and then let it on a commercial lease, but it is thought that most commercial developments will remain as leasehold. In Sydney, it is estimated that about 17% of commercial units are held under the New South Wales equivalent of commonhold – some 40 years after its introduction.

INDEX

References are to paragraph numbers.

Access
  construction of means of   2.2.2
  landlord's right   17.2.8
    alterations, to inspect   20.4
    to do repairs   17.2.8, 28.1.2
  site for development, to   7.3.5
  sub-lease, and   25.3.4
  trunk or classified road, to   2.2.2
Accommodation
  alternative, provision of suitable   33.8.4
  shop with, whether 'house'   38.2.1
Address for service   33.8.3
Administration   Chapter 23, 29.3
  application for order   29.3
  forfeiture right, and   29.5, 29.5.2
Administrative receiver   29.4
Administrator   29.3
Advertisement
  costs, recovery by landlord   24.4.1
  display of
    tenant, by, landlord's control   20.4
  local planning authority, by   3.4.5
  notification of planning application, by   3.4.4,
    see also Notification
  planning control
    display of, when material change of use
      2.1.2
    painting exterior of building as   2.2.2
  planning obligation discharge or modification
    application, of   4.5.2
Agreement for lease   26.1 *et seq*
  construction of building, example   26.3
    collateral warranties   26.3.9
    completion date   26.3.5, 26.3.6
    conditions of sale, incorporation of
      26.3.13
    damage prior to completion of lease
      26.3.10
    damages to tenant   26.3.8
    defects   26.3.9
    delays   26.3.5–26.3.8
    design flexibility   26.3.2
    force majeure clause   26.3.7
    insurance   26.3.9, 26.3.10
    landlord's works, extent   26.3.1
    lease, form of   26.3.11
    merger of agreement and lease   26.3.15
    plan and specifications annexed   26.3.1
    'practical completion' certificate   26.3.5
    premises, description in   26.3.12
    remedies against constructors etc, landlord's
      26.3.8, 26.3.9
    rent commencement date   26.3.8

rights and obligations set out in   26.3.13
    risk, passing of   26.3.10
    skill and care, standard of   26.3.3
    supervision by surveyor   26.3.4
    termination   26.3.8
    title deduction   26.3.14
    variation   26.3.2
  contractual obligations in, continued operation of
    26.3.15
  drafting of   26.1
  protection of, by land charge, notice or caution
    26.1
  registration   26.1
  stamp duty   10.2, 26.1
  uses of   26.2.
Agricultural Holdings Certificate   3.4.3
Agricultural lease
  alterations   20.3.2
  relief from forfeiture   30.5.3
  security of tenure exclusion   31.1.3
Agriculture
  operations on land used for   2.2.2
Airspace   13.2
Alienation   18.1 *et seq*, 25.3, *see also*
    Assignment; Charge; Sub-lease
  covenant against   18.2
Alterations   20.1 *et seq*
  see also Improvements
  agricultural lease   20.3.2
  ancillary provisions   20.4
  compensation
    claim from landlord   20.5
    payment to landlord   20.3.2
  consent to   20.3.2, 20.3.3
    refusal of, reasonableness   20.3.2
  covenant
    absolute   20.3, 20.3.1
    assignee, and   20.2.2
    drafting of   20.2.2
    fully qualified   20.3, 20.3.3
    injunction to prevent   28.1.3
    landlord's concerns   20.2.1
    length of lease, and   20.2.1
    need for   20.2.1
    qualified   20.3, 20.3.2
    tenant's concerns   20.2.2
  fire escape, for   20.3.1
  improvement, when is   20.3.2
  mining lease   20.3.2
  planning permission, and   19.4
  regulation of, apart from lease   20.1
  reinstatement at end of lease   20.4
  shops   20.3

Alterations *cont*
structural   20.3, 20.3.1
waste distinguished   20.4
Alternative accommodation
ground for opposition to new lease   31.5.4
Animal
Annoyance
repossession for   33.8.4
Appeal (planning)   1.2.3, 1.3.3, 3.7, 3.8, 3.9, 3.10
appellant   3.7.1
certificate of lawful use, on   5.3.4
challenge to decision   3.10, *see also* High
Court
circumstances for   3.7
conditions, on imposition of   3.6.2, 3.6.3
copy documents for   3.7.2
costs   3.9
enforcement notice, against   5.10
appellant   5.10.3
costs   5.10
documentation   5.10
fee   5.10
forum   5.10
further appeals   5.10
grounds for   5.10
inquiry, as   5.10
lodging of appeal, deemed planning
application   5.10.1, 5.10.4
procedure   5.10
time-limit   5.10
written representations, by   5.10
fact and degree questions   1.2.3, 2.1.2
forum   3.8.4, 5.10.4
grounds
form, set out in   3.7.2
hearing   3.8.3,
inquiry   3.8.2, 3.8.5
form   3.8.2
procedure   3.8.5
reason for   3.8.4
procedure   3.7.2, 3.8
form   3.7.2
reasons for refusal or conditions, on   3.5.4
third party influence   3.8.1, 3.8.4
time-limits   3.7.2
types   3.8
written representations, by   3.7.2, 3.8.1,
5.10.4
appropriateness   3.8.4
cost advantage of   3.8.1, 3.8.4
costs   3.9
evidence for   3.8.1
Arbitrator
rent review, for   16.6.4
Architect   8.2.3
appointment of   8.2.2, 8.2.3
agent, as   8.2.2

certificate of practical completion, by   8.2.2,
8.2.3, 26.3.5
negligence   8.3.2
plans, licence for use of   7.1
standard of care   8.2.5
Assault
landlord, of tenant   36.4.2
Assignment
bankruptcy of assignee   29.1.3
lease, of   12.3, 18.1.1
absolute covenant   18.2.1
administrator, by   29.3
application for consent   27.1–27.3
breach of covenant, as   27.1, 30.5.3
conditions to be satisfied for   18.2.3,
18.2.5, 18.2.7, 27.3
consent to   18.2.3, 18.2.4–18.2.7, 27.1
contract conditional on   7.2.1
costs of   27.1
covenants, and   9.2, 12.2, 12.3, *see also*
Covenant
covenant restricting   18.2, 27.1
death or bankruptcy, and   18.1.1
discrimination, and   18.2.4
'excluded', no release of assignor   12.3.2,
12.4.3, 27.1
forfeiture for   30.5.3
guarantor for assignee   12.4.6
injunction to prevent   28.1.3
involuntary   29.1.1
licence to assign, preparation, duration, etc
27.2, 27.3
notice of   18.3
original tenant's liability, *see* Liability of
parties to lease
qualified covenant   18.2.2, 27.1
reasonable refusal of consent   18.2.4,
18.2.5
receiver, by   29.4
references   18.2.5
refusal of consent   18.2.4,
18.2.5
registration fee   18.3
repayment of rent deposit   12.5
sub-letting is not   18.1.1
usual form of covenant   18.2.3
rights, of   8.4.2
Assured shorthold tenancy   34.1 *et seq*
anti-avoidance provision   34.2.1
breach   34.7
break clause   34.2.1
concept of, when established   32.5
definition   34.2.1
expiry of fixed term   34.3.2, 34.5–34.7
fixed term, must be   34.2.1
forfeiture clause   34.2.1
grant, initial   34.2.1
meaning   34.2.1

Assured shorthold tenancy *cont*
  new 34.3
    definition 34.3.1
    lettings to existing assured tenants 34.3.2
    lettings which will not be 34.3.2
    practical implications 34.3.2
    provision stating that tenancy is not shorthold
      34.3.2
    Rent Assessment Committee application
      34.4
    tenancies excluded by notice 34.3.2
  non-payment of rent 34.7
  notice prior to grant of 34.1
    interval between service and entry into
      agreement 34.2.1
    joint tenants, on 34.2.1
    prescribed form 34.2.1, 34.3.2
    specimen 34.2.1
  old shortholds 34.1, 34.2
    further let to same tenant 34.2.1
  possession 34.5, 34.6, 34.7
    grounds for 34.7
    see also Possession action
  rent 34.4
    reference to Rent Assessment Committee
      34.1, 34.4
  security of tenure 33.8.1
  6-month minimum 34.2.1
  statutory periodic tenancy arising after 34.5
  term of, minimum, etc 34.2.1
  termination 34.6, 34.7, *see also* possession
    above
  termination during first 6 months 34.2.1
  termination notices, formalities 34.6
  type of assured tenancy, as 34.2.1
Assured tenancy 32.5, 33.1 *et seq*
  absences 33.2.6
  alternative accommodation, repossession ground
    33.8.4
  anti-social behaviour 33.8.4
  breach of covenant, repossession for 33.8.4
  business tenancy exclusion 33.3.4
  company let 33.2.5
  death of tenant 33.6, 33.8.3
  definition 33.2
  demolition, repossession ground 33.8.3
  deterioration due to waste, etc, repossession for
    33.8.4
  dwelling house, meaning 33.2.2
  employee, former, repossession from 33.8.4
  end to any of requirements, effect 33.2.4
  exclusions 33.3
  false statements 33.8.4
    fixed term possession 33.8.2
    protection on end of 33.8.1
    see also Assured shorthold tenancy
  furniture, damage to, repossession for 33.8.4
  holiday let

  exclusion 33.3.6
    out of season, repossession 33.8.3
  individual 33.2.5
  landlord owner/occupier, possession where
    33.8.3
    just and equitable dispensation of notice
      requirement 33.8.3
  lodger, deterioration, damage, etc, due to
    33.8.4
  minister of religion, let to, repossession
    33.8.3
  mixed user 33.3.4
  mortgagee exercising power of sale, possession
    for 33.8.3
  nuisance, repossession for 33.8.4
  periodic
    death of sole tenant 33.6
    notice to quit 33.8.1
    statutory 33.8.1
  possession order 33.8.2
    anti-social behaviour 33.8.4
    conduct, relevance 33.8.4
    false statements 33.8.4
    grounds for, discretionary 33.8.4
    grounds for, mandatory 33.8.3
    just and equitable dispensation of notice
      requirement 33.8.2, 33.8.4
    notice on tenant 33.8.2
  pre-Housing Act tenancy 33.3.1, 35.5
  principal home 33.2.6
  rate/rent limits 33.3.2
  rent 33.1, 33.5
    arrears, repossession for 33.8.3, 33.8.4
    initial 33.5
    persistent delay in paying 33.8.4
    substantial arrears 33.8.3
  Rent Act tenancy, arising after 35.5
  resident landlord let 33.3.7
    exclusion of, general rule 33.3.7
  security of tenure 33.8
  separate dwelling, let as 33.2.3
  sharing of essential features 33.2.3
  shorthold, *see* Assured shorthold tenancy
  spouse, statutory succession to 33.6
  status can change 33.2.4
  student let
    out of term, repossession 33.8.3
    when excluded 33.3.5
  sub-let 33.7
    company, by 33.2.5
    deterioration, damage, etc, due to sub-tenant
      33.8.4
  succession 33.6
  tenancy, must be 33.2.1
  termination by landlord 33.8.1
  transitional provisions 33.4
  winter lets 33.8.3

Authorised guarantee agreement   12.3.2, 18.2.7,
    27.3
    benefit passing to assignee   12.2.2, 18.2.7
    condition for consent, may be   18.2.7
    disclaimer of lease on bankruptcy, effect
        29.1.3
    guarantor, and   12.4.2, 12.4.4, 29.1.3
    overriding lease, right of guarantor to   28.1.4

Bailiff   28.1.1
Bankruptcy
    see also Insolvency
    tenant, of   29.1
        disclaimer of lease by trustee-in-bankruptcy
            29.1.2, 29.1.3
        effect on leasehold interest   29.1.1
        forfeiture   29.5.1
        guarantor, effect on   12.4.3, 29.1.3
        stay of proceedings on   29.5.1
Bath
    repair of installations for   37.3.2, 37.3.4
Battery   36.4.2
Block of flats
    bad management, compulsory acquisition for
        39.3
    collective enfranchisement right, *see* Collective
        enfranchisement
    first refusal of freehold, tenant's right of
        39.1–39.3
        criminal sanctions   39.2.5
        excluded tenants   39.2.3
        landlord   39.2.2
        nominee for tenants   39.2.4
        notice on tenant, as offer   39.2.4
        premises   39.2.1
        proposed disposal, when 'relevant'   39.2.4
        tenants, qualifying   39.2.3
    repair
        common parts, of, *see* Common parts
        installations for water, gas etc, heating, of
            37.3.4
Breach
    see also Contract; Covenant; Damages; Distress;
        Forfeiture
    lease term, of
        ground for opposition to new lease   31.5.3
        re-entry for   Chapter 23
        sub-tenant, by   25.1
        surrender, effect on   30.6.1
Breach of condition notice   5.1, 5.6
    compliance period   5.6.2
    contents   5.6.2
    effect   5.6.3
    offence   5.6.3
    person served   5.6.1
    use of   5.6, 5.6.1
Break clause   11.3.5, 14.2, 30.1, 30.4

    conditions, fulfilment date   30.4
    effect on sub-tenant   14.2.3
    exercise of   14.2.2
    incorrect date in   14.2.2, 30.4
    rent review, and   16.6.1
    who has option   14.2.1
Building
    contract   8.2.2
        assignment of benefit   8.4.2
        defect remedy   8.4.2
    defect in   8.3, 17.2.4, 17.2.6
    demolition, *see* Demolition
    erection
        outline permission   3.3.1
    exterior, painting of   2.2.2
    land, as   13.3
    listed   1.2.1
    part of, *see* Lease of part
    temporary   2.2.2
Building contractor   8.2.2
    skill and care, duties   8.2.2
Building operations   2.1.1, 2.1.3
Building society
Business
    meaning for security of tenure   31.1.2
Business tenancy, *see* Lease
    assured tenancy exclusion   33.3.4
    collective enfranchisement exclusion   40.2.6
    first refusal of freehold provisions, exclusion
        39.2.3
Business use   2.1.3

Case-law (planning)
    change of use, and   2.1.2
    importance of   1.2.3
Ceiling   24.3.1
Certificate of lawful use or development   2.3.2,
    5.3
    application for
        existing development   5.3.2
        false statement, etc, offence   5.3.4
        notification of decision, time for   5.3.4
        proposed development   5.3.3
    contents   5.3.4
    effect   5.3.2–5.3.4
        existing development   5.3.2
        proposed development   5.3.3
    issue   5.3.2, 5.3.3
    lawful, meaning   5.3.1
    proof of lawfulness   5.3.2
    refusal of   5.3.2
    appeal   5.3.4
Change of use   2.1
    see also Planning permission
    development, when is   2.1.2, 2.1.3
    material, what is   2.1.2
    permitted   2.2.2

Change of use *cont*
  'planning unit'   2.1.2
  resumption of previous use   2.2.1
  single dwelling house, to use as   5.2.2
  shopping mall   2.1.2
  use class, within   2.1.2, 2.1.3
Charge
  lease, on   18.1, 18.1.2
    charge for consent   18.2.6
    consent of landlord to   18.2.3–18.2.5
Charitable housing trust
  demolition ground for repossession, and
    33.8.3
  landlord is, exclusion from collective
    enfranchisement right   40.2.6
Chattel   13.3
Child
  succession to, of Rent Act tenancy   35.5
Clean-up works   6.2.2, 6.2.3, 6.2.4, 6.2.5, 6.2.6,
    6.2.7, 6.3, 6.4, 7.3.3
  'appropriate person'   6.2.4
  indemnity from seller   6.4
  information, sold with   6.2.5
  remediation notice   6.2.6
  tenant, by   6.2.7
Client   8.2.1
  instructions from   32.6
Cohabitee   33.6, 35.5
Collateral warranty   8.4.1, 26.3.9
  action on   8.4.1, 26.3.9
  sub-contractor, from   8.4.1
  time for   8.4.1
Collective enfranchisement   40.1 *et seq*
  access   40.2.9
  background   40.1
  compensation to freeholder   40.2.16
  'flat'   40.2.5
  housing association let, and   40.2.11
  lease-back   40.2.11, 40.2.12
  long lease   40.2.5
  low rent   40.2.5
  market value   40.2.14
  marriage value   40.2.15
  non-qualifying tenant, flat let to   40.2.11
  notice on landlord   40.2.3
  opposition by landlord, redevelopment ground
    40.2.4
  parking   40.2.9
  premises   40.2.1, 40.2.9
    definition   40.2.7
    exclusions   40.2.8
  price   40.2.13
  qualifying tenants   40.2.1, 40.2.5
    company as   40.2.5
    exclusions   40.2.6
  resident landlord
    flat occupied by   40.2.11
    premises with   40.2.8

  right to   40.2.1
    excluded interests   40.2.10
    exercise of   40.2.3
    included interests   40.2.9
    nature of   40.2.2
  surrounding grounds   40.2.9
  'tenant'   40.2.5
  valuation   40.2.13–40.2.16
Commercial lease, *see* Lease
Common parts   11.3.2, 17.1
  insurance of   22.2
  repairs to   37.2.1, 37.3.3
Commonhold   41.1 *et seq*
  creation of   41.7
    conversion of existing developments
      41.7.2
    new developments   41.7.1
  history   41.3
  ombudsman scheme   41.8
  termination of   41.9
  working of   41.4, 41.10
Commonhold association   41.5
  definition   41.5.1
  duties   41.5.2
  rights   41.5.2
Commonhold community statement   41.6
  contents   41.6.2
  definition   41.6.1
  effect of   41.6.3
Commons register, search of   7.3.4
Company
  administration order, and claim for rent, etc,
    against   29.6
  assignee, as   18.2.3
  group member as tenant   31.1.2
  guarantor, as   12.4.1
  liquidation   29.2, 29.5.2, 29.7
    re-entry by landlord   29.5.2
  receivership   29.5.2, 29.6
Company let   33.2.5, 40.2.5
  address for service   33.8.3
Compensation   11.3.5, 31.6
  see also Damages
  alterations to premises, for   20.3.2, 20.5, *see
    also* Improvements
  breach of covenant, requirement in notice of
    30.5.3
  failure to obtain new lease, for   31.6
  revocation of planning permission, for   3.3.3,
    3.5.2
  stop notice prohibition, in respect of
    5.9.6
Completion notice   3.5.3
Compulsory acquisition
  freehold of flats, of, for bad management, etc
    39.3
Condition (of premises)
  see also Repairs

Condition (of premises) *cont*
    deterioration in, as repossession ground
        33.8.4
Condition, planning permission subject to, *see*
    Planning permission
Conditional agreement   7.2.1
    certainty of condition   7.2.1
    time for fulfilment   7.2.1
Conditions of sale
    agreement for lease, in   26.3.13
    contract of sale, in   7.1, 7.2.1
Conducting media, *see* Pipes and conduits
Consent (of landlord)
    alterations, to   20.3.2, 20.3.3
    assignment or sub-let, to   18.2, 27.1
        'reasonableness'   18.2.5
        refusal of   18.2.4, 18.2.5
    user, to change in   19.3.2, 19.3.3
Conservation area
    demolition in   2.1.1
    dwelling house in   2.2.2
    legislation on   1.2.1
Construction
    agreement for a lease prior to, *see* Agreement for
        lease
    contract   8.2.2
    personnel involved with   8.2
Constructor
    see also Building contractor; Sub-contractor
    landlord's remedies against   26.3.8, 26.3.9
Consultation
    prior to planning application, with LPA officer
        3.2
Contaminated land   6.1
    blighted land   6.2.1
    'brownfield sites', recycling of   6.2.2
    conditional contract, use of   6.4
    damage caused by, liability   6.2 *et seq*
    definition   6.1
    enquiries to discover   6.3, 7.3.2
    'harm'   6.1
    register of remediation notices   6.3
    repairing covenant covering   17.2.1
    searches   7.3.1
    warranty   6.4
Contents
Continuation tenancy, *see* Renewal lease
Contract
    see also Agreement for lease; Contract of sale
    assignment of rights   8.4.2
    breach   8.2.5, 8.3
    building   8.2.2
    collateral warranty action   8.4.1, 26.3.9
    enforcement of rights under, forced   8.4.2
    eviction or harassment as breach   36.4.2
    law, relevance   32.2
    lease as, construction rules   11.2

licensee under, eviction protection   36.2.1, *see*
        also Licence; Licensee
    sub-tenant's covenant with landlord as   25.1
    third party protection   8.3.1, 8.4, 25.4
    third party rights   8.3.1, 25.4
Contract of sale   7.1 *et seq*
    conditional   7.2.1
    lease, *see* Assignment
    option agreement   7.2.2
    standard conditions   7.1,
        7.2.1
    terms   7.1
    types of   7.2
Conversion, tort on   36.4.2
Costs
Council house tenant, *see* Secure tenant
County court
    injunction application to   5.7
County planning authority   1.4.1
    see also Structure plan
    'county matters'   1.4.1
Covenant
    lease, in   7.1, 7.3.5, 9.2, 11.3.4
        alterations, controlling, *see* Alterations
        assignee, by   9.2, 12.3, 18.2.3
        breach by landlord   28.2.1, 28.2.2
        breach by tenant   12.2, 12.3, Chapter 23,
            28.1.1, 28.2, *see also* Damages; Forfeiture;
            Injunction
        dealings, against, *see* Dealings
        decorations, as to   17.5, 20.4
        indemnity, *see* Indemnity
        insurance   22.1–22.4, 22.7.2, 22.7.3
        liability under   9.2, 12.2, 12.3, 31.1.6, *see*
            also Liability of parties to lease
        no derogation from grant   28.2.2
        original parties' liability, new leases
            9.2.2
        privity of contract   9.2.1, 9.2.2, 12.2.1,
            12.3.1
        privity of estate   9.2.1
        quiet enjoyment, for   21.1, 21.2, 28.2.2
        release from   12.2.2, 12.3.2
        rent, for payment of   15.1
        repair   8.4.2, 12.3.1, *see also* Repairs
        schedules to lease   11.3.6
        surety, *see* Guarantor
        touching and concerning the land   12.3.1,
            12.3.2
        user, as to, *see* User
    superior title, in   19.1, 20.1
Covenant for quiet enjoyment
    breach of   36.4.2
Crown let   33.3.8
Curtilage
    meaning   2.2.2

Damage
  see also Defect; Insurance
  demised premises, to   11.3.5, 15.5, 22.7
    effect on lease   22.7
    liability for   8.3, 8.3.1, 22.7
    suspension of rent   22.7.2
  risk passing on exchange   7.1
  term prohibiting tenant causing   *see also*
    Waste
Damages
  agreement for lease, under   26.3.8
  breach of contract, for   8.2.5, 8.3
  breach of covenant by landlord   28.2.1
  breach of covenant by tenant (other than rent or
    repair)   28.1.3
  breach of repairing covenant, for
    landlord, by   28.2.1
    tenant, by   17.6, 28.1.2
  eviction for harassment remedy   36.1,
    36.4.1
  insolvency and claim for   29.6
  tort, in   8.3
Dampness   37.1
Dangerous items or activities
  insurance, and   22.3, 22.8
Dealings
  see also Assignment; Charge; Sub-lease
  covenant restricting   18.2
  absolute   18.2.1
  breach of, damages   28.1.3
  qualified   18.2.2
  usual   18.2.3
Death   *see also* Succession
  covenant against assignment, and   18.1.1
  effect on guarantee   12.4.3
  tenant
    assured tenancy, of   33.6
    protected or statutory tenancy, of   35.5
Decoration
  see also Repairs
  lease of part, in   24.3.1
  sub-tenant, by   25.3.3
  tenant's obligation   17.5, 20.4
    relief from forfeiture for breach provision
      30.5.3
Defect
  see also Repairs
  agreement for lease, and protection for tenant
    26.3.9
  building, in   8.3, 17.2.4
    defective premises obligations   17.3
    inherent, and tenant's repairs   17.2.6
    latent, insurance against   8.4.2
    protection against   8.4
  fixture, in   13.3.1
Defect liability period   8.4.2, 26.3.9
Demolition
  development, as   2.1.1

ground for opposition to new lease   31.5.6
landlord seeking possession for   33.8.3
permitted   2.2.2
Deposit   7.1, *see also* Rent deposit
Derogation from grant   28.2.2
Design and build contract   8.2.2
Developer
  see also Client
Development
  see also Change of use; Development site
  commencement, meaning   3.5.3
  completion notice   3.5.3
  covenant against   19.4
  dwelling house, and, *see* Dwelling house
  meaning   2.1, 2.1.1, 2.1.2
  not requiring planning permission   2.2
  operations   2.1.1
    lawful   5.3.1
  permitted   2.2
    Article 4 Direction limiting   2.2.2
    conditions restricting   3.6.3, 3.6.4
  planning permission for, *see* Planning permission
  project
    financing, *see* Finance
  regulation of, in lease   11.3.2
  time-limit for   3.5.3
  unclear cases   2.3
    determination by LPA   2.3.2
    options   2.3.1
  VAT on, *see* Value added tax
Development Order, *see* General Permitted
    Development Order; Special development order
Development plan   1.5
  constituents of   1.5.1
  copy of relevant part   3.2
  importance of   1.5.2, 3.2, 3.5.1
  interpretation in PPG 1   1.5.3, 3.5.1
  purpose and uses of   1.5.2
  regional policy guidance, and   1.2.2
Development site
  agreement for lease pending construction, *see*
    Agreement for lease
  buyer's searches, *see* Searches
  use of option agreement for   7.2.2
Disaster
  landlord's implied repairing covenant, and
    37.3.6
Disclaimer of lease
  effect generally   29.1.3
  guarantor, effect on   12.4.4, 29.1.3
  liquidator, by   12.4.3, 12.4.4, 29.2
  sub-leases   29.1.3, 29.2
  trustee-in-bankruptcy, by   12.4.3, 12.4.4,
    29.1.2, 29.1.3, 29.6
  effect of   29.1.3
  vesting order for predecessor tenant   29.1.3
Distress
  availability of remedy   15.4, 28.1.1, 29.6

District planning authority   1.4.1
    local plan preparation   1.5.1
Drainage   7.3.1, 7.3.2, 7.3.5
Dwelling house
    demolition   2.1.1
    development within curtilage   2.2.2
    entry, exercise of right of, notice of   5.4.1
    meaning   33.2.2
        GPDO, for   2.2.2
    permitted development   2.2.2
    repairs, statutory implied terms   37.3, *see also*
        Repairs
    use as (single)   5.2.2
    use class   2.1.3

Easement   7.3.3, 7.3.5
    alterations not to infringe   20.1
    reservation of   7.1
Education body
    let by   33.3.5, 33.8.3
Electrical supply
    see also Services (utilities)
    covenant not to tamper with   20.4
Employee
    assured tenancy, repossession from former
        33.8.4
Employer, *see* Developer
Encroachment
Enforcement (planning)   5.1 *et seq*
    breach of condition, *see* Breach of condition
        notice
    breach of planning control
        apparent, meaning   5.8.2
        immunity for   5.2.2
        liability, when arises   5.8.1
        meaning   5.2.1, 5.8.2
    enforcement notice, *see* Enforcement notice
        (planning)
    enquiry as to lawfulness of use, *see* Certificate of
        lawful use or development
    injunction, by   5.1, 5.7, 5.8.9
    local authority powers   5.1
    planning contravention, *see* Planning
        contravention notice
    right of entry   5.4
        obstruction, offence   5.4.3
        with warrant   5.4.2
        without warrant   5.4.1
    'taking enforcement action'   5.2.1
    time-limits   5.2.2, 5.8.3
Enforcement notice (planning)   5.8
    appeal against   5.10
        effect of, on the notice   5.10.4
        see also Appeal (planning)
    challenge to issue   5.8.2
    contents   5.8.4
    criminal liability, and   5.8.1, 5.8.7

    date of effect of   5.8.4
    documents accompanying   5.8.4
    effect   5.8.7
    error in   5.8.6
    expediency of   5.8.2, 5.8.4
    'issue'   5.8.2
    'local planning authority' for   5.8.2
    non-compliance   5.8.7, 5.8.9
        power of entry of LPA   5.8.9
    nullity, when is   5.8.6, 5.8.9
    pre-requisites for   5.8.2
    service
        non-service, defence   5.8.9
        persons and time for   5.8.5
    steps to be taken, details in   5.8.4, 5.8.6
    time-limits   5.8.3, 5.8.5
    validity   5.8.6
    variation   5.8.8, 5.9.6
        appeal, on   5.10.4
    withdrawal   5.8.8
        appeal, on   5.10.4
Enfranchisement, collective, *see* Collective
    enfranchisement
Enfranchisement (long lease house)   38.1
    et seq
    assignment of lease, and   38.3.1
    building converted into flats   38.2.1
    conditions   38.2
    death of tenant, successor's right   38.2.3
    desire notice   38.3.1
    disputes
        price, as to   38.5
        terms of conveyance, as to   38.4
    extended lease, acquiring   38.1, 38.3
    freehold, acquisition of   38.1, 38.3
        price   38.5
        terms of conveyance   38.4
    'house'   38.2.1
    'long lease'   38.2.2
    marriage value   38.5
    'member of family'   38.2.3
    shop with living accommodation   38.2.1
    tenant, residence, etc requirements   38.2.3
    trust property   38.4.2
    valuation   38.5
Engineer
    negligence   8.3.2
    standard of care   8.2.5
    structural, etc   8.2.5
Engineering operations   2.1.1
Enquiries, pre-exchange
    local authority   7.3.1
    seller, of   7.3.2
Environment Agency
    enquiries of   1.2.2
    report on contaminated land   1.2.2
Environmental matters, *see* Contaminated land;
    Pollution

Environmental protection, *see* Public health

Estate contract
  desire notice for enfranchisement, as   38.3.1

Eviction   36.1 *et seq*
  breach of quiet enjoyment covenant, as   21.2, 28.2.2
  civil proceedings   36.4
  court order for   36.4.2
  criminal offences   36.2.1, 36.3
    occupiers protected   36.2.1
  statutory tort   36.4.2,

Exclusive possession   33.2.3

Execution on tenant's goods   Chapter 23

Expert
  rent review, for   16.6.4

Expiry   30.1, 30.2

Exterior
  meaning   37.3.3

Fair rent   35.1, 35.4
  application for   35.4.2
  assessment of   35.4.1
  register of   35.4.1

Family
  see also Spouse; Succession

Fee
  enforcement notice appeal, for   5.10.4
  planning application, for   3.4.2

Fence   2.2.2

Financial and professional services, use class
    2.1.3

Fire
  escape
    alterations for   20.3.1
    insurance against   22.5, 22.7.3, 22.8
    landlord's implied repairing covenant, and
      37.3.6

First refusal
  tenant's right of, for freehold   39.1–39.3, *see also* Block of flats

Fitting out
  rent-free period for   15.1

Fixed charges   28.1, 28.1.4

Fixed-term tenancy   14.1, 30.2
  assured, *see* Assured tenancy; Assured shorthold tenancy
  repairs, implied terms   37.3.1, 37.3.2
  security of tenure   31.1.1, 31.1.3, 31.2, *see also* Security of tenure
  waste, tenant's liability for   37.2.1

Fixtures   13.3
  removal of   13.3.2
  repair of   13.3.1
  tenant's or landlord's   13.3.2

Flat(s)
  collective enfranchisement right, *see* Collective enfranchisement

repair, etc, *see* Block of flats
  meaning, for collective enfranchisement right
    40.2.5

Floors   24.3.1

Food and drink
  change of use from   2.2.2
  use class   2.1.3

Forfeiture   Chapter 23, 30.5, 31.2
  assignment in breach of covenant, on   27.1
  breach of covenant (except rent payment)
    30.5.3
  decorative repairs, internal, relief for   30.5.3
  enforcement of right   30.5
  insolvency of tenant, on   Chapter 23, 29.5, 30.5.3
    leave of court, whether required   29.5.1
    relief provision   30.5.3
    stay on proceedings   29.5.1, 29.5.2
  meaning   30.5
  non-payment of rent, on   30.5.2
  notice ('s 146')   30.5.3
  relief from   30.5.2
  repairing covenant, counter-notice provision
    30.5.3
  waiver of right   30.5.1

Freehold
  see also Collective enfranchisement;
    Enfranchisement (long lease house);
    Reversion, sale/transfer of
  compulsory acquisition for bad management, etc
    39.3
  right of first refusal   39.1–39.3, *see also* Block of flats

Freeholder, *see* Landlord

Frustration   15.5, 22.7

Furnished house
  relief from forfeiture provision   30.5.3

Furnished lettings
  liability for repairs   37.2.1

Furniture
  damage, etc, to
    repossession for   33.10.4
    tort action for   36.4.2
  deprivation of occupier of use of   36.4.2

Gate   2.2.2

General Permitted Development Order
  certificate (Article 6)   3.4.3
  consultation duties of LPA   3.4.5
  permitted development   2.2.2
    limitations and restrictions   3.6.4

Goods
  trespass to   36.4.2

Goodwill
  disregarded for
    renewal lease rent   31.7.3
    rent review   16.5.4

Greater London   1.4.2
   development plan in   1.5.1
Green field site   7.1
   VAT on sale   10.1, 10.1.1, 10.1.2
      option to waive exemption   10.1.3
Guarantor   11.3.1, 12.4
   assignee, etc, for   12.4.6, 18.2.3, 18.2.7
      effect of new regime   12.4.6,
         18.2.7
   authorised   18.2.7, 27.3, 29.1.3
   bankruptcy of tenant, and   12.4.3,
      29.1.3
   co-guarantor   12.4.3
   death of   12.4.3, 12.4.4
   discharge   12.4.3
   extent and duration of guarantee   12.4.2,
      12.4.5
      abolition of privity of contract, effect 12.4.2,
         12.4.3
      guarantee agreement, ensuring not bound
         under   12.4.5
   financial status   12.4.1
   independent advice for   12.4.1
   insolvency of   12.4.4
   liability   12.4.2, 12.4.4, 12.4.5
   meaning of surety, in lease   11.3.3
   notice of claim to   28.1
   obligations   12.4.4
      disclaimer, effect on   12.4.4, 29.1.3, 5.2.2
   overriding lease, right to   28.1.4
   party to lease, as   12.4.4
   provisions in lease on   12.4.4, 12.4.5
   release   12.4.3, 12.4.4
   renewal lease, and   31.7.3
   tenant as, on assignment   18.2.7, 27.3

Habitation, fitness for   37.2.1
Harassment
   see also Damages; Injunction
   civil proceedings for   36.4
      causes of action   36.4.2
      interlocutory remedies   4.7.3, *see also*
         Interlocutory injunction
      reason for   36.4.1
   criminal offences   36.2.2, 36.3
      occupiers protected   36.2.2
Hazardous substance   1.2.1, 1.4.1
Heating system
   lease of part, in   24.3.1
      service charge, and   24.4.1
High Court
   enforcement notice appeal
      further appeal to   5.10.6
      order in   5.10.4
   injunction application to   5.7
Highway   7.3.1
Holiday let   33.3.6, 33.8.3

House
   meaning for enfranchisement right   38.2.1,
      see also Enfranchisement (long lease house)
Housing association landlord   33.3.8
   demolition ground for repossession, and
      33.8.3

Immoral or illegal user
   covenant against   19.4
Improvements   11.1.11, 18.4.1
   alteration distinguished   20.3.2
   compensation for tenant   20.5
      amount of   20.5
      authorisation   20.5.2
      qualifying improvement   20.5.1
      time-limits   20.5.4
   covenant against, and consent of landlord
      22.3.2, 20.5
   permission, statutory mechanism for   20.5,
      20.5.2
   renewal lease, and   31.7.3
   rent review, and   16.5.4
   repair contrasted with   17.2.5, 24.4.1
Indemnity
   implied   12.3.1
   landlord, for   12.2.1
   sub-tenant, by   25.3.5
   tenant or assignee, for   12.3.1, 12.3.2
Industrial premises   *see also* Pollution
Industrial use   2.1.3
Injunction
   enforcement notice breach, for   5.1, 5.7, 5.8.9
   eviction or harassment remedy   36.1, 36.4.1,
      interlocutory, *see* Interlocutory injunction
   landlord, for, mandatory or prohibitive   28.1.3
   tenant, for, for landlord's trespass   28.1.2
Inquiry, *see* Appeal (planning)
Insolvency   29.1–29.7
   assignee, of   12.3.1, 18.2.7, 29.1.2
   buyer, of   7.1
   guarantor, of   12.4.4
   landlord, of   29.7
      rent deposit, and   12.5
   proceedings, initiation of for rent arrears
      28.1.1
   tenant, of   12.3.1, 12.4.3, 12.5
      administration   29.3
      bankruptcy   29.1
      forfeiture, and   29.5
      guarantor, effect on   12.4.3,
         12.4.4
      liquidation   29.2, 29.5.2
      re-entry right   Chapter 23
Inspection   7.3.3
   see also Access
   reasons for   7.3.3
Inspector, *see* Appeal (planning)

Installations
  repair of   37.3.2, 37.3.4
Institutional lease, *see* Investor
Insurance   22.1–22.9
  latent defects, against   8.4.2
  lease, under   11.3.2, 22.1 *et seq*
    ancillary provisions   22.8
    breach of covenant   28.1.3
    definition of insured risks, importance of
      22.7.1, 22.7.2
    excess liability   22.8
    fire, and   22.5, 22.7.3, 22.8
    invalidation of policy   22.7, 22.8
    joint names preferable   22.4, 22.7.3, 22.9
    payment for   22.3
    premium level   22.3
    proceeds, covenant as to application of
      22.7.3
    proceeds unused   22.7.4
    reinstatement   22.7.3, 22.7.4, 22.9
    responsibility for   22.2, 22.9
    risks covered   22.5
    sum insured   22.6
    valuation for   22.8
  original tenant liability, against   12.3.1
  part let   24.6
  professional   26.3.9
  rent suspension, against   22.7.2
  subrogation   22.4
Insurance company
Interest
  rate of   15.6
  rent, etc, on   11.3.2, 15.6
  rent deposit, on   12.5
Interim rent   15.1, 16.2, 31.4
  alternative to   31.4.3
  amount of   31.4.2
  need for   31.4.1
Inventory   13.3
Investor
  purchaser of reversion, as *see* Reversion,
    sale/transfer of
  requirements as to lease   11.1

Joint tenants
  death of one, assured tenancy succession   33.6
Joint venture
Judicial review   3.5.5
  appeal decision, of   3.10, 5.10.6

Land
  see also Agriculture
  contaminated, *see* Contaminated land
  curtilage of dwelling house   2.2.2
  definition   13.3
  entry on to, right of   5.4

  law, relevance   32.2
  recovery of, *see* Possession action
  use of open   2.2.2
Landlord
  see also Charitable housing trust; Housing
    association; Lease; Local authority
  address for service   33.8.3
    change during currency of tenancy   33.8.3
  assault by, on tenant   36.4.2
  change of
  common parts liability, *see* Common parts
  consent to assignment of lease, *see* Assignment
  covenants   28.2, *see also* Covenant, Liability
    of parties to lease; Repairs
  demolition, intention   31.5.6
  derogation from grant   28.2.2
  disconnection of services, *see* Services
  entry on to demised premises   17.2.8, Chapter
    23, 28.1.2, 30.5.2
  family of, *see* Family; Spouse
  harassment by, *see* Eviction; Harassment
  insolvency   29.7
    liability on   9.2, 12.2
  joint and several liability   11.3.3
  occupation of premises, intention   31.5.7
    five-year rule   31.5.7
  original, liability of   12.2.2, *see also* Liability
    of parties to lease
  party to lease, as   12.2
  possession order, obtaining, *see* Possession action
  privity of contract   12.2.1
  quiet enjoyment covenant   21.1, 21.2
    breach of   28.2.2
  remedies   28.1, *see also* Damages;
    Forfeiture
  repairs
    obligations   37.2.1, 37.3
    see also Repairs
  resident, assured tenancy exclusion   33.3.7
  right of first refusal, meaning for   39.2.2
  service on   33.8.3
  successor to, possession of
Lease
  agreement for, *see* Agreement for lease
  alienation, *see* Assignment; Sub-lease
  ambiguity in   11.2
  assignment, *see* Assignment
  attestation clause   11.3.7
  break clause, *see* Break clause
  business use, end of   31.2
  commencement   11.3.1, 11.3.4, 14.1
  construction rules   11.2
  costs of grant   10.1.5
  covenants, *see* Covenants
  definitions   11.3.2
  distinguished from licence   32.1
  drafting   11.1 *et seq*
    amendments   11.1

Lease *cont*
  drafting *cont*
    'institutional' form, need for   11.1, *see*
        also Investor
    length   11.1
    see also Contract
  exceptions   11.3.4, 11.3.6
  exclusive possession   9.4
  execution   11.3.7
  expiry   30.2
  fixed charges   28.1, 28.1.4
  fixed term   14.1, 30.2, 31.1.1
  fixtures   13.3
  forfeiture, *see* Forfeiture
  grant of
    consideration for *see* Premium
  guarantor   11.3.1
  habendum clause   11.3.4
  implied grant, limits on   11.3.5
  improvements
    rent review, and   16.5.4
    see also Improvements
  inducements   15.1
  'institutional'   11.1, 16.1, 16.2, 35.2
  insurance   11.3.2
  interest   11.3.2
  interpretation clause   11.3.3
  licence, distinguished from   9.4
  misrepresentation, and   11.3.5
  mistake in   11.2
  notice to quit   30.1, 30.3, 31.1.1
  notices   11.3.5, 14.2.4
  operative words   11.3.4
  parcels clause, *see* Parcels clause
  part of building, of, *see* Lease of part
  parties   11.3.1, 12.1 *et seq*, *see also*
      Guarantor; Landlord; Tenant
  periodic   14.1, 30.3
    termination where protected   31.2.1
  perpetuity period   11.3.5
  personal qualifications of tenant important,
      forfeiture and   30.5.3
  pipes and conduits   11.3.5, 13.4
  premises
    damage to, position of parties *see also*
        Damage
    description of   11.3.2, 11.3.6, *see also*
        Parcels clause
    see also Premises
  privity of contract   9.2.1, 9.2.2, 12.2.1, 12.3.1
  privity of estate   9.2.1, 12.3.1
  provisos   11.3.5
  rectification   11.2
  reddendum   11.3.4
  renewal   14.3
  rent, *see* Rent
  rent-free period   15.1
    VAT, and   10.1.5

  rent review, *see* Rent review
  repair, terms in   37.2.1, 37.2.2
    implied by statute   37.3
  repairs, *see* Repairs
  reservations   11.3.4
  reverse premium   10.1.5
  reversion, *see* Reversion, sale/transfer of rights
    landlord's   13.4
    tenant's   11.3.6, 13.4
  sale   27.1–27.3
    see also Assignment
  schedules   11.3.6
  security of tenure   9.3, 30.1, 34.1 *et seq*
    contracting out   9.3, 9.4, 11.3.5
    see also Security of tenure
  service charge, *see* Service charge
  sham agreement   9.4
  stamp duty   10.2
  sub-lease, *see* Sub-lease
  term of   11.3.2, 11.3.4, 14.1–14.3
    commencement date   14.1
    liability for covenants, and wording of
        31.1.6
    tenant's liability, and   12.3.1, 12.3.2
  termination, *see* Termination of lease
  terms
    investor's requirements as to, *see* Investor
  user, *see* User
  VAT, and   10.1, 10.1.4
    defining in   11.3.2
  variation   12.4.3, 31.7.4
  void for uncertainty   14.1
  waiver   11.3.5, 30.5.1
Lease back   40.2.11, 40.2.12
Lease of part   11.3.2, 24.1
  see also Parcels clause
  identification of premises   11.3.2, 13.1
  insurance   24.6
  lifts   24.4.1
  management   24.4.1
  refuse removal   24.4.1
  repairs, landlord's expense of   24.4.1
  repairing obligations   17.1, 17.2, 17.3,
      24.3
    definitions   24.3.1
    drafting matters   24.3.1
    lease silent, position where   24.3.2
    ownership, and   24.3.1
  service charges, *see* Service charge
  sub-lease   18.1.4.
  walls   24.3.1
  windows
    cleaning   24.4.1
Leasehold Valuation Tribunal
  collective enfranchisement, and leaseback terms
      40.2.12
  price of freehold for enfranchisement, reference
      to   38.5

Legal costs
  alterations, of consent to   20.3.2
  assignment or sub-lease, of consent to
    18.2.6
  contract of sale, term in   7.1
    VAT on   10.1.5
  part let   24.4.1
Liability of parties to lease   12.1 *et seq*
  new leases, under
    assignee of tenant, of   12.3.2
    excluded assignments, no release   12.3.2,
      12.4.3, 27.1
    guarantee from outgoing tenant, 18.2.7
    guarantor, effect of regime on   12.4.2,
      12.4.3
    increase in rent, effect of   12.3.1, 12.4.3
    original landlord, of   12.2.2
    original tenant   12.3.2
    successor to landlord, of   12.2.2
  old regime, under
    assignee of tenant, of   12.3.1
    original landlord, of, and indemnity covenant
      12.2.1
    successor to landlord, of   12.2.2
    tenant, of, and indemnity covenant   12.3.1
  overriding lease, right to, and   28.1.4
  renewal lease, and   31.7.4
Licence (for occupation)   9.4, 18.1.2, 18.1.3
  see also Licensee
  distinguished from lease   32.1
Licence (liquor, etc)
  see also Public house
  covenant against lapse   19.4
  disregard of value for renewal lease   31.7.3
Licence (permission)
  assignment, for   27.2, *see also* Assignment
Licensee
  eviction or harassment protection   36.1
  let   33.3.8, *see also* Secure tenancy
  statutory tort protection   36.4.2
  tort action by   36.4.2
Limitation period   8.4.1
Liquidation
  see also Insolvency
  landlord of   29.7
  tenant, of   29.5, 29.6
    liquidator's powers as to lease   29.2
Listed building
  demolition   2.1.1
Local authority
  contaminated land
    enquiries of, by purchaser   6.3
    powers and duties as to   6.1
Local authority searches   7.3.1
  contract conditional on   7.2.1
  optional enquiries   7.3.1
Local plan   1.5.1
Local planning authority   1.4

  see also Planning application; Planning
    permission
  breach of condition notice   5.1
  certificate of lawful use or development
    2.3.2, 5.3
  completion notice   3.5.3
  consultation
    by applicant, with   3.2
    guidance from DoE   1.2.2
  inducement to, *see* Planning gain
  injunction application   56.1, *see also*
    Injunction
  notification by   3.4.5, 3.5.1
  payment to   3.6.2, 4.2.1, 4.3.1, 4.3.2
  planning contravention notice   5.1, 5.5
  publicity by   3.4.5
  register of applications   3.4.5
  register of enforcement and stop notices
    5.9.1
  right of entry   5.1
Lodger
  nuisance or acts of waste, etc, by   33.10.4
Long lease
  flat, of
  acquisition of, by qualifying tenant   40.3, *see*
    also 'new lease, tenant's right to' *below*
  right to buy freehold, *see* Collective
    enfranchisement
  house, of, right to buy freehold, etc, *see*
    Enfranchisement (long lease house)
  new lease, tenant's right to   40.3
    collective enfranchisement, interaction with
      40.3.1, 40.3.6
    compensation   40.3.5
    effect of grant   40.3.6
    entitlement   40.3.2
    marriage value   40.3.5
    not exercisable, circumstances   40.3.3
    premium   40.3.5
    qualifying tenant   40.3.2
    redevelopment, reservation of right
      40.3.4
    security of tenure   40.3.6
    terms   40.3.4

Managing agent
  employment costs   24.4.1
Market
  see also Rent; Rent review
  state of, effect on rent   16.4
Merger   30.7
  agreement for lease, and lease   26.3.15
Metropolitan area   1.4.2
  development plan in   1.5.1
Mineral
  planning   1.4.1

Mining lease
      alterations, and   20.3.2
      exclusion from security of tenure   31.1.3
      relief from forfeiture   30.5.3
Mining operations   2.1.1
Minister of religion
      let for, repossession   33.8.3
Monument, scheduled
      demolition   2.1.1
Mortgage
      enfranchisement of long-lease house, effect on
            38.4
      lease of
            by way of sub-lease   18.1.2, 30.5.4
            consent of landlord   18.2.5
            forfeiture relief for lender   30.5.4
Mortgagee
      exercising power of sale   33.8.3
      planning obligation, consent to   4.2.3

National Park
      'county matters', and   1.4.1
      dwelling house in   2.2.2
Negligence
      builder, architect, etc, of   8.3
            economic loss, liability for   8.3.2
            establishing liability   8.3
            physical damage, liability for   8.3.1
      solicitor, of   7.3.4
Non-residential use   2.1.3
Notice
      breach of condition, *see* Breach of condition
            notice
      completion   3.5.3
      enforcement, *see* Enforcement (planning);
            Enforcement notice (planning)
Notice to quit   30.1, 30.3
      length of notice   30.3
Notice(s)   13.3.5, 14.2.4
      assignment or sub-let, of   18.3
      assured shorthold, prior to grant   34.1
      breach of covenant, of forfeiture   30.5.3
      disrepair, of   17.2.8, 17.3
      service, method for *see* Service
      statutory, to terminate protected tenancy
            21.2.1, 31.2
            content   31.2, 31.2.1
            see also Notice to quit
Notification
      local planning authority, by application, of
            3.4.5
            decision, of   3.5.1
      owner or agricultural tenant, of planning
            application   3.4.4
Nuisance
      alterations, and   20.1
      meaning   33.8.4

tenant, by, repossession for   33.8.4
user, and   19.1, 19.4

Occupation
      landlord's intention, as opposition to new lease
            31.5.7
      premises fit for   22.7.2
      rights   7.3.3
      security of tenure, for   31.1.2
Occupier
      see also Licensee; Tenant
      eviction, meaning for protection from   36.2.1
Office
      partitions   20.3
Office of the Deputy Prime Minister   1.1, 1.3
      appeal against decision of, *see* High Court
      appeal to, *see* Appeal (planning)
      circulars   1.2.2, 1.3.2
      functions
            planning   1.3
      powers (planning)
      policy guidance dissemination   1.2.2, 1.3.2
      quasi-judicial   1.3.3
      SIs and directions, for   1.3.1
      Wales, position in   1.3.4
Open market rental valuation   16.4
Operations
      see also Development
      meaning   2.1.1
Option
      see also Break clause
      renewal, as to   14.3
Option agreement   7.2.2
      legal nature of   7.2.2
      stamp duty   7.2.2
      terms of   7.2.2
      uses   7.2.2
Outstanding natural beauty, area of
      dwelling house in   2.2.2
Overriding lease   28.1.4
Owner
      meaning   3.4.4

Parcels clause   11.3.4, 13.1–13.4
Parking
Particularly long term
      meaning   40.2.5
Particulars delivered   10.2
Partnership
Pension fund
Periodic tenancy
      assured tenancy as, *see* Assured tenancy
            see also Notice to quit
      repairs
      statutory implied terms   37.3.1, 37.3.2
      tenant's common law liability   37.2.1

Permitted development, *see* Development; General
   Permitted Development Order
Pipes and conduits   11.3.5, 13.4
   see also Services (utilities)
   lease of part, in   24.3.1
Plan
   outline planning permission, for   3.3.1
Planning agreement   4.1
Planning and Compulsory Purchase Bill 2003
   1.5.3, 3.3.5
Planning application   3.1 *et seq*
   see also Planning permission
   applicant   3.4.3
   decision on   3.5
      development plan, and   3.5.1
      matters affecting   3.5.1
      notification   3.5.1, *see also* Appeal
         (planning)
      time-limit for   3.5.1
   development plan, at variance with   1.5.3,
      3.5.1
   fee   3.4.2
   form   3.2
      submission   3.4.1
   notification to other owner/tenant   3.4.3, 3.4.4
   outline permission, for   3.3.1
   pre-application discussion with officer   3.2
   procedure   3.4
   refusal of determination on, power   3.5.5
Planning authority
   see also Local planning authority
   county and district   1.4.1
Planning contravention notice   5.1, 5.5
   contents   5.5.1
   duty to reply to   5.5.2
   effect   5.5.3
   information required   5.5.1
   offences   5.5.2
   person served   5.5.2
Planning control, *see* Enforcement (planning);
   Planning permission
Planning gain   4.3
   inducement, when legitimate   4.3.1, 4.3.2
   meaning and use of term   4.3.1
   permission subject to conditions compared
      4.3.2
Planning obligation   4.1 *et seq*
   agreement for   4.2
   condition imposition contrasted   4.3.2
   conditional   4.2.1
   costs of   4.4.1
   deed, need for   4.2.2
   discharge or modification of   4.4.2, 4.5
      agreement or application, by   4.5.1
      appeal against decision on   4.5.4
      applicant   4.5.2
      determination of   4.5.3
   drafting points   4.4

developer, for   4.4.2
local planning authority, for   4.4.1
duration   4.2.1
enforcement   4.2.3, 4.2.4, 4.4
   injunction, by   4.2.4
   local planning authority carrying out works
      4.2.4
   sums due, as charge on land   4.2.4
form of   4.2.1
function   4.3.1
Guidance   4.3.2
inducements   4.3
'material consideration' for LPA, test   4.3.3
meaning and effect   4.2.1
person bound by   4.2.3
'person interested in land'   4.2.1
'planning gain' derived from   4.3.1
planning permission conditions, and   4.4.2
reasonableness and relevance of   4.3.2, 4.3.3
registration of   4.2.2
restrictive covenant
   breach of   4.2.4
   drafting point on   4.4.2
   imposition by   4.2.1
undertaking for   4.6
   circumstances for   4.6.3
   DETR guidance on   4.6.2
   effect of   4.6.3
   reason for use of   4.6.1
unilateral   4.6
use of   4.1
validity   4.3, 4.4
Planning permission   3.1 *et seq*
   see also Development; Local planning authority
   abandonment   3.5.2
   alterations, for   20.1
   application for
      tenant, by   20.4
   automatic grant of   2.2.2
      limitations   2.2.2
   benefit of   3.5.2
   breach   5.1 *et seq*, *see also* Enforcement
      (planning)
   change of use, for   2.1, 2.1.2, 2.1.3
   condition   3.5.1, 3.5.4, 3.6
      appeal   3.5.4, 3.6.2, 3.6.3, *see also* Appeal
         (planning)
      application to develop without complying
         with previous   3.6.4, *see also* Appeal
         (planning)
      breach, and   3.6.4, 5.2.2, 5.3.1, *see also*
         Breach of condition notice; Enforcement
         (planning)
      burden of   3.5.2
      challenge to, out of time   3.6.4
      criteria for   3.6.3
      negative or positive, distinction
         3.6.2

Planning permission *cont*
   condition *cont*
      purpose of   3.6.1, 3.6.2
      reasons for   3.5.4, 3.6.3
      removal of   3.6.4
      restrictions on   3.6.2
      validity of   3.6.2, 3.6.3
      void, effect   3.6.2
   contract conditional on   7.2.1
   covenant in lease not to apply for   19.4
   demolition
      ground for opposing new lease, and
         31.5.6
   development
      lease, regulation in   11.3.2
   development plan, importance of   7.3.1, 1.5.2,
      3.5.1
   duration   3.5.3
   effect   3.5.2
   effective date of   3.5.3
   enforcement   19.4, *see also* Enforcement
      (planning)
   full   3.3
   grant of   3.5
      what constitutes   3.5.1
   lapse   3.5.3
   limitation   3.5.2
      breach of   5.2.2, 5.3.1, *see also* Breach of
         condition notice; Enforcement (planning)
   modification   3.5.2
   nature of   7.1
   operations, for   2.1, 2.1.1
   outline   3.3.1–3.3.4
      approval of reserved matters   3.3.4, 3.5.3
      effect of   3.3.3
      refusal or approval of reserved matters, *see*
         Appeal (planning)
      reserved matters   3.3.2, 3.5.1
      revocation of   3.3.3
      time-limits   3.5.3, 3.6.4
   permissive nature of   3.5.2
   personal   3.5.2
   plan on which based, licence for use   7.1
   preliminary steps for solicitor   3.2
   refusal of   3.5.4, *see also* Appeal (planning)
   renewal   3.5.3
   revocation   3.3.3, 3.5.3
   tenant's compliance with   20.1, 20.2.1, 23.2
   time-limits   3.5.3
   use of premises under lease, and   11.3.5, 19.1
Planning policy guidance notes   1.2.2
Planning unit   2.1.2
Plant and machinery
   part let   24.3.1, 24.4.1
Pollution   20.1
   see also Contaminated land
   'material consideration' for planning permission
      3.5.1

Possession
   see also Sub-lease
   forfeiture, and   33.8.2
      where tenant seeking reimbursement for
         mandatory grounds warning   32.3.17
   order, procedure for, *see* Possession action
   sharing or parting with   18.1.3, 18.2
Possession action
   assured tenant, against
      notice on tenant   33.8.2
   rent arrears, for   33.8.3, 33.8.4
Post
   appeal time-limit, and   5.10
Power lines   7.3.3
Pre-emption right
   tenant, of, for freehold   39.1–
      39.3
Premises
   see also Industrial premises; Shop
   condition of
      access to ascertain   17.2.8, *see also*
         Access; Repairs
      description of, in lease   11.3.2, *see also*
         Parcels clause
      part, dealing with, controls on   18.1.4, 18.2,
         see also Lease of part
      rental valuation, factors affecting   16.4
Premium
   new long lease, for   40.3.5
      Stamp duty on   10.2
      VAT on   10.1.5, 10.2
Private sector let   32.5
Privity of contract   9.2
   abolition of   9.2.2, 12.1, 12.3.2
   leases before January 1996   9.2.1
   release of original tenant   12.2.2, 12.3.2,
      12.4.2
Privity of estate   9.2.1, 12.3.1
Procedure
   certificate of lawful use or development, for
      2.3.2, 5.3
   enforcement notice appeal, for
      5.10.4
   planning application, for   3.4
Professional fees
   VAT on   10.1, 10.1.1, 10.1.5
Professional insurance   26.3.9
Property
   see also Dwelling house; Flat; House
Protected tenancy
   exclusions   35.2
   fair rent   35.4
   meaning   35.2
   new tenancy to protected tenant
      33.4
   security of tenancy after   35.3, *see also*
      Statutory tenancy
   termination   35.3

Protection from eviction, *see* Eviction
relief from forfeiture provision
30.5.3
Public sector tenancy 32.4
Publicity
see also Advertisement
planning application, of 30.4.5
Purchaser of reversion, *see* Investor

Quantity surveyor 8.2.4
standard of care 8.2.5
Quiet enjoyment covenant 21.1, 21.2
breach 28.2.2

Racial discrimination
local planning authority, by 3.5.1
Rates 15.1
Receiver
appointment 29.4
by tenant, to collect rents, etc 28.2.1
for tenant, landlord's re-entry right
Chapter 23
claim for rent or damages, and 29.6
forfeiture and receivership 29.5.2
powers 29.4
Reconstruction
ground for opposing new lease 31.5.6
Redevelopment
ground for collective enfranchisement
opposition 40.2.4
new long lease, reservation of right
40.3.4
Re-entry
corporate insolvency, on 29.5.2
proviso Chapter 23, *see also* Forfeiture
References
false statement in 33.10.4
unsatisfactory, of assignee 18.2.5
Registration
agreement for lease, of 26.1
certificate of lawful use, of 2.3.2
charge on rent deposit, of 12.5
new lease application, of 31.3.2
option to buy, of 7.2.2
planning obligation, of 4.2.2
sums due as charge on land, of 4.2.4
planning permission, of 3.4.5, 3.5.1
Reinstatement
alterations, after 20.4
damage, after 22.7.3, 22.7.4
Remediation notice 6.2.6
Renewal
repair contrasted with 17.2.5
Renewal lease 31.1.1, 31.7
order for 31.8
circumstances 31.7

revocation of 31.8
right to
agreement to defer 31.3.2
application to court 31.3.1, 31.3.2
compensation for failure to obtain 31.6
opposition, grounds for 31.5
registration of application 31.3.2
service of counter-notice, and 31.2.3,
31.3.1
time-limit adherence 31.3.2
time-limit after request to terminate
31.2.2, 31.3.1
terms 31.7
agreement of parties 31.7, 31.7.4
court jurisdiction 31.7, 31.7.4
disregards for rent assessment 31.7.3
disrepair, effect 31.7.3
duration 31.7.2
guarantors, provision for 31.7.3
lease of less than holding 31.7.1
premises 31.7.1
rent 31.7.3
rent review clause 31.7.3
variations to original lease terms,
circumstances 31.7.4
Rent 15.1
action to recover 28.1.1
advance or arrear 15.3
amount of 15.1, 18.3.3
factors affecting 18.2.1
arrears Chapter 23, 28.1.1, 29.6
notice of claim for 28.1
re-entry or forfeiture for 30.5.2
see also Interest
assured shorthold, under 34.4
assured tenancy, under 33.5, *see also* Assured
tenancy: rent
covenant 15.1
'touching and concerning' demised premises
12.3.1
damage to premises, effect on 22.7.2
date from which payable 14.1, 15.3
deduction of sums from 15.1, 28.2.1
defining 11.3.2, 15.1
fair rent, *see* Fair rent
increase or decrease, *see* Rent review
insolvency of tenant, and claim for 29.6
interim 15.1, 16.2, 31.4
low, meaning for enfranchisement right
12.2.3
non-payment 28.1.1
re-entry or forfeiture for 30.5.2
other payments reserved as 15.4
payment
address for service, and 33.8.3
persistent delay, statutory ground for opposition
to new lease 31.5.2
rebate or allowance, *see* Housing benefit

Rent *cont*
   reservation of   11.3.4
   service charge, *see* Service charge
   standing order or direct debit   15.3
   sub-lease rent   16.3.3
   substantial arrears   33.8.3
   suspension   15.5, 22.7.2
   time for payment   15.3
   turnover rent   16.3.3
   VAT   10.1.3, 10.1.4, 10.2
Rent Act protection   35.1 *et seq*
   fair rent system   35.4
   succession   35.5–35.5.3
   tenancy granted after Housing Act, for   33.4,
      35.1
   tenancy having, *see* Protected tenancy; Statutory
      tenancy
Rent Assessment Committee
   reference to   34.1, 34.4
Rent deposit   12.5
   default triggering access   12.5
   drafting of deed   12.5
   obligation to return   12.5
Rent officer   35.4.1
Rent review   16.1 *et seq*
   ancillary provisions on   16.7
   break clause, interrelation with   16.6.1
   conduct of, methods   16.6
      negotiation, by   16.6.2
      preferred method   16.6.3
      third party reference   16.6.4
      trigger notices, by   16.6.3
   dates for   16.2, 16.6.1
   fixed   16.3.1
   frequency   16.2
      5-yearly review common   16.2
   independent valuer, use of   16.3.4
   index-linked basis   16.3.2
   late   16.6.1, 16.7.1
   need for clause   16.1
   open market basis   16.3.4, 16.4–16.6
   penultimate day review   16.2, 31.4.3
   presence of clause, effect on rent   16.5.2
   record of   16.7.2
   schedule, as   11.3.6
   surveyor, status for   11.6.4
   time, whether of essence   16.6.1
   turnover based   16.3.3
   types of clause   16.3
   valuation
      assumptions   16.5.2, 16.5.3
      comparables, use of   16.5.2
      consideration and inducements, effect
         16.5.2
      date for   16.5
      disregards   16.5.4
      goodwill, and   16.5.4
      hypothetical letting   16.5
      improvements, and   16.5.4
      interest to be valued   16.5
      length of term   16.5.2
      market for   16.5.2
      occupation of tenant, effect   16.5.4
      principles   16.4
      rent-free period, effect of   16.5.2
      terms of lease, effect   16.5.2, 16.5.4,
         20.2.2
      user covenant, and   16.5.2
      vacant possession assumption   16.5.2
   wording of clause   16.5.1, 16.5.2
Repairs   17.1 *et seq*, 37.1 *et seq*
   access by landlord for   17.2.8, 28.1.2
   covenant   8.4.2, 17.1 *et seq*
      breach by landlord   28.2.1
      breach by tenant   28.1.2
      building erected after lease   17.2.1
      contaminated land, and   17.2.1
      decoration, as to   17.5, 17.6
      insured risks, and   22.7.1
      landlord's   17.3
      leave for landlord to sue for breach   28.1.2
      tenant's   17.2
      to yield up in repair   17.4
   damages for tenant's default   17.6, 28.1.2
      intention to demolish, etc, effect   28.1.2
   default by landlord   28.2.1
   default by tenant   17.2.8, 28.1.2
      expenses of putting right a debt   28.1.2
      statutory ground for opposition to new lease
         31.5.1
   defective premises, and
      landlord's duty   17.3
   disrepair   17.2.3, 17.2.4, 17.2.7
      notice of   17.2.8, 17.3
   express covenant   37.2.2
      statutory terms conflicting   37.2.1, 37.2.3
   'fair wear and tear' proviso   17.2.7
   fixtures, of   13.3.1, 17.2.1
   implied obligations   17.1
   improvement or renewal distinguished   17.2.5
   inherent defects   17.2.6, 17.2.7
   insurance, and   17.2.7, 22.7.1
   liability for   37.2
      common law, at   37.2
   meaning of 'repair'   17.2.5
   notice, requirement for   37.3.6
   part of building, let of   17.1, 17.2.1, 17.3, 24.3
   receiver, appointment to carry out   28.2.1
   schedule of condition   17.2.7
   service charge, *see* Service charge
   specific performance of obligation   28.1.2,
      28.1.3, 28.2.1
   standard of   17.2.4
   statutory implied terms   37.3
      common parts of block of flats   37.3.3,
         37.3.4

Repairs *cont*
    statutory implied terms *cont*
        dwelling house, for   37.3.1
        fire, etc, exception   37.3.6
        installations for water, gas etc, heating
            37.3.2, 37.3.4
        lease or agreement for, length of   37.3.1
        standard of repair   37.3.5
        structure and exterior   37.3.2, 37.3.3
        tenant's repairs and fixtures excluded
            37.3.6
Reserve fund   24.5
Reserved matters
    outline planning permission, under   3.3.2,
        3.5.1
Resident landlord
    exclusion from first refusal of freehold provisions
        39.2.2
    let by, assured tenancy exclusion   33.3.7
    meaning   33.3.7
Residential occupier
    meaning for eviction protection   36.2.1
Residential use   2.1.3, 2.2.2, *see also* Dwelling
    house
Restrictive covenant, *see also* Covenant
    planning obligation imposing   4.2.1, 4.4.2
        breach, enforcement powers   4.2.4
Reversion, sale/transfer of
    indemnity covenant   12.2.1, 5.4.2
    investment fund, to   11.1
    lease terms, requirements of purchaser as to
        11.1, 16.1, 35.2, *see also* Investor
    purchaser, *see* Investor
    release of original landlord   12.2.2
Right of way
    see also Access; Easement
    discovery of   7.3.1, 7.3.3
Road
    see also Highway
    access to   2.2.2
    obstruction of users' view   2.2.2
Roof   24.3.1

Sale of lease, *see* Assignment
Sale of freehold, *see* Reversion, sale/transfer of
Satellite antenna
    installation   2.2.2
Searches
    see also Local authority searches
    special   7.3.4
Security
Security of tenure   9.3, 30.1, 31.1–31.8
    assured tenancy, under   33.8, *see also* Assured
        tenancy
    breach of covenant, liability for   31.1.6
    'business'   31.1.2
    compensation for tenant   31.6

        amount   31.6.2
        availability   31.6.1
        contracting out   31.6.4
        double   31.6.3
    'competent landlord'   31.1.4
    conditions for   31.1.2
    continuation lease   31.1.1, 31.1.6
        rent   31.1.6
    contracting out   9.3, 9.4, 11.3.5, 31.1.3, 31.1.5
    counter-notices   31.2.3
    exclusions   31.1.3
    fixed term, notice to terminate   31.2
    forfeiture   31.2
    'holding'   31.1.4
    interim rent   15.1, 16.2, 31.4
        alternative to   31.4.3
        amount of   31.4.2
        need for   31.4.1
    mixed user   31.1.2
    new lease, right to and terms, *see* Renewal lease
        'occupation' for   31.1.2
    protection afforded   31.1.1
    service tenancy   31.1.3
    statutory grounds for opposition   31.5
        alternative accommodation   31.5.4
        demolition or reconstruction   31.5.6
        landlord's intention to occupy   31.5.7
        persistent delay in paying rent   31.5.2
        repair failure   31.5.1
        sub-lease of part   31.5.5
        substantial breaches of obligations   31.5.3
    statutory notice   31.2, 31.2.1
    counter-notice   31.2.3
    statutory tenancy, under   35.3
    surrender   31.2
    'tenancy'   31.1.2
    tenant no longer in business occupation
        31.2
    tenant's request to terminate   31.2, 31.2.2
        content   31.2.2
        counter-notice   31.2.3
        reasons for   31.2.2
        when not permitted   31.2.2
    termination methods   31.2
    user in breach of covenant   31.1.2
Service
    address for landlord for   33.8.3
    enforcement notice, of   5.8.5, 5.8.9
    notice to quit, *see* Notice to quit
    prescribed shorthold notice, of   34.2.1
    renewal lease, and, *see* Renewal lease
    stop notice, of   5.9.2
Service charge   8.4.2, 11.3.6, 24.4
    additional rent, reserved as   15.4, 24.4
    adjustments   24.4.4
    advance payment   24.4.4
    apportionment methods   24.4.3
    certification   24.4.4

Service charge *cont*
  decoration   24.4.1
  estimates   24.4.1
  fairness   24.4.2
  final payment   24.4.4
  improvement distinguished from repair
    24.4.1
  insurance costs recovered through   22.3,
    24.4.1
  investor's requirements
  landlord's covenant to perform   24.4.2
  notice of claim for   28.1
  payment   24.4.4
  provision of services, reasonable care and skill
    implied   24.4.2
  purpose of   24.4
  receiver appointed where default in service
    provision   28.2.1
  repair expenses recovered through   17.1,
    24.4.1
  services provided   24.4.1
  sinking or reserve fund   24.5
  suspension of   22.7.2
    provision for   15.5
  tenant's contribution   24.4.3
Service tenancy   31.1.3
  repossession ground   31.10.4
Services, provision of
  see also Service charge
  care and skill of supplier   24.4.2
Services (utilities)
  see also Drainage
  disconnection by landlord
    breach of contract, as   36.4.2
    harassment, as   36.2.2
  landlord's right to use, lease of part   27.3.2
  right to connect with   13.4
Set-off   15.1
Sharing
  construction of, as licence or lease   33.2.3
Shop
  living accommodation, with, whether 'house'
    38.2.1
  precinct, in
    alterations, landlord's control   20.3, *see
      also* Covenant
    insurance, note of tenant's interest   22.4
    plate glass, insurance of   22.8
    sale signs, etc, in   20.4, *see also*
      Advertisement
    user, landlord's control   19.1.1
    windows   22.8
  'shop within a shop' arrangement   18.1.3
  units in mall   2.1.2
  use as   2.1.3
Short lease
  problems arising   32.1

Shorthold, *see* Assured shorthold tenancy; Protected
    shorthold tenancy
Shower, *see* Bath
Sign, *see* Advertisement
Sinking fund   24.5
Solicitor
  see also Client
  contaminated land, awareness of signs of   6.3
  fees, VAT on   10.1.5
  landlord, for
  planning permission, involvement in   3.1, 3.2
  report to client before exchange of contracts
    7.4
  service at office of   33.8.3
Solicitors' office
  use class   2.1.3
Special development order   2.2.2
Specific performance   28.1.2, 28.1.3, 28.2.1
Spouse
  succession
    assured periodic tenancy, to   33.6
    meaning for   33.6, 35.5
    protected or statutory tenancy, to   35.5,
      35.5.3
Staff
  employment cost of landlord   24.4.1
  agreement for lease, on   10.2, 26.1
  lease, on   10.2
    VAT element, and   10.2
  option agreement, on   7.2.2
  particulars delivered   10.2
Statement
  false, inducing grant of tenancy
    33.8.4
Statutes   32.3
Statutory tenancy   35.3
  fair rent   35.4
Stop notice   5.1, 5.9
  compensation   5.9.6
  contents   5.9.2
  date takes effect   5.9.2
  expediency of   5.9.2
  non-compliance   5.9.4
  offences   5.9.4
  person for service   5.9.2
  procedure   5.9.2
  restrictions on   5.9.3
  service   5.9.2, 5.9.4
  site notice   5.9.2, 5.9.4, 5.9.5
  use of   5.9.1
  withdrawal   5.9.5
Storage or distribution, use class
    2.1.3
Structure
  meaning   37.3.3
Structure plan
  authority for   1.4.1
  meaning   1.5.1

Student accommodation
    educational body landlord   33.3.5,
        33.8.3
Sub-contractor
    collateral warranty from   8.4.1
    contractual liability   8.2.2
    nominated or domestic   8.2.2
Sub-lease   18.1.2, 18.1.4, 25.1–25.4
    access rights   25.3.4
    alienation, prohibition in   25.3.3
    alternative to assignment, as   25.2
    assignment by sub-tenant   27.1
    breach of covenant by head landlord, and
        25.4
    circumstances for   18.1.2
    consent to   18.2.3–18.2.5, 25.4
        charge for   18.2.6
        discrimination, and   18.2.4
        reasonableness of refusal   18.2.5
        refusal of consent   18.2.5
    covenant by sub-tenant with head landlord
        25.1, 25.4
    covenant restricting creation   18.2
    covenants in   25.3.3
    decoration   25.3.3
    disclaimer of headlease, effect   29.1.3, 29.2
    drafting matters   25.3
    headlease
        forfeiture of   30.5.4, 31.2
        inspection, need for   25.1, 25.4
        merger of lease   30.7
        notice of contents of   25.1
        surrender of   30.6.1
    indemnity   25.3.5
    insurance
        policy endorsement   25.4
        reimbursement   25.3.3
    liability of sub-tenant   25.1
    notice of   18.3
    notices, provision as to   25.4
    part, of   18.1.4.
        ground for opposition to new lease   31.5.5
    premises, definition for   25.3.3
    qualified covenant against, implied   25.3
    quiet enjoyment, and   25.3.4, 25.4
    reasons for   25.2
    rent   25.3.2
        payment to superior landlord   28.1.1
    rent review   25.3.2
    repair   25.3.3
        breach of covenant   28.1.2
    security of tenure   25.3.1
        tenant or sub-tenant, for   31.1.2
    term, length of   25.3.1
    termination, break clause in headlease, and
        30.4
    terms of   18.2.3, 25.3.3
    VAT, and   25.3.2

Sub-let
    assured tenancy, of   33.7
Sub-tenant
    nuisance, etc, or acts of waste, etc, by   33.8.4
Subrogation   22.4
Succession
    assured tenancy, to   33.6
    Rent Act tenancy, to   35.5
        death of first successor, on   35.5.3
        death on or after 15 January 1989   35.5.2
        death prior to 15 January 1989   35.5.1
    right to enfranchise, and   38.2.3
Sunday trading
Surety, *see* Guarantor
Surrender of lease   30.6, 31.2
    effect   30.6.1
    express   30.6
    guarantor, position of   12.4.3
    operation of law, by   30.6
    prior to assignment, etc, offer of   18.2.5
    security of tenure, and   30.6, 31.1.5
    VAT, and   10.1, 10.1.5
Survey   7.3.3
    tenant, for   8.4.2
Surveyor
    chartered   7.3.3
        certification of service charge   24.4.4
        construction supervision where agreement for
            lease   26.3.4
    see also Survey; Valuer
    quantity   8.2.4, 8.2.5

Taxation   10.1 *et seq*
    see also Value added tax
Tenancy
    see also specific tenancies
    contractual, *see* Protected tenancy
    meaning for security of tenure provisions
        31.1.2
Tenancy agreement
    repairs, as to   37.2.1, 37.2.2
Tenant
    see also Lease
    agricultural, meaning for GDPO   3.4.4
    assignee   12.3, *see also* Assignment
    breach by   12.2, 12.3, Chapter 23, 28.1, 28.2,
        see also Damages; Forfeiture
    clean-up works, responsibility for costs   6.2
    company, as   33.2.5, 40.3.2
    compensation   11.3.5, 31.6
    covenants, liability on
        post-1995 lease   9.2.2, 12.3.2
        pre-1996 lease   9.2.1, 12.3.1
        see also Covenant; Repairs
    defect liability period   8.4.2
    first refusal of freehold, right of   39.1,
        39.3

Tenant *cont*
    first refusal of freehold, right of *cont*
        anti-avoidance measures   39.2.5
    goods, removal after termination   11.3.5
    guarantee for assignee   18.2.7
    indemnity   12.3.1
    insolvency   29.1, 29.2
    joint and several liability   11.3.3
    notice of claim to   28.1
    original, liability of   12.3, 12.3.1
        see also Liability of parties to lease
    overriding lease, right to   28.1.4
    privity of contract   12.3.1
    protection of, overview   32.1
    qualifying, for enfranchisement right   38.2.3
    remedies   28.2
    rent, *see* Rent
    repairing covenant   8.4.2, *see also* Repairs
    repairs, liability for   37.2.1, 37.2.2
    request to terminate   31.2, 31.2.2
    rights, schedule of   11.3.6
    user, *see* User
    VAT on rent   10.1.3, 10.1.4
    waste by, *see* Waste
Termination
    see also Notice to quit, Security of tenure
    assured shorthold, *see* Assured shorthold tenancy
    assured tenancy, of   33.8.1
    common law, at   30.1–30.7
    expiry, by   30.2
    lease, of   9.3, 30.1 *et seq*, 31.2
    prescribed methods, where tenancy protected
        31.2
    protected tenancy, of   35.3
Terms, *see also* Tenancy agreement
Terrorism
    insurance and risk of   22.5
Third parties
    right to enforce contract   8.3.1, 25.4
Time-limit
    appeal (planning), for, *see* Appeal (planning)
    compensation claim, after stop notice   5.9.6
    development under planning permission, for
        3.5.3
    enforcement of planning, for   5.2.2, 5.8.3
    two limits   5.2.2
    extension of, approval of reserved matters, etc
        3.6.4
    planning application decision, for   3.5.1
Title, investigation of   7.3.5
    agreement for lease, and   26.3.14
    prior to planning application   3.2
Toilet
    repair of equipment   37.3.2, 37.3.4
Tort   8.3, 8.4.1, *see also* Negligence
    eviction or harassment action   36.4.2
    law of, relevance   32.2
    nuisance, *see* Nuisance

    statutory, under Housing Act   36.4.2
Tree preservation order   7.3.1
Trespass
    airspace, into   13.2
    land, person or goods, to   36.4.2
    landlord, by, into demised premises
        28.1.2
    quiet enjoyment covenant, and   22.1
Trust
    tenancy held on   31.1.2
Trust of rights   8.4.2
Trustee-in-bankruptcy   29.1.1, 29.6
    see also Disclaimer
Turnover
    rent based on   16.3.3

Underlease, *see* Sub-lease
Undertaking
    enforcement notice appeal, for damages
        5.10.4
    injunction application, for damages   5.7
    planning obligation entered into by   4.6
    tenant, by, as to costs   27.1
    unilateral, planning obligation as   4.6
Unitary council   1.4.2, 3.4.1
Unitary development plan   1.5.1
Use
    change of, *see* Change of use
    classes   2.1.3
        change of use within   2.1.2, 2.1.3, 2.2.2
        conditions restricting use within   3.6.4
        exclusions   2.1.3
    definition   2.1.2
    lawful   5.3.1
    resumption of previous   2.2.1, 3.5.2
    temporary   2.2.2
User
    ancillary provisions   19.4
    authorised use   *see also* Planning permission
    balancing act required   19.1
    consent to change   19.3.2
    covenant as to
        absolute   19.3.1
        breach, remedies for   19.1.3
        defining permitted use in lease   19.2
        full qualified   19.3.3
        injunction to prevent unauthorised   28.1.3
        naming tenant   19.2.2
        need for   19.1
        negative   19.2.3
        positive   19.2.3
        qualified   19.3.2
        rent review, and   16.5.2
    immoral or illegal   19.4,
    landlord's concerns   19.1.1
    mixed   31.1.2
    non-user   19.2.3

User *cont*
  non-user *cont*
    injunction against   28.1.3
    nuisance, and   19.1, 19.4
    planning permission, and   11.3.5, 19.4
    restrictions on, effect on rent   19.1.1
    superior title restrictions, and   19.1
    tenant's concerns   19.1.2
    use classes order, linked to   19.2.1

Vacant possession
  contract conditional on   7.2.1
  express term for   7.1
Valuation
  insurance, for, cost of   22.8
  interim rent application, prior to   31.4.2
  renewal lease rent, for   31.7.3
  rent review, for, *see* Rent review
  user restrictions, and advice on   19.1.1
Value added tax   10.1
  commercial development, and   10.1.2
  contract of sale, term on   7.1
  costs, on   10.1.5
  defining in lease   11.3.2
  election to waive exemption   10.1.3, 10.1.4
  insurance to include   22.6
  option agreement, and   7.2.2
  option to tax   10.1.3, 10.1.4
    election for   10.1.3
    limited disapplication   10.1.3
    revocation of election   10.1.3
  purchase price presumed to include   10.1.4
  rent, etc, on   15.7
  rent-free periods   10.1.5
  rent review, assumption for   16.5.3
  reservation as additional rent   15.4
  residential development   10.1.1
  reverse premium, and   10.1.5
  sub-let, and   25.3.2
  supplies in relation to property transaction   10.1
  surrender of lease   10.1.5
Valuer

  open market rent, of   16.3.4, 16.6.4
Variation
  agreement for lease, of   26.3.2
  enforcement notice requirement   5.8.8,
    5.9.6
    appeal on   5.10.4
  lease, of   12.4.3, 31.7.4
Vesting order
  predecessor tenant, for   29.1.3
Violence
  use or threats of   36.2.2, 36.4.2
    to secure entry   30.5, 36.3

Waiver   11.3.5
  right of forfeiture, of   30.5.1
Walls   24.3.1
  erection, etc   2.2.2
Warrant
  entry on to land, for   5.4.2
Warranty
  collateral   8.4.1, 26.3.9
  environmental   5.4.2
Waste, doctrine of   20.4
Waste
  planning application concerned with   3.4.1,
    3.4.5
  tenant, by
    common law position   37.3.1
    possession ground   33.8.4, 40.3.1
Water, *see* Services (utilities)
  supply
    repair of installations   37.3.2, 37.3.4
Water damage, insurance against   22.5
Water pollution   6.1
Water rates   15.1
Will, tenant at   30.2, 31.1.3
Window
  insurance of   22.8
  lease of part
    cleaning   24.4.1
Works
  see also Alterations; Improvements